THE ADVENTURES OF
ARTHUR CONAN DOYLE

Also by Russell Miller

THE ADVENTURES OF
ARTHUR
CONAN DOYLE

A BIOGRAPHY

RUSSELL MILLER

Thomas Dunne Books
St. Martin's Press
New York

THOMAS DUNNE BOOKS.
An imprint of St. Martin's Press.

THE ADVENTURES OF ARTHUR CONAN DOYLE. Copyright © 2008 by Russell Miller. All rights reserved.
Printed in the United States of America. For information, address St. Martin's Press, 175 Fifth
Avenue, New York, N.Y. 10010.

www.thomasdunnebooks.com
www.stmartins.com

Library of Congress Cataloging-in-Publication Data

Miller, Russell.
    The adventures of Arthur Conan Doyle : a biography / Russell Miller. — 1st U.S. ed.
        p. cm.
    Includes bibliographical references and index.
    ISBN-13: 978-0-312-37897-4
    ISBN-10: 0-312-37897-1
    1. Doyle, Arthur Conan, Sir, 1859–1930. 2. Authors, Scottish—19th century—Biography. 3.
Authors, Scottish—20th century—Biography. 4. Spiritualists—Great Britain—Biography. 5.
Physicians—Great Britain—Biography. I. Title.
    PR4623.M55 2008
    823'.8—dc22
    [B]

                                                                                    2008038631

First published in Great Britain by Harvill Secker,
a division of The Random House Group Limited

First U.S. Edition: December 2008

10 9 8 7 6 5 4 3 2 1

To Philip, a good friend

CONTENTS

PART THREE
THE SPIRITUALIST

FOREWORD

THROUGHOUT HIS LONG AND remarkable life, Sir Arthur Conan Doyle was an amazingly industrious correspondent, writing thousands of letters to friends, family, colleagues and acquaintances. He was a man more comfortable revealing his emotions on paper than by word or gesture. His adored mother received no fewer than 1,500 letters from her son, in one of which he confessed, for example, that he had fallen in love with another woman while his wife was dying of tuberculosis. Thereafter he kept her up to date with every intimate development of the affair. Conan Doyle's candid letters provide a unique insight into the man and form the backbone of this book, the first biography to enjoy virtually unlimited and unfettered access to his private papers.

The background to the Conan Doyle archive is complicated. During his lifetime Conan Doyle sold at least seven manuscripts to raise money for the Red Cross during the First World War and a further six Sherlock Holmes manuscripts were put up for auction at the American Art Galleries in New York in 1922. At his death on 7 July 1930, all his remaining papers – original manuscripts, research notes, journals and voluminous letters, almost his entire life's work – were lodged at Windlesham, his home in East Sussex. He left everything to his wife, who, over the next decade, added her own notes and memories to the collection.

When Lady Conan Doyle died in 1940, her three children – sons Adrian and Denis and daughter, Jean – shared the estate. While Jean would carve out a successful career, eventually becoming a Dame and Commandant of the Women's Royal Air Force, her two brothers were feckless playboys who rarely worked and shamelessly used their father's estate to finance their extravagant lifestyles. Adrian Conan Doyle, who liked to describe himself as a motor racing driver and big game hunter, was appointed executor and became the unlikely custodian of his father's memory, establishing at his chateau in Lucens, Switzerland, a Sherlock Holmes Museum. It was Adrian's absurd thesis, against all the evidence, that his father was the role model for Sherlock Holmes.

In the late 1940s Adrian invited the American thriller writer, John Dickson Carr, to write an authorised biography of his father, offering him use of the archive. Carr's book, *The Life of Sir Arthur Conan Doyle*, first published in 1949, included an appendix briefly listing the contents of a number of boxes in the archive, although little use appeared to have been made of the material in the narrative, almost certainly because Adrian Conan Doyle was exercising strict editorial control. Ten years later, a French scholar, Pierre Nordon, was also granted access for his Sorbonne thesis, later published as a similarly anodyne biography.

Through the 1950s and 60s Adrian Conan Doyle sold manuscripts and certain of his father's papers, mainly in the United States, where there was a ready market for Conan Doyle memorabilia. In 1969 he had the complete archive shipped secretly to New York with the intention of selling it in its entirety to a wealthy collector in Texas for a huge sum, but no agreement had been reached by the time of his death, from a heart attack, the following year. Thereafter the archive, amounting to 15 boxes, now somewhat disorganised but still containing all of Sir Arthur's personal papers, would be lodged in the offices of a London solicitor for nearly 25 years while legal squabbles between the family dragged on.

No one was more frustrated by these events than Richard Lancelyn Green, one of the world's leading experts on Sherlock Holmes and Conan Doyle. A prominent and popular member of the Sherlock Holmes Society of London, Lancelyn Green had devoted his life to collecting Conan Doyle memorabilia and had a reputation as a brilliant and witty raconteur with an encyclopaedic knowledge of his subject. He travelled widely, delivering lectures with theatrical flair to other Sherlock Holmes societies around the world and established his scholarly reputation in 1983 as co-editor of *A Bibliography of A. Conan*

Doyle, which was judged one of the most comprehensive and author-itative bibliographies ever produced, of any writer.

But the culmination of his life's work, a definitive biography, remained resolutely unachievable while the bulk of Conan Doyle's papers were the subject of continuing dispute within the family. The feuding finally ended in 1990, after the widows of both Adrian and Denis had died, when the estate was split between Dame Jean Conan Doyle and three cousins – the grandson of Conan Doyle's sister Ida and the grandchildren of his brother, Innes. Dame Jean's share included her father's letters to his mother, which she bequeathed to the British Library.

Lancelyn Green believed that the entire archive rightly belonged in the British Library and was thus dismayed to learn, early in 2004, that the three cousins intended to sell their share of the estate through Christie's auction house. An article in the *Sunday Times Magazine* about the forthcoming sale revealed that it was indeed a treasure trove being offered. It included fascinating correspondence with public figures including Winston Churchill, P. G. Wodehouse, Theodore Roosevelt and Oscar Wilde; Conan Doyle's tan lizard-skin wallet, its contents intact; the illustrated logs he kept as a surgeon on a whaling ship in the Arctic; an armband with a red cross which he wore as a doctor in South Africa during the Boer War; and the manuscript of an un-published novel, his first, written in the mid-1890s.

Lancelyn Green, alarmed at the prospect of this material being dispersed around the world, mounted a vigorous campaign to try and block the sale, contacting Members of Parliament and writing letters of protest to newspapers. But his efforts were to no avail and, seven weeks before the date of the auction, he was found dead, garrotted, at his Kensington home. A coroner recorded an open verdict, but many of Lancelyn Green's fellow 'Sherlockians' believe that he killed himself in despair.

The sale at Christie's went ahead in May, as planned. Had Lancelyn Green lived he would have been relieved that many of the most inter-esting lots were purchased by the British Library. Not long afterwards, it was announced that Lancelyn Green had left his own huge collec-tion of memorabilia, including rare first editions, letters and research notes, to the city of Portsmouth, where Conan Doyle once practised as a doctor and where he wrote the first two Sherlock Holmes stories.

The sudden and unexpected emergence of all this material into the public domain, combined with the generosity of Charles Foley, Conan Doyle's great-nephew and the current executor of his literary estate, make this book possible. While the British Library physically owns the most important letters, the copyright is still vested in the Conan Doyle Estate. Without Charles Foley's kind permission for me to make unlimited use of his great-uncle's papers, this book would be greatly diminished.

I was also the first biographer to have full access to the extraordinary Richard Lancelyn Green Collection at Portsmouth City Council and I particularly want to thank Sarah Speller, the project coordinator, for her help during the many hours my wife and I spent in the Guildhall going through box after box of papers. Grateful thanks, too, to Owen Dudley Edwards, who was generous with his time in Edinburgh, despite planning his own book on Conan Doyle. My dear friend Philip Norman suggested I should tackle Conan Doyle as a subject, just as, many years ago, he put forward the idea for my first book. I also want to thank Georgina Doyle, Christopher Roden, founder of the Arthur Conan Doyle Society, Caroline Hay of Christie's, Peggy Purdue at the Toronto Public Library, the helpful and friendly staff at the British Library, John Gibson, Jon Lellenberg, Roger Oldfield, my agent Michael Sissons and my superb editor, Stuart Williams. Renate, my wife, helped enormously with the research and read through many drafts of the manuscript with diligence, patience and good humour; as always, she is my loving first-line editor.

Russell Miller,
Brighton, 2008

PART I

THE DOCTOR

CHAPTER I

FAMILY PRIDE
AND FAMILY SHAME

T IS A PECULIAR IRONY that Sir Arthur Conan Doyle's birthplace in Edinburgh's Old Town, long since demolished, is not today marked with a statue of the writer himself but by a statue of his most famous creation – Sherlock Holmes, the character Conan Doyle came to believe was largely responsible for destroying his reputation as a serious literary figure. Perhaps it is understandable; after all, Holmes is the most famous man who never lived.

His aquiline profile, with deerstalker and pipe, is instantly recognisable, even in countries where people have the greatest difficulty pronouncing his name. It is picked out in ceramic tiles on the walls of Baker Street Underground station in London. It has featured on cigarette cards, tea towels, board games, dinner services, postage stamps, beer bottles, chewing gum, mouthwashes, computer games, Beecham's Pills and packets of Kellogg's Crunchy Nut corn flakes. Only Mickey Mouse and Santa Claus rival Sherlock Holmes for worldwide recognition.

He remains one of the few household names in English fiction, arguably the most famous character in literature after Hamlet, and one with whom the public has an extraordinarily intimate acquaintance. Everyone knows his catchphrase 'Elementary, my dear Watson!', although few are aware it is nowhere to be found in the stories. His eccentricities – pinning correspondence to the mantelshelf with a jackknife and keeping tobacco in the heel of a Turkish slipper, for example – are common knowledge. He is a valuable asset to the British tourist industry, known to 87 per cent of visitors to Britain, and is one of London's major attractions – indeed, Japanese and Russians often cite him as their main reason for visiting the city. Misguided souls still write to him at his Baker Street 'consulting rooms' in the hope that his genius may solve their problems, even though – had he ever existed – he would be long since dead.

Of course, to Sherlockians he *is* a real person. Holmes inspires a cult-like devotion among his fans which borders on the mystical. There are more than 400 Sherlock Holmes societies around the world which meet regularly to worship at the metaphorical shrine of the great detective. Members view late-nineteenth-century London, with its swirling fog and hansom cabs, as sacred territory. They study what they describe as 'the Canon' with forensic ardour, investigate the minutiae of Holmes's 'life', debate obscure textual conundrums, analyse the many glaring errors and inconsistencies in the stories, and dress up as characters. Apart from the holy books of the great religions, few texts can have been examined as microscopically as the Holmes canon. Thanks to Sherlockian 'scholarship', for example, we can know – if we care to – how many times Holmes is recorded as smiling (103).

More has been written *about* Holmes than any other fictional character – much more than Conan Doyle wrote himself – by those seeking to understand his enduring grip on public imagination as generation after generation fell under his spell. The fifty-four short stories and four novels have been translated into almost every living language, including Esperanto, have never been out of print and have been plagiarised, serialised, analysed and dramatised for screen, radio, television, stage and even a ballet.

Essential to every story is the symbiosis between the mercurial, eccentric, brilliant but bloodless detective and the affable and unflappable Doctor Watson, Holmes's 'rather stupid friend', as Conan Doyle once unkindly described him. Watson is the frequent butt of Holmes's sarcasm when he makes a simplistic deduction ('Excellent, Watson! You scintillate today') and cruelty ('After all you are only a general practitioner with very limited experience and mediocre qualifications'), but his loyalty never wavers. He is not rewarded until the very last series when, in 'The Adventure of the Three Garridebs', he is wounded and Holmes reveals his true feelings: 'My friend's wiry arms were round me and he was leading me to a chair. "You're not hurt, Watson? For God's sake say you are not hurt." It was worth a wound – it was worth many wounds – to know the depth of loyalty and love which lay behind that cold mask. The clear, hard eyes were dimmed for a moment, and the firm lips were shaking. For the one and only time I caught a glimpse of a great heart as well as of a great brain. All my years of humble but single-minded service culminated in that moment of revelation.'

Watson was the perfect foil for Holmes: their partnership has inspired more imitations than any other duo in literature and established an entire genre of detective fiction that endures today. Conan Doyle had no notion at the start that in Sherlock Holmes he was creating a colossus among cultural icons, yet when that realisation dawned it gave him no pleasure at all.

Doyle is a quintessentially Irish name, ranking twelfth in the list of the most common Irish surnames, said to be derived from the Gaelic *Dubh-Ghaill* ('dark foreigner'), the label the indigenous Celts gave to the Vikings who began settling in Ireland more than 1,000 years ago. The family of Arthur Conan Doyle, however, variously asserted its origins elsewhere. Conan Doyle himself first believed his ancestors came from Ulster, but he later took the view that the Irish Doyles were a cadet branch of the Staffordshire Doyles, who had taken part in the Anglo-Norman invasion of Ireland in 1169. In yet another version, the Doyles traced their roots to Pont d'Oilly near Rouen in France, and to the coat of arms adopted in the twelfth century by the Anglo-Norman family of d'Oilly, which had participated in the Norman invasion of Britain in 1066. An Alexander d'Oilly was indeed granted lands in County Wexford in 1333 by Edward III. Others within the family liked to boast that their earliest known ancestor was Foulkes D'Oyley, a comrade in arms of Richard Coeur de Lion.

Whatever their ancient origins, Doyles do not figure prominently in the early historical records of Ireland. In 1313 a Hercules Doyle was tried and hanged for burning down the manor of Fermoy and in 1642 a James Doyle of County Meath was accused of high treason. It was not until the eighteenth century that the Doyles began to make their mark on history with the emergence of six major generals – four of them baronets – a bishop, and the extraordinary dynasty founded by the painter and caricaturist John Doyle, born in Dublin in 1797, which would make significant contributions to the worlds of art and literature and become the only family in British history to warrant five separate entries in the *Dictionary of National Biography* within the space of three generations.

John Doyle's family had been impoverished by centuries of punitive laws against Roman Catholics and was finally dispossessed of its last small estate, in County Wexford, in 1762. The family fortunes plummeted; at the time of John's birth his father, James, was listed as a tailor living at 15 St Andrew Street. John's brother, James, would enter the priesthood and both his sisters became nuns, but John remained 'in the world', largely because he demonstrated, very early in life, a precocious artistic talent. He won his first medal at the age of 8 and studied at the Royal Dublin Society Drawing School, where he became a private pupil of the Italian landscape painter Gaspare Gabrielli, then based in Dublin, and the miniaturist John Comerford. The young John Doyle specialised in painting horses, an animal much loved, then as now, by the Irish, and in 1814, at the age of 17, he exhibited three portraits of horses at the Hibernian Society of Artists, receiving a number of commissions as a result. A keen horseman himself, he regularly rode out to hounds and could paint a horse from memory with extraordinary accuracy. Years later the Catholic journal the *Month* reported an occasion when Doyle commented on the similarity of a horse he had seen in England to one he had known many years earlier in Dublin; it turned out to be a direct lineal descendant of the Irish horse.

In February 1820, John Doyle, aged 23, married Marianne Conan, at St Andrew's Church in Dublin. The Conans believed themselves to be descended from the ancient ducal house of Brittany but, as with the Doyles, had fallen on hard times. Marianne's father was also listed as a tailor, living in Trinity Place, Dublin. (Some claim that the couple was invited to honeymoon at Arundel Castle, the home of the Duke of Norfolk, the first Catholic peer of the realm, but since the castle was uninhabited at that time it appears unlikely.) Within a year, Marianne had given birth to a daughter, Annette.

Dublin at that time could offer little to an ambitious young artist. Britain's attempt to solve the 'Irish problem' by the creation, in 1801, of the United Kingdom of Great Britain and Ireland had drastically reduced Dublin's status. It had been one of the wealthiest and liveliest cities in the British Empire, but the abolition of the Irish parliament marked the beginning of a long period of decline. John Doyle, like many of his compatriots, decided that a better future could be found across the water in London, which during the nineteenth century would be transformed into the world's largest city, the hub of a powerful empire and a global political, financial and trading centre.

The Doyles and their baby daughter probably arrived in London in 1822 and set up home in a rented house at 60 Berners Street, north of Soho, then a pleasant residential area popular with writers and artists. They brought few possessions, although they had contrived to retain some family heirlooms: silver plate engraved with the Doyle family crest, a sixteenth-century medical mortar also embossed with the Doyle arms and a half-length portrait of the Earl of Stafford, said to be by Van Dyck. (Thomas Wentworth, the Earl of Stafford, was a Protestant and one of Charles I's most influential advisers; he ruled Ireland on the King's behalf for seven years from 1633 but was executed in 1641 on trumped-up charges. How a staunchly Catholic family like the Doyles came to own a significant portrait of a prominent Protestant is unknown.)

The Regency period had drawn to an end when the Doyles arrived in London. In 1811, the recurring madness of King George III had led to his son, the Prince of Wales, being appointed Prince Regent. The short decade that took its name from his title amounted to the last gasp of Georgian exuberance before the staid morality of the Victorian era. The Prince, irreverently known as 'Prinny', set the tone with his louche and indolent lifestyle. His marriage to Caroline of Brunswick had been a disaster, and he cultivated a string of mistresses who grew older and fatter with him. When George III died in 1820, Prinny ascended to the throne as George IV and immediately tried to divorce his wife for adultery, leading to a scandalous trial which greatly entertained the nation and provided rich fodder for cartoonists.

Thanks largely to Prinny, the Regency era was the golden age of political caricature, exemplified by savage cartoons satirising his gross excesses. With no effective libel laws at that time, everything and everyone was fair game for famous caricaturists like Thomas Rowlandson and James Gillray, close friends who used their skills not just to entertain, but to influence public opinion and to campaign for social justice as well as to lampoon politicians, attack the morality of members of the court and highlight the contrast between royal extravagance and the plight of the poor. While Regency ladies showed off their finery at lavish balls, the theatre and the opera, and Regency dandies idled away their days in London clubs, agitation for political and social reform grew among the increasingly vocal working classes, mired in squalor and poverty in overcrowded, disease-ridden slums.

In Dublin the young John Doyle had enjoyed the occasional patronage of important figures such as the Marquis of Sligo, General Sir Edward Kerrison and the 2nd Earl Talbot, the Lord Lieutenant of Ireland. But in London he knew virtually no one. One of his first works was *The Life of the Race Horse* – a series of six pictures completed following a visit to Newmarket racecourse – after which he began painting portraits, mostly from memory, of prominent individuals. His first success was a portrait of the Duke of York on horseback.

But it soon became clear to Doyle that he would not be able to support a growing family – two sons, James William Edmund, born in 1822, and Richard, two years later – as a portrait painter. The popular art of caricature in journals and newspapers was an obvious alternative. And so, Doyle began visiting the public gallery of the House of Commons, taking with him a sketchbook. By 1827 he was selling political caricatures to a number of publications, notably *The Times*. His technique was completely different from the cruel, bawdy style of his Regency predecessors. Instead, he produced elegant, beautifully drawn and intelligent cartoons that satirised leading political and social figures without ever descending into coarse vulgarity. Avoiding any political affiliation, he was an amused spectator of the foibles of politicians, poking fun without malice or disfigurement; tellingly, he never made an enemy from his caricatures. 'My grandfather,' Arthur Conan Doyle would insist many years later, 'was a gentleman, drawing gentlemen for gentlemen, and the satire lay in the wit of the picture and not in the misdrawing of faces.'

Many of his pencil sketches are now considered the most lifelike representations in existence of the individuals portrayed. He signed his work 'H.B.', and guarded his anonymity jealously, insisted that his name never be revealed and delivered his drawings to the printer in a covered carriage to avoid detection. Thus, there was soon much speculation in fashionable drawing rooms about the identity of this intriguing new arrival, who was able to capture the essence of public figures with such skill and subtlety.

Doyle family lore held that when the news spread of a new set of H.B. lithographs, crowds would gather outside the publisher's offices and carriages jam the nearby streets. In July 1831 Thomas Macaulay, then a newly elected Member of Parliament, wrote to his sister that while waiting to see the Prime Minister Earl Grey at 10 Downing Street he was able to pass the time quite agreeably by looking through two portfolios of H.B. caricatures left in an ante-room. 'Earl Grey's face was in every print,' he noted. 'I was very much diverted. I had seen some of them before; but many were new to me and their merit is extraordinary.'[1]

His refusal to exploit his fame, or even reveal his identity, makes Doyle unjustly less well known than many of his contemporaries. The historian G. M. Trevelyan described him as 'an artist who has left to posterity a lively, exact and amusing record of the leading public figures in a great period of our domestic history'. The *Morning Post* reported that by the 1830s H.B.'s caricatures were no longer a luxury but a 'way of life'. Some 600 of his cartoons, representing a graphic political history of England in the early years of the reign of Queen Victoria, are now deposited in the Print Room at the British Museum.

In 1833 John and Marianne Doyle and their brood of children moved to 17 Cambridge Terrace, a large, comfortable house on a tree-lined avenue north of Hyde Park, now called Sussex Gardens. By then Annette, James and Richard had been joined by Henry Edward (born in 1827), Francis (1829), Adelaide (1831) and Charles (1832). Cambridge Terrace became the place where John Doyle entertained his growing circle of friends, among them the leading writers, politicians and artists of the day. Sir Walter Scott, Benjamin Disraeli, William Makepeace Thackeray, Dante Gabriel Rossetti, John Millais, Edwin Landseer and

Charles Dickens all graced the dinner table at one time or another. Charles Doyle left this account of a typical Sunday:

> The day was observed by all the children, great and small, Annette, James, Dick, Henry, Frank, Adelaide and myself going to Mass, celebrated at the French Chapel at 8 a.m. This in winter meant going from Cambridge Terrace up Edgware Road, down George Street, a couple of miles, often in the dark, and getting home to breakfast at 10. The after day was spent in perfect quiet until 8 in the evening when the camphor lamp and mole candles were lit in the drawing room, and guests began to arrive, often comprising the most distinguished literary and artistic men of London . . . Most delicious music was discoursed by Annette on the piano and James on the violincello till about 10 when the supper tray was laid, generally just cold meats and salad, followed by punch. We boys all retired when this appeared, but upstairs in bed I have often listened to indications of most delightful conversations till 1 or 2 . . .[2]

On 11 December 1839 Doyle's devoted wife, Marianne, died suddenly, at the age of 44, of a 'diseased heart', leaving Doyle to bring up their seven children alone, then aged between 7 and 18. Marianne's sister, Elizabeth, and brother, Michael Conan, a recently qualified barrister, were also living at 17 Cambridge Terrace at that time, and so Aunt Elizabeth and 18-year-old Annette took over the running of the household. Mainly tutored at home under their father's strict supervision, all the Doyle boys exhibited early artistic talent, manifested in the illustrated letters they were required to write their father once a week. Every Sunday all the children would gather for the 'show', at which they had to produce the week's artwork, usually a watercolour depicting some historical scene, which their father would review.

Despite an appearance of comfortable prosperity, the family lived close to the edge financially. Doyle's celebrity as 'H.B.' did not produce great riches, and there were occasions when Annette, who would eventually become a nun in the Society of the Daughters of the Heart of Mary in Kensington, would absent herself from the lunch table in order to ensure enough food to go around. Nevertheless, standards were rigorously maintained and the boys were coached in the gentle-manly pursuits of fencing, dancing and music.

Perhaps to help get over the loss of his mother, 15-year-old Richard ('Dicky') began work a few weeks after her death on an illustrated journal for the year 1840, now preserved in the British Museum. 'Dick Doyle's Journal of 1840' is a delight, packed with wry anecdotes and whimsical pen-and-ink vignettes depicting daily life at home and family outings to the opera, concerts, the zoo, the Royal Academy, the National Gallery and the Tower of London, along with sharply observed aspects of life in the capital early in Queen Victoria's reign. One illustration shows the three oldest boys, James, Dick and Henry, at their regular dancing lesson, which they all detested: they prance ineptly in front of their fiddle-playing teacher while their elder sister, Annette, looks on impassively. Also included is an account of a pantomime staged by Francis in which he played all the parts and which 'called forth such pangs of merriment from the wit displayed therein which was all brewed on the spot by the spirited manager, that I don't know what might not have happened if a supper had not been announced'.

Even after the death of their mother entertainment and laughter seemed ever present for the children at 17 Cambridge Terrace. Dicky's illustrated letter to his father, dated 17 July 1842, described a family concert which included pianoforte recitals by Annette and Adelaide, Dicky on the violin and a song from 'Master Charles Doyle' who 'entered, music in hand, to chant his favourite melody "Goodnight love, goodnight"', and *Non piu mesta,* arranged for two performers on the piano, played by 'Master Frank and Miss Adelaide'. This last 'trans-ported the audience, and so modest was the young gentleman [Francis] that he more than once made as though he was going to leave off in the middle of it, but being encouraged by the enraptured spectators he was prevailed to go on'.[3] Sadly, both Adelaide and Francis would be dead within a few years, Adelaide of consumption at the age of 13 and Francis before he reached 16 (the cause is not known).

Soon after *Punch* magazine was founded in 1841, both Richard and his father began contributing cartoons. Launched as a 'defender of the oppressed and a radical scourge of all authority', *Punch* was the mouthpiece of the emerging middle class and perfectly suited the

Doyles' satirical talents. Entertaining and provocative, it campaigned against the high cost of the monarchy, pointing out that Queen Victoria's consort, Prince Albert, enjoyed an annual allowance of £30,000 at a time when the total budget for educating the poor in England was only £10,000. Politicians were also a popular target of the magazine's caustic wit, particularly the Prime Minister, Sir Robert Peel, routinely referred to as 'Sir Rhubarb Pill'.

In 1843 Dick Doyle illustrated Thomas Hood's powerful poem 'The Song of the Shirt', a stinging indictment of capitalism and of the growing inequality between rich and poor. By 1848 Dick was producing almost a third of all the cartoons in the magazine, and the following year he designed the famous front cover featuring Mr Punch and his dog, Toby, which remained unaltered until well after the Second World War. But in 1850 a serious editorial rift led to his departure: a devout Roman Catholic like his father, he resigned in protest at what he perceived as *Punch*'s hostility to the Pope. The decision that year by Pope Pius IX to create an archbishopric and twelve bishoprics in England had been interpreted as 'papal aggression' by certain sections of the public and the media, including *Punch,* which energetically championed the Protestant cause.

Dick was particularly incensed by a cartoon portraying the then Prime Minister, Lord John Russell, as David, slaying Nicholas Wiseman, the future leader of the Roman Catholic Church in England, as Goliath. Wiseman was a close friend of the family. Dick refused all entreaties to stay on the staff, sacrificing a handsome salary of £800 a year. Thackeray was among those who tried to persuade him to change his mind, arguing that *The Times* had mounted similar attacks without its Catholic journalists resigning, but Dicky rebuffed the approach, claiming that it was 'all very well in *The Times*, but not in *Punch* . . . *The Times* is a monarchy whereas *Punch* is a republic.' After leaving the magazine he concentrated on book illustrations for Dickens, John Ruskin and Thackeray among others, and painting in watercolours: his romantic and fanciful pictures of elves and fairies being hugely popular to Victorian eyes.

Dicky was also a well-liked member of the 'Moray Minstrels', a group of artists, musicians and writers who met regularly at Moray Lodge in Campden Hill, the home of Arthur Lewis, a wealthy merchant and patron of the arts. It was probably at one such meeting that Dicky met the beautiful Blanche Stanley, with whom he fell deeply in love. He was heartbroken when, in 1851, she married the Earl of Airlie, and she appears in many of his pictures, notably his illustrations for Thackeray's *The Newcomes*. Dicky never reconciled himself to the loss and never married. On his death, in 1883, he was described as a 'singularly sweet and noble type of English gentleman',[4] this despite his strong Irish antecedents.

Richard's surviving brothers were similarly talented. James William Edmund Doyle was the scholar of the family. A tall, stooped figure with a black beard, and a frequent visitor to Holland House in Kensington, the home of the 3rd Baron Holland and the intellectual headquarters for English liberals and reformers, his studious demeanour earned him the soubriquet 'The Priest'. Modest and retiring, James was a respected historian and an expert on heraldry, as well as an artist. His best-known painting was *A Literary Party at Sir Joshua Reynolds*, and his colour illustrations for his own *A Chronicle of England, BC 55–AD 1485* are among his finest works. Towards the end of his life he spent thirteen years researching and writing *The Official Baronage of England*, the authorised textbook of the College of Arms, but died, in 1892, before he could complete it.

Henry Edward Doyle began his career as an art critic and painter – he was commissioned to paint frescoes of *The Last Judgement* for the Roman Catholic church in Lancaster – but achieved greatest prominence as Director of the National Gallery of Ireland in Dublin. Henry's flair, judgement and eye for a bargain played a major role in building the Gallery's present collection. He bought works by Giovanni Bellini, Antonio Allegri da Correggio, Jacob van Ruisdael and the English portrait painters Joshua Reynolds and Thomas Gainsborough before their reputations and prices soared. With an annual grant never exceeding £1,000, Henry turned the National Gallery of Ireland into a major institution, comparing favourably with any gallery in Europe. Three of his own pictures are included in its permanent collection – two portraits of his friend Cardinal Wiseman and a chalk drawing of his father, who bore a remarkable resemblance to the Duke of Wellington. (The old man was occasionally mistaken for the 'Iron Duke' when driving through Hyde Park in a carriage and greatly enjoyed being saluted by the populace.)

John Doyle died in January 1868. An obituary in the *Art Journal* noted his prepossessing manner and innate amiability, his noble cast of feature and his great repute ever ensuring him a welcome. 'There were few men,' it concluded, 'to whose sound sense and assured taste an appeal could be more safely made. He was one whom to know, even but little, was insensibly to esteem; to know much, to love much. In a word, he was from the hands of nature a rare gentleman . . .'

Charles Altamont Doyle, born on 25 March 1832, was the most enigmatic of John Doyle's talented sons. He undoubtedly suffered from being the youngest member of the family and from a sense of inferiority exacerbated by the brilliance of his three eldest brothers. His father, too, held out less hope for Charles. Doyle was in the habit of writing to the prime minister to put forward his ideas for improvements in public life, and would add news of his family. In a letter to Sir Robert Peel, dated 22 January 1842, he noted that while all of his five sons 'showed the strongest taste for the arts', it was the three eldest who 'evinced the most unequivocal promise'.[5] Charles was naturally close to Adelaide and Francis, who were only a few years older, and their premature deaths greatly affected him. Nevertheless, he had a happy childhood, enjoyed fishing with his friends on Paddington Canal and the Thames, and was very fond of animals. He had his own dog, Prinny, and a songbird, and arranged for a monkey to be sent to him from Ceylon although it died en route.

Perhaps believing that Charles was not likely to succeed as an artist, his father arranged for him to take a menial job in the civil service, at the age of 17, as one of three assistants to Robert Matheson, Her Majesty's Clerk of Works in Edinburgh, at an annual salary of £180. Accommodation was found for him in the heart of the elegant New Town in a house at 8 Scotland Street owned by Catherine Foley, an Irish Catholic widow; a local priest was charged with safeguarding his 'young morals and budding faith'. Charles seemed, at first, to be perfectly happy, writing enthusiastic letters home, illustrated, of course, with pen-and-ink drawings, about his work and his life in Edinburgh and 'interesting observations on that Scottish society, rough, hard-drinking and kindly, into which he had been precipitated at a dangerously early age, especially for one with his artistic temperament'.

In the summer of 1850, Charles, then 18, was proudly in charge of raising the flag on the roof of the Palace of Holyroodhouse, where his office was located, during Queen Victoria's visit to the city. Some biographers have claimed that Charles was responsible for designing a new stained-glass window for Glasgow Cathedral, but there is no confirmation of this in the cathedral records. Instead, his duties were largely confined to writing letters and making fair drawings; about the only evidence of Charles's contribution to the Department of Works are the drawings he prepared for a fountain in the forecourt of Holyroodhouse.

In July 1855, when he was 22, Charles married his landlady's 17-year-old daughter at St Mary's Roman Catholic Cathedral. Mary Josephine Foley was small and pretty, with fair hair parted in the middle, and had been partly educated in France. Catherine Foley did not entirely approve of the match, since she considered her daughter to be too young and Charles, a humble civil servant, to be unworthy of her, although he had at least gentility of birth, Irish parentage and Catholicism in his favour. Catherine Foley was born in Kilkenny in 1809, the daughter of William Pack, a grocer and wine merchant. She was inordinately proud of her heritage: the Packs, Protestants, claimed to trace their roots back to Oliver Cromwell's settling army; more recently, General Sir Denis Pack had commanded the Scottish Brigade at Waterloo. In the seventeenth century the Reverend Richard Pack married into the Percy family, allegedly establishing a link with the Plantagenet kings and the Dukes of Northumberland, although no documents exist supporting Catherine's claim to be descended from the Percys. Catherine was running a girls' boarding school with her sister in Kilkenny when she met and married William Foley, a doctor and graduate of Trinity College, Dublin, in 1835. Since the Foleys were a staunchly Catholic family – Foleys had been living at Lismore in County Wexford since the reign of Queen Elizabeth I – Catherine was obliged to renounce her faith and convert to Catholicism. But in 1841 her husband died suddenly, at the age of 33, leaving her with two young daughters to support. She returned to Kilkenny where she once again opened a girls' school, but it was not a success and in 1847 she took the courageous decision to start a new life in Edinburgh, then growing rapidly as Irish immigrants fled the potato famine. She started an agency supplying governesses and took in lodgers to help make ends meet. Despite her straitened circumstances, Catherine Foley clung tenaciously to past family glories, no doubt to compensate for present difficulties, and steeped her daughter in family history; thus Mary Doyle inherited in full measure her mother's pride in their lineage.

After their marriage, Charles and Mary lived for a time with Mary's mother before moving into a succession of rented apartments. They wasted no time starting a family and their first child, Ann Mary Frances Conan, known as Annette, was born in July 1856. Eight more children would follow, two of whom died in infancy. With so many mouths to feed on so little money, life was far from easy. Mary, strong-willed and intelligent, was losing the battle to keep up appearances as her highly-strung husband became increasingly disengaged from family life.

A gentle, melancholic figure, tortured by headaches and given to bouts of depression and periods of morbid introspection, Charles possessed the Doyle family charm in full measure, yet was frequently described as 'dreamy and remote', 'apathetic', 'naturally philosophic' or 'unworldly'. While he painted in his spare time, he was rarely able to sell his work, preferring to give it away rather than haggle over a price. So it was that the family struggled to survive on his salary, which never rose above £250 a year, plus an occasional bonus from book illustrations. Between 1858 and 1877 he contributed pictures to the *Illustrated Times, London Society* and *Graphic*, and illustrated a number of books, among them an edition of Daniel Defoe's *The Life and Surprising Adventures of Robinson Crusoe*, published in 1861, but earning a living as a full-time artist always hovered frustratingly out of reach.

Charles's unhappiness with his lot – exiled in Edinburgh, stuck in a dreary, dead-end job – can hardly have been helped by frequent letters from his brother Richard, describing his glamorous life in literary and artistic circles in London. 'I dare say,' Dick wrote, 'you heard of Smith and Elder [publishers] asking me to dinner to meet the author of "Jane Eyre," who is a delicate-looking but clever woman, about thirty, named Miss Bronte . . . Evans asked me to a Newsvendors' Benevolent Society dinner, Chas. Dickens in the chair, who made an admirable speech, Luck, Phiz, Lemon, Leigh, Etc., being present, which party and Mr Peter Cunningham afterwards went with Dickens to the Rainbow Tavern in Fleet Street and partook of burnt Sherry and Anchovy toast until a late hour . . .'

It was a life Charles could only imagine. He occasionally wrote to his sister Annette to ask about the possibility of getting a job in London and sometimes talked about taking off for Australia to dig for gold, but he was in a rut and he knew it. Pathologically withdrawn, neurotic, dogged by disappointment and a sense of failure, burdened by a house full of children he could barely afford to feed, Charles turned for solace to the bottle. In a city which nurtured a hard-drinking culture, his descent was rapid. Whisky was the drinkers' favourite tipple in Scotland, but Charles preferred burgundy and like all alcoholics was prepared to sink to any depth to find money for drink, even raiding the children's money boxes. When he was only 30 years old he suffered such a severe attack of delirium tremens that he was incapacitated and put on half pay for almost a year. Mary would later tell doctors that for months at a time her husband could only crawl, 'was perfectly idiotic [and] could not tell his own name'.[6]

Thereafter he lurched from one drunken crisis to another. In his desperation to procure alcohol, he not only secretly carried away everything of value in the family home but plunged them into debt by ordering goods from local tradespeople that he instantly converted into money. Such was his craving that one night he drank a bottle of furniture varnish.

After toiling for more than twenty-five years without promotion in the Office of Works, Charles was obliged to retire in June 1876, with a pension of £150 a year. It was noted on his records – very generously – that he had never been absent from work and that he had discharged his duties with 'diligence and fidelity'.

The following year he had a children's book, *Our Trip to Blunderland*, published and continued picking up occasional work as an illustrator, but while his occupation was listed in the city rolls as 'artist', his preoccupation was where to find the next drink. He became increasingly unstable, once stripping off his clothes and trying to sell them in the street.

In 1881 Charles and Mary Doyle effectively separated when he was institutionalised. Family and friends convinced her that he had to be removed from the home for his own good, and he was sent to

Blairerno House, a genteel, but secure, home for inebriates on the outskirts of the village of Drumlithie in Aberdeenshire. Blairerno advertised its services regularly in the *Medical Directory*: 'INTEM-PERANCE – Home for Gentlemen in Country House in the North of Scotland. Of very old standing. Home Comforts. Good Shooting, Trout-fishing and Cricket'. Charles joined seventeen male residents, among them a landowner, a tobacco manufacturer, a couple of retired army and naval officers, an MA from Edinburgh University and a music teacher.

Charles did not take well either to sobriety or confinement and frequently tried to escape. In May 1885 there was an 'incident' at Blair-erno: Charles managed to find alcohol, became violent when restrained by staff and broke a window. He was detained on criminal charges of violence and damage, and David Forbes, the owner, perhaps anxious to rid himself of this troublesome inmate, decided Charles had become a danger to himself and made arrangements to have him certified. There was no need to consult the family: under Scottish Lunacy Laws a patient destined for an asylum was required to be examined by two doctors, and, if their recommendation was confirmed by a local sheriff, committal proceedings could go ahead. Charles told one of the examining doctors that he was 'getting messages from the unseen world' and that God had told him to 'go away'; both signed certificates for the sheriff confirming 'the said Charles Altamont Doyle is a lunatic'.

Charles was committed to the Royal Lunatic Asylum at Montrose, sixteen miles to the south, under a detention order. When he was examined on arrival he had no memory and was found to be very confused and bewildered, hearing voices and convinced he was about to die. Years of excessive drinking had almost certainly resulted in brain damage. Mary Doyle certainly believed that if released he would drink himself to death and resigned herself to him remaining in a secure hospital, protected from himself. Six months later he had the first of a series of epileptic fits. Epilepsy was then little understood; it was untreatable and carried a considerable social stigma.

In some ways Charles was lucky – Montrose Royal Lunatic Asylum was the first of eight enlightened institutions built in Scotland mainly by public subscription to provide accommodation and treatment for mentally incapacitated patients desperately in need of protection and expert care. They established an unparalleled reputation for excellence in every regard and were far ahead of their time in the treatment of insanity. Not many years earlier, Londoners had been paying to watch the antics of those incarcerated in Bedlam.

Charles would remain a reluctant resident of Sunnyside House at Montrose Royal Lunatic Asylum for the next seven years, spending much of his time painting and drawing. He contributed numerous poems, articles and illustrations to the asylum magazine, the *Sunnyside Chronicle*, and painted a self-portrait, in watercolours, in which he is seated, in a pensive mood, while sinister and ethereal creatures writhe around him.

One of the haunting sketchbooks that he kept while at Sunnyside came to light in 1977. It had materialised in a job lot of books at a house sale in the New Forest; a London dealer recognised it as a major find and it was subsequently published as a book, *The Doyle Diary*. Rambling notes, captions and puns in Charles's neat handwriting accompany the surreal watercolours, quirky pen-and-ink cartoons and fantastical flights of fancy. They offer a moving insight into his tortured mind and terrible predicament, since he clearly believed he had been incarcerated unjustly. On the first page, dated 8 March 1889, he wrote in pencil: 'Keep steadily in view that this book is ascribed wholly to the produce of a MADMAN. Whereabouts would you say was the deficiency of intellect or depraved taste? If in the whole book you can find a single evidence of either, mark it and record it against me.'

That he felt he had been abandoned by his family was evident in another note, dated 22 May: 'I am not – well, I will put off writing what I was going to say till tomorrow – what I wanted to say was that I have now done a great many Vols. of ideas, but I am kept ignorant of what becomes of them. I asked them to be all sent to Mrs Doyle and submitted to publishers, but as I have never had a single book or drawing acknowledged by her or other relatives I can only conclude that they see no profit in them. In these circumstances I think it would be better that these books should be entrusted to the Lunacy Commissioners to show them the sort of intellect they think it right to imprison as mad . . .' Later he again asked for his sketchbooks to be sent to his 'poor, dear wife Mary' to show her he was thinking of her. 'God bless her and the rest of them,' he wrote, 'who I dare say all forget me now.' He added sadly, 'I don't them.'

Fairies and elves predominate in his sketchbook paintings. Often they prance among meticulously executed drawings of local flora and fauna, or confront animals and birds, disturbingly portrayed much larger than life. His pen-and-ink self-portraits reveal a tall man with a long, black beard and wire-rimmed spectacles; in one he is shown extending his right hand to the Grim Reaper, while an angel tries to draw him back. Death preyed constantly on his mind: he drew himself lying on a chaise longue in the grip of a 'tremendous headache' with an angel hovering above him. And his misery and frustration are apparent as he greets a skeletal, scythe-bearing figure of Death with a shake of the hand and the caption: 'I do believe that to a Catholic there is *Nothing* so sweet in life as leaving it.'

On other pages despair is tempered by affectionate doodles and verbal and visual puns which evince a childish sense of fun. A cleaner scrubbing the floor is captioned: 'Don't I wish I could cleanse my ways as she does here? Soapeariorly . . .' On a watercolour of a sycamore leaf he notes, 'In doing this I turne [*sic*] over a new leaf and no mistake. Altho' it's sicamore [*sic*] drawing more of it would make any one sicker.' A young girl shown with a sprig of fir sprouting from her head is 'A new branch of hairdressing', and a golfer using his elongated nose as a putter is captioned: 'Who nose what a Feature of Golf this would be.'

A little cartoon entitled 'Mary, my ideal home ruler' shows him sitting on a stool and gazing adoringly up at his wife, busy with her sewing. The subtitle says, 'No repeal of the union proposed in this case.' It is evident he was aware what was happening in the wider world, since the issue of Home Rule for Ireland was dominating British politics; here the subtitle obviously referred to his wistful hopes that his marriage remained intact.

In a long entry dated 5 June 1889, he returned once again to the anguished theme of his abandonment by family, friends and society:

> I am certain if my many Vols of, well, I'll say not serious work, were organised into some form submittable to the public they would tickle the taste of innumerable men like myself, and be the source of much money which I should like to bestow on my daughters, but imprisoned under most depressing restrictions, what can I do?

I believe I am branded as mad solely from the narrow
Scotch misconception of jokes. If Charles Lamb or Tom Hood
had been caught, they would have been treated as I am, and
the latter would probably have never written 'the Song of the
Shirt'.

He described himself as a 'harmless gentleman' and complained
bitterly about his continued incarceration. Charles's medical notes,
however, charted his inexorable mental deterioration: his memory
had virtually gone, he was obsessed by portents of death, he frequently
lay down as if to die and hallucinated that he was in hell, surrounded
by devils. He took refuge in religion – on one occasion he spent half
a day kneeling with his prayer book in the asylum's billiard room.

In January 1891 with his physical health declining – he was by now
having severe epileptic fits every few weeks – Charles Doyle was transferred for a 'change of scene' to the Royal Edinburgh Asylum as a
private patient. Records show that he was extremely thin, with greying
hair; he had serious memory loss and still suffered from hallucina-
tions. He spent his days sketching or reading religious books. He had
very little contact with his family – a letter from his wife to the superintendent refers to her 'poor, dear husband' but makes it clear that
she knew little of his condition and had not seen him for some time.
Sixteen months later he was transferred to the Crichton Royal Lunatic
Asylum, Dumfries, where a diagnosis of 'dementia' was recorded.
On his admission Mary Doyle wrote to the superintendent, Dr J.
Rutherford on 3 December 1892, revealing a well of affection for her
husband, despite the damage his alcoholism had done to the family.
She listed his symptoms as an alcoholic, including mendacity, but
stressed that he was a virtuous and decent man and that 'to know
him was to love him'.[7]

An entry by a doctor in his case notes on 3 October 1893 offered
a poignant glimpse into his essentially gentle character: 'Pleasant and
easily pleased. Solemnly presented me with an empty paper which
he assured me contained gold dust and was a reward for professional
attendance. He said he had collected it in the sunlight on the bed.'[8]

Charles Doyle died at Crichton seven days later, aged 61. Cause
of death was noted as epilepsy of 'many years standing'. A generous

obituary in the *Scotsman*, published on 23 October, mentioned both his celebrated family and his artistic talent and continued: 'Personally he was a likeable man, genial, entertaining and amusing in conversation. Possessed of a fertile imagination, it was always enjoyable to listen to his anecdotes. He was a great reader, and was in consequence well informed. His abilities and gentlemanly manner ensured to him a cordial welcome wherever he went, and few literary or artistic homes were without his occasional visit. Those who knew him will ever remember him with a warm and kindly thought.'

There was not a word about his years spent incarcerated in mental institutions, and only a brief mention that his son was 'the able novelist, Dr A. Conan Doyle'.

CHAPTER 2

CHILDHOOD

RTHUR IGNATIUS CONAN DOYLE was born at 11 Picardy Place, Edinburgh, on 22 May 1859 and baptised two days later in St Mary's, the city's massive Roman Catholic cathedral virtually adjoining his family home. His godmother was his great-aunt Catherine Doyle, a nun in the Presentation of Our Blessed Lady order in Killarney with the name of Mother Ignatius; his godfather was his great-uncle Michael Conan, now a literary, music and theatre critic based in Paris.

It was not a bad time to be born. The Victorian era, epitomised by national confidence and optimism, was approaching its zenith, and Britain had become not only the most industrialised nation in Europe but the possessor of a great and growing empire encircling the globe. Prosperity did not, however, filter down to the working classes. The old medieval centre of Edinburgh had long been notorious for its slums – Thomas Carlyle called it 'this accursed, stinking, reeky mass of stones and lime and dung' – and although the New Town, a stately city of grey stone, had been erected at the end of the eighteenth century, the overcrowded Old Town, within the city walls, remained a refuge for the poor, mainly Irish, and was given over to rats. 'Even in the chief thoroughfares,' Robert Louis Stevenson, a student at Edinburgh University, reported, 'Irish washings flutter at the windows, and the pavements are encumbered with loiterers.'[1] Disease, inevitably, was endemic and in 1866, when Arthur was 7, there were at least three outbreaks of cholera.

Never mind she already had a daughter, Annette (a second daughter, Catherine Amelia Angela, born on 22 April 1858, died at

the age of six months from hydrocephalus), Mary Doyle made no
bones that Arthur, her first son, was her favourite child: he was a
happy, rewarding baby, who smiled easily and cried little. Annette and
Arthur were the only two children to be given the compound surname
of Conan Doyle, and it would survive for only two generations:
Annette died young and childless, and Arthur's sons produced no
children to carry on the name. Not long after Arthur's birth, the family
moved to Wilson's Park, Portobello, then a small seaside resort outside
Edinburgh, where Mary Doyle's fourth child, a daughter also called
Mary, died at the age of two in the summer of 1863 after an attack
of laryngitis.

Diminutive Mary Doyle, like her mother fiercely proud of her
heritage, drummed into her son her fervent belief that they had
aristocratic ancestors and schooled him in the traditions and lore of
a bygone age, of chivalry and heraldry and knights in shining armour.
She would frequently challenge him to emblazon heraldic shields
and he could soon provide every detail. It was a welcome escape
from the spartan conditions, anxiety and genteel poverty in which
they lived, on an income that could barely support a family of five,
and provided the small boy with a sense of pride in his family's
history when their grinding daily struggle to survive offered no such
sense. Arthur never forgot sitting on the kitchen table while his
mother busied herself cleaning the hearth and expounding on the
past glories of her family and its connections with the Plantagenets,
the Dukes of Brittany and the Percys of Northumberland: 'I would
sit swinging my knickerbockered legs, swelling with pride until my
waistcoat was as tight as a sausage skin, as I contemplated the gulf
which separated me from all other little boys who swang their legs
upon tables.'[2]

Mary was also a natural storyteller and both thrilled and terrified
her children on long winter evenings around the fireside. 'In my early
childhood,' Arthur recalled, 'as far back as I can remember anything
at all, the vivid stories which she would tell me stand out so clearly
they obscure the real facts of my life . . . She had, I remember, an art
of sinking her voice to a horror-stricken whisper when she came to
a crisis in her narrative, which makes me goose-fleshy now when I
think of it. I am sure, looking back, that it was in attempting to

emulate these stories of my childhood that I first began weaving dreams myself.'³

In the light of their different circumstances, visits by Charles Doyle's more successful brothers can only have been an embarrassing ordeal. On one occasion Uncle Dicky is said to have brought with him the white-haired figure of William Makepeace Thackeray, author of *Vanity Fair*, who supposedly dandled Arthur on his knee and had his gold repeater watch strike one hundred for the little boy's entertainment. (It is on record that Thackeray visited the publisher John Blackwood in Edinburgh in 1859, but Arthur would have been a babe in arms; it might have been Annette the great man dandled on his knee.) Uncle Dicky drew a charming pencil portrait of Arthur at age 5, showing a serious child with huge dark eyes.

In 1865 Arthur posed for a formal *carte de visite* photograph with his father. Wearing a too-big knickerbocker suit with a white lace collar and boots, his hair parted in the middle, he holds his cap in one hand and stares solemnly at the camera, while his black-bearded father, in a three-quarter-length coat with light-coloured trousers, leans languidly against an aspidistra stand, his shiny top hat in one hand and his son's gloved hand in the other. It was a picture of pre-eminent Victorian respectability: no one looking at that photograph would ever have guessed that the elegant gentleman was already struggling with the alcoholism.

It was the indomitable Mary Doyle who counted the pennies, somehow ensured that there was always food on the table, that the children had clothes and boots to wear and that their father's drinking did not blight their young lives. Dicky described her as having 'fighting damn-your-eyes spirit' and not caring 'two pence for anybody's opinion'.⁴ As they moved from one dingy tenement apartment to another, it was Mary who tried to make a home, arranged beds with clean sheets, cheered the bairns by telling them stories around the fireside. And when her husband arrived home at night stinking of wine, she submitted, like a dutiful wife, to his advances, thus ensuring that she was almost continually pregnant.

If there was a bright spot in her existence, it was her beloved son, the focus of all her hopes. She loved her daughters, of course, but it was Arthur who was special. Encouraged by his mother, he learned to read early and soon discovered Sir Walter Scott's *Ivanhoe*, which he read over and over again, and the rollicking adventure stories of Captain Mayne Reid and Robert Michael Ballantyne. Once he started reading he could not stop. He devoured one book after another and so voracious was his appetite that his local library was obliged to inform him the rules stipulated that books could not be changed more than twice a day.

Long before his teens, in the company of Ballantyne and Reid, he had crossed every ocean, known the Rockies like the back of his hand, hidden under water breathing through a reed, shot rapids, leapt on the back of a charging buffalo, run a mile along a stream to throw bloodhounds off his scent, feigned madness to escape torture, dispatched any number of Indian braves in hand-to-hand combat, crossed the prairies with his trusty small-bore Kentucky rifle, strapped his moccasins on back to front to conceal his tracks, fallen from the topsail of a square rigger in the Pacific . . . there was scarcely an adventure he had not encountered in his imagination.

So it was perhaps inevitable that Arthur would try his hand at writing: his first attempt, at the age of 6, was a yarn about a Bengal tiger being pursued into a cave. He sent it, with enormous pride, to his godfather Michael Conan in Paris. 'It was written,' Conan Doyle later remembered,

> upon foolscap paper, in what might be called a fine bold hand – four words to the line – and was illustrated by marginal pen-and-ink sketches by the author. There was a man in it, and there was a tiger. I forget which was the hero, but it didn't matter much, for they became blended into one about the time when the tiger met the man. I was a realist in the age of the Romanticists. I described at some length, both verbally and pictorially, the untimely end of that wayfarer. But when the tiger had absorbed him, I found myself slightly embarrassed as to how my story was to go on. 'It is very easy to get people into scrapes, and very hard to get them out again,' I remarked, and I have often had cause to repeat the precocious aphorism of my childhood. On this occasion the situation was beyond me, and my book, like my man, was engulfed in my tiger.[5]

Arthur was enrolled at Newington Academy in Edinburgh at the age of 7. He would describe the spartan regime as being Dickensian, with a 'pock-marked, one-eyed rascal' of a teacher who beat the boys frequently. Arthur had been sent by his mother to stay with Mary Burton, a family friend, at Liberton Bank House, two miles from the city centre, and while the official reason for the move was that it was closer to the school, Mary Doyle undoubtedly wanted to protect her son from the increasing difficulties of their family life. Mary Burton was the sister of a prominent lawyer, bibliophile and historian John Hill Burton, whose son, William, would become one of Arthur's best friends. The boys fished together in the Braid Brae, a small, fast-moving stream at the bottom of the garden and William introduced his friend to the new science of photography. (Arthur would later dedicate his second novel, *The Firm of Girdlestone*, to him.) While Arthur was living with Mary Burton he acquired another sister, born in February 1866, and christened Caroline Mary Burton (Lottie) to mark Mary Doyle's gratitude to her friend.

Arthur stayed at Liberton Bank House for about two years, but rejoined his family when they moved again, to the top-floor apartment at 3 Sciennes Hill Place, a narrow, gloomy cul-de-sac, where the tall grey stone townhouses on one side of the street had been converted into apartments for poorer families, while the more prosperous folk lived in comfortable villas on the other, known as Sciennes Gardens. The Doyles' rent was £19 a year, only two-thirds of what they had been paying at Picardy Place, but a necessary economy when the head of the household valued alcohol above his responsibilities as a husband and father. The evils of the demon drink would be a recurring theme in his son's fiction, although Arthur never voiced a word of criticism of his father, rather sympathy that he had somehow missed the opportunities enjoyed by the rest of the family. Mary Doyle gave birth to their sixth child, Constance Amelia Monica (Connie), on 4 March 1868.

When a feud developed between the poor boys in Sciennes Hill Place and the boys in Sciennes Gardens, it was decided to settle it with a fist fight between one champion from either side. This was most likely Arthur's idea and as he was tall and strong for his age he was elected to represent the Sciennes Hill Place boys. He did not record who won, only that it took place in one of the villa gardens and was 'an excellent contest of many rounds'. He returned home greatly dishevelled and with a black eye, but when his mother commented on it retorted indignantly: 'You just go across and look at Eddie Tulloch's eye!'[6]

Always ready to put up his fists – on one occasion he was almost knocked senseless by an assailant wielding a heavy boot concealed in a bag – Arthur was acting out, in the grimy streets of the inner city, the heroic stories to which his mother had introduced him and which he later absorbed from books. Despite the brawling he remained his mother's boy and promised her that he would look after her once he could do so. 'When you are old, Mammie,' he liked to tell her, 'you shall have a velvet dress and gold glasses and sit in comfort by the fire.' It must have been an alluring prospect for a woman with a brood of children, very little money and a husband increasingly detached from reality. 'My father, I fear, was of little help to her,' Arthur would write in his autobiography, 'for his thoughts were always in the clouds and he had no appreciation of the realities of life.'

Michael Conan at least took his responsibilities as Arthur's god-father seriously and frequently sent him books in French. 'My dearest Laddie,' he wrote in a letter accompanying a book about the kings and queens of France, 'You will find gratification in studying these attentively, and I feel sure that, with the instruction of your dearest Mama who is so well acquainted with the French language, you will, at no distant time, become acquainted with it and thus read the text . . . Believe me to be, my dearest Laddie, your loving Godfather, M. E. Conan.'

———————◆———————

It was Conan who advised, not without some reservation, that the boy should be sent to a Jesuit school. For Catholic families who wanted their sons to go to public school in England there were really only two choices: Downside, run by Benedictines, and Stonyhurst in Lancashire, originally founded by Jesuits in St Omer, France, in 1593. The fees at both institutions would have been a serious drain on their meagre resources, but Stonyhurst offered Arthur a scholarship, waiving the £50 annual fee, perhaps in the hope that he would join the priest-hood. On 15 September 1867, at the age of 8, Arthur was enrolled at Hodder House, the preparatory school for Stonyhurst, some ten miles distant. Overcome with homesickness, he cried in the train all the way from Edinburgh to the border. At Preston station, he was met by a black-robed priest and driven, along with a handful of other boys, to the school.

For the next eight years he would usually only see his family during the annual six weeks of summer holidays, yet his devotion to his mother never wavered and he wrote to her frequently – a habit he would continue for the remainder of her life. His cheerful, uncom-plaining letters, now at the British Library, indicate that he settled in well at Hodder and chronicle his growing maturity. Although Arthur, in deference to his Irish antecedents, called his mother 'Mammy' and among the children she was always known as 'the Mam', he adopted a more formal style in his letters, usually addressing her as 'My dear Mama' and ending, stiffly, 'I remain your affectionate son, A. C. Doyle.'

While at Hodder House he wrote excitedly to tell her he had attended his first communion. The letter, written with a quill pen on blue paper with hand-drawn lines, begins in a handsome, if uncer-tain, copperplate but soon deteriorates into an untidy childish scrawl: 'My dear Mama, I hope you are quite well. I am glad to say that I have made my first communion. Oh Mama, I cannot express the joy that I felt on the happy day to rieceive [sic] my creator with [sic] my breast. I shall never thought [sic] I live a 100 years I shall never forget that day . . .' His precocious devotion to his faith would not endure the dour rigours of the Jesuit regime at Stonyhurst.

He was lucky to have as his form master a kindly monk, the Reverend Francis Cassidy, who was liked by all the boys. Cassidy loved to develop his pupils' potential, particularly if their interests were in creative writing, and encouraged Arthur's first attempts at poetry. Arthur retained a great affection for him long after he had left school and sent him copy of *Songs of Action*, his first book of verse, published in 1898, with a wry covering letter suggesting it was little more mature than his earlier efforts, although 'You might find your-self in the dilemma which I was in lately when a young author sent me a volume of poems and essays (both very bad) with a direct request for my opinion of its merits. I told him in reply that "He was equally at home in prose and in verse."' Arthur's two years at Hodder were not unhappy. The teachers, he later noted, were 'more human than Jesuits normally are'. It would be different at Stonyhurst.

Jesuits fleeing from the Napoleonic wars in 1794 first established Stonyhurst school in a ramshackle medieval building in Clitheroe, Lancashire, which had been unoccupied for more than half a century. In the ensuing years it was only half-heartedly repaired, as the monks anticipated an eventual return to France. Approached by a long straight drive, with two towers of dark and menacing aspect, it might well have been the model for Baskerville Hall, the setting for Arthur's most famous novel, *The Hound of the Baskervilles*. Until 1851 there were no proper bathing facilities, the boys washing outside under a row of taps above a trough. There were fewer than 300 pupils when Arthur arrived, many of them Irish. The syllabus was rooted firmly in the classics, with Virgil, Cicero, Livy, Tacitus, Horace and Homer taking precedence over geography, mathematics and English. 'It was the usual public-school routine,' he wrote later, 'of Euclid, algebra and the classics, taught in the usual way, which is calculated to leave a lasting abhorrence of these subjects. To give boys a little slab of Virgil or Homer with no general idea as to what it is all about, or what the classical age was like, is surely an absurd way of treating the subject . . . My classical education left me with a horror of the classics, and I was astonished to find how fascinating they were when I read them in a reasonable manner in later years.'

Religion dominated life at Stonyhurst. Shortly after his arrival at the age of 10, Arthur completed a three-day retreat with 160 other boys during which none of them was allowed to speak a word. The days were spent in religious instruction, reading the Saints' lives and meditating before retiring to bed at nine o'clock. 'I can safely say,' he wrote to his mother, 'that there are very few boys who are not quite changed by the retreat.' He forbore to explain how.

It was the fervent hope of all the monks at Stonyhurst that every boy would leave deeply imbued with the Catholic faith, a faith that would sustain them for the rest of their lives. In the case of Arthur Conan Doyle the very reverse applied. The joy he experienced at his first communion at Hodder was short-lived. He quickly became disillusioned by the rigid doctrine, intolerance and hypocrisy of the Catholic church; he was appalled when a Jesuit priest at Stonyhurst declared unequivocally that 'eternal damnation' awaited everyone outside the church. So it was he arrived at Hodder with his faith intact and left Stonyhurst with it in tatters, a budding agnostic.

Nevertheless, he was not in the least daunted by the austere regime and esoteric rituals at Stonyhurst, although he confessed in a letter to a friend much later that he would never send his own son there because the Jesuits ruled 'too much by fear – too little by love or reason'.[7] Summer and winter, pupils were roused at five every morning by a policeman's rattle; there was little or no heating in winter in their dormitories and the wind whistled through cracks in the walls. It was the boys' firm belief that the cracks had been deliberately opened expressly to increase their discomfort. In his first winter a serious diphtheria epidemic swept the country; several boys at Stonyhurst succumbed, but Arthur, always hale and hearty, was unaffected.

Good order – and the strictest celibacy – was maintained by vigilant supervision: the boys were never left to themselves for a moment, with the priests taking part in all their activities, whether academic, sporting or social. Prefects were used as spies and informers and encouraged to report any rule breaking, particularly of a sexual nature. The Jesuits were appalled by the immorality said to be rife at Eton, Harrow and Winchester and were determined to guard against 'the special dangers of boarding school life'.

A range of humiliating punishments was available to discipline troublemakers: the so-called 'penance-walk' required transgressors to walk in silence up and down the playground for an hour, presumably to ponder their sins. Corporal punishment was frequently administered, either by the birch or by a vicious flat rubber paddle, about the size and shape of a thick boot-sole, known as a 'ferula', but called a 'tolley' by the boys. The maximum punishment was 'twice-nine' – nine whacks on each hand. 'One blow of this instrument,' Arthur reported, 'would cause the palm of the hand to swell up and change colour. When I say that the usual punishment of the larger boys was nine on each hand, and that nine on one hand was an absolute minimum, it will be understood that it was a severe ordeal, and that the sufferer could not, as a rule, turn the handle of the door to get out of the room in which he had suffered. To take twice nine upon a cold day was about the extremity of human endurance.'

Arthur was stubborn, untidy and self-willed, which won him no plaudits from the monks. When he once told a master that he hoped to be a civil engineer when he left school, he relished the reply: 'You may be an engineer, Doyle, but from what I have seen of you I should think it very unlikely you will be a civil one.'[8] He never mentioned being punished in his letters home, but in his autobiography he made it clear that he was a frequent candidate ('I think few, if any, boys of my time endured more of it'), and recalled that it was a point of honour among the boys not to show that they were hurt: 'If I was more beaten than others it was not that I was in any way vicious, but it was that I had a nature which responded eagerly to affectionate kindness (which I never received), but which rebelled against threats and took a perverted pride in showing that it would not be cowed by violence. I went out of my way to do really mischievous and out-rageous things simply to show that my spirit was unbroken. An appeal to my better nature and not to my fears would have found an answer at once.

Not long after he arrived at Stonyhurst, Arthur wrote a sad poem, 'The Student's Dream', describing his apprehension over an impending beating:

> The Student he lay on his narrow bed
> He dreamt not of the morrow
> Confused thoughts filled his head
> And he dreamt of his home with sorrow . . .
>
> He thought of the birch's stinging stroke
> And he thought with fear of the morrow
> He wriggled and tumbled and nearly awoke
> And again he sighed with sorrow.

There were compensations, however, like Father Rector's Day in the winter when a frozen pond in the college grounds was lit by Chinese lanterns and coloured torches, and the boys were allowed to skate on the pond while the masters added to the fun by throwing fireworks onto the ice. At the end of the day the school band played 'Rule, Britannia', cigars were passed round and everyone toasted the Father Rector's health with tumblers of hot punch. Academy Day was another cause for celebration: 'A capital spread, turkey and sausages, fruit and cakes, together with port sherry and Claret. Songs were sung by everybody.'

The *Punch* cartoonist Bernard Partridge was a contemporary of Arthur's at Stonyhurst and remembered him well: 'I recall him at Stonyhurst as a thick-set boy, with a quiet manner, and a curious furtive smile when he was visited with one of the school penalties, such as leaving his desk and kneeling in the middle of the classroom with his books. He was, I fancy, rather lazy in his studies, never taking a prominent place in his form: but his brain was very nimble, and he was constantly throwing off verses and parodies on college personalities and happenings.'[9]

As at all English public schools, great emphasis was placed on sport, not just as a means of developing team spirit and physical fitness but as a diversion from unhealthy urges of the flesh. Stonyhurst had its own versions of football and cricket, perhaps to maintain a distance from Protestant schools, which meant that for many years it was impossible to arrange fixtures with other schools. Stonyhurst football dated from Elizabethan times and was played with a smaller ball, goalposts only seven feet apart and virtually no limit to the number of players in each team, resulting in frequent and violent scrummages on the field. Its version of cricket used a stone for a wicket, a club-shaped bat, a hard sheepskin ball and a semi-circular crease. Fielders were called 'fags' and batsmen were obliged to raise the bat above the horizontal for every ball; one run was known as a 'there and back'. Later in his life Arthur would describe the 'freak games' played at British public schools as 'national misfortunes' on which promising young men wasted their energies when they could have been developing an aptitude for regular sports.[10]

Fortunately for Arthur, conventional cricket – called 'London cricket' by the boys – was added to the school's list of sports in 1860. Keen on all sports, he excelled at 'London cricket' and would captain the Stonyhurst eleven. 'It is a jolly game,' he wrote to his mother, 'and does more to make a fellow strong and healthy than all the doctor's prescriptions in the world.' Corpus Christi in early summer marked the opening of the cricket season, and on that longed-for day all the boys marched behind a band through triumphal arches with the school bells pealing. The Stonyhurst cricket uniform comprised white flannels, pink shirts and blue caps, exciting derision among conventionally attired opposing teams and serving to underline the school's individuality, not always with positive results. Religious discrimination was still widespread, and in 1874, while Arthur was at Stonyhurst, the Protestant newspaper *The Rock* attacked the masters of the nearby Rossall School, in Fleetwood, for arranging a cricket fixture with Stonyhurst: 'All these comminglings with papists act as so many enticements to idolatry, and the masters who do not see this are unfit to manage a Protestant school.'[11]

Arthur's letters home were often full of his feats on the cricket field – 'On Shrove Monday we played the match, and we won a glorious victory. They got III runs and we got 276, of which I contributed 51' – alternating with pleas for money. Asking for permission to buy a pair of cricket flannels, he pointed out, not unreasonably: 'It is almost impossible to keep playing cricket for four or five hours a day with my thick trousers on. I am one of the only fellows who have not got them [cricket flannels].' He was obliged to wear his father's cast-off trousers, which, he said, were 'rather worn out'.

Mary Doyle somehow found the money, but then received this: 'Mr Kellet told me to ask you to write him a short note through me to tell him what you wish done. He says that I am growing so rapidly that the clothes he is keeping for me will by the time of the vacation be much too small for me. He says I am also in want of a suit as I have grown out of my brown trousers, and the weather is now much too hot for my blue winter jacket . . . I would be quite willing to wear the clothes I have on until the end of the year, if Mr Kellet would allow me. My cricket clothes fit beautifully and are very nice . . .'

In April 1873 he reported encouraging news from his tutors: 'I had a talk with the rector yesterday. He said he was extremely pleased with the report he had to send home about me and especially that I had overcome all the sulkiness or ill-temper I used to have. He also said there was scarcely a boy in the school who had done better!'

In fact Arthur did not enjoy academic work, not even history, in which his mother hoped he would excel. His school report for the second term in his third year placed him tenth in a class of twenty boys, recording his best marks for 'religious duties' and 'diligence'. History did not come alive for him until he discovered, like a revelation, the works of Lord Macaulay. In 1873 Arthur wrote to his godfather in Paris to tell him that he had lost his well-thumbed copy of *Ivanhoe* when it had fallen into a stream and been swept away. Michael Conan responded by sending him Macaulay's *Lays of Ancient Rome*. Arthur was enthralled by the book – it was, he said, like 'an incursion into an enchanted land' – and it inspired him to write his own poem, 'The Passage of the Red Sea', in rhymed pentameter. He immediately sought out more works by Macaulay, which he read in the dormitory at night by the light of a surreptitious candle, and which would generate in him a lifelong fascination with history. He learned Macaulay's 'Lay of Horatius' by heart and could still recite it, almost verbatim, when he was 50. That year, too, he began reading Jules Verne in French – *Vingt Mille Lieues sous les Mers* and *Cinq Semains en Ballon* – and reported to his mother that he was getting to 'relish them quite as well as English books'.

Shortly before returning to 3 Sciennes Hill Place for the 1873 summer holidays, Arthur wrote a newsy and cheerful letter to his mother reporting progress with his wardrobe:

> I have been to the Taylor, and I showed him your letter, explaining to him that you wanted something that would wear well, and at the same time look well. He told me that the blue cloth he had was meant especially for Coats, but that none of it would suit well as Trousers. He showed me a dark sort of Cloth, which he said would suit a blue coat better than any other Cloth he has, and would wear well as trousers. On his recommendation I took this Cloth. I think you will like it, it does not show dirt, and looks very well, it is a sort of black and white very dark Cloth . . . My Examen is finished, so I have finished all my work for the year, but of course it is kept profoundly secret who has got a prize. I trust I am among the Chosen few.

I hope you and the bairns are making the best of your vacation, as I suppose you can scarcely call the time when I am at home vacation.

I have never known a year pass so quickly as this last one, it seems not a month ago since I left you, and I can remember all the minutest Articles of furniture in the house, even to the stains on the wall. I suppose I will have to perform for Frank [his newborn brother, John Francis Innes Hay] the office I have so often performed for Lottie and Cony [Lottie and Constance, aged 4 and 6], namely, that of rocking him to sleep. I suppose he is out of his Long Clothes now.

We are going to have bathing during schools this evening, which is a nice prospect. This is the Golden time of one's life at Stonyhurst, the end of the year. Every Thursday is a holiday, and we are having Splendid weather.

I will now say Good-bye and remain your Affece son
A. C. DOYLE.

Arthur was, indeed, among the 'chosen few' to win a prize – the 'Merenti Collegium Stonyhurst', a calf-bound copy of *The Pursuit of Knowledge Under Difficulties* by George Craik. He was already developing a strong literary bent and in November 1873 he and another boy, Arthur Roskell, launched a journal called the *Stonyhurst Figaro*, made up of poems and essays and written by hand in a two-penny exercise book. The contents of Volume 1 were listed as: 'The Figaro's Prospects (poem) by Arthur Roskell; Some wicked jokes by A Doyle; The Student's Dream (poem) by A Roskell; The Abbot by A Doyle (poem); Music of the day and music of the past (essay) by Roskell; Bluestocking court (essay) by Roskell; After the Battle (poem) by A C Doyle'. Intended to be a monthly publication, it is unclear if there was ever a Volume 2.

He was never short of ideas and told his mother that whenever he was stuck for a quotation for an essay he would invent a few lines of doggerel and attribute it to an anonymous poet. Thus one essay ended:

It is said that a mother ever loves best the most distorted and deformed of her children, but I trust the saying does not apply to the feelings of an author towards his literary child, otherwise it bodes ill for this poor foundling. I cannot however conclude better than by quoting those cheering lines of the poet:

> 'Fail or succeed, the man is blessed,
> Who when his task is o'er
> Can say that he has done his best
> Angels can do no more.'

Arthur was also involved in the school's amateur dramatics and was not above a little gentle boasting, tempered with some self-deprecating rider. After a small part as a farrier's boy in a smock and corduroys in a play called *The Omnibus*, he wrote home: 'I got cheered greatly not because I did well, but because the main point in my part was to look foolish and I feel that I did that to perfection. Both plays were relished extremely by the rest of the college. We had the good supper a week afterwards and it fully justified its epithet. Songs were sung as usual. I sang mine everyone declared it was capital and that they must have another. I declared I did not know one. A master, however, brought me "the best of wives" which I sang with the same success . . .'

As Christmas rolled around every year, Arthur usually found himself remaining at the school along with a handful of other students, most of whose parents were abroad. He never commented in his letters on why it was that he could not go home, as the great majority of his friends did; it was possible his mother wanted to shield him from his father's excesses or simply that they could not afford the fare. Yet it was, in truth, no great hardship for him to stay behind because the pupils entertained themselves with concerts and amateur dramatics, usually lurid Victorian melodramas, although *Macbeth*, *Rob Roy* and *L'Affaire du Courrier de Lyon* featured one winter, and parents ensured their offspring did not miss out on the traditional feasting. Arthur reported once that he and three friends consumed: 'Two turkeys, one very large goose, two chickens, one large ham and two pieces of ham, two large sausages, seven boxes of sardines, one of lobster, a plate full of tarts and seven pots of jam. In the way of drink we had five bottles of sherry, five of port, one of claret and two of raspberry vinegar; we also had two bottles of pickles.' This was in stark contrast to the unwholesome fare that constituted their daily diet: dry bread and watered milk for breakfast, a 'butcher's meat' stew at lunchtime and fish on Fridays, a snack of dry bread and beer at teatime, known by the boys as 'horrible swipes', and supper of hot milk, more bread – this time with butter – and, occasionally, potatoes. Arthur wrote that the 'beer' served in the afternoon was 'brown but had no other characteristic of beer'.

In 1874, when he was 15, Arthur's Aunt Annette invited him to spend Christmas in London, and he was given permission to leave the college for three glorious weeks. He stayed at his Uncle Dick's studio at 7 Finborough Road, Chelsea, and his father's brothers all set to entertain him. Uncle Dick took him to Hengler's Circus; he went with Uncle Henry to see the life-size model dinosaurs at the Crystal Palace in Sydenham; and Uncle James treated him to the theatre twice, the first time to the Lyceum, in a box, to see Henry Irving in *Hamlet*: 'The play was continued for three months,' he wrote to his mother, 'yet every night the house is crammed to suffocation by people wishing to see Irving act. Irving is very young and slim, with black piercing eyes, and acted magnificently.' Later they saw Tom Taylor's *Our American Cousin* at the Haymarket – the play Abraham Lincoln had been watching a few years earlier in Washington DC when he was assassinated. Nothing could have been more exciting for a boy accustomed to the grey regime of Stonyhurst than the bustle and glamour of a West End theatre. Arthur also visited Westminster Abbey, St Paul's, Madame Tussaud's waxworks (he told his mother he particularly enjoyed the Chamber of Horrors), and the Tower of London, where he recalled staring in awe at the enormous numbers of swords and bayonets and the instruments of torture, racks, thumbscrews and all the other artefacts of medieval brutality.

In his final year at Stonyhurst he edited the school magazine and discovered a talent for extempore storytelling, winning great popularity among the younger boys by spinning bloodthirsty yarns, stretching them out for weeks on end, with a cliff-hanging end for each episode, and accepting bribes of cakes and apples to keep the story going. He described his experience like this: 'On a wet half-holiday I have been elevated on to a desk, and with an audience of little boys all squatting on the floor, with their chins upon their hands, I have talked myself husky over the misfortunes of my heroes. Week in and week out those unhappy men have battled and striven and groaned for the amusement of that little circle . . . Sometimes, too, I would stop dead in the very thrill of a crisis, and could only be set agoing again by apples. When I had got as far as "With his left hand in her glossy locks, he was waving the blood-stained knife above her head, when . . ." or "Slowly, slowly, the door turned upon its hinges, and with eyes which were dilated with horror the wicked Marquis saw . . ." I knew that I had my audience in my power.'[12]

Despite his frequent letters home, he was not kept abreast of family affairs particularly closely. In May 1875 he confessed himself 'astonished' to learn that his older sister Annette had left for Portugal, where she was to work as a governess. 'When is she going to come back?' he asked plaintively, before going on to enquire if his brother Innes was talking and 'what does dear little Ida look like . . . I am very curious to know all about the little ones.' (Jane Adelaide Rose (Ida), the eighth of Mary Doyle's children, was born on 16 March 1875.) In a postscript to another letter he demanded that Lottie should write to him at once: 'She ought never to put off till tomorrow what she can possibly put off till the day after.'

In the spring of 1875 Arthur travelled to London with thirteen other Stonyhurst boys to sit the matriculation examination at London University. The results arrived at Stonyhurst in July and were taken to the office of the Rector, the Very Reverend Edward Ignatius Purbrick, while the nervous candidates awaited their fate. In the end, ignoring the protests of prefects, the candidates and their friends rushed along the gallery and up the stairs to the Rector's room, where they crowded round the door, pushing and yelling. When the door opened, the Rector could be seen inside, smiling and waving the results packet above his head. It was good news, and a great cheer rang out; many of the boys tossed their handkerchiefs into the air. After the commotion had subsided the old grey-haired prefect of studies clambered onto a chair and announced that of the fourteen who had gone up thirteen had passed, the best results in the school's history. Arthur had passed with honours, rather to everyone's surprise: 'I nearly got a hole worn in the back of my coat being clapped on it and some enthusiasts carried me round the play ground.'

Before starting at London University, it was agreed in the family that Arthur should spend a year at Stella Matutina, a famous Jesuit college in Feldkirch, in eastern Austria, both to perfect his German and to broaden his academic horizons. En route to Feldkirch he stopped in London to see his aunt and uncles and took time to make a personal pilgrimage – a visit to Macaulay's grave in Westminster Abbey. At Feldkirch he was in trouble on his first night when he was observed poking a boy in a nearby bed with a stick. His explanation that he could not sleep because his neighbour was snoring was not received sympathetically and he was admonished to behave.

The regime at Feldkirch was in fact much more relaxed than Stonyhurst's. 'I met with far more human kindness than at Stonyhurst,' Arthur recalled, 'with the immediate result that I ceased to be a resentful young rebel and became a pillar of law and order.' He learned to play the bombardon, an enormous brass-valved tuba, in the school band, being one of the few boys strong enough not just to lift it but get wind through it; it sounded, he said, like 'a hippopotamus doing a step-dance'. He tobogganed, developed a taste for German beer, played football on stilts and founded and edited a school newspaper, the *Feldkirchian Gazette*, with the motto: 'Fear not, and put it in print.' Written in violet ink, entirely in his own hand, in two exercise books, he described it as a 'scientific and literary magazine'. The cover of Volume II, dated November 1875, noted that it included 'four contributions by Conan Doyle including verses on "A Football Match", "Feldkirchian Notes", "The Song of the Bombardier" and "The Round-about Papers"'. It also featured a strong leader protesting at the injustice of the boys' letters being read by their teachers before being distributed – much too strong for the school, which promptly closed it down.

While in Feldkirch, Arthur also sent a sheaf of his poems and copies of the school newspaper to his godfather, Michael Conan, in

Paris. 'There can be no doubt,' Conan wrote to Charles and Mary Doyle in Edinburgh, 'of his faculty for that accomplishment. In each one of his more serious inspirations I found passages of thoroughly original freshness and excellent spirits . . . His "Feldkirch Newspaper" gives capital promise, and I suspect that it is his own from first to last.'

Among the poems Arthur sent to his godfather was a comic verse about the bombardon:

> There is an instrument whose power
> Does all others far surpass
> Far o'er the rest one sees him tower
> A mighty instrument of brass
>
> The soundest sleeper, far or near,
> I think would scarcely slumber on,
> If close to his unconscious ear
> You played upon the Bombardon.

Every fortnight the band played at the head of a school march: 'It is rather hard, I find,' he wrote to his mother, 'blowing and marching at the same time, but like everything else it can be acquired by practice. It affords me a feeling of satisfaction to observe the effect produced by my deep sonorous notes on the unmusical oxen we meet on the way, drawing the peasants' carts. I always blow in their ears as I pass and cause a fine disturbance.'

Out on hikes, walking three abreast, foreign students were always paired with two Germans to oblige them to speak the language, and Arthur blithely took the opportunity to expound on the glories of the British Empire, the invincibility of the British Navy and the exploits of British heroes like Captain Matthew Webb, who had recently become the first man to swim the English Channel. On one march they covered forty-two miles in fourteen hours with 'no difficulty except some insignificant blisters'.

During this period Arthur came across the works of the American writer and critic Edgar Allan Poe and was immediately captivated; he would later say that with the exception of Macaulay and Scott, no other author had such an influence over him. Poe's short story 'The

Murders in the Rue Morgue', featuring the eccentric and brilliant detective C. Auguste Dupin, had launched the genre of detective fiction. Published in *Graham's Magazine* in 1841, it established many of the literary devices that would become commonplace in detective fiction (see chapter 6). Poe described his three stories featuring Dupin as 'tales of ratiocination', whereby the truth is obtained by a complex process combining scientific logic, astute observation, inference and intuition. Although Dupin was not the first fictional detective, he was the prototype for many who followed, notably Sherlock Holmes, and Conan Doyle always generously acknowledged the debt he owed his creator.

Shortly before leaving Feldkirch, Arthur received a letter from his mother to tell him, without any further explanation, that his father was 'retiring'. 'I was indeed surprised and sorry to hear that papa is leaving the office,' he replied innocently. 'Has he been unwell? Or is there any other particular reason for it?' Having been away from home for the best part of eight years, he had been spared witnessing his father's mental and physical deterioration.

At the end of June 1876, Arthur left for home, via Paris, where he intended to call on his godfather. A roistering farewell supper with fellow students in Strasbourg left him very short of funds, and he arrived in Paris, on a sweltering summer day, with exactly two small coins in his pocket. Reluctant to hire a hansom cab at the station and then have to ask his uncle to pay the fare, he decided to walk to 65 Avenue de Wagram. Near the Arc de Triomphe, he saw a man selling what he thought were cold drinks from a tin he carried on his back. A cup cost him half his funds and to his horror he discovered it was liquorice water, but it refreshed him sufficiently to continue on his way.

Arthur found Conan sitting in his shirtsleeves in the garden. He spent three happy, but 'penurious', weeks with his great-uncle and his great-aunt, describing him as a 'dear old volcanic Irishman' and giving the impression that they engaged in fiery debates about artists and writers, an impression curiously at odds with Conan's obituary in the *Art Journal*, which described its former Paris correspondent as quiet and unobtrusive and 'rather averse to thrust his opinions upon others, and more disposed to listen than to talk'.

Arthur then set off for Edinburgh where his family had moved, yet again. With five children still at home, the youngest only 16 months old, Mary Doyle was finding the struggle to provide for the family even harder than usual and had taken in a lodger. 'I found that the family affairs were still as straitened as ever,' Arthur wrote. 'No promotion had come to my father, and two younger children, Innes, my only brother, and Ida, had arrived to add to the calls upon my mother . . . Annette, the eldest sister, had already gone out to Portugal to earn and send home a fair salary, while Lottie and Connie were about to do the same. My mother had adopted the device of sharing a large house, which may have eased her in some ways, but was disastrous in others.'

The 'disaster' was Dr Bryan Charles Waller.

CHAPTER 3

THE MEDICAL STUDENT

RTHUR WAS NOT AT all pleased to discover, on his return to Edinburgh, that his mother's lodger appeared to have assumed a significant role in the family in the effective absence of his father, by now spending most evenings in a search for conviviality, and perhaps oblivion, in the city's drinking dens. Indeed, Mary Doyle was not even at home when he arrived – she was visiting Bryan Waller's mother at Masongill, the family estate in Yorkshire. He could not but help be concerned that Waller, a comparative stranger, was usurping his father's position and not unreasonably resented having to share his mother's affection with someone he considered to be an interloper.

Waller was only six years older than Arthur, an Oxford graduate and a published poet. From the tone of Arthur's letters to his brother and his sister Lottie it was obvious, and troubling, to him that his mother had developed a great fondness their wealthy and cultured lodger. It was also clear that Waller's contribution to the rent had enabled the family to move from the previous gloomy environs to 2 Argyle Park Terrace, a light and airy apartment with a bow window overlooking the Meadows, the great tree-fringed park in Edinburgh's New Town, where the professional white-collar classes lived. For a self-reliant young man it must have been painful for Arthur to witness the extent to which his family was now relying on Waller's largesse.

When Waller enrolled as a medical student at the University of Edinburgh, he could easily have afforded to set himself up in his own house with a full complement of domestic servants. Instead he chose, for some mystifying reason, to move in with Mary Doyle, her drunken

husband and their noisy brood, where he quickly became a super-
numerary member of the family and de facto head of the household
as Charles Doyle gave himself over to the bottle.

Some biographers have suggested he was prepared to put up with
the overcrowded conditions because he was in love with Annette. In
a collection of poems published after his death in 1932, there is one
titled 'Annette's Music', a lyrical, unbearably mournful elegy about the
grief of lost love. But according to Arthur's letter from Stonyhurst, by
May 1875 Annette had already left Edinburgh to take up a post as a
governess in Portugal. Why did Waller not declare himself before her
departure? Certainly no suitor would have been more acceptable to
her mother. Perhaps Annette did not return Waller's ardour, and she
saw him for the cold, self-important snob he later revealed himself to
be. But if that was the case why did he continue to encumber his life
with the Doyle family?

Not long after Arthur's return, Mary Doyle found herself pregnant
again. Her ninth and last child was named after Waller, even though
she was a girl. Bryan Mary Julia Josephine (Julia was Waller's mother's
name), known as Dodo, was born on 2 March 1877. Where Charles
Doyle was at this time is not known, but he must have been absent
or too drunk, as Mary Doyle registered the birth herself (Charles had
registered all the previous births, and the two deaths). Dodo's god-
parents were Waller and his mother. The curious naming of Mary
Doyle's last child has prompted speculation that Waller was the father,
but there is no evidence of a sexual relationship, and it is unlikely
given their age difference that a 22-year-old medical student would be
attracted to a careworn woman approaching 40. Nevertheless, the
relationship between Mary Doyle and Bryan Waller certainly went
far beyond that of lodger and landlady and continued for many years.

An only child, born at Masongill in 1853, Waller claimed descent
from a knight who captured the French king's cousin at Agincourt, on
the strength of which his family coat of arms was quartered with that
of the French royal family. He also asserted family links with a General
Waller, who commanded Parliamentary troops in the English Civil
War; the poet Edmund Waller, who wrote poetry in support of both
Oliver Cromwell and King Charles; and Hardress Waller, who signed
the King's death certificate. Waller's uncle, Bryan Waller Procter, was

well known in literary London as an author and playwright –
Thackeray had dedicated *Vanity Fair* to him. It was small wonder that
Mary Doyle, defiantly proud of her own ancestry despite the miserable reality of her life, took to the new lodger despite his haughty
demeanour and crippling stutter.

Waller graduated in 1876 and just two years later was awarded
a doctorate – and a gold medal for his thesis – by which time he
had taken over the middle two floors of a substantial house at
23 George Square, then the finest residential square in the city,
where he had put up his plate and set up a practice as a 'consulting
pathologist'. All the Doyles – Charles and Mary and the children
still at home – moved in with him. Waller paid the entire annual
rent of £85. In 1879 he was appointed Lecturer in Pathology at the
Edinburgh University School of Medicine, a post he held for four
years before abruptly giving up medicine and returning to Yorkshire
to take over Masongill, which he had inherited on the death of his
father in 1877.

As a respected doctor and a permanent fixture in the family, Waller
may have played a role in persuading Mary, and perhaps Arthur, that
Charles should be institutionalised for his own good. In the census of
1881 Charles is listed as one of eighteen residents at Blairerno, while
Mary Doyle is listed as 'head of household' at 23 George Square, with
Arthur, 21, a 'student of medicine', John Innes, 8, Jane (Ida), 6, and
Bryan (Dodo), 4, and an Irish maid, Mary Kilpatrick, 17. Annette,
Lottie and Connie were all in Portugal.

In 1883 Mary Doyle left Edinburgh with her three youngest children and moved into Masongill Cottage – actually a reasonably sized
house – on Waller's estate, where she would live rent-free for more
than thirty years, resisting all attempts by her eldest son to have her
move south and live with him. While there Mary abandoned her
Roman Catholic faith and followed Waller into the Anglican church
– clear evidence of the extent of his influence over her. In 1896 Waller
married the daughter of a professor at St Andrew's University, but he
remained devoted to Mary Doyle, often taking his meals with her, to
the distress of his wife, and claiming that only Mary knew how to
cook his favourite curry.

Waller's marriage was childless and probably loveless. Aloof and arrogant – he insisted his tenants doff their caps as he passed and refused to allow children within sight of his house[1] – he showed his wife little of the affection he clearly felt for his former landlady. His wife, in turn, keenly resented Mary Doyle's presence on the estate and her relationship, whatever it was, with her husband. This curious menage would not end until 1917 when Mary finally relented and moved south to be closer to her now famous son. Waller went into a decline after her departure and took to insisting that his wife should read to him through the night, often until dawn. He died at Masongill in November 1932.

———————————◆———————————

Arthur's behaviour towards his mother's friend was proper, although notably cool. In his frequent letters to his mother he would often ask to be 'remembered kindly' to 'the Doctor' and would pass on his 'best wishes' to Mrs Waller, but it was likely he was more interested in pleasing his mother than being 'remembered kindly'. Waller, for all his importance in the life of the Doyle family, does not merit a single mention by name in *Memories and Adventures*, Arthur's autobiography, published in 1924. His only reference to his mother taking in a lodger is given above: it 'may have eased her in some ways, but was disastrous in others'. Years later, in a letter to his younger brother, Innes, who had recently visited their mother at Masongill, he said how much he would have liked to have joined him 'if that fellow's [Waller's] presence did not poison the air for me'.

It was Waller who suggested Arthur should follow his example and study medicine at Edinburgh University; he wrote to Arthur in Feldkirch with the proposal and included two useful volumes on mathematics and chemistry. Mary Doyle was certainly pleased when Arthur announced he had decided to stay in Edinburgh rather than continue his education at London University as originally had been planned. Her reasoning was perfectly sound: she was ambitious for him, medicine was a respected profession, Edinburgh University had one of the finest medical schools in the world and, happily, her beloved son would be at home after so many years away.

Waller coached Arthur for the entrance examination, which he passed comfortably and won a bursary of £40 to boot, to the delight of his mother. Unfortunately, when he went to collect the money he discovered there had been a mistake, and the bursary was only available to an arts student; by then it was also too late for him to apply for a corresponding science prize and he had to make do with a solatium of just £7.

Arthur entered the University of Edinburgh Medical School, in the gloomy, rat-infested Old Town, in October 1876 and began what he would later describe as the 'long weary grind at botany, chemistry, anatomy, physiology, and a whole list of compulsory subjects, many of which have a very indirect bearing upon the art of curing'. Always a keen sportsman, at the age of 17 Arthur was a little more than six feet tall, weighed over 15 stone, was broad-shouldered, enormously strong and sported the nascent moustache that would adorn his upper lip for the remainder of his life. He would play as a forward in the university rugby team until he decided his 'want of knowledge was too heavy a handicap', played cricket and football and was a keen amateur boxer. 'I had an eager nature which missed nothing in the way of fun which could be gathered, and I had a great capacity for enjoyment. I read much. I played games all I could. I danced, and I sampled the drama whenever I had a sixpence to carry me to the gallery.'

In the previous five years the Faculty of Medicine had been greatly enlarged, doubling the number of students to more than 1,000, but there was none of the collegiate pleasures of Oxford or Cambridge – no community life, no halls of residence, few social facilities – and students, who were responsible for organising their own studies, paid their fees directly to the lecturers. The rapid enlargement of the medical faculty had prompted some overworked professors to delegate lectures to student-assistants, making the quality of the teaching uneven. Students could choose which classes they attended and which examinations they sat. The lectures were long, examinations demanding, textbooks few, and there was little toleration for the idle and incompetent. Only by rigid self-discipline could students last the course and many fell by the wayside. Arthur calculated that only about 400 of every 1,000 graduated.

Lectures were held in the gas-lit surgical amphitheatre, lined with tiers of wooden benches overlooking an operating table in the centre of the room. It was here that Arthur first made the acquaintance of Dr Joseph Bell, the talented and charismatic man on whom he would model his most famous creation. A tall, angular figure with sharp features, a beak-like nose, piercing grey eyes – Arthur said he had a face 'like a Red Indian' – and the long, sensitive fingers of a musician, his appearance mirrored the description of Sherlock Holmes in *A Study in Scarlet*: 'In height he was rather over six feet, and so excessively lean that he seemed to be considerably taller. His eyes were sharp and piercing, save during those intervals of torpor to which I have alluded; and his thin, hawk-like nose gave his whole expression an air of alertness and decision. His chin, too, had the prominence and squareness which marked the man of determination. His hands were invariably blotted with ink and stained with chemicals, yet he was possessed of an extraordinary delicacy of touch, as I frequently had occasion to observe when I watched him manipulating his fragile philosophical instruments.'

Known behind his back by students as 'Joe', Bell was only 39 years old but already a legend among medical students as a master of observation, logic and deduction, possessing almost clairvoyant powers of diagnosis. A showman who loved centre stage, his showmanship had a serious purpose: to alert trainee doctors to the wealth of information a patient provided before opening his or her mouth, much of it invisible to the untrained eye.

One of Bell's favourite tricks was to invite new students to taste an amber liquid in a glass vial. It was, he explained, an extremely potent drug with a vile and bitter taste which they needed to be able to recognise. Since he would not ask students to do anything he would not be willing to do himself, he said that he would be the first. He removed the stopper, immersed a finger into the liquid and then put his hand to his mouth, shuddering as he sucked his finger. The students dutifully followed suit as the vial was passed round, all of them registering disgust. At the end, Bell invariably expressed his disappointment in their poor powers of observation. It was his index finger, he reminded his groaning class, that he had dipped into the noxious brew, but it was his middle finger that he had put into his mouth.

Bell gave frequent demonstrations of his own deductive powers, which, combined with inspired guesswork, enabled him to discover much about a patient without asking a single question. Seated at a table in the well of the amphitheatre with his interns and dressers around him, patients were shown in by the outpatient clerk, diagnosed at great speed and shown out again. Awed students would then stand with their mouths open as Bell launched into a narrative diagnosis, constructing a chain of reasoning from what he could observe. 'The patient,' Bell liked to tell his students, 'is likely to be impressed by your ability to cure him in the future if he sees you at a glance know much of his past.'

'I remember one young fellow gave what was evidently a false name,' wrote Clement Gunn, one of Arthur's classmates. 'But Joe Bell in writing the prescription calmly wrote down his real name and handed the paper to the patient. He blushed, looked sheepish, and departed. When he had gone, Joe said: "I daresay you all noticed what I did then; it was obvious that John Smith was not his real name, but I saw the true name on his shirt-band." Thus he trained us, his amateur "Watsons", in the habit of observation.'[2]

Arthur described an incident when Bell, surrounded by his usual retinue, was confronted with a patient and immediately deduced that he was a soldier, a non-commissioned officer recently discharged from a Highland regiment stationed in Barbados. The astonished patient agreed that all this was true. '"You see, gentlemen," he would explain, "the man was a respectful man but did not remove his hat. They do not in the army, but he would have learned civilian ways had he been long discharged. He has an air of authority and he is obviously Scottish. As to Barbados, his complaint is elephantiasis, which is West Indian and not British, and the Scottish regiments are at present in that particular island."'

Harold Emery Jones, another classmate of Arthur's, recalled Bell booming: 'Gentlemen, a fisherman! You will notice that, though this is a very hot summer's day, the patient is wearing top-boots. When he sat on the chair they were plainly visible. No one but a sailor would wear top-boots at this season of the year . . . Further, to prove the correctness of these deductions, I notice several fish scales adhering to his clothes and hands, while the odour of fish announced his arrival in most marked and striking manner.'[3]

Bell claimed the ability to differentiate between Scottish accents almost to identifying the county, and that every craft left 'a sign manual' on the craftsman's hands – a miner's scars were quite different from those of a quarryman and a carpenter's calluses were distinct from those of a mason. He also had a highly developed sense of smell and could sniff out an occupation, like a French polisher, or a habitual drinker. 'The precise and intelligent recognition and appreciation of minor differences is the real essential factor in all successful medical diagnosis,' he frequently asserted. 'Eyes and ears which can see and hear, memory to record at once and to recall at leisure the impressions of the senses, and an imagination capable of weaving a theory or piecing together a broken chain or unravelling a tangled clue, such are the implements of his trade to a successful diagnostician.'[4]

But Bell's *coups de théâtre* would occasionally backfire. 'You are a bandsman,' he asserted to one patient. 'Aye,' replied the sick man. Bell turned triumphantly to his students. 'You see, gentlemen, I am right,' he said. 'This man has paralysis of his cheek muscles, the result of too much blowing on band instruments.' Turning once again to the patient he demanded, 'What instrument do you play, my man?' 'The big drum,' he replied.[5]

Although Arthur never claimed to be more than an average student, he made a sufficient impression in his first year to be invited by Bell to become his surgeon's clerk at the Royal Infirmary. Working with Bell at close quarters gave Arthur ample opportunity to study his unusual diagnostic techniques, and he was able to use the experience to great effect when he came to create Sherlock Holmes. Arthur would dedicate *The Adventures of Sherlock Holmes*, published in 1892, to Bell and wrote to his former mentor: 'It is most certainly to you that I owe Sherlock Holmes and though in the stories I have the advantage of being able to place him in all sorts of dramatic positions, I do not think that his analytical work is in the least an exaggeration of some effects which I have seen you produce in the outpatient ward.'[6]

He also referred to Bell in a short story, 'The Recollections of Captain Wilkie', published in *Chambers's Journal* in 1895, in which the narrator noted:

I used to rather pride myself on being able to spot a man's

trade or profession by a good look at his exterior. I had the
advantage of studying under a professor at Edinburgh who
was a master of the art, and used to electrify both his patients
and his clinical classes by long shots, sometimes at the most
unlikely of pursuits, and never very far from the mark. 'Well,
my man,' I have heard him say, 'I can see by your fingers that
you play some musical instrument for your livelihood, but it
is a rather curious one – something quite out of my line.' The
man afterwards informed us that he earned a few coppers by
blowing 'Rule Britannia' on a coffee pot, the spout of which
was pierced to form a rough flute.

Bell was not the only illustrious name in the faculty at the University of Edinburgh. The oceanographer Sir Charles Wyville Thomson, recently returned from circumnavigating the globe in HMS *Challenger* in search of new forms of life, occupied the Regius Chair of Natural History; Dr James Young Simpson pioneered the use of chloroform as a clinical anaesthetic at the Royal Infirmary; and Joseph Lister, the founder of antiseptic medicine, was the professor of clinical surgery. Arthur recalled great rivalry between supporters of Lister's theories and those who favoured the traditional use of carbolic acid, with the latter deriding the former by shouting, 'Shut the door, ye'll let the germs oot!' He also remembered with some affection the professor of chemistry, Alexander Crum Brown, notorious for being terrified of his own experiments. Having mixed some potion that was designed to explode, he would shelter behind his desk; when, as frequently happened, no explosion was forthcoming, the students in unison shouted, 'Boom!'

The pioneering toxicologist Sir Robert Christison, known to students as 'Dignity Bob' from his tall, erect figure, commanding presence and cold, imperious manner, held a chair at the university for fifty-five years and wrote a paper on medical jurisprudence for the *Edinburgh Medical and Surgical Journal* in April 1829, which described beating corpses with a heavy stick in order to study the effect of bruises produced after death. Dr Watson noted, in *A Study in Scarlet*, that Sherlock Holmes tried something similar: 'He appears to have a passion for definite and exact knowledge. When it comes to beating the subjects in the dissecting rooms with a stick, it is certainly taking a rather bizarre shape.'

Even though he was far from entertaining a career as a writer, Arthur was already storing up characters and ideas that would appear later in his fiction. The eccentric Professor William Rutherford, a physiologist with a bushy black beard and a booming voice that could be heard long before he entered the classroom, would provide the inspiration for one of his great comic characters, Professor George E. Challenger, leader of the expedition to South America in *The Lost World*.

Among his contemporaries in the student body was J. M. Barrie, whose play *Peter Pan* still provides funds for the Great Ormond Street Hospital for Sick Children. Arthur liked to believe that he might also have brushed shoulders with Robert Louis Stevenson at Rutherfords tavern in Drummond Street, but the author of *Treasure Island* (and founder of the university's student newspaper), who studied law at Edinburgh, was called to the bar in June 1875, a year before Arthur enrolled.

Having planted the seed of medicine in Arthur's mind, Waller continued to play a quasi-paternal role in his life, writing frequently with advice and encouragement and signing himself 'Your affectionate friend, Bryan Charles Waller'. He congratulated Arthur on achieving a first and two seconds in his exams at the end of the first session, adding that this 'augurs well for future results'. In the same letter he urged Arthur to read Balfour's *Botany*: 'It is a great lumbering book, uninteresting, and I wish heartily that you could be spared the trouble of reading it, but that is impossible so you must make the best of it.' Arthur showed no sign of resentment in his replies, dutifully reporting on his progress. This on 9 September 1876: 'Dear Dr. Waller, I do a Latin and Greek exercise every day, learn a chapter of Livy and Simpson's Cyropaedia, and a certain quantity of Euclid and Algebra. In fact I seldom emerge from my cell except for meals and sometimes in the evening when I petrify our small Family circle by reading Poe's Tales.'

He had time, however, to ponder issues other than medicine and while at university the latent agnosticism nurtured in him at Stonyhurst hardened into firm conviction. 'I found that the foundations not only of Roman Catholicism but of the whole Christian faith, as presented to me in nineteenth-century theology, were so weak that my mind could not build upon them.' Under the influence of the some of the great thinkers of the nineteenth century, the naturalist Charles Darwin, proponent of the 'theory of evolution', his fellow evolutionists Thomas Huxley and John Tyndall, and philosophers Herbert Spencer and John Stuart Mill, he refused to accept any proposition that could not be proved and thus absolutely rejected the story of creation as presented in the Bible. 'Never,' he said, 'will I accept anything which cannot be proved to me. The evils of religion have all come from accepting things which cannot be proved.' He did not consider himself at this time an atheist, favouring the idea of a beneficent power, some greater force, but not necessarily God, and called himself a Unitarian. His beliefs, or lack of them as far as the family was concerned, would cause increasing tension: his three uncles remained devout, practising Catholics and Aunt Annette was a nun.

Money was a perennial problem and the cause of continual worry, his fees for surgical classes with Bell alone amounting to £4. 4s. a year. Arthur allowed himself twopence for his lunch, 'the price of a mutton pie'. But the pie shop was near a second-hand bookshop with a barrel outside filled with books and a sign reading 'Your choice for 2d'. The mutton pie was frequently sacrificed to satisfy his overpowering appetite for literature and over the months he built up a well-thumbed library, including Thackeray's *Henry Esmond*, the Earl of Clarendon's *History of the Rebellion and Civil Wars in England*, Washington Irving's *Conquest of Granada*, Jonathan Swift's *A Tale of a Tub*, and anything he could find by Sir Walter Scott, Macaulay and Poe. It was while rummaging in that tub that he discovered Oliver Wendell Holmes, the American writer and poet. He was spellbound by Holmes's collection of 'breakfast-table' essays, originally published in *Atlantic Monthly*, featuring an autocrat, professor and poet involved in a wide-ranging and largely one-sided dialogue with the residents of a New England boarding house. 'Never,' he would write later, 'have I so known and loved a man whom I had never seen.'

To relieve the financial burden on his family, Arthur took the decision in 1878 to compress a year's classes into six months and advertised his services as a doctor's assistant, hoping to make a little money while he was still at university. It was an inauspicious start to his medical career: his first job was in Sheffield with a Dr Richardson, who found his self-assured manner irritating and terminated his employment after three weeks, paying him nothing.

While he was looking for another post he visited his family in London, lodging with his Uncle Dick in Finborough Road, Chelsea. It was a temporary relief from his austere student life. On his nineteenth birthday he was taken to see Henry Irving in *Louis XI*, which he thought overdone; 'the death scene is an awful bit of dramatic art,' he reported to his mother. He watched the Trooping of the Colour on Horse Guards Parade and read Trollope's *American Senator* to Aunt Annette and Macaulay's *Life and Letters* for his own pleasure. He wrote to his mother that he had bought 'the doctor' a German pipe with a china bowl and long stem.

Arthur stayed for two months, spending time hanging around the docks in the East End, watching the ships come and go and talking to the sailors. He longed for adventure, longed to travel and even briefly considered joining the Royal Navy as a surgeon. 'I roamed about London for some time with pockets so empty that there was little chance of idleness breeding its usual mischief. I remember that there were signs of trouble in the East [the Second Afghan War began in November] and that the recruiting sergeants, who were very busy in Trafalgar Square, took my measure in a moment and were very insistent that I should take the shilling. There was a time when I was quite disposed to do so, but my mother's plans [for him to qualify as a doctor] held me back.'

He was soon to wear out his welcome with the family, who found his high spirits, practical jokes and forthright views on religion difficult to tolerate. There was undisguised relief when he found a position with a Dr Elliott in the curiously named Ruyton-of-the-Eleven-Towns, a village near Shrewsbury in Shropshire, where he stayed for four months, was given very little to do and spent most of his time reading. His confidence in his as yet untested medical skills received a boost one afternoon when an over-excited messenger arrived at the surgery, while the doctor was out, announcing an accident at a fete in the grounds of a nearby country house. An old cannon had burst during firing and a piece of shrapnel had lodged in the head of a spectator. Arthur hurried to the scene to discover that the shrapnel had exposed the injured man's skull. He managed to extract it without damaging the brain, then 'pulled the gash together, staunched the bleeding, and finally bound it up, so that when the doctor did at last arrive he had little to add. This incident gave me confidence, and, what is more important still, gave others confidence.'

Yet his relations with his employer were cool. Dr Elliott, he observed, while 'outwardly a gentleman' did not have a single original idea in his head and flew into a rage at the slightest prompting. One evening Arthur ventured the view that capital punishment should be abolished. The doctor, purple-faced with fury, told Arthur that he would not have such a thing said in his house, let alone in his presence. Unperturbed and bolstered by the arrogance of youth, Arthur retorted that he would express his opinions where and when he wanted.

At the end of his four-month contract the doctor offered his assistant neither wages nor expenses. When Arthur requested his train fare home, the doctor replied that since he had no salary he could not claim expenses and should consider himself to be 'a gentleman travelling for his own improvement'. Time mellowed Arthur's views and when he came to write his autobiography nearly fifty years later he claimed he had affectionate memories of his time at Ruyton-of-the-Eleven-Towns.

The following year, still a student, he worked as a (paid) assistant to Dr Reginald Ratcliffe Hoare, who owned a prosperous 'five-horse city practice' in Aston, Birmingham, generating an income of £3,000 a year by charging 1s. 6d. for a prescription and 3s. 6d. for a visit. Arthur's duties were to dispense the medicines Dr Hoare prescribed in large quantities. It was hard work and long hours – he sometimes made up as many as 100 prescriptions in an evening – and he was dealing with the poorest members of the community, but he was comparitively well paid. 'On the whole I made few mistakes, though I have been known to send out ointment and pill boxes with elaborate directions on the lid and nothing inside.'

Initially he was kept very much in his place. When lonely he would go into the drawing room to chat to the doctor's wife, but he was soon informed that this was not the custom and that the assistant was expected to keep himself to himself. Nonetheless Dr Hoare and his wife soon took a strong liking to Arthur and treated him like a son; in the evenings he was invited to smoke a pipe with the doctor while Mrs Hoare enjoyed a cigar. As always, he kept his mother closely in touch with what he was doing:

> Dearest Ma'am,
>
> I have been very busy lately and hardly had time to write. I assure you I earn my two pounds a month. In the morning, I generally go out with R.R. [Dr Hoare] in his gig and do the rounds till dinner at two. This is an innovation and deprives me of any leisure. From dinner till tea I brew horrible draughts and foul mixtures for the patients, (I concocted as many as 42 today). After tea, patients begin to drop in and we experiment on them until nearly nine, and then we have supper and comparative peace until twelve when we generally turn in; so you see we have plenty to do, and the life is none the worse for that. I visit a few patients every day and get a good deal of experience . . .

Later he complained of having very little time to study for his exams: 'I have been worked off my legs since Xmas. I have hardly opened a medical book or sat down save when I have been so fagged as to be unable to do anything. We have had a most confounded hard time of it – I have been at 3 confinements in one day, with a long list of patients to see and 60 bottles of Physic to make – and then been up all night after it. I see the force of what you say about holding on here as long as possible and I like the work but anything like systematic reading is simply ludicrous. I have made good use of my time, so far, when I had any, but now there is simply none.'

———————◆———————

It was in Birmingham under the Hoares' demanding but benign regime that Arthur started to write short stories for publication. Finding the time, on top of his studies as a medical student and his duties as an assistant, required the iron discipline that would mark his entire career. He sent his first story, 'The Haunted Grange of Goresthorpe', written

in flawless copperplate on 24 lined pages in an exercise book, to
Blackwood's Edinburgh Magazine, where it was promptly filed and
forgotten.[7] Undeterred, he dashed off 'The Mystery of the Sassassa
Valley', borrowing heavily from his favourite writers – Poe and Bret
Harte, another American who made his name with rip-roaring
accounts of pioneer life in California. Set in South Africa, a country
he had yet to visit, it was a fast-moving yarn about a demon with
glowing eyes which terrified local villagers; it had many of the hallmarks of his later work – pace, a neatly worked plot, a strange and
uncanny theme and an exotic setting. He offered it to *Chambers's
Journal* in Edinburgh, a popular middlebrow literary magazine which
had first published Thomas Hardy's work. To his astonishment and
delight, it was accepted for a fee of three guineas – more than he
was earning for a month's hard labour in the surgery at Aston – and
appeared in the issue dated 6 September 1879. His next few submissions to *Chambers's Journal* were all rejected, but he did not lose
heart. 'I knew that whatever rebuffs I might receive – and God knows
I had plenty,' he would tell an interviewer later in his life, 'I had
once proved I could earn gold, and the spirit was in me to do it
again.'[8]

He was soon able to place a second story, 'The American's Tale',
in *London Society*, a magazine to which his father had earlier contributed
illustrations and which offered 'Light and Amusing Literature for the
Hours of Relaxation'. Arthur wrote the draft in Edinburgh, in both
pen and pencil, in a medical notebook entitled 'Notes on Medicine
Sessions 1879–80', perhaps indicating he was not paying as much attention to his classes as he might. In the front were clinical notes on
various patients, 'The Constitutional Complications of Gout' and
'Treatments for Rheumatism', and in the back, narrated by Jefferson
Adams, was the gothic, cautionary tale of Joe Hawkins of Montana
('Alabama Joe as he was called thereabouts. A regular out and outer
he was, 'bout the darndest Skunk as ever man clapt eyes on . . .').
Alabama Joe picks a quarrel in a bar with a foreigner, Tom Scott, and
gets beaten in a bare-knuckle fight. Intent on revenge, he lies in wait
for Scott in Flytrap Gulch. But when Alabama Joe's friends discover
he is missing and Scott is still alive, they vow to hang the foreigner
by the great flytrap in the gulch. A ghastly scene greets them as they

arrive: 'One of the leaves of the flytrap . . . was slowly rollin' back upon its hinges, so to speak. There, lying like a child in a cradle, was Alabama Joe in the hollow o' the leaf. The great thorns had been driving through his chest as it shut upon him.'

James Hogg, the editor of *London Society*, was so impressed with Arthur's work that he advised him to quit medicine to concentrate on writing, although not so impressed that he was willing to pay more than £1. 10s. for his contribution. In a letter to his mother, Arthur let drop, immodestly, that Mr Hogg viewed him as 'one of the coming men in literature'.

He also frequently composed doggerel as a mnemonic for his studies, scrawling on the inside page of 'The Essentials of Materia Medica and Therapeutics' the following:

Opium

I'll tell you a most serious fact
That opium dries a mucous tract
And constipates and causes thirst
And stimulates the heart at first
And then allows its strength to fall
Relaxing the capillary wall.
The cerebrum is first affected,
Contracted pupils are detected
On tetanus you mustn't bet
Secretions gone except the sweat
Lungs and sexuals don't forget.

In the same month that his first story appeared in *Chambers's Journal*, Arthur was proud to have a letter published in the *British Medical Journal* under the heading 'Gelseminum as a Poison', in which he described experiments he had carried out on himself to 'ascertain how far one might go' with the drug, the dried rhizome and root of yellow jasmine, then used to treat neuralgia. He subjected himself to an increasing daily dose of the tincture, carefully recording the side effects. On the third day he experienced giddiness, on the fourth 'difficult eye accommodation', on the fifth severe headaches and diarrhoea. He persisted until the seventh day, by which time he was taking ten millilitres and suffering from severe depression, among other symptoms. His experiment conclusively disproved the theory that half that dose would prove fatal.

In later years Arthur would insist that he was no more than a passable medical student and indeed his grades were hardly stellar. Between 1878 and 1881 he was awarded S (satisfactory) grades in all subjects except clinical surgery, for which he received an S–. Nevertheless, in an interview with *Pall Mall Gazette*, Bell would claim that Arthur was one of the best students he ever had: 'He was exceedingly interested always upon anything connected with diagnosis, and was never tired of trying to discover those little details which one looks for.' A fellow student, one D. Marinus, remembered him for another reason: 'Arthur impressed me chiefly by his very kind and considerate manner towards the poor people who came to the out-patients department, whom I am afraid some of us were in the habit of treating somewhat cavalierly.'[9]

Arthur cannot have been helped in his studies by events at home. He only referred very briefly in his autobiography to his father's 'illness', yet it can only have been devastating to see his father's deterioration. 'During all this time our family affairs had taken no turn for the better, and had it not been for my exertions and for the work of my sisters we could hardly have carried on. [Waller's help is not mentioned.] My father's health had utterly broken down, he had to retire to that convalescent home in which the last years of his life were spent, and I, aged twenty, found myself practically the head of a large and struggling family.' He admitted his father had 'weaknesses' but insisted that 'hard fate' had 'thrown him, a man of sensitive genius', into an environment which he was unfit to face.

Arthur's anguish would soon find expression in his fiction, in which themes of incarceration, mania and the perils of drink abound. In 'The Surgeon of Gaster Fell' (1885) a young surgeon is thought to have incarcerated an elderly man in a sinister cage, possibly for a cruel experiment, but the prisoner turns out to be the surgeon's own father, whom he is trying to keep from being committed to an asylum: 'He has an intense dread of madhouses, and in his sane intervals would beg and pray so piteously not to be condemned to one, that I could never find the heart to resist him.' A Charles Doyle figure also makes an appearance in 'A Sordid Affair' (1891) in the form of a disaffected artist and former clerk 'whose long course of secret drunkenness had ended in a raging attack of delirium tremens, which could not be concealed from his employers, and which brought his instant dismissal from his situation'. Married to a dressmaker, he steals an important copy of a dress in a West End Store and pawns it for alcohol. Eventually his wife finds him drunk in the gutter surrounded by a crowd of jeering boys. 'She caught a glimpse of a horrid crawling figure, a hatless head, and a dull, vacant, leering face . . . His coat was covered with dust and he mumbled and chuckled like an ape.'

Early in 1880 Arthur's thirst for adventure was assuaged when a friend named Claude Currie walked into his room at Edinburgh while he was cramming for an examination and asked him if he would be interested in a trip to the Arctic as the surgeon on a whaler. Currie had accepted the job but had just discovered that he could not go and was looking for someone to take his place. He probably chose Arthur because they were about the same size and weight and would fit the heavy clothing and leather boots Currie had bought. Nothing could have been more alluring to the young medical student, not just for the adventure but the money – £2. 10s. a week, plus a bonus of 3s. per ton of whale oil. In less than a fortnight he was at Peterhead with his friend's kit, a bag of books, a journal and two pairs of boxing gloves, reporting for duty on the SS *Hope*, a 307-ton steam whaler built in 1872 and owned by Captain John Gray, a member of one of the most prominent whaling families in the area.

Whaling in the late nineteenth century was in decline: the great fleet of whalers operating from Peterhead had been reduced to just seven ships as a result of both petroleum products replacing whale oil and the declining numbers of whales caused by over-fishing. Although the oil was still used for soaps and lubricants, the animals were now primarily hunted for baleen – the long bony plates of keratin hanging from their upper jaws – which was used for everything from kitchen utensils to corset stays. The curvaceous waistlines of Victorian ladies owed much to the whale.

Hunting techniques had changed little over the centuries. When a whale was sighted, a number of small boats were lowered and rowed silently towards the prey. Once within range, the gunner in the lead boat would fire a harpoon from a cannon. If the whale was hit, the trick was to keep it tethered by the rope attached to the harpoon, even if the animal dived to great depths or turned to attack the boats. It was a dangerous game – some harpooned whales had been known to crush both boat and crew in their jaws. But once the whale had tired, the hunters would move in to finish it off with lances, after which it would be towed back to the ship, lashed to the side and processed, the blubber being rendered in huge iron pots and the baleen stripped from the carcass, cleaned and bundled.

The *Hope* sailed from Peterhead on the afternoon of 28 February 1880, bound first for the Shetland Islands, where it would enlist 'Shetland hands' to help in the hunt for seals and whales. On the first night at sea, Jack Lamb, the ship's steward, noticed Arthur stowing his boxing gloves under his bunk and suggested a match. Certainly, Arthur agreed, but when? Right now, Lamb replied, pulling on a pair of the gloves. Not wishing to seem cowardly in front of his shipmates, Arthur had little choice but to follow suit. Lamb, bandy-legged, tough and wiry, was a street fighter with no knowledge of, or interest in, the Queensberry Rules; Doyle had learned boxing at university as a 'gentlemanly art'. (The sport would appear in several of his stories; a boxing medical student is the hero of 'The Croxley Master'.) Lamb flew at his opponent with a flurry of blows, most of which Doyle, his guard up, managed to block. While Lamb continued to throw punch after punch, Doyle, much the bigger of the two, kept him at a distance and waited for him to tire. But the little steward showed no sign of wilting, and in the end, after an experimental jab or two, Doyle flattened him with a tremendous hook to the head. Lamb emerged with a black eye and Arthur won the respect of his shipmates, Lamb included. Later Arthur heard Lamb talking through a cabin partition: 'He's the best surgeon we've ever had – he's blacked my eye.'

In contrast to his pugilistic talents, the steward had a fine tenor voice and would sing sentimental ditties in the galley, usually about women, which Arthur confessed filled him with 'a vague sweet discontent'. Lamb also engaged in a long-running feud with the ship's fiery chief mate, Colin McLean. When both men had had too much rum, one would inevitably pick a fight with the other, requiring Arthur to step in and separate them. 'I have a vivid recollection of an evening which I spent in dragging him [McLean] off the steward, who had imprudently made some criticism upon his way of attacking a whale which had escaped. Both men had had some rum, which made the one argumentative and the other violent, and as we were all three seated in a space of about seven by four [feet], it took some hard work to prevent bloodshed.'

Arthur enjoyed the company of the sailors, honest, hard-working men, and listened intently to stories about their lives and adventures. He was fascinated to discover that several, particularly those from the Shetland Islands, claimed to have had spiritual experiences both at home and at sea. Most were members of break-away Presbyterian churches in which alcohol was strictly forbidden, so they could not have been drunk when they claimed to have had visions. At one point he wondered if they were making fun of him, but concluded after extensive questioning that they were telling the truth. It was another early experience to which he would return later in life, both in fiction and in the propagation of spiritualism.

The *Hope* narrowly made the safe harbour at Lerwick in the Shetlands before a ferocious storm broke. From there Arthur wrote a long and affectionate letter to his mother:

> Dearest Ma'am,
>
>   Here goes by the aid of a quill pen and a pot of ink to let you know all the news from the north. The mail steamer came yesterday with your letter . . . And first of all you will be glad to know that I never was more happy in my life. I've got a strong Bohemian element in me, I'm afraid, and the life just seems to suit me. Fine honest fellows the men are and such a strapping lot . . . There are nearly 30 sail of whalers in Lerwick Bay now. There are only two Peterhead ships, the *Windward* and the *Hope*. There is a lot of bad blood between the two sets, Gray and Murray [Captain of the *Windward*] being both looked upon as aristocrats. Colin McLean our 1st mate was at the

Queen's on Saturday when half a dozen Dundee officers
began to run down the Hope. Colin is a great red bearded
Scotchman of few words so he got up slowly and said 'I'm
from the Hope myself' and began to run a muck [sic]
through the assembly. He floored a doctor and maimed a
captain and got away in triumph. He remarked to me in
the morning, 'It's lucky I was sober, doctor, or there might
have been a row'. I wonder what Colin's idea of a row may
be . . .

We just got in in time to avoid the full fury of that gale
the other day. The Captain says that if we had stayed out,
we would have lost our boats and bulwarks, possibly our
mast . . .

It was 10 March before the *Hope* was able to continue and even
then the wind was so fierce they were obliged to seek shelter for a
day and a night in the lee of one of the outlying islands. Arthur kept
a meticulous daily log of the voyage, illustrated with cartoons, maps
and pen-and-ink sketches of the wildlife and the daily routine on board
but he still had sufficient time to read and to begin a short story, 'A
Journey to the Pole'. In truth there was little to do as the *Hope* ploughed
steadily northwards; Arthur took part in boxing contests, sing-songs
and games of draughts. He was fascinated by the bird life of the Arctic
and read widely – Boswell, Carlyle, Laurence Sterne's *Tristram Shandy*,
which he thought 'coarse, but very clever', and William Scoresby's
classic book on whaling, *An Account of the Arctic Regions with a History
and Description of the Northern Whale Fishery*. He urged members of
the crew to borrow his Macaulay volumes, with varying degrees
of success; the first mate was not alone in being illiterate.

His excitement at entering the ice fields was evident: 'I awoke one
morning to hear the bump, bump of the floating pieces against the
side of the ship, and I went on deck to see the whole sea covered
with them to the horizon. They were none of them large, but they
lay so thick that a man might travel far by springing from one to the
other. Their dazzling whiteness made the sea seem bluer by contrast,
and with a blue sky above, and that glorious Arctic air in one's nostrils,
it was a morning to remember.'

The first seals were sighted on 18 March, but under an agreement between Britain and Norway hunting was prohibited until 3 April; nevertheless, numerous ships were gathering in the area. On the day that seal hunting began, a strong swell was running, making conditions on the shifting ice exceptionally dangerous, and Captain Gray ordered his inexperienced ship's surgeon to stay on board. Furious at being excluded from the action, Arthur sat disconsolately on the gunwale with his legs dangling over the edge until the *Hope* suddenly rolled and pitched him overboard. He disappeared into the water between two blocks of ice and only managed to clamber back on board with some difficulty, whereupon Gray observed sarcastically that if he could fall into the water from the ship he might 'just as well be on the ice'. Arthur happily changed his clothes and joined the hunt. He quickly discovered that it took 'a lot of knack' to know which ice would bear his considerable weight, and he took some time to acquire it, since by 6 April he had fallen into the water so often that Captain Gray nicknamed him 'The Great Northern Diver'.

Shooting grown seals and clubbing the pups to death was a bloody business which Arthur at first found hard to stomach. 'Those glaring crimson pools upon the dazzling white of the icefields, under the peaceful silence of a blue Arctic sky, did seem a horrible intrusion,' he wrote. 'But an inexorable demand creates an inexorable supply, and the seals, by their death, help to give a living to the long line of seamen, dockers, tanners, curers, triers, chandlers, leather merchants and oil-sellers, who stand between this annual butchery on the one hand, and the exquisite, with his soft leather boots, or the savant, using a delicate oil for his philosophical instruments, upon the other.'

Later in the voyage there was another mishap that could have cost him his life. He was working on the ice skinning a seal some distance from the other hunters when he stepped backwards and fell into the water, and found he could not pull himself back up, despite his physical strength, since he had nothing to grip. He knew well that he would be dead in minutes from hypothermia unless he could get out of the water and finally caught hold of the flipper of the dead seal, managed to get a knee over the edge of the ice and roll onto it. By the time he reached the ship his clothes had frozen solid, like a suit of armour, crackling as he clambered aboard.

On 7 April, he sat down to write a gripping account of his adventures for his mother, noting at the top of the letter that the SS *Hope* was at 'Lat 73 N Long 2 E':

Dearest Ma'am,

Here I am as well and as strong and as ugly as ever off Jan Meyer's Island in the Arctic Circle. We started from Shetland on 10th March & had a splendid passage without a cloud in the sky, reaching the ice upon the 16th. We went to bed with a great stretch of blue water before us as far as the eye could reach, and when we got on deck in the morning there was the whole sea full of great flat lumps of ice, white above and blue-ish green below all tossing and heaving on the waves. We pushed through it for a day but saw no seals, but on the second day we saw a young sea elephant upon the ice, and some schools of seals in the water swimming towards NW. We followed their track and on the 18th saw the smoke of six steamers all making in the same direction, in the hope of reaching the main pack. Next morning eleven vessels could be seen from the deck, and a lot of sea elephants or bladdernose seals were laying about. These always hang on the skirts of a pack of true seals so we felt hopeful. You must know that no blood is allowed to be shed in the arctic circle before April 3rd. On the 20th we saw the real pack. They were lying in a solid mass upon the ice, about 15 miles w by 8, literally millions of them. On the 22nd we got upon the edge of them and waited. 25 vessels were in sight doing the same thing. On the 3rd the bloody works began and it has been going on ever since. The mothers are shot and the little ones have their brains knocked out with spiked clubs. They are then skinned where they lie and the skin with blubber attached is dragged by the assassin to the ships side. This is very hard work, as you often have to travel a couple of miles, as I did today, jumping from piece to piece before you found your victim, and then you have a fearful weight to drag back. The crew must think me a man of extraordinary tastes to work hard and with gusto at what they all consider the most tiring task they have, but I think it encourages them. By the way in the last four days I have fallen into the sea five times which is a pretty good average . . . I have enjoyed my voyage immensely, my dear and only hope you are all as cheery. I don't think you would have recognised me as I came into the cabin just now – I'm sure you wouldn't. The Captain says I make the most awful looking savage he ever saw. My hair was on end, my face covered with dirt and perspiration, and my hands with blood. I had my oldest clothes on, my sea boots were shining with water and crusted with snow at the top. I had a belt around my coat with a knife in a sheath and a steel stuck in it, all clotted with blood. I had a coil of rope slung round my shoulders, and a long gory polar axe in my hand. That's the photograph of your little cherub, madam. I never knew before what it was to be thoroughly healthy. I just feel as if I could go anywhere and eat anything.

Now, my dear, don't be uneasy during the next month or two. If ever a round peg (not pig) got into a round hole it is me . . .

On 22 May, Arthur celebrated his 21st birthday, his coming of age, on the *Hope*. 'Rather a funny sort of place to do it,' he noted. The weeks of seal hunting had bagged 3,614 skins (Arthur's own 'game bag' was 55 skins), and by mid-June they were in the whaling grounds. For a young man brought up on tales of adventure, the thrill of the hunt, the battle in the wilderness between man and monster, stirred his passions as never before. 'No man who has not experienced it,' he wrote in his entry for 20 June, 'can imagine the intense excitement of whale fishing. The rarity of the animals, the difficulty attending any approach to its haunts, its extreme value, its strength, sagacity and size all give it charm.' He nevertheless experienced some qualms: 'Yet amid all the excitement . . . one's sympathies lie with the poor hunted creature. The whale has a small eye, little larger than that of a bullock, but I cannot easily forget the mute expostulation which I read in one, as it dimmed over with death within hand's touch of me.'

On one terrifying occasion, a wounded whale raised its huge fin over Arthur's boat, blocking out the sun, and threatening to crush them. 'One flap would have sent us to the bottom of the sea,' he recalled, 'and I can never forget how, as we pushed our way from under, each of us held one hand up to stave off that great, threatening fin, as if any strength of ours could have availed if the whale meant it to descend.' Fortunately the animal was in its death throes and the fin slipped harmlessly under the water as it rolled away.

Such dangerous experiences did nothing to dampen Arthur's enthusiasm, and his natural gifts as a writer shine through the pages of his journal, both in evoking atmosphere and meticulous attention to detail. His description of being at the oars in a small boat in pursuit of a quarry was typical:

> It is exciting work pulling on to a whale. Your own back is turned to him, and all you know about him is what you read upon the face of the boat-steerer. He is staring out over your head, watching the creature as it swims slowly through the water, raising his hand now and again as a signal to stop rowing when he sees that the eye is coming round, and then resuming the stealthy approach when the whale is end on. There are so many floating pieces of ice, that as long as the oars are quiet the boat alone will not cause the creature to dive. So you creep slowly up, and at last you are so near that the boat-steerer knows that you can get there before the creature has time to dive – for it takes some little time to get that huge body into motion. You see a sudden gleam in his eyes, and a flush in his cheeks, and it's 'Give way, boys! Give way, all! Hard!' Click goes the trigger of the big harpoon gun, and the foam flies from your oars. Six strokes, perhaps, and then with a dull greasy squelch the bows run upon something soft, and you and your oars are sent flying in every direction. But little you care for that, for as you touched the whale you heard the crash of the gun, and know that the harpoon has been fired from point-blank into the huge, lead-coloured curve of its side. The creature sinks like a stone, the bows of the boat splash down into the water again, . . . and there is the line whizzing swiftly

from under the seats and over the bows between your outstretched feet.

And this is the great element of danger – for it is rarely indeed that the whale has spirit enough to turn upon its enemies. The line is very carefully coiled by a special man named the line-coiler, and it is warranted not to kink. If it should happen to do so, however, and if the loop catches the limbs of any one of the boat's crew, that man goes to his death so rapidly that his comrades hardly know that he has gone. It is a waste of fish to cut the line, for the victim is already hundreds of fathoms deep.

Despite his reservations, Arthur evidently gloried in the contest. He enjoyed lancing because it was a more prolonged experience than harpooning, noting that the whale appeared to feel no pain and spoke of the hunt as a great sport. 'Who would swap that moment [the death of the whale],' he wrote, 'for any other triumph that sport can give?'

In fact six weeks' hunting only netted the *Hope* two Greenland whales and by the end of July she was heading home to Peterhead. 'I shall never again see the great Greenland floes,' Arthur ruminated in his log on 31 July, 'never again see the land where I have smoked so many pensive pipes . . . Who says thou art cold and inhospitable, my poor icefields? I have known you in calm and in storm and I say you are genial and kindly.'

Arthur never forgot his adventure in the Arctic, the stark beauty of the ice, the startling blue of the water, the peculiar mewling of the seal pups, the heart-stopping majesty of a breaching whale, the crisp, cold air and the intoxicating feeling of standing on the brink of the unknown. He went aboard the SS *Hope*, he admitted, a 'big, straggling youth' but disembarked a 'powerful, well-grown man'. He would also, like Jack London in *The Call of the Wild* and Joseph Conrad in *Heart of Darkness*, draw extensively on his experiences to add authentic colour to the stories he would later write.

Arthur claimed he returned to Edinburgh with fifty gold sovereigns hidden in various pockets so that 'the Mam' might 'have the excitement of hunting for them'. He resumed study for his finals, perhaps with a certain weariness after his beguiling taste of adventure in the Arctic. The family had moved again, this time to a secluded first-floor apartment at 15 Lonsdale Terrace, back overlooking the Meadows, and Waller continued to pay the rent of £60 a year. Charles Doyle's drunken behaviour may have made the move from George Square necessary, and in March 1881 he was finally sent to Blairerno. Arthur made the best of it in a letter to Lottie, writing euphemistically, 'We have packed Papa off to a health resort in Aberdeenshire.'

Back at university, nerves inevitably became frayed as the finals approached. Arthur described the scene as a crowd of students waited outside to be called in for a *viva voce*: 'It was painful to observe their attempts to appear confident and unconcerned as they glanced round the heavens, as if to observe the state of the weather, or examined with well-feigned archaeological fervour the inscriptions upon the old University walls. Most painful of all was it when someone, plucking up courage, would venture upon a tiny joke, at which the whole company would gibber in an ostentatious way, as though to show that even in this dire pass the appreciation of humour still remained with them. At times, when any of their number alluded to the examination or detailed the questions which had been proposed to Brown or Baker the day before, the mask of unconcern would be dropped, and the whole assembly would glare eagerly and silently at the speaker.'

Arthur passed his finals by his account with 'fair, but not notable, distinction' and qualified as a Bachelor of Medicine and Master of Surgery. On his graduation in August 1881, he drew a portrait of himself in pen-and-ink, jumping for joy, waving his diploma in his left hand, above the ironic caption 'Licensed to kill'.

CHAPTER 4

THE AMAZING DOCTOR BUDD

T THE AGE OF 22, the newly qualified Dr Conan Doyle was the Victorian embodiment of a 'fine figure of a man'. He carried his bulk lightly and walked with a purposeful gait, as if he always knew exactly where he was going. His wavy hair, slicked down with oil, was parted on the left, and he now sported a luxuriant walrus-like moustache, waxed into points, which covered his entire top lip. His Edinburgh accent was pronounced, but he spoke slowly so that he was easily understood and looked whomever he was addressing directly in the eyes.

Conan Doyle was anxious to find paid employment as soon as possible after graduating, if for no other reason than to make his family less beholden to Bryan Waller. His first hope was for a hospital appointment, but no openings were available. He then applied for a position as ship's surgeon on a passenger liner. When he had heard nothing for several weeks, he considered joining the Army, Navy, or even the Indian Service, from where he could send money home. But before a decision became imperative, a telegram arrived offering him the post of ship's medical officer, at a salary of £12 a month, on the African Steam Navigation Company's *Mayumba*. Hoping to repeat the excitement and romance of his trip to the Arctic he jumped at the opportunity. He had visions, he wrote, of exotic ports, steaming jungles, mighty rivers, cloud-capped mountains and 'the haughty grace of the untamed savage as he trod his native wilderness, or yearned in his simple untutored way for a slice out of the calf of your leg . . .'[1] The reality would be very different.

The *Mayumba*, lying in the port of Liverpool, was a 1,500-ton steamer which had certainly seen better days after twenty years' plying the west coast of Africa, carrying passengers, mail and mixed cargo on the outward journey, and palm oil, nuts and ivory on the return. Among the thirty or so passengers on board when Conan Doyle joined the ship were a number of wealthy African traders who appeared to have spent all their money in Liverpool on drink and women. When the *Mayumba* sailed, on 22 October 1881, one of them, Conan Doyle drily observed, was seen off by 'a choice selection of the *demi-monde*'.

Conan Doyle was not above a little judicious literary embroidery. He would claim in his autobiography that he saved the ship from running into rocks off the Irish coast only a few hours into the voyage when, in thick fog, he alone caught sight of the Tuskar lighthouse through the murk and alerted the first mate that they were heading straight for it. Yet he made no mention of this incident in his letters, nor in an article about the voyage published in the *British Journal of Photography* shortly after his return (his friend, William Burton, a keen photographer, had introduced him to the editor). In the same article he described in some detail the extensive photographic equipment he took with him, although there is no evidence he took a single picture. Nor, indeed, did he explain how an impoverished, newly qualified doctor could have acquired such expensive paraphernalia. But he would certainly have known he would not be able to interest the *British Journal of Photography* in his article unless there was a strong photographic connection.

For the first few days at sea, the *Mayumba* wallowed through a heavy storm in the Bay of Biscay and Conan Doyle was kept busy treating the passengers for seasickness. His cabin was flooded and remained ankle-deep in water until the storm abated. Further south the weather cleared and the ship made two enjoyable stops, at Madeira and the Canaries, where a number of the passengers disembarked. Some were ladies whom Conan Doyle was sorry to see go, since they had generated fun on board. Personable and well-liked, comfortable among women, he discovered one night they had made an apple-pie bed for him; he retaliated by hiding a flying fish in one of their night-gowns.

The first port of call on the coast of Africa was Freetown, in Sierra Leone, a truly dreadful place, he noted, of death and despair where the luckless white expatriates sought refuge from their surroundings in the bottle. A year stationed in Freetown, he noted, seemed to be about the 'limit of human endurance' and he wondered if such colonies were really worth the price being paid in human suffering.

Next stop was Monrovia, the capital port of Liberia, founded by the American Colonisation Society in 1822, where the black abolitionist leader Henry Highland Garnet, recently appointed the US consul, was headed. Born into slavery in Maryland, Garnet was a leading member of the generation of black Americans who led the abolitionist movement away from moral persuasion and into political action. Conan Doyle had enjoyed his company on board and engaged in lively discussion with him about English and American literature. 'This negro gentleman did me good,' he wrote, adding that he was 'the most intelligent and well-read man' he had met during the whole trip.

By and large, Conan Doyle was unimpressed by the expatriate communities he encountered: they lived miserable and fearful lives, he thought, constantly under threat of succumbing to disease, and drank too much. He admitted that he drank quite freely himself during this period but realised that 'the unbounded cocktails of West Africa' were a danger and cut down on them 'with an effort'. Like many of his contemporaries, he was similarly unimpressed by the natives: 'A great deal has been said about the regeneration of our black brothers and the latent virtues of the swarthy races. My own experience is that you abhor them on first meeting them, and gradually learn to dislike them a very great deal more as you become better acquainted with them.'[2]

Cheerful chaos marked the *Mayumba*'s slow passage down the west coast. On one occasion the ship weighed anchor while around a hundred native traders were on board, and they were obliged to dive off the ship and swim to their canoes, one carrying a tall hat, an umbrella and a religious poster he had bought from the crew. At another 'minor port', short of time, they threw a consignment of barrel staves overboard in the expectation that they would wash up on the shore. 'How the real owner could make good his claim to them I do not know,' Conan Doyle observed.

When the *Mayumba* dropped anchor off Cape Coast in what is

now Ghana, Conan Doyle decided to try to escape the intolerable heat by taking a swim in the warm waters of the Gulf of Guinea. He plunged in, swam in a leisurely fashion around the ship and then climbed out. While he was drying himself, he noticed the dorsal fin of a large shark cutting through the water as if in search of him. The sight, he recorded, made his blood run cold: 'Several times in my life I have done utterly reckless things with so little motive that I have found it difficult to explain them to myself afterwards. This was one of them.'

At Lagos in Nigeria, once a notorious centre for the slave trade, he was felled by a fever, probably malaria, and lay in his bunk for several days, wondering if he would live or die. He remembered staggering to his bunk and promptly passing out. As he was the only doctor on board, there was no one to care for him and he counted himself lucky to have survived, particularly when he discovered that another crew member who had gone down at the same time had died.

At the inappropriately named Bonny, in the Niger Delta, he wrote home to a friend:

> Never was there such a hole of a place, it is good for nothing but swearing at. I am just recovering from a smart attack of fever, and am so weak that the pen feels like an oar though I was only on my back for three days. It is our summer here, and while you are having crisp frosty mornings (it makes my feet tingle to think of them) we have an apoplectic looking sun glaring down on us in a disgusting manner, while there is never a breath of air, save when a whiff of miasma is borne off the land. Here we are steaming from one dirty little port to another dirty little port, all as alike as two peas, and only to be distinguished by comparing the smell of the inhabitants, though they all smell as if they had become prematurely putrid and should be burned without unnecessary delay . . .[3]

On the *Mayumba* steamed, as far as Old Calabar, a British colony sixty miles up the Calabar River in what is now Nigeria, along a channel so narrow the trees brushed the side of the ship. Conan Doyle sat on deck with a rifle, hoping to bag an alligator, but saw only swirls in the muddy water. While at Old Calabar he and another crew member took a canoe and paddled upstream through murky swamps to the ramshackle village of Creektown. 'Dark and terrible mangrove swamps lay on either side with gloomy shades where nothing that is not horrible could exist. It is indeed a foul place. I saw an evil-looking snake, worm-coloured and about three feet long. I shot him and saw him drift downstream. I learned later in life to give up killing animals, but I confess that I have no particular compunction about that one.'

When they alighted at Creektown, the natives informed them that they must report immediately to the King. Imagining themselves ending up in the King's cooking pot, they hastily returned to their canoe and paddled nervously back down the river. In fact a Presbyterian mission had been long established at Creektown and King Eyo Honesty VII probably desired nothing more than a courtesy call. In one expatriate's house Conan Doyle visited in Old Calabar, he was delighted to find a copy of *London Society* with his 'The American's Tale' in it. But the heat continued to sap his energy. 'It is too hot to say anything funny or interesting,' he wrote in his journal. 'Oh for a pair of skates and a long stretch of ice . . .'

Conan Doyle was generally unmoved by Africa – the stifling heat, the disease, the alien natives, were a world away from the stark beauty of the Arctic wastelands that he had so much enjoyed. 'The death-like impression of Africa grew upon me. One felt that the white man with his present diet and habits was an intruder who was never meant to be there, and that the great sullen brown continent killed him as one crushes nits.' The captain of the *Mayumba* only encouraged this view by telling him stories about natives offering up human sacrifices to the sharks, of hearing the screams of the victims as they were dragged towards the water and of seeing human skulls protruding from anthills. The swamp-like climate was particularly oppressive: 'When you feel your napkin at meals to be an intolerable thing, and when you find that it leaves a wet weal across your white duck trousers, then you know that you have really arrived.'

His boredom was exacerbated by a lack of intellectual stimulation. Although he had acquired a copy of *L'Atmosphere*, a book by the French astronomer Camille Flammarion, as a fee for ministering to a young Frenchman dying of fever, he was forced to keep rereading the books he had been able to bring: Macaulay most importantly, but also Shakespeare, Ouida, Charles Lever, Marryat, Henry Kingsley,

Carlyle and Wendell Holmes. Carlyle, he noted in his journal, was a 'grand rugged intellect' but 'I fancy Poetry, Art and all the little amenities of life were dead letters to him.' Whist and cribbage with other members of the crew occupied the remainder of his spare time, but, as restless as ever, he also wrote an account of the voyage for the *Sierra Leone Gazette*.

From Old Calabar the *Mayumba* headed for home, stopping at the same ports to collect oil and ivory to take back to Britain. The only excitement was a fire in one of the coal bunkers; with only a thin bulkhead separating the burning coal from the hold where the flammable palm oil was stored, there was a serious risk of a catastrophic explosion which would have sunk the ship. At one point, part of the hull glowed red-hot and thick black smoke poured through the ventilators. The captain ordered the lifeboats to be prepared prior to abandoning ship and told Conan Doyle to rouse the passengers and 'keep them calm' – not an easy task. But the fire was finally brought under control, and the *Mayumba* limped back into Liverpool, still smouldering, on 14 January 1882. Conan Doyle collected his pay and left the ship without regrets, any lingering notion of pursuing a career as a ship's surgeon now firmly rejected.

'I don't intend to go to Africa again,' he wrote to his mother, who had suggested he spend a couple of years with the African Steam Navigation Company to save enough to start a private practice. 'The pay is less than I could make by my pen in the same time, and the climate is atrocious. I trust you will not be disappointed by my leaving the ship, but this is not good enough.'

————◆————

Conan Doyle had not long been back in Edinburgh when a letter arrived from his Aunt Annette, inviting him to London to discuss his 'future' with the family. Recognising that the family, as influential Catholics, was guardedly offering to pull strings for him, he felt obliged to warn her that he no longer shared her faith. Annette replied promptly to say the family was deeply disturbed by his letter, wondered if he was not being precipitate and headstrong, and asked him again to pay them a visit, as a favour, so they could discuss matters face to face.

This fateful family meeting probably took place at 54 Clifton Gardens, Maida Vale, the home of the dour Uncle James and his wife, Jane Henrietta. It was evidently a difficult and painful confrontation for all concerned. For James and his brothers the Roman Catholic church was a pillar of their lives, inextricably interwoven with their proud heritage; while Arthur was at Stonyhurst, James had sent him sermons to study. It was impossible for them to understand how their nephew could abandon the faith that had sustained the family for generations, but Arthur steadfastly stood his ground, explaining that his agnosticism was based on reason and a refusal to accept any theory or philosophy that could not be proven beyond doubt. He could not share their blind faith and thus could not practise as a Catholic doctor with any integrity. His aunt and uncles made no secret of their disappointment in him and the meeting ended more in sorrow than in anger. Before Arthur left London, Uncle Dicky took him to lunch at the Athenaeum in a final attempt to persuade him of the advantages of accepting the family's patronage, but he would not be moved, demonstrating the strength of personal conviction and stubborn confidence in his beliefs that he would exhibit for the rest of his life.

In the absence of any other job offers, Conan Doyle returned to Aston to work as Dr Hoare's assistant, writing uncertain fiction in whatever spare time he could find. His lack of confidence is clear in this letter to the editor of *Blackwood's* magazine: 'I venture to submit to your notice the accompanying tale "The Actor's Duel". I once before trespassed upon your valuable time by sending up a sketch which did not come up to your standard – I trust that this may meet with a better fate. However defective the working out may be, I am conscious that the denouement is original and powerful, worthy, I hope, of the traditions of your magazine. Will you do me the favour not to destroy the ms in case of rejection . . . faithfully yours, A. Conan Doyle MD.'[4] His manuscript was returned on 24 March 1882. But, persistent as ever, he then sent it to the *Boy's Own Paper*, where it was again rejected. It was finally accepted by *Bow Bells* under title 'The Tragedians'.

In non-literary matters Conan Doyle was asserting himself with growing assurance. On a visit home around this time he was involved in an altercation with Waller which apparently ended in a fist fight. The cause is unknown, and Arthur never referred to it in letters to his mother but in a note to Annette written in April 1882 he boasted that he had 'frightened his immortal soul out of him' and 'made such a mess of him that he did not leave the house for 23 days'. He added that he 'fancied it will make him a better fellow', and while they had subsequently had a 'nominal reconciliation' they did not 'love each other very much yet'.[5]

While he was still in Birmingham, he was offered a job out of the blue by his friend, George Turnavine Budd, a remarkable individual who would subsequently make an unwitting contribution to many of the characters in Conan Doyle's fiction. They had first met at university and despite having little in common had become firm friends. Budd was ugly, unpredictable, aggressive, mercurial, brilliant, mad and, if so inclined, enormously good company. Five feet nine inches tall, heavily set, a fearless forward in the university rugby team, he had a red face, skin not dissimilar to the bark of a tree, beetle brows, spiky yellow hair protruding from his scalp like the bristles of a brush, a lantern jaw and bloodshot blue eyes set too close, which could twinkle with good humour or glisten with malevolence.[6] Although he rarely seemed to study and paid little attention in lectures, he sailed through exams and effortlessly won an important anatomy prize for which more diligent students had competed keenly.

Energetic, ingenious and exhausting, he could hold forth on any subject under the sun, dazzle an audience with his theories, no matter how dotty, and carry any argument, no matter how dubious. Having won his position, he would drop the subject and move on to another, usually unrelated. He was also full of money-making ideas, taking out patents on inventions that would revolutionise daily life and make fortunes. Like all of Budd's circle, Conan Doyle was swept up by his enthusiasm and awed by his genius: 'His mind is so nimble,' Conan Doyle wrote, 'and his thoughts so extravagant, that your own break away from their usual grooves, and surprise you by their activity. You feel pleased at your own inventiveness and originality, when you are really like the wren when it took a lift on the eagle's shoulder.'[7]

Conan Doyle, solid and sensible in every fibre, secretly admired the way his reckless friend careened through life. Once, during a crowded lecture, Budd, infuriated by a student in the front row making facetious comments, warned him to hold his tongue. The student unwisely suggested that Budd should make him do so. Budd needed no second invitation. He was sitting in one of the rear tiers and all the aisles were blocked: he simply stepped from desktop to desktop and dropped down in front of the student who promptly hit him full in the face. Budd threw himself at the other man, grabbed him by the throat, dragged him out from behind his desk and bundled him out, after which as Conan Doyle recalled, 'there was a noise like the delivery of a ton of coal'. Budd returned alone to the classroom, with a burgeoning black eye, to general applause.

Budd rarely drank alcohol, but when he did, it had an immediate effect, making him even more extrovert. After one or two glasses he was ready to fight anybody, to play the fool, to make everyone his friend or his enemy. On one occasion he assaulted the ticket clerk at Edinburgh station for a perceived slight and was arrested after a ludicrous chase through the streets. In court the next morning he defended himself with such shameless panache that he was let off with a small fine, whereupon he invited all the witnesses, including the police officers, to join him in a nearby pub.

His relations with women were equally fraught. He once threw himself out of a third-floor window to avoid compromising a lover when her husband returned home unexpectedly: a laurel bush broke his fall and he crept away unharmed and unabashed. When he decided to marry, his intended bride was not only a ward in Chancery, but also under age. Budd eloped with her after locking her governess in a room and dyeing his hair black, not entirely successfully, to avoid detection. The lovers spent their honeymoon in a small village inn, where his startling black and yellow hair excited some comment, not to say hilarity.

Not long after they returned to Edinburgh, Budd met Conan Doyle in the street and took him off to meet his bride in a small, sparsely furnished apartment they had rented above a grocer's shop. Conan Doyle found the new Mrs Budd to be a slight, timid, sweet-natured girl utterly in the thrall of her husband. They lived in only three of the four rooms since Budd had decided that the fourth harboured disease, and had locked the door and sealed the cracks with sticking tape. Conan Doyle was convinced that the smell was nothing more than the cheese in the grocer's shop below, but kept his counsel. Thereafter he was a frequent visitor, and spent many evenings sitting on a pile of magazines (there being only two chairs) while his friend paced the room, gesticulating and declaiming loudly. 'What did we care,' Conan Doyle recalled later, 'any one of the three of us, where we sat or how we lived, when youth throbbed hot in our veins, and our souls were all aflame with the possibilities of life? I still look upon those Bohemian evenings, in the bare room amid the smell of cheese, as being the happiest I have ever known.'[8]

After Budd graduated they lost touch for some time until a telegram arrived from Bristol: 'COME AT ONCE. I HAVE URGENT NEED OF YOU. BUDD.' Ever the loyal friend, he set off by train and was met at the station by Budd, who seemed in his usual ebullient high spirits, talking about everything other than the reason for the telegram, mainly a madcap scheme to equip soldiers with lightweight bullet-proof shields which would net him a profit of three-quarters of a million pounds. Budd was living in a large house standing in its own grounds and the door was opened by a liveried footman; he was, it seemed, doing well in private practice. Conan Doyle thought his wife looked tired and drawn, but they had an enjoyable supper rather reminiscent of the evenings in the flat, and afterwards retired to a small sitting room where the men lit pipes and Mrs Budd smoked a cigarette.

After jumping up and wrenching the door open to ensure that no one was listening at the keyhole, Budd finally blurted out: 'Doyle, what I want to tell you is that I am utterly, hopelessly and irretrievably ruined.' He explained that he had taken over the practice of his late father, who was a well-respected physician in the city, and set himself up in a fine house with liveried servants to attract the most wealthy patients, but they had simply not materialised. He was £700 in debt, owed £200 in rent and had total assets of less than £10. Conan Doyle hastily pointed out that he was in no position to help; the only advice he could offer was for his friend to call a meeting of his creditors and declare bankruptcy. Budd agreed, and seemed to cheer up.

Later that evening, after his wife had retired, Budd began drinking whisky, with inevitable results. The conversation turned to boxing and Budd suddenly suggested a few rounds. Conan Doyle, expecting a little friendly sparring, agreed, but Budd was more intent on relieving the pent-up rage generated by his financial problems. He rushed at Conan Doyle, pummelling him with furious punches, driving him back until he tripped over a footstool and, as he went down catching him with a blow to the ear. Conan Doyle had had enough: he got to his feet, waited for an opening and then hit Budd full in the face, bloodying his nose, and he followed up with a powerful jab to Budd's jaw that put him down. Budd, now even angrier, roared at Conan Doyle that he wanted to continue the fight with bare knuckles; luckily, Mrs Budd appeared, caught sight of the blood and demanded to know from Conan Doyle what was going on. Budd, suddenly all smiles, stepped in and assured her that there was nothing to worry about.

Next morning, all was forgiven and Budd was in fine form, pacing the room to expand upon one hare-brained money-making scheme after another. His flow was only interrupted by furious cursing as he watched patients arriving at the door of the doctor on the other side of the street. Conan Doyle could not stop himself laughing through most of this discourse: Budd suggested at one point that Conan Doyle should pretend to drop dead on his (Budd's) doorstep. Budd would be called, obviously, and would miraculously bring him back to life in front of the onlookers who had gathered. This would undoubtedly make headlines and Budd thereafter would be famous and probably rich. Conan Doyle chuckled most of the way back to Edinburgh. Later he heard that Budd had convened a meeting of his creditors and produced a bravura performance, reducing some to tears with the heart-wrenching story of his struggles and obtaining their agreement to give him time to pay off his debts.

He heard nothing further from Budd until the spring of 1882 when he received another telegram, this time from Plymouth: 'STARTED HERE LAST JUNE. COLOSSAL SUCCESS. MY EXAMPLE MUST REVOLUTIONISE MEDICAL PRACTICE. RAPIDLY MAKING FORTUNE. HAVE INVENTION WHICH IS WORTH MILLIONS. UNLESS OUR ADMIRALTY TAKE IT UP SHALL MAKE BRAZIL THE LEADING NAVAL POWER. COME DOWN BY NEXT TRAIN ON RECEIVING THIS. HAVE PLENTY FOR YOU TO DO.'

Mindful of Budd's last summons, Conan Doyle replied cautiously, pointing out that he was quite comfortable working for Dr Hoare and would not leave unless he could be sure of a permanent job.

Budd's response, ten days later, was typically bombastic: 'YOUR
LETTER TO HAND. WHY NOT CALL ME A LIAR AT ONCE? I
TELL YOU I HAVE SEEN THIRTY THOUSAND PATIENTS IN THE
LAST YEAR. MY ACTUAL TAKINGS HAVE BEEN OVER FOUR
THOUSAND POUNDS. ALL PATIENTS COME TO ME. WOULD
NOT CROSS THE STREET TO SEE QUEEN VICTORIA. YOU CAN
HAVE ALL VISITING, ALL SURGERY, ALL MIDWIFERY. MAKE
WHAT YOU LIKE OF IT. WILL GUARANTEE THREE HUNDRED
POUNDS THE FIRST YEAR.'

Well, it was tempting and Conan Doyle was tempted. He left for
Plymouth, despite his mother's strong opposition and against the
advice of Dr Hoare, who warned his young intern that by associating
with someone as shallow and unethical as Budd he could damage his
future prospects.

Budd was again waiting on the platform, in great good humour,
when his train arrived. Thumping his friend on the back, he guided
him to a fine carriage and pair standing outside the station. As they
clambered in, the coachman enquired of his master which of his
houses he should go to. Budd, ensuring the point had not been lost
on Conan Doyle, grandly asked to be driven to the 'town residential'.
On the way, he cheerfully bragged about the huge numbers of patients
he was attracting, how his waiting rooms were jammed from morning
to night and how other doctors in the town were being put out of
business.

The 'town residential' turned out to be a huge corner house near
Plymouth Hoe. Number 6 Elliott Terrace had once been a gentleman's
club until the members could no longer afford the rent. But trifling
considerations like paying rent did not bother Budd, who proudly
showed Conan Doyle round. The house had some thirty bedrooms,
few of which were furnished, but the ground-floor rooms were enormous and fitted out in considerable style. Conan Doyle's bedroom,
however, contained only a small iron bed and a washbasin on a packing
case; Budd explained that he was going furnish each room with the
best that was available, and so he was reluctant to put in a £40 bedroom
suite only to have to turn it out to make room for a £100 suite.

Dinner was delayed while his host conducted Conan Doyle on a tour
of the ground floor, boasting how much he had paid for everything.

He even grabbed the serving girl by the arm, demanding of his friend, to her great embarrassment, if he had ever seen a prettier maid. Halfway through the meal, Budd suddenly rushed from the room and returned with a bag full of cash, which he emptied onto the table. It was, he said, the day's takings, and amounted to £31. 8s. 0d. Conan Doyle ventured how his creditors in Bristol must be pleased and Budd's sunny mood immediately darkened: he became surly and defensive. He refused, he said, to be 'crippled' by debts owed to the tradesmen of Bristol'. Conan Doyle shrugged, and chose not to pursue the matter.

After dinner, Budd took Conan Doyle into the back room where he conducted his 'experiments'. His latest plan was to equip warships with powerful magnets towed on rafts astern which would attract incoming gunfire. It was incomprehensible to him that the Admiralty had shown no interest. When Conan Doyle failed to exhibit suitable enthusiasm, Budd insisted on a demonstration. He loaded a small pistol with a steel cartridge and took aim at a blob of sealing wax attached to the wall four inches above a magnet. When he fired, the cartridge hit the magnet rather than the sealing wax. To further convince his friend, he offered to put a magnet in his wife's bonnet and allow Conan Doyle six shots at her face. Conan Doyle demurred.

The next morning they drove to Budd's surgery in Durnford Street, where numerous waiting rooms were, as promised, packed. In his consulting room, he explained his unusual technique to his new partner. First principle, he explained, was never to be polite to patients. By way of demonstration, he strode to the door and bellowed down the stairs: 'Stop your confounded jabbering down there! I might as well be living above a poultry show!' Silence ensued. You see, he continued, a thoroughly insulted patient is the best advertisement you can have. He said he once threw a man down the stairs after an argument about his condition, and the man talked about it so much in his village that virtually the entire population came to see him. Patients had to realise that he condescended to see them; sometimes he showed up in the morning and sent them all packing, informing them imperiously that he had decided to spend the day in the country. Although consultations were free, Budd made his money through prescriptions, dispensed by his obliging wife. He scribbled a note on the prescription as to how much the patient was to be charged and

Mrs Budd collected the money. Another useful earner was to charge half a guinea to any patient who wanted the jump the queue. Budd reckoned he could make upwards of 20 guineas a day that way.

Conan Doyle listened to all this with an incredulity which turned to amazement when the unfortunate patients began to be ushered in. Budd roared at them, prodded them, pushed them about, refused to allow them to speak, made his diagnosis, wrote a prescription and then shoved them out of the door. 'A morning with him,' Conan Doyle wrote, 'when the practice was in full blast was as funny as any pantomime.' Budd told one bemused old lady that she was drinking too much tea and made her swear on a copy of *Taylor's Medical Jurisprudence* that she would only drink cocoa for fourteen days. Another dignified gentleman was about to explain his symptoms when Budd grabbed him by his waistcoat, hustled him down the stairs and out into the street, shouting after him that he ate too much, drank too much and slept too much. A woman who complained of a 'sinking feeling' was advised, if the medicine did not work, to swallow the cork as there was 'nothing better than cork if you were sinking'.

Conan Doyle struggled to keep a straight face throughout these histrionics, but recognised that behind the tomfoolery and showmanship Budd had considerable diagnostic skills, even if he prescribed alarming quantities of pills and potions, often for no other reason than to make money. 'He used drugs in a heroic and indiscriminate manner,' Conan Doyle noted, 'which produced dramatic results but at an unjustifiable risk.' When they walked home that evening, Budd jingled the bag containing the day's takings – £32. 8s. 6d. – as they passed other doctors' consulting rooms.

While Conan Doyle disagreed fundamentally with Budd on almost everything – and certainly on his philosophy that medical etiquette should be 'thrown to the devil' – he agreed to stay on in Plymouth and was given a consulting room opposite Budd's, where, for the first three days, he sat alone twiddling his thumbs and listening to his partner ranting across the passage. On the fourth day he received his first patient, an old soldier with a cancerous growth on his nose caused by the smoke from his short clay pipe. He successfully cut out the growth – his patient was blissfully unaware that it was the doctor's first operation – and thereafter his list began to grow. He made

£1. 17s. 6d. in his first week, £2 in the second, £2. 5s. in the third and £2. 18s. in the fourth.

In between running his chaotic practice, Budd kept busy. He tried to persuade Conan Doyle to help him set up a weekly newspaper; invented the 'Budd Spring-Shutter Screen', an ingenious device designed to prevent ships from sinking by plugging any hole in the hull with a spring-activated shutter; and, almost on a daily basis, came up with new schemes for coining money. He complained about only being able to make three or four thousand pounds out of the poor in Plymouth; he needed a continent to operate in and talked about emigrating to South America and specialising in eye surgery. There was a fortune to be made in eyes, he liked to say. A man begrudged having to pay for medicines, he reasoned, but he would give his last penny to save his sight – a dictum Conan Doyle later took to heart.

Conan Doyle helped his partner build a stable at the back of the surgery and was present on one memorable occasion when Budd decided to buy a horse being sold by an army officer who had bought it for £150 but was willing to part with it for £70 because he considered it to be dangerous. It was just the kind of challenge Budd relished. Conan Doyle's hilarious account of what transpired was a gem of descriptive prose:

> It was a beautiful animal, coal black, with a magnificent neck and shoulders, but with a nasty backward tilt to its ears, and an unpleasant way of looking at you . . . Budd clambered up upon its back and formally took possession of it by lamming it between the ears with the bone handle of his whip . . . The beast justified his reputation; but Budd, although he was no horseman, stuck to him like a limpet. Backwards, forwards, sideways, on his fore feet, on his hind feet, with his back curved, with his back sunk, bucking and kicking, there was nothing the creature did not try. Budd was sitting alternatively on his mane and on the root of his tail – never by any chance in the saddle – he had lost both stirrups, and his knees were drawn up and his heels dug into the creature's ribs, while his hands clawed at mane, saddle, or ears, whichever he saw in front of him. He kept his whip, however; and whenever the brute eased

down, lammed him once more with the bone handle. His idea, I suppose, was to break its spirit, but he had taken a larger contract than he could carry through. The animal bunched his four feet together, ducked down his head, arched his back like a yawning cat, and gave three convulsive springs into the air. At the first Budd's knees were above the saddle flaps, at the second his ankles were retaining a convulsive grip, at the third he flew forward like a stone out of a sling, narrowly missed the coping of the wall, broke with his head the iron bar which held some wire-netting, and toppled back with a thud into the yard.[9]

Budd leapt up with blood streaming down his face, staggered into the half-built stable to grab an axe and launched himself at the horse, clearly intending to wreak his revenge, but Conan Doyle grabbed him by his coat tails and managed to restrain him long enough for the chalk-faced dealer to run off with the animal.

Not long afterwards, these two unlikely friends fell out. While Conan Doyle's roster of patients was steadily increasing, he noticed a subtle change in the attitude of the Budds towards him, as if they were beginning to resent his presence. (He later learned that they were in the habit of reading letters from his mother, in which Mary Doyle criticised the Budds and her son for associating with them, which cannot have helped.) Eventually Budd stalked into Conan Doyle's consulting room one morning in a black mood and accused his friend of damaging the practice. His patient numbers had been falling, he said, ever since Conan Doyle had put up his plate. It was not just that Conan Doyle was taking his patients, but that if people saw two plates outside, they were not sure they would be able to see the doctor they wanted. Conan Doyle, furious, said he could easily put the matter right. He picked up a hammer in the yard, prised his plate off the wall and announced he was leaving. The Budds made little attempt to persuade him to stay, although Budd fell ill the following day and Conan Doyle nursed him, and the practice, for three weeks until he was back on his feet. As a measure of his gratitude, Budd offered his departing partner a stipend of £1 a week to help establish him in a new practice; Conan Doyle swallowed his pride and accepted the offer.

After first considering, and then rejecting, starting a practice in Tavistock, he settled on Portsmouth, a naval town like Plymouth, where he believed he might find sufficient numbers of patients. Although he may not have known it, Portsmouth also had strong literary connections – both Dickens and George Meredith were born there, it was home at one time to Sir Walter Besant and Rudyard Kipling, and H. G. Wells was working in a drapery establishment in nearby Southsea.

In June 1882 Conan Doyle packed his worldly possessions in a small trunk and boarded an Irish steamer bound for Portsmouth, curiously elated at the prospect of striking out on his own for the first time, despite the formidable difficulties he faced.

CHAPTER 5

A STRUGGLING PRACTICE

HE YOUNG DOCTOR ALIGHTED from the steamer at Clarence Pier in Southsea, a suburb of Portsmouth which had developed into a popular seaside resort with hotels, a pier, ornamental gardens and bathhouses. He left his trunk on the pier and took a tram into town to find lodgings with just £10 in his pocket. The conductor directed him to an area where there were a number of lodging houses in a 'shabby-genteel kind of thoroughfare'. He rang the bell of the first place that took his fancy and agreed to rent a room for 10s. 6d. a week.

That evening, out taking the sea air, Conan Doyle claimed to have encountered a commotion on the street – a noisy crowd had gathered round a burly, red-faced drunk kicking his wife, despite the baby in her arms. Conan Doyle pushed his way through, intending to try and reason with the man, but he whirled round and punched Conan Doyle in the throat. 'I found myself, within a few hours of my entrance into this town, with my top hat down to my ears, my highly professional frock-coat, and my kid gloves, fighting some low bruiser on a pedestal in one of the most public places, in the heart of a yelling and hostile mob! I ask whether that was cruel luck or not?'[1] In the event, a sailor was suddenly pushed between them and the drunk, little caring who he fought, turned his attention on the sailor. Conan Doyle took the opportunity to extricate himself, picked up his walking stick and hurried away, thankful, he said, that he was not going to spend the first night in his new home town in a police cell.

Next morning he began, with admirable diligence, a search for somewhere to set up a practice. He bought a shilling map of the town from the post office, laid it out on a table in his room and planned a series of walks. Each day he set out after breakfast and trudged the streets, making a note of every physician's brass plate. He usually managed a decent lunch for three pence and returned to his room at about four o'clock, where he marked the plates on his map with a circle. 'At the end of that time I had a complete chart of the whole place, and could see at a glance where there was a possible opening, and what opposition there was at each point.'[2]

He eventually settled on 1 Bush Villas, Elm Grove, Southsea, a narrow, unoccupied three-storey red-brick house with eight rooms, sandwiched between the Bush Hotel and St Paul's Baptist Church, which he was able to rent for £40 a year, unashamedly using his Uncle Henry's name – Henry had by then been made a CB (Companion of the Order of the Bath) for his work as Director of the National Gallery in Dublin – as a reference to avoid paying a cash deposit. 'It was my own house – all my very own! I shut the door again, the noise of the street died down, and I had, in that empty, dust-strewn hall, such a sense of soothing privacy as had never come to me before. In all my life it was the first time that I had ever stood upon boards which were not paid for by another.'

He ordered, on tick, £12 worth of ointments, powders, pills, infusions and tinctures. At an auction sale in nearby Portsea he acquired two small tables, three chairs, an umbrella stand, a square of red drugget, curtains, a small iron bed, a fender, a toilet set and three pictures for his consulting room for an outlay of little over £4. Half a pound of tea, a pound of sugar, a tin of Swiss milk and a tin of corned beef reduced his assets to less than £2.

An ironmonger supplied and fixed, at the side of the front door, a splendid brass plate engraved 'Dr Conan Doyle, Physician and Surgeon'. Later, he would creep out to polish it under cover of darkness, so that the neighbours would not realise he had no domestic staff. Most of the furniture went into the consulting room to give a reasonable impression of prosperity, but behind the curtain that separated it from the rest of the house the reality of his situation was all too evident. His 'kitchen' comprised a small frying pan with which he learned to cook on the single jet of a gas light, although there were times when he had nothing to eat but dry bread and water. In his first ten months of medical practice he lost ten pounds in weight. His cabin trunk served as both food locker and table, at which he sat on a small stool. Upstairs, only one bedroom was furnished, with a bed and a basin and jug balanced on a packing case he had found in the garden. On his first few nights he slept in his overcoat on the iron springs, with a copy of Bristowe's *Principles of Medicine* as a pillow, but his mother later sent down blankets, sheets and pillows and he made a mattress out of the straw and sacking in which his medical supplies arrived.

On 1 July 1882 Conan Doyle placed a small advertisement in the *Portsmouth Evening News*, curiously in the 'Miscellaneous Wants' column, announcing: 'Dr. Doyle begs to notify that he has removed to 1, Bush Villas, Elm Grove, next to the Bush Hotel.' The wording was crafty, implying that he had transferred his practice from some other location. With a red lamp, purchased on credit and hung in the front window to signify a doctor was in residence, he settled back to wait for patients: 'No patients yet,' he wrote to his mother a few days later, 'but the number of people who stop and read my plate is enormous. On Wednesday evening in 25 minutes 28 people stopped in front of it, and yesterday I counted 24 in 15 minutes.'[3]

His first caller was the local curate, who wanted to know if he would be attending divine service. Conan Doyle assured him he would not and explained precisely why, sending the shocked priest on his way. When the bell rang again, a bearded man in a top hat was waiting outside. Conan Doyle opened the door, as he explained years later, 'with an air of insouciance, as though I happened to find myself in the hall, and did not care to trouble the maid to ascend the stairs', showed his visitor into his consulting room, invited him to take a seat and divined, from his nervous coughing that he had a bronchial problem. He was wrong. The cough was because the man had come from the gas company to collect 8s. 6d. still owing from the previous tenant.

His first bona fide patient was, he recorded, 'a little anaemic old maid, a chronic hypochondriac, I should judge, who had probably worked her way round every doctor in the town, and was anxious to sample this novelty . . . She said that she would come again on Wednesday, but her eyes shifted as she said it. One and sixpence was as much as she could pay, but it was very welcome. I can live three days on one and sixpence.'

In a letter to an Edinburgh friend he said he waited six days for another patient, who wanted a vaccination: 'I had to pay 2s 6d for the vaccine in London, and could only screw 1s 6d out of the woman, so that I came to the conclusion that if I got more patients I would have to sell the furniture.' A little later he wrote again to say that patients 'swarm in at the rate of about two a week'.[4]

Conan Doyle kept careful accounts, working out his daily expenditure to the nearest farthing: his daily ration of tea, sugar and milk cost 1 penny, a loaf of bread was 2 pence 3 farthings and dinner – usually fried fish, saveloys or corned beef – was tuppence. He was obliged to give up his pipe, which he sorely missed, but could not resist the luxury of the halfpenny evening newspaper to keep abreast of world affairs, particularly in Egypt, where the Royal Navy had besieged Alexandria and Britain would soon be engaged in a brief war to safeguard access to the new Suez Canal which halved the journey time between Britain and India. He also discovered that pouring water on his top hat induced a temporary shine and gave the impression of prosperity when he was out and about in town.

Not long after signing the lease for Bush Villas, Conan Doyle received an exasperating letter from his former partner in Plymouth, withdrawing his offer of £1 a week. 'When the maid was arranging your room after your departure,' Budd wrote, 'she cleared some pieces of torn paper from under the grate. Seeing my name upon them, she brought them, as in duty bound, to her mistress, who pasted them together and found that they formed a letter from your mother to you, in which I am referred to in the vilest terms, such as "a bankrupt swindler" and "the unscrupulous Budd". I can only say we are astonished that you could have been a party to such correspondence, and we refuse to have anything more to do with you in any shape or form.' Conan Doyle was positive he had not left any of his mother's letters behind and realised that Budd must have been reading his mail while he was in Plymouth. He assumed his former partner never had any intention of paying the stipend and had waited until he had made financial commitments before reneging on his promise, the better to ensure Conan Doyle's financial ruin. He replied, saying that Budd's letter had been a 'source of gratification', as it removed the only cause for disagreement between his mother and himself. 'She had always thought him a blackguard, and I had always defended him; but I was forced now to confess that she had been right from the beginning.'[5]

(Despite all this, Conan Doyle could not help retaining some affection for Budd, perhaps because he provided such rich material for his fiction. When Budd died in 1899, in his early 30s, he was being investigated by the General Medical Council for his unorthodox practices. Inevitably, he had left his wife and four daughters virtually penniless; Conan Doyle, as a matter of honour, quietly provided for them for many years.)

Conan Doyle sorely missed the money that Budd had promised and was forced, against every instinct, to ask his mother for assistance on several occasions. Once he wrote saying he had only two shillings left, and so 'if you happen to be at all flush just remember the poor'. Despite her meagre resources and perhaps with the help of Bryan Waller, she somehow managed to provide some money. The quid pro quo was that Conan Doyle agreed to look after his younger brother Innes, then 9 years old. Conan Doyle was happy to have the 'little knicker-bockered fellow', both for company – he admitted to being lonely during his first few months in Southsea – and to help his mother, who now had only the two youngest girls, Ida and Dodo, to worry about. 'The sooner Innes comes the better,' he wrote. 'He shall have plenty of good food – now that the rent is off my mind we will not be so scrimpy. I have to sit up nearly to midnight every night in order to polish my two door plates without being seen. Have no gas yet but candles.'

As for Innes, known in the family as 'Duffy', he was delighted to be united with his greatly admired older brother and blithely unbothered by the spartan conditions at Bush Villas – he could remember worse in Edinburgh. He quickly settled in, enrolled in the local school – Hope House in Green Road (the 'house of desolation' where Kipling had been a pupil a few years earlier) – took over the plate-polishing duties, ran errands, answered the door in a page's uniform when Arthur was busy with a patient and sent cheerful, misspelled letters home to his mother. 'The patients are crowding in,' he wrote on 16 August 1882, perhaps embellishing the truth a little.

> We have made three bob this week. We have vax enated a
> baby and got hold of a man with consumtion and today

a gypsy's cart camp up to the door selling baskets and chairs so we determined not to let the man ring as long as he liked. After he had rong two or three times Arthur yelled out at the pitch of his voice, Go a way, but the man rang again so I went down to the door and pulled open the letter box and cried out Go a way. The man began to swere at me and said he wanted to see Arthur. All this time Arthur thought that the door was open and was yelling Shut that door. Then I came upstairs and told Arthur what the man had said so Arthur went down and we found out that the gypsy's child had measles . . . After all we got sixpence out of them.

Innes could not help but be aware of their circumstances and sometimes his excitement at the prospect of a new patient got the better of him. Once when he answered the door, he took one look at the woman standing outside and shouted up the stairs: 'Arthur! Hooray! It's another baby!'

Money remained tight for some time and Dr Conan Doyle was a familiar figure to the local pawnbroker, to whom he had to sacrifice his watch on more than one occasion. He made barter arrangements with local tradesmen, exchanging his services for goods, particularly with an epileptic grocer who provided butter and tea in return for treatment. The irony of this 'ghoulish compact' was not lost on him, whereby he enjoyed butter and bacon every time the grocer was ill, but was reduced to dry bread and saveloys when the unfortunate man was well.

It seems that he had learned something about self-promotion from the bombastic Budd: after a riding accident outside his front door in November 1882, he sent Innes off to the *Portsmouth Evening News* with a report which it obligingly published: 'An accident, which might have led to serious consequences, occurred this afternoon in Elm-grove as Mr Robinson, of Victoria-road, was riding in front of the Bush Hotel, his stirrup leather snapped, and he was thrown to the ground, the animal rearing at the same time and falling partially upon him. He was conveyed to the house of Dr Conan Doyle, of Bush Villas, and that gentleman was able to pronounce that, though considerably shaken and bruised, there was no injury of any consequence.'

His uncles and aunt in London were not so disaffected with him that they were unwilling to help his nascent practice, and Uncle Dick sent him an introduction to the Catholic Bishop of Portsmouth, pointing out that there was no Catholic doctor in Portsmouth, but Conan Doyle, still determined not to accept the family's patronage, burned it. Slowly, agonisingly slowly, patients began to call. 'From the very beginning a few stray patients of the poorest class, some of them desirous of novelty, some disgruntled with their own doctors, the greater part owing bills and ashamed to face their creditor, came to consult me and consume a bottle of my medicine. I could pay for my food by the drugs I sold. It was as well, for I had no other way of paying for it.'

The sole advantage of waiting for patients to arrive was that Conan Doyle had time to write. He sold a story about a disreputable ghost hunter, 'The Ghosts of Goresthorpe Grange', to his new champion James Hogg at *London Society* magazine for £10, neatly covering his rent for the first quarter, and at the end of the year *Temple Bar* paid him 10 guineas – £10. 10s. – for 'The Captain of the Polestar', a powerful short story in diary form in which a lovelorn sea captain pursues the spirit of his lost love onto an ice floe, where he freezes to death. As his shipmates discover his body, a sudden gust of wind disturbs the snow. 'To my eyes,' the narrator records, 'it seemed but a snow drift, but many of my companions averred that it started up in the shape of a woman, stooped over the corpse and kissed it, and then hurried away across the floe.' His first attempt at 'serious' supernatural writing, it was an accomplished piece and one of a number of stories which drew on his experiences in the Arctic and in Africa. It also marked what would be a lifelong interest in the paranormal. He was clearly pleased with it, using it as the title for his first collection of short stories, published in 1890.

Conan Doyle was fortunate in that popular magazines were thriving in the late Victorian era, with new titles springing up and editors competing to find writers. He was able to place stories in *Boy's Own Paper*, *All The Year Round* (founded by Charles Dickens), *Harper's*

Weekly and *Good Words*. In 'Life and Death in the Blood', an early science-fiction short story he wrote for *Good Words*, he invited readers to imagine a man reduced in size to less than one thousandth of an inch travelling through the bloodstream and describing what he encountered. But he also collected a fair number of rejection slips and it rarely occurred to him during this period that he might have a future as a full-time writer; for the present he was grateful for the 'casual pocket money' writing provided and without which he might have gone under.

Filling out his tax return for the year 1882, Conan Doyle recorded a total income of only £154, which left him, fortuitously, with no tax to pay. The disbelieving inspector marked it 'Most unsatisfactory' and sent it back. When he re-submitted it Conan Doyle could not resist adding, 'I entirely agree.' A subsequent inspection of his ledgers failed to unearth any further income and the return was eventually accepted.

By the beginning of 1883, however, business had improved sufficiently for him to hire a housekeeper, at last absolving him from the necessity of cooking and the hateful chore of cleaning and laying the fires, 'the most heart-breaking task that a man can undertake'. She turned out to be a gem, quickly summed up her employer's situation and became adept at convincing patients that the doctor was in great demand, consulting imaginary lists to see when they could be fitted in. With donations from his mother and Aunt Annette, Bush Villas began resemble the home of a successful doctor: a bust of his grandfather, John Doyle, stood on a table in the hall, there was new carpet up the stairs and African mats on the floor, and his consulting room proudly boasted twenty-one pictures, some by his unfortunate father, and eleven vases.

Conan Doyle was obviously in intermittent contact with his father by mail. In a letter to his mother referring to some sketches he had received from his father, he scribbled in the top left-hand corner, 'Papa in his letter seemed fairly content with his lot.' He said he was sending the drawings to be framed and was glad to be able to assist his housekeeper in improving the drawing room, adding that he had written to his father to thank him. Quite how 'content' Charles Doyle was was open to question, as events would prove.

Somewhat belatedly, it dawned on Conan Doyle that waiting for patients to come to him was no way to build a profitable practice and that it would be useful to get out and about to meet people and potential patients. Sport was his obvious entrée to the social life of Southsea, so with characteristic vigour he joined Southsea Bowling Club and Portsmouth Cricket Club, where he would eventually captain the First Eleven. He also helped establish a Portsmouth Football Club, and played in goal and as a back under the pseudonym of A. C. Smith, as football was not considered at that time to be a gentleman's game – a fact that bothered him not at all.

More in keeping with his station, he became a member of the Portsmouth Literary and Scientific Society, which met on alternate Tuesday evenings, and whose members were drawn from the upper middle classes, largely professional men with intellectual aspirations. The President was Major General Alfred W. Drayson, author of several astronomical works, dozens of articles in *Boy's Own Paper* and *Every Boy's Magazine*, and a committed spiritualist, who would later be instrumental in introducing Conan Doyle to spiritualism.

The young doctor learned the art of public speaking at the Society, though he was initially so nervous that his legs shook before he stepped to the lectern. He lectured the society on favourite writers, including Edward Gibbon, George Meredith and one of his great heroes, the Scottish historian and philosopher Thomas Carlyle. Two hundred and fifty people turned up on 4 December 1883, to listen to his address at the Penny Street Lecture Hall on 'The Arctic Seas', which he illustrated with animal specimens borrowed from a local taxidermist, not all of them indigenous to the Arctic. Many in the audience assumed that he had shot them himself; the speaker chose not to disabuse them and thus gained a reputation in Portsmouth society as a hunter of some considerable ability.

Conan Doyle scored his first major literary success the same year with the publication of 'J. Habakuk Jephson's Statement' in the highly regarded *Cornhill Magazine*, once edited by Thackeray. This acceptance made him realise, he noted in a letter to his mother, that he was ceasing to be what he described as a 'hack writer'. He was paid a fee of 29 guineas, enough to cover a large proportion of his year's rent, and stirred up considerable controversy, which he greatly enjoyed. 'J.

Habakuk Jephson's Statement' was based on the mystery of the *Mary Celeste*, the two-masted brigantine found drifting, deserted by her crew off the coast of Portugal eleven years earlier. In Conan Doyle's fictional account, the ship was commandeered by a group of passengers who murdered everyone else on board, sailed her to Africa and then set her adrift.

So convincing was his story that many readers mistook it for a factual report: there were public protests at such an outrage and the US consul to Gibraltar, Horatio J. Sprague, asked *Cornhill Magazine* to investigate the origins of what he described as a fraudulent article. Such was the furore that Frederick Solly Flood, Her Majesty's Proctor and Attorney General at Gibraltar, who had been in charge of the *Mary Celeste*'s salvage, was obliged to issue a statement pointing out that the story was 'a fabrication from beginning to end', adding rather confusingly that Mr Jephson's opinions might well damage England's relations with foreign countries. Conan Doyle was delighted that his fiction could be mistaken as a true account, but even more pleased when the *Illustrated London News* compared it to the work of Edgar Allan Poe and also suggested that the author might be Robert Louis Stevenson, whose *Treasure Island* had appeared to great acclaim only the year previously and who was a regular contributor to *Cornhill Magazine*. Flushed with success, Conan Doyle sent further submissions to *Cornhill*, all of which were summarily rejected.

He refused to allow this to dent his confidence and was irritated when he failed to win a competition in *Tit-Bits* for the best Christmas story – the prize was a £400 house called 'Tit-Bits Villa' – primarily because he considered the winning entry far inferior to his own. Unwisely, he wrote to the editor, suggesting a wager: his entry and the winning entry should be submitted to an impartial judge, such as the editor of *Cornhill Magazine*. If his entry was deemed the better, he'd win £25, if the decision went against him, he would lose the money. The editor of *Tit-Bits* chose not to reply.

Conan Doyle first met James Payn, the editor of *Cornhill Magazine*, when to his surprise and undisguised pleasure, he was invited to a contributors' dinner at the Ship Inn in Greenwich. 'All the authors and artists were there,' he wrote, 'and I remember the reverence with which I approached James Payn, who was to me the warden of the sacred gate. I was among the first arrivals, and was greeted by Mr Smith, the head of the firm, who introduced me to Payn. I loved much of his work [Payn was a successful novelist] and waited in awe for the first weighty remark which should fall from his lips. It was that there was a crack in the window and he wondered how the devil it had got there.' Payn, sometimes described as the 'father' of the younger writer, would often review his work and was always supportive.

Conan Doyle made no secret of his gratitude: 'Mr James Payn wasted hours of his valuable time in encouraging me to persevere. Knowing as I did that he was one of the busiest men in London, I never received one of his shrewd and kindly and mostly illegible letters without a feeling of gratitude and wonder.'[6]

In the matter of love, Arthur had become taken by Elmore Welden, a dark-eyed Irish girl whom he had met during a rare holiday with his cousins in Lismore in the summer of 1881. 'By Jove,' he noted. 'Such a beauty! We have been flirting hard for a week . . .' He was forced to admit that Miss Welden, whom he called 'Elmo', was a little on the heavy side, but she would hold his heart strings for some time, and he was able to see her frequently when she left Ireland to live at Ventnor, on the Isle of Wight, just across the water from Portsmouth. At one point he was seriously considering marrying her. 'She *is* a dashing girl,' he wrote to his mother, 'and I am more fond of her than ever.' She also had a £1,500 inheritance due from an aged aunt who annoyingly showed little inclination to die. 'I wish her money was not tied up,' he mused. 'If I could marry it would fetch the practice up with a rush.' In the summer of 1882 he took Elmore to London, where they saw a production of Gilbert and Sullivan's *Patience* and introduced her to his Aunt Annette, but they argued frequently and their relationship soon ended.

If he was heartbroken, he forbore to mention it, and in a letter to Lottie, he indicated that he was very much the carefree bachelor: 'I went to a ball the other night and by some mischance got as drunk as an owl. I have a dim recollection that I proposed to half the women in the room – married and single. I got one letter next day signed

"Ruby", and saying the writer had said "yes" when she meant "no"; but who the deuce she was or what she had said "yes" about I can't conceive.' This recollection may well have been coloured for his sister's entertainment since it was very much out of character; in those early years in Southsea, Conan Doyle behaved like an eminently respectable medical man, aware that his position in society demanded sobriety, even without the example of his father as a warning.

Ministering largely to the poor, Conan Doyle saw plenty of suffering among his patients and their families and won a reputation as a hard-working, compassionate and proficient young doctor, but he never lost his well-developed sense of humour. He described treating one dignified old lady who spent most of her days observing the comings and goings outside her house with haughty disdain until, every two months or so, she would get roaring drunk, open the window and 'skim plates' at passers-by. Dr Conan Doyle was the only person able to control her; eventually he could restrain her just by the look in his eye when he reached her garden gate. She was grateful for his ministrations and insisted on rewarding him with items from her extensive collection of china jugs, statues and curios so that he found himself 'staggering out of the house like one of Napoleon's generals coming out of Italy'. The moment sobriety returned, the lady would send a porter round with a note asking for their return. On one occasion when she had been 'particularly troublesome, I retained the fine lava jug, in spite of her protests'.

At the end of his second year in practice, Dr Conan Doyle's accounts indicated that he had made £250, a considerable improvement on his first year. He was enjoying both the pleasure of seeing his work in print and the extra income it provided, but like most ambitious young writers he had set his sights on a full-length novel. His first attempt, *The Narrative of John Smith*, written in Southsea, was lost in the post in its initial submission to a publisher. (The original handwritten manuscript, in four exercise books, surfaced at a Christie's sale in 2004.) It described six days in the life of the eponymous narrator, who was confined to his lodging house with an attack of rheumatic gout ('the hybrid form of torture . . . which unites the disadvantages of both diseases to a dash of malignancy of its own') and ranged widely over the fields of history, religion, philosophy, medicine, science, music and prophecy, including the possible futures of China, Great Britain and the United States. It was very much a personal statement of Conan Doyle's precocious social and political philosophy and later in his life he confessed that its publication might have been embarrassing: 'My grief at its loss would be as nothing to my horror if it were suddenly to appear again, in print.'[7]

In 1884 he began work on a second novel, *The Firm of Girdlestone*, an uncertain pastiche of Dickens and Thackeray drawing on his experiences as a medical student and his trip to Africa. Conan Doyle also wrote and submitted a steady stream of short stories to magazines. In 'Crabbe's Practice', the story of how a young, eccentric and unscrupulous doctor established his practice in a provincial English town, published in the Christmas 1884 edition of *Boy's Own Paper,* his former friend George Budd made his first, thinly disguised appearance in Conan Doyle's work.

Combining writing with his duties as a doctor was never easy as, years later, he would explain in an American magazine:

> How often have I rejoiced to find a clear morning before me, and settled down to my task, or rather, dashed ferociously at it, as knowing how precious were those hours of quiet. Then to me enters my housekeeper, with tidings of dismay.
>
> 'Mrs Thurston's little boy wants to see you, doctor.'
>
> 'Show him in,' say I, striving to fix my scene in my mind that I may splice it when this trouble is over.
>
> 'Well, my boy?'
>
> 'Please, doctor, mother wants to know if she is to add water to that medicine?'
>
> 'Certainly, certainly.' Not that it matters in the least, but it is well to answer with decision. Exit the little boy, and the splice is about half accomplished when he suddenly bursts into the room again.
>
> 'Please, doctor, when I got back mother had taken the medicine without water.'
>
> 'Tut, tut!' I answer. 'It really doesn't matter in the least.' The youth withdraws with a suspicious glance, and one more

paragraph has been written when the husband puts in an appearance.

'There seems to have been some misunderstanding about that medicine,' he remarks coldly.

'Not at all,' I say, 'it really didn't matter.'

'Well, then, why did you tell the boy it should be taken with water?' And then I try to disentangle the business, and the husband shakes his head gloomily at me. 'She feels very queer,' says he, 'we should all be easier in our minds if some one came and looked at her.' So I leave my heroine in the four-foot way with an express thundering towards her, and trudge sadly off, with the feeling that another morning has been wasted, and another seam left visible to the critic's eye in my unhappy novel.

———————◆———————

In 1885 Dr Doyle's practice would deliver an extremely unexpected prize. In March Dr William Royston Pike, a friend and fellow member of the Southsea Bowling Club, had called him for a second opinion on the condition of a desperately ill young man, recently arrived from Gloucestershire with his older sister, Louisa, and widowed mother, Mrs Emily Hawkins. When Conan Doyle arrived at their guesthouse, he immediately understood that he was being consulted only as a gesture to the family – John Hawkins had cerebral meningitis and clearly had only a short time to live. Louisa stood by with tears in her eyes, as the mother asked Conan Doyle if it would be possible for him to care for John as a resident patient. He was too ill to remain at the lodging house, and hospitals, in the days before antibiotics, were best avoided. Conan Doyle agreed, returned to Bush Villas and asked his housekeeper to prepare a spare room immediately.

John Hawkins only lived a few days longer; he died, aged 25, on 25 March. He had been examined on the previous evening by Dr Pike, who confirmed that his colleague had done everything possible, thus avoiding awkward gossip and a potential investigation; a funeral taking place from a doctor's house was bad enough, the worst possible advertisement for his services.

After the funeral, Conan Doyle asked permission to call on Louisa
Hawkins, ostensibly to help comfort her in her grief, at the lodging
house. She accompanied him on his evening walks and listened, spellbound, to the stories of his travels and adventures. Louisa, known
as Touie, was 27 years old, almost two years older than Arthur, sweet
natured, round faced, with brown curly hair and blue-green eyes; like
all well-brought-up young women, she was an accomplished needle-
woman and a competent pianist. Born in Dixton, a village near
Monmouth, in 1857, she was the sixth child and youngest daughter
of Jeremiah Hawkins, a farmer and landowner who died in 1873. Mary
Doyle paid a visit to her son to assess his new lady friend and indicated her approval; in April they became engaged. The speed of their
courtship, extraordinary in the Victorian era, was never explained. In
his memoirs, Conan Doyle only said that the Hawkins family was
'naturally grieved at the worry to which they had quite innocently
exposed me, and so our relations became intimate and sympathic,
which ended in the daughter consenting to share my fortunes'.

During May and June Conan Doyle found time – between courting
Touie, running his practice and tinkering with *The Firm of Girdlestone*
– to write a thesis for his MD degree, entitled 'An Essay upon the
vasometer changes in *tabes dorsalis* and on the influence which is
exerted by the sympathetic nervous system in that disease'. He
returned to Edinburgh for his oral examination in July and was duly
awarded a doctorate. Some ungenerous biographers would later claim
that Conan Doyle turned to literature because he failed as a doctor,
but there is little evidence to support this. His handwritten thesis –
lodged at the University of Edinburgh Library – asserted that syphilis
played a role in the aetiology of *tabes dorsalis,* a degenerative disease
of the spinal cord. This was an unfashionable and minority view at
the time but was later proved correct. The thesis also, as might be
expected, was written with considerable literary flair, referring to
patients 'finally recognising the demon which had seized them had
not relaxed its grip and suffering years of torture before seeing the
shades of death gather round'.

In a letter to the *Lancet* a year earlier, he had reported gout occurring in three generations of a single family and suggested it was the
cause of side effects like eye disease and psoriasis – another link not

proven conclusively until much later. He also campaigned for compulsory vaccination for soldiers against illnesses such as typhoid and smallpox, and forecast that his 'children's children' would see a time when the bacteriological causes of disease would be eliminated. He was in blistering form when calling for the reinstatement of the Contagious Diseases Act, which had granted powers for compulsory examination of women suspected of harbouring venereal disease, but which had been suspended in April 1883 as a distasteful abrogation of human rights. In a letter to the *Medical Times,* Conan Doyle railed mightily against the 'champions of the modesty of harlots' and the prostitutes in Portsmouth who tempted servicemen returning from overseas.

> I say that if an unfortunate soldier, coming home to his native land after an absence of years, and exposed to such temptations, should yield to them, and entail disease upon himself and his offspring, the chief fault should not lie at his door. It surely emanates logically from those hysterical legislators who set loose these bearers of contagion, and their like, upon society. For fear delicacy should be offended where no touch of delicacy exists, dreadful evils are the result, men to suffer, children to die, and pure women to inherit unspeakable evils. Loose statements and vague doctrines of morality may impose upon hasty thinkers, but surely, when the thing is reduced to its simplest terms, it becomes a matter of public calamity that these Acts should be suspended for a single day.

It was typical of Conan Doyle that his sympathies should lie with soldiers and sailors rather than with the rights of 'harlots', but he was by no means a misogynist and would later champion the cause of divorce law reform.

Conan Doyle would be a prolific and cogent letter writer all his life, campaigning on an extraordinary variety of issues as well as maintaining diligent correspondence with school and university chums, family friends, his brother and sisters and particularly his mother, to whom he would write lovingly at least once a week – usually addressing her as 'Dearest of Mams' or 'My dearest Mamma' – keeping her abreast of every aspect of his life and revealing his innermost hopes and fears. 'Your last letter did me good,' he wrote in an undated note from Bush Villas, 'I think that if I had a wife who could sympathize and stimulate as you do, I would be a better man. Sometimes I am confident, at others very distrustful. I know I can write small stories in a taking way, but am I equal to a prolonged effort – can I extend a plot without weakening it – can I preserve the identity of a character throughout – these are the questions which vex me . . .'

———————————◆———————————

In May 1885 shortly after his engagement Conan Doyle received the devastating news that his father had been detained on criminal charges of violence and damage, formally certified by the State and committed to the Royal Lunatic Asylum at Montrose.

There is no record of any of the Doyle family visiting Charles Doyle after he had been committed. In a telling letter to his mother apologising for not visiting her in Yorkshire because of cricketing engagements, Conan Doyle added: 'Besides I shall see your dear self before very long and *there is nothing else which would lead me north . . .*' (author's italics). It seems the only member of the family with a conscience about Charles Doyle was Annette who, correctly anticipating her early death, left instructions that her meagre savings should be devoted to her father's 'use and benefit during his lunacy'.

His plight certainly did not affect his son's wedding plans. On 6 August 1885 Arthur Conan Doyle and Louisa Hawkins were married at the parish church of Thornton-in-Lonsdale, near Masongill, where Mary Doyle now lived on Bryan Waller's estate. Waller gave the bride away. Conan Doyle never revealed what he felt about Waller adopting the de facto role of host at his wedding, but if Mary Doyle had insisted the ceremony take place near Masongill, her son would never have opposed her. Guests were kept to a minimum as the Hawkins family was still offically in mourning. The witnesses were the mothers of the bride and groom, Innes and Connie, Waller and his mother. Charles Doyle was obviously not present to see his son marry. His existence was only recognised by being listed ('Charles Doyle, artist') as the groom's father on the marriage certificate.

After a honeymoon in Dublin, which Conan Doyle cannily

contrived to combine with a cricket tour by the Stonyhurst Wanderers, the old boys' team, the newly-weds returned to Bush Villas and settled down to married life.

Conan Doyle's financial pressures were eased by the fact that Touie had a private income of £100 a year, a legacy from her father. In addition his practice was generating some £300 a year, although it would never exceed that figure, and he was firing off short stories in all directions and earning an average of about £4 for each one published. He continued to play cricket in the summer and football in the winter – the *Portsmouth Evening News* described him as 'one of the safest Association backs in Hampshire' – and Touie devoted herself to caring for her husband.

Marriage unquestionably agreed with him. 'After my marriage,' he reported, 'my brain seems to have quickened and both my imagination and my range of expression were greatly improved.' He had an extra spring in his step and filled notebook after notebook with ideas for stories, quotations, comments, anecdotes and epigrams. But he still craved recognition as a novelist: 'About a year after my marriage . . . I realised that I could go on doing short stories for ever and never make headway.'

At the end of January 1886 his labours over *The Firm of Girdlestone* finally ended and the manuscript was dispatched to a publisher, from whence it soon returned with a rejection slip. Conan Doyle was not greatly surprised: he had little confidence in it. 'It interested me extremely at the time,' he would say later, 'though I have never heard that it had the same effect upon anyone else.' Muddled, crammed with university reminiscences, it was enlivened only by his natural talent for humorous observation, as in this description of dancers at a ball: 'Their faces wearing that pained and anxious expression which the British countenance naturally assumes when dancing, giving the impression that the legs have suddenly burst forth in a festive mood, and have dragged the rest of the body into it very much against its will.'

The Firm of Girdlestone had been rejected by a second publisher when he began work on another novel in March. 'I felt now I was capable of something fresher and crisper and more workmanlike. Gaboriau [Emile Gaboriau, the pioneer of modern detective fiction] had rather attracted me by the neat dovetailing of his plots, and Poe's masterful detective, M. Dupin, had from boyhood been one of my heroes. But could I bring an addition of my own? I thought of my old teacher Joe Bell, of his eagle face, of his curious ways, of his eerie trick of spotting details. If he were a detective he would surely reduce this fascinating but unorganised business to something nearer to an exact science . . .' He decided that the hero of the story would be called Sherlock Holmes and that he would solve his cases by pure deduction and not, as was commonplace in popular detective fiction, because of an absurdly convenient coincidence which, he said, 'struck me as not a fair way of playing the game'.[8]

It did not take him long to finish it, as in April Touie wrote to Lottie: 'Arthur has written another book, a little novel about 200 pages long, called "A Study in Scarlet". It went off last night. We have no news of "Girdlestone" yet, but we hope that no news is good news. We rather fancy that "A Study in Scarlet" may find its way into print before its elder brother.'[9]

A Study in Scarlet was not, in fact, published for more than eighteen months. The world had to wait a little longer before being introduced to one of the most enduring characters ever created in the English language.

CHAPTER 6

ENTER SHERLOCK HOLMES

ITH THE ESTABLISHMENT OF organised police forces around the world – London's Metropolitan force was set up in 1828 – it was perhaps inevitable that the detective would emerge as a popular literary hero. Early 'true crime' stories popularised by the *Newgate Calendar* – originally a monthly bulletin of executions produced by the keeper of the notorious London prison in the late eighteenth century – tended to focus on the criminal as a sympathetic hero, but with rising crime in ever more crowded towns and cities, the emphasis shifted towards those who captured the criminals, the pursuer rather than the perpetrator, and capitalised on the burgeoning Victorian fascination with crime and detection. Such was the insatiable public appetite for crime and mystery stories in the first half of the nineteenth century that publishers began churning out lurid novels – 'pulp fiction' – written with little regard to literary merit. In Britain they were known as 'penny dreadfuls' or 'shilling shockers'; in America 'dime novels'.

Real-life detectives were not slow to capitalise on the popularity of their fictional counterparts by selling their reminiscences. One of the first was the extraordinary adventurer Eugène François Vidocq. The son of an Arras baker, Vidocq, according to his own colourful account, had a chequered and licentious career as a soldier, acrobat, smuggler and thief until, in 1796, he was sentenced to eight years for forgery. He contrived to escape, joined a band of highwaymen and then became a police informant, in which role he casually betrayed his highwaymen confrères. He was considered so useful to the French authorities that when a Brigade de Sûreté was formed in Paris in 1812

he was asked to take charge. He proved to be an innovative and energetic police officer, started an early card-index system, was adept at
disguise and was a pioneer in taking casts of footprints. But he was
obliged to retire early, at the age of 52, under suspicion of organising
many of the burglaries that his department was investigating.

Unabashed, he employed two ghostwriters and produced a racy
autobiography which became a best-seller. *Les Vrais Mémoires de Vidocq*
ran to four volumes, published in 1828 and 1829, and was hugely popular,
not least because the ghostwriters had been given a free hand to let
their imaginations run riot – M. Vidocq had a Gallic disregard for literal
truth and was anxious to be portrayed as a brilliant sleuth with
astounding powers of detection. This is how he described his days as
a police spy: 'I frequented every house and street of ill fame, sometimes under one disguise and sometimes under another, assuming,
indeed, all those rapid changes of dress and manner which indicated
a person desirous of concealing himself from the observation of the
police, till the rogues and thieves whom I daily met there firmly believed
me to be one of themselves.' The success of *Mémoires* led to a rash of
British imitators: *Scenes in the Life of a Bow Street Runner, Recollections
of a Detective Police Officer, Experiences of a Real Detective* and many more.

Detective thrillers were not regarded as a respectable literary genre
until 1841 when Edgar Allan Poe introduced Chevalier C. Auguste Dupin
in 'The Murders in the Rue Morgue', a locked-room mystery solved
by the 'peculiar analytical ability' of its hero. Enigmatic and eccentric,
Dupin was a sophisticated, highly intelligent individual equally capable
of discussing the classics or science; he possessed powers of observation second to none and techniques of deductive reasoning never previously employed in fiction. After Dupin, academic brilliance would
become almost de rigueur for gentlemen (amateur) detectives.

Poe's genius in his tales of ratiocination was to lay down the
essential elements of classic detective fiction: a brilliant, charismatic
leading character, a bumbling partner, a baffling crime, a client wrongly
accused, a trail strewn with false leads and an unlikely perpetrator
finally brought to justice. The plot of 'The Murders in the Rue Morgue'
became the template for hundreds of detective stories. First there was
an account of the crime; then Dupin's visit to the scene and his musings
on the clues that his admiring companion signally failed to observe;

then police botch the investigation; and finally the mystery is solved and explained by Dupin, who accuses the authorities of falling into the 'gross but common error of confounding the unusual with the abstruse. But it is by these deviations from the plane of the ordinary, that reason feels its way, if at all, in its search for the true. In investigations such as we are now pursuing, it should not be so much asked "what has occurred," as "what has occurred that has never occurred before".'[1]

The young French writer Emile Gaboriau, a great admirer of Poe, followed closely in his literary footsteps and created his own gentleman detective, Inspector LeCoq, partly inspired by Eugène Vidocq, in the 1860s. Gaboriau did much to popularise courtroom drama and was a master of suspense. LeCoq was a shrewd observer, like Dupin and Holmes, but unlike them he was part of the police system and not an amateur. His ability to construct a mental picture of the criminal by the examination of a few small clues which lesser mortals failed to notice was revolutionary in detective fiction and certainly influenced Conan Doyle.

The first British literary detective emerged in 1852 in the form of Inspector Bucket in Charles Dickens's novel, *Bleak House*, albeit in a minor role. While Bucket could not boast Dupin's powers of intellectual detection – he was a plodder relying on legwork rather than intellect – he established a pattern for the detective as an outsider, a figure with an uncertain status in society, standing halfway between respectable company and the criminal fraternity. Dickens reputedly based Bucket on a real policeman, Inspector Charles Field of the London Detective Force, who had featured in an article Dickens had written for his magazine, *Household Words*, the previous year.

Dickens's protégé, Wilkie Collins, made his reputation in 1860 with the first great mystery novel, *The Woman in White,* but *The Moonstone*, published in 1868 was later described by T. S. Eliot as 'the first, the longest and the best of English detective novels'. During the 1870s and 80s, any number of second-rate imitators corrupted the genre with 'blood and thunder' murder mysteries aimed at the barely literate working classes, mainly in London. They relied on formulaic plots, clichéd characters and cases being solved either by a combination of ludicrous coincidences or last-minute confessions, or by the stupidity of the criminal in making ridiculous mistakes. Sometimes suspense was maintained by withholding vital evidence from the reader; rarely was the reader made privy to a believable investigative process.

Conan Doyle was to eschew such techniques and sought, with Sherlock Holmes, to create a new and unique hero figure, a scientific detective who would succeed as a result of his exceptional skills, which the reader could admire, if not always understand until the denouement. Considering that *A Study in Scarlet* would set the stage for some of the best-loved detective stories ever written, its literary debut was hardly auspicious. Conan Doyle began writing the book in March 1886, and finished it in six weeks. Its first title was 'A Tangled Skein' and its two main characters were originally a 'sleepy-eyed young man', variously called Sheridan Hope or Sherringford Holmes, and Ormond Sacker, but they were to emerge in the final version as Sherlock Holmes and his faithful Boswell, Dr John Watson.

The curious worldwide community of Conan Doyle enthusiasts who call themselves 'Sherlockians' and like to believe that Holmes and Watson were real people have long debated the origin of their heroes' names. It is generally agreed that Holmes was based on Oliver Wendell Holmes, a writer whom Conan Doyle greatly admired. Sherlock might have derived from two Nottinghamshire cricketers of the 1880s, the bowler T. F. Shacklock and the wicketkeeper Mordecai Sherwin, although Conan Doyle also had a classmate at Stonyhurst called Patrick Sherlock, and a William Sherlock features in Macaulay's *History of England*, one of his favourite books. A Doctor James Watson was among the members of the Portsmouth Literary and Scientific Society (although Conan Doyle may not have met him until after he wrote *A Study in Scarlet*), and a Doctor Patrick Heron Watson assisted Joseph Bell at the Edinburgh Royal Infirmary.

A Study in Scarlet did not, initially, attract much interest. It was rejected first by *Cornhill*; Payn called it 'capital' but said it was too long for a single issue and too short for serialisation, and considered it too much in the style of a 'shilling shocker'. Arrowsmith of Bristol returned it unread, as did Fred Warne & Co. 'My poor "Study",' Conan Doyle wrote despairingly to his mother, 'has never even been read by anyone except Payn. Verily literature is a difficult oyster to open. All will come well in time, however.'

His confidence would be rewarded. On 30 October 1886 a letter of acceptance came from Ward, Lock & Co. which offered £25 for the copyright so long as the author did not object to *A Study in Scarlet* being held over until the next year as 'the market is flooded at present with cheap fiction'. The author perhaps objected more to the miserly fee and his work being described as cheap fiction than to the delay and replied asking for a small royalty on the sales. In a letter dated 2 November Ward, Lock & Co. politely refused, explaining that his story would be included with others in an annual and that allowing him to retain a percentage would therefore give rise to 'confusion'. In the absence of any other offers, Conan Doyle had little choice but to accept. 'I never at any time received another penny for it,' he noted sourly in his autobiography. Around this time he also accepted a commission, from the *Gas and Water Review,* to translate a contribution in German which duly appeared under the headline 'Testing Gas Pipes for Leakage'. He would joke that it was a turning point in his literary career – the first time a magazine had requested his services rather than the reverse.

A Study in Scarlet, a dark tale of murder and revenge, described the momentous meeting between Holmes and Watson, set the blueprint for all future Holmes adventures and introduced readers to the bohemian world of the great detective: Victorian London's murky gaslit cobbled streets swathed in fog, its rattling hansom cabs, its urchins and ragamuffins, and its endless mysteries. After being introduced by a mutual friend, the two men agree to share lodgings at what would become one of the most famous addresses in English literature: 'We met next day as he had arranged, and inspected the rooms at No. 221B, Baker Street, of which he had spoken at our meeting. They consisted of a couple of comfortable bedrooms and a single large airy sitting-room, cheerfully furnished, and illuminated by two broad windows. So desirable in every way were the apartments, and so moderate did the terms seem when divided between us, that the bargain was concluded upon the spot, and we at once entered into possession.'

It was the start of a symbiotic and timeless friendship, although in truth no two men could have more different. Holmes was an arrogant, unashamedly narcissistic misogynist, a cold, calculating, analytical ascetic who admitted to few emotions: 'I am a brain, Watson. The rest of me is a mere appendix.' Watson was a warm, loyal, salt-of-the-earth chap with a weakness for gambling and pretty women, utterly in thrall to his friend's brilliance. Holmes was, demonstrably, a man apart. 'You see,' he tells Watson, 'I consider that a man's brain originally is like a little empty attic, and you have to stock it with such furniture as you choose. A fool takes in all the lumber of every sort that he comes across, so that the knowledge which might be useful to him gets crowded out, or at best is jumbled up with a lot of other things, so that he has difficulty in laying his hands upon it . . . Depend upon it there comes a time when for every addition of knowledge you forget something that you knew before. It is of the highest importance, therefore, not to have useless facts elbowing out the useful ones.'

Holmes quickly reveals an apparently impressive ability, just like that of Dr Joseph Bell, to read the significance of mannerisms and appearance. Witness his first words to Watson: 'How are you? . . . You have been in Afghanistan, I perceive.' Watson, astonished, replies: 'How on earth did you know that?' But when Holmes gets round to explaining his deduction it hardly stands up to much scrutiny: 'Here is a gentleman of a medical type, but with the air of a military man. Clearly an army doctor, then. He has just come from the tropics, for his face is dark, and that is not the natural tint of his skin, for his wrists are fair. He has undergone hardship and sickness, as his haggard face says clearly. His left arm has been injured. He holds it in a stiff and unnatural manner. Where in the tropics could an English army doctor have seen much hardship and got his arm wounded? Clearly in Afghanistan.'

(Well, not necessarily, my dear Holmes. Why not South Africa, where British forces had recently been engaged in the Zulu War? And since when has Afghanistan been in 'the tropics'? And what is a 'gentleman of a medical type'? Holmes was certainly correct in identifying that Watson had been wounded in the shoulder, although he never clarified why it was, in subsequent stories, that the wound mysteriously travelled to his leg. Most readers, however, remained unbothered by this and other inconsistencies that riddle the Holmes stories, and it was left to dedicated Sherlockians to devise explanations: one suggested that Watson might have been shot from below while answering a call of nature and that the bullet first entered his leg and then his shoulder. Brilliant!)

The adventure begins, as most do, with a visitor to 221B Baker Street. Watson first spots him from the front window looking for a house number and carrying a blue envelope. He points him out to Holmes who immediately and correctly identifies him as a 'retired sergeant of Marines': an anchor tattoo on the back of the man's hand speaks of the sea, his military bearing and side whiskers indicate a marine, his age and air of command point to him being a non-commissioned officer. 'Wonderful!' an admiring Watson breathes. 'Commonplace,' his companion snorts.

The sergeant delivers a letter from Scotland Yard requesting Holmes's help in investigating the death of a well-dressed American found in an empty house in Brixton, in south London, with the word RACHE written in blood on the wall. Holmes instructs Watson to get his hat and together they set off in a hansom cab driving furiously for the Brixton Road. Holmes, of course, solves the case, but the crime is rooted in the fundamentalist Mormon community in Utah, and the second half of the book is taken up with a lengthy and melodramatic flashback during which Holmes is entirely absent and sorely missed.

The story owed much to Poe, and some of Holmes's techniques – following footsteps, the use of plaster of Paris, the significance of dust – were lifted almost verbatim from Gaboriau. Long after Sherlock Holmes became a household name Conan Doyle would readily acknowledge his debt to Poe, even though the insufferably egotistical Holmes would mischievously dismiss Dupin as 'a very inferior fellow', and Emile Gaboriau's LeCoq as a 'miserable bungler'.[2] In reality, Conan Doyle was a great admirer of both writers, but having one fictional character comment on another was an ingenious device which made both seem more real. As well as their shared deductive abilities, both Dupin and Holmes were outsiders, both were prone to periods of moody reverie, both were accompanied in their investigations by pliant companions courageous in dangerous situations, both had a low opinion of their official police colleagues and both employed newspaper advertisements to trap their quarries.

Some of Conan Doyle's plots also drew parallels with Poe. In 'The Murders in the Rue Morgue', the murderer was an orang-utan, while in one of Sherlock Holmes's locked-room mysteries, 'The Speckled Band', it is a snake. Poe's 'The Gold Bug' (1843) revolved around deciphering a code left by the pirate Captain Kidd on the basis that 'e' is the most commonly used letter in the English language; Conan Doyle used precisely the same technique in 'The Adventure of the Dancing Men'. He made no bones about his admiration for Poe, who he said was 'the originator of the detective story', and whose work was second only to Macaulay on the list of books that had influenced his life: 'You want strength, novelty, compactness, intensity of interest, a single vivid impression left upon the mind, Poe is the master of all.'[3]

A Study in Scarlet finally appeared in the 1887 Beeton's Christmas Annual as the main feature, with Holmes portrayed on the frontispiece as an anonymous figure stooped over a corpse. The Annual had been founded in 1860 by Samuel Orchart Beeton, a director of Ward, Lock & Co., whose wife wrote the famous 'household management' book bearing her name. Priced at one shilling and bolstered by advertisements for patent medicines and products like 'Steiner's Vermin Paste, A Sure and Certain Destroyer of Rats, Cockroaches, Mice and Black Beetles' it quickly sold out. Conan Doyle's contribution was generally reviewed with enthusiasm. 'This is as entrancing a tale of ingenuity in tracing out crime as has been written since the time of Edgar Allan Poe,' said the Scotsman. 'The author shows genius. He has not trodden in the well-worn paths of literature, but has shown how the true detective should work by observation and detection. His book is bound to have many readers.'[4]

While waiting for A Study in Scarlet to be published, Conan Doyle embarked on what he considered a much more ambitious and worthwhile project: Micah Clarke, a historical novel narrated in the first person, focused on political and religious turmoil at the time of the Monmouth Rebellion. It synthesised fact and fiction and would, Conan Doyle believed, 'test my powers to the full' as indeed it did. 'I chose a historical novel for this end, because it seemed to me the one way of combining a certain amount of literary dignity with those scenes of action and adventure which were natural to my young and ardent mind.' He might have added that all the major novelists in the nineteenth century – Scott, Dickens, Thackeray, George Eliot, Hardy among them – wrote historical fiction and that it was considered the proper work of any serious novelist. Conan Doyle wanted to join the club.

He had, of course, always been fascinated by history, largely thanks to Macaulay, and the ill-fated attempts by the Duke of Monmouth to unseat the 'papist' King James II in 1685 were of particular interest to a man who had been brought up in the Roman Catholic faith. But straining to produce a major work resulted in much of his prose being stilted and lifeless, unlike when he was writing Sherlock Holmes's adventures and simply told the story directly, unbothered by artistic considerations, history, fashion or the notion of 'fine writing'. A year's reading and research and five months' writing went into *Micah Clarke*. Conan Doyle kept a record in his journal of everything he read and made long lists of technical details. This from the entry for 10 January 1888:

> Chaufron (or chaupron). The iron mask of a charger.
> Aspen arrows – goose or peacock feather. Every archer had 24. They fought in open lines, like the teeth of a harrow.
> Light infantry wore skull caps, quilted jackets, iron gloves. Knives.
> A crake was the early name for a cannon. Greek fire was made of nitre, sulphur, naphtha.

He completed the novel a few months later. Its full title indicated what followed in the verbosity of the age it depicted:

> Micah Clarke His Statement as Made to His Three Grand-Children Joseph, Hervas & Reuben During the Hard Winter of 1734 Wherein is Contained a Full Report of Certain Passages in His Early Life Together with some Account of His Journey from Havant to Taunton with Decimus Saxon in Summer of 1685. Also of the Adventures that Befell Them During the Western Rebellion, & of their Intercourse with James Duke of Monmouth, Lord Grey, & Other Persons of Quality Compiled Day by Day from His Own Narration, by Joseph Clarke, & Never Previously Set Forth in Print. Now for the

First Time Collected, Corrected & Re-Arranged from the
Original Manuscripts by A. Conan Doyle.

Written in the form of a narrative related by an old man about
his adventures as a youth, *Micah Clarke* was a homage to the ringing
prose of Macaulay and Scott, but while Conan Doyle provided factual
insights into everyday life in late seventeenth-century England, many
of the characters were bland, cardboard figures. He was at his best, as
always, describing action and sweeping battle scenes: 'Out of the haze
which still lay thick upon our right there twinkled here and there a
bright gleam of silvery light, while a dull thundering noise broke upon
our ears like that of surf upon a rocky shore. More and more frequent
came the fitful flashes of steel, louder and yet louder grew the hoarse
gathering tumult, until of a sudden the fog was rent, and the long line
of Royal cavalry broke out from it, wave after wave, rich in scarlet and
blue and gold, as grand a sight as ever the eye rested upon . . .'

Micah Clarke did not set the publishing world on fire. The usually
supportive James Payn enquired why he was wasting his time and his
'wits' on historical novels; *Blackwood*'s snootily informed him that 'many
of your characters, for instance, strike us as belonging more to the 19th
than to the 17th century'; and Bentley and Company advised him that
his novel lacked 'the one great necessary point for fiction, i.e. interest'.
When he offered it for serialisation in the *People* newspaper, the rejection letter, dated 13 August 1888, was addressed to 'Dr A. Corran Boyle':

> Dear Sir,
>   The gentlemen who read our Tales for us have carefully
> perused your Micah Clarke, and, whilst fully admitting that
> it is written well, and has much interest of a kind, is not
> from the nature of its subject or its style suitable for serial
> publication in a popular newspaper like *The People*.
>   I may just mention that one great failure in it is the fact
> that it has next to no attraction for female readers who
> form undoubtedly a large percentage of our subscribers.
> Again it is hardly sensational enough.
>   I thank you for the offer, and am sorry that we cannot
> make use of the MS. How and where shall we send it?
>   Yours faithfully . . .[5]

Conan Doyle persevered with *Blackwood's*, penning a grovelling letter to the editor on 8 March 1888, asking if there was any way he could change their mind, pointing out the success of *A Study in Scarlet* and offering *Micah Clarke* for publication free of charge in return for a division of the profits 'in such a way as may seem equitable'.[6] *Blackwood's* remained unmoved, but to his great relief *Micah Clarke* was eventually accepted for publication by Longmans.

Conan Doyle was always extraordinarily persistent in chasing editors to make a decision about his submissions. As an Edinburgh man, he was determined to be published in *Blackwood's,* an Edinburgh publication, and sent the magazine a short story 'A Physiologist's Wife' at the beginning of 1890. When, by April, he had heard nothing, he wrote: 'I should be glad to hear if my little story "A Physiologist's Wife" is likely to see the light soon. I should also like stipulated that my name should be attached to it when it does happen. Yours very truly, A Conan Doyle.' He wrote again on 7 July: 'I should be glad to hear that my little yarn "A Physiologist's Wife" is in print. I think it has been with you about 15 months.' Two weeks later, enclosing stamps: 'I have no doubt that you have rather an "embarrass des richesses" [*sic*] of short stories just now, so perhaps it would be as well if you would send back my little tale "A Physiologist's Wife" which I sent you more than a year ago.'[7] His determination was not in vain: *Blackwood's* did publish 'A Physiologist's Wife' in its September issue.

On 28 January 1889 Louisa gave birth to their first child, delivered by her husband, at Bush Villas, whom they named Mary Louise. Conan Doyle wrote to his mother in jovial mode to give her the good news:

> Toodles produced this (Monday) morning at 6.15 a remarkably fine specimen of the Toodles minor, who is howling her head off in the back bedroom. I must say that I am surprised at the conduct of the young woman, seeing that both her parents are modest sort of people. She came evidently for a long visit, and yet she has made no apology for the suddenness of her arrival. She had no luggage with her nor any possessions of any kind, barring a slight cough and a voice like a coalman. I regret to say that she had not even any clothes and we have had for decency's sake to rig her out with a

wardrobe. Now one would not mind doing all this for the
sake of a visitor, but where the said visitor does nothing but
sniffle in reply, it becomes monotonous. She has frank and
engaging manners, but she is bald which will prevent her from
going out into society for some little time . . .

A month later *Micah Clarke* was published, dedicated to 'The
Ma'am'. It was an immediate success, requiring three reprintings
within ten months, and while some critics pointed out Conan Doyle's
tendency to take liberties with history, the reviews were generally
positive. 'The first and strongest impression which "Micah Clarke"
creates,' R. E. Prothero wrote in *Nineteenth Century* magazine, 'is that
it is an excellent story excellently told. Subsequent reflection shows
that it is also an admirable piece of imitative art, a tour de force of
correctness and vigour, a faithful yet dramatic picture of an historical episode . . .' As a work of art, he added, it was probably superior
to R. D. Blackmore's *Lorna Doone*. The *Scotsman* described it as 'a
powerfully conceived and clearly delineated picture of one of the
most stirring episodes of English history'.

In the lonely fastness of Montrose Royal Lunatic Asylum, Charles
Doyle was aware of his son's burgeoning literary career. In a corner
of his 1889 sketchbook, on a page filled with typically whimsical
cartoons, he wrote: 'Arthur's novel Micha [*sic*] Clarke – Reviewed on
Scotsman 4th March 1889. Highly favourable, Glasgow Herald, 19th
April 1889.' Underneath he painstakingly copied out a review, in the
Literary World, dated 11 January 1889, of his son's 'The Mystery of
Cloomber', for which he had provided an illustration. Conan Doyle
had also persuaded Ward, Lock & Co. to commission his father to
provide illustrations for a 'shilling shocker' edition of *A Study in Scarlet*,
published in July 1888. He produced six crude pen-and-ink drawings,
far below his usual standard of draughtsmanship, and either completely
ignored the text or did not bother to read it properly. He drew Sherlock Holmes somewhat in his own likeness, with a moustache and
beard, whereas Holmes was supposed to be clean-shaven. He similarly showed the street urchins who comprised the 'Baker Street Irreg-
ulars' being instructed by Watson, rather than Holmes.

At that time there was no copyright agreement with the United

States – copyright protection for foreign authors was not introduced until July 1891 – and almost as soon as a book was a success in London it was pirated in America. Thus it was that *A Study in Scarlet* swiftly appeared there, where it received excellent reviews. When Joseph Marshall Stoddart, publisher of *Lippincott's Magazine*, arrived in London from Philadelphia in August 1889 seeking to recruit new writers for a British edition, James Payn suggested he should talk to Conan Doyle and a young Irish writer Oscar Wilde, then working on *Women's World* magazine, but already notorious for his poetry and essays, no less than for his ostentatious wit and personality.

On 30 August Stoddart invited both Conan Doyle and Wilde to dinner at the elegant Langham Hotel, later to feature in three Sherlock Holmes stories, along with Thomas Patrick Gill, a former magazine editor and then an Irish Member of Parliament. It was a convivial evening, although it would be hard to find two men more different than a louche dandy like Wilde, who dressed, the actress Lillie Langtry observed, 'as probably no grown man in the world has ever dressed before', and a solid young gentleman like Conan Doyle, with his ruddy complexion, walrus moustache and tight-fitting tweed suit. As writers, too, they were poles apart: the avant-garde Wilde being champion of the 'art for art's sake' movement, and Conan Doyle being the exemplar of good, old-fashioned storytelling. Wilde told Conan Doyle that he had read *Micah Clarke* and enjoyed it very much, although it is hard to imagine he was being entirely truthful.

Conan Doyle was certainly impressed by Wilde: 'It was indeed a golden evening for me . . . His conversation left an indelible impression upon my mind. He towered above us all, and yet had the art of seeming to be interested in all that we could say. He had delicacy of feeling and tact, for the monologue man, however clever, can never be a gentleman at heart. He took as well as gave, but what he gave was unique. He had a curious precision of statement, a delicate flavour of humour, and a trick of small gestures to illustrate his meaning, which were peculiar to himself.' They would meet again years later, when Wilde's play *A Woman of No Importance* was playing to packed houses in London, and Conan Doyle formed a rather different opinion. Wilde asked him if he had seen the play and when he replied he had not, Wilde insisted he should do so: 'You must go. It is wonderful. It

is genius!' Conan Doyle, unaccustomed to such flamboyant immod-
esty, concluded that Wilde was 'mad'. He was sympathetic, however,
when Wilde was sent to prison in 1895 for 'gross indecency', not
because he was in any sense unusually tolerant for the time but because
he believed homosexuality was 'pathological' in nature and that 'a
hospital, rather than a police court, was the place for its consideration'.

Stoddart commissioned books from both men, signing a contract
with each that evening for a promised fee of £100 for 'not less than
40,000 words' – much more than Conan Doyle usually earned in a
year from his pen. Wilde, after first protesting that 'there are not
40,000 beautiful words in the English language', produced *The Picture
of Dorian Gray*, his only novel, which shocked Victorian society with
its homoerotic overtones. 'The newspapers seem to me to be written
by the prurient for the Philistine,' he wrote in a reply to Conan Doyle's
letter of congratulation. 'I cannot understand how they can treat *Dorian
Grey* as immoral. My difficulty was to keep the inherent moral subor-
dinate to the artistic and dramatic effect, and it still seems to me that
the moral is too obvious.' Wilde attempted to emulate Conan Doyle's
red-blooded prose style in *Dorian Gray* but had to admit defeat. 'I can't
describe action,' he admitted privately, 'my people sit in chairs and
chatter.'

For his part, Conan Doyle offered Stoddart *The Sign of Four*,
Sherlock Holmes's second appearance, which took him just two
months to write. Set in London, a city Conan Doyle barely knew –
'It must amuse you,' he wrote to Stoddart on 6 March 1890, 'to see
the vast and accurate knowledge of London which I display. I worked
it all out from a Post Office map'[8] – the story fleshed out the relationship between Holmes and Watson and their comfortable bachelor
lives at 221B Baker Street with Mrs Hudson, their redoubtable housekeeper, fussing over them: two friends, cocooned from the outside
world but ready to sally out and do battle with the forces of evil.

The Sign of Four finds Holmes at the peak of his powers, unravelling a mystery of robbery, betrayal and revenge rooted in the
Indian Mutiny and involving a beautiful woman with a shadowy past,
a man with a wooden leg and an evil dwarf with a blow pipe. It ends
with a thrilling boat chase on the Thames. Conan Doyle made a
number of elementary mistakes – all three Sikh characters were given

Muslim names, for example – but readers were swept along by the fast-moving action and the brilliance of Holmes's deductions.

The story also shockingly revealed that the great detective, if not an addict, was a regular user of cocaine, much to the disapproval of Dr Watson. 'Why should you,' Watson asked, 'for a mere passing pleasure, risk the loss of those great powers with which you have been endowed?' In fact there had been hints that Holmes was a drug user in *A Study in Scarlet*: 'For days on end he would lie upon the sofa in the sitting-room, hardly uttering a word or moving a muscle from morning to night. On these occasions I have noticed such a dreamy, vacant expression in his eyes, that I might have suspected him of being addicted to the use of some narcotic, had not the temperance and cleanliness of his whole life forbidden such a notion.'

The opening scene in *The Sign of Four* erased any doubt: 'Sherlock Holmes took his bottle from the corner of the mantelpiece, and his hypodermic syringe from its neat morocco case. With his long, white, nervous fingers he adjusted the delicate needle, and rolled back his left shirtcuff. For some little time his eyes rested thoughtfully upon the sinewy forearm and wrist, all dotted and scarred with innumerable puncture-marks. Finally, he thrust the sharp point home, pressed down the tiny piston, and sank back into the velvet-lined armchair with a long sigh of satisfaction.'

Largely imported from South America, cocaine at that time was frequently used as an anaesthetic and a nerve tonic, and was widely and legally obtainable, but the drug's dangerous addictive qualities were becoming recognised and Conan Doyle soon realised that Holmes would have to change his ways. In 'The Adventure of the Missing Three-Quarter' Watson reveals that he has managed to wean his friend from 'that drug mania which had threatened once to check his remarkable career. Now I knew that under ordinary conditions he no longer craved for this artificial stimulus, but I was well aware that the fiend was not dead, but sleeping . . .'

Some readers were appalled that a man of Sherlock Holmes's intellect and strength of character would inject himself with drugs, but Conan Doyle always wanted to distance his detective from the plodding image of a policeman: languid, bohemian, aesthetic, eccentric, Holmes viewed the science of criminal investigation as an art form and, as an artist, why should he not enjoy the pleasures of the needle?

Oscar Wilde wrote to congratulate Conan Doyle on *The Sign of Four*: 'I am conscious that my own work lacks those two great qualities that your work possesses in so high a degree – the qualities of strength and sincerity. Between me and life there is a mist of words always: I throw probability out of the window for the sake of a phrase, and the chance of an epigram makes me desert truth.'[9]

When *The Sign of Four* appeared in *Lippincott's* in February 1890, one admiring critic called it 'the best story I ever read in my life'. It appeared at the end, however, that Holmes and Watson would go their separate ways when Watson admits he has fallen in love with their client, Mary Morstan, who, with her 'sweet and amiable' expression and 'singularly spiritual and sympathetic' blue eyes resembles Touie. She had, he told Holmes, 'done me the honour to accept me as a husband in prospective', and thus their recently concluded investigation would be their last – a prediction happily unfulfilled.

CHAPTER 7

VIENNA INTERLUDE

OON AFTER CONAN DOYLE had finished working on *The Sign of Four* tragic news arrived from Lisbon: on 13 January 1890, his sister, Annette, died of influenza at the age of 33. She had spent her whole adult life working to support the family, Conan Doyle noted sadly, 'dying just as the sunshine of better days came into our lives'. Annette had been devastated by her father's alcoholism and left her life savings of £420 to her mother, 'the wife of Charles Altamont Doyle (now a lunatic) the natural and lawful Father and next of kin of the said Annette for his use and benefit during his lunacy'.

Conan Doyle's reference to the 'sunshine of better days' coming into their lives alluded to the extra income he was generating as a writer and with which he was always ready to help his family. In the enforced absence of his father, he had assumed the nominal role of head of the family, adopting a quasi-paternal attitude towards his younger brother, then at Richmond School, and writing to him frequently, addressing him as 'Dearest Boy', 'Dear Old Chap' or 'My Dear Laddie', and urging him to concentrate on his studies:

Dearest Boy,

I never hear anything about your work and it makes me uneasy. I do hope that you are pegging into it – for it would be a very serious thing if you fail to pass. Remember that if you do go through you will have all your life then for sport or riding or cricket or what you will, but that the success of your whole life depends upon the use that you make of just

these few months that are passing. If you are weak on any
subject then work from morning to night, holidays or no
holidays, at that one until you are strong at it. You have lots
of brains, as I know well, and all you want is steady
undeviating industry. Think of nothing else, then, I beg you,
until this is done . . . Goodbye dear boy, your affectionate A

He followed up with a postcard:

Dear Boy – Go at it day by day and don't let one slip, for it
is all important. Work with the same eager energy that a
man puts into a football match, for that is the secret of
success. On the other hand, my boy, if when the exam
comes and you have done your best you should be unlucky
enough to fail, don't be cast down, but go at it again.
Yrs, ACD.

His family responsibilities, however, did not weigh so heavily to
prevent him succumbing, in November 1890, to 'an irresistible impulse'
to go to Berlin in the hope of meeting Robert Koch, a German bac-
teriologist who had caused a sensation at the International Medical
Congress in August by announcing a 'remedy' for tuberculosis, then
known as consumption. As he had no particular interest in the disease
and was always sceptical of 'miracle cures', Conan Doyle's sudden
decision was probably due more to ennui than to any genuine medical
curiosity. While he always insisted that he was perfectly content in
Southsea with Touie and the baby, with his writing and his practice,
he was at heart just as much a man of action as his literary characters, and a trip to Berlin was exactly what he needed to break the
monotony. Touie meekly raised no objection. En route through
London he visited W. T. Stead, editor of the *Review of Reviews*, picked
up a commission to write a profile of Koch and collected letters of
introduction to the British Ambassador in Berlin and the correspondent of *The Times*. Much good would it do him.

Koch, the director of the Institute of Hygiene at Berlin University, was the greatest medical detective of his generation and had
become a household name after successively discovering the micro-
bial causes of anthrax, tuberculosis and cholera. His announcement

that he had found a remedy for tuberculosis, then a deadly disease, made headlines around the world. Doctors from all over Europe flocked to Berlin to see demonstrations of his technique, the so-called 'lymph-inoculation cure', which claimed to destroy the tissue in which the germs settled so that the entire diseased area would be sloughed off and expelled through coughing.

Conan Doyle was hoping to attend a demonstration on 17 November, the day after his arrival in Berlin, by Koch's close colleague, Doctor Ernst von Bergmann. But he quickly discovered that tickets were 'simply not to be had', and neither of his contacts was able, or willing, to help. Undaunted, he tried calling at Koch's home, but got no further than the front hall, where he watched a postman empty a sack of letters onto a desk. He realised, with a sense of shock, that they were mostly from desperately ill people who had heard about Koch's cure and believed he was their last hope. The newspapers were also full of stories about consumptives making their way to Berlin, some so sick they died en route. Since Koch's findings remained to be verified it seemed to the sceptical Conan Doyle that 'a wave of madness had seized the world.'

The next day he attempted to enter the demonstration by bribing a porter but only managed to get into the outer hall, where he stood utterly frustrated as ticket holders streamed past him into the auditorium. Finally he spotted von Bergmann approaching, trailed by a respectful entourage of assistants and researchers. In desperation he 'threw' himself across the great man's path and, artfully exaggerating the real distance between London and Berlin, said, 'I have come a thousand miles . . . May I not come in?' Von Bergmann stopped in his tracks, glared at Conan Doyle, then sneered, 'Perhaps you would like to take my place?' Turning to make sure his associates were listening, he shouted, 'Yes, yes, take my place by all means. My classes are filled with *Englishmen* already.' He pronounced 'Englishmen' with particular scorn and continued on his way without a backward glance.

Henry J. Hartz, an American doctor in Bergmann's group, was appalled by the German's rudeness and quietly offered to meet Conan Doyle later that day and share his notes on the demonstration; had it not been for his help, the trip would have been an utter waste of time. Hartz also gave Conan Doyle an unofficial tour of von

Bergmann's clinical wards, after which Conan Doyle spent the remainder of the day analysing all the clinical data before coming to the precocious conclusion that Koch's treatment was 'experimental and premature'.

In his room at the Central Hotel, he composed a letter to the *Daily Telegraph* elaborating his views: 'It may, perhaps, be not entirely out of place for an English physician who has had good opportunities of seeing the recent development of the treatment for tuberculosis in Berlin to say something as to its present treatment and probable results. Great as is Koch's discovery, there can be no question that our knowledge of it is still very incomplete, and that it leaves large issues open to question. The sooner that this is recognised the less chance will there be of serious disappointment among those who are looking to Berlin for a panacea for their own or their friends' ill health.' Koch might have been forgiven for concluding that this high-handed pronouncement by an unknown and inexperienced British doctor with no specialist knowledge, who had not even attended one of his demonstrations and whose 'good opportunities of seeing the recent development' were highly questionable, bordered on the insulting. But Conan Doyle turned out to be right: the healing power of Koch's technique was greatly exaggerated, although he did go on to win a Nobel Prize for physiology. Early in 1891, after several patients receiving the cure had died, Koch retracted his initial claims, asserting that while his discovery was an excellent diagnostic tool, an actual cure was nowhere in sight.

The trip did, however, set Conan Doyle on a new career path. Somewhere along the way, perhaps on the night train to Berlin, he had fallen into conversation with Malcolm Morris, a Harley Street skin specialist and 'a very handsome and courteous man'. Morris had been a provincial doctor, like Conan Doyle, but saw there was little future in a small country practice and had trained in dermatology and moved to London, where he had prospered. Morris convinced Conan Doyle he was wasting his time in Southsea and should set up a practice in London, where he could have a vibrant social life and still find time for writing. Morris suggested specialising in ophthalmology, as Conan Doyle had had some experience at Portsmouth Eye Hospital, where he had worked part-time, correcting refractions.

Vienna, then the political and cultural capital of the Austro-Hungarian Empire, was the best place in the world to study ophthalmology.

Conan Doyle returned to Southsea greatly enthused. He would later speculate that had it not been for the trip to Berlin he might well have stayed in practice in Southsea for the rest of his life. Naturally, he talked it over with Touie, and compliant as ever, she offered no opposition when her husband suggested leaving the baby with her mother for six months while she accompanied him to Vienna. There were no difficulties about disposing of his practice, since it was too small and personal to be sold – he simply handed it over to a Doctor Claremont, a neighbouring doctor with whom he had a covering arrangement.

On 12 December 1890 the Portsmouth Literary and Scientific Society held a farewell dinner for the Conan Doyles at the Grosvenor Hotel. In his speech, Dr Doyle paid tribute to the warm-hearted friends he and his wife had made in Southsea and contrasted it with his first night in the town, when he was involved in a scuffle. He was sorry to leave such congenial companions but consoled himself with the knowledge that 'London nowadays was after all a suburb of Southsea, or vice versa.' Mr A. H. Wood, a master at Portsmouth Grammar School, spoke of the loss that Dr Doyle would be to the local football and cricket teams. ('Woodie' would later become Conan Doyle's business manager and secretary.) It was a convivial evening and Conan Doyle admitted to regret at abandoning his practice; it would leave a gap in his life and that of his wife, 'who was universally popular for her amiable and generous character'.

After spending Christmas with 'the Mam' at Masongill and dropping off the baby with Louisa's mother, who now lived in the Isle of Wight, the Conan Doyles travelled to Vienna, where they arrived, in the middle of a blizzard, late on 5 January 1891. He reported their safe arrival to his mother in a letter written from the Hotel Kummer: 'We drove to this hotel and were quite fresh by 12 o'clock when we got up. We then had a good meal and started house-hunting together . . . we eventually settled upon a Pension which is very stylish indeed. Madame Bomfort, Universitaet Strasse 6, Vienna, is our address from tomorrow. I think that it will do very well indeed . . .'

They had their own room overlooking one of Vienna's main streets, furnished with two narrow beds, a writing table, wardrobe and sofa and heated by a large white porcelain stove. The rent was £4 a week, which included meals taken with the other residents, mostly English and American students. The university hospitals were close by and Conan Doyle initially had every hope of making a success of the trip, but although he had learned German during his year at Feldkirch, he quickly discovered his command of the language was insufficient to cope with specialised scientific lectures.

According to a note in his diary he started work on a novella, *The Doings of Raffles Haw*, which had been commissioned by *Answers* magazine, almost as soon as he arrived in Vienna. (Conan Doyle's diaries, which he kept meticulously for around twenty years, shed little light on his day-to-day activities and no insight into his feelings; he briefly recorded cricket scores, books he had read, fees paid by magazines and publishers, and dates when he started and finished various stories.) It is clear he spent much of the first week in Vienna writing *The Doings of Raffles Haw*, which he finished on 23 January and for which he was paid £150 on 3 February. This was more than generous, since it was possibly his worst work: a feeble tale about an alchemist, who, having discovered how to turn base metal into gold, devotes himself to helping the needy and in the process corrupts an entire community by breeding universal discontent. Conan Doyle described it as 'not a very notable achievement', the main value of which was that it enabled him to pay his current expenses. But that the magazine accepted such an inferior work was clear evidence that editors were beginning to buy his work on the strength of his name alone.

In his autobiography, Conan Doyle claimed he spent four months in Austria, mixing in 'gay Viennese society', skating on the Danube, sipping *Kaffee* with *Sachertorte* in crowded cafes and enjoying the heady decadence of the Austro-Hungarian Empire's penultimate decade. His diary tells a different story for by 9 March the Conan Doyles were on their way home, via Venice, Milan and Paris, arriving back in England on the 24th.

Notwithstanding the debacle of his so-called studies in Vienna, Conan Doyle remained determined to set up a practice as an ophthalmologist in London. He found lodgings in Bloomsbury – three rooms at 23 Montague Place – for himself, Touie and little Mary, who had had her second birthday while her parents were in Vienna, and rented a consulting room, with part use of a waiting room, at 2 Upper Wimpole Street, two blocks from Harley Street, where London's best, and most expensive, doctors practised. The rent was £120 a year. Despite his best efforts to put his name around – he joined the Ophthalmologic Society of the United Kingdom and made his presence known to the nearby Royal Westminster Eye Infirmary – he claimed that not a single patient crossed his threshold for about a month. He would wryly remark years later that both the rooms he had rented were waiting rooms: 'I waited in the consulting room and no one waited in the waiting room.'

With time weighing heavily on his hands, hanging around for patients who never arrived, he spent most of his time writing. 'Every morning I walked from the lodgings at Montague Place, reached my consulting-room at ten and sat there until three or four, with never a ring to disturb my serenity. Could better conditions for reflection and work be found? It was ideal, and so long as I was thoroughly unsuccessful in my professional venture there was every chance of improvement in my literary prospects.' He told a rather different story in a contemporary interview a year later, saying that his duties as a doctor left him too little time for writing, so that in the end he resolved to 'throw physic to the dogs'.[1]

He was able to put the finishing touches to *The White Company*, another ambitious historical romance, which he had started the previous year. Set in the reign of Edward III, it followed the adventures of a group of 'manly and true' bowmen, led by a 'gallant, pious' knight called Sir Nigel Loring, during the Hundred Years' War, which Conan Doyle considered the greatest epoch in English history. He said he spent nearly two years researching and writing the novel, reading 150 books, in both French and English, and absorbing a vast amount of material. He carefully cross-indexed his research, filling dozens of notebooks with tiny copperplate writing interspersed with diagrams and sketches. Under the heading of 'Archer', for example, he listed everything he could discover about archery lore, what oaths they might have used, where they had fought, how they trained. He did the same for all the other character groups, hoping in this way to recreate viable dialogue between archers and monks, monks and armourers, or armourers and knights.

The White Company unquestionably reflected the passion for heroism, honour and chivalry that had been instilled in him at his mother's fireside: indeed, Mary Doyle could easily have been the model for Lady Tiphaine, the wife of a French nobleman, who keeps the bowmen spellbound with her stories: 'The mind had gone out of them and they could but look at this woman and listen to the words which fell from her lips – words which thrilled through their nerves and stirred their souls like the battle-call of a bugle . . .'

While it was stirring stuff ('Now order the ranks, and fling wide the banners, for our souls are God's and our bodies the King's, and our swords for Saint George and for England!'), and provided a vivid sense of life in England and France in the fourteenth century, The White Company was over-researched and burdened by tedious information: 'In front stood the bowmen, ten deep, with a fringe of under-officers, who paced hither and thither marshalling the ranks with curt precept or short rebuke. Behind were the little clump of steel-clad horsemen, their lances raised, with long pensils drooping down the oaken shafts. So silent and still were they, that they might have been metal-sheathed statues, were it not for the occasional quick, impatient stamp of their chargers, or the rattle of chamfron against neck plates as they tossed and strained . . .' It was a historical romance in which the author allowed history to overwhelm the romance, and only when he gave his imagination free rein in the action sequences, as in Micah Clarke, did the book really come to life – his stunning description of a battle in Spain, in which the White Company fights a valiant but ultimately futile action, is worthy of Dumas.

When he finally finished The White Company, Conan Doyle reported that he enjoyed 'a wave of exultation and with a cry of "That's done it!" I hurled my inky pen across the room, where it left a black smudge upon the duck's-egg wallpaper. I knew in my heart that the book would live and that it would illuminate our national traditions.' He was convinced that it was his best book yet and wrote to Lottie: 'You will be pleased, I am sure, to know that I have finished my great labour, and that "The White Company" has come to an end. The first half is very good, the third quarter pretty good and the last quarter very good again. So rejoice with me, dear, for I am as fond of Hordle John and Samkin Aylward and Sir Nigel Loring as though I knew them in the flesh and I feel that the whole English-speaking race will come in time to be fond of them also.'[2]

He offered it first to *Blackwood's* as a serial, expressing a willing-ness to accept £300 from 'a good magazine' rather than the £500 he could expect from a syndicate. It was, he promised, 'a long way the best thing I have ever done. The scene is medieval, but it is full of love, fighting and go, so that it would make a good serial. I will answer for it that it is better from every point of view than "Micah Clarke" . . .' Written in pencil on the letter someone at *Blackwood's* has scrawled, 'What will I say about this man's offer?' In fact James Payn at *Cornhill* magazine bought the rights before *Blackwood's* made up its mind, Payn expressing the view he had read nothing so good since *Ivanhoe*.

The White Company was serialised in 1891, before appearing as a three-volume novel. Conan Doyle earned £200 for the serial rights and a further £350 for the book, which quickly became a best-seller, despite mixed reviews. The *Spectator* claimed there was 'not a vestige of plot' and the characters were 'wooden dolls moved by mechanism and not particularly distinguishable from one another save by the costumes they wear'. Conan Doyle was primarily disappointed that book was praised as a rip-roaring adventure for boys, rather than as the important historical work he believed it to be – he thought it would become the standard work on the period – and which he hoped would establish his reputation as a serious writer. 'There is hardly a boy who would not delight in following the adventures of Sir Nigel Loring,' said the *Daily Graphic*, while the *National Observer* felt it would 'endear its author to the hearts of British boys and men'. 'They treat it too much as a mere book of adventure,' Conan Doyle complained bitterly in a letter to his mother, 'as if it were an ordinary boy's book – whereas I have striven to draw the exact types of character of the folk then living and have spent much work and pains over it, which seems so far to be under appreciated by the critics.'

Nevertheless, *The White Company* went through more than fifty editions in Conan Doyle's lifetime and remained in print long after his death and was available, despite paper shortages, during the Second

World War, as it was considered to be a national morale booster. In 1905, when Conan Doyle had tired of writing about Sherlock Holmes, a prequel, *Sir Nigel*, appeared. Conan Doyle was proud of both as portraying 'an accurate picture of that great age' and said that taken together they formed 'the most complete, satisfying and ambitious thing that I have ever done'.

By the time *The White Company* was published, Conan Doyle had acquired a literary agent, A. P. Watt, to relieve him of what he described as 'hateful bargaining'. Alexander Pollock Watt, an enterprising Scottish advertising manager, had begun working as a literary agent in 1875 after a friend asked him to negotiate a contract with a London publishing company. By 1881 he had incorporated his business as the world's first literary agency, and A. P. Watt would eventually have the world's finest writers on its books, including G. K. Chesterton, Joseph Conrad, Charles Dickens, Thomas Hardy, Rudyard Kipling, H. G. Wells and P. G. Wodehouse.

While Conan Doyle was still in Vienna, Watt had sold one of his short stories, 'The Voice of Science', to the *Strand Magazine*, launched in January 1891 by the publisher George Newnes, a former home-furnishings salesman who had made a fortune out of a penny weekly called *Tit-Bits*. Originally *Tit-Bits From All the Most Interesting Books, Periodicals and Newspapers in the World*, it was packed with diverse stories culled from other publications. A mixture of fact and fiction, humour and human interest, interspersed with pictures and cartoons, it was so popular that within months a number of imitations were on the market. But *Tit-Bits* always had the edge, largely because Newnes combined an acute business sense with a showman's flair for promotion – at one point he offered free life insurance to any reader killed in a railway accident while carrying a copy of his magazine.

He came up with the idea for the *Strand* after studying the US magazine market, which he considered 'smarter, livelier and more interesting'. The choice of the title pandered to the aspirations of its middle-class readership: The Strand, with its numerous theatres, restaurants and public houses was a raffish, busy thoroughfare at the heart of metropolitan London, with Trafalgar Square at one end and the Inns of Court at the other, a street where journalists and barristers rubbed shoulders with actors and vaudeville artists.

Newnes intended the *Strand Magazine* to be a much more upmarket, serious literary endeavour than *Tit-Bits*, and promised it would 'cost sixpence and be worth a shilling' and feature the very best writers and illustrators. 'The editor of *The Strand Magazine* respectfully places his first number in the hands of the public . . .' he wrote in an introduction to the first issue: 'the past efforts of the Editor in supplying cheap, healthful literature have met with such generous favour from the public, that he ventures to hope that this new enterprise will be a popular one . . . Will those who like this number be so good as to assist, by making its merits, if they are kind enough to think that it has any, known to their friends.'

The launch issue set the format for decades to come. With an illustration on virtually every page – an entirely new concept in British publishing – fiction from major writers including Voltaire, Pushkin, Paul Heyse and Grant Allen was intermingled with reportage – 'The Metropolitan Fire Brigade; Its Home and Its Work' and 'At the Animals' Hospital' – and what would become a regular feature, 'Portraits of Celebrities at different times of their Lives'.

The *Strand* was the publishing success of the decade. The first issue of 300,000 copies was in the shops by Christmas 1890 and sold out. By the turn of the century the magazine would be selling almost half a million copies every month and would include among its regular contributors, Wells, Kipling, Rider Haggard, Edith Nesbit, Arnold Bennett and, of course, Arthur Conan Doyle. Queen Victoria was said to be an avid reader. The magazine editor and critic W. T. Stead ascribed its popularity to its lightweight editorial mix: 'The phenomenal success of *The Strand* . . . shows that the peculiar genius of Mr George Newnes is as great in putting together monthly illustrated articles as in compiling weekly *Tit-Bits*. *The Strand* is light reading from cover to cover; bright, entertaining, illustrated matter, admirable for passing the time, and quite safe against suggesting forbidden speculations; nor does it provoke its readers to too great exercise of thinking.'[3]

Although Newnes was nominally the editor, the magazine was effectively run by its literary editor, Herbert Greenhough Smith, a Cambridge graduate in his mid-30s who had written a number of unsuccessful novels, was a fine poker player and an expert on French poetry. It was Greenhough Smith who accepted 'The Voice of Science', agreeing the payment with A. P. Watt at the rate of £4 per thousand words. The story appeared in the March 1891 issue without a byline. It is a slight piece set around a *conversazione* organised by Mrs Esdaile, a lady of remarkable scientific attainment about whom it was whispered that, on the occasion of the delivery of a lecture entitled 'On the Perigenesis of the Plastidule', she was 'the only woman in the room who could follow the lecturer even as far as the end of his title'. In the story, her pretty daughter, Rose, is saved from the attentions of a bounder when his indiscretions are unexpectedly exposed.

Around this time Conan Doyle identified a fundamental truth about the magazine market: he argued that a series, as distinct from a serial, made more sense for the majority of readers. 'Considering these various journals with their disconnected stories, it had struck me that a single character running through a series, if it only engaged the attention of the reader, would bind that reader to that particular magazine. On the other hand, it had long seemed to me that the ordinary serial might be an impediment rather than a help to a magazine, since, sooner or later, one missed one number and afterwards it had lost all interest. Clearly the ideal compromise was a character which carried through, and yet instalments which were each complete in themselves, so that the purchaser was always sure that he could relish the whole contents of the magazine. I believe I was the first to realise this.'

To test this theory, Conan Doyle submitted to the *Strand* in the spring of 1891 two short stories featuring Sherlock Holmes. Greenhough Smith, a rather gloomy figure with a wintery smile and a clinically detached manner, would later provide a number of unlikely accounts of his excitement at finding the handwritten manuscripts for 'A Scandal in Bohemia' and 'The Red-Headed League' on his desk: 'I at once realised that here was the greatest short story writer since Edgar Allan Poe. I can still remember rushing into Mr Newnes' room and thrusting the stories before his eyes . . . Good story writers were scarce, and here, to an editor jaded with wading through reams of impossible stuff, comes a gift from heaven, a godsend in the shape of a story that brought happiness into the despairing life of this weary editor . . . There was no mistaking the ingenuity of plot, the limpid clearness of style, the perfect art of telling a story. The very hand-writing, full of character, and clear as print . . .'⁴ Greenhough Smith immediately offered Conan Doyle a contract to write four more Holmes stories at a handsome fee, 30 guineas each, greatly bolstering not just his finances but his confidence in his abilities as a writer. It was the moment he realised that in Sherlock Holmes he had not only found an enduring character but one that could probably sustain a literary career.

Before he could settle down to work, Conan Doyle very nearly succumbed to a virulent influenza epidemic then sweeping London. On the morning of 4 May 1891, he was walking to his consulting room when he began to shiver; he recognised the symptoms and turned round but was barely able to make it back to his lodgings. In the days before antibiotics, influenza was a killer – Annette had died of it – and there were moments when Conan Doyle thought he would not pull through. But nursed by the faithful Touie and helped by his strong constitution, he recovered within a couple of weeks.

It was while he was convalescing that he made the fateful decision to give up trying to combine a literary and medical career: 'I saw how foolish I was to waste my literary earnings in keeping up an oculist's room in Wimpole Street, and I determined with a wild rush of joy to cut the painter and to trust for ever to my power of writing. I remember in my delight taking the handkerchief which lay upon the coverlet in my enfeebled hand, and tossing it up to the ceiling in my exultation. I should at last be my own master. No longer would I have to conform to professional dress or try to please anyone else. I would be free to live how I liked and where I liked. It was one of the great moments of exultation in my life. The date was in August 1891.'

Had he consulted his diary, he would have found the date was in May.

PART II

THE WRITER

CHAPTER 8

THE GREAT DETECTIVE
AND THE *STRAND*

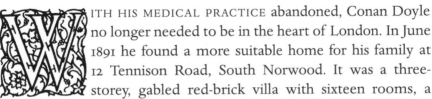ITH HIS MEDICAL PRACTICE abandoned, Conan Doyle no longer needed to be in the heart of London. In June 1891 he found a more suitable home for his family at 12 Tennison Road, South Norwood. It was a three-storey, gabled red-brick villa with sixteen rooms, a balcony at the front and a walled garden, in the southern suburbs of London, not far from open country in Surrey and the Crystal Palace, built for the Great Exhibition in 1851.

There we settled down, and there I made my first effort to live entirely by my pen. It soon became evident that I had been playing the game well within my powers and that I should have no difficulty in providing a sufficient income . . . The difficulty of the Holmes work was that every story really needed as clear-cut and original a plot as a longish book would do. One cannot without effort spin plots at such a rate. They are apt to become too thin or to break. I was determined, now that I had no longer the excuse of absolute pecuniary pressure, never again to write anything which was not as good as I could possibly make it, and therefore I would not write a Holmes story without a worthy plot and without a problem which interested my own mind, for that is the first requisite before you can interest anyone else.

'A Scandal in Bohemia' appeared in the July issue of the *Strand*. Curiously, it would be the only Holmes story in which he was beaten

– and by a woman to boot, one Irene Adler, a young opera singer and 'well known adventuress'. It offers a hint that Holmes was not quite the misogynist he sometimes appeared. Dr Watson began thus: 'To Sherlock Holmes she is always *the* woman. I have seldom heard him mention her under any other name. In his eyes she eclipses and predominates the whole of her sex. It was not that he felt any emotion akin to love for Irene Adler. All emotions, and that one particularly, were abhorrent to his cold, precise but admirably balanced mind.'

The story opened with a masked visitor to Baker Street, whom Holmes quickly identifies as the hereditary King of Bohemia. The King wants Holmes to recover a compromising photograph of himself with Miss Adler to avoid a scandal before his forthcoming marriage. By the use of disguise and a brilliant ruse, Holmes finds out where Miss Adler has hidden the picture, but when he attempts to retrieve it he discovers not only that it has gone, but that Miss Adler has been aware of his identity and his plan all along.

The *Strand's* art editor, W. H. J. Boot, decided to commission Walter Paget, who had illustrated *Treasure Island* and *Robinson Crusoe*, to portray Holmes in pen-and-ink, but the project was passed in error to Walter's lesser known brother, Sidney, also a commercial artist. One story has it that Boot wrote to Sidney because he had forgotten Walter's first name; another that Sidney opened Boot's letter because it was addressed to 'Mr Paget the illustrator'. As Charles Doyle had done before him, Paget more or less ignored Conan Doyle's description of Holmes in *A Study in Scarlet* and used his good-looking brother, Walter, as a model, producing a figure, according to one critic, 'only a shade less elegant in person and appearance than a popular matinee idol'. Conan Doyle evidently had not imagined Holmes as this handsome chap but admitted that 'from the point of view of my lady readers it was as well'. It was Sidney Paget who, in 'Silver Blaze', provided Sherlock Holmes with the famous Inverness cape and deerstalker which would fix his popular image in the public imagination.

Following publication of 'A Scandal in Bohemia' it was rumoured that Conan Doyle had based Irene Adler and her admirer on real people, and there was much speculation as to their true identities. Prominent candidates included Lillie Langtry, whose affair with the Prince of Wales had been the subject of endless gossip; another was a singer, Ludmilla Hubel, allegedly the lover of Archduke John Salvator of Austria, the nephew of Emperor Franz Joseph; a third was Lola Montez, former mistress of Ludwig I of Bavaria. Even the great Australian soprano, Dame Nellie Melba, was mentioned. It was all grist to the publicity mill.

The August 1891 issue of the *Strand* featured 'The Red-Headed League', a wonderfully ingenious and sometimes hilarious story in which a criminal gang attempts to lure a shop owner from his premises in order to tunnel into the adjoining bank. The gang places an advertisement in a newspaper inviting all red-headed men to apply to an address in Fleet Street for membership in the Red-Headed League, which offered a salary of £4 a week 'for purely nominal services'. The only remarkable aspect of Jabez Wilson, the owner of the shop, is his 'blazing red head'. Holmes solves the case with masterly ease, making a number of startling deductions along the way, observing about Wilson: 'Beyond the obvious facts that he has at some time done manual labour, that he takes snuff, that he is a Freemason, that he has been in China, and that he has done a considerable amount of writing lately, I can deduce nothing else.'

As soon as Conan Doyle had delivered the first six stories, Greenhough Smith commissioned six more, thus a Sherlock Holmes story appeared every month in the *Strand* until June 1892. Somewhat to his creator's bewilderment, the detective had by then captured the imagination of readers like no other fictional character had done before: they queued at newsagents on the day a new issue was due, and by the time the first series had ended Holmes was well on the way to becoming a cultural icon. Within two years a delighted George Newnes would estimate that Conan Doyle's name on the cover of the *Strand* boosted circulation by as much as 100,000 copies.

The superhero of the Victorian era, a knight errant with Watson as his Sancho Panza, Holmes appeared on the scene at a time when the British Empire was at its zenith and London, his home, was the political and economic capital of the world. 'Science' was the new obsession and Holmes was the embodiment of the scientific investigator, pursuing abstruse twists and turns in the trail, picking up obscure clues from seemingly impenetrable puzzles and producing a final, triumphant solution. He frequently chided Watson for failing to recognise that investigation was merely a 'scientific exercise'. Those who looked for scientific proof of Holmes's brilliance could quote many examples. For instance his discovery in *A Study in Scarlet* of a reagent for haemoglobin which foreshadowed use of antisera in precipitin tests. In *The Sign of Four* he referred to his 'monograph upon the tracing of footsteps, with some remarks upon the use of plaster of Paris as a preserver of impresses'. This predated the publication in 1891 of Hans Gross's seminal textbook on criminality, *Criminal Investigation,* in which he recorded experimenting with six methods of preserving footprints and concluding that plaster of Paris was the best. In 'The Reigate Squires' Holmes sets out criteria which are the scientific basis for handwriting comparison today.

No writer conjured up London in the late Victorian era more evocatively than Conan Doyle, an achievement made even more impressive by the fact that when he wrote the first two stories he only had a passing knowledge of the city from a handful of family visits. Here is Conan Doyle at his best, setting the scene in *The Sign of Four*: 'It was a September evening and not yet seven o'clock, but the day had been a dreary one, and a dense drizzly fog lay low upon the great city. Mud-coloured clouds drooped sadly over the muddy streets. Down the Strand the lamps were but misty splotches of diffused light which threw a feeble circular glimmer upon the slimy pavement. The yellow glare from the shop-windows streamed out into the steamy, vaporous air, and threw a murky, shifting radiance across the crowded thoroughfare.'

While Orson Welles would memorably describe Holmes as 'the world's most famous man who never was', many readers believed him to be a real person and attempted to seek his advice at 221B Baker Street, only to discover there was no such address. Conan Doyle received many letters asking if he could obtain Holmes's autograph, and a press-cuttings agency wrote to enquire if Holmes might like to avail himself of its services.

The pairing of Conan Doyle and Sherlock Holmes was propitious in every way. Conan Doyle preferred to refer to himself as a storyteller rather than an author, explaining to friends that his sole purpose was to tell a story well, lucidly and with sufficient pace to entertain. The secret, he liked to say, was rhythm and control. In Sherlock Holmes

Conan Doyle found the perfect medium for his extraordinary ability to devise labyrinthine plots that only the great detective could unravel. Readers followed his adventures with missionary fervour and delighted in quoting Holmes' favourite aphorisms, like 'When you have eliminated the impossible, whatever remains, however improbable, must be the truth', and 'It is a capital mistake to theorize before one has data.' The novelist John Le Carré has described the Holmes stories as 'a kind of narrative perfection: a perfect interplay between dialogue and description, perfect characterisation and perfect timing'.[1]

In October 1892 the twelve stories in the first series were collected in *The Adventures of Sherlock Holmes*, which became an instant best-seller. Nearly a quarter of a million copies of *Adventures* were sold in its first three years in print. It was admiringly reviewed in the *Bookman* by the man who had inspired Holmes, Dr Joseph Bell: 'Dr Conan Doyle in this remarkable series of stories has proved himself a born story-teller. He has had the wit to devise excellent plots, interesting complications; he tells them in honest Saxon-English with directness and pith; and above all his other merits, his stories are absolutely free from padding. He knows how delicious brevity is and he has given us stories that we can read at a sitting between dinner and coffee, and we have not a chance to forget the beginning before we reach the end.'

Conan Doyle was naturally gratified by his success but increasingly concerned that Holmes was damaging his aspirations to be considered a serious writer. As early as November 1891, only four years after Holmes's first appearance in print, he had written to his mother revealing that he was thinking of 'slaying' Holmes in the final story of the first series. 'He takes my mind from better things,' he explained.[2] Mary Doyle was horrified that he should think of eliminating the source of such a handsome income and urgently advised him to reconsider. Conan Doyle could consider killing off Holmes because he had become acutely aware of his value in the publishing market, as he reported to his mother in a follow-up letter:

> I have been having a correspondence with Arrowsmith of Bristol. He wanted me about 24 months ago to do a book for his shilling series, and offered to pay a royalty on it – I wanted

£100, and on that we quarrelled, he sending me a rather imper-
tinent card, of which I took no notice. End of Act I. A year
ago he wrote offering me £100 in advance on such a book. I
answered that my price was now £200. End of Act II. Last
week he wrote asking me to do the book (60,000 words) at
that price. I replied that my price was now £400. Frantic howls
came from Bristol, with much repentance as to the past. So
now I have agreed to do a 50,000 worder for £250 as an advance
on a 20 percent Royalty, I to retain American & continental
rights. MS to be delivered in August, which will give me lots
of time. I have therefore my hands full for '92.

In his diary at the end of 1891 Conan Doyle noted that he had
made £1,500 from his pen during the year and had written 210,000
words – 30,000 were the first 150 pages of *The Refugees: A Tale of Two
Continents,* which he had started at the beginning of December and
would finish by the end of February 1892. A novel heavily influenced
by Dumas and built around the suppression of the Huguenots in
France in the seventeenth century and their subsequent flight to North
America, it first appeared as a serial in the *Strand,* before being
published in book form. *Harper's New Monthly Magazine* called it, 'A
brilliant and fascinating story . . . One does not easily recall a more
vivid picture of the court of Louis the Great, with its splendour, its
misery, its meanness, its dignity, its culture, its ignorance, its intrigues,
and its bigotry . . .' Conan Doyle's mother told him not long afterwards that on a visit to France the tour guide at the Château de
Fontainebleau had recommended *The Refugees* as a book that would
give the reader an understanding of the court of Louis XIV. Conan
Doyle was delighted: 'I expect the guide would have been considerably astonished had he then and there been kissed by an elderly English
lady, but it was an experience which he must have narrowly missed.'[3]
   Freed from any pretence of having to follow a medical career,
Conan Doyle was now writing at a furious pace, as if all the ideas
that had been bottled up while he working as a doctor could no longer
wait to take shape. His versatility, he wrote dozens of stories, was
incredible: medical, historical, sporting, weird, ingenious, funny,
horrible, pathetic. It seems there was no subject he could not tackle.

After *The Refugees* he plunged into yet another historical novel, *The Great Shadow*, a gory tale set in the Napoleonic era at the time of the Battle of Waterloo, described in bloodthirsty detail: '[a cannonball] knocked five men into a bloody mash, and I saw it lying on the ground afterwards like a crimson football. Another went through the adjutant's horse with a plop like a stone in the mud, broke its back and left it lying at close quarters like a burst gooseberry.'

Long before the *Strand* had finished publishing *The Adventures of Sherlock Holmes*, Greenhough Smith was pleading with Conan Doyle for a second series. At first he resisted because he wanted to concentrate on what he considered more serious work, and sought to deter Greenhough Smith by demanding £1,000 – a truly phenomenal sum at the time – fully expecting Smith to refuse. He did not. With the deal agreed, Conan Doyle wrote to Lottie to persuade her to return home: '*The Strand* want 12 more Sherlock Holmes stories – for which I have charged them £1000. Altogether I ought to earn a clear £3000 this year, so it would be funny if I were to leave my sisters in a foreign land.'[6] Both Connie and Lottie would return from Portugal in 1892, courtesy of their brother's generosity; he would eventually pay Lottie an allowance to act as his literary assistant in South Norwood. Innes, who was training for a commission in the Army at the Royal Military Academy in Woolwich, also received financial help, and only when he indicated a desire to join the elite Royal Horse Artillery did his brother baulk at the cost.

Since Conan Doyle seldom took more than a week to complete a Sherlock Holmes story, his fee was generous in the extreme. His technique was to map out the problem and its solution, draw up a rough outline and sketch in the characters before sitting down to write the finished story. He worked at a flat-topped desk in a corner of his study, which overlooked the garden. The walls were hung with his father's watercolours and mementoes of his trip to the Arctic were all around – whaling harpoons, a stuffed Icelandic falcon and the skull of a polar bear. It was his habit to write from breakfast until lunch every morning, then from five to about eight o'clock in the evening, usually averaging 3,000 words a day – a prodigious output any writer would envy. Many of his ideas were dreamed up in the afternoons, walking or cycling with Touie, or playing tennis or cricket. Once he had finished a story he had no further interest in it. As he would explain in a letter to G. K. Chesterton, his work might be improved by editing, but not by him. He had given all in his first effort and any further tinkering would be 'gratuitous and a waste of time'.[4]

Although he had a typewriter, Conan Doyle preferred to work by hand, writing by pen in a neat legible script, with few corrections. He also kept an Ideas Book in which he annotated ideas as they were used or discarded:

> The Bourse story and the tale of the man with the hereditary taint. (This should be very strong).
>
> Idea of the Beggar near Change and the disappearance of Mr Easton Brown. (Done).
>
> The woman who was capable of icing good claret and of warming good champagne.
>
> The old nun who in her extreme old age sees the man for whose sake she entered the convent. (Used).
>
> Of all the ruins on Earth that of a man is saddest. (End of Cullingworth – used.)

He was always on the lookout for new ideas and receptive to suggestions from others. 'I think that a fine thing might be done about a bacteriological criminal,' he wrote in response to a suggestion from Bell, 'but the only fear is lest you get beyond the average man, whose interest must be held from the first and who won't be interested unless he thoroughly understands. Still even so I think that something might be done on those lines, I should be so glad if you should find yourself with ten minutes to spare if you would give me an idea of the case which you speak of, and indeed I should be very grateful for any "spotting of trade" tips, or anything else of a Sherlock Holmesy nature . . .'[5]

Compared to the diligent research that he put into his historical novels, the Holmes stories were churned out carelessly, riddled with glaring errors and inconsistencies. Credibility was tested: readers were invited to believe that Holmes was able to disguise himself in a matter of minutes so convincingly that not even Watson could recognise him.

Then there was the mystery of Watson's disappearing dog. When Holmes and Watson are discussing, in *A Study in Scarlet*, individual shortcomings that might affect their ability to share lodgings, Watson declares that he has a pet, 'a bull pup'. But it is the animal's only mention in the canon. There was a prize howler in 'The Man With the Twisted Lip', when Watson's wife refers to him as James although his name is John. In 'The Adventure of the Speckled Band' – Conan Doyle's favourite Sherlock Holmes story – a 'swamp adder . . . the deadliest snake in India', trained by bowls of milk and recalled by a whistle, slithers down a bell pull, kills a sleeping woman and returns to its master by climbing up the bell pull and entering the adjoining room through a ventilator. There is no such reptile as a 'swamp adder', there are no adders in India, snakes do not like milk, are completely deaf, and no snake could climb a bell pull.

Holmes, too, is full of puzzling contradictions. Initially, he rises early and has 'invariably breakfasted and gone out' before Watson emerges; not many stories later he is 'usually very late in the mornings'. In *The Sign of Four* he has never heard of Thomas Carlyle; later he discourses at length about him. He expresses no interest in philosophy at one point; yet at another is quoting obscure philosophers and explaining philosophical systems. His sometime colleague, Inspector Lestrade of Scotland Yard, transmutes from a 'little sallow, rat-faced, dark-eyed fellow' in the very first story into a 'small, wiry bulldog of a man' in another. More mystifyingly Holmes appears in 'The Adventure of Wisteria Lodge' at a time when he was supposed to have been travelling incognito in Tibet and was presumed by the world to be dead.

Conan Doyle, however, was blithely untroubled by such trifles. 'In short stories,' he declared, 'it has always seemed to me that so long as you produce your dramatic effect, accuracy of detail matters little.'[6] When an editor wrote to tell him there was no railway line at a particular place, he replied: 'I made one.' In truth, he probably never bothered to keep track of what he had written, first, because he didn't see Holmes as an immortal, iconic character, and secondly, because although he earned large sums of money, he cared little for the work that did little, he believed, to enhance his literary stature.

The demands of a second Holmes series did not prevent him

from another project: adapting his short story 'A Straggler of '15' – the reminiscences of a 'gaunt, bent and doddering' corporal in the Napoleonic wars – into a one-act play which he sent to Henry Irving, his boyhood actor idol. Conan Doyle described it as a 'moving picture of an old soldier and his ways. My own eyes were moist as I wrote it, and that is the surest way to moisten those of others.' Irving asked his friend Abraham (Bram) Stoker, soon to become famous as the author of *Dracula*, to read it. Stoker was at the time the business manager at Irving's Lyceum Theatre: 'As he [Irving] came hurrying out to the stage, after putting on the soft broad-brimmed felt hat for which he usually exchanged his topper during rehearsals, he stopped beside my table where I was writing, and laying a parcel on it said "I wish you would throw an eye over that during rehearsal. It came this morning. You can tell me what you think of it when I come off."'[7]

After the rehearsal Stoker told Irving that the play was absolutely made for him, that he should on no account allow it to go elsewhere and that he ought to own it at any price. Irving agreed and immediately bought the rights for £100 and sent a congratulatory note to Conan Doyle on 7 March 1892: 'A delightful and remarkable little play, which I should very much like to have the opportunity of acting at some time.' Irving would later play the protagonist, Corporal Gregory Brewster, when, re-named *A Story of Waterloo*, the play opened in Bristol on 21 September 1894 and later transferred to the Lyceum in London.

Conan Doyle's newfound celebrity as a novelist, dramatist and short-story writer meant his social life was much expanded. He joined the Reform Club, home to a prominent literary circle headed by Sir John Robinson, editor of the *Daily News*, and was invited to literary dinners hosted by Jerome K. Jerome, editor of *The Idler* and author of *Three Men In A Boat*, published to great acclaim in 1889. Conan Doyle occasionally contributed to *The Idler*, which published an eclectic mix of fiction, essays, cartoons, poetry and interviews. His faintly dour offerings – his first contribution featured the apparition of a dead man appearing to his wife – were rather at odds with the magazine's humorous tone, but were welcome nonetheless, and the other contributors warmed to him. Jerome's convivial afternoon teas usually extended into the evening, when stronger drink would be served, and sometimes ended with guests sleeping on the floor in the magazine's offices.

It was at an *Idler* dinner that Conan Doyle met J. M. Barrie, several years before he became famous as the author of *Peter Pan,* and struck up an immediate friendship. The two men had much in common – both were Scots, both had attended the University of Edinburgh and were passionate about cricket. Barrie had his own team, the 'Allahakbarries', a play on his name and an Arabic phrase for 'Lord help us', which Conan Doyle joined. The 'Allahakbarries' played mainly for fun and were alarmed by the ferocious pace of his bowling and his flailing bat. After a particularly vigorous performance, a fellow team member expressed surprise over the 'surprisingly low death rate'.

Jerome K. Jerome also became a good friend and dedicated his *Novel Notes* in 1893: 'To Big-Hearted, Big-Souled, Big-Bodied Friend Conan Doyle'. He remembered Conan Doyle as a tremendous worker: 'He would sit at a small desk in a corner of his own drawing room, writing a story, while a dozen people round about him were talking and laughing. He preferred it to being in his study. Sometimes, without looking up from his work, he would make a remark, showing he must have been listening to our conversation; but his pen never ceased moving.'[8]

Jerome accompanied Conan Doyle with a party of family and friends on a trip to Norway in the summer of 1892, organised as a treat for Touie, who was pregnant again. Jerome was rather taken by the vivacious Connie ('A handsome girl, she might have posed as Brunhilda'), who alone among the women did not succumb to seasickness on the crossing. The rough sea, he wrote in his memoirs, 'added to her colour and gave a delightful curl to her hair. She had a sympathetic nature, and was awfully sorry for the poor women who were ill. She would burst in on them every now and then to see if she could be of any help to them. You would have thought her mere presence would have cheered them up. As a matter of fact, it made them just mad. "Oh do go away, Connie," I heard one of her friends murmur, while passing the open door, "it makes me ill to look at you".'[9] (Connie did not return Jerome's interest and went on to marry the novelist E. W. Hornung.)

Jerome reported with delight that Conan Doyle's overconfidence in his ability to speak Norwegian resulted in an embarrassing incident. Conan Doyle had started learning the language on the ship and apparently picked it up so quickly that he missed no opportunity of airing his knowledge. One day the party went up to a rest-house in the mountains on *stoljas* – single-person carriages drawn by sturdy ponies. During lunch a young officer came up to their table and spoke to them in Norwegian. Conan Doyle immediately took over and after a brief conversation – incomprehensible to the rest of the party — the young officer bowed and took his leave. 'We all watched the conversation,' Jerome wrote. 'The young Norwegian officer was evidently charmed with Doyle, while Doyle stood ladling out Norwegian as though it had been his mother's tongue.' When asked what they had talked about, Conan Doyle became uncharacteristically reticent and vague. Of course, he admitted, he had not understood *everything*, just about someone who had hurt his leg. After lunch the *stoljas* were brought round to the front but Conan Doyle's was missing. When he enquired as to its whereabouts, a waiter informed him that he had lent it to the young officer, whose own pony had gone lame. Are you sure, Conan Doyle demanded. Absolutely said the waiter. You said 'Certainly, with pleasure' and 'Don't mention it' several times. Conan Doyle was less inclined to speak Norwegian thereafter.

Back in South Norwood, journalists who arrived to interview Conan Doyle almost always expressed surprise at his appearance and demeanour. Perhaps they had no clear idea what to expect, but certainly not a large hale and hearty man, invariably dressed in tweeds, who looked more like a gentleman farmer than the usual idea of a writer. In a measure of his growing celebrity, Harry How spent 'A Day With Dr Conan Doyle' for the August 1892 issue of the *Strand*. 'I found him totally different from the man I expected to see . . .' he wrote. 'There was nothing lynx-eyed, nothing "detective" about him – not even the regulation walk of our modern solver of mysteries. He is just a happy, genial, homely man; tall, broad-shouldered, with a hand that grips you heartily, and, in its sincerity of welcome, hurts. He is brown and bronzed, for he enters liberally into all outdoor sports – football, tennis, bowls, and cricket . . . But in exercise he leans most towards tricycling. He is never happier than when on his tandem with his wife and starting on a thirty mile spin; never merrier than when he perches his little three-year-old Mary on the wheels, and runs her round the green lawn of his garden.'

One of the photographs accompanying the feature showed Conan

Doyle, in tweed knickerbockers and a peaked cap, on a tandem tricycle outside the front door with Touie perched uncertainly on the front seat in a long black dress and a perky hat. Even when not pregnant, Touie, who was not strong, could never manage the distances that Conan Doyle regularly covered on his tricycle. In a letter to his mother he told how, on a ride into the Weald of Surrey with Innes and Connie, Touie had to be sent home by train because she could no longer continue.

On 15 November 1892 Touie gave birth to Arthur Alleyne Kingsley. (Alleyne Edricson was Sir Nigel Loring's squire in *The White Company*, but the boy was always known in the family as Kingsley.) Conan Doyle was overjoyed to have a son in whom he could instil the manly virtues of which he was so proud, not to mention teaching him cricket and boxing.

That month the *Strand* trumpeted the exciting news that another series of Sherlock Holmes stories would be starting in December and sought to explain why Holmes had been absent for some months: 'His [Conan Doyle's] reason for refraining from writing any more stories for a while is a candid one. He is fearful of spoiling a character of which he is particularly fond, but he declares that already he has enough material to carry him through another series, and merrily assures me that he thought the opening story of the next series of "Sherlock Holmes", to be published in this magazine, was of such an unsolvable character, that he had positively bet his wife a shilling that she would not guess the true solution of it until she got to the end of the chapter!'

Conan Doyle had admitted in a letter to Joseph Bell that he was in 'great dread' of the new series failing to match the standard of the first, but he need not have worried. 'Silver Blaze', the first story, was Conan Doyle at his ingenious best and would become one of the best known sporting mysteries ever written, perhaps most famous for a brief exchange between Holmes and the local police inspector, who suspects the detective knows more than he is letting on:

> [Inspector:] 'Is there any other point to which you would wish to draw my attention?'

> [Holmes:] 'To the curious incident of the dog in the night-time.'

'The dog did nothing in the night-time.'

'That was the curious incident.'

While Conan Doyle was toiling on the remaining stories he was contracted to write, Barrie got in touch to ask a favour. He had fallen ill while writing the libretto of *Jane Annie*, a comic opera for the impresario Richard D'Oyly Carte and asked Conan Doyle to help him finish it. 'Of course I was very happy to serve him in any way,' Conan Doyle wrote later. 'My heart sank, however, when, after giving the promise, I examined the work. The only literary gift which Barrie has not got is the sense of poetic rhythm, and the instinct for what is permissible in verse. Ideas and wit were there in abundance. But the plot itself was not strong, though the dialogue and the situations also were occasionally excellent. I did my best and wrote the lyrics for the second act, and much of the dialogue, but it had to take the predestined shape.'

In turn, Barrie remembered Conan Doyle as being rather too good natured. 'If we lost him at rehearsals he was sure to be found in a shrouded box writing a new song for some obscure member of the company. They had only to plead with him, "I have nothing to say, Mr Doyle, except half a dozen lines in the first act", when he would reply, "Oh, my poor chap, too bad", and retire into a box, from which he emerged almost instantly with a song.'[10]

Jane Annie opened at the Savoy Theatre on 13 May 1893, with Barrie and Conan Doyle sharing a box, and soon wishing they could be elsewhere. The audience grew more and more hostile as the production stumbled on, and at the end one female lead was so upset she refused to leave her dressing room for the curtain call. There were certainly no calls for the authors, and when a mutual friend came into their box and Conan Doyle asked him why he did not cheer, he replied, 'I didn't like to, when no one else was doing it.' Barrie and Conan Doyle quietly crept away to lick their wounds over dinner at the Athenaeum Club.

The reviews were devastating, with most critics expressing dismay that two such talented writers should produce something so bad. George Bernard Shaw, writing in the *World*, excoriated Barrie and Conan Doyle: 'It would ill become me, as a brother of the literary craft, to pretend to congratulate them seriously upon the most unblushing outburst of tomfoolery that two responsible citizens could conceivably indulge in publicly . . .' Several critics suggested, to Conan Doyle's intense irritation, that the libretto might have been improved by the presence of Sherlock Holmes.

That summer Conan Doyle was invited to Lucerne in Switzerland with Touie to lecture on 'Fiction as a Part of Literature'. In the garden of the Hotel de l'Europe, overlooking the lake, the Conan Doyles met Silas E. Hocking, a minister of the United Methodist Free Church and fellow author. Like so many others, Hocking was surprised to find the writer of the Sherlock Holmes stories was a big, bluff, good-humoured Englishman 'such as one would find on any cricket pitch'.

From Lucerne, the Conan Doyles travelled to Meiringen, where they visited the Reichenbach Falls, a place soon to assume enormous importance in the folklore of Sherlock Holmes. (Meiringen still has a Sherlock Holmes Museum, in the basement of the English church, on Conan Doyle Place.) They met up again with Hocking's party in Zermatt, staying at the Riffel Alp Hotel, in the shadow of the Matterhorn. Hocking later described a conversation he had with Conan Doyle when they both climbed the Findelen glacier, during which Conan Doyle reiterated his wish not to be remembered simply as the creator of Sherlock Holmes and revealed that he intended to kill him off at the end of the year. 'The fact is,' he said, 'he has got to be an "old man of the sea" about my neck, and I intend to make an end of him. If I don't he'll make an end of me.' Hocking asked how he was going to do it and Conan Doyle replied that he had not yet decided. 'Why not bring him out here and drop him down a crevasse?' Hocking suggested. Conan Doyle laughed and said, 'Not a bad idea.'[11]

Not long after their return from Switzerland, Touie fell ill, complaining of a cough and a pain in her side. He called in a local doctor, who diagnosed 'galloping consumption'. Touie's lungs were badly damaged, the doctor said, and there was little hope of a permanent cure 'considering her record and family history'. (Her father, Jeremiah Hawkins, was probably diabetic, and her sister Mary as well as her brother had died young.) Distraught, Conan Doyle sought a second opinion from Sir Douglas Powell, the acknowledged expert in the field; he confirmed the diagnosis, and said Touie might only

have a few months to live. Diagnosis of consumption in the late nineteenth century was a death sentence, and there was a widespread
belief that it was contagious. It was frowned on socially, regarded as
the scourge of the lower classes, and many tended to keep well away
from sufferers.

Conan Doyle wrote from the Reform Club to pass on the bad
news to his mother in measured tones:

> My Dearest Mam,
>
> I am afraid we must reconcile ourselves to the diagnosis.
> I had Douglas Powell, who is one of the first men in
> London, out on Saturday and he confirmed it. On the other
> hand, he thought that there were signs of fibroid growth
> around the seat of the disease and that the other lung had
> enlarged to compensate. He seemed to think that mischief
> must have been going on for years unobserved, but if so, it
> must have been very slight . . .
>
> Well, we must take what fate sends, but I have hopes
> that all may yet be well . . . Touie drives out on fine days
> and has not lost much flesh. The cough is occasionally
> troublesome and the phlegm very thick – no haemorrhage
> yet, but I fear it.
>
> Goodbye, dearest, many thanks for your kind
> sympathy . . .

It is curious that Conan Doyle, a trained doctor who only three
years earlier had travelled to Berlin to study tuberculosis, had failed
to diagnose the disease in his wife. In truth, he was under considerable stress. He had suddenly become famous for work he privately
held in low esteem and worried constantly about his reputation. In
the previous eighteenth months he had written more than twenty
Sherlock Holmes stories, three novels, a number of other short
stories and articles for newspapers, not to mention his ill-fated
collaboration with J. M. Barrie. He was in demand as a lecturer
and sportsman and still made time to socialise in literary circles. It
was all too much and his family life suffered. He was intermittently
moody and bad-tempered, suffered from insomnia and wrote to his
mother complaining that he was troubled by his nerves 'more than

most people know'. Any guilt he might have felt about failing to diagnose Touie's condition was perhaps assuaged by the fact that she lived for another thirteen years, due in part to the care he provided.

Hard on the heels of the devastating news about Touie came word that his 61-year-old father had died at Crichton Royal Asylum in Dumfries. As Charles Doyle had virtually disappeared, many had assumed he was already dead, an assumption the family never corrected. Conan Doyle knew that his father's condition was steadily deteriorating. When Charles Doyle had been moved to Crichton in May 1892, his son had signed the transfer certificate and agreed to pay the fees of £40 a year. On the certificate he stated the cause of his father's condition was 'dipsomania' and in answer to a question whether he was dangerous to others he replied, emphatically, 'Certainly not'. But there was no chance of his father ever rejoining the family, and while his death was a matter of great sadness, it must have been tinged with relief that he had been released from his miserable existence.

A rare insight into the horror of Charles's alcoholism was provided by his wife in a candid letter to Dr James Rutherford at the Crichton Royal Asylum, written on 3 December 1892, in which she described the attacks of delirium tremens he frequently suffered and the desperate lengths to which he would go to get drink: 'Every article of value he or I possessed [was] carried off secretly, debts to large amount contracted to our trades people, bills given, etc – all for goods which never entered our doors, but were converted at once into money . . . He would strip himself of all his underclothes, take the very bed linen, climb down the water spout at risk of his life, break open the children's money boxes. He even drank furniture varnish . . .' She added ruefully that there was a public house in Edinburgh where 'I am told they have a most valuable collection of his sketches, given for drink.'[12]

Themes of incarceration and alcoholism occur repeatedly in Conan Doyle's work. In 'The Japanned Box', written in 1899 six years after the death of his father, Sir John Bollamore, a chronic alcoholic, kept a phonograph message from his wife in the titular box, made as she lay dying and imploring him never to drink again. Sir John could have been Conan Doyle's father: 'I began to understand that strangely human look in his eyes, those deep lines upon his careworn face. He was a man who was fighting a ceaseless battle, holding at arm's length from morning till night, a horrible adversary, who was for ever trying to close with him – an adversary which would destroy him body and soul could it but fix its claws once more upon him.'

Years later, in an interview with *New York World*, as if to make amends for the family's neglect, Conan Doyle would belatedly insist that his father was a 'great unrecognised genius'. He claimed his father 'drifted' to Edinburgh from London and so 'lost the chance of living before the public eye. His wild and strange fantasies alarmed, I think, rather than pleased the stolid Scotchmen of the early 50's and 60's. His mind was on strange moonlight effects, done with extraordinary skill in water colours; dancing witches, drowning seamen, death coaches on lonely moors at night, and goblins chasing children across churchyards.'[13]

Conan Doyle had little time to grieve for his father, since he needed to get his wife away from the damp and cold of an English winter. In the Arctic he had noted the 'marvellous invigorating properties' of the air, and he remained a firm believer in the therapeutic value of breathing clean, crisp air. As tuberculosis spread across Europe, a number of sanatoria had opened high in the Swiss Alps, where the climate offered both some alleviation from the condition and the hope of a cure. A contemporary medical journal suggested that the Alpine air could 'purge and rejuvenate' afflicted lung tissue. Conan Doyle swiftly made arrangements for Touie to spend the winter at the Kurhaus Hotel in Davos, where, he wrote, 'there seemed the best chance of killing this accursed microbe which was rapidly eating out her vitals'. She left with her older sister, Emily (Nem), on 1 November; her mother had once again agreed to look after the children. Conan Doyle remained behind temporarily, to supervise the closing down of the house and to fulfil his contract for the *Strand*.

He had, by then, become entirely disillusioned with Sherlock Holmes, morosely blaming the voracious public appetite for the great detective's adventures for obscuring his more important work – his historical novels, plays and poems – and preventing him assuming what he believed was his rightful place in the literary pantheon. When a publisher suggested he should write a preface for a new edition of *A Study in Scarlet*, he haughtily replied that 'so elementary a form of fiction as the detective story hardly deserves the dignity of a preface'.

In December 1893 he solved the problem, scrawling two words in his Ideas Book: 'Killed Holmes.'

CHAPTER 9

A PREMATURE DEATH

HEN THE DREADFUL NEWS spread that Sherlock Holmes had plunged to his death over the Reichenbach Falls in the Bernese Oberland, locked in combat with his arch-enemy Professor Moriarty, no one was prepared for the dismayed reaction amongst his huge army of admirers. Not since the death of Dickens's 'Little Nell', fifty-two years earlier, had a fictional character's demise unleashed such an outpouring of public grief and outrage. A collective gasp of horror, one newspaper reported, could be heard from Land's End to John O'Groats. The *Strand* lost 20,000 subscribers and furious letters poured into the their offices by the sackload, many abusing Conan Doyle, others pleading with George Newnes to deny the report and promise more stories. One lady reader called Conan Doyle a 'brute', another allegedly swatted him with her handbag. The Prince of Wales was said to be particularly anguished. In the City of London, workers sported black armbands or wore black mourning crepe tied round their top hats; in New York 'Keep Holmes Alive' societies sprang into being. In an increasingly scientific age, people yearned for romance, fantasy and adventure, and were furious at being deprived of their hero. 'It was as if a god had been destroyed by treachery,' the critic Vincent Starrett noted.

'The news of the death of Sherlock Holmes has been received with most widespread regret,' the *Strand* declared, 'and readers have implored us to use our influence with Mr Conan Doyle to prevent the tragedy being consummated. We can only reply that we pleaded for his life in the most urgent, earnest and constant manner. Like hundreds of correspondents, we feel as if we have lost an old friend whom we could ill spare. Mr Doyle's feeling was that he did not desire Sherlock to outstay his welcome, and that the public had had enough of him. This is not our opinion, nor is it the opinion of the public; but it is, we regret to say, Mr Doyle's.'

Holmes's terrible fate was recorded by a heavy-hearted Watson in 'The Final Problem', published in the *Strand* in December, 1893. Those readers not overcome with shock and horror and still capable of analysing the story might have concluded that Conan Doyle could hardly wait to dispose of his creation. He did not, for example, bother to devise a mystery for Holmes to solve with his usual brilliance. Instead, Moriarty was briskly introduced: 'He is the Napoleon of crime, Watson. He is the organiser of half that is evil and nearly all that is undetected in this great city. He is a genius, a philosopher, an abstract thinker. He has a brain of the first order. He sits motionless, like a spider in the centre of its web, but that web has a thousand radiations, and he knows well every quiver of them . . .' Considering that by his own account Holmes had devoted much of his career to breaking up Moriarty's criminal network, dedicated readers might have been surprised to have heard nothing of him before.

It quickly becomes evident the two men are each bent on destroying the other. For reasons not entirely clear, Holmes absents himself from London and invites Watson to accompany him to the Continent where Moriarty secretly pursues them to the village of Meiringen, near the Falls. Watson is lured away on the false pretext of being urgently needed to treat an English woman in Davos dying from consumption (a hint from Conan Doyle, perhaps, that he had more on his mind than devising more Holmes stories) and Holmes and Moriarty end up struggling on a precipitous granite ledge overlooking the Falls. Sidney Paget's stirring gothic drawing of them teetering on the brink, with the Falls roaring behind, is redolent of doom. 'Any attempt at recovering the bodies was absolutely hopeless,' Watson concluded, 'and there, deep down in that dreadful cauldron of swirling water and seething foam, will lie for all time the most dangerous criminal and the foremost champion of the law of their generation.' It was, Conan Doyle drily observed, 'a worthy tomb for poor Sherlock, even if I buried my banking account along with him'.

Many readers were genuinely puzzled that an author would want to dispatch such a popular, not to mention lucrative, character. 'I have been much blamed for doing that gentleman to death,' Conan Doyle would say in a speech to the Author's Club in 1896, 'but I hold that it was not murder, but justifiable homicide in self-defence, since, if I had not killed him, he would certainly have killed me.'[1] He went on to explain that after writing twenty-six Holmes stories, dreaming up new plots and chains of inductive reasoning had become a 'trying occupation'.

'Poor Holmes is dead and damned' he wrote to a friend. 'I couldn't revive him if I would (at least not for years), for I have had such an overdose of him that I feel towards him as I do toward *pate de foie gras*, of which I once ate too much, so the name of it gives me a sickly feeling to this day.'

Conan Doyle himself missed much of the furore surrounding Holmes's death. After closing down the house in South Norwood, he joined his wife and sister-in-law in Davos in time for Christmas. He brought Lottie, who was very close to Touie, with him, but decided that the children should remain in England. Touie, who feared she might never see them again, was greatly distressed: she too had few illusions about her prognosis.

Davos had been transformed in the mid-eighteenth century from a remote farming community into a thriving health spa, particularly popular with well-to-do English families, who made up almost half the population and had their own newspaper and church. Set 5,000 feet above sea level, in a spectacular valley between the snow-capped peaks of two mountain ranges, it had recently been connected to the rest of Switzerland by a steam railway, but sleighs, toboggans and carriages predominated on the streets, their bells mingling with those from churches and chapels, from goats, cows and sheep. Facilities for the ever increasing numbers of tuberculosis patients arriving to 'take the air' included shops, spas, restaurants, sports facilities, even a concert plaza and theatre.

While Touie spent her days in a wicker bath chair on the hotel balcony, wrapped in rugs and furs and enjoying the winter sunshine, her husband buried himself in his work, not just as a form of therapy (Holmes to Watson: 'Work is the best antidote to sorrow'), but because he needed money to pay for Touie's treatment and the considerable expenses of their stay in Switzerland. Liberated at last from the burden of devising more puzzles for Holmes to solve, he had begun work on a semi-autobiographical novel. On 23 January 1894 he wrote to his mother: 'I am nearing the end of my book – could end it this week easily. I cannot imagine what its value is. It will make a religious sensation if not a literary – possibly both. I really don't think a young man's life has been gone into so deeply in English literature before. Willie [Hornung] will read it before it reaches Jerome [K. Jerome]. I shall be most interested to know what he thinks. I am going to lead the life of a savage when it is finished – out of doors on snow shoes all day. We think "The Stark-Munro Letters" is the best title . . .'

The Stark Munro Letters, Being a Series of Twelve Letters Written by J. Stark Munro, M.B. to His Friend and Former Fellow-Student, Herbert Swanborough, of Lowell, Massachusetts, During the Years 1881–1884, Edited and Arranged by A. Conan Doyle tells the story of a recently graduated doctor whose father, a country doctor 'with a touch of gout', is suffering a terminal illness. The old man instructs his son to find employment as soon as possible in order to support the family. 'Of course I could only answer that I was willing to turn my hand to anything. But that interview has left a mark upon me – a heavy, ever-present gloom away at the back of my soul, which I am conscious of even when the cause for it has for a moment gone out of my thoughts.' With the 'heavy, ever-present gloom at the back of my soul,' Conan Doyle probably never got closer to admitting guilt about his father's incarceration in a lunatic asylum.

Disguised as James Cullingworth, his former friend George Budd figures prominently. Maddening, mercurial, cunning, ferocious, ingenious and charming, his antics provided the opportunity for Conan Doyle to deliver a tour de force of comic writing, somewhat uncomfortably interspersed with long theological and philosophical musings, variously indicating the author's disaffection with the dogma and hypocrisy of the Roman Catholic church, the futility of organised religion and his emerging belief in spiritualism. 'Whatever theory of belief we may hold about the soul, there can, I suppose, be no doubt that the body is immortal. Matter may be transformed . . . but it can never be destroyed.' Catholic theology, on the other hand, is castigated as being so backward as to be 'somewhere about the Early Pliocene'.

By then it was widely known that Conan Doyle had become interested in the burgeoning spiritualist movement, which had been founded in the United States some forty years earlier and claimed spirits of the dead could communicate with the living. That the creator of Holmes, the cool, calculating master logician could align himself with dubious spirits from a world beyond the grave seemed distinctly curious to many people. It was not a conundrum that Conan Doyle could appreciate however – he never saw any contradiction between his literary career and his beliefs, or thought it in the least odd that he should espouse a cause many people considered to be risible, if not downright fraudulent.

Almost everything in *The Stark Munro Letters* was true to Conan Doyle's life: Cullingworth secretly reading his mother's letters; the street brawl the night he arrives in Birchespool (Southsea); setting up a practice in 1 Oakley Villas (1 Bush Villas), having his young brother Paul (Innes) come to stay; the accident outside his front door; the epileptic grocer who kept him in food; the gypsy with the sick baby; the man who developed cancer of the cheek from smoking a short-stemmed pipe; his great regard for America and Americans. He described tetchy quarrels with his father over the subject of religion: 'You know how I admire him, and yet I fear there is little intellectual sympathy between us. He appears to think that those opinions of mine upon religion and politics which came from my inmost soul have been assumed either out of indifference or bravado. So I ceased to talk on vital subjects with him, and, though we affect to ignore it, we both know that there is a barrier there.'

Stark Munro's mother, conversely, is depicted as a saintly figure: 'You must remember her sweet face, her sensitive mouth, her peering, short-sighted eyes, the general suggestion of a plump little hen, who is still on the alert about her chickens. Ever since I can remember her she has been the quaintest mixture of the housewife and the woman of letters, with the high-bred spirited lady as the basis for either character.' Like Mary Doyle, she also possesses an unbending will and great strength of character: 'I have often heard her say (and I am quite convinced that she meant it) that she would far rather see any one of us in our graves than know we had committed a dishonourable action. Yes, for all her softness and femininity, she could freeze iron hard at the suspicion of baseness; and I have seen the blood flush from her white cap to her lace collar when she has heard of an act of meanness.'

The Stark Munro Letters was published in 1895 to mixed reviews. 'The vehicle of fiction,' the *Spectator* sniffed, 'does not readily lend itself to the precision of thought and language which is essential to useful discussion of these great themes.' G. W. Smalley, in the *New York Herald*, agreed: 'It is his creator's fortune to be himself a medical man, and his misfortune to have views upon religion and upon various social problems. The book is full of the slang of surgery, enlivened by interpolated disquisitions on subjects which are beyond the writer's reach.' The *Speaker* was kinder: 'Allowing for altered days and changes in style, *The Stark Munro Letters* remind us not a little of Defoe and of Defoe at his best.'

When Conan Doyle finished *The Stark Munro Letters*, he put work aside, and, as he had told his mother, spent time enjoying the sporting facilities on offer in Davos. He went tobogganing, skating on the large Davos ice rink, took sleigh rides to St Moritz and hiked mountain trails, all without complaint from Touie, who assured him she was happy resting at the hotel. They moved hotels twice, first to the Grand and then to the Belvedere, where Robert Louis Stevenson had stayed ten years earlier to seek a cure for his consumption and Thomas Mann would follow many years later.

Writing to a friend from his Southsea days he reported that Touie was improving, 'but it will take *at least* two more winters to set her right. What an infernal microbe it is! Surely science will find some way of destroying it. How absurd that we who can kill the tiger should be defied by this venomous little atom . . . They gnaw at you as cheese-mites do into cheese . . . Could we not impregnate every tissue of the body so that they could not live? One can keep parasites out of wood and out of cloth.'[2]

Nevertheless, Touie remained resolutely cheerful and seemed to rally in the crisp Alpine air, so much so that Conan Doyle felt no guilt about learning an exotic and unusual new sport: skiing, or ski-running as it was then known. Winter sports like tobogganing, skating, curling, ice hockey and sledding were already popular in Switzerland, but downhill skiing was virtually unknown, although Tobias Branger, a local saddle maker, and his brother Johannes, a mountain guide, had been experimenting with skis brought from Norway for some time. Initially they had no idea how to use them and their first attempts on the slopes on the unwieldy eight-foot long planks of wood attracted so much ridicule that they practiced under the cover of darkness. By the time Conan Doyle arrived in Davos they had more or less mastered the technique and were willing to teach him.

Like the millions who would follow him, Conan Doyle discovered that learning to ski was a frustrating experience. 'There is nothing peculiarly malignant in the appearance of a pair of skis . . .' he wrote in the *Strand* later that year. 'But you put them on, and you turn with a smile to see whether your friends are looking at you, and then the next moment you are boring your head madly into a snow-bank, and kicking frantically with both feet, and half rising only to butt viciously into that snow-bank again, and your friends are getting more entertainment than they had ever thought you capable of giving.'[3]

It was not in his nature to be defeated by any sport and he persevered. By 23 March 1894 he had become sufficiently proficient to accompany the Branger brothers on a crossing from Davos to the town of Arosa, in a parallel valley, via the 9,000 feet Mayerfelder-Furka Pass, a perilous 12-mile trek which the Brangers had proved was possible in winter only a year earlier. They left before dawn carrying their skis on their shoulders under 'a great pale moon in a violet sky', trekking for two hours through virgin snow sometimes knee-deep. As the sun rose, they strapped on the makeshift leather bindings of their skis, which had been fitted with rudimentary nets to stop them sliding backwards. At one point they traversed a 50 or 60 degree slope which ended in a sheer precipice. 'A slip might have been serious,' Conan Doyle noted with masterly understatement. The Branger brothers cautiously skied some way below him, ready to break his fall.

When the slopes were more favourable, he found descending on skis through deep powder was a joy. 'The real sport of snow-shoeing,' he reported, 'provided a pleasure which boots can never give. For a third of a mile we shot along over gently dipping curves, skimming down into the valley without a motion of our feet. In that great untrodden waste, with snow-fields bounding our vision on every side and no marks of life save the tracks of chamois and of foxes, it was glorious to whiz along in this easy fashion. A short zig-zag at the bottom of the slope brought us, at half past nine, into the mouth of the pass, and we could see the little toy hotels of Arosa away down among the fir woods, thousands of feet beneath us.'

But they still had to negotiate a slope too steep for skis. The Brangers lashed their skis together to form crude toboggans and headed off. When Conan Doyle attempted to follow suit, his skis promptly 'flew away like an arrow from a bow', leaving him stuck on the side of the mountain with only one way to join the Brangers hundreds of feet below – on his backside. He lowered himself over a ledge and slithered down with arms and legs extended to check his momentum, ending up in a flurry of snow at the Brangers' feet. The incident, he noted, thoroughly disproved his tailor's theory that 'Harris tweed cannot wear out', and in Arosa in his tweed knickerbockers with a threadbare seat he was 'happiest when nearest the wall'. Arriving at the Hotel Seefeld in time for lunch, Conan Doyle was tremendously proud when Tobias Branger added the word 'Sportesmann' after his (Conan Doyle's) entry in the hotel register.

The following day he wrote to his mother: 'My dearest Mam. Yesterday I performed a small feat by crossing a chain of mountains on snowshoes (Norwegian Ski) and coming down to Arosa. Two Swizz accompanied me. I am the first Englishman who has ever crossed an Alpine pass in winter on snowshoes – at least I think so. We left at four in the morning and were in Arosa at 11.30. It created quite a little excitement . . .'

Conan Doyle was very upbeat about the possibilities offered by this new sport. 'I am convinced,' he predicted in the *Strand*, absolutely correctly, 'that the time will come when hundreds of Englishmen will come to Switzerland for the "ski"-ing season. I believe I may claim to be the first, save only two Switzers, to do any mountain work . . . but I am certain I will not, by many thousands, be the last.'[4] In the same article he also claimed that he was responsible for getting the Branger brothers interested in skiing after reading an account of Fridtjof

Nansen's epic crossing of Greenland in 1888. He must have known it was not true; it was a rare occasion when his instinct for fiction overcame his talent as a reporter and as a result it has been widely and incorrectly reported that Conan Doyle 'introduced' the sport of downhill skiing to Switzerland. According to Sir Arnold Lunn's authoritative *History of Skiing* that distinction belongs to a Norwegian, O. Kjelsburg in 1889. But there is no doubt that Conan Doyle's article in the *Strand*, accompanied by eight photographs and reprinted many times, made a major contribution to popularising the sport. Indeed, within ten years the Davos English Ski Club had been formed, marking its birth as an international ski resort. The residents of Davos would later show their gratitude by erecting a commemorative plaque next to their sports arena, thanking Conan Doyle for 'bringing this new sport and the attraction of the Swiss Alps in winter to the attention of the world'.

In April Touie, who was feeling considerably stronger, begged to be allowed home to see the children. Her doctors and her husband agreed. She stayed with her mother while Conan Doyle lodged at the Reform Club in London, where, characteristically, he buckled down to work. Under the title *Round The Red Lamp: Being Facts and Fancies of Medical Life*, he assembled a ground-breaking collection of mainly medical stories, warning readers in a preface that some of the stories dealt with the 'darker side' of medical life. 'It is the province of fiction,' he explained, 'to treat painful things as well as cheerful ones. The story which whiles away a weary hour fulfils an obviously good purpose, but not more so, I hold, than that which helps to emphasise the graver side of life.' It was too much for the critics. 'Ought the tragic realities and the painful common-places of the sick-room and death-bed be made the theme of fiction?' the *Spectator* demanded. The *Nation* deemed the stories 'disgusting', and the *Catholic World* pointed out that only those 'not easily nauseated' would be able to 'wade through professional horrors so ghastly in their way as anything that the feverish imagination of Edgar Allan Poe conjured up in a less sickening school'.

Conan Doyle's growing fascination with the paranormal was evident in several of the stories. 'Lot No. 249', described a 'reptilian' student of arcane law who buys a mummy at an auction and brings it to life to carry out his evil desires, while 'The Parasite' was a macabre tale of a doctor who falls under the spell of a female mesmerist: 'She can project herself into my body and take command of it. She has a parasite soul; yes, she is a parasite, a monstrous parasite. She creeps into my frame as the hermit crab does into the whelk's shell. I am powerless. What can I do? I am dealing with forces of which I know nothing.'

One of the less graphic contributions, 'The Doctors of Hoyland', shed an interesting light on Conan Doyle's attitude towards women. A doctor in a small Hampshire village is concerned to discover that a new and highly qualified rival has put up his plate in the same village. He pays a courtesy call and is greeted by 'a little woman, whose plain, palish face was remarkable only for a pair of shrewd, humorous eyes'. Assuming she is the doctor's wife he is astonished when she explains that she is unmarried and that *she* is the doctor. 'He had never seen a woman doctor before, and his whole conservative soul rose up in revolt at the idea. He could not recall any biblical injunction that man should remain ever the doctor and the woman the nurse, and yet he felt as if a blasphemy had been committed.' At first deeply aggrieved, he finds himself falling in love and eventually proposes marriage, but she proves her feminist credentials by putting her career first and her superior talents as a doctor by moving to Paris to undertake medical research.

Conan Doyle was soon drafting ideas for another historical series, set in the Napoleonic era and featuring the dashing Brigadier Etienne Gerard of the Hussars of Conflans: 'gay-riding, plume-tossing, debonair, the darling of the ladies and of the six brigades of light cavalry'. Gerard was inspired by *The Memoirs of Baron de Marbot*, originally published in Paris in 1844, which Conan Doyle regarded as 'the first of all soldier books in the world', while admitting at the same time that a certain 'robust faith' was required to believe it all. The vain and pompous baron had served under Napoleon, and his innumerable, if unlikely, 'hairbreadth escapes and dare-devil exploits' fired Conan Doyle's imagination, satisfied his craving to write historical fiction and provided him with a new hero more fun than Holmes who could romp through a series of adventures, first for magazine publication and then collected in a book.

Gerard made his debut in the December 1894 issue of the *Strand* and would prove to be one of the funniest, most endearing and popular characters Conan Doyle ever created. Both likeable and ludicrous, a buffoon and a braggart never reluctant to sing his own praises, he was described by his commanding officer as 'all spurs and moustaches, with never a thought beyond women and horses'. There were elements of Budd about the Brigadier in his mad courage, his vainglorious verve, his frequent humiliations and his unerring ability to recover from potentially disastrous misjudgements. Sent on impossible missions, he invariably managed, by a combination of braggadocio, sheer stupidity and good fortune, to extricate himself from perilous battlefield situations. Richly comic and ranging from satire to burlesque, the sixteen short stories rattled along at a furious pace, were packed with action and unburdened by the mass of technical detail that had clogged Conan Doyle's historical novels, demonstrating again that he was far more accomplished and comfortable as a short-story writer than he was as a novelist. Although Conan Doyle tended to dismiss them as a 'little book of soldier stories', he admitted to a fondness for Gerard and could often be persuaded to read aloud from them. The biographer Frederick Whyte recalled Conan Doyle reading to a 'rather listless' audience at the Hampstead Conservatoire without much reaction until he started on 'How the Brigadier Slew the Fox', which 'ended with the entire room in convulsions and Conan Doyle himself laughing so much he could scarcely continue'.[5]

On 21 September 1894 *A Story of Waterloo*, the play he had sold to Henry Irving, opened at the Prince's Theatre in Bristol, with Irving in the lead role as Corporal Brewster, reminiscing about his experiences in battle. Such was the interest that a special train was arranged to transport the London critics to Bristol. Most were impressed, with the exception of a venomous George Bernard Shaw, who noted that Irving only managed to depict 'with convincing art the state of an old man's joints'.

After the opening night Bram Stoker wrote in his diary: 'New play enormous success. H.I. fine and great. All laughed and wept.

Marvellous study of senility. Eight calls at end.'[6] Ellen Terry wrote to Conan Doyle the following day: 'A thousand congratulations upon the success of your *perfect* little play . . . it moved me strangely.'

Conan Doyle, however, was faintly aggrieved that many reviewers heaped praise on Irving's performance at the expense of his contribution: 'Several critics went out of their way to explain that the merit lay entirely with the great actor and had nothing to do with the indifferent play.' The role of Corporal Brewster became a favourite with Irving. He performed the play 343 times during the next decade and sent a guinea to Conan Doyle after each performance, having initially acquired the rights for only £100. 'It was a good bargain for him,' Conan Doyle noted, 'for it is not too much to say that Corporal Gregory Brewster became one of his stock parts and it had the enormous advantage that the older he got the more naturally he played it.'

With Touie still 'holding her own', Conan Doyle had agreed to undertake a lecture tour in the United States and Canada that autumn. He justified his absence by claiming that Lottie's nursing skills and the steady improvement in Touie's condition gave him 'renewed liberty of action'. In reality, he probably relished the prospect of a respite from the sickroom and visiting America had been a cherished ambition ever since he was a boy, when he was captivated by the frontier yarns of James Fenimore Cooper and Mayne Reid. He had often written, in letters to newspapers, of his dream that the 'English-speaking races' would one day be united in an empire made up of Great Britain and the United States.

Before his departure, he expanded on his views in an interview with the *Cincinnati Commercial Gazette* in which he claimed, perhaps stretching the truth a little, that there was no subject on which he took a keener interest than creating closer ties between Britain and the United States: 'I believe the English-speaking races must either coalesce, in which case the future of the world is theirs, or else they will eternally neutralize each other and be overshadowed by some more compact people, as the Russians or the Chinese. They should pool their fleets and their interests. What a lot of minor questions would be settled instantly, by their doing so! It would be the first great step towards the abolition of war and the federation of mankind.'[7] It was a theme to which he would frequently return.

Conan Doyle invited Innes, who had recently finished his military training with the Royal Artillery in Woolwich, to accompany him on the trip. Innes was delighted and had no trouble getting leave of absence. The brothers arrived in New York on 2 October, on board the German 'express steamer', the *Elbe*. (Five months later it would sink, with the loss of 332 lives, after a collision with a British ship in the North Sea.) On the crossing both men were aware of a certain hostility towards them from the German passengers and crew. One night at dinner at the captain's table, which was bedecked by German and American flags, they drew a Union flag on a piece of paper and ostentatiously hung it above the others.

The promoter of the tour was Major James Pond, a Civil War veteran with a goatee beard who had made his name promulgating the 'improving talk' as a form of entertainment and who numbered Mark Twain among his clients. The Major had advertised the visit of the celebrated creator of Sherlock Holmes as 'The Latest Platform Attraction for the Season of 1894–5'[8], so it was that a posse of reporters was waiting on the dockside to greet them. To judge by an effusive report in the *New York Times,* Conan Doyle made an exceptionally favourable impression: 'He is tall, straight, athletic and his head that his blue eyes make radiant with affability must have been modeled by Energy herself, so profoundly impressed is it with her mark. His forehead is not colossal, yet it is as if it were built of the same marble as the Titans. His look is merry, quick, curious, inventive, and resolutely fixed on the things that happen, and not on an invisible star.'[9]

Conan Doyle had originally planned three lectures: English fiction, the novels of George Meredith and a third on his own work, titled 'Readings and Reminiscences'. In the end he abandoned the first two and concentrated, if a little reluctantly, on his reminiscences. 'It is naturally repugnant for a man to stand up on a public platform and talk about himself and his own work,' he told his audiences, '. . . before I came to this country, however, it was pointed out to me that if anybody should come to hear me lecture, it would not be because they want my criticism on this or that, but because something I have written has come in their way and they want to make a bond of sympathy between us.'

That bond was forged at his first engagement, at the 1,500-seat

Calvary Baptist Church in New York, on 11 October. 'His lecture was interesting, exceedingly so,' the *New York Recorder* reported, 'for while it lasted his audience listened intently to every word, followed care- fully his explanations and digressions, and enjoyed not only the subject of his discourse but also the very sound of his voice. There are few physical gifts that are so delightful as a hearty, cheery, sympathetic voice, and such a voice is one of Dr Doyle's most charming powers.'

Apart from his deep bass voice and his Scots accent, it was his natural British reserve, personal warmth and enthusiasm for everything American that won him much support. 'Few foreign writers who have visited this country have made more friends than A. Conan Doyle,' Hamilton W. Mabie gushed in the *Ladies' Home Journal.* 'His personality is a peculiarly attractive one to Americans because it is so thoroughly wholesome . . . Simple, sincere, unaffected and honest, Dr Doyle has that background of old English qualities which united with great kindliness of spirit and courtesy of manner, makes friends and holds them.' [10] Innes, too, greatly enjoyed himself, particularly when he was described in one newspaper as a 'handsome young fellow' who could easily be mistaken for the author.

In truth, many attended Conan Doyle's lectures just to get a look at him. It was always a surprise: since he was associated so closely with Sherlock Holmes, there was a curious expectation that he would resemble his creation, whereas he strode onto the stage in his untidy tweeds as if he had just arrived from a long walk in the country. He loved to quote one newspaper which spoke of a 'thrill of disap- pointment' running through the audience as he emerged to deliver his lecture. 'I learned afterwards that they expected to see in me a cadaverous-looking person with marks of cocaine injections all over him.' But neither did he look like a writer. Anthony Hope, then working on his classic *Prisoner of Zenda,* said that Conan Doyle wrote good books, 'yet looked as if he had never heard of such a thing in his life'. Frederic Whyte memorably described him as 'looking like two policemen rolled into one'.

Women in the audience were further disappointed when he absolutely refused to socialise after the event: as soon as he had finished his lecture he would make a beeline for the stage door. 'I remember that I made a promise to a group of very prominent New

York ladies,' Major Pond recalled, 'who had made a special request to meet the Doctor after his reading, that they could have the privilege of being introduced to him. While in the wings as he was stepping onto the stage I told the Doctor what I had done and asked him to please wait and meet them. He replied "Oh Major, I cannot, I cannot. What do they want of me? I haven't the courage to look anybody in the face".' ¹¹

Inevitably, Conan Doyle was questioned about Sherlock Holmes, and he did his best to conceal both his disaffection with the character and his paradoxical lack of regard for the stories. At one press conference he was asked if he had been influenced by Poe when he set out to create Sherlock Holmes. A nervous hush fell as many of the reporters present thought he might take offence, 'Oh, immensely!' he replied cheerfully, 'his detective is the best in fiction.' ¹² Interviewed by a reporter from the *Union and Advertiser* in Rochester, New York, he adamantly denied he was going to resuscitate Holmes: 'I have been reported as saying in nearly every city I have visited that I would write more Sherlock Holmes' stories. This statement I wish to absolutely deny. I had to kill the omnipresent Sherlock in sheer self defense. The strain was something I could not endure any longer. Of course, had I continued I could have coined money, for the stories were the most remunerative I have written, but as regards literature they would have been mere trash.' ¹³

This notwithstanding, Conan Doyle had the good sense to realise that he should introduce Holmes to his audiences like a close friend: 'At this period [recalling his early years in Southsea], a gentleman appeared in my life who certainly has been a very good friend to me, and to whom I think I afterward behaved in a very ungrateful manner – I mean the late Sherlock Holmes of Baker Street.' He continued with readings from a number of the stories, thus ensuring that audiences felt they had received good value.

Major Pond was a hard taskmaster and had booked Conan Doyle to give talks and readings in thirty cities, some of them on more than one occasion. In one hectic 24-hour period Conan Doyle found himself lecturing in New York, Princeton and Philadelphia. He was frequently forced to sleep on trains to maintain the exhausting schedule and in addition he was obliged to pay his own travelling expenses.

Conan Doyle had one favourite tongue-in-cheek story about his trip to America which he would tell friends for the rest of his life. He claimed that a cab driver who had dropped him at a lecture venue requested a ticket for the event instead of a fare. Conan Doyle, surprised, asked how the driver had recognised him. This was the alleged reply:

> If you will excuse me, your coat lapels are badly twisted downward, where they have been grasped by the pertinacious New York reporters. Your hair has the Quakerish cut of a Philadelphia barber, and your hat, battered at the brim in front, shows where you have tightly grasped it, in the struggle to stand your ground at a Chicago literary luncheon. Your right shoe had a large block of Buffalo mud just under the instep; the odour of a Utica cigar hangs about your clothing and the overcoat itself shows the slovenly brushing of the porters on the through sleepers from Albany. The crumbs of the doughnut on the top of your waistcoat could only have come there in Springfield. And, of course, the labels on your case give a full account of your recent travels – just below the brass plaque reading 'Conan Doyle'.[14]

On 11 November, in the middle of the punishing tour, Rudyard Kipling wrote to Conan Doyle from Naulakha, his home in Brattleboro, Vermont, with an invitation to visit over Thanksgiving:

> Dear Doyle,
>   I've been reading 'The Red Lamp' at one fascinated sitting . . . The Mummy tale gave me a bad dream for all I had read it before in the magazines . . .
>   Don't shorten your programme, which I know is likely to be full, but if you can head this way with your brother let us know before you come . . .
>   Ever yours, Rudyard Kipling.[15]

Conan Doyle rated Kipling as 'England's best novelist since Dickens' – *The Jungle Book* had been published that year – but was discomforted by Kipling's vocal criticism of the United States expansionism and antipathy towards the concept of democracy. Nevertheless he welcomed the invitation if only as respite from his schedule. Once they were able to shift the conversation away from the merits or otherwise of America, they discovered many shared interests, including photography, medicine and the paranormal. Conan Doyle had brought his golf clubs and attempted to teach Kipling the game in a nearby field, watched from afar by 'New England rustics . . . wondering what on earth we were at, for golf was unknown in America at the time'. By the end of the visit they were firm friends; and afterwards Conan Doyle sent Kipling a pair of skis as a gift, with the suggestion that he sample another form of exercise other than golf. He wrote an enthusiastic account of the visit to his mother: 'I have been staying two days with Kipling and we had a great time and golf and much high converse. He is a wonderful chap.'

Back in New York, staying at the Aldine Club on Fifth Avenue, Conan Doyle was visited by Samuel S. McClure, the owner and editor of *McClure's Magazine*, which had published a number of his stories. McClure apologised for not making contact sooner, but explained that his magazine, founded the previous year, was in deep financial trouble. He was losing $1,000 a month and owed British contributors, among them Conan Doyle, around $5,000. Only that morning as he left his home on Long Island he had asked his wife to pray for some kind of salvation. She said he should pray too, but he had replied that she was better at it.

In his autobiography, McClure said that Conan Doyle immediately offered to put some money into the magazine, saying he believed both in McClure and his magazine. They lunched at the club, then walked across to the magazine's offices where Conan Doyle wrote out a cheque for $8,500.[16] (About £1,700 at that time.) Conan Doyle's version was that he stumbled into McClure's office and found him down on his knees in prayer, having been reduced to 'his last farthing', and when he heard of the publisher's desperate financial plight he offered to invest £1,000 – the total profit from his tour. Whatever the amount, Conan Doyle claimed he made a tidy profit when he sold his stake in *McClure's* twenty years later.

The brothers left New York on 8 December, on the Cunard Line's *Etruria*. Major Pond had tried to persuade Conan Doyle to stay longer, but he had refused, explaining that he had an invalid wife with whom he had promised to spend Christmas. It had been agreed that Touie would return to Davos for the winter, and that this time she would take the children with her, along with their French nurse and Lottie. Mary was then five years old and Kingsley would celebrate his second birthday in Davos. The *Etruria* docked at Liverpool on 15 December: Conan Doyle and Innes immediately caught a train for London, where, driving down the Strand in a hansom cab, they learned from a news-paper billboard that Robert Louis Stevenson was dead, having succumbed to a stroke at his home in Samoa, aged 44 and at the height of his creative powers. His novella *The Strange Case of Dr Jekyll and Mr Hyde*, with its vivid interplay of good and evil, had stunned Victorian London when it was published in 1886 and become an instant best-seller. Conan Doyle, who had been corresponding with Stevenson for some time, was distressed by the news: 'Something seemed to pass out of my world,' he noted.

Conan Doyle hurried on to the Grand Hotel Belvedere in Davos. The weather was appalling, not at all conducive to Touie's well-being, and he resolved to find somewhere warmer for the next winter. While continuing work on the remaining Gerard stories, he threw himself into social and sporting activities, gave talks to the Davos and English Literary Society, participated in a billiards tournament, entered a tobogganing contest, played goalkeeper in an ice hockey match between Davos and St Moritz, and even, in the spring, laid out a simple golf course, despite 'the curious trick the cows had of chewing up the red flags'.

The family would stay in Switzerland for most of 1895, though Conan Doyle made several trips home. During one he met the Cana-dian writer, Grant Allen, who also suffered from consumption. They became good friends: both were independent thinkers unafraid of controversy. The year they met, Allen had outraged male Victorian society with his sexually explicit book *The Woman Who Did*, a story about an early feminist who flatly refused to marry her lover because she believed the marriage laws were unfair to women. Allen had built a house at Hindhead, a village in Surrey, where he swore the air was particularly beneficial, so much so that the area was becoming known as the 'Little Switzerland' of Surrey. Conan Doyle was so convinced that before returning to Switzerland, he acquired a four-acre site in Hindhead for £1,000 and engaged Joseph Henry Ball, an architect friend from Portsmouth, to design a large house. Touie was delighted when Conan Doyle gave her the news. The thought of returning to England, he wrote, 'brought renewed hope to the sufferer'.

Touie and the children had a peripatetic existence that year, travelling, immersing themselves in the art, architecture and history of Europe, sometimes with Conan Doyle, sometimes without. From Davos they moved to Maloja, a resort in the beautiful Engadine valley, and then to Caux, a village high above Montreux overlooking Lake Geneva. At Caux, Conan Doyle started work on *Rodney Stone*, a novel set in the Regency times of Beau Brummell which focused on the brutal sport of bare-knuckle boxing. Conan Doyle loved boxing, although by the time he took it up at school the Marquis of Queensberry had long imposed rules that required fighters to wear gloves. But he could see nothing wrong with the old days and was stirred by the idea of a bare-knuckle bout as a gladiatorial contest. 'Better,' he noted, 'that our sports should be a little rough than that we should run the risk of effeminacy.' He once confessed to a friend that he would much rather have earned a living as a sportsman than a writer.

On 7 September 1895, he wrote to his mother from the Maloja Hotel: 'You will be glad to hear that I have finished my book. I am going over it again but in a week or so I hope to have it in its final form. I think of calling it "Rodney Stone. A Reminiscence of the Ring." On the whole, I am satisfied with it. It contains some scenes which are as good as I have ever done, and although I don't think it has the "go" of "The White Company" or the thought of "The Stark Munro Letters" it at least strikes a healthy manly patriotic note and deals with matter which is, I think, new to British Fiction. It might make a big hit and it will certainly do me no harm . . .'

It was a correct assessment. Conan Doyle's position as an author was assured. Although he received not infrequent maulings from the critics, he remained extraordinarily popular with the public. At the *Strand* there had been fears that the circulation would plummet after the death of Holmes, but it actually increased when Brigadier Gerard made his debut. By the mid-1890s the magazine's editors realised that Conan Doyle's name on the cover virtually guaranteed that the issue would sell out. If Conan Doyle was occasionally boastful, particularly to his mother, he had much to boast about: during the last decade of the nineteenth century, he would publish no fewer than eleven novels and five collections of short stories and could lay claim to being one of the most successful – if not respected – writers in literary history.

CHAPTER 10

THE 'HONORARY WAR
CORRESPONDENT'

ITH NO PROSPECT OF the house in Hindhead being ready for some time, Conan Doyle decided to spend the winter of 1895–6 in Egypt, where he hoped the hot, dry climate would suit his wife. The children were sent home to stay with Granny Hawkins, in Reigate. Conan Doyle, Touie and Lottie travelled south through Italy, staying for a few days in Rome before moving on to Brindisi to catch a boat for Cairo, where they checked into the Mena House Hotel, a former royal lodge overlooking the pyramids.

The climate in Egypt certainly helped Touie's condition, and she improved sufficiently to join her husband in enjoying Cairo's exotic social life: parties at the Turf Club, camel races, polo matches at the Gezira ground and picnics under the palm trees. 'Touie seems much better for the change,' he wrote to his mother, 'and we are settling down to our new life very comfortably. It is a charming hotel and the air is splendid. I go for a ride every morning – of all things on this earth the last I should ever have prophesied is that I should ride on the Sahara desert upon an Arab stallion. Yet it is so.'

Riding in the desert was not without its hazards, as he soon discovered. On one occasion his horse – 'a black devil . . . with a varminty head, slab-sided ribs, and restless ears' – threw him and kicked him in the head, leaving him with a permanent and noticeable droop in his right eyelid. He arrived back at the hotel leading his mount, with blood pouring from a wound over his eye. 'A pretty sight I presented as I appeared before the crowded veranda!' he noted in his Egyptian journal. 'Five stitches were needed, but I was thankful, for very easily I might have lost my sight.'

Conan Doyle and Lottie climbed the Great Pyramid at sunset, an experience he vowed not to repeat. While the view from the top was unforgettable – the Nile delta, the distant minarets of Cairo, the scattered villages, the camel trains and the great Saharan sand sea stretching into the distance – every step was the height of a table and both were exhausted by the effort. Unlike most tourists, he was unimpressed by the pyramids, which he considered 'childish'. He played golf on a rudimentary links in front of the hotel where he joked that if you sliced the ball you might easily find it bunkered in some ancient tomb. In one round with Sir Horatio Kitchener, then the 'Sirdar', commander-in-chief, of the Egyptian Army, Conan Doyle observed that as his ball was teed, Kitchener's black caddie pointed two fingers at it and spat. He learned that his ball had been cursed for the remainder of the game and subsequently enjoyed an intimate acquaintance with every hazard on the course, although he admitted that 'I have accomplished that when there was no Central African curse upon me.' [1]

In the New Year the three of them took a Thomas Cook's tour 400 miles up the Nile on a sternwheel paddle steamer, the *Nitocris*, making frequent excursions ashore to explore the relics of Egyptian civilisation. 'There is nothing like this in the world,' Conan Doyle wrote. 'The Roman and British Empires are mushrooms in comparison.' As an aspiring spiritualist, however, he viewed the Egyptian custom of preserving earthly bodies in mummified form as a quaint aberration: 'What a degraded intelligence does it not show! The idea that the body, the old outworn greatcoat which was once wrapped round the soul, should at any cost be preserved is the last word in materialism.'

'Today we have been over the three great temples of Luxor, which are called the ruins of Karnak,' he recorded in his journal on 7 January. 'So vast are they that it would take weeks to gain, and hours to write, anything but the most general impression. I certainly think that the great temple of Karnak must have been the greatest building which has, as far as I know, ever existed upon this earth. The rows of monstrous pillars extending away in vistas, and the huge blocks of stone with which they are crossed look like the work of giants. When they were all painted in the gorgeous colours which still linger in parts the appearance must have been most brilliant and wonderful . . .'

Conan Doyle could also not fail to be impressed by 'the broad café au lait coloured river' as their steamer churned the muddy waters: 'Sunset left a long crimson glow over the Libyan desert. The river ran as smooth as quicksilver, with constant drifts of wild duck passing between ourselves and the crimson sky. On the Arabian side it was blue-black until the edge of the moon shone over low mountains.'

They travelled as far as Wadi Halfa, on the Sudanese border, headquarters of the Anglo-Egyptian force preparing to recapture Sudanese territory taken by the Mahdi after the fall of Khartoum. Mahdi Muhammad Ahmad was the charismatic religious leader of a rebel army which in 1884 had overrun large parts of the Sudan, then occupied by the British and laid siege to Khartoum, where British General Charles Gordon commanded a garrison of 7,000 Egyptian and loyal Sudanese troops. Gordon's plight excited great concern in the British press, but a relief expedition under the command of Sir Garnet Wolseley arrived too late to prevent 50,000 rebels crossing the Nile in January 1885 and capturing the town. The entire garrison was slaughtered. Gordon was said to have been speared to death on the steps of the governor's residence, earning a place in history as a martyr and hero. After the fall of Khartoum the Mahdi ('the guided one') controlled the whole of Sudan and established an Islamic state under strict sharia law, a situation the British government could not tolerate.

'We are now within the area of the Mahdi forces,' Conan Doyle noted in his journal on 13 January, 'and when we saw the Southern sky all slashed with the red streaks . . . it seemed symbolical of that smouldering barbaric force which lies there.' Although they were travelling on a guided tour, Conan Doyle admitted to some concern about the political situation, and was acutely aware that the party would be helpless if attacked by rebel tribesmen. 'If I were a Dervish general,' he wrote on 16 January, 'I would undertake to carry off a Cook's excursion party with the greatest of ease.'

The trip was the inspiration for *The Tragedy of the Korosko*, in which a party of tourists, also travelling under the auspices of a well-known travel agency, falls prey to a gang of desert bandits. Conan Doyle often used fiction to articulate his world view or argue a political, moral, religious or philosophical point. Writing to Greenhough Smith after his return from Egypt with 'a few particulars' about *The Tragedy of the Korosko*, he expressed the hope that it would 'make the man in the bus realise what a Dervish means, as he never did before'.

Conan Doyle was usually ready to dismiss most forms of organised religion after his years at Stonyhurst, but in *The Tragedy of the Korosko* he recognised the power of Islam, writing presciently as the tourists watched their captors pray: 'Who could doubt as he watched their strenuous, heart-whole devotion, that here was a great living power in the world, reactionary but tremendous, countless millions all thinking as one from Cape Juby to the confines of China? Let a common wave pass over them, let a great soldier or organiser arise among them to use the grand material at hand, and who shall say that this may not be the besom with which Providence may sweep the rotten, decadent, impossible, half-hearted south of Europe, as it did a thousand years ago, until it makes room for a sounder stock?'[2]

Back in Cairo, Conan Doyle left Touie and Lottie to relax in the hotel while he went off on a typically energetic jaunt to a famous Coptic monastery in the desert, some fifty miles distant, at the Natron lakes. His companion was Colonel David Lewis, a British officer seconded to the Egyptian Army who was a fitness fanatic and chose, for much of the journey, to run along behind their carriage – an extraordinarily ornate horse-drawn golden coach which had been built for the use of Napoleon III in expectation of his opening the Suez Canal in 1869. (Actually it was opened by his wife, the Empress Eugenie, from the Imperial yacht.) The two adventurers set out brimming with enthusiasm and confidence, but without a guide were soon lost in the featureless sands. Fortunately, as night fell they came across a German surveyor sitting outside his tent drawing by the light of a hurricane lamp. Conan Doyle's lumbering arrival with a gilded coach 'with a full colonel as carriage dog' must have been one of the surveyor's more memorable Egyptian experiences. He gave them detailed directions, whereupon they set off again and an hour or so later thankfully spotted a light they assumed was the monastery – it was the German surveyor. With further directions they finally arrived at their destination.

On returning to Cairo Conan Doyle discovered that war had been declared, and the Anglo-Egyptian Nile Expeditionary Force, assembled under General Horatio Kitchener, was ready to begin operations. 'Egypt had suddenly become the storm centre of the world,' Conan Doyle noted, 'and chance had placed me there at that moment.' The imminent departure of the Expeditionary Force with orders to reconquer Sudan and crush the power of Khalifa Addallah, the Mahdi's successor, electrified Conan Doyle and offered him the chance of realising a long-cherished ambition to become a war correspondent, although he was aware that Touie could not remain very much longer in Egypt before the heat became too great. Sweet-natured and obliging as ever, she assured him that she would be happy to stay until the end of April; Lottie would look after her and the two of them would be fine. While the long separation from her children must have pained her deeply, she had a strong sense of duty and always put her husband's interests first.

Conan Doyle telegraphed the *Westminster Gazette* in London and soon had himself appointed 'honorary war correspondent'. Kitted out with a khaki coat, riding breeches, an Italian revolver with 100 cartridges and a wooden water-bottle, 'which gave a most horrible flavour of turpentine to everything put into it', all purchased in Cairo, Conan Doyle set out for Aswan with Sir Julian Corbett of the *Pall Mall Gazette*, travelling by train and boat. Corbett was a retired lawyer and the author of Elizabethan historical novels on his first – and only – assignment as a foreign correspondent. They found Aswan alive with the 'stir and bustle of warlike preparation' and at the Aswan Hotel joined forces with three more experienced war correspondents: Frank Scudamore of the *Daily News,* E. F. Knight of *The Times* and Arden Beaman of the *Standard*.

In his memoirs Conan Doyle would recall the young officers' stoicism in the intolerable dust and heat of the desert at Aswan. Four of them insisted on remaining at their posts despite high fevers and cheered themselves up with a daily lottery: every morning they would each pitch a coin into a hat – the man with the highest temperature that day won. Conan Doyle recalled only one occasion when there was any excitement. Returning to the hotel, which had been commandeered as a general headquarters, he found a group of officers gathered round a notice board craning their necks to see a telegram. He assumed it was news of impending action. Actually, it was the result of the Oxford and Cambridge University Boat Race. (Oxford won.)

When the Press party was offered the opportunity of accompanying a group of cavalry officers travelling along the banks of the Nile to Wadi Halfa, Corbett and Conan Doyle decided to take their chances with the Fleet Street professionals who, despite the risk of falling into the hands of marauding Dervishes, opted to make the journey independently on camels to avoid the 'insufferable' dust kicked up by a great body of horsemen. Scudamore, who could speak fluent Arabic and Turkish, was designated to purchase the camels, a process of considerable drama with much haggling and arm-waving.

The party – five correspondents, eleven camp followers, ten camels, five horses and a native cook – left Aswan on 2 April, travelling by night. It was an unforgettable journey. 'I am still haunted,' Conan Doyle wrote in 1924, 'by that purple velvet sky, by those enormous and innumerable stars, by the half-moon which moved slowly above us, while our camels with their noiseless tread seemed to bear us without effort through a wonderful dream world.'

His wry observations on the camel were classic Conan Doyle, who could see humour in the most unlikely situations: 'It is the strangest and most deceptive animal in the world. Its appearance is so staid and respectable that you cannot give it credit for the black villainy that lurks within. It approaches you with a mildly interested and superior expression, like a patrician lady in a Sunday school. You feel that a pair of glasses at the end of a fan is the one thing lacking. Then it puts its lips gently forward, with a far-away look in its eyes, and you have just time to say, "The pretty dear is going to kiss me," when two rows of frightful green teeth clash in front of you, and you give such a backward jump as you could never have hoped at your age to accomplish.'

En route they encountered a death adder, a tarantula and a Nubian tribesman in the early dawn. 'A more sinister barbaric figure one could not imagine,' he wrote, 'and he was exactly the type of those Mahdi raiders against whom we had been warned.' This 'barbaric figure'

would eventually feature in a short story called 'The Three Correspondents', although it is possible he may have been no more than a
figment of Conan Doyle's fertile imagination.

After eight days they reached Korosko, then boarded a stern-
wheeler for Wadi Halfa where Major Francis Wingate, the director of
military intelligence, informed them that no civilians would be allowed
to travel further for any purpose. Conan Doyle did, however, meet
Kitchener, and was invited to dinner. Kitchener warned Conan Doyle
that nothing was going to happen for some time; the advance had
stalled and before the war could begin in earnest he needed to reor-
ganise the army and build a railway line from the Red Sea to ensure
that supplies and reinforcements could be brought to the front. Conan
Doyle had little inclination to wait, since he knew time was running
out for Touie. Bitterly disappointed at seeing no action, he returned
to Cairo on a cargo boat, subsisting on a diet of bread and tinned
apricots and reading Rousseau's *Confessions,* which he had somehow
acquired on his journey and did not much enjoy.

Conan Doyle's stint as a war correspondent in Sudan was not
especially productive. Unable to observe any action beyond troop
movements, he was limited to describing Wingate ('the man who knows
more about the true inwardness of the Sudan and its movements than
anyone else alive') and Slatin Pasha (an Austrian adventurer serving
under Kitchener), and enjoying the company of his fellow correspondents. But his 'Letters from Egypt' in the *Westminster Gazette* were
as inconsequential as the campaign at that stage.

Back in Cairo they packed their bags and left almost immediately for
Britain, arriving at the end of April for a happy reunion with Mary
and Kingsley. Since the new house at Hindhead was still not ready,
they rented Greyswood Beeches, in nearby Haslemere, where, to the
delight of the children, there were rabbits and chickens in the garden.
Living together as a family for the first time in many months, Conan
Doyle made an uncharacteristically saccharine list of anecdotes about
his children's behaviour, seemingly for his own amusement, which
provided a rare insight into their family life.

Their play nearly always takes the form of acting – Doctor and patient, church, visiting, etc. Very fond also of dressing up.

When romping with me Tootsie [Mary] called to Boysie [Kingsley], 'Sit on his head. Make yourself quite at home on his head!'

When watching me burying a puppy Tootsie said, 'Daddy, are you planting puppies – wouldn't it be better to put it in a flower pot?'

'Why doesn't that man put his shirt inside his trousers?' asked Boysie after being taken to high church.

Tootsie, to the dancing mistress, 'You should not speak so loud, or some day you may frighten some little girl . . .'

Daddy asked Tootsie what family mushrooms belonged to. Tootsie replied: 'These mushrooms belong to our family.'

Tootsie is to have lime-juice every day that begins with a P, so she has invented a new day called Punday that comes between Saturday and Sunday.

'Why is Daddy so absurdly anxious that we should not be spoiled? I rather like it than otherwise.'

On looking at me before I had shaved Boysie said; 'Where did you get that fur?'

Tootsie asked for the ground-floor of the loaf.

'What is that coffin?' 'That is Mr Jones going to God.' Half an hour afterwards: 'No doubt God is now unpacking Mr Jones.'

'I like to sit on Daddy's head. When you have been working hard and running about all day, it is so nice to have something soft to sit upon.' [3]

Sadly, in later life Mary would recall her father as a distant, unapproachable, somewhat awe-inspiring figure. Her relationship with her mother, whom she described as 'the background of all our happiness', was much closer. She remembered her as a tiny woman with dainty hands and feet and 'shadowy' eyes that seemed to see beyond what she was looking at: 'There was a gentle all-lovingness about her that drew the simple folk, children, and animals to her, as to a magnet. She had the quiet poise that comes rather from the wisdom of the spirit, than from knowledge of the world, and there ran through her a bright ripple of fun, that would glint in her eyes, and hover round the mouth. It was a sense of fun rather than the more sophisticated sense of humour, because Mother never smiled at a joke at anyone else's expense. At such moments a shadow passed over her face, and her silence would rebuke the joker. But she loved the comical aspects of life and the unconscious humour in people and things.' [4]

If Conan Doyle was distant to his children, he was endlessly patient and considerate to his wife. Mary never forgot one occasion when her mother stretched a hand across a page of her father's newly written manuscript, smearing the ink with her cuff. It was, she said, 'the kind of maddening incident that could make some men fly off the handle. But he just smiled at her vexation and set to work, to re-copy the page.' [5]

Towards the end of 1896 *Rodney Stone* was published as a book after serialisation in the *Strand*. It earned its author the then enormous sum of £5,500: £4,000 as an advance from Smith, Elder & Co. for the book rights and £1,500 from the *Strand* for the serialisation. Newnes provided Greenhough Smith with an extraordinary budget to reward contributors; from the mid-1890s onwards, the *Strand* never paid Conan Doyle less than £100 per thousand words. In June 1896 he was able to buy a house in Portsmouth – Southview Lodge, 50 Kent Road – as a rental investment for £1,800. He put £500 down as a deposit and obtained a mortgage of £1,300, which he had repaid in full by 1901.

One critic called *Rodney Stone* 'the best story of the ring ever written', but a precocious 23-year-old Max Beerbohm, later a prominent parodist and caricaturist, begged to differ. Writing in the *Saturday Review* he mercilessly teased the author for being a doctor with gold-rimmed glasses who had carried his 'bedside manner into literature'. The slight plot, he said, bobbed up only at the beginning and end of the book, 'and yet he is quite pleased with himself, this obstinate medico . . . No, no, Doctor Doyle! You're a very good general practitioner, I've no doubt. But you bungled the post-mortem. Operations of this kind require great special knowledge and most delicate handling. Come! Roll down your shirt-sleeves! Put on your coat! It's a pity for your professional reputation that you ever undertook the case. You had far better have stuck to your ordinary practice. Pack up your instruments, my good sir! Jump into your brougham!'[6]

Conan Doyle responded, curtly, in a letter to the magazine, highlighting Beerbohm's 'historical and social errors', and complaining that he had confused Pitt the Younger with his father and that he had disputed certain characteristics of Beau Brummell which could be authenticated by contemporary sketches: 'He may be upon safe ground when he refers to my bedside manner and gold-rimmed glasses, but he is very ignorant of the period about which he writes.'[7] Beerbohm was not to be outdone and refuted Conan Doyle's assertions one by one. It was an exchange thoroughly enjoyed by the literary world and would be resurrected to general glee the following year.

In January 1897 the family moved to Moorlands, a house in Hindhead close to their new home. Construction delays and a problem with a right of way through the property meant the house would not be ready until later in the year, well after the celebrations for Queen Victoria's Diamond Jubilee in June, which marked the longest reign in the history of the British monarchy and had seen the creation of the most powerful empire since Rome. Tens of thousands of people lined the streets of London to watch the Queen's procession to St Paul's Cathedral for a service of thanksgiving. 'No one ever, I believe,' she noted in her diary, 'has met with such an ovation as was given to me . . . The cheering was deafening and every face seemed to be filled with real joy. I was much moved and gratified.' As part of the celebrations a special performance of A Story of Waterloo was staged for colonial troops at the Lyceum Theatre.

Towards the end of 1897 the Conan Doyles were at last able to move into their new home. 'Undershaw' – the name chosen by Conan Doyle was derived from Anglo-Saxon and meant a place under a hanging grove of trees – was a substantial gabled red-brick mansion, which reflected the fame and status of its owner. Adjoining Hindhead House, owned by the philosopher John Tyndall, it was completed at a cost of around £10,000, and was one of the first properties in the area to have its own power plant for electric light.

A winding drive led to the front door, which opened onto a double-height entrance hall dominated by an enormous stained-glass window depicting the family crests of Conan Doyle's ancestors. The house was designed for entertaining, with a large billiards room hung with original Sidney Paget drawings of the Sherlock Holmes stories, a dining room capable of seating thirty, eleven bedrooms and servants' quarters. Touie now had a large domestic staff to manage, including a butler, and her mother, who lived in a nearby cottage, assisted.

All the principal rooms on the ground floor, including Conan Doyle's study, faced south with glorious views across a valley and heathland to the distant Downs. In the wood-panelled drawing room was a piano, a small Broadwood upright, for Touie; sporting trophies, including the bat with which Conan Doyle had scored a century at Lords, and souvenirs from his travels were prominently displayed. There was a lodge, stabling for six horses, a coach house and tennis court in the grounds. Bram Stoker was an early visitor and was complimentary: 'It is so sheltered from cold winds that the architect felt justified in having lots of windows, so that the whole place is full of light. Nevertheless, it is cosy and snug to a remarkable degree and has everywhere that sense of "home" which is so delightful to occupant and stranger alike.'[8]

All this notwithstanding, Conan Doyle confessed to suffering 'bouts of melancholy' around this time. 'I had everything in those few years,' he wrote in his memoir, 'save only the constant illness of my partner. And yet my soul was troubled within me.' Conan Doyle nursed his ailing wife with patience and devotion, sitting by her bedside for long periods, reading her passages from his latest work and chatting about their mutual friends. She enjoyed literary gossip and her husband recounted endless anecdotes about Jerome K. Jerome's struggle to keep his magazine, the *Idler*, afloat and about socialising with other writers. But it was by necessity an incomplete marriage, as medical advice at the time strongly advised against sexual relations with patients suffering from tuberculosis. Conan Doyle accepted that that part of his marriage was at an end. Few of his friends would have rebuked him if he had resorted to prostitutes – a not unusual solution for men in his position – but there is no evidence that he did so.

With Touie defying the medical odds and the family at last settled in their own comfortable home, the Conan Doyles might have expected a period of stability in their lives, but fate was to intervene. Something happened that no one, least of all Conan Doyle, could have anticipated. This Victorian gentleman with a highly developed sense of honour and a deep reverence for propriety would fall hopelessly in love with another woman.

CHAPTER II
CONAN DOYLE IN LOVE

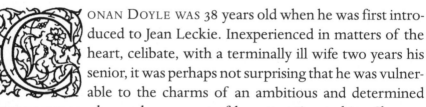ONAN DOYLE WAS 38 years old when he was first intro-
duced to Jean Leckie. Inexperienced in matters of the
heart, celibate, with a terminally ill wife two years his
senior, it was perhaps not surprising that he was vulnerable to the charms of an ambitious and determined
young woman who made no secret of her attraction to him. She was
22, the daughter of wealthy Scottish parents. Strikingly good looking,
with curly dark blonde hair and green eyes, she was widely read and
entertaining company, a trained mezzo-soprano who had only recently
returned from singing lessons in Florence, and an accomplished horse-
woman who rode to hounds.

Precise details of where and when they were introduced are not
recorded. One version is that she was at a party in Southsea in late
1896 attended by Conan Doyle and Innes, and since she and Innes,
who was unmarried, were of similar age she was invited to visit Undershaw and became a family friend. Another is that they met on 15
March 1897, at an unknown location and that Conan Doyle was
instantly smitten, later marking the anniversary every year by
presenting her with a single snowdrop.

Although in his memoirs Conan Doyle was circumspect about the
early stages of his relationship with Jean – 'There are some things
which one feels too intimately to be able to express' – he never denied
he had fallen in love almost from the moment he first laid eyes on her.
At the same time he was a man who lived by a strict moral code, the
very model of a Victorian gentleman, who held chivalry and honour
in high esteem and who regarded the bonds of marriage as inviolable.

He determined to stay faithful to Touie and to shield her from any pain or dishonour. Even when he and Jean had admitted their mutual attraction, he warned her that there could be no question of a divorce.

From his diaries and letters, it is clear Conan Doyle fervently believed that Touie never knew what was going on, but it stretches credulity to think that that he did not betray by some word, gesture or glance, something of his feelings for this young woman, particularly as she was being drawn inexorably into the family's social circle, presumably at his instigation. She was certainly in the family party that attended the Albert Yacht Club Ball at the Portland Hotel in Portsmouth in July 1897. 'Very grand,' Innes noted in his diary, '1,200 people. The Vernon Fords, Miss Driver, Miss Lecky [sic] at our party.' She was also included in the Conan Doyle table at the Goodwood Ball the same month. By the end of 1897, judging by Innes's diary, Leckie was a frequent visitor to Undershaw:

Friday 26 November. Miss Lecky [sic] dined.

Monday 6 December. Walked to Waggoner's Wells in afternoon with Miss Halahan, Miss Leckie and Arthur. Brought them all in to tea.

Wednesday 22. Arthur, Paget, Miss Leckie and Miss Halahan went hunting to Elstead. The ladies dined with us after.[1]

'Paget' was Sidney Paget, the artist who had made a name for himself as the illustrator of the Sherlock Holmes stories in the *Strand*. He was staying at Undershaw to paint Conan Doyle's portrait, a fine study in which the unsmiling subject, seated on an armchair with his legs crossed, a notebook on his lap and a pen in his right hand, stares straight out of the canvas through slightly hooded eyes. With his large waxed moustache and tight double-breasted jacket he looked more like a Victorian banker than a writer, a man who took life seriously – certainly not a man approaching middle age and obsessed by a forbidden love.

Around this time Conan Doyle took up hunting, probably to impress Jean Leckie since he had hitherto exhibited a marked distaste for blood sports. He bought two horses, Brigadier and Korosko, and rode to hounds with the Chiddingfold. He also evinced a renewed interest in music – he had last played in the student band in Feldkirch

– by attempting to learn the banjo, although it was an unlikely instrument on which to accompany a mezzo-soprano. And he risked revealing his ardour to colleagues, writing to Gerald Christy, his English lecture agent, asking him to consider advancing Jean's career: 'That young lady to whom I introduced you has a quite remarkable mezzo-soprano voice and contemplates a professional career.'[2]

In spite of his emotional turmoil, Conan Doyle's output remained as prolific as ever. The main outlet for his work continued to be the *Strand,* which remained as loyal to him as he was to it. When, in 1898, rival publishers attempted to challenge its domination of the sixpenny magazine market by launching threepenny illustrated journals, including *Royal Magazine* and *Harmsworth's Monthly Pictorial,* Conan Doyle wrote to Greenhough Smith: 'I hope your old ship is weathering the storm caused by all these cheap imitations . . . They are always pestering me, but I do not even answer their letters now. My ambition is always to stand by the old craft.'[3]

Conan Doyle's relationship with Greenhough Smith was friendly, but always formal. He usually began his letters 'My dear Smith' and signed himself 'A. C. Doyle'. He rarely encouraged anyone to call him by his first name and would bridle noticeably if anyone was presumptuous enough to address him, uninvited, as 'Arthur'. His reserve was palpable; even the most well-meant slap on the back was unwelcome familiarity. This is not to say that he was unpopular, far from it. Flora Thompson, who would later make her name with the enchanting memoir *Lark Rise to Candleford,* was assistant postmistress in the nearby village of Grayshott where Conan Doyle was a frequent customer: 'Scarcely a day passed without his bursting like a breeze into the post office, almost filling it with his fine presence and the deep tones of his jovial voice. As he went about the village he had a kindly greeting for all, rich and poor, known and unknown alike. He was probably the most popular man in the neighbourhood. Practically everyone had read at least one of his books and many of the local readers fully believed him to be the greatest of living authors.'[4]

He was also well respected as a local sportsman, playing golf and cricket regularly and founding Undershaw Football Club, the first in Hindhead, which played on a field behind the Royal Huts Hotel, opposite his home. Greenhough Smith, on a visit to Undershaw, remembered sitting around the fire on a cold winter evening when a sudden squall drove a hail of rain against the window. As if to prove his credentials as a lover of the outdoors, Conan Doyle immediately suggested a walk. Greenhough Smith thought he was joking and demurred, but his host managed to recruit a younger member of the party, and, equipped with caps and waterproofs, they set out into the night, returning an hour later pink-cheeked and dripping. Having rid himself of his 'dank weeds' Conan Doyle then challenged Greenhough Smith to a game of billiards and wiped him out with a break of 100. 'Truly,' Greenhough Smith observed, 'such versatility has an annoying side to it sometimes.'[5]

Equally versatile professionally, Conan Doyle had not abandoned the notion of being a war correspondent and when, in the autumn of 1898, tension between Britain and France escalated, he contacted a press agency, Central News, offering his services should war be declared. His telegram was acknowledged by the manager on 3 November confirming that in the event of war, 'we shall ask you to go to the Mediterranean to join our dispatch boat'.[6] The cause of the tension was the 'Fashoda Incident' when, during the imperial scramble for Africa, both France and England claimed the strategic town of Fashoda, in the eastern Sudan, France to extend its influence from the Atlantic coast and Britain to further its ambition to dominate Africa from Cairo to the Cape. Both countries began to mobilise their fleets in preparation for war, but in the end, faced with overwhelming military supremacy in the area, France quietly withdrew and there was nothing for Conan Doyle to report, much to his disappointment.

In December 1898 with Touie still in reasonable health – she tired easily, needed to rest every day, but was otherwise up and about – the Conan Doyles hosted a grand fancy-dress ball for 200 family and friends at the Hindhead Beacon Hotel, which went on until 5 a.m. 'Elaborate preparations had been made,' the *Surrey Advertiser* reported, 'to make the ballroom and the ball in keeping with the brilliant costumes worn by all the dancers, and entire success crowned the event.' Conan Doyle went as a Viking, complete with winged helmet and double-bladed axe; Touie was a 'poudre' of the court of Louis XIV. The newspaper reported the names of all the guests and noted their costumes: halfway down the list was Jean Leckie, 'one of the Queen Maries'. Innes noted in his diary: 'Dance a great success. All costumes wonderfully good. Nearly 200 people. Everything right except that the band stole all the cigars.' He mentioned, without comment, that 'Miss Lecky' (he never seemed sure of the spelling) was among the party staying at the hotel.

Conan Doyle's feelings for Jean Leckie were very much in the forefront of his mind when in the New Year he wrote an intriguing letter to Greenhough Smith: 'I have a book on the stocks so queer that there is nothing anywhere like it. I don't want to speak of it or to sell it until it is done for only then can I tell whom it will suit – or if it will suit anyone. It is the most purely natural and spontaneous thing I have ever done. With all kind regards, yours very truly, A. Conan Doyle.'[7]

A Duet with an Occasional Chorus was published in March 1899. Quite different from anything he had previously written, it was a love story about a blissfully happy marriage threatened suddenly by the emergence of a former lover. While not exactly analogous to his own situation, it involved a strikingly similar troika and, in its radical divergence from all his work to date, was surely inspired by his own romantic entanglement. Conan Doyle described the book as a 'domestic study' focused on the 'subtle, indefinable, golden-tinted atmosphere of love'.

The central character, Frank Crosse, meets Maude Selby, who 'had come like an angel of light across the shadowed path of his life' – an apt description, perhaps, of Jean Leckie. But after their marriage he receives a letter from Violet Wright, with whom he had enjoyed a 'premarital experience', threatening to expose him unless he meets her once more in the 'dingy little room' above a restaurant in Covent Garden where they used to make love. Frank agrees, but manages to resist Violet's wiles:

> 'Frankie, you have not kissed me yet.'
>   She turned her smiling face upwards and sideways and for an instant he leaned forward towards it. But he had himself in hand again in a moment. It gave him confidence to find how quickly and completely he could do it. With a laugh, still

holding her two hands, he pushed her back into the chair by the table.

'There's a good girl!' said he. 'Now we'll have some tea . . .'

The picture of Frank heroically resisting temptation accurately reflected Conan Doyle's determination not to succumb to his growing lust for Jean Leckie and his warm portrayal of marriage was almost certainly drawn on his early years married to Touie, before she became sick. 'There are parts of this book also which are personal experiences,' the author admitted in a preface, 'though the greater part is an imaginative attempt to draw average British Life and experience.' Frank, who inherits an artistic and literary bent from his mother, was perhaps how Conan Doyle now saw himself in his unaccustomed role as a ladies' man: 'There was sometimes just a touch of the savage, or at least there were indications of the possibility of a touch of the savage, in Frank Crosse. His intense love of the open air and of physical exertion was a sign of it. He left upon women the impression, not altogether unwelcome, that there were unexplored recesses of his nature to which the most intimate of them had never penetrated . . .'

After his initial uncertainty, Conan Doyle grew very optimistic about the book's prospects and felt it could out-live almost everything he had previously written. He urged the publisher, Grant Richards, to order a first edition of between 12,500 and 15,000 copies. It was a mistake. Many readers were genuinely shocked by *A Duet* because it went beyond the borders of propriety: a woman enticing a former lover to continue their affair after his marriage was a scandalous matter in the late Victorian era. Reviewers were similarly shocked, but shocked that Conan Doyle could produce something so banal, and scorned the work as overly sentimental and naive. 'The result is a book which is certainly quite unworthy of Mr Conan Doyle's reputation,' wrote one, 'and which, indeed, considering the sort of work that he has accustomed his numerous admirers to expect from him, is, we cannot refrain from saying, a rather daring experiment on the docility of his public.'[8] 'It may be vulgar taste,' said Andrew Lang, one of Britain's most influential critics, 'but we decidedly prefer the adventures of Dr Watson with Sherlock Holmes.'[9]

Depressed by the reviews, Conan Doyle was understandably furious when he discovered that several were the work of William Robertson Nicoll, editor of the *Bookman*, who wrote under different pseudonyms for a number of publications. Nicoll had been prominent among the critics who had flayed *Uncle Bernac* as 'thin, quite unexciting, and does not contain a single surprise in word or deed'. His opinion of *A Duet* was even more withering. Writing as 'Paternoster Row' in the *British Weekly*, Nicoll expressed the view that it would have been better if the book had not been published because of the chapter – Violet's attempted seduction of newly married Frank – that 'taught the devil's own lie'. He judged it to be merely 'passable' and 'very stuffed out' and suggested that Conan Doyle should henceforth be considered a 'doubtful author' whose works would need to be carefully scrutinised before being admitted into respectable British households. Then as 'O.O.,' in the 'Literary Lounger' column in the *Sketch*, he was equally caustic, dismissing the two main characters as 'particularly uninteresting young people', claiming it was marred by inanities, crude jokes and 'one chapter neither conceived nor written in good taste'. Conan Doyle, he concluded, had no qualifications for entering into the 'complexities of humanity' and would be well advised to refrain from similar attempts in the future.

Conan Doyle was furious and claimed the practice of 'multiple reviewing' was tantamount to a fraud on the public. In an angry letter to the *Daily Chronicle*, he pointed out that this 'growing scandal' made it appear that his book had received a slew of bad reviews and called for an end to the 'pernicious system' by which 'what to the uninitiated might seem to be a general burst of praise or blame may really, when analysed, prove to be the work of a single individual . . . It becomes year by year a more crying evil. It is not too much to say that the property of authors and of publishers comes in this way to be at the mercy of a very small clique of men.'

Nicoll responded by readily admitting that he wrote in various publications under 'recognisable pseudonyms' but asserted his right to criticise Conan Doyle's latest book as 'unworthy of his genius'. Conan Doyle returned to the fray, suggesting that Nicoll, as an adviser to the publishing house of Hodder & Stoughton, might have a financial interest in the success of its books and favour them in his reviews. 'I have hesitated,' Nicoll replied coldly the following day, 'as to whether Dr Doyle's supplementary letter would be answered more properly in a court of law than a newspaper.' He insisted he received no financial advantage from reviews and recommended to Conan Doyle 'the wise saying' of the theologian and critic Richard Bentley: 'No man was ever written out of reputation but by himself.' A month later, writing as 'Claudius Clear' in the *British Weekly* about the pleasures of reviewing, Nicoll made a snide reference to Conan Doyle's 'excited imagination'.

It was irritating to Conan Doyle that no other writers came forward to support him. 'I wonder if you have followed my expose of Robertson Nicoll?' he asked the novelist Thomas Anstey Guthrie in an undated letter written from Undershaw.

> This nonconformist clergyman, a narrow man with pecuniary interests bound up in a house of publishers, *is* practically British Criticism at present. I have now traced him to 11 different methods of expression. There are not more than 30 or 40 in London, so that by throwing himself into it, he can sway it in any way he likes, and within certain limits holds every man's immediate career in his hands. And yet, in my public exposure of this monstrous thing, I have been left to fight single-handed. What I despise are the 'leaders' of our profession, the men with the money and fame whose selfish dignity is so dear to them that they will not descend to right a wrong. Selfishness and Cowardice are the curses of our profession – so much so that when a man does take up a public cause it seems to be taken for granted that he must have a selfish reason for doing so – an argument which a self-respecting man will not even condescend to deny . . .

It may be his fellow authors mostly agreed with Nicolls's opinion of *A Duet with an Occasional Chorus*, but Conan Doyle doggedly refused to accept the critics' verdict. He fervently wanted to believe that all his 'serious' work was destined for immortality. In letters to his mother he admitted being initially disheartened but he was still convinced this book would endure beyond many of his other works, as it had 'a quality of heart which is rare in English literature'. *A Duet*'s lukewarm reception did not stop him from having a copy specially bound as a gift for Jean Leckie hoping perhaps that she would recognise herself as the ravishing Maude and him as the faithful Frank.

By this time Conan Doyle, who could keep nothing from his mother, had confessed to her that he had fallen in love with Jean Leckie, while emphasising his decision to stand by his ailing wife: 'I have nothing but affection and respect for Touie . . . I have never in my whole married life had one cross word with her, nor will I ever cause her any pain.' The Mam approved, both of his decision and of Jean, indicating her support by presenting Jean with a family heirloom, a bracelet that had once belonged to Conan Doyle's Aunt Annette, and by acting as chaperone on occasions when the couple wanted to spend time together. On 22 May he thanked his mother for her understanding: 'Many thanks for your very sweet letter, dearest. I love to hear your impression of life because I respect your judgement and know your sincerity. It is charming – the way you put it. Well, I am 40 today but my life has grown steadily fuller and happier . . .'

It seems that in June Conan Doyle wrote to Innes, who had been posted to India three months previously, to tell him about Jean and that Innes expressed some concern. Neither letter has been found, but Conan Doyle responded: 'My last letter about my private affairs must have surprised you rather. You need not fear however that any harm will arise from it or that any pain will ever be given to Touie. She is as dear to me as ever, but, as I said, there is a large side of my life which was unoccupied but is no longer so. It will all fit in very well, and nobody be the worse and two of us be very much the better. I shall see to it very carefully that no harm comes to anyone. I say all this lest you, at a distance, might fear that we were drifting towards trouble . . .' He quickly moved on to the safer territory of cricket: 'I am developing into a hitter in my old age. I have been too conscientious always. Last week I made 67 in an hour v East Gloucestershire and 42 in ¾ hour next day v Cheltenham College, so I think my tactics are right . . . My bowling is much improved. On my 40th birthday I took 53 and 10 wickets. How's that? Your loving brother A.'

In referring to 'a large side of my life which was unoccupied but is no longer so', was Conan Doyle trying to tell his brother that his relationship with Jean had been consummated? His original letter might have shed some light on the question, but without it one can only speculate. Conan Doyle himself always insisted he remained faithful to Touie until her death and he was a man with a great regard for moral values and gentlemanly behaviour. Would it have been the act of a gentleman to take another woman to bed while his wife was dying? Certainly not. But then perhaps a gentleman would have resisted falling in love, although in the literary world few eyebrows would have been raised had Conan Doyle decided to conduct a discreet affair – two other acclaimed English men of letters, H. G. Wells and Charles Dickens, were known to have had mistresses and illegitimate children.

Because none of Touie's letters survive – it is possible they were destroyed after Conan Doyle's death because Jean wanted to be seen as the great, unrivalled, love of his life – most biographers have assumed that Conan Doyle's evident fondness for Touie paled in comparison to his passion for Jean, that his first marriage provided no more than amiable companionship while his second was an enduring affair of the heart. If that was the case, perhaps Conan Doyle was simply telling his brother he was in love.

Other members of the family, including Lottie, who had joined Innes in India to keep house for him, were brought in on the secret, as were Jean's parents. The Leckies were probably not too happy, but liked Conan Doyle and accepted the situation. 'Did I tell you,' he wrote to his mother, 'that Mr and Mrs Leckie gave me a beautiful diamond and pearl pin-stud for Xmas? It must have cost 15 guineas at least.' Even Mrs Hawkins, Touie's mother, was made aware and, by her silence, implicitly condoned the relationship. The result of all this manoeuvring was that the Leckies and their charming daughter were added to the roster of the Conan Doyles' friends and all those in the know pretended not to know, including probably Touie, who played the role of gracious hostess at Undershaw, frequently welcoming Jean Leckie to family parties without ever giving a hint of anything untoward.

In the summer of 1899 Sherlock Holmes appeared on the London stage, played by the American actor William Gillette, in an eponymous production promoted as a 'hitherto unpublished episode in the career of the great detective'. In fact it was a compilation of different stories put together by Gillette for dramatic effect. Conan Doyle had initially written the first version of the play in 1897, and sent it to Herbert Beerbohm Tree, actor-manager of Her Majesty's Theatre, half-brother of Max Beerbohm and probably the most famous thespian in England after Henry Irving. Fresh from his triumphant performance as Svengali in *Trilby*, Tree expressed an interest, and visited Undershaw to discuss the project. He declared himself enthusiastic but required major alterations to the script. Conan Doyle by then had begun to have grave reservations about putting Holmes on the stage at all, worrying that it might draw attention to 'my weaker work which has unduly obscured my better'. Faced with a demand for Holmes's part to be completely rewritten, Conan Doyle quietly put the play away, until he heard that Gillette was interested.

William Gillette was both a playwright and an actor and had achieved extraordinary success in the United States starring in his own plays, notably *Held by the Enemy* and *Secret Service*. It was as a writer that he initially approached Conan Doyle, pointing out certain diffi-culties in staging *Sherlock Holmes* and asking for permission to revise the script. This time Conan Doyle agreed, perhaps because he was not being asked to do the rewriting himself. Gillette crafted the play into a conventional melodrama, with a strong romantic interest. When he wrote to Conan Doyle asking if, for the purposes of the play, Sherlock Holmes could marry, Conan Doyle famously replied by telegram: 'You may marry him, murder him, or do anything you like to him.'

In May 1899 Gillette arrived in England to read the script for Conan Doyle and obtain his final approval. The American decided to dress the part, and donned a long grey cape and deerstalker cap for the journey to Hindhead, where he was met by Conan Doyle. There is a story, perhaps apocryphal, that as he stepped off the train he whipped out a magnifying glass, looked Conan Doyle, in his usual tweeds, up and down and remarked: 'Obviously an English author'. Conan Doyle is said to have roared with laughter.

Any anxiety Gillette may have had about tampering with the words was dispelled when, after the reading, Conan Doyle thought for a moment, then nodded and said: 'It's good to see the old chap again.' He did not even cringe when Holmes declared his undying love for the heroine, Miss Alice Faulkner: 'Your powers of observation are somewhat remarkable, Miss Faulkner, and your deduction is quite correct. I suppose, indeed I know, that I love you.'

Sherlock Holmes, a drama in four acts, opened at the Garrick Theater in New York on 6 November, with great success. He would play Holmes for more than 1,300 performances, and as a result he became the physical embodiment of the detective in many people's minds, particularly since the American artist Frederick Dorr Steele drew on a likeness of the actor to illustrate a number of the later stories in *Collier's*. Over the years Gillette and Conan Doyle became good friends and Conan Doyle made no secret of his admiration for the actor. 'My only complaint,' he wrote in a tribute to Gillette's farewell performance, '[is] that you make the poor hero of the anaemic printed page a very limp object as compared with the glamour of your own personality which you infuse into his stage presentment.'

Curiously, *Sherlock Holmes* had a poor reception from the critics when it opened in London at the Lyceum in September 1901. One thought it predictable, another described it as 'crude and commonplace' and a third condemned Gillette's portrayal of Holmes as 'mere burlesque'. The public, however, disagreed. *Sherlock Holmes* played for eight months, including a royal command performance during which the King summoned Gillette to his box in the interval and kept him talking for so long that the start of the second half was delayed. By the time its run ended, four touring companies were taking it around the country. Gillette returned to London in 1905 with 16-year-old Charlie Chaplin in the role of 'Billy', the Baker Street pageboy.

In his memoirs Conan Doyle would describe the latter part of 1899 as being a placid period in his life: 'My wife was holding her own in winter as well as in summer. The two children, Mary and Kingsley, were passing through the various sweet phases of our human development, and brought great happiness into our lives.' In a revealing question-

naire he completed around this time he listed 'unaffectedness' as his
favourite virtue, 'manliness' as his favourite virtue in another man,
'work' as favourite occupation, 'time well filled' as his ideal of happiness, 'men who do their duty' as favourite heroes in real life, and
'affectation and conceit' as his pet aversions. In reality his life was far
from placid. Torn between loyalty and passion, Conan Doyle was
under considerable stress at home. Normally the most equable of
men, he became moody, distracted and quick-tempered, particularly
with his children. Whereas once he was happy to have the children
playing in a corner of his study while he worked, they were now
instructed to tiptoe past his closed door so as not to disturb him. He
was stiff and withdrawn with friends, took offence easily and was
curt with staff.

The children, both now at school in Hindhead, were of course
completely unaware that Miss Leckie was anything other than a
family friend, and neither suffered unduly from his moodiness,
although Mary later admitted that she was occasionally frightened
of her father and remembered how she would be reduced to silence
when he lowered his newspaper and glared angrily at her for something she had either said or done wrong – she was often unsure
what. Yet at the same time she was proud and pleased when he
arranged to have a short story she had written, 'A Visit to Heven',
published as a book in a limited edition of 200 copies. Conan Doyle
did not correct his ten-year-old daughter's spelling, adding greatly
to the story's charm: 'As I entered my dear little cosey home I
thought what fun it would be to sale up to heven . . . Mother and
Daddy kept waving towls in the air and the last I saw of Undershaw was a little black speck in the distans . . .'

In a letter to his mother Conan Doyle confessed that he was
tired of the 'sick room', and he took every opportunity to get away
from Undershaw, staying in London at the Reform Club or travelling around the country on public speaking engagements. He filled
his time with lecture tours, literary and social functions and, of
course, sport. One laconic entry from his diary gives an indication
of his schedule: 'Tomorrow I go up to dine at one of Sir Henry
Thompson's octave dinners, on Friday I dine with Nugent Robinson,
on Monday we entertain the Bishop of London at the Author's Club,

on Thursday I dine with the Royal Society. I will not, at least, die of hunger.'

At the beginning of 1899 Conan Doyle had a passing flirtation with pacifism. The Tsar of Russia had convened a peace conference at The Hague in an attempt to limit armaments and establish an international tribunal to resolve disputes between countries before resorting to war. Meetings were being held all over Europe to discuss the Tsar's proposals; Conan Doyle chaired one such gathering in Hindhead and spoke enthusiastically in support. He had invited George Bernard Shaw to participate, expecting unequivocal encouragement, but to his surprise Shaw dismissed the idea of arms limitation.

> All the statesmen of Europe, the very men who are now ordering torpedo boats, are also expressing approval of the Tsar's Rescript. Every one knows that if the French submarine boats are a success, this country will at once order them, Germany will order them, and the Tsar himself will not have the power to prevent Russia from ordering them. No good will be done by repeating the platitudes which we put on our Christmas cards every year. We must face the situation by making a sharp distinction between two sets of proposals now before the world. One of these is that war should be less terrible than it is at present. But I cannot too strongly insist that it is not armaments or ironclads that fight, but men, and that if we do away with all the weapons of war and reduce men to the aboriginal weapons of their fists, teeth, and claws, they will fight just as horribly.

Afterwards, Shaw told the writer Hesketh Pearson that he had converted Conan Doyle from 'Christmas-card pacifism to rampant jingoism' but added that he (Shaw) might have 'overdone it'. Certainly Conan Doyle had discarded all thoughts of pacifism by the end of the year when he announced his intention to go to South Africa to fight in the Boer War.

CHAPTER 12

THE BOER WAR

ONAN DOYLE HAD FOLLOWED the unfolding events in South Africa with increasing concern through the early months of 1899, and when war was declared in October he was, like most of his countrymen, entirely convinced that right was on Great Britain's side. The judgement of history would be less certain.

The Dutch, German and Huguenot ancestors of the Boers had first settled on the Cape of South Africa as early as 1652. After Great Britain claimed the colony in 1814 to secure a vital port on the route to India, the Boers were reluctant to submit to foreign colonial rule and began leaving the Cape. In 1836 ten thousand Boers, today known as Afrikaners, headed north in ox-drawn wagons on what was called the Great Trek – still a potent symbol of Boer pride – first to Natal and then to the highlands, where they set up the Orange Free State and the Transvaal Republic, imagining they would at last be free from British imperial ambitions. They were wrong.

In 1877 Britain annexed the Transvaal. Three years later, the Boers, led by the imposing figure of Paul Kruger, rebelled. As vice president of the Transvaal Republic, he had made two trips to Europe to attempt a negotiated settlement; when that failed he became leader of the resistance movement. In December 1880 the Boers ambushed and destroyed a British army convoy at Bronkhorstspruit and then laid siege to British garrisons across the Transvaal. At this time the British army uniform still used scarlet tunics, making them easy targets for Boer snipers.

On 28 January 1881 the Natal Field Force, under the command of Major General Sir George Pomeroy Colley, attempted to break through

Boer positions to relieve British garrisons but was beaten back. A month later, at the Battle of Majuba Hill, Colley was killed and the British routed. The first Boer War ended in humiliating defeat on 23 March 1881, when Prime Minister William Gladstone agreed a truce and granted the Boers self-government in the Transvaal.

Six years later the largest gold field in the world, more valuable even than South Africa's fabled diamond mines, was discovered in the Transvaal, at Witwatersrand, a 60-mile-long ridge south of Pretoria. Kruger, by then president, presciently predicted that the discovery would lead to disaster: 'Instead of rejoicing you should weep, for this gold will cause our country to be soaked in blood.'

Thousands of *uitlanders* (foreigners), mainly British, streamed over the border from the Cape Colony in a migration reminiscent of the great Gold Rush in California nearly forty years earlier. The city of Johannesburg sprang up as a shanty town almost overnight but the church-going Boers, nervous and resentful of the presence in their country of so many foreigners, denied the settlers voting rights, obstructed mining developments and imposed swingeing taxes on the gold industry. Great Britain would make the denial of enfranchise-ment to its citizens in the Transvaal a major issue, but in truth the *uitlanders* were more interested in prospecting than in politics, and Britain was more interested in extending its imperial influence than protecting the so-called rights of the prospectors, described by a contemporary as 'a loafing, drinking, scheming lot' who would 'corrupt an archangel'.

The continuing failure to gain improved rights for the *uitlanders* was used by the British Government as spurious justification for a major military build up in the Cape. In September 1899 Joseph Chamberlain, the Colonial Secretary, sent an ultimatum demanding full citizenship rights for British settlers in the Transvaal only for Paul Kruger to respond with his own ultimatum demanding the withdrawal of all British troops from the Transvaal border within forty-eight hours. The British government was certainly not minded to consider ulti-mata and when the deadline passed with no response from the British, the Boers declared war on 12 October. A week after hostilities began, the bellicose Colonial Secretary explained to the country what Britain was defending: 'The first principle is that if we are to maintain our existence as a great power in South Africa, we are bound to show we are both willing and able to protect British subjects everywhere when they are made to suffer from oppression and injustice . . . The second principle is that in the interests of the British Empire, Great Britain must remain the paramount power in South Africa.' Conan Doyle, the arch patriot, heartily agreed.

Great Britain was at the zenith of her power and prestige; Victorian Britons were the most patriotic citizens in the world, comfortable with their supremacy and certain of their right to rule far-flung countries around the world. Queen Victoria was undaunted by initial reverses in South Africa, declaring, 'We are not interested in the possibilities of defeat; they do not exist.' Her subjects unques- tionably concurred; anyone voicing criticism of Britain's motives was ridiculed or branded 'pro-Boer'; music halls stoked the jingoism with songs like 'My Lulu is Half-Zulu' and recitations of Kipling's poem 'Absent Minded Beggar', a plea to remember the common soldier:

> When you've shouted 'Rule Britannia',
> When you've sung 'God save the Queen',
> When you've finished killing Kruger with your mouth,
> Will you kindly drop a shilling in my little tambourine
> For a gentleman in khaki ordered South? . . .

In London it was not expected that the war would last long. Some newspapers dubbed it the 'Teatime War'. In fact it proved to be the longest (nearly three years), the costliest (more than £200 million), the bloodiest (at least 22,000 British, 25,000 Boer and 12,000 African lives lost) and the most humiliating war of the century.

British military commanders in South Africa, who expected little opposition from a rabble of farmers, seriously underestimated the threat. The Boers, who would later be described by Conan Doyle as 'one of the most rugged, virile, unconquerable races ever seen upon earth', were fighting on their home soil, were well-drilled, fast and mobile, willing to adopt modern defensive innovations including the slit trench and barbed wire, and were equipped with modern German weapons. By contrast, the British Army had little experience of the harsh conditions on the veldt, struggled to adjust to the Boer strategy and was trained in tactics of formation and advance that had changed little since the battle of Waterloo – mounted troops were still equipped with swords and lances.

During a single week in the middle of December, later known as 'Black Week', the British suffered a series of devastating losses at Stormberg, Magersfontein and Colenso. Advancing in close formation in all three battles, as they had done in the Napoleonic wars, they stood no chance. They were short of arms and ammunition and poorly equipped – few units were kitted out with the new khaki uniforms which would have provided a modicum of concealment on the veldt, and their boots fell apart in the heat.

Reinforcements under the command of Field Marshal Lord Roberts were immediately sent, and a call went out for volunteers, vigorously supported by Conan Doyle in a letter to *The Times*: 'The suggestion comes from many quarters that more colonials should be sent to the seat of war. But how can we in honour permit our colonial fellow-citizens to fill the gap when none of our own civilians have gone to the front? Great Britain is full of men who can ride and shoot. Might I suggest that lists should at least be opened and the names taken of those who are prepared to go if required – preference might be given to those men who can find their own horses? There are thousands of men riding after foxes or shooting pheasants who would gladly be useful to their country if it were made possible for them. This war has at least taught the lesson that it only needs a brave man and a modern rifle to make a soldier.'[1]

Conan Doyle was certainly ready to put his own name down. In fact he had determined a month earlier that he should take part in the war. When he wrote to tell his mother of his plans, she was appalled, replying on 22 November:

My own dearest and very naughty son.

How dare you – what do you mean by it? Why your very height and breadth would make you a simple and sure target, and is not your life, to say the least, of more value, even to your country – at home?

You owe it to us all, to care for your life as a great treasure, and it is just a fever you have, dear One – the old fighting blood – Percy and Pack, Doyle and Conan, all

struggling to push you on to what, noble as it looks, to
what would be, if stripped to the core, a real crime, and a
great and useless folly.

For God's sake, listen to me . . . even at your age I am
God's representative to you. You may have other relations
of every kind, but only one Mother. Do not go Arthur, that
is my first and last word. If these politicians and journalists
who so lightly drift into war had to go right away to the
front themselves they would be a great deal more careful.
They pushed the country into this horrific war and now
you shall not be their victim if I can help it. My love to you
all – Oh! you naughty darling son.

Your own M.

To emphasise her determination to dissuade him, she scrawled,
in red ink capitals at the top of the letter: 'The Matriarch Speaks'.
She was 62 years old, as feisty as ever and well versed in world affairs.
She took the view that the war was about gold and greed and did not
want her son to make a sacrifice for an ignoble cause.

But Conan Doyle, as stubborn and determined as his mother,
was not in the least deterred. After his letter to *The Times* he wrote
to her to say he felt 'honour bound' to be among the first to volunteer; whatever his value as a soldier, he believed he could be of use
as a 'role model'. 'What I feel is that I have perhaps the strongest
influence over young men, especially young athletic sporting men,
of any one in England, (bar Kipling). That being so, it is really important that I should give them a lead . . . As to the merits of the quarrel:
from the day they invaded Natal that becomes merely academic. But
surely it is obvious that *they* have prepared for years and that we have
not . . . I had grave doubts before war broke out, but ever since I
have been sure that it was a righteous war and well worth sacrifices.'
Quite why he believed he exerted any influence over the youth of
Great Britain is hard to understand, as there is no evidence that he
was able to influence young people, nor indeed that he ever sought
to do so.

In truth Conan Doyle was not entirely motivated by pure patriotism:
he was attracted by the possibility of writing a history of the war

from first-hand knowledge. He had already assembled a comprehensive file of newspaper cuttings and interviewed military officers involved in the early battles. All his life he had craved adventure and had long hankered to experience war at first hand. Touie's health had forced him to leave Egypt before he had had an opportunity, as a correspondent, to witness a campaign at close quarters. (He had heard of Kitchener's great victory at the Battle of Omdurman in the Sudan in September 1898 while watching the Army's summer manoeuvres on Salisbury Plain and bitterly regretted not being there.) Here, at last, was his chance to take part in a war on the side of justice and righteousness, for the honour of the British nation and to experience what he had spent so much time writing about – action on a battle-field.

He sent off enlistment applications first to the War Office, then to the Imperial Yeomanry in South Africa and the Middlesex Yeomanry, where he had friends. But at his age, with no soldiering experience, he was hardly prime recruit material. When interviewed about his military experience, he replied that he had had an 'adventurous life' and had seen 'a little of military operations in the Sudan'. It was, he privately admitted, 'stretching it about as far as it would go' but claimed that a gentleman was permitted 'two white lies' – to protect a woman or 'to get into a fight when the fight is a rightful one'.

Conan Doyle was placed on a waiting list but given little hope. It seemed he was to be thwarted until he ran into John Langman, a friend and a wealthy philanthropist, who was equipping and dispatching a 100-bed hospital unit to South Africa at his own expense. Langman's son, Archie, whom Conan Doyle knew from Davos, was to be the general manager, but Langman suggested that Conan Doyle might like to join the unit as a 'supplementary medico'. Conan Doyle leapt at the opportunity. 'I think I have found a way of reconciling my duty with your desire,' Conan Doyle wrote to his mother, 'and will not volunteer further unless the emergency there should be excessive – which it won't be now . . . My precious carcass would be safe enough there – and I will be serving my country also. I very badly want an absolute change at present and this is a great chance. I shall be much better in the long run.'

He spent the next week helping to recruit the remaining personnel
– surgeons, dressers, nurses and ancillary staff – although he was
unable to dissuade John Langman from appointing another friend, Dr
Robert O'Callaghan, as chief surgeon. Conan Doyle took a dislike to
him, sneering in his memoirs that he was a gynaecologist, 'a branch
of the profession for which there seemed to be no immediate demand',
although he must have known it was not true: O'Callaghan was a
Harley Street specialist in abdominal surgery. Conan Doyle was
happier with two 'really splendid young surgeons' Charles Gibbs and
H. J. Scharleib. Although Langman had guaranteed to pay for the
upkeep of the hospital for six months, the War Office insisted that a
military officer should accompany them and posted Major Maurice
Drury, RAMC, a wonderfully louche Irishman who claimed that his
only ambition in life was to leave the service and 'marry a rich widow
with a cough'.

Mary Doyle remained determined to block his plans and threatened to contact the Langmans to ask that he should be relieved. 'Don't
write to the Langmans at all about it like a good little mother,' her
son wrote in an imploring letter which revealed yet another reason
why he was so keen to go. 'I know exactly what I am doing and why
and there is lots of method in my actions. Nothing could fit into my
life better. I have lived for six years in a sick room and Oh how weary
of it I am! Dear Touie! It has tried me more than her – and she never
dreams of it and I am very glad she does not . . . May 1900 bring us
all, including the country, better luck!'

While waiting for permission to leave for South Africa, Conan
Doyle made idiosyncratic preparations by experimenting with a technique for dispatching snipers hiding behind rocks by firing a rifle into
the air and dropping bullets onto the enemy. He thought it might be
possible to make a sighting device that would 'turn a rifle into a
portable howitzer' and tested his ideas at nearby Frensham Pond.
Standing in the reeds at the edge of the pond, he pointed a rifle into
the air, tilted it slightly forward and fired. The bullet, he reported,
very nearly landed on his own head; it was so close he could hear it
thud into the ground. He continued firing until an obviously angry
man marched up to him and asked if he would like to know where
his shots were falling because 'they have been dropping all round *me*'.

Conan Doyle abandoned the experiment but still thought the idea potentially 'epoch-making' and worthy of bringing to the attention of the War Office. The reply to his letter was frosty: 'With reference to your letter concerning an appliance for adapting rifles to high-angle fire I am directed by the Secretary of State for War to inform you that he will not trouble you in the matter.' Undaunted, Conan Doyle thought this typical bureaucratic short-sightedness and wrote to *The Times*: 'No wonder that we find the latest inventions in the hands of our enemies rather than ourselves if those who try to improve our weapons meet with such encouragement as I have done.' [2]

Before its departure, the Langman hospital unit was inspected in February 1900 by the elderly Duke of Cambridge, who indicated his extreme disapproval that none of Conan Doyle's tunic buttons was engraved with any regimental marks. This notwithstanding, the unit sailed for South Africa from Tilbury on the 28th, aboard the chartered P&O liner *Oriental*. Jean Leckie arranged to have his cabin filled with flowers but did not come on board to say goodbye, choosing to remain anonymous in the milling crowd on the dockside.

The *Oriental* first called at Queenstown in Ireland, to pick up the 3rd Militia Battalion, Royal Scots Fusiliers, then steamed south. During a routine stop at Cape Verde island, Dr Conan Doyle was picked for a cricket team under the captaincy of Lord Henry Scott which defeated a team from the Atlantic telegraph station and which boasted it had previously beaten all the visiting teams from passing transports. The *Oriental* reached Cape Town on 22 March, stayed for four days then continued to East London, where the Royal Scots Fusiliers and the Langman hospital disembarked.

Conan Doyle had been entrusted with funds to distribute in South Africa for 'charitable purposes', and one of the first duties he carried out on landing was to visit Boer prisoners. On the train to Bloemfontein, the capital of the Orange Free State, which had been captured on 15 March, he was clearly intoxicated by the strange exhilaration of war. 'There were nights on that journey which I shall never forget – the great train roaring through the darkness, the fires beside the line, the dark groups silhouetted against the flames, the shouts of "Who are you?" and the crash of voices as our mates cried back, "The Camerons", for this famous regiment was our companion. Wonderful is the atmosphere of war. When the millennium comes the world will gain much, but it will lose its greatest thrill.'

In Bloemfontein he watched the brigade commanded by Horace Smith-Dorrien march into the city and wrote a jingoistic account in the *Friend*, a newspaper produced by correspondents in South Africa, which reflected his boyish glee at being present.

> If it could have passed, just as it was, down Piccadilly and the Strand it would have driven London crazy. I got down from the truck, which we were unloading, and watched them, the ragged, bearded, fierce-eyed infantry, straggling along under their cloud of dust. Here are clumps of Highlanders, their workmanlike aprons in front, their keen faces burned black with months on the veldt. It is an honoured name that they bear on their shoulder-straps. 'Good old Gordon!' I cried as they passed me. The sergeant glanced at the dirty enthusiast in the undershirt. 'What cheer, matey!' he cried, and his men squared their shoulders and put a touch of ginger in their stride . . . What splendid fellows there are among them! Here is one who hails me; the last time I saw him we put on seventy runs together when they were rather badly needed, and here we are, partners in quite another game.[3]

His exhilaration, however, did not endure. Bloemfontein was soon in the grip of a virulent typhoid epidemic which would cost 5,000 lives and create conditions of almost indescribable horror. The British had failed to secure the waterworks, 23 miles outside the city, and the Boers cut off the town's water supply. Soldiers on strict water rations soon began looking elsewhere to quench their thirst and filled their water bottles from the nearby Modder river, contaminated by animal carcasses and sewage from a Boer camp upstream.

Conan Doyle's unit camped on the ground of Bloemfontein Ramblers' Cricket Club and hastily converted the pavilion into a ward. For a month they lived, he wrote, in the midst of death in its 'vilest, filthiest form'. Equipped to deal with 100 patients, they had more than double that number, with the dead and dying lying between the beds. Latrines were installed, incongruously, on a stage still set up with a scene from the last amateur production, *HMS Pinafore*, but few patients had the strength to stagger to the stage. 'Four weeks may seem a short time in comfort, but it is a very long one under conditions such as those, amid horrible sights and sounds and smells, while a haze of flies spreads over everything, covering your food and trying to force themselves into your mouth – every one of them a focus of disease . . . Our hospital was no worse off than the others, and as there were many of them the general condition of the town was very bad.'

Coffins were out of the question and the dead were wrapped in brown blankets and lowered into shallow graves at the average rate of sixty a day. A sickening smell hung over the stricken town. On one occasion Conan Doyle rode out on horseback to take a break; he was about 6 miles from the town when the wind changed and the familiar stench suddenly filled the air all around him.

Mortimer Menpes, a war artist commissioned by *Black and White* magazine, visited the Langman Hospital specifically to sketch Conan Doyle at work. He found him with his sleeves rolled up, tired and overworked, but coping admirably. It was difficult, Menpes reported, to associate the exhausted and blood-spattered doctor with the creator of Sherlock Holmes; he was simply a doctor, and an enthusiastic one too: 'I never saw a man throw himself into duty so thoroughly, heart and soul.' Menpes asked Conan Doyle if he intended to write a book about his experiences but he claimed at that moment he had far too much to do to think about literary matters. As proof he pushed open the door of a ward. 'What I saw baffles description,' Menpes wrote later.

> The only thing I can liken it to is a slaughter house. I have seen dreadful sights in my life; but I have never seen anything quite equal to this – the place was saturated with enteric fever, and patients were swarming in at such a rate that it was impossible to attend to them all. Some of the cases were too terrible for words. And here in the midst of all these horrors, you would see two or three black-robed Sisters of Mercy going about silently and swiftly, doing work that would make a strong man faint: handling the soldiers as through they were infants; bandaging and dressing and attending to a thousand little

details, all in a calm, unruffled way, never appearing in a hurry. 'What superb women!' I exclaimed involuntarily. Dr Doyle smiled as he watched them. 'They are angels,' he said simply. [4]

It had been years since Conan Doyle had practised medicine but the conditions tested his character as much as his medical skills. He stayed grimly at his post, uncomplaining, and trying to function in circumstances worse than anything he could have imagined in fiction. It became too much for Dr O'Callaghan, who soon planned to return to London. The playboy Major Drury sought solace in the bottle, while the two young surgeons did their best, helped by the arrival of two Red Cross nurses. On 20 April Conan Doyle found time to write to his mother, sparing her by admitting only that the atmosphere and surroundings were 'pretty fetid'. But, he said, he remained very fit and confident he had sufficient strength to resist infection. He did, however, complain about O'Callaghan and Drury – 'the one thinks of nothing but himself and the other of nothing but whisky' – and added that he would be 'very glad to see the last of his [O'Callaghan's] fat body'. The Mam probably had a fair idea of what was happening because Unionist MP William Burdett-Coutts, on assignment as a war correspondent for *The Times*, had sent home a series of caustic dispatches which shocked the nation and led to the setting up of a Royal Commission to investigate the care of the sick and wounded in South Africa.

Conan Doyle estimated that in the first month of the epidemic between 10,000 and 12,000 soldiers fell ill, noting that enteric (as it was then called) was a persistent and debilitating fever which required very careful nursing to prevent its spread. More than 50 men were dying everyday and at least 1,000 new graves had been dug in the city cemetery. Staff at the Langman Hospital suffered too, despite having been inoculated. Of the six nurses, one died and three others contracted typhoid; one of the eighteen orderlies died and eight more went down, as did two of the five dressers.

Conan Doyle was full of praise for his colleagues:

No one served their country more truly than the officers and men of the medical service, nor can any one who went through the epidemic forget the bravery and unselfishness of those

admirable nursing sisters who set the men around them a
higher standard of devotion to duty ... All through the
campaign, while the machinery for curing disease was excellent, that for preventing it was elementary or absent. If bad
water can cost us more than all the bullets of the enemy, then
surely it is worth our while to make the drinking of unboiled
water a stringent military offence ... It is heart-rending for
the medical man who has emerged from a hospital full of
water-borne pestilence to see a regimental water cart being
filled, without protest, at some polluted wayside pool.[5]

Conditions only began to improve when, after nine weeks of
epidemic, a British force captured the waterworks. Conan Doyle went
along to watch the action, with Archie Langman and two journalists.
He spent the night before the anticipated battle huddled underneath
a wagon, 'colder than I can ever remember being in my life'. But by
dawn the Boers had retreated and British troops were able to take
control unopposed. With clean drinking water, the epidemic was
under control within a few weeks, and Conan Doyle was organising
a series of morale-raising inter-hospital football matches.

News of the war from elsewhere was more encouraging. On 18
May after a siege lasting 217 days, Mafeking was relieved, provoking
scenes of wild jubilation on the streets of London, and Pretoria, the
capital of the Transvaal, fell on 5 June. As the British Army under
Field Marshal Lord Roberts began its advance on Pretoria, Conan
Doyle, anxious to see something of the war and gather material for
his book, obtained permission to spend a week with the troops in the
front line. He left Bloemfontain on horseback with Archie Langman
and joined the long lines of infantry marching across the veldt,
supported by artillery. He saw plenty of action, not all of it admirable
– British troops routinely looted Boer farms in their path – spent two
hours sheltering from an artillery duel and took copious notes in his
journal. He watched Lord Roberts's army crossing the river Vet 'the
whole 10,000 men ... rolling slowly like an irresistible lava stream
over the plain' and had an unerring eye for colourful detail. When he
came across a British soldier sitting on a looted wagon playing 'Home
Sweet Home' on his harmonica at a sacked Boer farmstead, he noticed

a number of photographs scattered on the ground, one a wedding picture of the couple 'whose menage had become such an irreparable ruin'.

Even on the battlefield, his fame preceded him. Seeing two men bringing a wounded soldier back from the line he rode out to meet them; the injured man had been shot in the arm and stomach but the bullets were just under the skin and Conan Doyle assured him he would live. He opened his eyes for a moment and said, 'I have read your books' before he was carried off. On another occasion at the Langman Hospital a patient had asked him which was his favourite Sherlock Holmes story; Conan Doyle was so distracted or exhausted he could not even remember the title, saying he had always liked 'the one about the serpent'.

Despite the danger, he made no secret of the fact that he enjoyed the whole experience of war: 'I felt happy because I had always wanted a baptism of fire and now I had had a fairly good one. As far as I could judge my own sensations I felt no nervousness at all – or at least far less than I should have expected – but my mind kept turning on other things all the time. For example I was so annoyed at the loss of my haversack that I really for some time forgot about the shells altogether as I bustled about looking for it.' He would later include a rip-roaring account of his adventures on the front line as a chapter in his autobiography laying himself open to charges of glorifying war, but his intent was almost certainly to highlight the bravery of the fighting man, as celebrated in his fiction, rather than to conceal or ignore the grim realities of the battlefield.

Back at the hospital unit, he was struck down with a fever, probably a mild form of typhoid, but continued working, although he would complain years later that he still had something 'insidious' in his system. An over-enthusiastic tackle during a football match also left him with severely bruised ribs. 'I was getting too old,' he admitted, 'for the rough handling which I could have smiled at in my youth.' It was virtually the end of his footballing career; thereafter he would only play very occasionally.

Conan Doyle would claim in the preface to his book on the war that the majority of it was 'written in a hospital tent in the intervals of duty during the epidemic at Bloemfontein' and that his only source material were the convalescing officers and men under his care. This was clearly stretching the truth somewhat – he had little time for writing during the epidemic and he conducted extensive interviews once the worst of the crisis had passed.

When conditions in Bloemfontein had improved, he was able to write a long letter to the *British Medical Journal* about the epidemic, which he described as 'a calamity the magnitude of which had not been foreseen, and which even now is imperfectly appreciated . . . It was appalling in its severity, both in quantity and quality. I know of no instance of such an epidemic in modern warfare.' He argued that had inoculation been made compulsory, many more lives would have been saved and was full of praise for both the heroism and dedication of the orderlies and the stoicism of the soldiers: 'They are uniformly patient, docile, and cheerful, with an inextinguishable hope of "getting to Pretoria". There is a gallantry even about their delirium, for their delusion continually is that they have won the Victoria Cross. One patient, whom I found the other day rummaging under his pillow, informed me he was looking for "his two Victoria Crosses" . . .' [6]

When a relief doctor arrived in the city Conan Doyle felt he had discharged his duty, but first he wanted to visit the army headquarters in Pretoria to interview senior commanders, most notably Lord Roberts, the commander-in-chief. On 23 June he wrote to his mother from Bloemfontein: 'I am just starting for Pretoria . . . Now that the Boers are giving up their arms as rapidly, I cannot think that much work lies before us and my true work now is my history, which will explain at least to some of the doubters how righteous is the position of my country. My duty I think lies in London rather than here. I go by train as far as Kroonstadt and then I hope to get a truck . . .'

He described the journey, under constant threat of attack from marauding bands of Boers, as one of the strangest in his life. The train stopped continually in the middle of the veldt, sometimes for five minutes, sometimes for five hours, with no clue as to when it would start moving again. They passed a down train with all its windows 'shattered' and heard that 'twenty folk had been injured in a Boer ambuscade'. At Roodeval, where a few days earlier the Boer commander General Piet De Wet had 'cut up' the Derbyshire militia and captured a huge store of ammunition, provisions and mail, the line was under repair and the train stopped long enough for the passengers to disembark. For Conan Doyle it was a golden opportunity to go over the ground, littered with empty shell cases, where the battle had been fought. De Wet had ordered all the mailbags to be burned – 'one of his less sportsmanlike actions,' Conan Doyle observed – and thousands of fragments of charred letters were blowing around. Conan Doyle made out the postscript of one letter scrawled in an unpractised feminine hand: above several rows of kisses, the unknown woman wrote: 'I hope you have killed all them Boers by now'. As soon as he arrived in Pretoria, he wrote to his mother: 'We had a great journey of three days . . . very picturesque all the way, telegraph posts burned down, stations in ruins, charred heaps where our mails were destroyed, pickets and patrols everywhere. The town here is pretty pleasant and I am in a comfy hotel. There are many Boers about, I smoked and argued with some of them. They are not bad chaps but easily led and very ignorant . . .'

On 27 June he was granted an interview with Lord Roberts ('urbane and alert . . . eyes were full of kindness and intelligence, but they had the watery look of age') and spent much of his remaining time in the capital collecting first-hand accounts of the campaign. He visited a Boer prisoner-of-war camp where a few weeks earlier British troops had been held and had been busy digging an escape tunnel with spoons. He posed for a photograph standing up to his waist in the half-completed tunnel and posted copies to friends inscribed 'Getting out of a hole, like the British Empire'. As souvenirs he carried away a Boer carbine, a band triangle, a half-knitted sock made with needles fashioned from barbed wire and a set of leg fetters.

From Pretoria Conan Doyle travelled south to Cape Town, where he met Sir Alfred Milner, the British High Commissioner and the chief architect of the war, and on 11 July 1900, he sailed for home on board the Cunarder RMS *Briton*. Although he spent most of his time compiling notes and writing in his cabin, he remembered it as a 'very joyous' voyage largely because of his amiable fellow passengers. In the first-class dining room Conan Doyle shared a table with two correspondents who had been in South Africa covering the war – Bertram Fletcher Robinson of the *Daily Express,* who would later be given credit for inspiring one of the most famous of the Sherlock Holmes stories, *The Hound of the Baskervilles*, and Henry Nevinson of the *Daily Chronicle*. Nevinson remembered Conan Doyle with great fondness as 'a large, loosely-made man with big grey eyes that turn on you when you speak to him with a trustful friendliness like a big dog's . . . Indeed, in voice and character he has always reminded me of an affectionate St Bernard or Newfoundland dog.'[7]

Only one incident marred the voyage, when a French officer alleged in Conan Doyle's presence that the British forces had habitually used soft-tipped dumdum bullets, which exploded in the body on impact. It was a charge that had been frequently levelled at both sides and generated considerable controversy. Conan Doyle, who completely accepted the British government's denial, and had already taken a great dislike to the way the man talked so indiscreetly about his experiences, promptly called him a liar. The man turned and walked out. Later, Fletcher Robinson knocked on Conan Doyle's door and explained that the man had reconsidered his position, decided he was wrong and asked if Conan Doyle would accept an apology. Conan Doyle gruffly replied that he would not, since it was the Army that had been insulted. The two men avoided each other for the remainder of the voyage.

As the RMS *Briton* steamed closer to home Conan Doyle's thoughts, after five months away, turned towards what awaited him. In a final letter to his mother from Pretoria he had written: 'There are only two things for which I wish to return to England. One of them is to kiss my dear mother once more . . .'

He did not identify the second thing but it was unlikely to be the thought of returning to the side of his sick wife.

CHAPTER 13

THE PARLIAMENTARY CANDIDATE

N HIS RETURN FROM South Africa Conan Doyle ran straight into a family row caused by his burning desire to see Jean Leckie. A few days after being reunited with Touie and the children at Undershaw, he left for London, ostensibly to fulfil his cricketing commitments – four fixtures at Lord's and a game against the London County Cricket Club, captained by W. G. Grace, at Crystal Palace. Instead of staying at the Reform Club, as was his usual habit, he checked into Morley's Hotel in Cockspur Street. Being in an anonymous hotel enabled him to spend more time with Jean.

It was perhaps inevitable that they would be seen together and it happened at Lord's. Willie Hornung, his brother-in-law, was also in the crowd and was shocked to observe Conan Doyle strolling around the ground with a woman who was not his wife, unconscionable behaviour at that time. Conan Doyle was aware that he had been spotted and that evening called on Hornung and Connie at their home in Kensington in an attempt to explain. He was received graciously and, it seemed, sympathetically, as he insisted that his relationship with Jean Leckie was entirely platonic and would remain so while Touie was alive. After hearing him out Hornung declared himself satisfied, while Connie agreed, in an act of conciliation, to meet her brother and Jean for lunch at Lord's the following day.

But next morning, Conan Doyle received a telegram claiming that Connie had a toothache and would no longer be able to make lunch. Unconvinced by this excuse he returned to Kensington, where he found Hornung in a truculent mood and now unwilling to condone his brother-in-law's behaviour. He had decided that Conan Doyle's insistence that his relationship with Jean was platonic made little real difference: the fact that there *was* a relationship and their willingness to flaunt it at Lord's was not only a betrayal of Conan Doyle's wedding vows, but an affront to Touie.

Conan Doyle was furious, but did his best to control his temper. He absolutely refused to accept that Touie's honour had been impugned, insisting that the difference between a chaste and an unchaste relationship was the difference between 'guilt and innocence'. Thus he was innocent. Hornung would not be moved. Declining to discuss 'so sacred a matter' any further, Conan Doyle stormed out. The following day he wrote a plaintive letter to his mother describing what had happened: 'I suppose their hearts spoke first and then they were foolish enough to allow their heads to intervene. Willie's tone was that of an attorney dissecting a case, instead of a brother standing by a brother in need . . . I left the house not angrily but in a serious frame of mind which is more formidable. When have I failed in loyalty to any member of my family? And when before have I appealed to them?'

Obstinate and untroubled by self-doubt, Conan Doyle could see no merit in Hornung's position and viewed himself as the wronged party, betrayed by those closest to him whose duty was to support him. He found it absurd that Connie and Willie should censure him when his mother, his other siblings and even Touie's mother, had all acquiesced to the friendship. As de facto head of the family for many years, he clearly expected his siblings to reciprocate the loyalty he had shown them. What most upset him, he told his mother, was the effect that the row had on Jean Leckie, who apparently blamed herself: 'The dear soul gets these fits of depression (it is her artistic nature), and then her remorse is terrible and she writes, poor soul, as though she had done some awful thing. I never love her more than at such moments. Dearest, I don't know how to thank you for all your goodness to us.' Eventually the row blew over: 'I have written a polite note to Connie, which, between ourselves, is more than she deserves.'

Conan Doyle's protestations that his relationship with Jean remained chaste are supported by numerous letters to his mother over the years, in which he devised elaborate travel plans for trysts with Jean during which his mother would act as chaperone. 'I fear the Paris plan won't work,' he wrote once, 'but I have a wider and more comprehensive one which I think I could carry through without any danger at all. Was there ever such a love story as ours since the world began!' At the same time, he believed as a gentleman that there was such a thing as a 'permissible lie' – one which protected the honour of a woman – and on his frequent visits to London he stayed in hotels rather than at the Reform, where it would have been impossible to entertain a woman not his wife, or the Athenaeum, which did not admit women. In 1902, Conan Doyle's literary agent delivered to the *Strand* the last of a new series of Sherlock Holmes stories, 'The Adventure of the Second Stain'. It had been written at the Golden Cross Hotel, near Trafalgar Square, and Greenhough Smith was surprised to discover that part of the manuscript was in another hand: Jean Leckie's.[1]

Conan Doyle had little time to fret over the rift with the Hornungs, since he had agreed to stand for Parliament as Liberal Unionist candidate for Central Edinburgh in the 'khaki election' called by the Prime Minister, Lord Salisbury, on the back of the victories in the Boer War. In August he had written to Joseph Chamberlain, leader of the Liberal Unionists, suggesting his 'experience in South Africa' and his role as a historian would make him an ideal candidate.

There had been speculation for some time in the press that Conan Doyle would be offered a safe seat in Parliament. His fame as an author, his popularity, his prominent involvement in public issues, his fervent patriotism and his reputation untainted by the faintest whiff of scandal – no one outside the immediate family knew that he had fallen in love with another woman – made him an attractive candidate, and both the Conservative and the Liberal parties had made approaches to him. He had, however, joined the Liberal Unionists more than ten years earlier, in the mid-1880s, when Home Rule for Ireland dominated the domestic political agenda.

Home Rule was promoted by William Gladstone's Liberal Party

as the only means of ending the troubles between the nationalists and the unionists, but many in the party did not agree and formed an offshoot called the Liberal Unionists, which Conan Doyle supported, despite his Irish antecedents. For him there was no paradox: it was a simple matter of patriotism, since he regarded Ireland to be an integral part of Great Britain, just as much as Scotland or Wales. In June 1886 Gladstone's Home Rule Bill, offering limited self-government, was defeated in Parliament and the country faced its second general election in the space of seven months.

On the eve of the election, Major General Sir William Crossman, then the leader of the party, was forced to cancel an appearance at a rally at the Amphitheatre in Portsmouth and Conan Doyle was asked to stand in for him. Despite admitting to nerves, he spoke for twenty-five minutes and roused the audience to cheers with his thunderous rhetoric, ending his speech with a colourful parody of the marriage service: 'England and Ireland are wedded together with the sapphire wedding ring of the sea, and what God has placed together let no man pluck asunder!' The following month he was elected vice chairman of the Portsmouth branch of the Liberal Unionists, further increasing his public profile in the city. Local newspapers made much of an incident, a little later, when the future Prime Minister, Arthur Balfour, visited the city to deliver a speech on Ireland. Two anti-Unionists attempted to heckle him, but Conan Doyle clamped his hefty hand over one heckler's mouth; the other, furious, promptly whacked Conan Doyle over the head with a walking stick and collapsed his top hat.

In the 1900 general election, questions about Home Rule and Free Trade took second place to the continuing Boer War. The ruling Conservative party favoured seeing the war through to the end and mounted an unashamedly jingoistic campaign, claiming 'every seat lost to the government is a seat sold to the Boers', while the opposition Liberal party was hopelessly divided, with many of its MPs expressing fervent opposition to the conflict. For his part, Conan Doyle whole-heartedly approved of the Liberal Unionists forging an alliance with Conservatives on the basis of continuing the war. His influence would, if he wished, have guaranteed him a safe seat, but he chose instead to fight in Edinburgh, then held by the Liberals.

Later in his life he was never able adequately to explain his decision to try and enter politics. It was certainly not, he said, from any 'burning desire to join that august assembly' (the House of Commons). It was more to do, arguably, with a sense of not having fulfilled his potential. He was rich, famous and successful, but what had he achieved for the greater good? Imbued with the belief that he had been put on earth for some 'big purpose', politics seemed, at least at that time, to offer not just an opportunity to test himself but to find his mission in life. 'I am 41,' he noted in his journal. 'If I miss this election the chances are that it will be seven years before another. That would make me 48. Rather late to begin. So it is now or never.'²

Towards the end of September he took a train to Edinburgh for a first meeting with the Liberal Unionist agent, E. Bruce Low, and the chairman of the local party, John Cranston. They were dismayed to discover that their candidate was extremely ill equipped to answer questions on local issues, and had only a vague grasp of the party's policies and little idea of its wider aims. They offered to write a manifesto for him as a briefing document but he politely declined and embarked with gusto on ten days of intensive campaigning. 'I was fresh from the scene of war and overflowing with zeal to help the army, so I spared myself in no way,' he wrote in his memoirs. 'I spoke from barrels in the street or any other pedestal I could find, holding many wayside meetings beside my big meetings in the evening, which were always crowded and uproarious.' He learned, quickly, how to handle noisy hecklers, who were numerous, many of them addressing him sarcastically as 'Sherlock Homes'. In truth, his evening meetings were crowded with people who only wanted to see the famous author, but his enthusiasm never flagged. He gave as many as ten speeches a day, often starting at dawn, addressing workers leaving the night shift, and not finishing until after midnight.

Conan Doyle's election platform rested on the importance of the Empire, military reforms, national defence and the vital need to support the Unionist Conservative alliance in order to carry on the war. It would be madness, he told one gathering, to 'swop horses in the middle of a stream'; to another he said that focusing on local issues would be 'like a man wanting to tidy his sitting room while his house was on fire'. On most social and local issues, he said he agreed with his Liberal opponent, a wealthy publisher named George Mackenzie Brown. It was on whether or not to pursue the war that they differed and on this one question the electorate should cast its votes. He referred frequently to his own experience in South Africa and to how he had returned ever more convinced of the 'justice and necessity' of the struggle.

To judge by its report on a speech delivered before several hundred foundry workers, the *Scotsman* was generally impressed: 'He spoke to them as an Edinburgh man to Edinburgh men. He was born and bred in the city and it was a great joy to him to be amongst them again, and it was his proudest ambition to serve his fellow-townsmen in Parliament.' At another meeting the newspaper reported that 'The heckling of the candidate was carried on with great liveliness, his ready and straight replies being received with loud cheers.' On 29 September, he wrote to his mother: 'Dearest, They say this is the fight in Edinburgh which is exciting the people most since the days of Lord Macaulay – it is tremendous. I had the Operetta House packed, they followed me in crowds to the Hotel, Prince's Street was blocked, and I had to speak from the steps of the Hotel, I did 14 speeches in 3 days – pretty good!'

The culmination of Conan Doyle's campaign would be a rally at Edinburgh Literary Institute. An hour beforehand crowds had gathered outside and the police had to be called to deal with a gang of 'unenfranchised youths' threatening to cause trouble. When the doors opened there was a rush for seats, but many had to stand. There was wild and sustained cheering when Conan Doyle walked onto the stage, and some moments passed before he could quieten the crowd sufficiently to begin. Amid more cheering he told the assembly that the colonists in South Africa were looking to Edinburgh for deliverance; the excitement 'in all the little towns' was intense, and all across the country 'their brethren' would be gathering where the election results would be displayed. He appealed to everyone in the hall to make it possible for South Africa to say, on the morning after the election: 'Thank God, Edinburgh has gone straight!'

This artful rhetoric nearly brought the house down, but Conan Doyle had one more trick up his sleeve. He might be unable to produce Sherlock Holmes, as his hecklers had consistently demanded, but he could produce the man on whom his famous detective had been based

– Dr Joseph Bell, now 63 years old. Bell stood alongside his former pupil and declared that he had probably known Conan Doyle for longer than anyone in the audience. 'If Conan Doyle does half as well in Parliament as he did in the Royal Edinburgh Infirmary,' he asserted to applause and more loud cheering, 'he will make an unforgettable impression on English politics.'

After the undoubted success of this rally, Conan Doyle could have been forgiven for thinking that he was heading for certain victory, but he was to be sabotaged at the very last moment. On the night before polling day, a group called the 'Dunfermline Protestant Defence Organisation', run by one Jacob Plimmer, plastered 300 posters across the city impugning Conan Doyle as a 'Papist conspirator; a Jesuit emissary and a Subverter of the Protestant Faith' whose candidacy constituted an assault on 'everything dear to the Scottish heart'.

Conan Doyle did his best to repair the damage, accusing Plimmer of running a smear campaign and being an 'Evangelical fanatic', but he could hardly deny being raised as a Catholic and educated by Jesuits, despite stressing that he 'doubted that anyone in the world held broader views' on the subject of religion. His opponent gallantly issued a statement denouncing Plimmer's 'slanderous attack', but Conan Doyle lost by 569 votes (2,459 votes against Brown's 3,028, cutting the Liberal majority by around 1,500), although the Conservatives and Liberal Unionists, under the leadership of Lord Salisbury, secured a large overall majority across the country. He was convinced that Plimmer was responsible for his defeat, noting in his autobiography that he 'very narrowly missed' winning the seat and was only beaten 'by a few hundred votes'.

In an attempt to set the record straight, he wrote to the *Scotsman* pointing out that he not been a practising Roman Catholic since his school days, that for more than twenty years his strongest convictions had been in favour of complete liberty of conscience and that he regarded 'hard and fast dogma of every kind as an unjustifiable and essentially irreligious thing putting assertion in the place of reason, and giving rise to more contention, bitterness, and want of charity than any other influence in human affairs'. There was, he said, not one word of truth in the false and malicious placards distributed around

Edinburgh and the fact that they vitally influenced the election was a 'very grave public scandal'. He had been advised that he could take legal action but preferred to have the facts on record and hope the publicity would prevent the 'recurrence of so gross a scandal'.[3]

Conan Doyle was not quite so unruffled as he appeared. He wrote to Bruce Low from Undershaw offering to pay for the services of a private detective to investigate Plimmer and suggested threatening him with legal action to force him to divulge who was behind his activities. When he knew all the facts, he said, he would write an exposé in the *Scotsman* that would make his opponent squirm: 'He will find I can fight without the gloves. Tell me any way I can help you and I'll do it. Brown may be guiltless but his wire pullers must have been in it.'[4] Eventually, however, he let the matter drop.

When Conan Doyle had time to reassess his brief flirtation with politics he changed his view. 'Looking back,' he wrote in his autobiography, 'I am inclined to look upon Mr Plimmer as one of the great benefactors of my life. He altered the points at the last moment and prevented me from being shunted on to a sideline which would perhaps have taken me to a dead end. I could never have been a party man, and there seems no place under our system for anyone else.'

Back at Undershaw, Conan Doyle put the finishing touches to *The Great Boer War*, which he dedicated to John Langman and was obliged to present as an 'interim history', as the war itself was still raging. Published before the end of 1900 and packed with detailed accounts of innumerable battles, complete with maps, the 552-page book was a remarkable achievement, bearing in mind he had not long returned from South Africa and had stood for Parliament in the meantime. It was testimony to Conan Doyle's extraordinary work ethic, his powers of concentration and ability to absorb information quickly and transform it into lucid, readable and vigorous prose. *The Great Boer War*, enlarged and revised, would go through seventeen editions, although the author threatened to 'destroy' the second when he discovered to his horror that the publisher, Thomas Nelson & Sons, had used his photograph, with the bristling points of his waxed moustache extending beyond his cheeks, as the frontispiece. He insisted it should be replaced, 'as was proper', by one of Lord Roberts.

Conan Doyle would claim later that £27,000 was spent on compiling an official history of the war, but proudly asserted there was nothing in it 'which I had not already chronicled, save for those minute details of various forces which clog a narrative'. When he asked the chief official historian whether *The Great Boer War* had been of use he apparently replied 'very handsomely' that it was the spine around which the official history had been built.

Considering Conan Doyle's trenchant views on the war, his narrative was scrupulously fair and admirably even-handed, even if it was too impressionistic to be considered a serious military history. He conceded that the Boer claim to territory for which they had 'travelled far, work hard, and fought bravely' had merit, but the fact that the British settlers, who outnumbered the Dutch, were denied any voice in government provided unquestionable moral justification for the conflict. Human rights, he said, not just British rights, were being violated. Moreover, soldiers from many parts of the Empire had rallied to the cause, proving that the Empire was not simply a conglomeration of disparate colonies but a world force capable of confronting global problems and solving them.

It was the book's final chapter, in which Conan Doyle advocated sweeping military reforms, which caused most stir. Excerpted in *Cornhill* two months before publication with the title 'Some Military Lessons of the War', his proposals were deemed as verging on the revolutionary, particularly within the military, yet in retrospect they were amazingly perceptive, and within two decades most had been put into effect.

The British Army, he said, was hidebound by tradition and committed to methods which had outlived their usefulness: it needed to modify its entire approach to modern warfare. Mounted troops armed with lances and swords – not unlike his character Brigadier Gerard – had been sent to South Africa and proved singularly ineffective. He had seen them in action and concluded that the only place for lances and swords was in a museum. He suggested that the best thing to do with the cavalry was to 'abolish it altogether'. This submission alone must have caused apoplexy in the officers' messes of cavalry regiments across the country, particularly when Conan Doyle went on to demand an end to the 'frippery' of the officer class, with its extravagant uniforms, luxurious quarters and unnecessary expenses like running a string of polo ponies which made it difficult for an individual without substantial private means to take a commission.

Infantry tactics, too, were outdated. The idea that a foot soldier was a 'pikeman' had never quite evolved; thus infantrymen, although armed with rifles, were still expected to march in step and advance shoulder to shoulder, just as pikemen did in the seventeenth century to protect the musketeers. 'All this,' he wrote, 'is medieval and dangerous.' He put forward the militarily sacrilegious idea that the infantry should spend more time learning how to shoot than how to drill on a parade ground and called for the recruitment of volunteer militia units to provide home defence, enabling the regular army to be deployed abroad in the defence of the Empire.

He expanded his ideas in a letter to the *Westminster Gazette*: 'Let the island be defended by the million of militia, volunteers, and riflemen, who could easily be raised if the public were taught that they were to rely entirely upon themselves for self-protection. We should then be stronger both at home and abroad than we are at present, and in war time we should have an enormous reserve of men who knew something of the use of weapons, and who could rapidly be turned into good soldiers. It is deplorable that our young men should all be playing games or shooting rabbits when they might so easily be doing something to strengthen their country . . .' [5]

At Undershaw Conan Doyle turned words into action by founding the Undershaw Rifle Club, supplying weapons and ammunition, holding training sessions twice a week and offering prizes at regular shooting competitions. There was no red tape, no swagger and no uniform, other than a broad-brimmed hat with a badge. His hope was that within a year or two there would not be a 'carter, cabman, peasant or shop-boy' in the village who was not a trained marksman and that the idea would spread to surrounding villages until the district was full of 'possible fighting men'.[6] His club soon had 300 members and was the model and pioneer of dozens of similar clubs which sprang up all over the country and would prove their value in the First World War, providing the army with recruits who already knew how to shoot. (All his life Conan Doyle liked nothing better than a cause, no matter how eclectic: he soon turned his attention to the plight of shopworkers in the grocery trade, writing to *the Grocers' Assistant* to condemn the 'crying evil' of shop assistants working too hard and to support its campaign for shorter working hours.[7])

On 21 January 1901 Queen Victoria died, at the age of 81, after the longest reign in British history. Her death plunged the nation and the Empire into mourning and brought to an end an era of confidence and perceived invincibility. She had presided over a great age of industrial expansion, economic progress and the growth of an empire on which, it was frequently said, the sun never set. Every writer of note felt moved to mark her passing with suitably sombre prose, and after the funeral and burial next to her beloved Prince Albert at Windsor, Conan Doyle penned an emotional valediction for the *New York World*:

> The Great Mother has gone down alone upon the dreary road which leads to the black portal. With reverent silence we have seen her this day pass through us, and never more shall the eyes of her people look upon her. Of all the millions who lined her course, how many would have given their own lives to have her back? But we watched in helpless sorrow while through the black banks of the mourners, down the valley of white faces, the Great Queen swept onward out of the sunlight into the gloom. The little body on the dark gun carriage yonder, frail and fragile, scarcely larger than a child's, is that to which 400,000,000 of us who dwell under the red-crossed flag looked, as the centre of all things, the very heart of our lives, our inspiration, our standard of duty, the dear mother of us all. But there came one who summoned her, and amid an awful hush in crowded London, she passed on into the shadow . . . [8]

Public support for the war in South Africa began to wane rapidly. It had been assumed in Great Britain that the capture of Bloemfontein and Pretoria would end the war, but the rebellious Boers waged a protracted guerrilla campaign, blowing up trains and ambushing British army columns. The conflict became more brutal as time wore on. The British Army was accustomed to fighting set-piece battles with large military formations, whereas the Boer commando units were fast and highly mobile, employing hit-and-run tactics, inflicting mounting British losses and making use of new smokeless cartridges in their German Mauser rifles which helped conceal their positions.

To crush the Boer guerrillas, Lord Kitchener – appointed commander of the Army shortly after the 'khaki election' – built fortified blockhouses across the country to restrict guerrilla movements and flush Boers into the open, and formed new regiments of irregular light cavalry to hunt down and destroy the enemy. In March 1901 he switched to a scorched earth policy and began seizing livestock, torching crops and farms, poisoning wells and forcibly herding Afrikaner families into what were dubbed 'concentration camps' – an unwelcome addition to the English language if ever there was one. Conditions in the camps rapidly deteriorated and overcrowding, inadequate diet, meagre medical care led to many deaths, particularly among children. Conan Doyle remained an unapologetic hawk and suggested in a letter to *The Times* that putting a truck full of Boer 'irreconcilables' behind every railway engine in South Africa might dissuade their comrades from derailing trains.[9]

As the war dragged on, costs and casualties mounted and reports from front-line correspondents, particularly in foreign newspapers, were increasingly critical of Kitchener's strategy and the dreadful conditions in the concentration camps. Accusations surfaced that British troops were committing atrocities, rape and torture. For the first time in a generation the British began to wonder if right was on their side, goaded by commentators such as W. T. Stead, editor of the *Review of Reviews*, who frequently fulminated against the war: 'Night and day the whole hellish panorama is unrolled in South Africa, and we know that before sunset British troops carrying the King's commission will be steadily adding more items of horror to the ghastly total.'[10]

Stead was a particularly influential figure, the great crusading journalist of his time, who became famous in 1885 for a series of articles in the *Pall Mall Gazette* exposing child prostitution and white slavery after he had 'bought' a 13-year-old girl from her mother. Conan Doyle was infuriated by Stead's vocal opposition to the war and in a letter to his mother described him as a 'scoundrel' who 'traduces our Soldiers most foully'. He was in no doubt that Stead's charges were false: 'He says, for example, that the number of women raped by our soldiers is so numerous that it can never be computed. Now no case of rape has actually occurred in the whole campaign. If one did the offender would be instantly shot, as both Boers and British know well.' He insisted, in another letter, that the behaviour of the British troops had been 'perfectly astonishingly good'.

Conan Doyle found himself in a diminishing minority. Prominent politicians, including Lloyd George and Keir Hardie, joined the Stop the War Committee, and many Irish nationalists sympathised with the Boers, regarding them as another people oppressed by British imperialism. During a speech in Parliament, Lloyd George, the Liberal MP for Caernarfon (and a future prime minister), quoted devastatingly from a letter by a British officer in South Africa: 'We move from valley to valley, lifting cattle and sheep, burning and looting, and turning out women and children to weep in despair beside the ruin of their once beautiful homesteads.'

In January 1902 the Boer general J. C. Smuts, later Prime Minister of the Union of South Africa, published a report accusing Kitchener of carrying out a policy of 'unbelievable barbarism and gruesomeness which violates the most elementary principles of the international rules of war . . . the basic principles of Lord Kitchener's tactics has been to win, not so much through direct operations against fighting commandos, but rather indirectly by bringing the pressure of war against defenceless women and children'.

An armchair strategist typical of the clubmen of the day, Conan Doyle was deeply concerned at the growing international hostility towards the war and took it upon himself to defend his countrymen. 'For some reason,' he explained, 'which may be either arrogance or apathy, the British are very slow to state their case to the world. In view of the persistent slanders to which our politicians and our soldiers have been equally exposed, it becomes a duty which we owe to our national honour to lay the facts before the world.'

Fired by patriotism and indignation, he wrote a robust defence of his country in *The War in South Africa: Its Cause and Conduct*. It was a direct appeal to world opinion, sold for sixpence in Britain and distributed free throughout Europe, after an appeal for funds in *The Times*. Conan Doyle called it 'an incursion into diplomacy' and wrote to his mother, 'You'll see your son single-handed trying to swing round the whole opinion of the world.'

'There never was a war in history,' he began, 'in which right was absolutely on one side, or in which no incidents of the campaign were open to criticism. I do not pretend that it was so here. But I do not think that any unprejudiced man can read the facts without acknowledging that the British Government had done its best to avoid war, and the British Army to wage it with humanity.' He responded systematically to all the charges levelled against Britain. He made a good case refuting accusations that British soldiers were guilty of rape, looting and brutality, but was on less sure ground in asserting that the concentration camps were, in reality, merely refugee camps set up to accommodate women and children displaced by the war, and that it was better to give them shelter than to abandon them to die of starvation and disease in the veldt. He admitted the mortality rate in the camps was high but pointed out that it was because of disease rather than bad treatment. He argued that the 'natural instinct' of Boer mothers to cling on to their children and prevent them from being moved into quarantine was more responsible for the excessive mortality among minors than the overcrowded conditions. He also absolutely denied, though he was later proved wrong, that the British, in violation of international law, had used dumdum bullets. He accused the Boers of being wholly committed to a disregard for the 'recognised rules of warfare', and said considering their dastardly tactics, including torture and summary executions, it was surprising that British troops did not behave in a more uncivilised manner.

It was all too much for opponents of the war. John M. Robertson, a member of the Ethical Society, which maintained that Britain was fighting an unjust war, produced his own pamphlet, *The Boer Struggle for Freedom*, in which he roundly denounced Conan Doyle for misrepresentation, asserting he was 'an amateur' and a 'menace' basing his opinions on 'comic opera evidence'. Conan Doyle's pamphlet should be 'consigned to the waste-paper basket without more ado', and his history of the war was 'the most worthless, the most careless, the most faithless history of an important international episode that has been published in our time'.[11]

Nevertheless, *The War in South Africa* was, by and large, well received: 300,000 copies were sold in Britain within a few months, but, more importantly, foreign translations helped soften opinion abroad. Conan Doyle sent copies to Boer officers interned in prison camps in St Helena and Cyprus. 'There was a rapid and marked change in the tone of the whole Continental press,' he noted in his memoirs, 'which may have been a coincidence, but was certainly a pleasing one. In the case of many important organs of public opinion there could, however, be no question of coincidence, as the arguments advanced in the booklet and the facts quoted were cited in their leading articles as having modified their former anti-British views.'

At home Conan Doyle found himself stopped in the street by former soldiers and civilians alike who wanted to shake his hand; the new King Edward VII, a fan of Sherlock Holmes, invited him to dinner and sat him at his side. Profits from the pamphlet were distributed to a number of good causes, including military charities, a famine appeal in India and a fund for distressed Boers. Conan Doyle chose to give much of the credit to Jean: because of her he had cancelled a planned trip to India and thus became available to write the pamphlet which he described in a letter to his mother as 'the greatest public work of my life . . . this alone is enough to show that this is a high and heaven-sent thing, this love of ours'.

The Boer War ended in May 1902 when the last of the Boer commandos, left without food, clothing, ammunition or hope, were forced to surrender. The cost had been horrendous: around 75,000 lives were lost, about a third of them civilians in concentration camps; British casualties were 22,000, mostly from disease; nearly 120,000 men, women and children were forcibly moved into concentration camps; 30,000 farmhouses and 40 small towns were destroyed. Six days after the signing of the treaty ending the war, Lord Kitchener was created Viscount Kitchener of Khartoum, of the Vaal in the Colony of the Transvaal and of Aspall in the County of Suffolk.

That summer Conan Doyle heard that in recognition of his unofficial role as chief propagandist for the war he was being considered for a knighthood in the Coronation honours. To his mother's dismay, he insisted he could not possibly accept, arguing that his work for his country would be tainted if he accepted a 'reward' and calling a knighthood 'the badge of the provincial mayor'. Touie now featured very low in his priorities, as was clear in a letter to his mother: 'I assure you that if Jean and Lottie and you – the three people whom I love most in the world – were all on their knees before me I could not do this thing.' But, forceful as ever, the Mam would not countenance the idea of her beloved son not being publicly recognised for his work. She insisted that he should accept, eventually persuading him that a rejection would appear a calculated insult to the King.

The coronation of King Edward VII took place at Westminster Abbey on 9 August 1902. On 24 October Arthur Conan Doyle was knighted for his services to the Crown and appointed a deputy lieu-tenant of Surrey. 'Dearest boy,' he wrote to Innes. 'It is a Knighthood – seems funny, but the terms in which it was offered would not permit refusal. They have also made me Deputy Lieutenant of Surrey. I feel like a new married girl who is not sure of her own name . . .'

He told his mother that in his deputy lieutenant's uniform he looked as if he had 'escaped from the top of a barrel organ'. In the same letter he informed her that Touie was 'bright and well' and then blithely suggested that the Mam take a break and join him at a hotel in Norfolk. 'We could have a pleasant time together and talk of many things . . . and if we then had a visitor [Jean] for a few days there could be no harm.'

CHAPTER 14

THE RETURN OF HOLMES

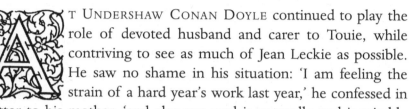T Undershaw Conan Doyle continued to play the role of devoted husband and carer to Touie, while contriving to see as much of Jean Leckie as possible. He saw no shame in his situation: 'I am feeling the strain of a hard year's work last year,' he confessed in a letter to his mother, 'and also my soul is naturally and inevitably rather wrenched in two all the time. I am most careful at home and I am sure that at no time have I been anything but most considerate and attentive. But the position is difficult, is it not? Dear J [Jean] is a model of good sense and propriety in the whole thing. There never was anyone with a sweeter and more unselfish nature.' Some might have thought this last sentence might equally have referred to Touie lying day after day on her sickbed and almost certainly aware of her husband's infatuation with another, younger, woman.[1]

It was, inevitably, a strain on all parties in this unhappy troika. Touie pretended she knew nothing of what was going on; Conan Doyle pretended nothing *was* going on; Jean Leckie pretended to be no more than a family friend. Conan Doyle, increasingly given to black moods at home and short-tempered with his children, agonised over continuing his relationship with Jean and even gallantly suggested to her that it might be better if she found a younger, unattached partner. She would not hear of it: she assured him she was content to wait. But behind her patience there lurked the gruesome truth that both of them knew what they were waiting for. They were waiting for Touie to die.

Despite his emotional turmoil, Conan Doyle continued to work and in March 1901 he wrote to Greenhough Smith at the *Strand* to tell him he had a 'real creeper' of a story to sell him. 'It is full of surprises, breaking naturally into good lengths for serial purposes. There is one stipulation. I must do it with my friend Fletcher Robinson, and his name must appear with mine. I can answer for the yarn being all my own, in my style without dilution, since your readers like that. But he gave me the central idea and the local colour, and so I feel his name must appear. I shall want my usual £50 per thousand words for all rights if you want to do business.'[2]

Greenhough Smith was always happy to 'do business' with Conan Doyle, even though he might have had some misgivings about him collaborating with a friend. Bertram Fletcher Robinson, known to his friends as 'Bobbles', was the young journalist Conan Doyle had met on board the *Briton* when returning from South Africa the previous year. They took a short golfing holiday together at the beginning of March at the Royal Links Hotel in Cromer, on the north coast of Norfolk, during which Robinson talked about the folklore legends of his native Devon. There was the 'Black Dog of Dartmoor', a spectral hound with flaming red eyes said to chase coaches crossing the moor at night, and the mysterious Dewer, a huntsman who terrorised the countryside with his pack of hounds hunting for the souls of unbaptised babies. The stories immediately fired Conan Doyle's imagination. In his next letter to his mother he spoke of planning a 'small book' with his friend Robinson. He even had a title; he was going to call it *The Hound of the Baskervilles* – the 'real creeper' he would soon offer to Greenhough Smith.

Sherlockians have debated the genesis of *The Hound of the Baskervilles* for years. There is no shortage of diabolical hellhounds in British folklore: Yorkshire offers the 'barghest', a monstrous goblin-dog with huge teeth and claws whose appearance was a portent of death; in Wales, there was the Dog of Darkness, the Gwyllgi, a mastiff with baleful breath and blazing red eyes; in the Isle of Man a spectral hound called Mauthe Doog; in Jersey the Tchico, the Black Dog of Death; and in Suffolk, in 1577, Black Shuck, the size of a calf, was said to have burst through the doors of Blythburgh church during a service and caused the church tower to collapse. Thus there were myriad sources of inspiration that Conan Doyle could have called upon for his hound. That Robinson was initially involved there is no doubt, but whether the story really originated from his Devon childhood is not established, as Greenhough Smith avowed that Robinson had told him he had read the story in a Welsh guidebook. Still other accounts claim the story was based on the legend of an evil squire, Richard Cabell of Buckfastleigh, whose death was followed by a pack of black dogs, breathing fire, racing across the moor and howling.

Conan Doyle himself had sketched a similar idea in a short story 'The King of the Foxes', published in *Windsor Magazine* in 1898. A young gentleman, out riding to hounds, gets ahead of the hunt and encounters a monstrous fox which turns out to be a grey Siberian wolf escaped from a local menagerie. As the hounds go in for the kill the wolf pounces: 'At the same instant, a creature the size of a donkey jumped on to its feet. A huge grey head, with monstrous glistening fangs and tapering fox-jaws, shot out from among the branches; and the hound was thrown several feet into the air, and fell howling among the cover. Then there was a clashing snap like a rat-trap closing, and the howls sharpened into a scream and then were still . . .'

Whatever the inspiration, Conan Doyle and Robinson could soon be found striding together across Dartmoor, the desolate and windswept moorland plateau in Devon, which provided a home to Britain's most notorious and remote prison, sometimes covering 14 miles a day. Robinson had invited the author to stay at his house at Ipplepen, on the edge of the moor, to 'soak up the atmosphere'. They visited the Stone Age ruins scattered across the moor and Fox Tor Mire, the treacherous bog that was the model for the Great Grimpen Mire, in the book, where one false step meant 'death to man or beast'.

Robinson thoroughly enjoyed Conan Doyle's eight-day visit: 'One of the most interesting weeks that I ever spent was with Doyle on Dartmoor. The great wilderness of bog and rock that cuts across Devonshire . . . appealed to his imagination. He listened eagerly to my stories of the ghost hounds, of headless riders and of the devils that lurk in the hollows – legends upon which I had been reared, for my home lay on the borders of the moor.'[3]

Robinson's coachman recalled seeing the two men 'writing and talking' together in the billiard room late into the night, although it is unlikely Robinson made much of a contribution to the actual composition. Conan Doyle's previous attempts at collaboration had been notable failures, but he still thought of the project as 'our book', as he pointed out in a letter to his mother, written from Rowe's Duchy Hotel in Princetown, Devon, on 2 April 1901: 'Here I am in the highest town in England. Robinson and I are exploring the moor over our Sherlock Holmes Book. I think it will work out splendidly – indeed I have already done nearly half of it. Holmes is at his very best, and it is a highly dramatic idea – which I owe to Robinson.'

The Hound of the Baskervilles is arguably the most popular of all the Sherlock Holmes stories – it has been filmed no fewer than eighteen times – yet Holmes was not included in its original conception. Only when Conan Doyle realised that he needed a strong central character to hold the plot together did he decide to resurrect Holmes by setting the story in 1889, before he plunged over the Reichenbach Falls. Conan Doyle also had an eye to commercial considerations, recognising that introducing Sherlock Holmes would be a popular move at the *Strand*. Quite unabashed, he suggested in a letter to Greenhough Smith that his fee should be doubled. 'As far as I can judge,' he wrote, 'the revival of Holmes would attract a great deal of attention . . . Suppose I gave the directors the alternative that it should be without Holmes at my old figure or with Holmes at £100 per thou., which would they choose?' The *Strand* unhesitatingly plumped for the latter, and publisher George Newnes was delighted to announce at the company's annual general meeting that, after trying for a number of years, they had at last managed to 'resuscitate their deceased friend Sherlock Holmes'.

Conan Doyle was nothing if not canny about money. With *The Hound of the Baskervilles* he consolidated his status as one of the world's highest-paid authors, receiving between £480 and £620 for each instalment. Enclosing the fourth and fifth instalments along with another letter to Greenhough Smith, he warned that the story might run to more than the 50,000 words originally promised and assumed he would not be 'debarred' from charging for them.[4]

The first cliff-hanging episode appeared in the *Strand* in August 1901. Word had spread that the great detective was back, and on the morning of publication a queue had formed outside the magazine's office. To Greenhough Smith's delight, circulation increased by 30,000 copies; it was the only occasion in the magazine's ten-year history that a seventh printing was required to meet the demand. In America, 50,000 copies of the US edition were sold in the first ten days.

Robinson did not get equal billing, as Conan Doyle had first demanded. Instead, a small acknowledgement was inserted under the first column of text: 'This story owes its inception to my friend, Mr Fletcher Robinson, who has helped me both in the general plot and in the local details.' When *The Hound* first appeared in book form in April 1902, Robinson received a generous dedication: 'My dear Robinson: It was your account of a west country legend which first suggested the idea of this little tale to my mind. For this, and for the help which you gave me in its evolution, all thanks.' Robinson's contribution would, however, be steadily eroded, for when the book appeared in the United States, Conan Doyle expressed his gratitude to his friend only for having 'suggested the idea', and later, in an omnibus edition of Holmes stories, he acknowledged merely that the story 'arose from a remark' by his friend and declared that 'the plot and every word of the actual narrative was my own'.

Robinson himself was ambivalent about his contribution. He made no claims to authorship before the book appeared, but afterwards was occasionally promoted in bylines as the 'joint author' of *The Hound of the Baskervilles,* perhaps prompting Conan Doyle's subsequent assertion that every word of the narrative was his own. The reality is that no one but Arthur Conan Doyle could have written *The Hound of the Baskervilles*. It begins, in classic form, with a visitor arriving at the Baker Street consulting rooms and asking Holmes to investigate the recent death of Sir Charles Baskerville and its possible connection with a curse on the Baskerville family. Having described the circumstances under which Sir Charles came to be found, the visitor adds that he had observed a strange cluster of markings around the body. Holmes asks if they were footprints and his visitor agrees.

'A man's or a woman's?'
    Dr Mortimer looked strangely at us for an instant, and his voice sank almost to a whisper as he answered:
    'Mr Holmes, they were the footprints of a gigantic hound!'

The Hound of the Baskervilles was lauded by some critics as the greatest mystery novel of all time. Conan Doyle was at the height of his descriptive powers, building a sense of foreboding and menace as events unfolded in the bleak environment of the moor, with its swirling mists, half-shadows, loneliness and a silence broken only by the anguished baying of a spectral hound. 'A hound it was, an enormous coal-black hound, but not such a hound as mortal eyes have ever seen. Fire burst from its open mouth, its eyes glowed with a smouldering glare, its muzzle and hackles and dewlap were outlined in flickering flame. Never in the delirious dream of a disordered brain could anything more savage, more appalling, more hellish be conceived than that dark form and savage face which broke upon us out of the wall of fog.' Ironically, Conan Doyle himself did not rate *The Hound of the Baskervilles* particularly highly, telling his mother it was 'not as good as I should have wished'.

Perhaps to take his mind off events at home, around this time Conan Doyle enrolled in a 'muscular development' course with Eugen Sandow, a German-born vaudeville strongman turned entrepreneur who became a pioneer of body building. He still played cricket regularly for the MCC and J. M. Barrie's Allahakbarries, taking seven wickets for 51 runs for the MCC against Cambridgeshire. But his finest moment was at Crystal Palace when, with the first delivery of his third over, he bowled out the legendary W. G. Grace, the cricketer who transformed the game into a national institution. Grace got his revenge the following year, dismissing Conan Doyle for 43. One match provided the inspiration, much later in his life, for a short story – 'The Story of Spedegue's Dropper' – when Conan Doyle was bowled out by the England cricketer A. P. (Bunny) Lewis with an extraordinary ball that rose 30 feet into the air and dropped behind his back onto the bails.

In April, 1902, Conan Doyle paid a visit to his sister Ida and her husband, Nelson Foley, on Gaiola, travelling by sea to Naples on the RMS *Austral* from Tilbury. They had married in December 1895; Foley was a cousin of Mary Doyle and a widower who had been appointed naval architect to the King of Naples.

This time Jean accompanied him on board to say goodbye. 'It was quite safe,' he wrote his mother, 'for there was a great crowd and bustle, no one knowing anyone and everyone very busy. She decorated my cabin with flowers and kissed my pillow on both sides. I last saw her face in the shadow of the shed as she tried to hide that she was crying. I tell you these things, Ma'am, because you have insight and you know how the little things count in life.' He was always anxious to convince his mother of the strength of his passion for Jean, perhaps to expiate his guilt. Later in the year he went so far as to send her one of Jean's love letters 'that you may see how fresh still are our feelings after the searching trial of years encompassed with difficulty'. He asked her, after she had read it, to either burn it or tear it up and scatter it among flowers: 'Only in those two ways would I ever have any note of hers disposed of.'

The Foleys had a villa just off the unspoiled Posillipo peninsula, with unrivalled views across the bay of Naples to Mount Vesuvius. Conan Doyle was fond of Italy and had been decorated a Knight of the Order of the Crown by King Umberto I several years earlier, most likely on the recommendation of Prime Minister Francesco Crispi, who was a great fan of Sherlock Holmes. He made the most of the break, visiting Sicily and Venice, then travelling to the Italian lakes in the north, before heading for Switzerland and home.

While Conan Doyle was in Italy he began work on a new series of roistering adventures featuring the valiant and conceited Hussar, Brigadier Gerard. Three stories in the new series appeared in the *Strand* before the end of the year; a further five in 1903. He always took great interest in how his work was presented and complained to Greenhough Smith about the false economy of spoiling a '£200 story by the intrusion of a 3 guinea engraving'. He was particularly irritated that the illustration for the last of the Brigadier Gerard stories gave away the denouement: 'My whole object is to give the reader a stunning shock by Napoleon lying dead at the crisis of the adventure. But the story is prefaced by a large picture of Napoleon lying dead, which simply knocks the bottom out of the whole thing from the storyteller's point of view.'[5]

In November 1902 Innes returned home from South Africa after more than four years' service abroad. He was met from the boat train at Waterloo by his mother, brother and sister Connie, and the four of them caught a train to Haslemere – the nearest station to

Undershaw – where a considerable welcome had been arranged. As their train pulled in, Haslemere Town Band struck up 'Home Sweet Home'.

A carriage conveyed them to Hindhead, where the horses were unhitched and 40–50 volunteers pulled the carriage to Undershaw by ropes, accompanied by torchbearers and the Grayshott Brass Band. Free drinks for all were served in the Royal Huts Hotel, opposite the house. The grounds of Undershaw, the *Surrey Advertiser* reported, were 'prettily illuminated with fairy lamps and Chinese lanterns, and close to the Hindhead Post Office a string of flags had been placed across the road'. Family friends waited to greet Innes at the front door, but it was a cold, wet night, and Touie was obliged to remain indoors. At least Conan Doyle had the sensitivity, on this occasion, not to invite Leckie to join the welcoming party.

In the spring of 1903 Conan Doyle acquired a toy which he hoped would give him a 'new interest in life' – a motor car. He purchased, from the recently established Wolseley Tool and Motor Car Company in Birmingham, a five-seater 10-horsepower model with dark blue livery and red wheels; Jean accompanied him to Birmingham to place the order. He had sent his coachman, Holden, to Birmingham for three weeks' driving instruction but had little intention of allowing him to spend much time behind the wheel. Kitted out in a peaked cap and goggles, Conan Doyle drove the 140 miles from Birmingham back to Hindhead, accompanied for much of the way by furiously barking dogs. A small crowd gathered outside Undershaw to witness his triumphant arrival, as the Wolseley chugged through the gates with the famous author sitting upright at the horizontal steering wheel.

Despite the success of this maiden journey, it took him some time to master the intricacies of motoring. Showing off the car's paces to his mother he rounded a bend and frightened the horses drawing two farm wagons loaded with turnips. The leading horse whirled round in a panic and ran up a bank whereupon its cart overturned and poured turnips all over the other wagon. Conan Doyle sprang out to help the enraged farmer and while trying to sort out the chaos happened to glance back at his mother, who, unimpressed, was still sitting in the car calmly knitting.

Not long afterwards, sweeping through the gates of Undershaw with Innes after a round of golf, the Wolseley clipped the gatepost, careered up a grassy bank out of control and rolled over on top of them, pinning Conan Doyle and Innes to the ground. The high steering wheel broke the impact and undoubtedly saved their lives. Innes was quickly able to scramble clear, but before Conan Doyle could follow the steering wheel column collapsed and the full weight of the car settled across his spine, just below the neck, pressing his face onto the gravel with such force that he could not utter a sound. Fortunately a number of men came running to the scene and lifted one side of the car, enabling Conan Doyle to wriggle free, bruised but unscathed. Innes made a laconic note in his diary later that day: 'Golf at Hankly. Upset motor car – marvellous escape. A and I both underneath.'[6]

Conan Doyle was not in the least deterred from motoring, either by that accident or by the brakes' alarmingly frequent failures, usually when negotiating hills. On 15 April 1905, he entered a motoring speed trial at Hindhead and came first, covering a distance of 2 miles, 1,500 yards from a standing start in 9 minutes and 56 seconds. It might have gone to his head: in September of that year the *Hampshire Telegraph* reported that Sir Arthur Conan Doyle had been fined £10 for speeding at Folkestone magistrates' court. He had been caught driving at an estimated 26 miles per hour along Cheriton Road, Folkestone, and admitted a previous conviction for a similar offence in Guildford.

Later this enthusiastic motorist, with an eye to the defence of the realm, would call for motor car owners to be mobilised in the event of an invasion: 'My suggestion is that a thousand motorists, a number which I am sure could be trebled or quadrupled, should organise themselves, and should pledge themselves, on the first news of such an invasion, to instantly fill up their cars with picked riflemen drawn from their own immediate neighbourhood, and to convey them, with a week's food, their rifles, and their ammunition, to the danger point . . .'[7]

To Conan Doyle, motoring, when not deployed thwarting an invasion, was an adventure to be enjoyed, among many others. In 1902 he had ridden as a passenger in a hot air balloon, which had taken off from Crystal Palace in London, risen to an altitude of 6,500 feet and

Arthur, aged six, with his father, Charles Altamont Doyle. Charles was already in the grip of alcoholism when this picture was taken in 1865

Mary Doyle, Arthur's formidable mother, aged 55. She was known to all her children as 'the Mam'

Arthur's three sisters, Annette, Lottie and Connie, in Lisbon, 1881. All three girls worked as governesses in Portugal and sent money home to help support the family

Arthur, third from the left, during his whaling expedition to the Arctic in 1880. He fell in the water so frequently he was nicknamed 'The Great Northern Diver'

'Touie', Conan Doyle's first wife, with their children Mary and Kingsley. Touie would die of tuberculosis in 1906

Dr Joseph Bell, the inspiration for Sherlock Holmes

The family pictured at Conan Doyle's home at Hindhead in 1904. Back row (left to right):
Innes, Connie, her husband E.W. Hornung, Mary, Arthur, Lottie, Captain Leslie Oldham
(Lottie's husband), Dodo, Cyril Angell (Dodo's husband). Middle row: Oscar Hornung
and Kingsley. Front row: Nelson Foley (Ida's husband), his son Percy, Touie, Brandford
(the Angells' son), 'the Mam', Ida holding her son Innes

Conan Doyle and his second wife, Jean Leckie,
on their wedding day in 1907

Conan Doyle dandling Denis,
his son from his second marriage

The proud father second time around, posing outside Windlesham with Jean and his sons Denis and Adrian (in pram)

Conan Doyle in the 'wondrous khaki garb' he designed for himself to visit the front in the Great War, in the garden at Windlesham with his sons Denis and Adrian

Conan Doyle standing by his car during the Prince Henry Motor Tour in 1911

Kingsley Conan Doyle, who died two weeks before the Armistice was signed in November 1918

Conan Doyle's younger brother, Innes, survived the Great War only to succumb to the pandemic of Spanish influenza in February 1919

Conan Doyle outside Windlesham, his home for more that twenty years

A family group in the garden, (left to right) Jean, Denis, Conan Doyle holding baby Jean, Adrian and Mary, his daughter from his first marriage

On board the SS *Olympic* en route to the United States for a spiritualist crusade

Conan Doyle at the grave of his brother, Innes, who would make many appearances at seances after his death

A 'spirit photograph' of Conan Doyle with an image purporting to be that of his son Kingsley

The garden at Bignell Wood, where Conan Doyle waited patiently for fairies to appear

Gnomes in the garden positioned by Conan Doyle
to encourage fairies

Conan Doyle with the daughter of the
gardener at Bignell Wood in one hand
and a portable gramophone in the other;
he hoped both would entice the fairies

floated for an hour and 45 minutes before landing safely in a field near Sevenoaks, 25 miles away. 'The first time I went up in a balloon I was terribly frightened,' he told a young journalist called P. G. Wodehouse, who interviewed him for the *Victoria Club* magazine in 1903. 'It was pleasant enough at first, with all the spectators cheering, and so on. But when we had been rising for some minutes, and were about a mile from the ground, and I looked over the side – I was never in such a miserable fright in my life! To see people running about, looking the size of dogs, and to feel that there was only a sort of strawberry-basket between me and *that!* It was a long time before I would let go of the ropes. But after I had been up a little while I became quite used to it, and I suppose that is what happens to everyone.' Later he talked about how he would like to make a parachute jump, just for the sake of 'one great experience'. He thought the first man to have tried out a parachute must have been the 'pluckiest on earth'.[8]

Conan Doyle also acquired a Roc motorcycle, prompting a visit to Undershaw from a new magazine called *The Motor Cycle.* 'I cannot leave Undershaw without referring to my old friend Sherlock Holmes,' the reporter said. 'May I ask whether we can expect to hear the famous detective hunting down his quarry, accompanied by the faithful Watson, both mounted on the newest and finest type of motor cycle?' 'No,' Conan Doyle replied unhesitatingly. 'In Holmes' early days motor bicycles were unthought of. Besides, Holmes has now retired into private life.'[9]

Actually, Holmes was very far from retired. Such was the success of *The Hound of the Baskervilles* that there had been a renewed clamour, from readers and publishers alike, in London and New York, for more stories. In 1903 Conan Doyle's agent, A. P. Watt, wrote to tell him that *Collier's Weekly* magazine in the United States had offered a truly phenomenal sum for a new series: $25,000 for six stories, $30,000 for eight or $45,000 for thirteen. This was just for American rights: George Newnes was prepared to pay a further £100 per thousand words for British rights. (It was a veritable fortune: £100 in 1903 is equivalent to around £7,000 today; $45,000 then would be worth about £500,000.) The opportunity to earn such huge sums from stories he could churn out in a few weeks proved irresistable. Conan Doyle replied to Watt, on a postcard: 'Very well. A.C.D.'

The first problem was that Holmes was dead. Conan Doyle was reluctant to set a whole new series in a period pre-dating Holmes's fatal struggle, and so he devised an audacious plan. Only Conan Doyle could have got away with it. In 'The Adventure of the Empty House', the first of thirteen stories that would be collected under the title *The Return of Sherlock Holmes*, Watson bumps into an 'elderly, deformed' man in the street, knocking the books he has been carrying out of his hand. He endeavours to apologise but the elderly man turns on his heel 'with a snarl of contempt' and scurries away. A few minutes later, returning to his home in Kensington, the maid announces an unexpected visitor. 'To my astonishment, it was none other than my strange old book collector, his sharp, wizened face peering out from a frame of white hair, and his precious volumes, a dozen of them at least, wedged under his right arm.' The old man suggests that Watson might like to buy some books to fill an untidy gap on his bookshelves. Watson instinctively turns to look at the gap and when he turns back he finds the wizened old bookseller has been miraculously transformed, in a trice, into a smiling Sherlock Holmes, back from the dead. Watson promptly – and understandably – faints, 'for the first and last time in my life'.

Holmes's explanation, when Watson recovers, is no more convincing than his transmogrification. Only Moriarty had fallen to his death at the Reichenbach Falls; with the help of baritsu, a 'Japanese system of wrestling, which has more than once been very useful to me', Holmes had managed to slip from his grasp. 'Baritsu' would have very much surprised the Japanese, since it did not exist. Conan Doyle probably meant 'bartitsu', a system of self-defence with a walking stick invented by an English martial arts exponent, Edward Barton-Wright, and described by him in January 1901 in *Pearson's* magazine, to which Conan Doyle also contributed.

As Moriarty went over the edge with 'a horrible scream', Holmes had realised that if it was presumed that he, too, was dead it would be easier for him to track down and destroy the professor's partners in crime. Only his 'much cleverer' brother, Mycroft, who was required to provide him with funds, knew the truth. In fact he had not managed to mop up the Moriarty gang but had spent an interesting three years, wandering Tibet and visiting the Dalai Lama in Lhassa, before passing through Persia and Mecca and paying a 'short but interesting visit to the Khalifa at Khartoum'. He had ended up in France researching coal-tar derivates at a laboratory in Montpellier and had only returned to England to investigate an intriguing new case.

None of it was particularly plausible, but few readers cared how Holmes had survived. What was important was that he was back. In the autumn of 1903 both the *Strand* and *Collier's Weekly* carried prominent advertisements trumpeting the news of Holmes's return. 'Readers have a vivid recollection of the time when Sherlock Holmes made his first appearance before the public,' the *Strand* declared, 'and of the Adventures which made his name a household word in every quarter of the world. The news of his death was received with regret as at the loss of a personal friend. Fortunately, the news, though based on circumstantial evidence which at the time seemed conclusive, turns out to be erroneous. How he escaped from his struggle with Moriarty at the Reichenbach Falls, why he remained in hiding even from his friend Watson, how he made his reappearance, and the manner he signalised his return by one of the most remarkable of his exploits will be found in the first story of the New Series . . .'

'The Adventure of the Empty House' was published in the October 1903 issue of the *Strand*. Queues formed at newsagents and libraries and the scenes at railway bookstalls were reminiscent of the January sales as readers pushed and shoved to get their hands on a copy. Holmes's return generated a fresh flood of letters addressed to him at the magazine care of Sir Arthur Conan Doyle. Most were requests for autographs and many enclosed gifts of tobacco, pipe cleaners and violin strings.

Twelve more stories appeared at monthly intervals with the final story, 'The Adventure of the Second Stain', featured in the December 1904 issue. Conan Doyle set the entire series between 1894 and 1898 to avoid involving Holmes with modern devices like telephones, motor cars or trams, and Watson was conveniently available to move back into the Baker Street consulting rooms because of a recent 'sad bereavement', presumed to be his wife.

Now relieved from 'the excuse of absolute pecuniary pressure' Conan Doyle was determined to make every story as good as possible, but claimed that he still found it difficult to come up with ideas; at one point he wrote to Greenhough Smith expressing his 'intense disinclination to continue', worrying that there was a 'certain sameness and want of freshness' about the stories and suggesting that it might be wise to limit the number to eight.[10]

In fact he found ideas wherever he could, even from the pages of the *Strand*: the central deceit in 'The Adventure of the Priory School' was inspired by a description of ancient counterfeit horseshoes from its 'Curiosities' page in May 1903. Conan Doyle said he had the idea for 'The Adventure of the Dancing Men' from watching the landlord's son draw stick men while he was staying at the Hill House Hotel in Happisburgh, Norfolk, although Edgar Allan Poe also had some input. Poe's short story, 'The Gold Bug', described how to decipher a code in exactly the same way. None of the thirteen stories in *The Return of Sherlock Holmes* disappoints, although as before it is sometimes evident from continuity errors or errors of fact that they had been written carelessly, or in haste.

───────────◆───────────

At Undershaw Touie continued to hold her own: Conan Doyle reported to his mother that she was 'very well, bright and happy and full of interest'. Whenever he was away – often meeting Jean – he always returned with a posy of flowers or a gift. Once he gave her a diamond bracelet with a card on which he had written: 'Here's brightness for your wrist dear wife, But you put brightness in all my life.' There was no longer any question of large-scale entertaining. If the weather was warm she would occasionally go out for a carriage ride with her mother, and in May 1904 she was well enough to go to the theatre in London with her sister. Innes, home on leave from a second tour in South Africa, took both of them to His Majesty's Theatre to see *Darling of the Gods*, starring Herbert Beerbohm Tree, and then to dinner at the Grand. Innes also noted in his diary that he had paid a visit to Sheringham, on the north Norfolk coast, with 'A', where they had been joined by some 'members of the Leckie family'.

Family correspondence around this time indicates clearly the extraordinary extent to which Jean had been integrated into the family circle. Conan Doyle's sisters were in regular contact with her, Lottie in particular, who wrote as early as 1899 hoping 'that next time we meet you will call me Lottie . . . I hate being Miss Doyle to anyone I like'. On Boxing Day 1904 Lottie wrote from Undershaw to tell her about their 'very bright' Christmas, how Arthur was the 'heart and soul' of the festivities and how he and her husband, Leslie, were getting exercise every morning by boxing in the new 'motor house'. For the benefit of Touie, the entire family maintained the charade that Jean was no more than a family friend.

The strain of Conan Doyle's double life was eased by the Mam's cooperation, although the logistics of deceit were always complicated. He was obliged to make complex hotel and travel arrangements while concealing them from his wife and children. In the summer of 1904 while he was on a cricket tour, he asked his mother if she would join him in lodgings in Leamington while Jean was staying. 'We can work out the details as time approaches,' he wrote from Undershaw. 'I see no reason why I should say anything to anyone about you being there, I am simply away on a cricket tour.'

During Innes's leave there was a major family reunion, and the Mam gathered her surviving children and her grandchildren for a memorable photograph. Lottie and her husband, Leslie Oldham, had returned from India, and Ida and Nelson Foley were in London on a visit from Gaiola. Seated in the centre are Touie, with a bow in her hair, and her mother-in-law, wearing a lace cap and looking very much like Queen Victoria. On Touie's right sits grey-bearded Nelson Foley and on Mary Doyle's left is Ida Foley, with her baby, Innes, on her lap. Ranged behind them is the remainder of the family, all the men sporting fine moustaches. On the left is Innes, standing with his hand on Oscar Hornung's shoulder, then Connie and Willie Hornung, Kingsley, aged 12, and Mary, aged 15, Arthur Conan Doyle, unsmiling, in a high-buttoned double-breasted jacket, Lottie Oldham in a saucy curly-brimmed hat and her husband Leslie, and Dodo with her clergyman husband Cyril Angell. Sitting cross-legged at the front are Percy Foley and Branford Angell. No one would guess from the photograph that Touie, smiling and looking directly at the camera, was either ill or suffering emotionally.

In April 1905 Conan Doyle returned to Edinburgh to receive an honorary doctorate (LLD) from his alma mater. The Laureation Address was given by Professor Sir Ludovic J. Grant, Dean of the Faculty at Law, and was appropriately laudatory: 'If the chief function of the novelist be to entertain his reader, Sir Arthur yields place to no contemporary writer of fiction. Some may prefer his historical romances, with their brilliant studies of distant days . . . others his tales of modern hazard and adventure . . . [or] the trail of some latter-day mystery of the very Argus of detectives . . . Let us not forget that he has proved himself no less capable as a writer of serious history.'

That summer Conan Doyle began work on another historical novel, *Sir Nigel*, a prequel to *The White Company*, which he still con-sidered his best work. It traced the early career of Sir Nigel Loring, how he had learned chivalry and heraldry at the feet of his grand-mother, Dame Ermyntrude, before sallying forth on his knightly adventures. While the narrative was packed with action – jousts, brawls in taverns, encounters with damsels in distress, castles under siege, etc. – it was also packed with too much detail about the morals and manners of the age, just like *The White Company*.

He finished writing *Sir Nigel* in October and was pleased with his efforts. 'I have put into it every ounce of research, fancy, fire and skill that I possess,' he wrote to Greenhough Smith. 'It rises to the very highest I have ever done.'[11] William Taylor, editor of Associated Sunday Magazines, which paid $25,000 for first serial rights in the United States, was optimistic that *Sir Nigel* would increase the combined circulation of the nine newspapers that took his magazine by a quarter to 1,250,000. He sent Conan Doyle copies of the advertising and pro-motional material along with a fawning letter: 'We think "Sir Nigel" is the greatest of all historical romances . . . I hope you will be pleased with our exploitation and presentation of the story, so well pleased in fact that you will be kindly disposed towards our little magazine when your next work is ready for publication.'[12]

Once again, to Conan Doyle's intense irritation, critics viewed *Sir Nigel* as a boys' adventure book rather than the 'high-water mark in literature' that he considered it to be. A review in the *Bookman* was typical: 'There is nothing novel or ambitious about the book; this kind of work has been done often enough before, though rarely with such spirit and gusto as Sir Conan Doyle brings to the task. But after the psychological miasma of much modern fiction of the Ibsenical sort, it is like a breath of fresh air to find ourselves once more in the open, riding side by side with these simple-hearted knights, who batter each other so cheerfully . . . In short, "Sir Nigel" is the boys' book of the year.'[13]

Although the book sold well – and Kipling wrote saying he had devoured it 'at one gulp' – Conan Doyle could not conceal his chagrin and frustration. 'It received no particular recognition from critics or public,' he noted morosely, 'which was, I admit, a disappointment to me. In England versatility is looked upon with distrust. You may write ballad tunes or you may write grand opera, but it cannot be admitted that the same man may be master of the whole musical range and do either with equal success.'

Towards the end of 1905, Conan Doyle once again became involved in politics. In September 1903 Joseph Chamberlain had resigned as Colonial Secretary to be free to advance his ideas for tariff reform, to transform the British Empire into a united trading block. Consolidating the Empire into an imperial federation was, he argued, the only way for Britain to remain a great power in the face of increasing challenges from the United States, Germany and Russia. Fundamental to his objectives was the need to have a system of preferential trade with the Empire, necessitating tariffs on imported foreign goods. The issue of free trade versus tariff reform would split the ruling Conservative party and lead to the Liberals winning a landslide victory in the 1906 general election. As a staunch supporter of the Boys' Empire League – 'to promote and strengthen a worthy Imperial spirit in British boys all over the world' – Conan Doyle was a committed tariff reformer, lectured on the subject several times and offered his speeches to Joseph Chamberlain's campaign.

It was Chamberlain who persuaded a reluctant Conan Doyle that his most useful contribution would be to stand again for Parliament; thus he became the Unionist candidate for the so-called 'Border Burghs' – Hawick, Galashiels and Selkirk, textile manufacturing towns in the Borders. It would be Conan Doyle's final, and not exactly enthusiastic, attempt to enter politics. He put up a reasonable fight, but with little of the fire that accompanied his first campaign in Edinburgh.

He soon reached the conclusion privately that electioneering was a 'vile business', that the Scot was so innately conservative he would rather change his religion than his voting allegiance and that mischievous heckling aimed at making the candidate look foolish or ignorant precluded any sensible political debate.

Since his Liberal opponent hardly bothered to hold any election meetings, Conan Doyle's were the only fun to be had. 'Before the meeting the packed house would indulge in cries and counter-cries with rival songs and slogans, so that as I approached the building it sounded like feeding-time at the zoo. My heart often sank within me as I listened to the uproar, and I would ask myself what on earth I meant by placing myself in such a position. Once upon the platform, however, my fighting blood warmed up, and I did not quail before any clamour.' A local newspaper produced a picturesque report of a noisy meeting at the Volunteer Hall at Galashiels, where Conan Doyle faced forty minutes of continuous heckling. '"Is the candidate prepared to grant universal female suffrage?" "No, I am not." (Cries of "Oh, oh.") "Will the candidate tell us why not?" (Cheers.) "Certainly I will. When a man comes home from his day's work, I don't think he wants a politician sitting opposite him at the fireside." (Cheers, hisses, and general uproar.)'

During the campaign Innes visited his brother in Hawick and commented on how curious it would be if his real career should prove to be political rather literary. Conan Doyle replied, off the cuff: 'It will be neither – it will be religious', making both burst out laughing at the absurdity of the notion. But later Conan Doyle would regard this exchange as deeply significant, an example of the 'unconscious power of prophecy which is latent within us'.

On the stump Conan Doyle stuck closely to the tariff reform agenda set by Chamberlain, hoping to persuade the textile workers that their best interests would be served by a tax on foreign imports. He liked to use Ireland as an example of the iniquities of free trade: 'Ireland had manufacturers, and British laws killed them. Then she had a flourishing agriculture, and again British laws – the law of free trade – let the produce of the whole world in, and swamped her home market . . . Don't you see the advantage if all our dominions, in spite of geography, were welded as close together as are the states of America?'

They did not. On 17 January 1906 Conan Doyle was not in the least surprised, or disappointed, to be defeated by his Liberal opponent, Thomas Shaw, by 3,133 votes to 2,444. He would never again entertain politics as a career. Among the letters he received regretting his defeat was one from a woman, consoling him with the thought that 'If the Ladies had had but votes I am sure you would have got in by a huge majority.'

In the spring of 1906, Touie's health began deteriorating rapidly. The tuberculosis had spread to her throat and she could now only speak in a whisper, yet she remained, as far as her children were concerned, serene and cheerful. 'There was still the brave, gay little smile,' Mary recalled, 'and never a word of complaint. Her only thought was for our happiness, and to this end she encouraged us more and more to go out with our friends, assuring us that she was happy and content doing the needlework she enjoyed, and was very gifted at.'[14]

Mary remembered, during a whispered conversation at her mother's bedside weeks before she died, her mother telling her that she thought it was wrong for wives to expect their husbands to cherish their memory after they were gone. All that mattered, she said, was her father's happiness. She did not want her daughter to be either surprised or shocked if her father should choose to marry again and if he did so it would be with her blessing. It was then that Touie dropped a bombshell and informed her daughter that her new stepmother was quite likely to be Jean Leckie.[15] At the time, Mary told no one what her mother had said. Only 17, she perhaps did not understand the full import – that her mother knew, and had possibly known for a long time, that her father was in love with Jean Leckie. Touie never hinted to her husband that she knew, and she was unfailingly grateful for his nursing; if he plumped her pillows or helped her to a more comfortable position, she would always thank him with 'Bless you, dear' or 'That's the ticket'.

On 29 May Touie was well enough to accompany Innes to the theatre in London. It would be her last outing. During June Conan Doyle sent out regular one-line bulletins to Innes: 'T. holds her own well'; 'Touie better'; 'Better; sat up for tea; I hope for the best.' On 30 June he read her a letter about the marriage in Naples of Claire Foley, Nelson's daughter and Ida's stepdaughter, and she appeared to understand what he was saying, but that night he wrote to Innes: 'Dear old Chap, It may be days, or it may be weeks, but the end now seems inevitable . . . She is painless in body, and easy in mind, taking it all with the usual sweet and gentle equanimity.'

Mary and Kingsley were summoned from boarding schools to be with their mother. 'When the sad hour of parting came,' Mary wrote later, 'my father sat by the bedside, the tears coursing down his rugged face, and her small white hand enfolded in his huge grasp. As I bent down to kiss her she murmured "Take care of Kingsley" and soon afterwards her lovely spirit passed away.'[16]

Touie died at 3 a.m. on 4 July, with her husband and her beloved sister, Nem, at her bedside. She was 49. After her funeral, Conan Doyle wrote to his mother: 'I tried never to give Touie a moment's unhappiness; to give her every attention, every comfort she could want. Did I succeed? I think so. God knows I hope so.'

Her death merited one short paragraph in his autobiography.

CHAPTER 15

A REAL-LIFE
SHERLOCK HOLMES

OST ACCOUNTS OF CONAN DOYLE's life claim he went into a steep decline after Touie's death, consumed by grief and racked by guilt over falling in love with another woman. Laid low by a recurrence of the intestinal disease he had picked up in South Africa, it was said he could neither work, eat nor sleep and did little but visit Touie's grave and mourn alone at Undershaw.

Innes's diary tells a rather different story. At the beginning of August 1906, less than a month after Touie's death, Conan Doyle moved into the Ashdown Forest Hotel, on a golf course at Forest Row, not far from the new Leckie family home at Monkstown, Crowborough. On 10 August Innes joined his brother and that night they dined with the Leckies, presumably with Jean present. Barely a month later Conan Doyle was in Scotland with 14-year-old Kingsley, who was soon to start at Eton. They stayed at the Roxburgh Hotel in Dunbar, where they were again visited by Innes; the actor Lewis Waller dropped by for tea with some friends on his way to Edinburgh.

While in Dunbar Conan Doyle was invited, after Innes and Kingsley had left, to spend a few days with Lord Balfour, the former Prime Minister, who was hosting a house party on his family estate at Whittinghame, not far away. He was deeply impressed by the Sunday evening service, when the whole staff of the house, maids and grooms, some twenty in all, gathered with the family and guests for prayers read by the statesman. 'It was fine to hear the groom and statesman praying humbly together,' he noted, 'that they may be forgiven the sins of the day, and merging all earthly distinctions in the presence of that which is above all.' This was an uncharacteristic sentiment for Conan Doyle, who frequently railed against conventional religion. Only a few days before he had caused outrage by writing to the *Daily Express* decrying the notion that 'any form of ritual, including the ritual of going into a large stone building for the purpose of communion with the great Unseen, has any bearing upon true religion'. Conan Doyle recalled Balfour as being a charming host and good listener, who 'laughed heartily at small provocation, and talked always very frankly and modestly of himself. After my long solitude I was more loquacious, I remember, than is my way, but he bore it with good humour.'

Actually Conan Doyle had had numerous social engagements in the two months since Touie's death. Mary spent time with him at Undershaw because she remembered that they would take long walks together when she was home from boarding school immediately after her mother's death. He talked freely to her about his views on life, and she was often surprised by his radicalism. He told her that he did not agree with the perceived wisdom that women should marry at all costs, since he was certain that spinsterhood was infinitely preferable to marrying the wrong man. On the subject of what constituted a gentleman he was considerably more conventional. There were, he said, three hallmarks: chivalrous treatment of the opposite sex, courtesy to those in a lower social status and diligence in repaying loans. October found Conan Doyle enjoying a round of golf at Hindhead with Innes, Fletcher Robinson, his secretary Alfred Wood ('Woodie' to all the family) and Wood's nephew, Sholto. And the next day, Sunday, 21 October, Innes and Conan Doyle motored to Godalming, where Mary was at school, to take her out to tea. 'Long solitude' was clearly not an apt description for this period in his life.

There was no shame in this honourable man not being prostrate with grief. His wife had been a semi-invalid for years, and he could take some pride in that she confounded the grim diagnosis for so long due in part to his care and diligence: 'At least we had held the vital fort for thirteen years after every expert had said that it was untenable.' But he was in love with another woman and cannot have avoided the thought that the death of his wife left the way clear for him to consummate that passion. Miss Jean Leckie, too, who had been waiting with exemplary patience for so long, could have been forgiven for meeting Touie's death as much with relief as grief.

———————————◆———————————

Whatever Conan Doyle's true state of mind, if he was suffering from a debilitating lethargy it certainly lifted in November, when he received a letter from George Edalji, a young solicitor fighting to clear his name after being convicted and imprisoned for the bizarre offence of wounding a pony. It was not unusual for Conan Doyle to receive requests from all parts of the world – occasionally from police officers faced with insoluble crimes – to look into true-life cases of perceived injustice or missing persons, sometimes offering him substantial sums of money. He had always publicly disclaimed possessing any of Holmes's detective skills and usually replied explaining that he was no more a consulting detective than he was a fourteenth-century English bowman or a valiant French cavalry officer in the service of Napoleon. But the Edalji case was different. For the first time in his life – but not the last – Conan Doyle used his influence to mount a national campaign and prove the young man's innocence, in just the way that Sherlock Holmes saw justice triumph and injustice foiled. 'Fair play' was a tenet of Conan Doyle's life, not just on the sporting field. He was instinctively on the side of the underdog and it was entirely in character for him to take up cudgels on Edalji's behalf and wage a protracted battle against officialdom to try and clear his name.

The Reverend Shapurji Edalji, a Parsee who had converted to Christianity, was the vicar of St Mark's Church in Great Wyrley, a mining village in South Staffordshire. He had originally arrived in Britain from Bombay to attend a training course for prospective missionaries, but stayed on when it was decreed that only Europeans should spread the Christian gospel on the subcontinent. He accepted a number of temporary posts in the church and while acting as a curate in Liverpool met Charlotte Stoneham, the youngest daughter of the vicar of Ketley. The couple became engaged with the blessing of Charlotte's parents and married in 1874. Charlotte's uncle, the vicar of St Mark's, was about to retire because of ill health and arranged, as a 'wedding gift', for Edalji to take over the parish. He and his wife went on to have three children, of whom George, a shy, lonely boy with few friends, was the eldest, born in 1876.

In an introverted and suspicious community like Great Wyrley, a 'black' vicar was something of an aberration; it was rigorously assumed that it was the sacred duty of white men to evangelise the blacks, not the other way round. Some parishioners could not understand how an Asian could be a minister in a Christian church and were reluctant to shake his hand after morning service. Inevitably, the family suffered racial abuse, and the children were taunted at school, which greatly exacerbated George's nervous disposition. Although local newspapers often praised his sermons, the Reverend Edalji did not help his position by being high-handed and brusque with his flock, a stickler for the rules with a tendency to ignore local sensitivities.

In 1888, when George Edalji was 12, his father began receiving poison pen letters. He ignored them, but they became more menacing in tone, and their 17-year-old maid, Elizabeth Foster, was also targeted, one letter threatening to shoot her while the 'Black man' was out. The vicarage windows were smashed and graffiti denouncing the Edaljis as 'wicked' was daubed on the walls. Eventually the Reverend Edalji called in the police, who checked the handwriting of everyone in the vicarage and decided that Elizabeth was the likely author, writing decoy letters to herself to thwart any investigation. She adamantly denied that she was responsible, but on the advice of her solicitor was persuaded to plead guilty to a reduced charge when she appeared at Cannock Police Court in January 1889. She was bound over to keep the peace, but continued to insist her innocence and swore that she would one day wreak revenge on the Edaljis, who had little alternative but to dismiss her.

The letters stopped for a while, but in 1892 the poison pen campaign was resumed with a vengeance. Dozens of anonymous letters descended on the vicarage, apparently written in three different hands by individuals harbouring a malignant and diabolical hatred for the Edaljis. Many seemed to be the work of a deranged religious maniac, invoking 'the Almighty', the 'Prince of Darkness' and 'God-Satan', and ranting incoherently: 'I long, yes I long, to be . . . rotting in the flames of Hell fire that shall never be quenched, never, never, never

. . . Oh God thou knowest why I have blasphemed . . .' George was the object of particular malice: 'I swear by God that I will murder George Edalji soon. The only thing I care about in this world is revenge, revenge, sweet revenge I long for, then I shall be happy in hell . . .'

It was not long before the matter came to the attention of the Chief Constable of Staffordshire, Captain the Honourable George Anson, the second son of the Earl of Lichfield. He quickly developed an obsessive antipathy towards the Edaljis, almost entirely based on racial prejudice, enquiring how it was that a 'Hindoo who could only talk with a foreign accent came to be a clergyman of the Church of England in charge of an important working class parish'.[1]

When the Edaljis found brown-paper packages containing excreta on the vicarage doorstep, the police agreed to maintain a watch on the house. On 12 December 1892 one officer found a large key on the back doorstep which, it later was discovered, had been stolen from Walsall Grammar School. No one had been seen to go in or out of the vicarage between the time George arrived home from school and when the key was found, and on this fact alone he became a prime suspect. Anson, behaving in a manner reminiscent of Conan Doyle's unflattering portrayals of the pedestrian Inspector Lestrade, wrote to the Reverend Edalji, in an apparent attempt to get his son to confess and adding: 'I may say at once that I shall not pretend to believe any protestations of ignorance which your son may make about this key.'[2]

Meanwhile, the persecution of the Edaljis entered new dimensions. Advertisements appeared in local newspapers purporting to be a public apology by George Edalji and another boy for writing the anonymous letters: 'We, the undersigned, G.E.T. Edalji and Fredk. Brookes, both residing in the parish of Great Wyrley, do hereby declare that we were the sole authors and writers of certain offensive and anonymous letters received by various persons during the last twelve months.' After corrections were published more hoax advertisements appeared offering rooms for rent at the vicarage, and the services of the vicarage as a marriage bureau, with a number of desirable ladies available for eligible bachelors. The Edaljis were inundated with goods that they had not ordered: encyclopaedias, live geese, wagon-loads of coal, crates of champagne, gallons of paint, furniture, medicines, clothes and musical instruments. A postcard signed 'S. Edalji' was sent to a clergyman in Essex: 'Unless you apologise at once and by telegram for the outrageous hints you give in your sermons concerning my Chastity, I shall expose your adultery and rape.' A dressmaker arrived from Stafford to measure George's little sister, Maud, for a wedding dress. An undertaker turned up to collect a body. A female detective was asked, allegedly by Mrs Edalji, to investigate her husband's infidelity. As Conan Doyle would later observe, the hoaxes demonstrated considerable ingenuity and daring and 'might have seemed comic had it not been for the tragedy of such a persecution'.

The family's misery continued for three relentless years, with the police apparently making no progress. Relations between the Reverend Edalji and the Chief Constable continued to deteriorate as it became clear that Anson still viewed George as the likely culprit, despite the fact that his father protested that his son was often sitting with him when the letters were pushed under the front door. One depicted the Reverend as a 'hellish bastard' whose 'loathsome carcase still defiles the soil'.

In December 1895 the letters, the hoaxes, the unwanted deliveries, all suddenly stopped. Life for the Edaljis returned to something approaching normality. George enrolled at law school in Birmingham, graduated with flying colours and became articled to a firm of solicitors in the same city. In 1898 he was awarded second-class honours and a bronze medal by Birmingham Law Society in the solicitors' final examinations and set himself up in practice with a small office in Birmingham, commuting every day by train from Great Wyrley.

Four years later he found himself in financial difficulty, largely as a result of his naivety and trusting nature. He had agreed to stand surety for a solicitor friend, John William Phillips, who had been accused of misappropriating clients' funds. Unfortunately Phillips absconded. In order to honour the bond, Edalji first borrowed from moneylenders at an exorbitant rate and then speculated on the stock market. Desperate to avoid bankruptcy, which would have ended his legal career, he circulated begging letters to various notable individuals in the area – this came back to haunt him when he sorely needed to prove his reputation was spotless.

Between February and August 1904 there was a mysterious outbreak of horse and cattle mutilation in and around Great Wyrley.

Sixteen animals were found mutilated, slashed by a sharp instrument across their stomachs and left to bleed to death. At the same time the police began receiving letters, signed with a false name, suggesting that a gang was responsible. Among those named as members was 'Edalji the lawyer'. Official alarm stepped up when a letter arrived warning that the gang was going to 'start on little girls' and 'do twenty wenches like the horses before next March'.

When, on the morning of 18 August, a pit pony was found lying in the muddy Plant Pit Meadow not far from the vicarage with its belly ripped, the police arrived demanding to examine George's clothes. They took away a case of four razors, a pair of mud-spattered boots and a damp coat (it had been raining hard the previous night) on which they claimed they had found horse hairs. The Reverend Edalji swore that his son had not been out the previous night – they slept in the same room – but the police officers were unimpressed. George Edalji was arrested in his Birmingham office later that day and taken into custody.

Under questioning, Edalji insisted he had nothing to do with the mutilations. He had arrived home from work the previous evening at half past six, had gone out for a walk, as was his habit, returned to the vicarage for supper and then retired to bed. He confirmed that he slept in the same room as his father and did not leave the room until twenty minutes to seven the following morning. His father always locked the bedroom door and had he tried to leave the creaking of the lock would undoubtedly have disturbed the old man, who was a light sleeper.

The arrest of the 'weird' son of the 'black' vicar of Wyrley after so many months of gossip about who might be responsible stoked the fires of racial hatred. Crowds gathered to hurl abuse as Edalji was driven to and from the preliminary hearings at the magistrates' court. A reporter from Birmingham's Daily Gazette made no attempt to hide his naked racism when he described Edalji in court: 'He is 28 years of age but looks younger. He was dressed in a shrunken black and white check suit, and there was little of the typical solicitor in his swarthy face, with its full, dark eyes, prominent mouth, and small round chin. His appearance is essentially Oriental in its stolidity, no sign of emotion escaping him beyond a faint smile as the extraordinary story of the prosecution unfolded.' His guilt was blithely assumed and everyone had a suggestion to make about why he did it, as the Wolverhampton *Express & Star* reported: 'Many and wonderful were the theories I heard propounded in the local ale-houses as to why Edalji had gone forth in the night to slay cattle, and a widely accepted idea was that he made nocturnal sacrifices to strange gods.'

Dr Butter, a police surgeon, testified that he had found twenty-nine short brown hairs on the coat removed from the vicarage and that when examined under a microscope, they matched in every regard the hairs on the mutilated pit pony. But the most damning witness was a handwriting expert, Thomas Henry Gurrin, who asserted that Edalji was indeed the author of the letters sent to the police accusing himself of the crime. In his closing address the prosecuting counsel addressed the lack of motive and suggested that the defendant was driven by self-importance, a longing for notoriety, a desire to outsmart the police and to prove himself superior to the rest of society. In took the jury just forty minutes to find Edalji guilty. He was sentenced to seven years' hard labour.

Not long afterwards another animal was mutilated in Wyrley and further anonymous letters were sent to the police. One might have thought that these incidents would have raised official doubts about Edalji's guilt, but the official explanation was that he was the obvious ringleader of a gang and that its members were still at large and intent on causing trouble.

Nevertheless, there were growing public misgivings about his conviction. The notion that a meek solicitor, the son of a churchman, was the leader of a ruthless gang that mutilated animals at night for no reason seemed, to many, patently absurd. *Truth* magazine took up his case and Sir George Lewis, the pre-eminent criminal lawyer of the day, publicly expressed the view that the conviction was fatally flawed. The Reverend Edalji published an eloquent and closely argued pamphlet asserting his son's innocence. R. D. Yelverton, the former chief justice of the Bahamas and a zealous legal reformer, helped organise a petition with 10,000 signatures, which was presented to the Home Office calling for the case to be reviewed, to no avail. Then, in October 1906, after three years in prison, Edalji was suddenly freed, without explanation and without a pardon, meaning he could no longer practise law or receive any compensation. He was a discharged convict, still under police supervision.

Desperate to clear his name if for no other reason than to return to work, Edalji, who had devoured the Sherlock Holmes stories while he was in prison, wrote to Conan Doyle for help. Conan Doyle read his letter, and the enclosed press cuttings, with a sense of mounting outrage. To him, the issue was utterly simple: if Edalji was guilty he deserved every day of his seven-year sentence; if he was not, then he deserved a pardon, restitution and an apology for the ordeal of his arrest, trial and three years in prison. On the strength of what he had read, Conan Doyle was inclined to think he was innocent, but he wanted a meeting with the young man before finally making up his mind.

Conan Doyle dictated a reply to Edalji, suggesting they meet in the lobby at the Grand Hotel, Charing Cross. Uncharacteristically, Conan Doyle was late. Immediately recognising the dark-skinned young man reading a newspaper in an armchair, he was about to stride across the room with an apology when something checked him. Instead, he stood for several minutes observing that Edalji was holding the newspaper very close to his face, at a slight angle. It was evident he was extremely short-sighted. When he introduced himself, Conan Doyle's first question, after explaining that he had once studied to be an eye surgeon, was to ask Edalji if he suffered from astigmatic myopia. Edalji admitted he had always had very short sight. Was this not, Conan Doyle enquired, a factor in the trial? Edalji smiled ruefully and said his counsel did not think it necessary to call an optician as a witness, since the evidence against him was so slight he could imagine no other outcome than an acquittal.

Conan Doyle arranged for Edalji to be examined at his expense by a leading London eye specialist, Kenneth Scott. He was also by then more or less satisfied that Edalji was probably the victim of a dreadful miscarriage of justice. 'I realised,' he wrote in his memoirs, 'that I was in the presence of an appalling tragedy, and that I was called to do what I could to set it right.' Scott's report supported his view: Edalji was suffering from eight dioptres – a measurement of the eye's refractive power – of myopia. Poring through the trial documents, Conan Doyle learned that the prosecution's key witness, the graphologist Gurrin, had once before been responsible for sending an innocent man to prison.

Conan Doyle wanted to view the scene of the crime and contacted Anson to arrange a visit, mentioning that he intended to write an article about the case for the *Daily Telegraph*. The Chief Constable, flattered by the famous author's interest and confident that he would be able to convince him of Edalji's guilt, offered to help in any way he could, even extending the hospitality of his own home, and added that he would be interested in 'what Sherlock Holmes might have to say about a real life case'. (This last remark would have grated on Conan Doyle.)

On 3 January 1907 Conan Doyle travelled to Great Wyrley, where he interviewed the Reverend Edalji and traipsed from the vicarage to Plant Pit Meadow, over very rough ground that involved crossing the London and North-Western Railway tracks and skirting clumps of gorse which confirmed Conan Doyle's theory that Edalji, with his chronically short sight, could never have made the same trip on a dark, wet night. The mud in the field was of a yellow-reddish hue, quite different from that found on Edalji's boots. And whoever was responsible would also have had to sidle up close enough to strike; Edalji had no experience with animals of any kind. His squint, he added, 'gave the sufferer a vacant, bulge-eyed, staring appearance, which, when taken with his dark skin, must assuredly have made him seem a very queer man to the eyes of an English village, and therefore to be naturally associated with any queer event'.[3]

After talking to a number of other residents he went on to meet Captain Anson, who had promised a full briefing. Anson wasted no time in setting Conan Doyle right about the Edaljis. It was necessary, he said, to delve behind the veneer of George Edalji's life: while he seemed a respectable young solicitor, he was in fact dishonest and mired in gambling debts; he had accused the police of stealing two £100 notes from his office which he was later seen cashing at a bank in Birmingham; he was responsible for writing the poison pen letters – and his father had lied in the witness box. His eyes had been examined in prison and little was found to be wrong with his sight; in any case, Anson was positive he could have found his way blindfolded to Plant Pit Meadow. (Conan Doyle did not mention the tests he had had carried out on Edalji's sight.) Anson's *coup de grâce* was slyly to suggest there was a sexual motive to the sleeping arrangements at the vicarage, saying he 'presumed' there was a good reason for George to sleep with his father. Conan Doyle was appalled; he was more than ever convinced that Edalji was innocent and the likely victim of racial prejudice.

'What aroused my indignation,' he wrote later, 'and gave me the driving force to carry the thing through, was the utter helplessness of this forlorn little group of people, the coloured clergyman in his strange position, the brave blue-eyed, grey-haired wife, the young daughter, baited by brutal boors and having the police, who should have been their natural protectors, adopting from the beginning a harsh tone towards them and accusing them, beyond all sense and reason, of being the cause of their own troubles and of persecuting and maligning themselves.'

Back in London, Conan Doyle's sense of fair play prevailed, and he wrote to Anson to warn him that publication of his article was imminent and that the Staffordshire police would not come well out of it. He explained he was 'honour bound' to do justice to his enquiries. He disclosed the results of Edalji's eye test and pointed out that if Anson had taken the trouble to make the walk himself from the vicarage he would never have described it as easy. He also absolutely rejected claims that the Edaljis were liars and reprimanded Anson for his insinuation about the sleeping arrangements. He could see nothing suspicious in it and cautioned Anson that 'if similar reports have gone to the Home Office and stand in the way of justice, then the Edaljis must find some public way of showing how baseless they are. In this they have my sympathy.'[4] Anson soon denounced Conan Doyle publicly as an 'absolutely dishonest and unscrupulous man', 'an utter fool' and 'a knave'.[5]

On 11 January the *Daily Telegraph* published the first instalment of an 18,000-word article spread across 14 columns over several pages, and titled 'The Case of Mr George Edalji' by Arthur Conan Doyle. 'I hope that the effect of my narrative,' he began, 'will be to raise such a wave of feeling in this country as will make some public reconsideration of his case inevitable.' He went on effectively to demolish the prosecution case, spoke bitterly of the injustice involved, attacked the police prejudice and inefficiency, and called for a pardon. Underlying the whole messy affair was racism, he wrote, and while it was possible to excuse the feelings of uneducated countrymen, it was less easy to excuse the Chief Constable, whose dislike of the Edaljis had infected the entire force.

'I have examined a very large number of documents,' he stated, 'and tested a long series of real and alleged facts. During all that time I have kept my mind open, but I can unreservedly say that in the whole research I have never come across any considerations which would make it, I will not say probable, but in any way credible, that George Edalji had anything to do, either directly or indirectly, with the outrages or with the anonymous letters.' Edalji's 'footprints', allegedly found close to the mutilated pony, were actually obtained – long after the field had been trampled by police officers, passing miners and sightseers – by pressing one of Edalji's boots into the mud alongside a likely-looking print, then measuring both and concluding they were the same. Conan Doyle maintained that whoever carried out the attack would have been covered in the pony's blood, yet the two bloodstains on the sleeve of Edalji's coat were insignificant: 'The most adept operator who ever lived would not rip up a horse with a razor upon a dark night and have only two threepenny-bit spots of blood to show for it. The idea is beyond all argument.' And the horse hairs on the coat could easily be explained by the fact that it was bundled up, as evidence, with a sample of skin cut from the dead pony.

'These wrongs would have been almost comic had they not had so tragic an upshot. If the whole land had been raked, I do not think that it would have been possible to find a man who was so unlikely, and indeed so incapable, of committing such actions.' Edalji was of 'irreproachable character'; his former schoolmaster 'testified to his mild and tractable disposition'. He had served his time with a Birmingham solicitor, who gave him the highest references. He had never shown traits of cruelty . . . Finally, he was a total abstainer, and so blind that he was unable to recognise anyone at the distance of six yards. It was clear that the inherent improbability of such a man committing a long succession of bloody and brutal crimes was so great that it could suggest insanity. Yet there had never 'been any indication even of eccentricity in George Edalji. On the contrary, his statements of defence were measured and rational', and he had survived experiences 'which might well have unhinged a weaker intellect'.[6]

Conan Doyle likened it to the squalid Dreyfus case. Captain Alfred Dreyfus, a promising young artillery officer in the French army, had been arrested in 1894 on trumped-up espionage charges, found guilty of treason and sent to Devil's Island in French Guyana. Emile Zola's famous open letter to the French president, 'J'accuse', focused public attention on the case, and Dreyfus was finally exonerated in July 1906, but the affair exposed bitter divisions in French society. The similarities were striking: both involved the manipulation of evidence by authorities positive they had the right man, and both involved forgery, a miscarriage of justice and racial prejudice. In both cases a famous writer came to the rescue.

Dreyfus had been made a scapegoat because he was a Jew, Conan Doyle pointed out; Edalji because his father had been born a Parsee. And this in England, the home of liberty and the same country that had expressed horror over the Dreyfus affair. All official remedies to right the wrong done to Edalji were exhausted. 'The door is shut in our faces,' Conan Doyle concluded. 'Now we turn to the last tribunal of all, a tribunal which never errs when the facts are laid before them, and we ask the public of Great Britain whether this thing is to go on.'

Overnight, the case became a national cause célèbre. 'England soon rang,' Conan Doyle recalled, 'with the wrongs of George Edalji.'[7] The letters page of the *Telegraph* was dominated by outraged readers expressing their disgust at Edalji's plight, and other newspapers, both at home and abroad, quickly picked up the story, many of them focusing on Conan Doyle turning into Sherlock Holmes. A leader in the *Daily Chronicle,* for example, suggested that at last Sherlock Holmes was engaged on a real investigation: 'It is a tribute to the force with which he [Conan Doyle] has impressed the personality of his hero upon the reader's mind that one instinctively merges the creator in his creation, and thinks of this special investigation as the work of the great Sherlock.'

At Undershaw Conan Doyle was swamped by letters of congratulation, many suggesting further leads. Not all of them were entirely complimentary: 'A.C.' wrote from the Junior Garrick Club: 'Of course you know the miscreant, felon & convict, your own associate, and bosom friend, the brute "Edalji", he, and he alone, is the foul fiend . . . the infernal hell-hound.' But George Meredith wrote on 14 January praising Conan Doyle for the 'great public service' he had performed. 'I shall not mention the name which must have become wearisome to your ears,' he added, 'but the creator of the marvellous Amateur Detective has shown what he can do in the life of breath . . .' J. M. Barrie chimed in a few weeks later: 'I could not doubt that at all events Edalji had been convicted without any evidence worthy of the name.'

The media furore and public outcry forced the government to take action. England was virtually the only civilised country in the world not to have a criminal appeal court, and so the Home Secretary, Herbert Gladstone, announced the setting up of a committee of inquiry to look into the case. Unfortunately one of the three men appointed to the commission, Sir Albert de Rutzen, Chief Magistrate of the Metropolitan Police Courts, was a second cousin of Captain Anson.

For his trouble, Conan Doyle began receiving deranged letters in the same hand as those addressed to the Edalji family. 'I know from a detective of Scotland Yard,' his anonymous correspondent wrote, 'that if you write to Gladstone and say you find Edalji is guilty after all they will make you a lord next year. Is it not better to be a lord than to run the risk of losing kidneys and liver. Think of all the ghoulish murders that are committed why then should you escape?' The letters insisted that it was Edalji who had written the earlier missives: 'The proof of what I tell you is in the writing he put into the papers when they loosed him out of prison where he ought to have been kept along with his dad and all black and yellow faced Jews . . . Nobody could copy his writing like that, you blind fool.'

Undeterred, Conan Doyle continued his own investigation, now determined to find the real culprit and provide complete exoneration for George Edalji. A schoolteacher in Great Wyrley had written with valuable new information, claiming that a retired teacher in Walsall had been the victim of a very similar poison pen campaign.

Accusations entirely without foundation had created a poisonous atmosphere of innuendo which made it virtually impossible for him to carry out his duties; in the end he resigned. He suspected, but could not prove, that the author of most of the letters was a boy called Royden Sharp, an incorrigible troublemaker. Among Sharp's misdemeanours at school, before he was expelled, was forging letters.

Conan Doyle employed a private detective agency to carry out further enquiries. It was discovered that Sharp, who had previously worked for a butcher, had a hankering to go to sea and found a berth on a ship out of Liverpool in 1895, when the hoaxes and the letters ceased, and he did not return until Christmas 1902, shortly before the first horse was maimed. During 1902 he had served on board a cattle ship and had thus become familiar with working with animals. Wilfred Greatorex, Sharp's guardian, testified that Sharp had shown his wife a horse lancet, an instrument used for blood-letting which Conan Doyle thought exactly the kind of weapon to inflict the peculiar injuries on the maimed animals – shallow incisions through the skin and muscles but which had not penetrated the gut. Sharp had apparently boasted to Mrs Greatorex that it was used to kill cattle, and she told him to put it away, saying, 'You don't want me to think you are the man, do you?' Sharp's name had been given to the police as a possible suspect when the spate of animal mutilations began, but no action had been taken. 'The case against my quarry is already very strong,' Conan Doyle wrote in a letter to the Mam dated 29 January 1907. 'But I have five separate lines of inquiry on foot by which I hope to make it overwhelming. It will be a great stroke of luck if I can lay him by the heels!'

Now in full Sherlock Holmes mode, he compiled a detailed dossier entitled 'Statement of the Case Against Royden Sharp' in which he claimed that Sharp was 'in all respects peculiarly fitted to have done these crimes' and that there was much evidence which should cause him to be 'regarded with the gravest suspicion'. The report traced Sharp's early life and alleged he had shown marked criminal tendencies from a young age, including setting fire to a hayrick at the age of 12 and slashing upholstery on trains with a knife. His record at Walsall Grammar School (where the key had been stolen) was dismal: he was caned almost daily for misbehaviour, was caught cheating, was suspected of writing anonymous letters threatening violence and was eventually expelled. Conan Doyle made great play of the fact that Sharp was apprenticed to a butcher, 'thus learning how to use a knife on animals' and that the letters and hoaxes ceased while he was away at sea. The letters had named people unknown to the Edaljis but known to the Sharp family. Sharp was said to be affected by a new moon and the first four cattle maimings occurred immediately following a new moon. And a handwriting expert confirmed that Sharp was responsible for the anonymous letters Conan Doyle had received.

To Conan Doyle, his case was conclusive, but he would have done well to have abided by the Holmes dictum in 'A Scandal in Bohemia': 'It is a capital mistake to theorise before one has data. Insensibly, one begins to twist facts to suit theories, instead of theories to suit facts.' In truth, Conan Doyle's hypothesis about the guilt of Royden Sharp was deeply flawed, being based almost entirely on local gossip in a community rife with rumour and tainted by his deep antipathy towards the disreputable Sharp family, whom he considered mentally and morally degenerate without having met them. His dislike of Anson and the single-minded fervour of his desire to exonerate Edalji further prejudiced his views. But as so often in his life, once he had made up his mind, nothing would change it.

Conan Doyle submitted the dossier, complete with witness statements, to Gladstone's committee of inquiry. It fell on stony ground: Conan Doyle was informed by Sir Charles Matthews, a Whitehall mandarin appointed to consider Conan Doyle's allegations, that the 'evidence' he had presented was so insubstantial that the case would be thrown out by any judge.

Anson, of course, was delighted by the rejection of Conan Doyle's dossier and wrote a crowing note to inform him that one of his principal informants had been removed to a lunatic asylum suffering from 'acute religious mania, after making two attempts at self-destruction'. He would later point out that Conan Doyle had not produced 'one scrap of real evidence . . . nor has any single convincing reason been adduced for believing him [Sharp] to have been guilty of any letter writing of a criminal nature . . . a great part of the statements of Sir Arthur are grossly inaccurate'. He was particularly incensed that Conan

Doyle had forwarded his letters to the Home Office along with the suggestion that Anson was alleging the Reverend Edalji and his son were committing sodomy. Anson indignantly denied ever having made allegations of immorality and accused Conan Doyle of behaving like a 'contemptible brute'.[8] Conan Doyle was eventually obliged to withdraw the accusation, but the vitriolic feud between the two men continued for years, with each complaining to the Home Office about the other.

In May 1907 the findings of the committee of inquiry were made public. It decided that Edalji's conviction on a charge of horse maiming was unsafe and thus he would be granted a pardon, but added that it believed Edalji had indeed written the anonymous letters: 'We think it quite likely that they are the letters of an innocent man, but a wrong-headed and malicious man, indulging in a piece of impish mischief, pretending to know what he may know nothing of, in order to puzzle the police, and increase their difficulties in a very difficult investigation.' To that extent, the commission concluded, he had brought his troubles on himself and would not therefore be offered any compensation.

While the Law Society readmitted Edalji to the roll of solicitors with leave to practise, Conan Doyle was irate that he had not been completely exonerated. It was, he asserted, a 'wretched decision'. He wrote again to the *Daily Telegraph*, complaining that the commission's conclusions were 'absolutely illogical and untenable', offered to demonstrate in half an hour that Edalji could not have written the letters and asked if anything could be more un-English than a free pardon without reparation. Edalji's father also wrote, describing his son's treatment by both the police and the Home Office as 'most shocking and heartless'. This might have been diplomacy, he added, 'but it is not what they would have done if he had been the son of an English squire or an English nobleman'.

The *Daily Telegraph* set up an appeal fund for Edalji which raised £300 and Conan Doyle continued to write articles about the injustice, prompting questions to be asked in Parliament of the Home Secretary. Was there any precedent for not paying compensation to someone wrongly convicted and subsequently granted a free pardon? Would a new inquiry be set up to look into the question of the handwriting?

Would all police reports and communications on the subject of the Edalji case be made public? And was Mr Edalji being thus treated 'because he is not an Englishman'? On all questions Mr Gladstone declined to answer.

George Edalji left Great Wyrley, took up a position with a firm in London and practised as a solicitor for many years. He never married and from the early 1930s lived with his sister, Maud, in Welwyn Garden City until his death in 1953 at the age of 77. The anonymous letters continued intermittently for twenty-five years, as did further outbreaks of animal mutilation. In 1934 Enoch Knowles, a labourer at an iron works in Wednesbury, was arrested, admitted writing the letters and was sent to prison. But no one else was ever arrested for mutilating animals in Great Wyrley.

Throughout the early stages of the Edalji campaign, Conan Doyle had contrived to spend as much time as he decently could with Jean Leckie. After Touie's death she was quickly assimilated into Conan Doyle's family life, visiting Undershaw with her brother, Malcolm, as chaperon, when the children were home for the holidays. The rift between Conan Doyle and the Hornungs had evidently been healed, since in July 1907 Jean was invited to the Hornungs' home in Kensington for the Mam's 70th birthday party and accompanied the family group to dinner at the Gaiety and then to the theatre.

There was, of course, no question of Conan Doyle remarrying within a year of his wife's death, but Jean was not of a mind to wait much longer than the customary twelve-month period of mourning, and a date in September for the wedding had been agreed. Conan Doyle accepted the impossibility of starting a new life with her at Undershaw, which was so redolent of his first wife, and bought a substantial Victorian villa called Little Windlesham, on the edge of the Ashdown Forest in Crowborough, not far from her parents.

On 18 September 1907 Sir Arthur Conan Doyle and Miss Jean Leckie were quietly married at St Margaret's church in Westminster, with only close relatives and a few friends present. The groom was 48 years old, the bride 32. His brother-in-law, the Reverend Cyril Angell, conducted the ceremony and Innes Doyle was best man. Conan Doyle wore a traditional frock coat, striped trousers, a white gardenia in his buttonhole and, according to one newspaper report, a 'beaming smile', while the bride was in a 'particularly beautiful' dress of ivory silk and Spanish lace and held a bouquet of 'choice white exotics'. After the ceremony, Conan Doyle carried his bride up the red-carpeted stairs to the Whitehall Rooms at the Hotel Metropole for a reception attended by 250 guests, among them Jerome K. Jerome, Bram Stoker, J. M. Barrie, George Newnes, Greenhough Smith – and George Edalji. (Mr and Mrs Bryan Waller were notably absent.) The happy couple left for a two-month honeymoon in Paris, Berlin, Venice, Rome and Constantinople.

The marriage was reported across the world, from Berlin to Buenos Aires, although no dispatch was more mystifying than that in Belgium's *La Chronique*: 'Conan Doyle, the English writer who invented the genial type of detective, Sherlock Holmes, has just been married. A French journalist tells us that the young lady was enthralled into marriage by the extraordinary adventures of the king of detectives.'

CHAPTER 16

A NEW LIFE WITH JEAN

HERE WAS LITTLE DOUBT THAT Conan Doyle was besotted with his bride and would remain so for the rest of his life. Whenever they were apart, he would write adoring notes to her, sometimes twice a day, addressing her as 'my own darling', 'my angel', 'my own love', 'my wonderful brave girl', 'my little girlie'. On a lecture tour of the United States in 1923, at the age of 64, his letters were reminiscent of those of a lovelorn teenager: 'Oh girlie, it will be good to put my arms around you'; 'You darling, I do want you so!'; 'Don't forget, my heart's darling, that you are the best thing that ever happened to me. It must be joy to be a woman when a man can say that with a full heart.' [1] This elderly Victorian gentleman even alluded, on occasion, to s-e-x: 'It will be a weary old jumper who comes back to you. His first jump will be into your arms. His next one into bed. Goodbye my sweet one. I hunger for your kiss . . .'

The new Lady Conan Doyle, for her part, made it clear she worshipped her husband and expected everyone else to do the same. An excellent organiser and accomplished hostess, she swiftly took charge of the household at Windlesham and of his life. She had always craved the limelight (she was given to theatrical gestures, perhaps as the result of her operatic training) and revelled in her new role, on centre stage at last, as the wife of a famous and titled author. Rather less welcome was her role as stepmother to Mary and Kingsley, then aged 18 and 14 respectively.

Kingsley was safely ensconced at Eton, but Mary had finished school and assumed she would be making her home with her father and her new stepmother at Windlesham. Jean had other ideas and in the summer of 1907 Mary found herself rapidly dispatched to study music in Dresden. She had absolutely no desire to go and was certain that her stepmother simply wanted her out of the way, but her father, seemingly in thrall to his manipulative wife, was not inclined to listen to Mary's protests. No sooner had she arrived in Dresden than she began fretting in a series of plaintive letters to her brother about whether she would be allowed home for Christmas: 'My boy – if I don't come home for Xmas there will be *words* – for the girls I travelled out with are returning for 3 weeks, and coming back again after. So there are people to conduct me both ways. Surely if *they* can return, I can . . .'

A few days later she speculated for the first time that perhaps her father and his new wife actually did not *want* her to return: 'I do – oh so hope I shall come home for Xmas. Because there is no reason why I shouldn't, unless they want to clear us both out of Windlesham, and have it to themselves for Xmas. We're a bit of a mistake now. But never mind old chap, *we'll* stand together whatever happens.' Mary agonised about when she should ask her father for permission to return, but when she did finally pluck up courage she was told it was out of the question. In an indignant letter to Kingsley she said her father had told her he did not expect to see her again for another nine months; he had accused her of weakness of character for even asking if she could return, leaving her 'awfully low and depressed'. She added a sad little note: 'I can't think why my father is so hard – I have not had one gentle word, or sign of love from him since Mother died. One would have thought it would be otherwise. But no – life has all gone to make him a very hard man . . .'[2]

In fact, judging from another long letter to her brother, Mary managed to enjoy Christmas in Dresden despite her disappointment. She described her various presents and added without comment: 'This morning I got a line from Jean with a Postal Order for £1 to get whatever I wanted.' She was embarrassed at not being allowed home and felt she had to lie to her friends to explain why she was being ignored by her father and stepmother. 'It has hurt my pride to be put in such a position,' she said. 'It's for all the world as if they didn't care. Well I suppose that is the truth just at present. But at least they might hide it more decently . . .'

Kingsley was sent to spend the holidays with the Hornungs. He visited Windlesham before returning to Eton but evidently to no warm welcome and wrote to Mary about it. 'Dear old Boy,' she replied, 'I feel alternately angry and sad for you. I consider the least Daddy and Jean could have done, considering they denied you me – your natural companion – was to have made you as at home and happy in the New Life as possible. And in neglecting you like that, I consider they have let slip a very important duty. I'm disappointed in both of them.'

Mary was both confused and angry but recognised she was helpless to influence events. When her brother wrote to tell her that their father was upset because he had been ill – he had been suffering from haemorrhoids – and she had not bothered to write to him, she replied that she had been sending letters every day. She wondered if his secretary, Woodie, had had the 'colossal cheek' put them to one side because they would be full of 'money matters and complaints', but she could scarcely credit it. She did not speculate that her stepmother might have been involved.

Jean's influence was almost certainly behind Conan Doyle's sudden and completely uncharacteristic concern about the expense of keeping his daughter in Dresden. Now a wealthy man, he had always been extraordinarily generous to his family, but when Mary asked him if he would pay for her to go to Berlin to see an opera she had been studying, he sent her a cheque for £10 and enclosed a note explaining that he could not afford, at the same time, to pay for Kingsley to visit her, as had been arranged. He suggested, unkindly, that she should choose between the opera and her brother's visit, although in the end he relented.

In the summer of 1908 Mary was at last allowed home but the visit was not a success. She wanted to show her father and stepmother what she had learned in Dresden and offered to sing for them. Jean pointedly refused to accompany her on the piano and so Mary accompanied herself. Later Jean told her husband privately that his daughter's singing was flat and that she stood no chance of forging a career in music. Conan Doyle waited until Mary was back in Dresden before passing on the bad news, saying that while she had a sweet voice it would never stand out from others and that her ear was by no means infallible: 'We both sing flat without knowing it . . . and it is not knowing it that makes our cases bad.'

Mary was indignant and realised that her father, who had little interest in, or knowledge of music would hardly have presumed to criticise her musical ability without input from the 'trained mezzo-soprano' who was his wife. The scales had fallen from her eyes and she could hardly wait to tell Kingsley: 'Well my dear, do you know what it all amounts to? Simply this – Jean wants the coast clear for herself, and she doesn't want any rivalry or competition. I might possibly in the future put her in the shade, therefore I'm politely invited to leave it alone! . . . Jean wants to reign supreme in her one Art, therefore I am at all hazards to be discouraged.'[3] She added sadly that she now realised that in all future dealings it was Jean, and not her father, with whom she would have to reckon and that if Jean considered her tuition an unnecessary expense she was 'done for'. It would break her heart, she said, if she was forced to give up singing.

Mary wisely kept her counsel and was unfailingly polite towards Jean in her letters home. When Conan Doyle wrote in October to tell her that Jean was pregnant, she replied immediately: 'I can't tell you how much the thought of it gladdens me . . . Best love and a special kiss for Jean. Ever your affectionate, Mary.'[4]

———◆———

Conan Doyle wrote very little fiction during the first year following his wedding. He was too bound up in his new life to think of work. He produced 'The Adventure of Wisteria Lodge', a two-parter which launched a new, occasional Holmes series in the *Strand*, but otherwise occupied himself with his marriage, while supervising major extensions to Windlesham, working in the garden, playing golf and being dazzled by Jean's talents as a hostess. They entertained frequently. The enormous billiard room at Windlesham, which ran from the front to the back of the house, was also used as a ballroom and could comfortably accommodate 150 couples. At one end was a harp and Jean's grand piano – and at the other was Conan Doyle's billiard table. Over one huge fireplace was the Van Dyck painting of the Earl of Stafford, inherited from his grandfather, John Doyle, and over another a stag's head draped with a bandolier he had brought back from the Boer War. Animal-skin rugs were strewn across the polished wood floor. Here the new Lady Doyle held court, charming her husband's many influential friends at dinner parties and dances while he looked on proudly, smiling indulgently as she sparkled. 'Jean is simply splendid,' he wrote to his mother. 'She is as energetic as ever, gives dinner parties and has become quite the society queen here. Everyone admires and loves her. The more I see her, the more wonderful does she seem . . .'[5]

At the invitation of the *Daily Mail*, Conan Doyle covered the marathon at the 1908 Olympic Games in London and was sitting in the front row when the plucky little Italian athlete Dorando Pietri wobbled into the stadium on the point of total exhaustion, turned right instead of left, collapsed, was helped up by doctors and fell three more times before being half carried across the finishing line by race officials, to the cheers of the huge crowd. A few hours later, it was announced that he had been disqualified for receiving assistance. Like almost everyone else in the stadium, Conan Doyle thought Pietri deserved the gold medal for guts alone and started a subscription for him in the *Daily Mail* which raised £300, enough for him to start a baker's shop in his Italian village.

On 17 March – St Patrick's Day – 1909, Jean gave birth to their first child, a boy they christened Denis Percy Stewart – the 'Percy' a concession to the Mam's insistence that the family descended from the illustrious Percy family of Northumberland.

By then Conan Doyle was back at work and in June *The Fires of Fate*, a play he adapted from *The Tragedy of the Korosko*, opened at the Lyric Theatre in London. Billed as a 'modern morality play', Conan Doyle had written it for his friend Lewis Waller, who played the leading role of Colonel Cyril Egerton, a debonair military man who learns that he has a rare illness that will kill him within a year. He briefly considers suicide, but then decides to lead a party of tourists on an adventurous expedition up the Nile. Inevitably he falls in love with a comely American, but his illness presents him declaring himself. When the party is captured by dervishes, Egerton receives a serious blow on the head but manages to escape and organise a rescue force. Conan Doyle, who stage managed the production, manoeuvred a happy, if unlikely, ending: the blow on the head miraculously effects a cure for the colonel.

Conan Doyle was never a good judge of his own work and told family and friends that he thought *The Fires of Fate* (despite its turgid and melodramatic plot) was by far the best thing he had done for the stage. The audience seemed to agree and was brought to its feet at the curtain call on the opening night. 'Such moments to a dramatist,' Conan Doyle noted, 'give a thrill of personal satisfaction such as the most successful novelist never can feel. There is no more subtle pleasure if you are really satisfied with your work than to sit in the shadow of a box and watch not the play but the audience.' He loved to recount the dubious story of how, at a later performance, a friend of Innes, an officer who had won both the Victoria Cross and the DSO, had to be restrained from clambering up onto the stage to help when the hapless tourists were being beaten by their Arab captors.

Paradoxically for a man so happily embarked on a new marriage, that same year Conan Doyle accepted an invitation to become president of the Divorce Law Reform Union, a campaigning group set up to press for equality for men and woman seeking to escape an unhappy marriage. Divorce in Britain was virtually impossible before 1857 but that year the government of the day, bowing to social, moral and political pressure, approved a law making divorce legal, although on very different terms for the sexes. While a man could obtain a divorce simply on the basis of his wife's adultery, a woman not only had to prove her husband's adultery, but also had to show either that she had been deserted by him for at least two years, or that she had been the victim of sustained and systematic brutality (men were allowed by law to 'chastise' their wives). Not only that, but divorce was expensive and the inheritance and property laws meant very few women had the resources to initiate divorce proceedings.

With his high regard for social justice, Conan Doyle recognised the system was manifestly unfair. He drew a characteristic analogy with the old days of chivalry, when young knights came to the rescue of damsels in distress. By supporting divorce law reform, he said, modern-day knights had the opportunity to rescue tens of thousands of women from 'hopeless lifelong misery, from the embraces of drunkards, from bondage to cruel men, from the iron which fetter locks them to the felon or the hopeless maniac'.

As president of the group he sought to motivate public opinion with a well-tried formula – the pamphlet. *Divorce Law Reform*, by Sir Arthur Conan Doyle, called for fundamental changes in the law, with no distinction between the sexes and extending the right to divorce when either party had been deserted for an uninterrupted period of at least three years. Anticipating opposition from the church, Conan Doyle went on the attack, asserting that the existing law was a 'wretched attempt to compromise between the crying needs of human life and the objection of theologians . . . Every church has a right, which none can deny, to prescribe conduct for its own members. None has the right to enforce its views upon the general public. If it pleases the ecclesiastical mind to consider that our present ethical customs should be regulated by its own particular interpretation of certain words uttered 2,000 years ago, then that is its own affair.' He further enraged churchmen by suggesting in a letter to the *Daily Telegraph* that bonding an innocent woman to a drunk by marital vows was not so much divine as degenerate. He was greatly amused to hear that he had been denounced from a multitude of pulpits as a man without Christian beliefs, incapable of understanding the moral and religious necessity of the institution of marriage.

Under Conan Doyle's leadership, the Divorce Law Reform Union persuaded the government to set up a Royal Commission of Inquiry which eventually adopted his principal recommendation, that 'the cause for divorce should be the same between the sexes'. It would, however, be 1923, before the church's fervent resistance could be overcome and the law reformed.

Conan Doyle had barely put down his pen after finishing the divorce pamphlet before he was picking it up again to write another, on a very different subject – a 'crime unparalleled in its horror'[6] taking place in the Congo. Africa in the late nineteenth century was effectively dismembered by white colonialists, and in 1885 at the Conference of Berlin a vast area, five times as big as France, was formally acquired by King Leopold II of Belgium and named the Congo Free State – a supreme irony since it was neither free nor a state, but the private fiefdom of the King. The Conference of Berlin was convened to guarantee free trade, suppress slavery and ensure the rights and religious freedoms of the natives. None of this came to pass, since the new Congo Free State harboured huge reserves of ivory and rubber in what were called 'vacant lands'. Exploitation of the rubber industry began immediately by tyranny, enslaving and terrorising the local population to provide ever increasing exports to Europe. Natives were deprived of all rights to work their own land, except under compulsion for the benefit of the state. Arbitrary quotas of rubber production were imposed by force and any resistance met with bestial measures. A private army, the Force Publique, spread terror by routinely amputating the limbs of men, women and children. Between 1885 and 1908 some ten million Congolese died from execution, abuse, overwork or disease.

The terrible events unfolding in the Congo were first brought to the world's attention in 1903 by a campaigning journalist, Edmund Dene Morel, sometime editor of the *West African Mail,* and Roger Casement, the British consul in the capital, Boma. Casement, who had arrived in the Congo in 1884 at the age of 20, travelled extensively through the region and sent a total of 43 reports to the Foreign Office in London detailing an appalling catalogue of torture, mutilation and summary executions inflicted on the native population, often working chained together, by the white overseers. Workers were lashed with a *chicotte*, a vicious whip made out of sun-dried hippopotamus hide, women were raped and children removed from their families. As a result of Casement's work, Britain launched a diplomatic initiative which forced Leopold to appoint a Commission of Inquiry. The members were chosen by the King himself and predictably found little fault, although the day after meeting members of the Commission the Belgian Governor General mysteriously committed suicide.

Meanwhile, Morel and Casement formed the Congo Reform Association to step up international pressure on Belgium. In 1908 Leopold was forced to cede the territory to the Belgian government, but little else changed and the Congo Reform Association canvassed prominent individuals for support, among them the writers Joseph Conrad, Rudyard Kipling and Arthur Conan Doyle. Conrad, who had witnessed the genocide at first hand as the captain of a Congo steamer and who had used the experience in his novella, *The Heart of Darkness*, a powerful indictment of the evils of imperialism, declined to help, claiming he was only 'a wretched novelist'. Kipling was concerned about the political implications of intervention and worried that Germany might 'fold her protective wings around Belgium'. Conan Doyle, the great crusader, willingly leapt into the fray. 'The duty which we owe to the weak,' he had written presciently in *Micah Clarke*, 'overrides all other duties and is superior to all circumstances.'

After meeting Morel in the summer of 1909 in the smoking room of a London hotel, Conan Doyle offered to help by speaking on behalf of the Association and by writing an account of events to date. 'I came away deeply stirred by the magnetism of his personality, touched and grateful,' Morel wrote later. 'Here was a friend, indeed. And right well did he prove it in the days to come. I pitched all my voluminous scribblings at his head and he set himself to master every detail of a most complicated and protracted struggle. For a couple of weeks, hardly a day passed without a letter from him. Then, when he had probed the whole thing to the bottom, he shut himself in his study and worked like a demon, hardly giving himself time to shave, as he put it.'[7]

As on other occasions when he had been fired by a 'burning indignation', Conan Doyle worked virtually non-stop and claimed to have written 45,000 words in just eight days, sleeping only for about four hours at night and drinking cup after cup of coffee. He set himself a target for the number of words he had to write each day and would stay up until dawn to compensate if he fell behind. Kipling counselled caution, writing to him on 29 August 1909: 'Dear Doyle, I knew you were keen on the state of affairs in the Congo, which is pretty bad and I am sure what you write will wake people up. But the way I see it is that we haven't anything resembling an efficient army *or* a navy to back up our representations with; and if England goes into the Congo business, isn't she liable to lay herself open to the humiliation of having her bluff called? Neither France nor Russia are able to help us and if Belgium chooses to tell us to mind our own affairs (with a few nasty remarks about India thrown in) what can we do?' Kipling warned that Germany might go to the aid of Belgium and 'the rest would be a simple sum in arithmetic of men, guns and efficient boats'.[8]

But Conan Doyle valued people above politics and *The Crime in the Congo* was a raw, passionate indictment describing in unflinching detail 'the sack of a country, the spoilation of a nation, the greatest crime in all history'. Using horrific first-person testimonies provided by Morel, he painted a picture of a regime which treated natives with barely credible barbarity and turned the Congo into 'a hell on earth'. Workers who resisted were summarily shot and then had their left hands cut off: 'The soldiers do not care who they shoot down, and they most often shoot poor, helpless women and harmless children. These hands – the hands of men, women and children – are placed in rows before the Commissary, who counts them to see the soldiers have not wasted cartridges.'

The Crime in the Congo was widely distributed throughout Europe and the United States, and the author sent personal copies to influential politicians and statesmen around the world, including Kaiser Wilhelm II, President Theodore Roosevelt and Winston Churchill, then President of the Board of Trade. He followed it up by writing a long circular letter to the editors of sixty American newspapers urging them to support intervention. The situation in the Congo, he said, was 'a mixture of wholesale expropriation and wholesale massacre all done under the guise of philanthropy, and with the lowest commercial motives as a reason. It is this sordid cause, and the unctuous hypocrisy which make the crime unparalleled in its horror . . . there is not a grotesque, obscene, or ferocious torture which diseased human ingenuity could invent which has not been used against these harmless and helpless people.'

After the publication of his treatise, Conan Doyle embarked on a speaking tour of Britain, delivering nine lectures around the country. His second London engagement, at the Albert Hall on 19 November, was chaired by the Archbishop of Canterbury. Conan Doyle had invited Cardinal Francis Bourne, the Archbishop of Westminster, but was rebuffed, the cardinal making it clear that he did not approve of the Association's activities and writing that a 'perusal' of *The Crime in the Congo* had only served to strengthen his distrust of the methods used by the Association and his reluctance to see Catholics identified with it in any way. The cardinal may have been influenced by the fact that he was educated at the University of Louvain, or by Conan Doyle's

attack on the church for failing in its secular duties by maintaining a
silence about the atrocities taking place. What was happening in the
Congo, he wrote, 'cast a strange light upon the real value of those
sonorous words Christianity and civilisation. What are they really
worth in practice when all the Christian and civilised nations of the
earth can stand around, and either from petty jealousy or from absolute
moral indifference can for many years on end see a helpless race,
whose safety they have guaranteed, robbed, debauched, mutilated and
murdered, without raising a hand or in most cases even a voice to
protect them?'[9] It was another blow to Conan Doyle's relationship
with organised religion.

Conan Doyle continued to lobby hard on behalf of the Association
and reforms were – eventually – instituted, but only very slowly and
only after King Albert succeeded to the Belgian throne. Edmund Morel
had no doubt that Conan Doyle played a very significant role, as he
explained to Arthur St John Adcock, the editor of the *Bookman*: 'Conan
Doyle's intervention at that time exercised a decisive influence on the
course of events. It provided the best antidote possible to the reactionary influences at work against us. It effectually prevented the most
fatal of all diseases to a movement of this sort, public lassitude. Yet
it was not his book – excellent as it was, nor his manly eloquence on
the platform, nor the influence he wielded in rallying influential men
to our cause, which helped us most. It was just the fact that he was
– Conan Doyle; and that he was with us. I do not think any other
man but Conan Doyle could have done for the cause just what Conan
Doyle did at that time.'[10]

Persuaded by the modest success of *The Fires of Fate* that he could
conquer the stage as easily as he had the short story, Conan Doyle
turned impresario and in the spring of 1910 took a six months' lease
on the Adelphi Theatre in London for £600 a week to stage a play he
had adapted from his prizefighting novel, *Rodney Stone. The House of
Temperly; A Melodrama of the Ring* was an ambitious production
entailing seven sets and 43 speaking parts. A boxing coach was hired
to train the actors for the fight scenes, which culminated with the

gallant Captain Temperly stepping into the ring to face the villainous 'Gloucester Dick', save the family honour and settle a £10,000 wager. No expense was spared in mounting the production and Conan Doyle was counting on a long run to recover the costs. To his dismay, on the opening night the audience sat through the first act in total silence – up in his box, he scribbled 'too anaemic' on his programme – but the play came alive when the fight scenes began, and when the curtain came down there were loud cheers for the author.

The reviews were generally good. 'Only those who attend a performance of the piece,' the *Athenaeum*'s critic noted, 'can have any idea how life-like these passages are made on the stage. Such zest cannot but affect an audience, and the play obtained the heartiest first-night reception of any of the year.' But the public disagreed and audiences quickly fell away – boxing, it appeared, was not a popular subject for the stage, particularly with women – and Conan Doyle soon realised he had an expensive flop on his hands.

On 6 May 1910 King Edward VII died at Buckingham Palace, immersing the nation in mourning less than ten years after the death of his mother: all theatres in the West End of London immediately closed as a mark of respect. Conan Doyle seized the opportunity to cut his losses on *The House of Temperly* and turned to the one man guaranteed to bring in the audiences – Sherlock Holmes. He shut himself away in his study at Windlesham and wrote a new play, based on 'The Speckled Band', one of his favourite Holmes stories, in a week. Within a fortnight of *Temperly* closing *The Speckled Band* was in rehearsal.

Considerable tension developed, however, between the author and the producer, the Shakespearian actor Lyn Harding, who also played the villain, Dr Grimesby Rylott (not Roylott as in the book). Harding wanted to make Dr Rylott a much more flamboyant character and kept adding embellishments, to the increasing irritation of Conan Doyle, who sat moodily in the stalls following the dialogue and objecting every time Harding departed from his lines or stage directions. Conan Doyle saw Rylott as a typically Victorian melodramatic figure, insisted that Harding should play the part as he had written it and complained that it was being 'burlesqued'. In the end, J. M. Barrie, a friend of both men, intervened and advised Conan Doyle to let the actor have his way, although the scene in the book where Rylott, in a rage, bends a poker only to see it effortlessly straightened by Holmes, had to be abandoned for want of a sufficiently flexible poker.

There was also a problem with the snake. The cast, quite reasonably, wanted a mechanical snake. Conan Doyle would not hear of it and acquired a rock python to play the part, but it turned out to be an uncooperative thespian, as did its understudies. In the climactic closing scene, having dispatched Rylott, it was required to uncoil itself from its victim's head and slither across the stage towards an unheeding Watson. 'They were all inclined,' Conan Doyle recorded, 'either to hang down from the hole in the wall like inanimate bell-pulls, or else to turn back through the hole and get even with the stage carpenter who pinched their tails in order to make them more lively.' In the end, an artificial version performed the role more reliably and perhaps convincingly. While a real snake was being employed, one critic had described it, to Conan Doyle's wry amusement, as a 'palpably artificial serpent'.

The Speckled Band opened at the Adelphi on 4 June and was a great success, with more than twelve curtain calls and particular acclaim for Lyn Harding. Conan Doyle graciously apologised to Harding by sending him a congratulatory note. Although the reviews were mixed and aficionados complained that Holmes did not explain his deductions on stage – a de rigueur element of every literary adventure – the play took £1,301 at the box office in its first week, generating a handsome profit of £650.

On 24 June Conan Doyle invited his colleagues from the Congo campaign, Edmund Morel and Roger Casement, to join him and Jean, who was pregnant with their second child, and Stewart Leckie, Jean's brother, for dinner at the Metropole and afterwards for the best seats in the house at the Adelphi. It was a convivial evening at the end of which no one in the party had any notion that Casement's night was only just beginning. After bidding farewell to his companions he went on the prowl, as usual, looking for male prostitutes, and noted in his diary that night: '1 a.m. H.B. 10/- & 1.45 A.M. Jamaica 6/6'. Casement's infamous 'Black Diary', meticulously recording in code his frequent homosexual encounters, would figure prominently when he was tried for high treason during the First World War.

The Speckled Band transferred to the Globe following its run at the Adelphi and closed on 10 October after a total of 169 performances. Despite its success Conan Doyle told a reporter that he was finished with the stage. 'I am not leaving stage-work because it does not interest me,' he said. 'It interests me too much. It's so absorbing that it draws your mind away from the deeper things of life. Don't misunderstand me! For those who can treat the deep matters of life dramatically it's different. But I recognise my own limitations. So I make an absolute pledge that I will not write for the stage again.'[11]

In truth, he had a great number of demands on his time. Besides his continued campaigning for divorce law reform, he was invited to attend numerous functions, make speeches, support causes and judge competitions. He had presided at the celebrations for the centenary of Edgar Allan Poe's birth in 1909 and in December that year received a letter from Irving Jefferson Lewis, managing editor of the *New York Morning Telegraph*, asking him to referee the Jeffries–Johnson world heavyweight title fight: 'It would . . . rejoice the hearts of the men in this country if you were at the ringside when the great Negro fighter meets the white man Jeffries for the world's championship.' He refused with the greatest of reluctance and missed witnessing Jack Johnson become the first black man to win the title.

Life at Windlesham settled down into a pleasant routine for the family. The original house had been greatly enlarged to include fourteen bedrooms and five reception rooms. Though Conan Doyle sometimes complained about being overcharged for the building works and wryly referred to the place as 'Swindlesham', he unquestionably enjoyed living there. His upstairs study overlooked the Downs which he liked to call 'the Highlands of Sussex'. Woodie, his secretary, worked in an adjoining room. In the summer, Conan Doyle would also write in 'the hut' – a small wooden summer house in the grounds – and there was an alcove off the billiard room where he liked to read. Among the many mementoes scattered about the house was the bat with which he had scored a century in his first game at Lord's. Neither of the children from Doyle's first marriage was living at Windlesham: Kingsley, who had finished at Eton, was in Lausanne for a year to study medicine; Mary was living in a flat in the recently completed Elgin Mansions in Maida Vale with 'Aunt Juey' – Julia Pocock, an elderly friend of the family who was effectively her chaperone and companion.

On 19 November 1910 Jean's second son, Adrian Malcolm, was born at Windlesham, an event which caused as much delight to Conan Doyle as the news that his brother, Innes, now promoted to major, was engaged to be married to Clara Schwensen, a Dane who was studying music in Berlin.

Sport remained a big part of Conan Doyle's life: he was captain of Crowborough Beacon Golf Club (although he regarded the game as more of an excuse for a stroll on the Downs than a competition); he still played cricket regularly, had only recently abandoned football and claimed he was 'good for three rounds with the gloves' when he got the chance.[12]

In the summer of 1911 he took part in the Prince Henry Motor Tour, a competition organised by Prince Henry of Prussia, head of the German Navy, ostensibly as a gesture of sporting goodwill in honour of King George V's coronation on 22 June. Fifty German automobiles competed against a similar number of British cars in a rally starting in Hamburg and ending, 2,500 miles later, in London. 'It is the reliability of the car and man that counts, not speed,' Conan Doyle told his mother. 'The team which drives best, and loses fewest marks for contretemps, will be the winner. I take Jean as a passenger. It should be a fine rush.'

At the beginning of July Conan Doyle arrived in Hamburg at the wheel of 'Billy', his sixteen-horsepower Dietrich-Lorraine landaulet, with a horseshoe attached to the radiator for good luck, Jean sitting beside him and Alfred Stiller, his chauffeur, recruited to the team as a mechanic, in the back. His arrival coincided with news that Germany had sent a gunboat and cruiser to Agadir, on the Atlantic seaboard of Morocco, to 'maintain and protect German interests'. Although at the time, Conan Doyle said he was impressed by the 'extreme kindness and sympathy' displayed by their German hosts, later he became convinced that the timing of the rally was no coincidence: 'The competition had been planned in Germany, and there can be no doubt in looking back that a political purpose underlay it. The idea was to create a false *entente* by means of sport.'

Tempers frayed quickly. The rules stipulated that each car would be accompanied by a military observer from the opposite country, so out of respect for Prince Henry, Britain sent high-ranking officers; Germany assigned youthful subalterns and captains, immediately creating tension. On 5 July the cars set off from Hamburg en route to Cologne, Munster and Bremerhaven, with considerable jostling and frequent complaints about the larger German cars attempting to force the smaller British competitors off the road.

On the steamer ferry from Bremerhaven to Southampton, the British teams assembled to compare notes and agreed that many of the German observers radiated hostility and talked frequently about the inevitability of war in Europe. The British were not entirely innocent in this regard. 'The only thing I want to do with these people,' one British officer noted, 'is to fight them.' As the rally headed north, Conan Doyle became concerned that the German observers had a secondary role – to act as spies. They all carried cameras and seemed intent on photographing as much of Britain as possible; in London his own observer suddenly disappeared to an hotel in the East End for no innocent reason that Conan Doyle could fathom.

The rally ended on 20 July at the Royal Automobile Club in London with a victory for the British team. Prince Henry presented the trophy, an ivory carving of a woman engraved with the word 'Peace', and made a pretty speech: 'We have seen a loveable country and a loveable people. The whole tour from beginning to end has been a great "thank you".' Next day the competitors gathered at the newly opened Brooklands motor-racing circuit in Surrey for a final event, at which a German monoplane appeared and flew over the track. 'I don't like the look of things,' Conan Doyle confessed in a note to Innes.

———————◆———————

Distracted by events at home, Conan Doyle was writing little around this time – the *Strand* had only published two Holmes stories in 1911, 'The Adventure of the Red Circle' and 'The Disappearance of Lady Frances Carfax', and none in 1912. The fact was that he was running out of ideas for new adventures and even suggested to Greenhough Smith, perhaps not entirely seriously, running a competition for the best short-story proposals. 'Probably,' he added gloomily, 'you would get no fish worth taking out of the net.'¹³

If his professional output was somewhat curtailed, his desire to vent his views in the press was undiminished, and in the spring of 1912 he became embroiled in a heated, and very public, argument with another distinguished man of letters, his friend and distant neighbour, George Bernard Shaw, over the circumstances surrounding the sinking of the *Titanic* on her maiden voyage. On the night of 14 April 1912, the White Star liner RMS *Titanic* had struck an iceberg in the north Atlantic and sunk with the loss of more than 1,500 passengers and crew. Among those who died was W. T. Stead, the editor of *Review of Reviews,* with whom Conan Doyle had crossed verbal swords over the Boer War. The tragedy made headlines around the world and for weeks the papers were full of stirring first-person accounts from the survivors, of the heroism on board, of those who sacrificed their places in the lifeboats that others might live, of the band that kept playing as the great ship slipped beneath the waves.

By the beginning of May, Shaw, for one, had had enough. He viewed the disaster as a shambles and a scandal and said so in a withering article published by the *Daily News and Leader* on 14 May. His thesis was that the tragedy had been distorted by the media into a romantic saga of national heroism rather than a shameful disgrace. The truth was that the captain had lost his ship 'by deliberately and knowingly steaming into an ice field at the highest speed he had coal for'; lifeboats which were not full had refused to go to the aid of those struggling in the water in cork-jackets; the band only continued playing to reassure the third-class passengers and prevent them rushing the lifeboats. 'What is the use of all this ghastly, blasphemous, inhuman, braggartly lying?' Shaw demanded. 'Here is a calamity which might well make the proudest man humble, and the wildest joker serious . . . The effect on me was one of profound disgust, almost of national dishonour.'

It was too much for an arch-patriot like Conan Doyle who, had he been travelling with his family on the *Titanic*, would no doubt have seen his wife and children safely into a lifeboat before calmly going down with the ship. On 20 May, the *Daily News* published his lengthy and emotional riposte. He accused Shaw of deliberately bending the facts to fit his thoroughly objectionable views. 'As to the general accusation that the occasion has been used for the glorification of British qualities,' he wrote, 'we should indeed be a lost people if we did not honour courage and discipline when we see it in its highest form.' He concluded with a personal sideswipe: 'Surely it is a pitiful sight to see a man of undoubted genius using his gifts in order to misrepresent and decry his own people.'

Shaw leapt back into the attack two days later: 'Sir, I hope to persuade my friend Sir Arthur Conan Doyle, now that he has got his romantic and warm-hearted protest off his chest, to read my article again three or four times, and give you his second thoughts on the matter; for it is really not possible for any sane man to disagree with a single word I have written.' His defence was spirited and unapologetic. 'The Captain of the *Titanic* did not, as Sir Arthur thinks, make "a terrible mistake". He made no mistake. He knew perfectly well that ice is the only risk that is considered really deadly in his line of work, and, knowing it, he chanced it and lost the hazard. Sentimental idiots, with a break in the voice, tell me that "he went down to the depths": I tell them, with the impatient contempt they deserve, that so did the cat.'

Conan Doyle was certainly not 'minded to have second thoughts on the matter' and closed the debate with a final insult: 'The worst I think or say of Mr Shaw is that his many brilliant gifts do not include the power of weighing evidence; nor has he that quality – call it good taste, humanity, or what you will – which prevents a man from needlessly hurting the feelings of others.'

The spat did not prevent them sharing a platform later in the year at a crowded meeting held in the Memorial Hall in Farringdon Street, London, where they both spoke in favour of Home Rule for Ireland (Conan Doyle had reversed his views on Home Rule, perhaps under the influence of his new friend Roger Casement) and attempted to calm fears that the Catholic majority would wage a campaign of persecution against the Protestant minority. (Ironically, as it turned out, the very reverse happened in the north after the separation of Ulster from the Republic.)

By then Jean, who had had a miscarriage the previous year, was once again pregnant. This time there were no complications and on

12 December, 1912 she gave birth to a daughter, Lina Jean, described by Conan Doyle in a letter to Innes as 'the very prettiest and sweetest babe I ever saw'. Her stepchildren were still notably absent from Windlesham. Kingsley, now enrolled at St Mary's Hospital Medical School, Paddington, had moved in to his sister's flat nearby.

Conan Doyle was still plagued by requests to help solve crimes, find missing persons or fight injustices. The Edalji saga had cast him in the not altogether welcome role as a people's champion, but it was not until the troubling case of Oscar Slater was brought to his attention in 1912 that he once again took up the cudgels. It was very much to his credit that in this instance he had little sympathy for the accused, whom he considered to be a 'blackguard'. But, as he wrote later, 'It is impossible to read and weigh the facts in connection with the conviction of Oscar Slater in May 1909, at the High Court in Edinburgh, without feeling deeply dissatisfied with the proceedings, and morally certain that justice was not done.'[14]

On the evening of 21 December 1908, a servant girl, Helen Lambie, was sent to buy a newspaper by her employer, Marion Gilchrist, a wealthy 82-year-old spinster who lived in an apartment in Queen's Terrace, Glasgow. Following instructions, the girl double-locked the door behind her, knowing that Miss Gilchrist feared being burgled. While she was away, Arthur Adams, a friendly neighbour who lived underneath the old lady, heard a thud on the ceiling and three distinct knocks. He went to investigate but could get no reply and still had his hand on the bell when the maid returned. As she entered the apartment a man emerged from the bedroom into the gaslit hallway, walked calmly to the door and then disappeared down the stairs. Adams only saw the man very indistinctly – he had not brought his spectacles – but had the impression that he was 'gentlemanly and well-dressed'. He also noted that the servant girl appeared to evince no surprise at the man's presence. Lambie went to deliver the newspaper and found the body of her employer lying on the floor in front of the fireplace in the dining room, bludgeoned to death. In a spare bedroom a wooden box containing her private papers lay broken open on the floor, the papers scattered, and her jewellery, which she kept hidden in a wardrobe, strewn on a dressing table. Only a small diamond brooch, in the shape of a crescent, was missing.

Both Lambie and Adams later described a man they had seen as being about 5 feet 6 inches tall, dark-haired, clean-shaven, wearing a light-grey overcoat and a dark cap. Next day a 14-year-old girl, Mary Barrowman, who had been walking past Miss Gilchrist's flat at the time of the murder said she, too, had seen a man, but described him as tall and quite young with a crooked nose, wearing a fawn cloak or mackintosh, a round hat and brown boots. After further questioning, she changed her mind and produced a description much like that of Helen Lambie.

The brutal murder of a defenceless old lady caused an outcry in Glasgow and the police were under enormous pressure to make a quick arrest. Within a few days they discovered that a dubious character called Oscar Slater had been seen in the city trying to sell a pawn ticket for a crescent-shaped diamond brooch. Moreover he had 'fled' from Glasgow to Liverpool, where he and his mistress had embarked on the *Lusitania*, bound for New York, travelling under false names. It was enough for Glasgow detectives to assume immediately that Slater, a known 'bad lot', was their quarry.

Oscar Slater was a German Jew, named Joseph Leschziner, who was born in Silesia in about 1870, the son of a baker. At the age of 15 he left home, worked in a bank in Hamburg and then moved to Britain, where he changed his name to Slater and earned an erratic living on the fringes of the criminal fraternity, on racecourses and in gambling halls. He married in around 1902, but abandoned his wife and moved in with a French woman who called herself a 'nightclub singer' – a profession she probably combined with that of the world's oldest. Six weeks before the murder of Miss Gilchrist, the couple moved to Glasgow.

Despite discovering that Slater's pawn ticket related to a different brooch, pawned more than a month before the crime, Glasgow detectives remained convinced that he was their man, and an official request was telegraphed to the New York Police Department that he should be arrested on arrival, pending extradition proceedings. For this, the three witnesses needed positively to identify him. A Scots police inspector travelled to New York with them and shamelessly stage

managed proceedings, ensuring they got a good look at Slater before
he was escorted into the courtroom. Both Lambie and Barrowman
identified him; the short-sighted Adams was less sure, but admitted
there was a resemblance.

Slater's American lawyer advised him to resist extradition on the
clear evidence that the brooch he had pawned was not Gilchrist's, but
Slater was convinced he could prove his innocence before a British
court and chose to return. His luggage, which had been sealed at the
time of his arrest, was searched as soon as he arrived back in Glasgow
by police looking for the murder weapon. All they found was a small
upholsterer's hammer, which Slater claimed to have bought with a
card of assorted tools from Woolworths, but it made do as the murder
weapon.

Slater was brought to trial in Edinburgh on 3 May 1909. His defence
was that he had never heard of Miss Gilchrist, had no idea where she
lived and had only been resident in Glasgow for six weeks. His pawn
ticket was for a brooch that was his own property. On the night of
the murder he was at home having dinner with his mistress. She would
testify to that fact, as would their servant. It made no difference.

Underlying the prosecution case was a nascent streak of anti-
Semitism: the fact that Slater was what many people referred to as a
'dirty Jew' did his case no good. Between 1890 and 1905 tens of thousands of Jews had arrived in Britain, victims of massive pogroms in
the Ukraine and Poland. They settled wherever they could, many in
Glasgow, and this led to the unleashing of racist phobias about
unnamed diseases they were carrying, or ideas of revolutionary
socialism that they were nurturing, or money-grubbing capitalism
they were practising, at the expense of non-Jews.

The prosecution produced a dozen witnesses who claimed they
had seen Slater loitering in the vicinity of Miss Gilchrist's house. A
police doctor gave evidence that about 40 blows from the upholsterer's
hammer could have caused the injuries sustained by the dead woman,
although no blood had been found on the weapon or on Slater's
clothing. The prosecuting counsel did not explain how the murderer
had entered the double-locked flat, nor how he knew that Miss Gilchrist
was wealthy and kept her jewellery in a wardrobe. The identification
witnesses, and the fact that the accused was both a German and Jew,

were sufficient. The jury pronounced him guilty. As the judge prepared to pass a death sentence, Slater cried out in protest. 'I know nothing about the affair, absolutely nothing! I never heard the name! I know nothing about the affair! I know nothing about it! I came from America on my own account!'

Slater was scheduled to hang at Glasgow prison on 27 May, but the antagonistic fever the case had generated in the city was replaced by a vague public unease about the flimsiness of the evidence against him. When Slater's lawyer started a petition calling for the death sentence to be commuted, some 20,000 decent Glaswegians stepped up to sign it. Two days before the execution was due to take place, the Secretary of State for Scotland announced that his sentence would be commuted to one of life imprisonment with hard labour.

Almost three years would pass before Conan Doyle became involved, somewhat reluctantly, at the instigation of Slater's lawyer, Alexander Shaughnessy. Once he began to delve into the case he could not conceive how Slater could have committed the crime for which he had been imprisoned. How did he gain access to the victim's apartment? Why steal only one brooch rather than a pocketful of the old lady's valuable jewellery? Why was the servant girl not surprised to see an intruder? 'I saw that it was an even worse case than the Edalji one,' he wrote, 'and that this unhappy man had in all probability no more to do with the murder for which he had been condemned than I had.'

The Case of Oscar Slater, by A. Conan Doyle, an 80-page sixpenny booklet published in August 1912, effectively demolished the prosecution case. Slater had not, for example, 'fled' from Glasgow; he had booked into a hotel in Liverpool using his own name. The upholsterer's hammer was too light to inflict the wounds on Miss Gilchrist and too long to be concealed about his person if indeed he had been seen leaving the flat. There was no blood on the hammer, or on Slater's clothing. The identification witnesses were asked to pick out his 'swarthy Jewish physiognomy' from among nine Glasgow policemen and two railway officials. Naturally, they did it without hesitation.

'I cannot help in my own mind,' Conan Doyle wrote, 'comparing the case of Oscar Slater with another, which I had occasion to examine – that of George Edalji. I must admit they are not of the same class. George Edalji was a youth of exemplary character. Oscar Slater was a blackguard . . . Thus one cannot feel the same burning sense of injustice over the matter.' Nevertheless, he appealed for the case to be reconsidered and suggested, rather uncharitably, that Slater's punishment thus far should be 'allowed to atone for those irregularities of life which helped make his conviction possible'.

Conan Doyle advanced alternative theories about what might have happened. Everything hinged on the double-locked door: either the murderer knew the victim and was admitted to the apartment by her, or had obtained duplicate keys with the connivance of someone who knew her. Perhaps, he speculated, it was not a jewel robbery at all. Was it a document he was after, a will perhaps, and did he just take the diamond brooch as a blind? The fact that the servant girl seemed unsurprised at encountering the murderer in the hallway clearly indicated that she had recognised him. She had also entered the spare bedroom, where it was obvious a robbery had occurred, and emerged without expressing any alarm. Only when Adams demanded, 'Where is your mistress?' was the body of Miss Gilchrist found.

'I leave the matter now,' Conan Doyle concluded, 'with the hope that, even after many days, some sudden flash may be sent which will throw a light upon as brutal and callous a crime as has ever been recorded in those black annals in which the criminologist finds the materials for his study. Meanwhile it is on the conscience of the authorities, and in the last resort on that of the community, that this verdict obtained under the circumstances which I have indicated shall now be reconsidered.'[15]

The media greeted publication of *The Case of Oscar Slater* half-heartedly. The *Scotsman* dismissed Conan Doyle as 'an outside spectator', the *Glasgow Herald* questioned his readiness to accept an alibi supported only by Slater's mistress and their servant, and *The Times* concluded that it was by no means certain that a revision of the case would result in the prisoner's favour. The *Westminster Gazette* was more supportive: 'If the evidence against Slater were no stronger than the creator of Sherlock Holmes shows it to be, then only an uncommon stupidity and a deliberate plot could have brought about the conviction.'

While Conan Doyle's treatise made little impact on the official

view of the case, two years later one of the investigating police officers, Detective Lieutenant John Thomson Trench, approached a
Glasgow solicitor David Cook to unburden himself. Unable to speak
out publicly as a serving officer, he testified, under a promise of immu-
nity from the Secretary of State, that evidence had been suppressed
during Slater's trial. What he had to say was explosive – the servant
girl, Helen Lambie, knew the murderer and knew that it was not
Slater. On the night of the murder she had run to the house of a Miss
Margaret Birrell, a relative of the dead woman, and confessed that
she had recognised the man. She had told this to the police, but had
been persuaded to make a second statement implicating Slater.

As a result of Trench's information a Commission of Inquiry was
appointed but met in camera and witnesses did not have to give
evidence under oath. Lambie and Birrell both denied Trench's
account, although it was revealed that the prosecution *had* concealed
evidence at the trial, notably the statement of a neighbour who
confirmed Slater's alibi. Nevertheless, the Secretary of State for Scotland concluded, on 27 June 1914, that there was no case to justify
interfering with Slater's sentence. Conan Doyle was furious. 'How
the verdict could be that there was no fresh cause for reversing the
conviction is incomprehensible,' he wrote in a letter to the *Spectator*.
'The whole case will, in my opinion, remain immortal in the classics of crime as the supreme example of official incompetence and
obstinacy.'

Slater remained more or less forgotten in Peterhead prison until
1925 when a fellow prisoner, William Gordon, was released and smug-
gled out a letter under his dentures. It was an appeal for help from
Conan Doyle: 'Gordon my boy, I wish you in every way the best of
luck and if you feel inclined, then please do what you can for me.
Give the English public your opinion regarding me personally and
also in other respects. You have been for 5 years in close contact with
me and so you are quite fit to do so . . . Farewell Gordon, we likely
may never see us again but let us live in hope that it might be otherwise. Your friend, Oscar Slater. P.S. Don't forget to write or see Connan
D. [*sic*] also communicate with my cousin in Germany.'[16]

Gordon forwarded Slater's letter to Conan Doyle with a covering
note: 'I have been an unfortunate inmate of Peterhead Prison where

I met Slater . . . I made a promise that I would see you and deliver a verbal message on his behalf. The enclosed is a written message he gave me a few hours before my discharge. I secreted it in my mouth and got it out safely . . .' Conan Doyle was appalled when he was reminded that Slater was still in prison and wrote to Sir John Gilmour, now the Secretary of State for Scotland, asking for Slater to be considered for a free pardon.

Meanwhile, a Glasgow journalist, William Park, had mounted an independent investigation and came to the same conclusion as Conan Doyle: that Miss Gilchrist had known her murderer and invited him into her home. Unable to name names because of libel laws, Park speculated that the killer was her nephew and that he had argued with his aunt about a document she possessed. During the course of the argument he had pushed her and she had fallen and injured her head on a coal box near the fireplace. He was then faced with a terrible dilemma – allow her to recover and charge him with assault, or finish her off? He chose to kill her. After the publication of Park's sensational 'The Truth about Oscar Slater', in July 1927, a number of newspapers revived the story.

The breakthrough came when the *Empire News* tracked down Helen Lambie in the United States and, under the headline 'Why I Believe I Blundered Over Slater', she confirmed that she had given the police the name and description of the man she had seen in the apartment on the night of the murder. He had visited Miss Gilchrist several times before and knew his way about the place, and she was normally sent out on an errand when he was due to arrive. The police had ignored all this and persuaded her to identify Slater as the visitor.

The *Empire News* published its exclusive interview on 23 October 1927. Conan Doyle was outraged and sent a note to his friend J. Cuming Walters, editor of the *Manchester City News*: 'I should have sent you Lambie's confession in the *Empire News,* but I guess you saw it. That should be final. What a story! What a scandal! She says the police MADE her say it was Slater. Third degree! What a cesspool it all is! But we have no words of hope from those wooden-headed officials. I shall put on the political screw and I know how to do it. I'll win in the end but it has been a long fight.'[17] He complained in another letter that he was 'up against a ring of political lawyers who could not give away the police without giving away themselves'.[18]

On 8 November the Secretary of State for Scotland announced that Slater was being released from prison, ostensibly for good behaviour. The official statement made no reference to his guilt or innocence: 'Oscar Slater has now completed more than eighteen and a half years of his life sentence and I have felt justified in deciding to authorise his release on license as soon as suitable arrangements can be made.'

Slater was released from Peterhead prison on 15 November. Conan Doyle immediately wrote to him: 'This is to say in my wife's name and my own how grieved we have been at the infamous injustice which you have suffered at the hands of our officials. Your only poor consolation can be that your fate, if we can get people to realise the effects, may have the effect of safeguarding others in the future.' Slater penned an effusive reply: 'Sir Conan Doyle, you breaker of my shackles, you lover of truth for justice sake, I thank you from the bottom of my heart for the goodness you have shown towards me. My heart is full and almost breaking with love and gratitude for you your wife dear Lady Conan Doyle and all the upright men and women who, for justice sake, (and that only) have helped me, *me an outcast*. To my dying day I will honour you and the dear lady, my dear, dear Conan Doyle, yet that unbounded love for you both, makes me sign plainly, Yours, Oscar Slater.'[19]

For Conan Doyle, Slater's freedom was not enough. He circulated to Members of Parliament an updated version of his *Case of Oscar Slater* pamphlet urging them to call for a retrial in order that Slater could be pardoned and generated sufficient support for a special Act of Parliament to be passed to enable the Scottish Court of Criminal Appeal to reopen the case. Conan Doyle covered the appeal hearing in Edinburgh for the *Sunday Pictorial* in June 1928 and met Slater for the first time. 'One terrible face,' he wrote, 'stands out among all those others. It is not an ill-favoured face, nor is it a wicked one, but it is terrible nonetheless for the brooding sadness that is in it. It is firm and immobile and might be cut from that Peterhead granite which has helped make it what it is. A sculptor would choose it as the very type of tragedy. You feel that this is no ordinary man but one who has been fashioned for some strange end. It is indeed the man whose misfortunes have echoed around the world. It is Slater.'

Slater was eventually cleared of all charges, but only on a technicality and awarded £6,000 in compensation for the eighteen years he had spent breaking rocks in Peterhead quarries. Conan Doyle assumed that Slater would repay the substantial loans he had received to cover his legal fees, but Slater thought otherwise. He claimed he had not sanctioned the appeal, had not given Conan Doyle or anyone else authority to act on his behalf and alleged – unjustly – that Conan Doyle had received large sums for articles he had written about the case.

'Had Slater lost,' Conan Doyle wrote to the *Empire News* on 5 May 1929, 'I would have cheerfully taken this heavy expense [of the appeal] upon myself, but as he has received £6,000 in compensation it seems a monstrous thing that these charges should be met by me . . . I shall be reluctantly driven to assert my right in a court of law unless this man has the common decency to pay his own debts of his own free will.' He was dissuaded by friends from taking legal action but severed all contact with the man he had done so much to help with a final, angry letter: 'You seem to have taken leave of your senses. If you are indeed responsible for your actions, then you are the most ungrateful, as well as the most foolish, person whom I have ever known.'[20]

CHAPTER 17

THE LOST WORLD

Y 1912 CONAN DOYLE HAD not written a novel for six years. To be sure, he had had many distractions – his new family, his campaign for justice in the Congo, his crusades on behalf of George Edalji and Oscar Slater, his commitment to the Divorce Law Reform Union, his brief career as an impresario and much else besides. Nevertheless, the critical indifference to his historical novels, *Micah Clarke, The White Company* and *Sir Nigel,* still rankled. He recognised it was time to try something new and an idea was already germinating. 'My ambition,' he wrote to Greenhough Smith, 'is to do for the boys' book what Sherlock Holmes did for the detective tale. I don't suppose I could bring off two such coups. And yet I hope I may.'[1] The result was *The Lost World,* an early science-fiction masterpiece which introduced a character almost as memorable and enduring in the public's affection as Holmes: the impossible, the pugnacious, the quixotic, the egocentric yet curiously lovable Professor George Edward Challenger.

The inspiration for *The Lost World* most likely dated back to the summer of 1910 when Conan Doyle had been invited to speak at a Royal Society luncheon in London welcoming Commander Robert Peary on return from his epic expedition to discover the North Pole. His theme was that explorers were uncovering so much of the globe that writers of romance were harder and harder pressed to find mysterious locations in which to set their stories. 'The question is,' he asked, 'where is the romance writer to turn when he wants to draw any vague and not too clearly defined region?' He already had an answer in mind.

The first decade of the twentieth century had seen a growing interest in palaeontology, which Conan Doyle naturally shared. Out walking near Crowborough he had discovered what he thought were the fossilised footprints of a large lizard in a rock quarry and had reported his find to the British Museum, which duly sent a palaeontologist to take impressions. In the billiard room at Windlesham were two large casts of iguanodon footprints, also found on the Downs, and a Stone Age flint arrowhead. Cruising the Aegean on his honeymoon in 1907, he had seen a creature in the sea which he remarked to Jean looked remarkably like a 'young ichthyosaurus', an early Jurassic fish lizard, about four feet long, with a long beak and tail and four flippers. It was probably a dolphin, which are common in the Aegean, and which vaguely resemble ichthyosaurus, but Conan Doyle preferred to believe it a dinosaur somehow stranded in the modern world.

All this combined to set his fertile creative powers working. Serialised in the *Strand* starting in April 1912, and published simultaneously as a book in Great Britain and the United States six months later, *The Lost World* is narrated by an amiable Irish journalist, Edward Dunn Malone, clearly based on E. D. Morel, the journalist with whom Conan Doyle had worked exposing the scandal in the Congo. Malone is in love with the delicious Gladys ('That delicately bronzed skin, almost Oriental in its colouring, that raven hair, the large liquid eyes, the full but exquisite lips – all the stigmata of passion were there') but she declares herself unwilling to marry anyone who is not famous and ostentatiously heroic. Thus when Malone has an opportunity to prove himself by joining an expedition in search of prehistoric life on a remote plateau in the South American wilderness, he jumps at it. (When he returns home in triumph, both famous and a hero, he discovers that Gladys has married a solicitor's clerk.)

The expedition is led by Professor Challenger, a dominating, doctrinaire character given to capricious mood swings. Conan Doyle himself claimed that his model was Professor William Rutherford, a physiologist with a booming voice who taught at Edinburgh University when he was a student, but other names have been mentioned, among them George Bernard Shaw and the eccentric and excitable Dr George Turnavine Budd. The two other members of the team are the argumentative and ascetic Professor Summerlee and a raffish, titled

white hunter, Lord John Roxton, probably based on Sir Roger
Casement into whose mouth Conan Doyle puts one of his abiding
beliefs: 'There are times, young fellah, when every one of us must
make a stand for human rights and justice, or you never feel clean
again.'

The four adventurers struggle through numerous hair-raising
mishaps en route to the plateau, where they discover, as Challenger
had promised, that 'the ordinary laws of nature are suspended' and
they enter a primeval world populated by dinosaurs and warring tribes
of cavemen and 'little red warriors'. Challenger and Summerlee bicker
throughout the expedition, often at moments of extreme peril, on such
subjects as whether the apemen should be classified as 'dryopithecus'
or 'pithecanthropus'. Lord John's opinion is slightly less academic: he
decides they are 'Missin' Links, and I wish they had stayed missin'.'

As in his historical novels, Conan Doyle was diligent in his research,
drawing details from Sir Edwin Ray Lankester's seminal *Extinct Animals*,
published in 1905. But once he had a grip on the technicalities, he
allowed his imagination to blossom, creating fantastic, terrifying
monsters, the stuff of nightmares: 'a great running bird, far taller than
an ostrich, with a vulture-like neck and a cruel head which made it
a walking death'; 'the toxodon, the giant ten-foot guinea pig with
projecting chisel teeth'; and a toad-like creature with a 'bloated, warty,
blood-slavering muzzle' which pursues Malone across moonlit country.

There is an exuberance about *The Lost World,* a sense that Conan
Doyle enjoyed every minute writing it: he would read aloud what
he had written during the day to Jean and any guests staying at
Windlesham and very often could not stop himself from laughing
out loud. He was certainly able to have more fun with Challenger
than he ever could with Holmes and perhaps identified more closely
with him, even posing as Challenger, in a false beard and eyebrows,
for a photograph to illustrate the book.

When the two professors are captured by the apemen, Challenger
gets special treatment, a fact Lord Roxton puts down to his marked
physical resemblance to their king. The team eventually escapes from
the plateau and returns to Britain, bringing back with them a pterodactyl as proof of what they have discovered. It is due to be produced
from a packing case at a scientific convention at the Queen's Hall in

London. 'Professor Challenger drew off the top of the case, which formed a sliding lid. Peering down into the box he snapped his fingers several times and was heard from the Press seat to say, 'Come, then, pretty, pretty!' in a coaxing voice . . . An instant later, with a scratching, rattling sound, a most horrible and loathsome creature appeared from below and perched itself upon the side of the case. Even the unexpected fall of the Duke of Durham into the orchestra, which occurred at this moment, could not distract the petrified attention of the vast audience . . .' The commotion in the audience disturbs the creature and it takes flight before Challenger can grab it. It flaps around the hall for a few minutes, beating against walls and chandeliers in a blind frenzy, until it chances upon an open window, 'squeezed its hideous bulk' through it and is gone.

While *The Lost World* owed something to H. G. Wells's *The War of the Worlds* and *The First Men on the Moon*, Jules Verne's *A Journey to the Centre of the Earth* and Daniel Defoe's *Robinson Crusoe*, it exemplified Conan Doyle at the top of his form as a writer of science fiction, seamlessly knitting adventure, humour and fantasy into a narrative that never palls. It would also influence much that followed. Willis O'Brien created the special effects for the first film version in 1924, honing the techniques he would use a few years later for the classic *King Kong*, and *The Lost World* unquestionably inspired, some eighty years later, *Jurassic Park*, the novel by Michael Crichton which was turned into a Hollywood blockbuster. (Crichton also commandeered Conan Doyle's title for his sequel.)

The critics were enthusiastic. *The Times* thought it was 'a highly interesting tale of outlandish adventure of a sort to stir the pulses and arouse the wonder of even the "jaded" novel reader'. According to the *Athenaeum* it was 'decidedly the most imaginative of the author's works', and to *The Times Literary Supplement* it was a 'glorious story': 'The pace is terrific; only a ski-runner, as Sir Arthur is, could have maintained it in such rough country without losing his balance. Indeed, the story is most deftly constructed, and one does not know which to admire most – the art with which a logical crescendo is preserved, or the high spirits which hurry the reader, laughing and panting, over any inconsistencies that may lie in his way . . .' '[It] is at once one of the most realistic and the most romantic of his books,' the *Bookman* concluded, 'its wild imagination wearing an air of sheer reality from the Defoe-like matter-of-fact manner of [the] narration.'

Sir Edwin Lankester was delighted that his scientific tome had helped inspire such exhilarating fiction and wrote to Conan Doyle to congratulate him on his 'perfectly splendid' story and expressing pride to have had a small part in its inception. The venerable zoologist's enthusiasm extended to making suggestions for a sequel: 'What about introducing a gigantic snake sixty feet long? Or a herd of pygmy elephants two feet high? Can four men escape by training a vegetarian pterodactyl to fly with them one at a time? Will some ape-woman fall in love with Challenger and murder the leaders of her tribe to save him?'[2]

A month after publication of The Lost World, the sensational discovery of the 'Piltdown man' – the so-called 'missing link' between apes and humans – electrified palaeontologists around the world. A labourer digging in a gravel pit near the village of Piltdown in Sussex had allegedly unearthed a piece of bone which he passed to a local amateur archaeologist, Charles Dawson, who verified it as a fragment of an ancient human skull and who began looking for a jawbone, which he soon found. He forwarded his discovery to the British Museum, where Sir Arthur Smith Woodward confirmed that while the skull had human features, the jaw was definitely ape-like. The fossil was named Eoanthropus dawsoni, Dawson's dawn man, but became known as 'the Piltdown man'.

Soon after The Times had reported the discovery, Conan Doyle visited the ongoing dig at Piltdown, only seven miles from Windlesham, and was introduced to Dawson, who later told a friend that the author was very excited by the work going on there and offered to drive the archaeologist anywhere he wanted to go in his motor car. In 1915 a second 'Piltdown man' skull was discovered only a couple of miles away, along with tools he had used and the fossilised remains of animals that had lived at the same time. It was taken as conclusive proof that apes had first evolved into humans in England. Dawson died the following year, but Sir Arthur Smith Woodward, Piltdown man's greatest advocate, spent the twenty years following his retirement from the British Museum digging at the Piltdown site in the hope of discovering more remains. He found nothing.

In 1953, to the enormous embarrassment of the British scientific community, 'Piltdown man' was exposed a hoax. He was literally half-ape, half-human: the skull was from a medieval human, and the jawbone and teeth were from an orang-utan. The appearance of age had been created by staining the bones with an iron solution and chromic acid and the teeth had been filed to fit. Over the next few years finding the hoaxer became a minor academic industry, and while Charles Dawson was the prime suspect – artefacts he had supposedly discovered and donated to a museum in Hastings also turned out to be forgeries – the name of Sir Arthur Conan Doyle was also mentioned, 'evidence' being cited from the pages of *The Lost World*.

Although the case against him would never have passed the scrutiny of Sherlock Holmes, the suggestion that Conan Doyle might have been the perpetrator was first made in *Science '83*, the official journal of the American Association for the Advancement of Science, by American academic John Winslow. Winslow cited the fact that Conan Doyle had 'haunted' the Piltdown site, that he was a doctor with extensive knowledge of the human anatomy and a keen interest in archaeology, that he was a writer gifted at manipulating complex plots and that he loved hoaxes, adventure and danger. Most important of all, Winslow claimed, he 'bore a grudge' against the British science establishment. He noted that *The Lost World* was crammed with geological and palaeontological references, including one to the Wealdean clay in which the Piltdown man was found. Finding a dinosaur footprint, Professor Challenger bellows: 'Wealden! I've seen them in Wealden clay!' Challenger also refers to his 'gifted friend' Lankester, the director of natural history at the British Museum, who had predicted, in 1906, the discovery of a 'missing link'. Deep significance was attached to a throwaway remark by Malone's news editor, who suggests that the dinosaur bones Challenger had found on his first visit to South America are not necessarily genuine: 'If you are clever enough and know your business, you can fake a bone as easily as you can fake a photograph.'

These obtuse clues, the location of the Piltdown gravel pit and Conan Doyle's medical training which would have helped him perpetrate the fraud represented the sum of the case against him. The suggestion that his motive was resentment against the scientific community, which by and large rejected the tenets of spiritualism, made no sense since in 1912 he was not actively crusading on its behalf. He was long dead by the time these charges were levelled, but it stretches credulity that a man who placed such high value on honour and probity would have remained silent, even in the highly unlikely event that he had initiated the saga as a practical joke which then got out of hand. The perpetrator of the hoax remains as elusive to this day as the 'missing link'.

Professor Challenger and his colleagues reappeared in 1913 in an uninspiring sequel, a novella called *The Poison Belt* in which a cloud of poison gas drifts slowly across the earth killing all life. Convinced there is no escape, Challenger arranges for his friends to gather in his wife's dressing room together with a supply of oxygen to witness the apocalypse through sealed windows. When the oxygen is about to run out, Challenger precipitates their demise by throwing his field glasses through a window when at that very moment, lo and behold, the gas dissipates. Just as the four adventurers come to accept that they have effectively witnessed the end of the world, normal life resumes: the reader is invited to believe that both humans and animals had been victims of a form of catalepsy.

Conan Doyle used *The Poison Belt* as an opportunity to introduce into his fiction a theme with which he was increasingly preoccupied – life after death. Locked in that claustrophobic chamber and facing certain death, Challenger suddenly steps out of character and waxes ethereally about nature building a beautiful door into the afterlife and hanging it with 'many gauzy and shimmering curtains to make an entrance to the new life for our wandering souls'. Challenger's odd musings reflected how spiritualism increasingly engaged Conan Doyle's thoughts and filled the pages of his journal. 'Even granting that Spiritualism is true,' he wrote, 'it advances but a little way. And yet that little way does solve the most important of immediate questions – does death end all? Fancy a London which went mad on Spiritualism as it recently did on glove fighting, and which flocked round a successful medium as round Georges Carpentier. What a nightmare it would be! What an orgy of fraud and lunacy would be cooked. We should all regard such an outbreak with horror. And yet it would still not be incompatible with a belief that all the Spiritualists claim is true.'[3]

Science fiction and spiritualism apart, some viewed *The Poison Belt* as a metaphor for Conan Doyle's fears about European political events and the increasing threat from Germany. In early 1913 he was genuinely shocked by *Germany and the Next War* by General Friedrich von Bernhardi which he saw as a open avowal of German aggression. Von Bernhardi argued that Germany had the right and responsibility to wage war to gain the power it deserved; negotiation between the Great Powers, he said, was pointless. Conan Doyle's trenchant response, published in the *Fortnightly Review* in February of that year, painstakingly refuted Bernhardi's case against England. 'Every one of his propositions I dispute,' he concluded. 'But this is all beside the question. We have not to do with his argument, but with its results. Those results are that he, a man whose opinion is of weight and a member of the ruling class in Germany, tells us frankly that Germany will attack us the moment she sees a favourable opportunity. I repeat that we should be mad if we did not take very serious notice of the warning.'

The 'German peril' was certainly a matter of pressing public concern. Two years earlier something like panic had swept the country when the First Lord of the Admiralty announced that the government had underestimated German naval growth, that thirteen German dread-nought battleships would be completed in 1911 alone and that German naval strength might soon overtake Britain's, a situation that no one had ever envisaged. In July 1912 Britain had withdrawn its battleships from the Mediterranean and put them on patrol in the North Sea in response to the continuing German naval build-up, following the break-down of Anglo-German talks to limit the arms race.

Conan Doyle, however, believed the real danger lay elsewhere and advanced the then extraordinary theory that the submarine was likely to present a formidable threat to Britain's survival in the event of a European war. When Britain launched its first submarine in 1901 the Admiralty had initially expressed reservations about their use in naval warfare, but by 1904 six were in service and such was the Royal Navy's confidence in the new craft that the Prince of Wales was taken on an underwater tour of Portsmouth Harbour. From the start, Conan Doyle believed that submarines, he called them 'these poisonous craft', were likely to play a major role in future wars and he was particularly concerned about their ability to mount a blockade of the British Isles: 'What effect a swarm of submarines, lying off the mouth of the Channel and the Irish Sea, would produce upon the victualling of these islands is a problem beyond my conjecture.'

His preferred solution was the construction of a tunnel under the English Channel linking Britain and France, an idea first mooted in 1802. 'The matter seems to me to be of such importance,' he wrote to *The Times* in May 1913, 'that I grudge every day that passes without something having been done to bring it to realisation.' A tunnel, he said, would cost the British taxpayer some £5 million and would take three years to build. In peacetime it could be used by tourists and at times of war it would not only guarantee supplies but would enable troops to be rapidly withdrawn from mainland Europe in the event of an invasion.

Innovative thinking of this kind was typical of Conan Doyle, but he received little support from either politicians or military experts, although a parliamentary commission was appointed to consider the tunnel project. Most, however, agreed with the Prime Minster, Herbert Asquith. 'The question of our power of feeding our people, or of preserving our communications across the Channel,' Asquith sniffed, 'is a question of whether or not we have got an invincible Navy and command of the sea.' Undeterred, Conan Doyle persevered. He wrote memoranda to the War Office, the Admiralty and the Council of Imperial Defence. He ignited a controversy in the correspondence columns of *The Times*, dismissing fears that a tunnel could be used by an invading force with withering logic: 'The idea of the invasion of a great country through a hole in the ground 26 miles long and as many feet broad seems to me to be a most fantastic one.' He spoke in public on the subject whenever and wherever he was able to do so, all to no avail.

Conan Doyle's letters to the press would, many years later, provide the material for a substantial book.[4] This was an age, before radio and television, when writers like Kipling, H.G. Wells, George Bernard Shaw, G.K. Chesterton – and, of course, Arthur Conan Doyle – wielded huge social as well as literary influence, were quoted as authorities on a whole range of subjects and were looked upon to provide a moral view of the world. Since Conan Doyle was one of the most visible literary figures in England it was almost to be expected that his opinions would fill the letters pages of both national and local newspapers, and he had opinions on everything, from literature to politics, from religion to science, from sport to international affairs.

Conan Doyle did not, perhaps, bolster the gravity of his case for a tunnel by encompassing his argument in an adventure yarn and writing an overtly propagandising short story for the July 1914 issue of the *Strand* called 'Danger! Being the Log of Captain John Sirius', in which 'Norland', a fictional country with a squadron of eight submarines, manages to sink sufficient British merchant ships to cause a famine in Great Britain. As Captain Sirius, commander of Norland's submarine squadron, observes: 'It is an amazing thing that the English, who have the reputation of being a practical nation, never saw the danger to which they were exposed. For many years they had been spending nearly a hundred millions a year upon their army and their fleet . . . Yet when the day of trial came, all this imposing force was of no use whatever, and might as well have not existed. Their ruin could not have been more complete or more rapid if they had not possessed an ironclad or a regiment.'

The author was clearly determined to score points against those who dismissed his theories. 'When they have a tunnel,' Captain Sirius notes, 'they can use their fine expeditionary force upon the Continent, but until then it might just as well not exist so far as Europe is concerned. My own country, therefore, was in good cause and had nothing to fear. Great Britain, however, was already feeling my grip upon her throat. As in normal times four-fifths of her food is imported, prices were rising by leaps and bounds. The supplies in the country were beginning to show signs of depletion, while little was coming in to replace it.' By picking up newspapers from passing ships, Captain Sirius was aware that social order was breaking down in Britain, with starving crowds clamouring for bread at municipal offices; within days Britain was forced to sue for peace. Captain Sirius was not above labouring a point: 'The true culprits were those, be they politicians or journalists, who had not the foresight to understand that unless Britain grew her own supplies, or unless by means of a tunnel she had some way of conveying them into the island, all her mighty expenditure upon her army and her fleet was a mere waste of money . . .'

Conan Doyle admitted that his intention in writing the story was not to entertain but to 'direct public attention to the great danger which threatened this country'. To this end the *Strand* sought the opinions of prominent naval officers and experts, which were published in the same issue. Most viewed the story as highly improbable – more like Jules Verne, said one critic. Few supported the idea of building a Channel tunnel – 'God made us an island,' Admiral Sir William Kennedy declared, 'by all means let us remain so' – but there was general agreement that Conan Doyle was right to focus attention on the precarious nature of the nation's food supply. Douglas Owen, a lecturer on naval warfare, eloquently addressed the issue of whether an adventure story was an appropriate medium to air such a controversial topic: 'By some it may be thought that for a popular writer to employ his talents in the creation of general alarm is to make ill use of them. If so, I think they will, on reflection, agree with those who hold, on the contrary, that a far-seeing citizen who places before his slumbering countrymen a graphic awakening picture of a danger hanging over them is rendering them the highest service.'

A retired admiral begged to differ. 'I do not myself think,' Admiral C. C. Penrose Fitzgerald huffed, 'that any civilised nation will torpedo unarmed and defenceless merchant ships.' Admiral William Hannam Henderson agreed: 'No nation would permit it.' Less than a year later, on 7 May 1915, the RMS *Lusitania,* on her 202nd Atlantic crossing, was torpedoed and sunk by a German U-boat with the loss 1,195 lives, marking the end of any delusions that 'civilised' warfare would endure into the twentieth century.

◆

In the spring of 1914, with the grim prospect of war in Europe looming larger, Conan Doyle and his wife accepted an invitation from the Canadian government to visit the National Reserve at Jasper Park in the Canadian Rockies. Leaving their three children in the care of a nanny and a close friend of Jean's, Lily Loder Symonds, they departed from Southampton on board the White Star liner SS *Olympic* – the sister ship to the *Titanic* – on 20 May. During the crossing, Conan Doyle jotted down ideas for speeches and snatches of hilar-

ious conversation with his fellow passengers. His ear for comic ver-
nacular was acute. Here is Mr Stevens Ulman, a bombastic American businessman, as recorded in Conan Doyle's 'America Canada
1914' notebook: 'I'm a man that gets around some. You see, sir, I'm
right in it. If there's anything you want at New York you come to
me. I've the pull there. Anything at all. Just come to me and you can
have it . . . I was speakin' to the Pope. He said "Why didn't you come
sooner?" I said "It was late when I got in." "My" said he "You should
have come right away." They like to talk with me, I guess. Maybe
I'm more truthful with them than some. I'm for speaking right out.
We're all men when all's said and done. That was what the French
President said to me . . .'[5]

Conan Doyle liked and admired America, its optimism and self-
confidence, and Americans generally liked and admired him, his gruff,
old-world gentlemanly charm, his love of sport and fair play, his battles
against injustice. Before leaving he told a reporter for the *New York
American*: 'Personally I regard the United States as a country with the
most remarkable destiny the world has ever known.'[6] He had long
harboured the dream of a union between the United States and the
United Kingdom, articulated by Holmes as early as 1892 in 'The Adventure of the Noble Bachelor': 'It is always a joy to meet an American,
Mr Moulton, for I am one of those who believe that the folly of a
monarch and the blundering of a minister in far-gone years will not
prevent our children from being some day citizens of the same worldwide country under a flag which shall be a quartering of the Union
Jack with the Stars and Stripes.'

As the *Olympic* steamed into the Hudson River, the famous American detective, William J. Burns, came out on a revenue cutter to greet
them. A former secret service agent, Burns was the founder of the
William J. Burns International Detective Agency. A combination of
good casework and an instinct for publicity had turned him into a
celebrity, sometimes described as the 'Sherlock Holmes of America'.
He had met Conan Doyle a year earlier, during a visit to Great Britain,
and had been entertained for the weekend at Windlesham. The two
men had got along famously and it was likely that Burns's stories of
his days as a private detective provided Conan Doyle with the inspiration for his last full-length detective novel, *The Valley of Fear*, about

an agent from the famous Pinkerton detective agency infiltrating criminal gangs in the coalfields of Pennsylvania.

Jean Conan Doyle kept a journal of their trip and was obviously delighted by everything. 'Arrived at New York early in the morning at about 8 o'clock,' she wrote on 27 May. 'Crowds of pressmen came on board and surrounded Arthur, photographing him and me! Mr Burns, the great detective, came on board to meet us. Other people came to the docks to see us. It was a great reception. All day long the telephone was ringing in our rooms and interviewers coming to interview A and me! . . . I am awfully impressed with New York and I like the people very much . . .'[7] She was particularly enthusiastic about the women: 'American women are charming. And so smart! I don't think any women anywhere are smarter. I can't help noticing the smart appearance everywhere I go; the shop-girls have it as well as the women one sees in the hotels and theatres.' Her breathless, wide-eyed tone did not conceal her delight at being treated like a celebrity.

The American media naturally wanted to know Conan Doyle's views on the issues of the day, particularly on female suffrage. At that time the struggle for female emancipation in Britain was making headlines around the world, and although Conan Doyle had campaigned vigorously for divorce reform, essentially a women's rights issue, he viewed the suffragette movement with some distaste, largely because of the increasingly violent tactics it employed. Militant suffragettes had taken to smashing shop windows in London's West End, fighting the police with hatpins and umbrellas, staging arson attacks and explosions, and painting 'Votes For Women' on public buildings. Suffragettes on hunger strike in prison were being force-fed, a gory process that involved shoving a steel tube down the inmate's throat and outraged public opinion. In February 1913 Emmeline Pankhurst went on trial on bomb charges and proudly accepted responsibility for what she described as the suffragettes' 'guerrilla warfare', and in June Emily Davison died when she ran in front of the King's horse at the Epsom Derby race meeting. In November protesting suffragettes fought a pitched battle with police outside Parliament and nearly 200 were arrested after another battle in Downing Street. *The Times* described the demonstrators as 'demented creatures'.

Conan Doyle was prominent among public figures denouncing the women's rampant militancy and for his trouble was booed at public events, was the victim of hate mail, had sulphuric acid poured through the letter box at Windlesham and was temporarily obliged to have a policeman posted at the gates. It was his view that women could not expect the right to vote until they paid their own taxes, and furthermore he doubted that women in general, outside the suffragette movement, were interested in politics. His own beloved wife certainly had no desire to vote and his equally beloved mother had proven, as far as he was concerned, that it was quite possible for a woman to hold her own in a man's world. Would either benefit from female suffrage? No. He considered that the suffragette movement was more likely to result in social chaos than equality for women.

It was not in his nature to dissemble and so when he faced the New York media, he did not hesitate to share his honest view that the patience of the British public had been strained to breaking point by the actions of the militant suffragettes. He would not be in the least surprised, he said, to hear that some of them had fallen victim to mob law; there could be a 'wholesale lynching bee' and if that happened the militants could only blame themselves. Conan Doyle was furious at the headlines which appeared the following day in some of the less respectable newspapers: 'SHERLOCK'S HERE; EXPECTS LYNCHING OF WILD WOMEN' (*New York World*): 'LYNCHING IS CONAN DOYLE'S SUFF REMEDY' (*New York Mail*); 'CONAN DOYLE SAYS: LET THE MILITANTS DIE OF STARVATION' (*New York American*). He attempted damage limitation in an interview with Louis Sherwin in the *New York Globe*: 'Really, you know, that sort of thing [inaccurate reporting] is perfectly monstrous. Why, some of my best friends are suffragettes and what will they think of me? That will be cabled right over to London, for they are keenly interested over there in everything that goes on in America . . . It puts me in a most uncomfortable position – makes it appear that I am coming over here to say things I should not dare to at home . . .'

In fact the fuss soon died down and they were able to enjoy a VIP tour of the city. 'Arthur and I went to the top of the Woolworth building – 59 stories high!' Jean wrote in her diary. 'We had a most wonderful view from the top. Arthur did the Tombs prison and then was the Guest of the Pilgrims Club to lunch. All the great men were there "to entertain him" . . . Arthur gave a splendid address – various people who were there told me it was fine . . . Drove to the Stock Exchange – it was such a fascinating sight – the shouting of the men was terrific. So many recognised Arthur.' At a reception that evening Conan Doyle was tickled to be introduced, by Joseph Hodges Choate, the former US ambassador to London, as 'the best known living Britisher'.

Conan Doyle was taken alone to visit the notorious Sing Sing prison on the banks of the Hudson river, where he arrived in time to watch a music-hall troupe entertaining the inmates. 'Poor devils,' he observed, 'all the forced, vulgar gaiety of the songs and antics of half-clad women must have provoked a terrible reaction in their minds! Many of them had, I observed, abnormalities of cranium or of features which made it clear that they were not wholly responsible for their actions.' He sat, briefly, in the 'electrocution chair', which he described as 'a very ordinary, stout, cane-bottomed seat, with a good many sinister wires dangling from it' and was locked up in a seven-by-four-foot cell. 'It was the most restful time I have had since I arrived in New York,' he joked, 'for it was the only chance I had to get away from the reporters.' Joking apart, he was shocked by the conditions in the jail and told the *New York Times* that he thought the place should be 'burned down'. 'It is nothing less than a disgrace,' he was quoted as saying, 'for a state so great and wealthy as New York to have a prison which is a hundred years behind the times.' He offered the view that a third of the inmates were 'defectives' whose cases called for medical care rather than incarceration, but at the same time he believed that habitual criminals should expect to be 'permanently segre-gated' from the community. The *New York Times* headline was unequiv-ocal: 'CONAN DOYLE WOULD BURN DOWN SING SING'.

On Tuesday, 2 June, the Conan Doyles left for Canada in a private railway carriage belonging to the president of the Canadian Grand Trunk Railway which had been put at their disposal. 'The car is delightful,' Jean wrote, 'there is a sitting-room at the end of the car with a sofa and four arm chairs – 2 tables with drapes on them and footstools – cushions etc – also a speedometer. There are four large windows & two at the back and a door (glass top) and when that is open there is a wire mosquito door to close – letting in all air and keeping out mosquitoes. We have each a very comfortable little cabin – as I call them – with a wide bed, a washing stand, a seat and a minute wardrobe and a drawer in it. There is a door between my cabin and Arthur's. Then comes a delightful little dining room, with a large bowl of flowers in the centre of the table. Breakfast was already laid for us . . .'

Wednesday 3 June: 'Fort William Henry . . . the scenery we have been through today has been beautiful – we coasted nearly all along Lake Champlain which is 100 miles long and in one place 12 miles broad. My darling has had a more restful day today – he is so sweet and kind. He said just now that he is quite silly when I am about! No man ever loved a woman more or showed it more at every turn in every way . . .'

From Montreal the Conan Doyles travelled on in their private railway carriage to Winnipeg and Edmonton where Jean noted in her diary: 'Arthur said yesterday that I have been such a wonderful comrade to him – that not one clouded or grey moment had he had since we started on the journey from England.' Jean liked nothing more than compliments, and it is clear from her journal both that she glowed in her husband's reflected glory and loved the attention of the media. Away from Windlesham and the children, travelling in style, she had her first taste of true celebrity and loved it.

As a goodwill ambassador, Conan Doyle did his duty diligently, admiring everything, delivering speeches, talking to reporters and posing for photographers. But he admitted privately, in a letter to Innes written on Grand Trunk Pacific notepaper from Winnipeg that he was far from taken with Canada and was 'frayed at the edges' from the incessant travel: 'My dear old Chap, We are sagging back on the old trail, the trail that is anything but new. I don't want to see Canada again. Their clubs and papers bore me, everything is raw, there is no history (save in the East) and nature is not kind.'[8]

One would never have guessed his disenchantment from his memoirs, in which he recalled being mightily stirred by his first glimpse of the Rockies: 'A line of low distant hills broke the interminable plain which has extended with hardly a rising for fifteen hundred miles. Above them was, here and there, a peak of snow. Shades of Thomas

Mayne Reid [one of his boyhood heroes], they were the Rockies –
my old familiar Rockies! Have I been here before? What an absurd
question, when I lived here for about ten years of my life in all the
hours of dreamland. What deeds have I not done among redskins and
trappers and grizzlies within their wilds! And here they were at last,
glimmering bright in the rising morning sun. At least, I have seen
my dream mountains. Most boys never do.'

Jean was not inspired to such emotional heights in her diary.
Wednesday 24 June: 'We got to Fort William at 1.30 where several
people came to meet us, among them the Mayor, who had brought
his car to take us for a ride. The outskirts of Fort William are beautiful – Arthur bought a plot of land with a small wooden house on
it – in one of the main streets – which ought to prove very valuable.
We got on to our car at 6.30 and one or two women turned up to
see Arthur. Then we dined and slept on the car, the car remaining in
the station all night and being put on to a train early in the morning.'

———◆———

She made no mention in her journal of the momentous events taking
place in Europe while they were away. On 28 June, the heir to the
Austro-Hungarian throne, the Archduke Franz Ferdinand, was assassinated by a 19-year-old Serbian student while on a visit to Sarajevo,
the capital of Bosnia. A wave of horror and indignation swept through
Europe in its wake. 'It shakes the conscience of the world,' *The Times*
declared. The *Daily Chronicle* described it as a 'clap of thunder' over
Europe. In Vienna students staged anti-Serbian demonstrations and
the foreign minister, Count Leopold von Berchtold, spoke of dealing
with the 'Serbian wasp's nest', even at the risk of provoking European
'complications'.

The Conan Doyles arrived home on board the SS *Megantic* to find
Europe moving inexorably towards war. On 5 July, while they were
still at sea, Kaiser Wilhelm II reaffirmed Germany's alliance with
Austria. On 23 July, the Austrian government issued an ultimatum
giving Serbia forty-eight hours to agree to a series of drastic and
humiliating demands. Events then unfolded with bewildering speed.
Serbia rejected Austria's ultimatum and ordered its army to mobilise.

In St Petersburg the tsar warned Germany that Russia would not remain indifferent if Serbia was invaded. On 28 July Austria declared war on Serbia. Great Britain's attempts to mediate were rejected by the Kaiser as 'insolent'. On 1 August, the tsar declared war on Germany, on 3 August, Germany declared war on France and on 4 August, Britain declared war on Germany. As news of the war spread, cheering crowds gathered outside Downing Street and Buckingham Palace, and young men flocked to the recruiting offices anxious to see action for fear it would be 'all over by Christmas'.

While he was in Canada, Conan Doyle admitted to a 'presentiment of coming trouble' but claimed he had never imagined that a world war was so close. Ironically, on 29 June, the day after the assassination of Archduke Ferdinand, the House of Commons had been scheduled to debate the question of a Channel tunnel.

CHAPTER 18

THE GREAT WAR

N THE DAY WAR BROKE out, Conan Doyle received a plaintive note from Mr Goldsmith, the village plumber, delivered by hand to Windlesham. 'There is a feeling in Crowborough,' he wrote, 'that something should be done.' Conan Doyle, man of action, heartily agreed. He had long believed in the need for a trained civilian home defence force and immediately had leaflets printed and distributed around the surrounding district, inviting anyone interested to attend a meeting that evening:

IMPORTANT

A Meeting
Will be held
To-night, August 4
In the
Oddfellows' Hall
To discuss the feasibility of forming a Local Company or Companies for Purposes of Drill and Efficiency, that we may be of service to our Country In this crisis.

Sir A. Conan Doyle D. L.
Will take the Chair at 8.30

Quite a crowd turned up. Conan Doyle outlined his ambitious plans under which every citizen, young and old, would be trained to carry arms, creating a 'great stockpot into which the nation could dip and draw its needs'. No one, he pointed out, would be the worse for being able to drill, handle a weapon and be assembled into organised units. He was the first to sign the roll of what they decided to name the 'Crowborough National Reserve Company'; 173 men followed. They met again at a local drill hall the next day to devise rules and choose non-commissioned officers capable of organising their training. Thereafter they began drilling every day.

Conan Doyle had the good sense to inform the War Office of the existence of his Civilian Reserve and to request official sanction. He was also careful to point out that no able-bodied young men who could reasonably be expected to join the Army would be recruited. Meanwhile, he wrote to *The Times* describing how he had set about forming the unit and how, if other towns and villages followed suit, the Civilian Reserve would free Britain's Territorial Army for active service. 'We have our own record of organisation,' he wrote, 'and I should be happy to send copies of our method to anyone who may desire to form other centres.' The response was extraordinary: some 1,200 requests for more information from towns and villages across Great Britain. Conan Doyle and Woodie spent a whole day sending off details.

Alarm bells began ringing in the War Office, however, at the prospect of hundreds of civilian militia units being set up without any central control, and telegrams were sent out, including to Conan Doyle, ordering all 'unauthorised bodies' to be disbanded immediately. The idea, however, was clearly considered a good one and a committee was established to organise a national volunteer force. Conan Doyle was invited to be a member and his Civilian Reserve eventually became the Crowborough Company of the Sixth Royal Sussex Volunteer Regiment with the honour, enshrined in the *Volunteer Gazette*, of being the first company in the country. At his own wish Conan Doyle would remain a private in the Crowborough Company for the remainder of the war, enthusiastically taking part in route marches, regular training and guard duties.

'Our drill and discipline were excellent,' he recalled, 'and when we received our rifles and bayonets we soon learned to use them, nor were our marching powers contemptible when one remembers that many of the men were in their fifties and even in their sixties. It was quite usual for us to march from Crowborough to Frant with our rifles and equipment, to drill for a long hour in a heavy marshy field, and then to march back, singing all the way. It would be a good fourteen miles, apart from the drill.' He thoroughly enjoyed mixing with the locals, being 'one of the lads', and nothing pleased him more than to be patronised by an inspecting officer and to enjoy his embarrassment when his identity was revealed.

It was typical of Conan Doyle that even though he was doing his bit in the Civilian Reserve and even though he was 55 years old, he should consider enlisting in the regular Army, despite being advised against it both by Woodie and his younger brother, then a temporary Lieutenant Colonel in command of 3rd County of Durham Brigade, Royal Field Artillery. It was also typical of him to think that by not serving he was missing a 'wonderful experience' – a delusion he shared with millions of men across the country. 'Dear old Boy,' he wrote to Innes on 28 August: 'Wood takes the same view that you do about my volunteering and yet I am not convinced. From a coldly reasonable point of view I am sure you are both right. But I have only one life to live and here is this grand chance of a wonderful experience which might at the same time have a good effect upon some others. I am sorely tempted. If disaster should come to us it will be still more difficult to keep still . . . Your affectionate brother, A.'

In the end he succumbed to the temptation and formally applied to the War Office for enlistment, shamelessly using the Civilian Reserve – and, curiously, his loud voice – to bolster his case:

> I have been told that there may be some difficulty in finding Officers for the New Army. I think I may say that my name is well known to the younger men of this country and that if I were to take a commission at my age it would set an example which might be of help.
>
> I can drill a company – I do so every evening. I have seen something of campaigning, having served as a surgeon in South Africa. I am fifty five but very strong and hardy, and can make my voice audible at great distances, which is useful at drill.
>
> Should you entertain my application, I should prefer a

regiment which was drawn from the South of England –
Sussex for choice. I am, Sir, yours faithfully,

Arthur Conan Doyle.

A few days later, on 21 August, his application was politely rejected.

Initial reports from the front were less than cheering: the German
Army had swept over most of Belgium, forcing both the British
Expeditionary Force (BEF) and the French Army to retreat, and
after a four-day battle at Tannenberg, on the border with East
Prussia, the Russian Army had suffered a terrible defeat, with 'severe
losses'. The family suffered its own first loss during the retreat from
Mons: Conan Doyle's brother-in-law, Captain Malcolm Leckie of
the Royal Army Medical Corps, was severely wounded. He
continued to treat other comrades until he died four days later. He
was awarded a posthumous DSO.

Denied active service from the start of the conflict, Conan Doyle
vigorously applied his pen to the war effort, writing a bellicose 32-
page propaganda pamphlet, *To Arms!*, in August in which he rammed
home the justice of the British cause. 'All our lives,' he wrote, 'have
been but a preparation for this supreme moment.' Germany, which
he once regarded with some affection, was now very definitely beyond
the pale, an upstart nation with no culture, utterly inferior in 'spiritual and intellectual matters'. (This conveniently ignored the large
numbers of German scientists, writers, composers and philosophers
whose books filled libraries around the world and the fact that the
first Nobel Prize for Physics had been awarded to a German.) Germans
had for years, he wrote, regarded the British Empire with 'eyes of
jealousy and hatred . . . a most bitter hatred, a hatred which long
antedates the days when we were compelled to take a definite stand
against them'. Britain was fighting the 'narrow bureaucracy and
swaggering Junkerdom of Prussia, the most artifice and ossified sham
that ever our days have seen'. Gung-ho, jingoistic and rabble-rousing,
To Arms! reflected Conan Doyle's blinkered, black-and-white view of
the war. Britain's nickname, 'perfidious Albion', had not been acquired
without some justification, but to Conan Doyle 'King and country'
were synonymous with irreproachable rectitude.

Published by Hodder & Stoughton, with a foreword by F. E. Smith,

Conservative MP and the future Lord Birkenhead, *To Arms!* was widely distributed in Great Britain and abroad, in the United States, Denmark, Holland and the Argentine. Conan Doyle wanted to produce a second pamphlet in German as an exercise in demoralisation to convince soldiers in the German Army they were on the wrong side, but there was no realistic way of distributing it.

It did not take long for Conan Doyle's dire prophecies about the danger of enemy submarines to be realised. Soon after dawn on 22 September 1914, a German U-boat, the U-9, on patrol in the North Sea under the command of Commander Otto Weddigen, torpedoed and sank three British cruisers, HMS *Aboukir, Hogue* and *Cressy*, in the space of little more than an hour, with the loss of 1,459 lives. 'A young German lieutenant with 20 men,' Conan Doyle fumed, 'had caused us more loss than we suffered at Trafalgar.'

Dismayed by the calamity, he launched a campaign in the media, notably the *Daily Mail* and the *Daily Chronicle,* to equip all sailors and troops embarking for France with inflatable rubber collars to help them stay afloat in the event of their ship being sunk. These would at least, he pointed out, 'hold the poor fellows above the waves until some help could reach them'. Such was his influence that the Admiralty put through a rush order for 250,000 such collars, which henceforth became standard equipment. 'The Navy has to thank Sir Conan Doyle for the new life-saving apparatus the Admiralty are supplying,' the *Hampshire Telegraph* reported. 'There is little doubt that this swimming collar will result in the saving of many lives, and the Admiralty are to be congratulated upon the promptitude with which they have adopted the suggestion of Sir Conan Doyle.'

Conan Doyle did not rest on his laurels. He then questioned the practice of ditching wooden lifeboats overboard during action to prevent them catching fire and setting an entire ship ablaze. It made no sense to him to provide sailors with inflatable collars if they could not be rescued by lifeboats. In rough sea at the height of winter, he argued, men would soon perish and the collars would only 'prolong their agony'. In a letter to the *Daily Mail* he suggested replacing wooden lifeboats with inflatable rubber boats: 'We can spare and replace the ships. We cannot spare the men. They *must* be saved, and this is how to save them. There is nothing so urgent as this. We can view all future disasters with equanimity if the ship's company has only a fair chance for its life.'

One of the few public figures to engage so pragmatically with the realities of war, he described his campaigning as 'agitation'. 'The final result of the agitation was the provision of collars, safety waistcoats, and (as I believe), of a better supply of boats. I need hardly say that I never received a word of acknowledgement or thanks from the Admiralty. One is not likely to be thanked by a Government depart-ment for supplementing its work. But it may be some poor seaman struggling in the water sent me his good wish, and those are the thanks that I desired. There was nothing in the war which moved me more than the thought of the helpless plight of the gallant men who were sacrificed when they could so easily have been saved.'

Other of his ideas were less welcome to the military authorities. He proposed 'something like a huge trident or toasting fork' fixed to the bows of Royal Navy ships to deal with the menace of mines. The device could be hauled up when it was safe but lowered in mine-infested waters to explode them ahead of the ship. He also pressed the War Office to consider issuing troops with body armour, a proposal he had first put forward at the time of the Boer War. 'It has always seemed to me extraordinary,' he wrote to *The Times,* 'that the innumerable cases where a Bible, cigarette case, a watch, or some other chance article has saved a man's life have not set us scheming so as to do systematically what has so often been the result of happy chance.'[1] In collaboration with Herbert Frood, owner of the Ferodo brake-lining factory in Derbyshire, a prototype was constructed of compressed asbestos with a woven textile surface. It was successfully tested against bullets, but nothing came of the research. The commander-in-chief, General Sir Douglas Haig, reportedly took the view that only cowards would want to wear it.

Conan Doyle might have reflected bitterly that armour might have saved members of his own family: his nephew Oscar Hornung, a Second Lieutenant in the Essex Regiment, died in action at Ypres at the age of 20 in July 1915; and his brother-in-law Leslie Oldham, Lottie's husband, was killed just three weeks later. Oscar's death was particularly poignant: a year earlier he had written to his uncle asking him to use his influence to have him accepted for active service. 'This is what I am aiming for,' he wrote, 'to get to the front if possible.'[2]

Jean's closest friend, Lily Loder Symonds, lost three of her brothers at Ypres, a fourth was killed in an accident and a fifth wounded and taken prisoner. When Conan Doyle discovered where Captain Willie Loder Symonds was being held – at a prison camp in Magdeburg – he began sending him news of the war by painstakingly pricking out letters with a needle on the pages of one of his books, starting with the third chapter. He enclosed a note: 'This may relieve your prison activity and afterwards be placed in the prison library. It is slow, but you might find the third chapter to be a little more interesting.'[3] A fellow prisoner of Loder Symonds got word back to Conan Doyle that he understood the message, but neglected to add that his efforts were unnecessary since they were being supplied with British newspapers.

Some light relief from the war was provided by the serialisation in the *Strand* of a new Sherlock Holmes novel, *The Valley of Fear*, a precursor of the crime thrillers that would enjoy huge popularity during the heyday of the prolific British novelist Edgar Wallace in the 1920s. Published in book form in Great Britain in June 1915, it was greeted by a reviewer in *The Times* as a welcome escape: 'We congratulate Sir A. Conan Doyle on the new field and on the old, and are grateful for both. His pen is one of the few that can help us forget the war for an hour or two.'

The Valley of Fear was actually two stories, only tenuously linked. The first part, 'The Tragedy of Birlstone', was a classic 'locked room' murder mystery described by the thriller writer John Dickson Carr as a 'very nearly perfect piece of detective-story writing'. The second part, 'The Scowrers', was an extended flashback about a Pinkerton detective who infiltrated the Molly Maguires, Irish secret societies operating in the Pennsylvania minefields in the 1860s and 70s, and other events that had led up to the crime committed in England. Unfortunately Sherlock Holmes was almost entirely absent from this part, disappointing many readers.

When Conan Doyle was reporting his progress with *The Valley of Fear* to Greenhough Smith, he scrawled an ominous note across the top of the letter: 'I fancy this is my swansong in fiction.' Greenhough Smith, much alarmed, asked him to explain and he replied that he had reached the point financially where he felt he could devote himself to historical work. Temporarily true to his word, by the time *The Valley of Fear* was published, he was well embarked on an extraordinarily ambitious project – a complete history of the war, even as it was being fought. Before the end of 1914 he had made contact with commanders-in-chief to ask for their cooperation in supplying him with regular eyewitness accounts of the campaign, letters, journals and reports of all kinds. He had soon secured the agreement of some significant figures, as he explained in a letter to Innes, who was in France and also served as a source: 'My hand is fairly cramped with writing history. I have had great luck. *Between ourselves* I have Smith-Dorrien's diaries and am promised Haig's, so on top of Bulfin's, I am pretty well informed. I shall now do a worthy book and it may well be my Magnum Opus for the subject will make it illustrious. I should be proud to do *the* record of this war. It can never be precise, but it will be true and, I hope, interesting . . .'[4]

General Edward Bulfin, a contemporary at Stonyhurst, was commander of the 28th Division; General Douglas Haig was then commander of the 1st Army Corps; and General Horace Smith-Dorrien was in command of the 2nd Corps. They were just the start: by the end of the war Conan Doyle was corresponding with nearly fifty generals and receiving at least five letters from senior officers by every post. An officer in the General Staff charged with collecting material for the official history of the war obligingly kept him posted with divisional reports and journals, but the War Office itself was reluctant to participate. Sir Reginald Brade, head of the censorship department, did not feel able to offer Conan Doyle access to the official archive and also warned the Chief of Military Intelligence that he was trying to extract confidential information from senior officers. Sir John French, commander-in-chief of the BEF, to whom Conan Doyle intended to dedicate the first volume, initially gave his approval then changed his mind. On 20 May 1915 Sir John's private secretary wrote to Conan Doyle to inform him that the Military Censor considered publication to be 'undesirable' and that Sir John 'would not wish the book if published to be dedicated to him as originally proposed'.[5]

Convinced that he was performing a valuable public service by using his literary talents to make a permanent record of the war for all time, Conan Doyle was undeterred. He went to great lengths to check his information with commanding officers in the field and sent out foolscap sheets with his notes on the left-hand side, asking for comments to be inserted on the right. Against his information concerning the battle of the Aisne: 'The British trenches were a mile and a quarter from a river. The position appeared serious as there was a river and the Aisne Canal behind the troops, and no supports all the way to Paris', an unnamed officer had written: 'Be careful how you make use of this, as it was a tactical error, probably avoidable, but still we must not give away the Generalship.' Some of his contacts took the opportunity, indiscreetly, to pay off scores. Smith-Dorrien was extraordinarily candid in his observations, for example, complaining that Sir John French would 'never admit he can be wrong' and denigrating his superior officer's abilities ('Sir J French was certainly not at his best in the days of Mons and Le Cateau').[6]

In February 1915 Conan Doyle was appalled to read a report in *The Times*, culled from German newspapers, suggesting that his story 'Danger!' might have given the Germans the idea of mounting a submarine blockade of Britain. He felt obliged to issue an immediate statement warding off the embarrassing possibility of being accused of offering aid to the enemy: 'I need hardly say that it is very painful for me to think that anything I have written should be turned against my own country. The object of the story was to warn the public of a possible danger which I saw overhanging this country and to show it how to avoid that danger.' He went on to explain that his story was set in the future: 'I am quite sure,' he concluded, 'in the present circumstances, that although we may possibly lose more ships, the German blockade can have no serious effect on the war.'[7]

As the war ground on and casualties increased, Conan Doyle was in the vanguard of stiffening the nation's backbone by depicting the Germans as monsters capable of any atrocity, from 'systematic murder' to the torture of prisoners of war. In a penny pamphlet published by the Central Committee for National Patriotic Organisation in May

1915, he unashamedly stoked the fires of prejudice, listing the bestial practices of the enemy to 'warm the hearts' of British soldiers in battle and to 'teach them that it is better to die on the field than fall into the cruel hands of German gaolers'. He suggested that relations with Germany were beyond repair: 'Never again in our time will a German visitor be welcome in our country. Never again should our students of music flock to Dresden, of art to Leipzig and Munich, or our invalids to the overrated spas of the Fatherland. A deep fissure will divide the two races . . .'

In a letter to *The Times* in October 1915, he suggested that 'avenging squadrons' of British aeroplanes should retaliate after every Zeppelin attack with raids on three German towns. The first Zeppelin raid on London in May 1915 had killed 28 people and injured 60. 'We should soon bring them to reason. I can well imagine that our airmen would find such work repugnant, but they must bear in mind that women and children have for a long time been sacrificed over here, and that all forbearance has been shown, and that no other methods but those of reprisal offer any assurance that we can save civilians from these murderous outrages.' He continued to press for increased retaliation against Germany. When it became known that Nurse Edith Cavell had been shot in October 1915 accused of helping Allied soldiers escape from occupied Belgium, he proposed executing three prominent German prisoners of war in response. When Charles Fryatt, the captain of a British merchant ship who had become a national hero after attempting to ram and sink a German submarine, was subsequently captured and executed, Conan Doyle suggested killing two German submarine captains. He later proposed shooting all captured enemy airman as 'these are the only arguments the German military can understand'.

Although more vocal than the man in the street, Conan Doyle was articulating the national mood of shock and horror at the events unfolding in France and German tactics. The notion that the war would be over by Christmas had long since faded, stories from the trenches gave little hope that it would end any time soon and the nation needed to be reminded it was fighting a just war against a bestial enemy: this was the role that Conan Dole sought to fulfil.

In Crowborough, Lady Conan Doyle was also doing her bit for the war effort, running a home for Belgian refugees at Gorselands, not far from Windlesham, where, on still winter nights, they could hear the distant thunder of the heavy guns in France. The Conan Doyles gave over a wing of the house to soldiers, entertained a large number of Canadian officers to dinner every week and cut the family's rations – but not those of their servants – by a quarter.

Mary had taken a job in the Vickers munitions factory and Kingsley, having confessed to her that he could not countenance fighting and killing whilst honouring the Hippocratic oath he would soon take as a doctor, joined the City of London Royal Army Medical Corps as a private. He was assigned to be an ambulance driver and sent to Malta, then known as the 'sick bay of the Mediterranean', where 25,000 beds had been allocated for the wounded. Conan Doyle undoubtedly believed that his son's place was at the front with other young men of his age – he described conscientious objectors with utter contempt as 'half-mad cranks whose absurd consciences prevented them from barring the way to the devil'[8] – and admitted in a letter to Innes that: 'I never feel I know him [Kingsley] in the least, he lives behind a very tight mask and all his real interests and thoughts are concealed from me. But I am sure they are good. His one fault is his extreme secretiveness.'[9]

After a year in Malta, however, Kingsley Conan Doyle experienced a change of heart and decided he could not allow other men to fight and die for him. It is unclear whether he knew of or was influenced by his father's disapproval, but Conan Doyle was no doubt delighted when his son took a commission in the Hampshire Regiment and was sent to France in April 1916. 'My big lad is in the Hampshires and yearning for the fray,' he wrote to Greenhough Smith. 'I wish to God they would let the Volunteers go. I believe we should do right well – indeed that we hold in our ranks some of the best material in England.'[10] In his memoirs Conan Doyle made no mention of his son initially joining a non-combatant unit and proudly described him as a 'soldier, first, last and all the time'.

Not long after Kingsley had left for France, it was announced that Conan Doyle had been 'invited' to visit the Italian front as an independent British observer. In fact he had initiated the visit himself. After adverse criticism of the Italian Army for its retreat from Trentino in May 1916 in the face of a massive Austrian offensive, Conan Doyle contacted the Foreign Office and offered to write a positive article about the Italians if he could be allowed to visit other fronts to conduct first-hand research for his history. It was made to look like an official invitation so that other correspondents with a better claim to facilities would not feel that Conan Doyle was being given preferential treatment.

When the Foreign Office informed him that he would need to be in uniform, he proudly pointed out that he already had one, as a private soldier in the Crowborough Company of the Sixth Royal Sussex Volunteer Regiment. The Foreign Office was unimpressed and gently suggested that he might be advised to travel as an officer. He decided to adapt the elaborate uniform that accompanied his honorary position as Deputy Lieutenant of Surrey, conferred on him when he was knighted in 1902. 'I went straight off to my tailor,' he recalled, 'who rigged me up in a wondrous khaki garb which was something between that of a colonel and a brigadier, with silver roses instead of stars or crowns upon the shoulder-straps.' He also had matching uniforms made for his sons Denis and Adrian, then 7 and 5 years old, and was photographed with them, all in their new uniforms, in the garden at Windlesham.

Togged up in his 'wondrous' attire and feeling, perhaps unsurprisingly, like 'a mighty imposter', Conan Doyle left for France on board a Royal Navy destroyer in the company of General Sir William Robertson, then the British chief of staff. At General Headquarters he found his unusual uniform excited considerable interest: 'I was still a rare specimen, and quite a number of officers of three nations made enquiry about my silver roses. A deputy-lieutenant may not be much in England, but when translated into French – my French anyhow – it has an awe-inspiring effect, and I was looked upon by them as an inscrutable but very big person with a uniform all of his own.'

Issued with a gas mask and a tin helmet he was conducted on a tour of the British lines – plodding through interminable muddy trenches – and was deeply impressed by the Army's 'extraordinary efficiency' and 'cheerful bravery'. He was offered a periscope to look across the rusting barbed wire to the German lines, 180 yards distant, and noted that the soldiers around him seemed genuinely relaxed: 'Who would dream, who looked at their bold, careless faces, that this was a front line, and that at any moment it was possible that a grey wave [the German forces] might submerge them?'

Later he was able to spend time with Innes, by then a Lieutenant Colonel and Assistant Adjutant General of the 24th Division, head-quartered at Bailleul. After dinner Innes took his brother up to a ridge to see the lights of Ypres Salient – the front line. 'I have seen nothing like it, but the nearest comparison would be an enormous ten-mile railway station in full swing at night, with signals winking, lamps waving, engines hissing and carriages bumping . . . Never shall I forget the impression of ceaseless, malignant activity which was borne in upon me by the white, winking lights, the red sudden flares, and the horrible thudding noises in that place of death beneath me.'

While in Flanders Conan Doyle also interviewed General Sir Douglas Haig, who arranged for Kingsley to be withdrawn from the trenches to meet his father in a village behind the line. They talked for an hour and Kingsley told his father that the 'big push' – the start of the great battle of the Somme – was expected at any time and that his battalion, the 1st Hampshires, would be in the vanguard. Conan Doyle learned later that before the battle started Kingsley had crawled out into no man's land on ten successive nights to mark, with white crosses (brown on the far side), areas where the German wire was intact, as a guide to British artillery. The BEF suffered 58,000 casual-ties, a third of them killed, on 1 July 1916, the first day of the Battle of the Somme, the worst day in the history of the British Army. Kingsley sustained two shrapnel wounds to his neck and spent two months in hospital.

From the Somme, Conan Doyle travelled by train to Paris, where he spent two days at the Hotel Crillon and found the city greatly subdued, before making for the Italian front. At their headquarters he found conditions very much like those in Flanders though with a more congenial climate. He was hoping to see the front-line trenches to make comparison with the British positions but was 'courteously but firmly warned off'.

Travelling with his escorts in an open car on the way to Monfalcone, a small dockyard town recently recaptured from the Austrians, they came under enemy artillery fire: '[T]here was a noise as if the whole four tyres had gone simultaneously, a most terrific bang in our very ears, merging into a second sound like a reverberating blow upon an enormous gong. As I glanced up, I saw three clouds immediately above my head, two of them white and the other of a rusty red. The air was full of flying metal, and the road, as we were told afterwards by an observer, was all churned up by it. The metal base of one of the shells was found plumb in the middle of the road just where our motor had been.' Fortunately they were travelling so fast that they were round a bend in the road and out of sight before another shell could be fired.

Subsequently Conan Doyle was allowed to visit the front at Trentino, where the Italians were experiencing a 'moment of depression'. He felt his presence helped lift their spirits. 'I may flatter myself when I think that even one solitary figure in a British uniform striding about among them was good at that particular time to their eyes . . . Certainly I was heartily welcomed there, and surrounded all the time by great mobs of soldiers, who imagined, I suppose, that I was someone of importance.' The throwaway caveat could not conceal Conan Doyle's pleasure. He usually did his best, in his gentlemanly way, not to appear vain, yet at the same time he clearly enjoyed his station in life.

He left Italy with 'sheaves of notes' which he hoped would make the British public more sympathetic to the Italian forces. Back in Paris he stepped out of a train to be informed by a British military policeman that Lord Kitchener was dead, drowned when the HMS *Hampshire*, on which he was travelling to Russia, struck a mine off the Orkneys. Kitchener, then Secretary of State for War, had recruited thousands of young men by pointing accusingly from posters: 'Your country needs you.' News of his death, Conan Doyle recalled, was like 'clods falling on my heart'. He was infuriated to find the Hotel Crillon full of 'sword-clanking Russians', since it was their 'rotten, crumbling country' Kitchener was visiting when he met his end.

Robert Donald, editor of the *Daily Chronicle*, was waiting to meet Conan Doyle in Paris. The *Daily Chronicle* had been publishing Conan Doyle's dispatches from the French and Italian fronts, and Donald, a

Scot with excellent contacts, had arranged for them to visit the French lines in the Argonne, where the battle of Verdun – which would be the longest in the war – was raging. In the trenches at Soisson they were shown a multitude of devices testifying to the ingenuity of the French. 'Every form of bomb, catapult and trench mortar was ready to hand. Every method of crossfire had been thought out to an exact degree.' When an artillery duel began above their heads, Conan Doyle noted that the French were firing three or four rounds to the enemy's one, thanks to the 'extraordinary zeal' of the French workers supplying the front with ammunition. At a dinner in his honour that night, with a special menu card embossed with a revolver and a violin, one French general fixed Conan Doyle with a steely glare and demanded: 'Sherlock Holmes, est-ce qu'il est un soldat dans l'armeé Anglaise?' Conan Doyle, momentarily nonplussed, replied: 'Mais, mon general, il est trop vieux pour service,' drawing a ripple of laughter from those around the table.

Conan Doyle returned to Britain deeply impressed with everything he had seen. Carried away by blind patriotism, barely a critical word passed his lips or emerged from his pen. The Allies were doing a superb job: the soldiers were cheerful, doughty and in fine fettle; the generals were all fine leaders, far-sighted, infallible and gifted tacticians. The front firing trench he described as 'surely the most wonderful spot in the world'. History would record a different verdict of trench warfare in the First World War, of the sheer futility of sending thousands of men 'over the top' to a certain death in the face of enemy machine-gun fire, but Conan Doyle was more patriot and propagandist than reporter. It was inconceivable to him that anything could be wrong with Allied tactics, just as it was inconceivable that he could not have witnessed the desperate conditions of the men in the trenches: he simply chose to ignore it.

He ended his report from France: 'Soldiers of France, farewell! In your own phrase I salute you! Many have seen you who had more knowledge by which to judge your manifold virtues, many also had more skill to draw you as you are, but never one, I am sure, who admired you more than I. Great was the French soldier, under Louis the Sun-King, great too under Napoleon, but never was he greater than today.' And in a slim volume published as a morale booster on his return under the title *A Visit to Three Fronts*, he paid fulsome tribute to the sterling qualities of the British soldiers he had met and admitted to a quiver in his stiff upper lip: 'I confess that as I looked at those brave English lads and thought of what we owed to them and their like who have passed on, I felt more emotional than befits a Briton in foreign parts.'

———————◆———————

During his absence in France, Conan Doyle's friend from his Congo campaign, Sir Roger Casement, had been arrested for attempting to ship weapons into Ireland to support an insurrection and sentenced to death for high treason. Conan Doyle was shocked by the sentence. Casement's guilt was not in doubt – he was recognised across the land as the 'foulest traitor ever to draw breath' – but Conan Doyle knew him to be an honourable man and convinced himself, without evidence, that Casement's actions were only explicable by some form of mental breakdown. Safely back at Windlesham he would participate in a vigorous campaign for a reprieve with his usual energy and certainty.

Knighted by King George V in recognition of his distinguished consular career, Casement had retired in 1912 because of ill health and returned to his homeland, where he became increasingly absorbed in militant nationalist politics. Irish revolutionary nationalists always looked to England's enemies for support and immediately after the outbreak of the First World War, leaders of Clan na Gael, a republican organisation of Irish-Americans in the United States, met the German ambassador in New York to outline how Britain's power could be broken by exploiting unrest in its vulnerable possessions, notably Ireland. They appealed for arms and military assistance to support an insurrection in the hope that a German-Irish alliance would result in securing full Irish independence. Casement became the central figure in negotiations and arrived in Berlin, via the United States, in October 1914, on an extraordinarily audacious mission. He proposed recruiting an Irish Brigade from among Irish prisoners captured on the Western Front and transporting them to Ireland to lead the fight for freedom, an attractive proposition for Germany, which would have required

Britain to divert troops from France and Belgium. On 20 November the German government declared its support for Irish independence and recruiting for the Irish Brigade began, but the response was disappointing. Many prisoners were disinterested in politics and many more refused to switch their allegiance, regarding Casement as an out-and-out traitor.

When the Irish Brigade failed to materialise the Germans lost interest in Irish nationalism until early in 1916 when word arrived from Dublin that a date had been set for the uprising – Easter. In response to an urgent request for arms and ammunition, Germany reluctantly agreed to ship 25,000 captured Russian rifles, ten machine guns and several million rounds of ammunition to southern Ireland on board the *Aud Norge,* a vessel masquerading as a Norwegian merchant ship. Casement was dismayed by the meagre support – the rebels had asked for 200,000 guns – and was convinced that the uprising was doomed. He arranged to return to Ireland on board a German submarine, determined to persuade the leaders to call it off.

Casement's submarine, the U-19, was due to rendezvous with the *Aud Norge* off the coast of County Kerry but the operation quickly degenerated into a fiasco. British intelligence had intercepted signals between the rebels and the German Embassy in New York and was thus anticipating the arrival of the ship. The *Aud Norge* was intercepted by a Royal Navy vessel and ordered into the port of Queenstown, but was scuttled en route by her crew. U-19, having failed to make the rendezvous, dropped Casement and two co-conspirators in a dinghy which overturned in the surf as they approached the beach in Ballyheige Bay. They struggled ashore, but Casement was too weak to continue. While his friends went for help, he rested near the remains of a Roman fort where he was discovered and arrested by a police constable who had seen the dinghy floating offshore. Three days later, on 24 April 1916, the Easter Rising began. It failed dismally, in part because of lack of arms, cost 450 lives and left much of Dublin in ruins.

Casement was imprisoned in the Tower of London before being tried for 'high treason' at the Old Bailey. On 29 June 1916, after a trial lasting three days, it took the jury less than an hour to find him guilty. Before sentencing, Casement spoke from the dock at some length claiming he was only guilty of being an Irishman who 'put Ireland first'. The judges were unmoved and sentenced him to death.

Clement Shorter, editor of the *Sphere*, was the prime mover in organising a petition addressed to the Prime Minister Herbert Asquith, calling on the government to show mercy, and it was Shorter who asked Conan Doyle to draft the wording. For once, Conan Doyle's facility failed him. As there was no doubt of Casement's guilt, he cast about vainly for reasons why the government might issue a reprieve; what he came up with was deeply unconvincing. In a hand-written letter to Shorter, dated 2 July, Conan Doyle offered three reasons why the 'extreme sentence of the law' should not be inflicted. He first postulated that Casement might be suffering from an 'abnormal physical and mental state' as a result of the many years he had been 'exposed to severe strain during his honourable career of public service', including enduring tropical fevers and two nerve-racking investigations in the Congo and the Amazon. Conan Doyle also called attention to an apparent 'violent change' in Casement's feelings towards Great Britain – from fervent British patriot to rabid Irish nationalist – as further evidence of his mental instability.

Secondly, Casement's execution, he argued, would only favour Germany by inflaming the situation in Ireland, and could be used as a weapon against Britain in the United States and other neutral countries. 'On the other hand, magnanimity upon the part of the British Government would soothe the bitter feelings in Ireland, and make a most favourable impression throughout the Empire and beyond.' Conan Doyle's third point was perhaps the least convincing, suggesting a reprieve could help solve the intractable 'Irish problem'. Drawing a comparison between the Easter Rising and the American Civil War half a century earlier, he 'respectfully reminded' the Prime Minister of the 'object lesson afforded by the United States at the conclusion of their Civil War'. None of the defeated leaders of the insurrection in the South had been executed and 'this policy of mercy was attended by such happy results that a breach which seemed to be irreparable has now been happily healed over'.[11]

In drafting the petition to Asquith, Shorter unwisely used Conan Doyle's letter verbatim. Many notable figures agreed to sign – among them Arnold Bennett, G. K. Chesterton, John Galsworthy,

Jerome K. Jerome, John Masefield and Beatrice and Sidney Webb – but many did not, some specifically citing the wording of the petition. Kipling was among those who declined with a brief note, dated 9 July 1916: 'Dear Mr Shorter, I find myself unable to sign the Petition you sent me re Roger Casement, and I return it accordingly. Yours sincerely, Rudyard Kipling.'[12]

Casement's solicitor, too, strongly objected to Conan Doyle's suggestion that his client might be unhinged. G. Gavan Duffy wrote to Shorter on 5 July. 'As Roger Casement's solicitor and confidant I cannot take part in the petition for his reprieve because I know that he welcomes the death sentence and that we would not ask the Government for any favour . . . Perhaps you will also allow me to say quite frankly that the introductory sentence of Sir Arthur Conan Doyle's petition seems to me quite unnecessary, not to put it higher, and that however flattering to the Empire may be the notion that my client's mind is affected, I think it is due to him to tell you that I have found no warrant for the assumption in the many conversations I have had with him during the past month.'[13]

The Foreign Office, perhaps alarmed that someone of Conan Doyle's stature was backing calls for a reprieve, summoned him to a meeting at which he was informed that Casement was a promiscuous homosexual who had kept graphic and explicit accounts of his sexual adventures in his private diaries. The government had been shamelessly exploiting Casement's so-called 'Black Diaries' to defuse any lingering public sympathy for his plight. Copies were sent to the King, the Archbishop of Canterbury and the Pope and circulated in Parliament. The *News of the World* reported that no one who ever read them would 'ever mention Casement's name again without loathing and contempt'.

Extracts were shown to Conan Doyle and others among Casement's prominent sympathisers to try and ensure his execution was unopposed. 'I have seen them and read them,' wrote the poet Alfred Noyes, 'and they touch the lowest depths that human degradation has ever touched. Page after page of his diary would be an insult to a pig's trough to let the foul record touch it.' Some were so shocked they shrank back from calls for clemency, but not Conan Doyle. To him, Casement's homosexuality was pathological, a sign of his 'mental disorder', as he explained in a note to Shorter: 'The summons to the F.O. proved to be about

Casement. They told me that his record for sexual offences was bad and had a diary of his in proof of it. I had of course heard this before, but as no possible sexual offence could be as bad as suborning soldiers from their duty, I was not diverted from my purpose. Nonetheless, it is of course very sad, and an additional sign of mental disorder. However I explained to the F.O. that this was all beside the question, for it was the political fortune of the Empire and not the man's life that I was anxious about . . .'[14] (Conan Doyle had little truck with those tolerant voices beginning to suggest that homosexuality was a predisposition rather than either a crime or an illness: in his memoirs he referred guardedly to the 'monstrous development' that ruined Oscar Wilde and to his belief that a 'hospital rather than a police court was the place for his consideration'.)

The petition failed. On 2 August 1916 Conan Doyle received a brief note from the Home Office: 'The Secretary of State has failed to discover any grounds which would justify him advising His Majesty to interfere with the due course of the law.' Casement was hanged at Pentonville prison the following day and became an instant Irish martyr. His executioner, Albert Ellis, said he was the 'bravest man it fell to my unhappy lot to execute'. For years there was a widespread belief, particularly in Ireland, that Casement's diaries had been forged as part of a diabolical British intelligence plot to discredit him, but in 2002 an independent forensic examination concluded unequivocally that all five diaries were the exclusive work of Roger Casement's hand.

———————◆———————

By the time of Casement's execution, the first part of Conan Doyle's history of the war was almost ready for publication. Loyal as always, Greenhough Smith paid Conan Doyle £5,000 for the serial rights to *The British Campaign in France and Flanders* which was promoted in the *Strand* as 'the inside story' of the war. With his boyish enthusiasm and his uncritical presentation, the early episodes set the tone for the remainder of the work. He was blind to the wanton disregard for human life on the part of the General Staff and their crass miscal-culations. Here he describes the opening day of the battle of the Somme: 'There was universal joy that the long stagnant trench life should be at an end, and that the days of action, even if they should prove to be days of death, should at last have come ... The preparations were enormous and meticulous, yet everything ran like a well-oiled piston-rod.' This was the day on which nearly 20,000 British soldiers died, 35,000 were wounded and 2,100 went missing. As Conan Doyle solemnly noted, the General Staff had not yet attained 'that skill in the avoidance of losses'. Other, younger writers – the poets Siegfried Sassoon, Wilfred Owen, Edmund Blunden and Robert Graves – soon came to the conclusion that what might have started out as a 'glorious adventure' had quickly degenerated into the mass slaughter of a generation. But Conan Doyle had a simplistic view of the conflict as the forces of good against the forces of evil, a heroic, epic struggle of the kind he had described in his medieval novels and he considered it his duty to assign dignity and splendour to the cause and to gloss over any blunders and incompetence of the leaders. He described Haig, for example, in glowing terms as 'the ideal man for a great military crisis' – a characterisation with which few military historians have since agreed. Kipling would offer a rather different perspective: 'If any question why we died, Tell them, because our fathers lied.'

Such was Conan Doyle's unswerving support for the war that he was approached to take over as director of the government propaganda programme. He pleaded lack of time because of his continuing work on his history of the war, and similarly refused when he was asked, after Lloyd George became Prime Minister in December 1916, to consider writing his official biography. Frances Stevenson, Lloyd George's confidential secretary and mistress, noted in her diary after lunching with Conan Doyle that he was 'a nice old gentleman, very courteous and interesting' but he was having difficulty obtaining material for his history and was only being given 'what they want him to know'. She added, prophetically, that he had a 'childlike idea of the infallibility of W.O. [War Office] officials'.[15]

Nevertheless, Lloyd George remained interested in Conan Doyle's history and invited him for breakfast at Downing Street in April 1917. Conan Doyle found the Prime Minister devoid of pretension: with no servants there, Lloyd George poured tea for them both and told Conan Doyle to help himself to bacon and eggs from a side table. While they ate Lloyd George prompted Conan Doyle to give his opinion of

various British generals, and Conan Doyle took the opportunity, once
again, to press his case for armour to be issued to front-line troops.
To Conan Doyle's astonishment, the Prime Minister then launched
into a savage attack on the late Lord Kitchener, whom he portrayed
as arrogant and 'usually stupid', quoting Violet Asquith, daughter of
the former prime minister, as saying Kitchener was not so much a
great man as a 'great poster'. Conan Doyle was so shocked that immediately after leaving Downing Street he returned to his room at the
Berkeley Hotel and made a note of Lloyd George's remarks: 'K (Kitchener) grew very arrogant. He had flashes of genius but was usually
stupid. He could not see any use in Munitions. He was against Tanks.
He was against Welsh and Irish Divisions. He refused the flags which
the ladies worked. He obstructed in all things and ruined the Dard-
anelles . . .'[16] When he came to write his memoirs some years later,
Conan Doyle discreetly toned down their conversation.

———————◆———————

In October 1917 a collection of seven Sherlock Holmes stories was
published under the title *His Last Bow*, a clear warning to fans that
their hero was about to go into permanent retirement. Six of the
stories had appeared in the *Strand* years earlier, but the title story was
new and was promoted in the September 1917 issue with a cover-line
'Sherlock Holmes outwits a German spy'. Its original subtitle was
'The War Service of Sherlock Holmes' and it was presumably intended
as just the tonic readers needed when losses on the Western Front
were mounting inexorably and national morale was slipping. But it
was an unusually lacklustre effort, as if Conan Doyle had dashed it
off without troubling to tease out the usual intricacies of plot.

Set in an English coastal village shortly before the outbreak of war,
it opens with two German spies discussing the numerous failings of
the British. One leaves for London while the other waits for Altamont,
an Irish-American agent who is to bring him the British naval codes.
Altamont arrives but delivers a copy of *The Practical Handbook of Bee
Culture, with some Observations upon the Segregation of the Queen* instead
of naval codes and clamps a chloroform pad over the face of the
German. Altamont is, of course, Holmes and his chauffeur is Dr

Watson, invited to witness the denouement of the adventure. Holmes explains that he has spent two years infiltrating the spy ring, but the story offers very little detail, no action and not much drama, suggesting that its author's interests were largely engaged elsewhere.

Readers were left in little doubt that it really was intended as the great detective's last bow: the story's subtitle was 'An Epilogue of Sherlock Holmes' (although there was in fact a further, final, series still to come). At the end of the story Holmes says to Watson: 'Stand with me here upon the terrace, for it may be the last quiet talk that we shall ever have.' Then he offers the promise of better times ahead: 'Good old Watson! You are the one fixed point in a changing age. There's an east wind coming all the same, such a wind as never blew on England yet. It will be cold and bitter, Watson, and a good many of us may wither before its blast. But it's God's own wind none the less, and a cleaner, better, stronger land will lie in the sunshine when the storm has cleared.'

In September 1918, towards the end of the war, Conan Doyle was invited by the Australian High Command to join a group of journalists visiting the sector of the front at Peronne, in the Somme, held by the famous Anzacs, the acronym for Australian and New Zealand troops. The party crossed the Channel on board a destroyer in the teeth of a gale and made their way to Peronne via Abbeville and Amiens, across country eerily familiar to Conan Doyle: 'Though I had not been over the ground before, I had visualised it so clearly in making notes about the battle that I could name every hamlet and locate every shattered church tower.'

On the day after his arrival he was reunited with Innes, who was serving with the 3rd British Corps on the left of the Australians. Innes drove over to Peronne for lunch and invited his brother back to his headquarters mess for dinner that night, a few hours before the final Allied offensive against the Hindenburg line that would end the war. As Innes was returning to Peronne Conan Doyle recorded that the entire eastern skyline was silhouetted by the artillery bombardment which was the prelude for the offensive.

Setting out for the front the following morning, they passed streams of wounded Australians returning, most of them, Conan Doyle noted, smiling grimly. Among them was a gaggle of German prisoners, 'hang-dog creatures with no touch of nobility in their features or their bearing' for whom he could muster no pity. When they could drive no further they left their car and continued on foot, through a deafening field-gun battery which had been hard at work for more than six hours, and under a 'screaming canopy of our own shells', to an advanced dressing station about 1,000 yards from the Hindenburg line. When an Australian gunner captain offered to 'rush them forward' to a vantage point even closer to the line, Conan Doyle immediately accepted, considering it to be a 'crowning bit of good fortune'. The vantage point turned out to be a tank which had broken down during the advance and Conan Doyle was initially disappointed that he could see little of the battle from the top of the tank, even through his field glasses. There was considerable noise and smoke, but no sign of 'that great fight where at last the children of light were beating down into the earth the forces of darkness'.[17]

Suddenly the German artillery opened up with a barrage clearly aimed in their direction, each salvo falling closer. They hastily made their way back to the trenches while the artillery barrage intensified all around them. Conan Doyle admitted he might have been more concerned had it not been for the 'chatty afternoon-tea' demeanour of the Australian troops around them, one of whom was casually trying to sell watches undoubtedly looted from German prisoners.

Finally able to recover their car, their adventures were far from over. Driving through the village of Templeux a stray shell burst just ahead of them and as they turned a bend in the road they were confronted with an horrific sight: 'There was a tangle of mutilated horses, their necks rising and sinking. Beside them a man with his hand blown off was staggering away, the blood gushing from his upturned sleeve. He was moving round and holding the arm raised and hanging, as a dog holds an injured foot. Beside the horses lay a shattered man, drenched crimson from head to foot, with two great glazed eyes looking upwards through a mask of blood. Two comrades were at hand to help, and we could only go upon our way with the ghastly picture stamped for ever upon our memory.'[18]

Further on they passed a column of about 900 German prisoners. Conan Doyle could not help but draw a prejudiced contrast between the 'keen, clear-cut, falcon faces' of the Australians and those of the

Germans, whom he described as 'uniformed bumpkins ... heavy-jawed, beetle-browed, uncouth louts'. The column, he said, was a 'herd of beasts, not a procession of men'. He greatly admired the 'reckless dare-devilry' of the Australians, and that evening had the opportunity of saying so, when, standing on a mound in pouring rain, he addressed some 1,200 Anzacs and told them what he thought of their 'splendid deeds', perhaps tactlessly reminding them that seventy-two per cent of the men engaged and seventy-six per cent of the casualties were Englishmen.

The visit figured prominently in Conan Doyle's ambitious 6-volume magnum opus, *The British Campaigns in Europe in 1914–1918*, which he hoped would establish his reputation as a war historian of the first order. In fact it signally failed to excite the public's imagination, with each succeeding volume attracting less attention and fewer sales. Readers were either exhausted by the war, or no longer able to see it, like he did, as a 'glorious adventure', or it was simply packed with too much detailed information. Conan Doyle was excessively proud of the fact that he was the first to describe 'the full battle-line with all the divisions, and even brigades, in their correct places from Mons onwards'.

A review in *The Times* of the final two volumes, published in 1920, was particularly dismissive: 'Here we have the two final instalments of Sir Arthur Doyle's history of the late war; and we are sorry to say that we find them no more satisfactory than their predecessors.' The reviewer pointed out the immense difficulties of covering, in a few hundred pages, a campaign that involved a succession of vast battles lasting weeks along fronts that were measured by scores of miles. 'Sir Arthur Doyle lacks the knowledge, for which he cannot be blamed, since official material is denied to him; and it is quite impossible that such a history as his should not be more or less hastily produced, so that he also lacks time. We fear that we must add, lastly, that he fails in literary skill. His maps are so defective that we closed the book in despair, unable to make head or tail of the operations. We cannot predict a long life for Sir Arthur's compilation. He has been much at the front, he has worked hard, and he has felt much; but it is not his metier to write military history.'[19]

Conan Doyle was shattered by the lukewarm reception of his great work, describing it as 'the greatest and most undeserved literary disappointment of my life'. In some respects he had every right to feel that his disappointment was undeserved since he had worked so diligently and had deployed all his skill to convey honestly and accurately the conditions endured by ordinary soldiers. His compassion for them shone out through the text. This from his account of the disastrous battle of Passchendaele in 1917: 'For four days and nights the men were in shell-holes without shelter from the rain and the biting cold winds, and without protection from the German Fire . . . So dark was the night and so heavy the rain that it took them eleven hours of groping and wading to reach the tapes which marked the lines of assembly. Then worn out with fatigue, wet to the skin, terribly cold, hungry, and with weapons that were often choked with mud, they went with hardly a pause into the open to face infantry who were supposed to be second to none in Europe, with every form of defence to help them . . .'

Most historians would later agree that the Battle of Passchendaele, which played out from 31 July to 6 November 1917, was a disaster: it achieved nothing and cost 325,000 Allied casualties. But Conan Doyle was as usual circumspect in his criticism, in this case of the architect of the operation, General Sir Douglas Haig, who was one of his principal sources. Assessing Haig's decision to continue the offensive in such hopeless conditions, Conan Doyle could only say: 'Looking back with the wisdom that comes after the event, one can clearly see that had the whole operation been stopped when the rain fell after the first day, it would have been the wisest course . . .'

Although neither was killed in action, Conan Doyle blamed the war for the loss of the two closest men in his life – his son and his brother. On 28 October, two weeks before the Armistice was signed and shortly before his 26th birthday, Kingsley Conan Doyle died of pneumonia at St Thomas's Hospital in London. He had been recalled from the front in November 1917 to resume his medical studies because of the desperate shortage of doctors in Britain, only to succumb to the virulent pandemic of Spanish flu that had broken out around the world and which would eventually kill more people than the war. His father believed the wounds he had sustained in the Somme made him more vulnerable to the infection. He was buried next to his mother in the graveyard of Grayshott parish church, close to Undershaw.

Less than four months later, on 19 February 1919, Innes died, in
Belgium, from the same pandemic, leaving a wife and two sons. A
Brigadier General and Assistant Adjutant General of the 3rd Corps,
he was, said his older brother, 'so worn out by his war duties that he
had no reserve power to meet the pneumonia'.[20]

However great Conan Doyle's grief, it was, however, assuaged by
a new certainty: that death was not the end of life and that his son
and brother had only crossed over to the 'other side' and would soon
be in contact. Bolstered by this certainty, he was ready to embark on
the last great crusade of his life, one that would consume his time
and wealth, subject him to considerable ridicule and ultimately damage
his reputation as a serious man of letters.

PART III

THE SPIRITUALIST

CHAPTER 19

THE PATH TO SPIRITUALISM

ONAN DOYLE HAD LONG BEEN moving towards a wholehearted acceptance of spiritualism, but it was the war which persuaded him that the time had come to go public, not just to announce himself as a fully-fledged spiritualist but to take the spiritualist message to an agonised world and, as he saw it, offer comfort to the millions of bereaved trying to make sense of their losses. 'It was borne in upon me that the knowledge which had come to me thus was not for my own consolation alone, but that God had placed me in a very special position for conveying it to that world which needed it so badly.' So it was that the most highly-paid fiction writer of his generation was virtually ready to abandon fiction and devote his pen – and his life – to a cause he fervently believed could change the world.

In truth Conan Doyle had been searching for a faith for most of his adult life, ever since his early rejection of the Roman Catholic church, and spiritualism appealed to both his love of drama and danger and his preoccupation with the macabre – its haunted houses, darkened rooms, sepulchral voices, moving tables, ghostly manifestations and array of psychic phenomena. Once he had made up his mind, nothing would shake his conviction and he became a zealous apostle for the salvation of mankind, which he believed spiritualism offered the world. It did not matter to him that mediums were forever being exposed as fraudsters. He had found the Truth: 'I seemed suddenly to see that this subject with which I had so long dallied was not merely a study of a force outside the rules of science, but that it was really something tremendous, a breaking down of the walls between two worlds, a direct undeniable message from beyond, a call of hope and of guidance to the human race at the time of its deepest affliction.'[1]

Spiritualism, defined in the *Oxford English Dictionary* as 'the belief that the spirits of the dead can hold communication with the living', began in the United States. Although the idea that it was possible to communicate with the dead had existed for millennia, the modern spiritualist movement was born in an allegedly haunted farmhouse in Hydesville, upstate New York. In March 1848 John Fox, a farmer from Canada, moved into the farmhouse with his wife and two daughters, Margaret, aged 14, and Kate, aged 11, while a house was built for them on land nearby. Within days the family began to be disturbed by strange noises in the night – banging, rattling and knocking. One night Kate woke up screaming that a cold hand had touched her face; another night her sister had the blankets pulled from her bed by unseen hands, and their mother swore she heard disembodied footsteps walking through the house and descending the stairs into the cellar.

John Fox was not a superstitious man and sought a rational explanation: he checked the floorboards for squeaks and the fitting of the windows and doors to see if they rattled in their frames. While he was knocking on the walls his daughter Kate realised that there was an echo from within the wall: however many times her father knocked on the walls, the same number would respond. She clapped her hands twice; two knocks replied. Similarly when she rapped several times on the table. Summoning her mother and sister, she told them she thought that something, or someone, was trying to communicate with them. Mrs Fox tried asking the 'spirit' questions that could be answered by numbers, such as the ages of her children. The 'answers' were accurate. Unsure what to do, John Fox invited his neighbours to witness the phenomenon. At first incredulous, they were astounded when their own questions were answered correctly. One neighbour, William Duesler, devised a simple alphabet using a series of knocks in order to attempt a 'conversation'. In this way they learned that the presence in the house was the spirit of a pedlar robbed and murdered there years earlier.

News quickly spread and the Fox daughters were not slow to cash in on their new fame. Claiming to possess 'mediumistic' powers, they began giving public demonstrations and were soon attracting large paying audiences. With an older sister, Leah, acting as their manager, they toured from city to city, staging ever more elaborate seances in which spirits appeared and tables levitated. Newspaper reports were generally sceptical, but the Fox sisters developed a large following of true believers and were embraced by celebrities, including the showman P. T. Barnum, the novelist James Fenimore Cooper, Judge John W. Edmonds, a respected member of the New York Court of Appeals, and Horace Greeley, founder of the *New York Tribune* and America's most famous newspaper editor. Greeley, still grieving the death of his son, invited the sisters to stay at his mansion in New York: he confirmed their honesty and his conviction that they were in touch with the spirit world in an open letter to his newspaper.

America, then as now a devoutly religious country, and the home of repeated religious 'revivals', was fertile ground for spiritualism. In 1854 a senator from Illinois presented a petition to Congress, signed by 15,000 of his constituents, demanding an investigation into the spirit world's apparent desire to communicate with the real one. The emergence of spiritualism as an independent religious belief in the United States owed much to the rise of the Apostolic Church, founded in the 1830s to preach the infallibility of the Bible, and the acceptance of 'speaking in tongues', or being taken over by the Holy Spirit. While ordained ministers lambasted spiritualism as the 'work of the Devil', many people recognised a clear connection between mysticism and religious fervour.

Meanwhile, numerous attempts were made to expose the sisters as impostors. It was variously claimed that they produced 'spiritual' phenomena by toe, knee and ankle cracking, or by ventriloquism, or by secret mechanical devices, but no trickery was discovered. A number of inquiries were set up to test their powers, usually by posing questions to the spirit world, and while the answers were often inconsistent, they were sufficiently impressive to convince many doubters. On one occasion, having been accused of making knocking sounds with their feet, they were bound tightly at the ankles but still managed to produce rapped answers to their questions. On another, a committee of women was asked to examine the sisters' undergarments to ensure nothing was concealed under their skirts. Leah was frequently accused of wheedling useful information from members of the audience and attempts to call up the famous were not always successful; when it was noted that Benjamin Franklin's spirit demonstrated a surprisingly poor grasp of grammar, Margaret angrily walked out.

Inevitably, as the fame of the Fox sisters spread, more individuals discovered mystical powers to communicate with the dead. Mediums, conducting seances in darkened rooms, became popular figures in American society. For some, a seance was no more than an amusing way to spend a long winter evening, but for others it was an intense, emotional experience, particularly after the Civil War, in which 600,000 people died, ended in 1865. The suggestion that it was possible to contact such a loved one offered considerable solace to grieving widows and mothers.

By the time of Conan Doyle's birth in 1859, more than 10,000,000 Americans had accepted the spiritualist faith; dedicated spiritualist churches had opened across the country; and some 25,000 'mediums' were conducting regular seances. Conan Doyle's hero, the poet Oliver Wendell Holmes, was among prominent voices speaking out against spiritualism, describing it as a 'plague': 'While some are crying out against it as a delusion of the Devil, and some are laughing at it as an hysteric folly, and some are getting angry with it as a mere trick of interested or mischievous persons, Spiritualism is quietly under-mining the traditional ideas of the future state which have been and still are accepted.'[2]

The fad soon spread to Britain, led by Daniel Dunglass Home, who arrived in London from the United States in 1855, mixed in aris-tocratic circles, developed a huge following and made spiritualism fashionable. Home was credited with extraordinary powers – he could levitate, materialise anywhere in the world at will and lift heavy objects without touching them. Three honourable gentlemen (Lord Dunraven, Lord Lindsay and Captain Wynne) were prepared to swear on oath that they had witnessed Home float out of one window and into another, 70 feet above the ground. Conan Doyle would later describe him as 'a truly great man' and believed that he would one day be canonised. He also accepted Home's claim that he was the illegitimate nephew of the Earl of Home; in fact he was the son of a labourer with a taste for drink.

Victorians were fascinated by the pseudo-sciences and were receptive to new ideas after the chaos and sweeping reforms of the Industrial Revolution. Spiritualism, phrenology, telepathy and mesmerism were all enthusiastically embraced as means of making sense of a confusing new world. That Queen Victoria and the Prince Consort approved and participated in seances greatly added to spiritualism's reputation. Victoria was interested in the occult very early on; in July 1845 she presented a watch to a female medium engraved 'for her Meritorious and Extraordinary Clairvoyance'. Despite the fervent opposition of the Salvation Army, which railed against spiritualism as one of a 'trinity of evils', along with gambling and ritualism, the movement flourished: mediums and crystal balls were in great demand and dubious entrepreneurs profited wherever they could – even marketing tables 'guaranteed' to tilt. By 1855, the first spiritualist newspaper, the *Yorkshire Spiritual Telegraph,* had been launched in Britain and within a decade four magazines dedicated to spiritualist matters were being published in London; one, a weekly called the *Spiritualist,* carried hints on how to summon the spirits: 'One or more persons possessing medial powers without knowing it are to be found in nearly every household . . .'

Predictably, spiritualism attracted innumerable charlatans, both in Europe and the United States, looking to line their pockets. Notable among them were Ira and William Davenport, brothers from Buffalo, New York, whose hair-raising supernatural demonstrations owed more to vaudeville than religion. The brothers, tied at hand and foot, were placed inside a huge wooden cabinet centre stage. As the lights dimmed, the doors to the cabinet were shut and ghostly manifestations began: unworldly music filled the theatre, instruments floated through the air and disembodied hands appeared through holes in the cabinet. When stagehands threw open the doors to the cabinet, the manifestations ceased instantly and the brothers would be seen, still trussed, heads bowed and eyes closed in deep concentration. In the audience one night was 13-year-old Ehrich Weiss who quickly deduced that the brothers had found a way to slip in and out of their bonds in order to manipulate the mysterious phenomena. It was a useful lesson to a youth who would later call himself Harry Houdini.

Despite one medium after another being exposed as a fraud, the bedrock beliefs of spiritualists remained unshaken, even after Margaret Fox publicly renounced spiritualism as a sham. The Fox sisters had not fared well: the stress of performing, of maintaining a charade, of being subjected to continuing investigation, took its toll and both Margaret and Kate turned to drink. In 1888 Kate was arrested in New York for drunkenness and her two sons taken into the custody of the welfare department.

Later that year Margaret booked the New York Academy of Music to make a sensational announcement. She walked nervously onto the stage and confessed that she and her sister had staged the entire drama at their home in Hydesville: the knockings were created with an apple on a string and later they tapped their toes on hard surfaces. 'We were led on unintentionally by my good mother,' she explained. 'She used to say when we were sitting in a dark circle at home "Is this a disembodied spirit that has taken possession of my dear children?" And then we would "rap", just for the fun of the thing, you know, and mother would declare that it was the spirits that were speaking.' Margaret roundly condemned the spiritualist movement: 'I have seen so much deception . . . that is why I am willing to state that Spiritualism is a fraud of the worst description.'

Margaret Fox's confession ought to have sounded spiritualism's death knell, but by then there were too many true believers. Dedicated spiritualists denounced her as an untrustworthy drunk. Kate continued performing as a medium when she was sober and Margaret later recanted her confession. Neither lived long: Kate literally drank herself to death, at age 56, in July 1892 – and eight months later Margaret died penniless at a friend's home in Brooklyn, at age 59.

———————◆———————

More than ten years before their ignominious demise, when he was 21 years old, Conan Doyle had attended a lecture in Birmingham titled 'Does Death End All?' given by an American spiritualist. He was interested, but deeply sceptical. 'I had at that time the usual contempt which the young educated man feels towards the whole subject which has been covered by the clumsy name of Spiritualism. I had read of mediums being convicted of fraud, I had heard of phenomena which were opposed to every known scientific law, and I had deplored the simplicity and credulity which could deceive good, earnest people into believing that such bogus happenings were signs of intelligence outside our own existence.'

One of his earliest stories, 'Selecting A Ghost', published in 1883, poked fun at the occult and exemplified his attitude to the subject. A wealthy grocer decides to hire a medium for no other reason than to audition prospective ghosts for his mansion: one of the ghostly candidates makes a pitch for the job by professing to be a 'great ethereal sigh-heaver'.

When he was in practice in Southsea, Conan Doyle still described himself as a 'convinced materialist' and a cynic, claiming to regard the subject of spiritual phenomena as 'the greatest nonsense upon earth'. He wondered 'how any sane man could believe such things'.[3] His attitude, he explained, was that when the candle burned out, the light disappeared.

Despite this, he was keen to investigate, in a spirit of scientific enquiry, the uncharted potential of the human mind. He read widely: in his Southsea notebooks he listed the titles of more than seventy books about spiritualism. He dabbled in telepathy, theosophy and mesmerism and explored occultism and Buddhism. He admitted to being 'deeply attracted' for a time by theosophy, a movement founded in 1875 by the notorious Madame Helena Blavatsky. Theosophy imposed no beliefs on its followers, who were united by a common quest for 'truth' and a desire to learn the meaning and purpose of existence. There were links between theosophy and spiritualism, notably a belief in spirits and the afterlife, but Conan Doyle eventually rejected theosophy because he required 'severe proof' rather than unquestioning faith. Madame Blavatsky was later exposed as 'one of the most accomplished and interesting impostors in history'.[4]

Between 1885 and 1888 he participated in 'table tipping' sessions at the homes of friends and received 'connected messages', not all of them nonsensical. Messages were received by the tedious process of reciting the alphabet and writing down the letter indicated by a tap of the table leg, but 'it seemed to me that we were collectively pushing the table, and that our own wills were concerned in bringing down the leg at the right moment'. When he asked, at one session, how many coins he had in his pocket as a test question, he received a testy rebuke from the spirit world: 'We are here to educate and elevate, not to guess riddles . . . The religious frame of mind, not the critical, is what we wish to inculcate.' On another occasion they received a long and detailed message from the spirit of a commercial traveller who had died in a theatre fire in Exeter and implored them to make contact with his family who lived in 'Slattenmere', in Cumberland. A dutiful Conan Doyle wrote to the family, but his letter was returned, address unknown. Unsurprisingly, these sessions achieved little, except to make him suspicious of his friends and ambivalent towards the whole subject. 'I was puzzled and worried over it, for they were not people whom I could imagine as cheating – and yet I could not see how the messages could come except by conscious pressure.'[5]

What did impress him, however, was the level of scientific support that spiritualism was apparently attracting, despite its legion of avowed sceptics. Those who, in later years, professed astonishment that someone as down to earth as Conan Doyle should espouse spiritualism failed to appreciate that the movement in the late Victorian era, far from being dominated by cranks and charlatans, attracted some of the country's leading scientific minds. In 1882 a distinguished group of Cambridge scholars formed the Society for Psychical Research to examine alleged paranormal phenomena in a rigorously scientific and unbiased manner. Among the members were the future Prime Minister Arthur Balfour, the philosopher William James, the naturalist Russell Wallace, the physicists William Crookes and Oliver Lodge and the astronomer Nicolas Flammarion. Crookes, inventor of the radiometer – an instrument for detecting radiation – had personally tested and endorsed both Kate Fox and Daniel Dunglass Home, while Wallace wrote a book, *Miracles and Modern Spiritualism*, in which he suggested that the 'spiritual essence' of human development could only be explained by 'the unseen universe of Spirit'.

There were also, of course, prominent names – Charles Darwin, Aldous Huxley, John Tyndall and Herbert Spencer among them – deriding the movement, believing it was too ridiculous to merit serious investigation. Charles Dickens was similarly unimpressed: 'I have not the least belief in the awful unseen being available for evening parties at so much a night,' he wrote to Frances Trollope. 'Although I shall be ready to receive enlightenment from any source, I must say I have very little hope of it from the spirits who express themselves through mediums; as I have never yet observed them talk anything but nonsense.'[6]

His doubts notwithstanding, Conan Doyle discussed spiritualism at length with a fellow member of the Portsmouth Literary and Scientific Society, Major General Alfred W. Drayson, who happened to be one of the pioneers of the movement in Britain. A distinguished soldier, military historian, theoretical astronomer, passionate card player and prolific author who had been published in some of the same journals as Conan Doyle, Drayson was a man Conan Doyle greatly respected despite his deeply eccentric views, including his peculiar theory about the language spoken by Jesus Christ and his belief that the globe was constantly expanding. Drayson sought to assuage Conan Doyle's doubts, particularly about 'messages' received from the beyond that were either inane or untrue. Every spirit passes over to the next world entirely unchanged, Drayson explained; just as this world is full of weak and foolish people, so is the next. And fraud, he added, did not necessarily invalidate spiritualist beliefs. Drayson's view was that trickery was a fact of life and that the spirit world simply mirrored the real world. Many Christians led deeply un-Christian lives, he said, but this did not diminish the faith. Drayson was later discredited for his insistence that psychic 'apports' – the term used by spiritualists to describe the physical materialisation of objects – occurred regularly at his seances.

Conan Doyle continued to attend table seances and often took detailed notes, particularly of descriptions of life beyond the grave. One spirit who 'came through' was a Dorothy Postlethwaite who had died in Melbourne at the age of 16, had been at school with one of the sitters and correctly spelled out the name of their headmistress. She explained she inhabited a place of light and laughter, where there were no rich or poor and the general conditions were far happier than on earth. They were free from bodily pain, but not mental anxiety, and enjoyed many pleasures, music among them. Conan Doyle noted that Miss Postlethwaite also informed them that Mars was inhabited by a race much more advanced than humans.

Conan Doyle was not able to maintain a detached interest indefinitely. In 1887 his scepticism was badly shaken when he attended a seance with a professional medium. After delivering a 'trance address', the medium scribbled a message, in 'automatic writing', for each of those present. Conan Doyle was flabbergasted by his: 'This gentleman is a healer. Tell him from me not to read Leigh Hunt's book.' Unknown to anyone but himself, Conan Doyle had recently been contemplating reading *Comic Dramatists of the Restoration* by the essayist James Leigh Hunt. 'I can only say that if I had to devise a test message I could not have hit upon one which was so absolutely inexplicable on any hypothesis except that held by Spiritualists . . . After weighing the evidence I could no more doubt the existence of the phenomena than I could doubt the existence of lions in Africa.'[7]

In a letter to *Light*, the journal of the London Spiritualist Alliance, Conan Doyle conceded that he was revisiting his initial doubts and beginning to view spiritualism as a redemptive force: 'Let a man realise that the human soul, as it emerges from its bodily cocoon, shapes its destiny in exact accordance with its condition; that that condition depends upon the sum result of his actions and thoughts on this life; that every evil deed stamps itself upon the spirit and entails its own punishment with the same certainty that a man stepping out of a second floor window falls to the ground; that there is no room for deathbed repentances or other nebulous conditions which might screen the evil doer from the consequences of his own deeds, but that the law is self-acting and inexorable. This, I take it, is the lesson which Spiritualism enforces, and all phenomena are only witnesses to the truth of this central all-important fact.'[8]

Having rejected the Catholic church and incurred the opprobrium of his family, Conan Doyle was warming towards the idea of embracing an alternative faith more in tune with his mindset, perhaps to fill some void in his life which had left him spiritually adrift. In the largely autobiographical novel *The Stark Munro Letters*, the protagonist confesses to feeling as if his 'life-belt had burst' when he left the church. 'I won't exaggerate and say that I was miserable and plunged into utter spiritual darkness. Youth is too full of action for that. But I was conscious of a vague unrest, of a constant want of repose, of an emptiness and hardness which I had not noticed in life before. I had so identified religion with the Bible that I could not conceive them apart. When the foundation proved false, the whole structure came rattling about my ears.' Conan Doyle insisted he was agnostic rather than atheist. He believed in the goodness of God, 'but I have no respect for the Old Testament, no conviction that Churches are necessary . . . I desire to die as I have lived, without clerical interference, and with that peace which comes from acting honestly up to one's own best mental convictions.'[9]

He continued to explore the entire range of emerging, and exotic, sciences. When, in February 1889, a Professor Milo de Meyer arrived in Southsea to give an exhibition of 'mesmeric force', Conan Doyle was one of a dozen or so local doctors and scientists in the audience. Mesmerism was named after Friedrich Anton Mesmer, an eighteenth-century Austrian physician whose theory of 'animal magnetism' was the forerunner of modern hypnotism. Through an interpreter the professor explained that his science was founded on the mysterious electric force emanating from magnets. As ten young volunteers, most likely stooges, who had already been hypnotised 'to save time', were produced from the wings, Conan Doyle stepped forward to join them, having offered, the *Portsmouth Evening News* reported, to 'swell the number of would-be subjects'. While Professor de Meyer demonstrated total control over the original volunteers – one man was unable to shut his mouth after opening it, another fell to his knees and could not rise again, and two others were obliged to act out 'an amusing scene' as dentist and patient – he had less luck with Conan Doyle: 'An attempt to magnetise Dr Doyle in a similar manner failed,' the newspaper noted, 'the Professor remarking, after making the attempt, that the process would take too long.'

This unpersuasive experience notwithstanding, mysticism still figured prominently on Conan Doyle's eclectic reading list. *Human Personality and Its Survival of Bodily Death*, the monumental two-volume work by F. W. H. Myers, co-founder of the Society for Psychical Research, made a deep impression. Myers argued that the soul was able to survive the death of the body and that the subliminal self was a vast psychic organism of which what was then understood as consciousness was only a small component. Conan Doyle thought Myers's work deserved a place alongside Francis Bacon's

Novum Organum and Darwin's *Descent of Man* and wrote to his mother to say he believed it would be a 'great root book from which a tree of knowledge will grow'.[10]

Myers reported on a series of experiments he said proved conclusively that 'mental telepathy' worked and which Conan Doyle attempted to replicate with his architect friend, Joseph Henry Ball. The two men sat back to back, each with a pencil and pad. One would draw a symbol and the other would attempt to draw the same image. Time and again Conan Doyle found it worked. 'I showed beyond any doubt whatever,' he observed with the conviction that would later mark his unreserved conversion to spiritualism, 'that I could convey my thought without words.'[11]

The more he read, the more impressed he became by the strength of the spiritualist position and by the 'want of all dignity and accurate knowledge which characterised the attitude of its opponents'. Sir William Crookes's attitude to psychic phenomena – 'It is incredible but it is true' – reflected Conan Doyle's own dawning convictions. Robert Louis Stevenson apparently shared his interest in the paranormal but seems to have taken the subject rather less seriously, addressing letters to Conan Doyle 'O frolic fellow-spookiest'.

On 9 May 1889 the *Portsmouth Evening News* published a long letter from Conan Doyle responding to a report about the pernicious influence of spiritualism, which had been described as 'an old snake of Satan's in a new dress'. In a trenchant defence, he stated his belief that spiritualism was capable of uplifting and invigorating humanity and that 'in the opinion of many', it was the strongest and most vital movement on the planet. He signed himself 'a Spiritualist', a very significant turning point and his first declared association with the movement. The following year, as honorary secretary of the Portsmouth Literary and Scientific Society, he presided over a lecture on the subject of 'Witches and Witchcraft', delivered, appropriately enough, on 1 April. The speaker referred to scientific experiments being conducted in Paris on mesmerism and clairvoyance and told the story of how a volunteer, having been hypnotised, was given a lump of sugar that he was told was arsenic and ordered to administer it in three months' time to his closest friend, which he did. Afterwards Conan Doyle observed that there must be something in witchcraft as it was a belief held in many countries for a long period of time; his view was that it was 'a case of preternatural power, used for malevolent purposes'.

A number of short stories emerged from Conan Doyle's fascination with the occult, exemplifying the curious schism in his work as a writer, between the logic and deductive skill of Sherlock Holmes on the one hand and dreamy mysticism on the other. In 'The Great Keinplatz Experiment', the protagonist, Professor von Baumgarten, might have been articulating the views of the author:

> It is evident that under certain conditions the soul or mind does separate itself from the body. In the case of a mesmerised person, the body lies in a cataleptic condition, but the spirit had left it. Perhaps you reply that the soul is there, but in a dormant condition. I answer that this is not so, otherwise how can one account for the condition of clairvoyance, which has fallen into disrepute through the knavery of certain scoundrels, but which can easily be shown to be an undoubted fact. I have been able myself, with a sensitive subject, to obtain an accurate description of what was going on in another room or another house. How can such knowledge be accounted for on any hypothesis save that the soul of the subject has left the body and is wandering through space?

The professor's ambition is to 'build a new exact science which should embrace mesmerism, spiritualism, and all cognate subjects'.

In November 1893, the year his wife was diagnosed with terminal illness and three weeks after his father died, Conan Doyle signalled his gradual metamorphosis from materialist to spiritualist by applying to join the Society for Psychical Research, whose newly elected president was Arthur Balfour. No one could have been welcomed more enthusiastically into the Society, as a member pointed out: 'He may be very useful as a doctor and as Sherlock Holmes, his testimony will have great weight with the public.'[12]

The following year Conan Doyle took part in his first paranormal investigation. Colonel Elmore, a veteran of the 1878–80 Afghan war, had allegedly asked the Society for Psychical Research to investigate the possible haunting of his home in Dorset. At night his family could hear what seemed to be chains being dragged across the floor and the low moaning of 'a soul in torment'. The dog refused to enter certain parts of the house and most of the Colonel's domestic staff had resigned. Three members of the Society – Conan Doyle, Dr Sydney Scott and Frank Podmore, a leading psychic investigator who had carried out a considerable amount of research into the case – spent the whole train journey reviewing the evidence.

To avoid alarming the Colonel's wife and adult daughter, it had been agreed that they would pose as old Army comrades and at dinner that night the conversation rarely strayed from various campaigns in Afghanistan. After a rubber of whist everyone retired to bed, but once the investigators were certain the Elmores were asleep they emerged from their rooms and began making preparations for the night's vigil, securing the doors and windows and stringing thread across the stairs and passages. They took turns to keep watch, but no psychic phenomena occurred and Dr Scott decided to return to London.

On the following night, however, a 'fearsome uproar' woke the entire house. 'It was like someone belabouring a resounding table with a heavy cudgel,' Conan Doyle reported later. 'It was not an accidental creaking of wood, or anything of that sort, but a deafening row.' Conan Doyle and Podmore rushed to the kitchen, which seemed to be the source of the noise, but found nothing. The Elmores emerged from their rooms having been disturbed, but could offer no explanation. Conan Doyle and Podmore stayed up for the rest of the night hoping there would be a repeat of the 'noise' but the house remained quiet.

The two investigators left Dorset the next day without having reached any firm conclusions about whether the house was haunted, or whether they had been the victims of a practical joke. Some years later, however, the house burned down and the skeleton of a child who had died about ten years old was found buried in the garden. For Conan Doyle this explained the haunting of the house: 'There is a theory that a young life cut short in a sudden and unnatural fashion may leave, as it were, a store of unused vitality which may be put to strange uses.'

Conan Doyle would later tell different versions of this story to friends. To James Payn he said the family consisted of a mother, son and daughter and that he concluded the son was responsible. Jerome

K. Jerome claimed Conan Doyle told him the so-called ghost was actually Colonel Elmore's daughter, 'an unmarried woman of about five and thirty'. He was initially suspicious of her when she claimed she had heard nothing and that everyone had imagined it. The next night he set a trap and uncovered her as the 'ghost': 'She was not mad. She protested her love both for her father and her mother. She could offer no explanation. The thing seemed as unaccountable to her as it did to Doyle. On the understanding that the thing ended, secrecy was promised. The noises were never heard again.'[13] Yet at spiritualist lectures all over the world Conan Doyle stuck to his original story and included it in his autobiography and various spiritualist tracts as hard evidence, from his own personal experience, of the existence of ghosts.

Although Conan Doyle had the good sense not to involve Sherlock Holmes in spiritualism, the idea of life after death was a recurring theme in other stories. 'Through the Veil', which appeared in the *Strand* in November 1910, explored the notion that flashes of past lives could intrude into an individual's present-day consciousness. In 'How it Happened' (1913), a motorist meets a deceased friend after a major car accident only to realise that he, too, has been killed. Shortly before writing this story, Conan Doyle had urged his friend, the novelist Rafael Sabatini, the future author of *Scaramouche*, to seek consolation in spiritual communication after his son had been killed in a motoring accident.

One of the most significant personal events for Conan Doyle was his wife's conversion during the early years of the war. Jean Conan Doyle had originally viewed spiritualism with nervous distrust: it was the one area in which they were not in total accord. He was always ready to explore and investigate psychic phenomena; she thought dabbling in the unknown was risky and unnatural. It was her close friend Lily Loder Symonds, who was instrumental in changing her mind.

Lily had been a bridesmaid at their wedding and had moved in with the Conan Doyles at Windlesham at the start of the war, ostensibly as a companion for Jean and to help look after the children, although her health was poor – she suffered from a severe bronchial condition – and it is more likely that Jean took her in as an act of friendship. Lily was a gifted medium who had developed a talent for automatic writing, a means of communicating with the other world which had existed since the early days of spiritualism. Automatic writing was attributed to spirits manipulating the pen of an intermediary, who was either in a trance or otherwise appeared to have no control over what was being written. Through this medium, in the late nineteenth century spiritualists around the world claimed to be in touch with everyone from Jesus Christ to Benjamin Franklin; 'literary spirits' dictated entire novels and thousands of lines of poetry, much of it lamentable. Conan Doyle was at first doubtful about its credibility. 'Of all forms of mediumship this seems to me to be the one which should be tested most rigidly,' he declared, 'as it lends itself very easily not so much to deception as to self-deception, which is a more subtle and dangerous thing.'[14] It was Lily Loder Symonds who convinced him that she was, indeed, receiving communications from the spirit world.

Lily obtained messages from her brothers, three of whom had been killed at Ypres, which included military information she was unlikely to have known otherwise. One mentioned the name of a Belgian who Conan Doyle subsequently discovered had indeed met one of the Loder Symonds. When the RMS *Lusitania* was torpedoed by a German U-boat on 7 May 1915, with the loss of 1,195 lives, her spirit guide prompted her to write: 'It is terrible, terrible, and will have a great influence on the war'. She also accurately foretold the arrival of an important telegram and even gave the name of the deliverer, but most significant of all, at least for Jean, was a message from her beloved brother, Malcolm, killed during the retreat from Mons. She never revealed its content, other than that it referred to a private conversation between her brother and her husband some years earlier, but it was certainly enough to persuade her that it had genuinely emanated from Malcolm and thereafter she became an enthusiastic supporter of her husband's crusade.

Lily Loder Symonds was a respectable woman from a good family and it is unlikely she was deliberately duping her friends, the Conan Doyles. If one accepts that she was not receiving messages from the spirit world, what was going on? First, there was the resurgence of interest in spiritualism directly linked to the war and the rising numbers being killed every day in the trenches. Within spiritualism, automatic writing was an accepted psychic phenomenon: anyone could take up a pen, sit before a clean sheet of paper and wait to see what happened. If the subconscious mind moved the pen to form words, or even a coherent message, then there were many ready to believe its origin was mystical rather than self-delusional.

In the case of Lily there was another significant factor. She adored, almost worshipped, Conan Doyle; some friends believed that she was secretly in love with him. It is therefore credible that, either consciously or subconsciously, she believed that conjuring up psychic phenomena would both please her host and help repay his hospitality. Certainly nothing could have pleased him more than that her skill in automatic writing should convert his wife. As for the alleged significance of the messages, much could be easily accounted for and not just by inspired guesswork. The military information could easily have been picked up at the dinner table at Windlesham, as Conan Doyle was in the habit of talking about his work in progress, then a history of the war; the 'Belgian' could have been mentioned by one of her brothers in a letter from the front written before Ypres; it hardly needed the prompting of the spirits to describe the sinking of the *Lusitania* as 'terrible', and it was Conan Doyle who decided that the remainder of the message foretold the entry of the United States into the war two years later. As for the private conversation between Malcolm Leckie and Conan Doyle, he would almost certainly have told his wife and there is no reason to think that she would not pass it on to her best friend.

Conan Doyle was oblivious to all this, as he was to Loder Symonds's feelings towards him – he had eyes only for his 'darling girl'. Lily's automatic writing offered objective proof of what he had wanted to believe for thirty years – that there was indeed a spirit world – and he set out to explore its religious significance. 'The objective side ceased to interest,' he noted, 'for having made up one's mind there was an end to the matter. The religious side was clearly of infinitely greater importance.'[15] Unlike the established church, Conan Doyle could see no conflict between religion and spiritualism; he argued that the latter could be a 'great unifying force' for organised religions and if the broad premises offered by 'teaching from beyond' were accepted, then the human race would have made a great stride towards religious harmony.

As losses mounted in France – 50,000 members of the British Expeditionary Force died in a pointless offensive in the Artois-Loos region in September 1915 – the *International Psychic Gazette* asked prominent figures what consolation they could offer to the bereaved. Conan Doyle's reply was terse and perhaps surprising: 'I fear I can say nothing worth saying. Time only is the healer.' It was evident he was not ready to declare himself publicly a spiritualist, otherwise he would surely have offered words of comfort to the effect that the bereaved would be meeting up with their loved ones in the other world. He had certainly by then embraced the belief in life after death. In May he had written to Lily Loder Symonds: 'You know what I think of death. It is a most glorious improvement on life, a shedding of all that is troublous and painful and a gaining of grand new powers which are a supreme happiness to the individual . . .'[16] Her health continued to fail; she died in January 1916 from influenza. Conan Doyle, now largely convinced of her ability to communicate with the spirit world, described her as a 'high soul upon earth'.

By then he was ready to see psychic phenomena all around him. Early in 1916 his son Adrian, aged 5, was seriously ill with pneumonia. Jean stayed by the boy's bedside day and night. She left him for a moment to retrieve something from the nursery where Adrian's older brother, Denis, jumped from a chair and accidentally stepped on some of Adrian's tin soldiers. When she returned to the sickroom, Adrian opened his eyes and said, 'Naughty Denis, breaking my soldiers!' Jean reported the incident to her husband, who concluded that Adrian's soul had left his body and accompanied his mother. 'I can only explain it by the supposition, which can be supported by a volume of evidence,' he wrote to *Light*, 'that the soul can be, and probably always is, out of the body at such times, and that occasionally under rare conditions which we have not yet been able to define, it can convey to the body the observations which it has made during its independent flight.'[17]

In October 1916 *Light* published another article by Conan Doyle in which he said that communicating with the dead was either 'absolute lunacy', or 'a revolution in religious thought, a revolution which gives us an immense consolation when those who are dear to us pass behind the veil'.

He was still not ready to go public, but was girding himself for the moment and was greatly encouraged to read a book written by his friend Sir Oliver Lodge, the eminent physicist, detailing conversations he had had, through a medium, with his son Raymond, killed in the trenches by a shell fragment near Ypres in 1915.[18] Sir Oliver described how the medium, Mrs Osborne Leonard, communicated with Raymond through a 'spirit control', a young Native American girl named Feda. (Mediums frequently claimed that their spirit controls were 'Red Indians'.) Raymond was able to tell his father that he was in a place called 'Summerland' where every home comfort was available, including whisky and cigars. In one message he said via Feda that there were laboratories in Summerland which manufacture all manner of things, 'not like you do, out of solid matter, but out of essences, and ethers, and gases'. Significantly, Sir Oliver was a world expert on ether and proposed that spirits had an 'etheric' body able temporarily to utilise terrestrial molecules as a means of materialising.

Although much of the book was a serious scientific study of the interaction between life and consciousness and the relation between mind and brain, Sir Oliver inevitably endured a good deal of ridicule from reviewers tickled by the idea of whisky and cigars in the afterlife. But Conan Doyle leapt to his defence: 'Raymond may be right or wrong, but the only thing which the incident proves to me is the unflinching courage and honesty of the man who chronicled it, knowing well the handle that he was giving to his enemies.'[19] Lodge wrote thanking him for his support: 'It is a good thing that somebody of importance lets himself go every now and then. In these days of heavy artillery that is the only way to progress, the long-standing entrenchments of prejudice cannot otherwise be broken down.'[20] The public was less inclined to cynicism than the critics, and Sir Oliver's book went through twelve printings in three years, an indication of the intense longing on the part of the war bereaved for what he was postulating to be true. As Sir Oliver pointed out: 'If we can establish the survival of any single ordinary individual, we have established it for all.'

The June 1917 issue of the *Strand* carried an article by Lodge titled 'How I Became Convinced of the Survival of the Dead', in which he explained that after trying many other hypotheses, he had been seduced by the evidence that it was possible under certain circumstances to hold conversations with, or receive messages from, the dead. The following month the magazine asked, 'Is Sir Oliver Lodge Right?' and published two opposing views. 'Yes' was by Conan Doyle, and 'No' by Edward Clodd, an anthropologist, former chairman of the Rational Press Association and an early follower of Darwin. Conan Doyle described in detail his slow metamorphosis from sceptic to believer, the years of 'amazed and reluctant reconsideration' which finally led him to absolute conversion as the evidence became stronger and his knowledge fuller. Clodd would have none of it and weighed in with devastating effect. Spiritualism was rooted in fraud, he said, and propagated by 'a pack of sorry rascals of both sexes, some of whom have been committed to prison, and rogues and vagabonds'. He ridiculed the fact that discarnate spirits had not managed to offer up a single ennobling thought and castigated messages from the other world as 'nauseating, frivolous, mischievous, spurious drivel'. To most readers Clodd won the debate resoundingly.

One persistent source of complaint was that 'spirits' chose curious ways to communicate – tilting tables for example, or banging tambourines – and that their messages were banal in the extreme. In a long letter to Innes, Conan Doyle theorised that we were still in a 'kindergarten stage' of contact with the other world and that the spirits were signalling for attention before preparing to deliver their divine message. 'Queer agents are chosen,' he admitted, 'but God's ways are often queer . . . Excuse my scribble – my thoughts ran away with me. This subject is offensive to many good people, tho' it should not be so. Your affectionate brother A.'[21]

Among those to whom the subject was offensive were some members of his own family, including his mother, sister Ida, daughter Mary and son Kingsley. Now a frail 80-year-old, the Mam had finally left Masongill and moved south, to Bowshott Cottage in West Grinstead, close to the Hornungs. For once, Conan Doyle blithely ignored his mother's outspoken antipathy and in a letter to her, dated 9 May 1917, he described himself as a 'convinced Spiritualist': 'Kingsley is in the front line but is kept at regimental HQ as bombing officer. However that means he is well in the front. I get the most cheery letters but I am naturally very anxious. I do not fear death for the boy, for since I became a convinced Spiritualist death became rather an un-caring thing, but I fear pain and mutilation very greatly. However, all things are ordained . . .'[22] He also told his mother he was helping bereaved parents get in touch with their loved ones. He had had a letter from the mother of a dead boy thanking him: 'She is the 13th within my knowledge. It is indeed a most marvellous thing . . .'

In November 1917 Kingsley wrote to his Aunt Ida from the Officers' Rest Room, expressing his doubts about spiritualism but adding 'however, I would not pretend to argue with Daddy on the subject'. Kingsley was a devout Christian, wrote to his sister at length about the importance of faith and thought that spiritualism dragged 'something beautiful and spiritual', like conventional religion, down to a human and material level. Mary agreed: 'I tried to go along with it, but couldn't . . . These personal demonstrations of survival were to me acutely embarrassing and painful. I could not get used to the idea of contacting a loved one through someone else's body – it was all queer and uncanny to me.'[23] (She would nevertheless have a change of heart later and embrace spiritualism under pressure from her father.)

Ida Foley wrote to Conan Doyle from Italy questioning the proposition that spirits were 'hanging about clamouring to communicate with earth'. She received a terse reply: 'Dearest Ida, Your view about the spiritland seem to me a little unreasonable . . . I am sorry you don't like the prospect but what you or I may like has really nothing to do with the matter. We don't like some of the conditions down here . . . I may be very limited but I can imagine nothing more beautiful and satisfying than the life beyond as drawn by many who have experienced it. We carry on our own wisdom, own knowledge, own art, music, architecture but all with a far wider sweep. Our bodies are at their best. We are free from physical pain. The place is beautiful. What is there so dreadfully depressing in all this?'[24]

By the autumn of 1917 Conan Doyle was finally ready to declare himself publicly. He chose a meeting of the London Spiritualist Alliance, chaired by Sir Oliver Lodge, at the British Artists' Gallery in Pall Mall on 25 October. He was careful to establish his credentials from the start as a man who had thought long and hard before sharing his beliefs. He admitted that his medical studies had left him a convinced materialist, that he did not believe in an anthropomorphic deity and had looked upon spiritualism as 'the greatest nonsense'. It was his personal experiences of psychic phenomena combined with the views of great men like Crookes, Wallace and Flammarion that had won him over. The war had compelled a reassessment of his values and made him appreciate fully the importance of a study that would break down the wall between the 'two worlds'.

He spoke confidently for more than an hour, describing the foundation of his beliefs and discussing how spiritualism could be reconciled with established religions. Like conventional religion, spiritualism required faith: 'When an inquirer has convinced himself of the truth of the phenomena there is no real need to pursue the matter further.' (Fans of Sherlock Holmes would have detected here an echo of his famous aphorism from 'The Adventure of the Beryl Coronet': 'It is an old maxim of mine that when you have excluded the impossible, whatever remains, however improbable, must be the truth.')

The new doctrine taught, he went on, that passing into the spirit world was easy and painless. The spirit body was analogous to the earth body. There was a period of oblivion or sleep before taking up the duties of the spirit life, a pleasant condition from which no one wished to return. The world beyond was no vague region of floating emotion, but a definite reality attested by a body of evidence nobody could reject. 'The real object of the investigation,' he concluded, 'is to give us an assurance in the future and spiritual strength in the present, to give us a clear perception of the fleeting nature of matter and reveal the eternal values beyond all the shows of time and sense – the things which are indeed lasting, going on and ever on through the ages in a glorious and majestic progression.'

What Conan Doyle did not say, but what he had come to believe, was that he was standing on the threshold of the greatest discovery in the history of mankind.

CHAPTER 20

THE APOSTLE

S IN EVERYTHING HE DID, once Conan Doyle made up his mind he was unstoppable, impervious to argument, blind to contradictory evidence, untroubled by self-doubt. There were few grey areas in Conan Doyle's life. There was black and white, there was right and wrong, clearly defined. You believed in something, or you did not. If you believed, you believed passionately – and you wanted others to believe.

So it was that he would espouse the cause of spiritualism with missionary fervour. He would in time be mocked, insulted and disparaged, but nothing would shake him from his beliefs, not the collapse of long-standing friendships, the uncovering of fraud or the exposure of mediums as confidence tricksters. To his friends and supporters he became the St Paul of the spiritualist movement. Critics would ridicule his extreme credulity and childlike enthusiasm, but none of it mattered to him. Once he had convinced himself that spiritualism had a valuable message for the world he took it upon himself to be the messenger with single-minded dedication.

Within a week of his lecture to the London Spiritualist Alliance, he was writing in *Light* about the meaning of death: '[It] makes no abrupt change in the process of development, nor does it make an impassable chasm between those who are on either side of it. No trait of the form and no peculiarity of the mind are changed by death but all are continued in that spiritual body which is in the counterpart of the earthly one at its best, and still contains within it that core of spirit which is the very essence of the man.'

Greenhough Smith was persuaded to allow his star contributor a platform in the *Strand*, and mystified readers, accustomed to ripping yarns, were soon obliged to digest various esoteric theories in Conan Doyle's new role as psychic investigator in a series called 'The Uncharted Coast'. In Part 5, published in the November 1920 issue under the title 'The Absolute Proof', he argued that 'ectoplasm', the peculiar white-ish substance that emanated from the bodies of some mediums, was the final proof of the existence of 'discarnate spirits'.

Conan Doyle described ectoplasm as differing from every known form of matter, being able to mould itself into a human face then disappear without trace. Ghosts were formed of certain types of ectoplasm: 'Utterly incredible as it may appear,' he wrote, when ectoplasm was moulded into a resemblance of a dead person 'the cord which binds it to the medium is loosened, a personality which either is or pretends to be that of the dead person takes possession of it, and the breath of life is breathed into the image so that it moves and talks and expresses the emotions of the spirit within.'

Understandably, Greenhough Smith appealed repeatedly to Conan Doyle to return to fiction, or at least to write something with more general, popular appeal. 'I wish I could do as you wish,' he replied, 'but, as you know, my life is devoted to one end and at present I can't see any literature which would be of any use to you above the horizon. I can only write what comes to me.'[1] For readers of the *Strand*, and indeed Conan Doyle fans around the world, it was hard to imagine how the creator of Sherlock Holmes, the very epitome of a cold, calculating logician, 'the perfect reasoning and observing machine', could embrace a cause which, frankly, required the *suspension* of logic. To the British public Conan Doyle was the pipe-smoking embodiment of common sense, a man who revered history, an adventurer in real life not given to flights of fancy. How could he be reconciled with the ludicrous doctrine, and the so-called 'wonders', of spiritualism?

'In a less practical man his belief in Spiritualism would have been fanatical,' said the playwright Arthur Rose. 'He carried it to extreme lengths, showing impatience with anyone who expressed the slightest doubt. Yet fanaticism is the last word I could attach to a man so solid. You would have judged him to have not the slightest spark of the mystic. Yet his eye would light with something like the mystic's when he spoke of the spirit land, and his devotion to the cause was nothing less than a crusade, to which he sacrificed money and all other interests as far as I know.'²

If anyone doubted his commitment they had only to read *The New Revelation*, a credo published in June 1918, in which he declared in ringing, apocalyptic prose that spiritualism would bring about 'the greatest development of human experience which the world has ever seen'. *The New Revelation* was dedicated to 'all the brave men and women, humble or learned, who have had the moral courage during seventy years to face ridicule or worldly disadvantage in order to testify to an all-important truth', brave folk among whom Conan Doyle would soon be numbering himself, in his new role as apostle.

The basis of his argument was that all psychic phenomena, from the table rapping to the 'inspired utterance of a prophet', were linked in a chain up which humanity could feel its way to the revelation that awaited. Conan Doyle offered readers a detailed, picturesque description of crossing into the other world, culled from a number of corroborating messages received during seances. At death the spirit body either stood or floated beside the old body, aware of it and of the surroundings. The spirit body was an exact counterpart of the physical body, he claimed, though free from all disease, weakness or deformity. Passing into the other world was easy and painless and was accompanied by an overwhelming feeling of peace and ease after having a long sleep which varied from a few days to several months, depending on how much hardship the deceased had experienced in life. There was no hell in the other world, merely 'probationary spheres, which should perhaps rather be looked upon as a hospital for weakly souls than as a penal community'. In conclusion Conan Doyle offered two explanations for the growth of spiritualism:

> The one supposition is that there has been an outbreak of lunacy extending over two generations of mankind, and two great continents – a lunacy which assails men or women who are otherwise eminently sane. The alternative supposition is that in recent years there has come to us from divine sources a new revelation which constitutes by far the greatest religious

event since the death of Christ . . . a revelation which alters the whole aspect of death and the fate of man. Between these two suppositions there is no solid position. Theories of fraud or of delusion will not meet the evidence. It is absolute lunacy or it is a revolution in religious thought, a revolution which gives us as by-products an utter fearlessness of death, and an immense consolation when those who are dear to us pass behind the veil.

The New Revelation, not surprisingly, received a mixed reception from the critics. The Daily Chronicle, to which Conan Doyle had contributed reports from the Western Front, thought it was 'very frank, very courageous and very resolute', and the Daily News considered it deserved respect, but The Times accused Conan Doyle of 'incredible naivety', counselling that he should perhaps take a moment to consider the arguments against spiritualism. The Nation concluded that the book left readers with 'a rather poor opinion of the doctor's critical abilities', and the Sunday Express asked in a banner headline: 'IS CONAN DOYLE MAD?' Its review was more sympathetic than the headline suggested, acknowledging Conan Doyle's achievements as a writer, historian and campaigner: 'It is not easy to reconcile these facts,' the columnist James Douglas admitted, 'with the hypothesis that he is stark, staring mad on the subject of the dead. He has established the right to be heard, and we may be wrong in refusing to hear him. There may be oceans of fraud and folly in Spiritualism, but there may be a grain of truth in it.'

Conan Doyle was blithely undaunted by his critics and launched into a series of lecture tours, first in the south of England and then in the Midlands, Leeds and Nottingham, which drew large audiences. He alternated between two basic presentations – a 'photographic' lecture in which he showed lantern slides of 'spirit photographs' in which ghostly apparitions had appeared on photographic plates, and a 'philosophical' lecture which was essentially a distillation of The New Revelation. His thesis was based on two principles: the failure of religion, or churches, to stem the mounting tide of materialism, and that a new 'science of religion' should be compatible with traditional religious teaching.

He was due to give his second lecture in Nottingham in October 1918 when a telegram arrived from Mary telling him that Kingsley had died. He had known his son had contracted pneumonia and was very ill, but had not felt that he could cut short his lecture tour. Neither did he cancel the lecture that evening, and when urged to do so he replied gruffly, 'No, under no circumstances would I break faith with the public. They have learned to trust me, and I must be worthy of that trust. Besides, Kingsley would wish it so.' In any case, as a committed spiritualist, he knew that Kingsley had simply 'crossed over' and that they would soon meet again, the message he confidently conveyed to the waiting audience. From the Victoria Station Hotel he wrote to Innes: 'Dear old boy, You will have heard our sad news. I must lecture tonight here and then get back to London tomorrow morning to take some weight off Mary who has been splendid. I suppose the dear boy will be buried on Thursday. I can hardly realise it and am stunned by the news. I rejoice to think we never had a word between us in his life. I know I have your sympathy, ACD.'[3] Mary organised the funeral and told her father afterwards that it was only his stern self-control that prevented her from breaking down.

During the next twelve months Conan Doyle gave forty lectures in Scotland and the north of England. In his study he kept a map of Great Britain marked with all the towns that had received his message and a bulging file on his desk containing invitations from more than a hundred spiritualist groups he had had to refuse because of lack of time. His brother's death in Belgium, in February 1919, though keenly felt, did not make a dent in his schedule. He reported his progress in frequent and optimistic letters to his mother, even though she had made it clear she was not in sympathy with his mission:

My dearest Mammie,
　　Tomorrow I go to London to give my address upon 'The New Revelation' which may, I think, be an acorn from which a tree will grow in days to come. So far as I know it

is the first attempt to show what the real meaning is of the
modern spiritual movement, and it puts into the hands of
the clergy such a weapon against materialism which is their
real enemy, as they have never had. I get plenty of abuse for
it but some of them will see the point and they will leaven
the lump. Any how I am doing what I feel to be my plain
duty, tho' not always an easy or a pleasant one . . .[4]

What spiritualists loved about Conan Doyle was his bravura, his
lack of caution, his certainty. Speaking at a memorial service at the
Albert Hall for the fallen, organised by the Spiritualists' National
Union, in April 1919, Conan Doyle drew loud cheers when he declared
that spiritualism was the greatest movement that had been seen for
the last 2,000 years. They had a 'Hindenburg line of ignorance and
theological barbed wire in front of them', but they were going to go
right through it because they had a cause that could not be beaten.
This was not a memorial service; it was a 'joyous reunion made possible
by the new knowledge which was theirs'.

Besieged with requests from bereaved parents and wives for help,
Conan Doyle sent out a standard reply: 'These things are true. Your
loved ones are alive. If you wish to get in touch with them go in a
reverent mood to a medium. I can recommend one; her charges will
be 10s 6d. You may get nothing but you may get something and
when you have been kindly let me know the result.' He explained he
had 'tested' the medium, claiming that 42 of the 50 people who
had consulted her had had success. Unfortunately he recommended
Mrs Annie Brittain, who had twice been convicted and fined for
fortune telling and was exposed by *Truth* magazine, which claimed
that her spirits appeared 'at the magic spell of half a guinea' and that
her clairvoyance was a 'venal vision cleared by seeing half a crown'.
The magazine attacked Conan Doyle as being the 'victim of his own
imagination'.[5]

Other critics suggested it was becoming rapidly evident that there
was nothing Conan Doyle could not believe and questioned how it
was he knew so much that the rest of the world did not? He claimed
personally to have witnessed the entire range of psychic phenomena:
direct voice contact, telekinesis (movements of objects at a distance),

apports (bringing objects from a distance), table tipping and rapping, levitation, automatic writing and materialisation of faces, limbs and complete bodies. He had seen a procession of figures, old and young, adults and children, emerging one at a time from a small cabinet, some of whom answered questions put to them; he had watched an illuminated trumpet whirling around a room and banging on the ceiling like a moth against a light; he had seen brilliant 'luminosities' shooting like a 'dazzling crown' out of a medium's head; he described a brilliant light that settled on his moustache like a firefly; he had participated in crystal gazing and seen dim faces appear one after another interspersed with fog. What sceptics failed to understand was that Conan Doyle was immoveable in his views because he was constantly encouraged by numerous messages from the other world praising his commitment. One was from Kinglsey, newly arrived, and rejoicing at the 'Christ-like message' his father was giving to the world. William T. Stead, who had gone down on the *Titanic*, described Conan Doyle's work as 'the Review of Divine Reviews' and added that he had 'looked into the eyes of the Christ with Cecil Rhodes by my side and he said tell Arthur that his work on earth is holy and divine'.

In August 1919 a second volume on spiritualism, *The Vital Message*, was published, proposing that there had been an 'inner reason' for the war: to 'shake mankind loose from gossip and pink teas, and sword-worship, and Saturday night drunks, and self-seeking politics and theological quibbles – to wake them up'. This was Conan Doyle the writer at his very worst – muddled, dogmatic and unfathomable. Much of *The Vital Message* was a reworking of *The New Revelation*, but Conan Doyle enlarged on the concept of the 'spirit body' in an attempt to invest the movement with scientific status. That someone trained as a doctor should propose a thesis founded at best on un-verified guesswork was an indication of the artless credulity with which he approached the whole subject.

The soul, he explained, was a complete replica of the body, down to the smallest pimple, but constructed of a light, tenuous material

he described as 'bound ether'. In ordinary conditions the two intermingled so that the existence of the finer one was entirely obscured.
At the time of death, 'according to the observation of clairvoyants
on this side and the posthumous accounts of the dead upon the other',
the soul disengaged itself from the heavier, physical body in a painless and natural process and stood at the deathbed aware of those
present but unable to communicate with them except through clairvoyants. While the 'cocoon' of the body was interred, the soul
continued on its journey to the other side, where it was remodelled
into a perfect state. Deformities were removed, the ugly would be
made beautiful, the weak strong, and so on. Soldiers who had lost
limbs in the war would have them replaced. The ageing process did
not exist, but children would grow up as usual, so that a 'mother who
lost a babe of two years old and dies herself twenty years later finds
a grown-up daughter of twenty-two awaiting her coming'.

While there was no physical love on the other side, and no child-
birth, there was deep comradeship between the sexes and everyone
found a soulmate. Sullen husbands and flighty wives were no longer
there to plague their spouses. God-given powers were carried over:
writers and artists were able to continue their work, intellectuals were
able to study and research, craftsmen continued their craft 'but only
for the joy of their work'. There were no poor and no rich; social
divisions and class enmity were non-existent. There were games and
sports of all kinds, and while food and drink 'in the grosser sense' did
not exist, everyone enjoyed the pleasures of taste. All in all, it was a
place of joy and laughter.

Conan Doyle's glib descriptions of the other world began to irritate
many serious spiritualists, who complained that his account made it
more like Hampstead Garden Suburb than heaven. 'All is sweet and
peaceful . . . Beautiful gardens, lovely flowers, green woods, pleasant
lakes, domestic pets – all of these things are fully described in the
messages of the pioneer travellers who have at last got news back to
those who loiter in the old dingy home.'[6]

If some spiritualists were irritated, the clergy were infuriated
both by Conan Doyle and by his claim that spiritualism represented
a religious revival that would humanise theology by reconciling it
with science and reason. In The New Revelation he had claimed that

Christianity had to accept spiritualism 'or perish' and that the certainty of life after death should be the basis of all religion, but in *The Vital Message* he mounted a swingeing attack on the Bible, and the Old Testament in particular: 'a document which advocates massacre, condones polygamy, accepts slavery and orders the burning of so-called witches'.

Reaction from the church was predictable. At a conference of the Catholic Young Men's Society of Great Britain, spiritualism was denounced as a 'menace' and Conan Doyle and his friend Oliver Lodge were accused of having lost their 'mental poise', possibly under the influence of some demonic force. 'I would rather be in prison for the rest of my life,' one speaker declared, 'than carry on the work that is being done by these two gentlemen.' At another debate in Bristol which attracted an audience of 3,000 people, Conan Doyle was cast as a 'trifler with divine realities and castigated for his 'wicked perversion' of the Scriptures; calls were made for the 'evil which he promulgates' to be exposed. James Boyd, a well-regarded religious poet, was among the speakers and was greeted with loud applause when he boomed: 'In this wretched book of Sir Arthur Conan Doyle's, scripture is twisted all out of shape to make it appear to agree with this abomination, and the object of the devil in doing this is the destruction of the souls of those who give themselves into his hands.'

In October 1919, at a Church Congress in Leicester, the Reverend J. A. Magee accused Conan Doyle of lowering the moral, mental and spiritual standards of the country. Conan Doyle travelled to Leicester a week later to deliver a speech in rebuttal. Every seat was taken and hundreds more people had to be turned away at the door. By then he calculated he had spoken to some 100,000 people at 50 lectures. Spiritualism, he said, had come as an ally to Christianity in confuting materialism and in proving the continuity of life and the evil effects of sin. This should merit some better return than ignorant clamour and accusations of necromancy. When a man had again and again, beyond all doubt and question, spoken face to face with the so-called dead, as he had done, how was it possible for him to yield to the arguments of those who had not had so sacred an experience?

'We represent a cause,' he cried, 'which for 70 years has been the
butt of every person who tried to be humorous, subjected to every
form of abuse, from accusations of devil worship down to the most
absurd joke . . . But anyone who knows our literature – unfortunately
these gentlemen of the Church Congress are ignorant of it – knows
we have proved that life goes on after physical death, carrying with
it a reasonable evolution of the human soul. That being so, if these
people were not blind they would say to us "Come in and help us
fight the materialism of the world."'

Conan Doyle's strengths as a public speaker were his patent
honesty, passion and evident sincerity. 'He spoke with the fire of
the prophet,' one reporter noted, 'with the eloquence of the
visionary and with the masterful assurance of a man who has
convinced himself late in life that his earlier attitude was mistaken.'
He also never ducked an issue, even the awkward subject of the
many mediums exposed as charlatans: 'Fraud? Of course we have
fraud. I could fill a book with it. We have had fraud because we
treat our mediums so badly. They are men with the most delicate
and beautiful gift that God ever put in the human frame and we
have turned them out to earn a living.' His explanation was that
mediums occasionally suffered a temporary loss of power and
that the expectation placed upon them by the public tempted
them to repeat by fraud what they had previously achieved by psychic
means.

Many fans of Sherlock Holmes rued Conan Doyle's metamorphosis from writer to prophet, as E. T. Raymond wrote in *Living Age*:
'One can imagine the devout Doylist wringing his hands over every
fresh appearance of Sir Arthur in the character of an exponent of
Spiritualism. For Sir Arthur the spiritualist makes cruel war on the
great legend of the perfect detective . . . Sir Arthur Conan Doyle, in
his new character, is the exact opposite of his creation. Instead of
common sense penetrated with glamour, we have here the wildest
mysticism tamed down and vulgarized by a dreadful ordinariness . . .
When good Dr Watson waxed too impossibly obtuse, Sherlock Holmes
used to rally him with a "Really, my dear Watson". Is there nobody
to bring up Dr Watson's creator with a friendly remonstrance of the
same kind? It appears to be called for.'[7]

At Windlesham Conan Doyle became accustomed to receiving hate mail, most of which he disregarded, but there was one particularly vituperative letter, dated 16 December 1919, from Lord Alfred Douglas, Oscar Wilde's former lover and a relatively recent convert to the Roman Catholic church: 'Sir, What a disgusting beast you are with your filthy caricatures of "Christ". The proper way to deal with such a man as you would be to give you a thrashing with a horse whip . . .' Douglas accused Conan Doyle of promoting spiritualism for the sake of money and notoriety, 'in short for the same purposes and with the same flat-footed low persistence as you worked your idiot "Sherlock Holmes" business'. He went on to prophesy that Conan Doyle's 'blasphemous ravings' would bring a 'dreadful judgement' on him and signed himself 'Yours with the utmost contempt'. Conan Doyle replied the following day, with a masterful and succinct dismissal: 'Sir, I was relieved to get your letter. It is only your approval which could in any way annoy me.'[8]

Windlesham was maintained by a large domestic staff – a butler, Mr Rogers, a cook and five maids in the house, two gardeners and a chauffeur outside, plus a garden boy who cleaned the boots and shoes and doubled as a pageboy, with a green bellhop uniform and pillbox hat, when the Conan Doyles were entertaining, which they did frequently. The gardeners directed visitors' cars where to park and the chauffeurs all gathered in the kitchen while the party was under way; two housemaids found their future husbands from among the chauffeurs they had first met in the kitchen. One of the last daily duties of the housemaids was to ensure the family's two dogs were given a drop of brandy in their bowl of milk to stop them howling at night.

The children of Conan Doyle's second marriage were greatly indulged, in noticeable contrast to the strict Victorian upbringing of Kingsley and Mary. Denis and Adrian, aged 11 and 9 in 1919, cajoled the staff to play games with them in the garden in their 'free hour' after serving lunch. On one occasion, the boys 'borrowed' a revolver their father had brought back from the Boer War for a game of cowboys and Indians, and while they were waving it about a shot was fired. 'We were all shocked, the boys included,' recalled James Payne, one of the gardeners. 'Sir Arthur strode from the house looking very angry, took the gun from the boys and pointed for them to go into the house. He immediately apologised for the boys' behaviour and the boys came to us to do the same.'⁹ This did not stop them, however, from persuading Payne's son, Roger, the garden boy, to hold a target in one hand while they practised with an air rifle. Inevitably, he got shot in the hand and Conan Doyle was obliged to remove the pellet with a pair of tweezers.

His daughter Jean remembered her father spending a lot of time with them, devising games and joining in. One of her earliest memories was of playing on the floor of her father's study and listening to the squeak of his pen as he worked. Yet his fascination with the dead could take precedence over the living. An ophthalmic surgeon who was asked to examine Jean when she was 6 years old was astonished that her father, as a doctor and ophthalmic specialist, had not noticed her extreme short-sightedness: 'I remember being shaken to the core that Sherlock Holmes had only just found out what must have been evident to the most casual observer for months, if not years, that the child was as blind as a bat because of her uncorrected myopia.'¹⁰

Seances became a regular feature of the Conan Doyles' social life at Windlesham. They were held behind closed doors in the old nursery, adjoining the billiard room; staff were warned that they were not to be disturbed and the telephone was taken off the hook lest an earthly communication disrupt their concentration. Conan Doyle kept a meticulous record of spirit 'contacts' and registered 60 successful contacts out of 72 attempts in the course of a year. At one seance Kingsley materialised, laid a heavy hand on his shoulder and told his father he was happy. At another, Innes spoke a few words in Danish, his wife's native tongue: 'I can solemnly declare,' Conan Doyle reported in a letter to *The Times*, 'that, using an unpaid medium, I have beyond all question or doubt spoken face to face with my son, my brother, my nephew by marriage, and several other close friends since their death. On each occasion there were six or more witnesses.'¹¹

Conan Doyle described the seance at which Kingsley appeared in a letter to Lodge. The medium was Evan Powell, a colliery clerk by trade who had made a name for himself in the spiritualist movement. Beforehand Powell was subjected to a rigorous search of his pockets and tied to a chair to avoid any risk of deception. As soon as the lights were extinguished, the medium began exhibiting signs of a 'manifestation', groaning and muttering:

> Then came a voice in the darkness, a whispered voice, saying 'Jean, it is I.' I heard the word 'Father'. I said 'Dear boy, is that you?' I had then a sense of a face very near my own, and of breathing. Then the clear voice came with an intensity and note very distinctive of my son, 'Forgive me!' I told him eagerly that I had no grievance of any kind. A large, strong hand then rested upon my head, it was gently bent forward. And I felt and heard a kiss just above my brow. 'Tell me, dear, are you happy?' I cried. There was silence, and I feared he was gone. Then on a sighing note came the words, 'Yes I am so happy.' A moment afterwards another gentle voice, claiming to be that of my wife's mother, recently deceased, was heard in front of us. We could not have recognised the voice as we could the other. A few loving words were said, and then a small warm hand patted both our cheeks with a little gesture which was full of affection. Such were my experiences.[12]

Prominent among Conan Doyle's critics was Joseph McCabe of the Rationalist Press Association, who characterised him as gullible and misguided, cruelly offering false hope to bereaved families. When McCabe suggested a public debate, Conan Doyle accepted immediately and a date was set for 11 March 1920, at the Queen's Hall in London. As soon as the event was announced people from all over the country applied for tickets, hoping to be present at what many considered would be either a defining moment for the spiritualist cause or the start of its demise. It sold out a month in advance.

'The debate is on Thursday,' Conan Doyle wrote to his mother.

This will in a way be the most important night of my life so
I pray you to think of me. It is rather touching to think that
in little villages in the hills of Wales and elsewhere, meetings
will be held that night to send me spiritual help. I hear of
such from all parts. On the other hand, McCabe takes the
floor as champion of all atheists, agnostics and materialists
of England, which is a large body. They are good men – the
thinking ones – but their creed is negative and hopeless. Well,
I go into battle in good heart. Fifty chosen spiritualists sit at
my right and fifty rationalists on his left. They could have
sold the house out three times over and as I think I told
you, titled people have been crammed into the gallery. Well,
we'll see . . .

There was palpable excitement in the audience when the two men
took to the stage. McCabe spoke first, forcefully excoriating spiritualism and everything it stood for. It was, he said, 'born in fraud, cradled
in fraud and was based to an alarming extent all over the world on
fraudulent   performances'.   The   mediums   Conan   Doyle   had
pronounced as genuine, McCabe would prefer to describe as 'not
found out'. 'I submit to this jury,' he thundered to the cheers of his
supporters, 'that, like every man who has gone into that dim supernatural world, he [Conan Doyle] has lived in clouds, in a mist. Whatever other witnesses there may be, you will find that distortion of
judgement, that blearing of vision, which occurs whenever a man
enters that wonderful world, that world of almost unparalleled trickery
in the history of man.' He questioned Conan Doyle's claim that spiritualism was supported by a large number of distinguished scientists
and scholars. 'I courteously challenge him in his first speech tonight,
to give me the names not of fifty, but of ten, university professors of
any distinction who have within the last thirty years endorsed or
defended Spiritualism.'

It was a challenge to which Conan Doyle was delighted to respond.
Now a polished and confident orator – the days in Southsea when he
shook with nerves before speaking in public were long gone – he
withdrew a small notebook from his pocket as he got to his feet. 'Mr
McCabe has shown that he has no respect for our intellectual position,'

he began, 'but I cannot reciprocate. I have a very deep respect for the honest, earnest materialist, if only because for very many years I was one myself.' Waving the notebook he continued, 'I have in this little book the names of 160 people of high distinction, many of them of great eminence, including the names of 40 professors . . . I beg you to remember that these 160 people whose names I submit to you are people who, to their own great loss, have announced themselves as Spiritualists. It never yet did a man any good to call himself a Spiritualist, I assure you . . .' (Conan Doyle was certainly speaking from experience at this point.)

He went on to defend the mediums whom McCabe had sarcastically categorised as 'not found out', and continued with an abbreviated version of his standard speech, detailing how he had once been a materialist but had slowly seen the light. At the end of the evening it was generally agreed there was no clear winner; both men acquitted themselves well and ended up respecting each other, even though neither budged from his original position. Conan Doyle was pleased.

'The debate was great,' he wrote to his mother shortly afterwards. 'They say there was never so fine a one, so orderly and on so high a level, in London before. Magnificent audience and very attentive and impartial. I don't dislike McCabe, who has had a hard fight. He is an ex-Franciscan priest and a very clever man. He seems all brain but wanting, perhaps, in heart.'[13] He added an optimistic postscript: 'Some close observers thought that McCabe faltered before the end.'

By the time of the McCabe debate, the Conan Doyles were planning their first great spiritualist crusade to the other side of the world, Australia and New Zealand. The expense was considerable – they took their three children, Woodie and Jakeman, Jean's maid – and the return fares alone accounted for £1,700, but money was less important to Conan Doyle than the mission.

On 29 July 1920 they were entertained at a farewell lunch in the Holborn Restaurant in London by a large group of supporters. Conan Doyle was presented with an illuminated address – a lavishly illustrated testimonial – in appreciation of his work for the movement and delivered a short speech. Three years had passed, he said, since he had determined to devote himself to the great cause and he had spoken in every part of Britain. He had had plenty of opposition from materialists, Bible-quoters and other critics but his resolve was undiminished. Lady Conan Doyle was in perfect sympathy with his views and together they intended to take whatever comfort they could to thousands bereaved by war in Australia and New Zealand. The whole world, he said, wanted the comfort that spiritualists had to give.

The party left on Friday, 13 August, on board the SS *Naldera*, a new P&O ship built specifically for the London to Sydney service. Woodie was in charge of organising entertainment and lessons for the children en route, a six-week journey which took them through the Suez Canal to Bombay and Colombo before arriving in Adelaide, the first port of call in Australia. Halfway across the Mediterranean, somewhere south of Crete, Conan Doyle addressed 200 first-class passengers on the subject of 'psychic religion'. Afterwards someone told him there had 'never been so much religion talked on a P&O ship since the line was started'.[14]

He was impressed by the Suez Canal as an engineering feat but appalled by the huge hoardings advertising whisky which lined the banks. Prohibition had recently been introduced in the United States, a measure of which Conan Doyle heartily approved after his experience with his father, and he considered it disgraceful that travellers passing through the canal should be assaulted with crude exhortations to buy alcohol. As they sailed further south the summer heat intensified; several stewards collapsed and one passenger died, but Conan Doyle repeated his lecture to the sweltering second-class passengers while crossing the Red Sea. Like the gentleman he was, he made no concessions to the climate: a photograph shows him sitting on a bench on deck wearing a heavy suit, collar and tie, and a trilby hat and writing the first chapter of *The Wanderings of a Spiritualist*, his 'memorial' of the trip.

The family disembarked in Adelaide, where on 25 September Conan Doyle delivered his first lecture to a packed audience of around 2,000 people at the Town Hall on the subject of the human and scientific aspects of spiritualism, beginning, as usual: 'I want to speak to you tonight on a subject which concerns the destiny of every man and woman in this room.' The Adelaide *Register* was impressed: 'The audience, large, representative and thoughtful, was in its calibre and proportions a fitting compliment to a world celebrity and his mission . . . It cannot be doubted, of course, that the brilliant literary fame of the lecturer was an attraction added to that strange subject which explored the "unknown drama of the soul". Over all Sir Arthur dominated by his big arresting presence. His face has a rugged, kindly strength, tense and earnest in its grave moments, and full of winning animation when the sun of his rich humour plays upon the powerful features . . .'

While he was in the city he attended several seances – he rarely missed an opportunity – and mounted an exhibition of psychic photographs of ghostly manifestations which, he claimed, 'stunned' and 'staggered' everyone. He also received plenty of abusive letters, one of which fervently wished that he would be 'struck dead' before he left Australia.

At his next stop, Melbourne, a public prayer meeting had been held, while they were en route to Australia on board the *Naldera*, at which Presbyterians prayed that he would never reach their shores. Unsurprisingly their welcome in Melbourne was cool. A 'few devoted souls' waited to greet them with flowers at the railway station, but they soon learned that the local newspaper, the *Argus*, had published a vituperative leader attacking spiritualism as a 'cranky faith' and 'black magic' and concluding that Conan Doyle represented 'a force which we believe to be purely evil'. He was not particularly concerned – 'The greater the darkness,' he observed, 'the more need of light' – but he was outraged by the newspaper's coverage of his first lecture which described in great detail the dress his wife was wearing, the colour of his spectacles and the tone of his voice, but omitted to report a single word he had said.

Despite the antagonism of the local media, he was heartened by the crowds who attended his lectures and delighted to meet Charles Bailey, a medium with an extraordinary reputation for introducing foreign objects into locked and sealed seance rooms. In the course of six seances he was said to have produced no fewer than 130 objects, including 87 ancient coins, 8 live birds, 18 precious stones, 2 turtles, 7 inscribed tablets, a leopard skin and a young shark tangled in seaweed. Bailey had recently been discredited when two birds appeared at one of his seances only for a local pet-shop owner to identify him as the man who had purchased the birds earlier that day. But Conan Doyle was always ready to believe the best and accepted Bailey's explanation that the bird incident was a rash act which he regretted and had only committed under pressure.

At a first seance with Bailey, faintly luminous hands appeared, but Conan Doyle was concerned by a 'disturbing suggestion' of distinctly unspiritual cuffs around the wrists. He was much more impressed at a second sitting when Bailey produced a perfectly constructed bird's nest containing a small white egg. Bailey's Hindu spirit control claimed it had come from India and was the nest of a bird called a jungle sparrow; a local museum confirmed to Conan Doyle that it was not the nest of any bird species found in Australia. He also took away with him one of the 'Assyrian' inscribed tablets that had materialised during one of Bailey's seances, but was disappointed when the British Museum later pronounced it to be a fake. It did not, nevertheless, alter his opinion that Bailey was a 'true medium, with a very remarkable gift for apports'.

The next stop was Sydney, where they received a much warmer welcome, the men cheering and waving their hats and the women carrying flowers. He was barracked at his first lecture at the Town Hall but was quite accustomed to dealing with hecklers. When he was describing how his son had returned to him during a seance, a voice shouted that it must have been the devil. Conan Doyle simply paused and, laughing, said that such a remark showed the 'queer working' of some people's minds, which produced loud cheers from the floor. Then someone at the back of the hall started repeatedly shouting 'Anti-Christ!' but was quickly bundled out by stewards.

Despite the doubters, Conan Doyle was establishing a strong personal following. Members of the Stanmore Spiritualist Church in Sydney presented him with an illuminated address bound in black Morocco leather and inscribed: 'We recognise in you a specially chosen Leader, endowed with power to command attention from the most obdurate minds, and we heartily rejoice to know that you have consecrated your life to the spread of our glorious gospel.' He admitted he was almost moved to tears when, at one meeting, 3,000 people got to their feet, waved handkerchiefs and sang, 'God be with you till we meet again.'

From Sydney Conan Doyle travelled alone to New Zealand, delivering eight lectures in fifteen days in Auckland, Wellington, Lyttelton, Dunedin and Christchurch. The clergy vigorously protested against his presence, variously describing spiritualism as a 'blasphemy nurtured in fraud', 'the abrogation of reason', 'an ancient delusion' and a 'foolish Paganism'. Conan Doyle relished the battle, as he made clear in a letter to his father-in-law, written from Warners Hotel in Christchurch on 16 December: 'Here I am charging like a mad bull down the length of New Zealand, only pausing to utter a prolonged bellow or to toss an occasional parson. They think (and say) that the devil has got loose and there will be a general jubilee when I disappear either over the sea or into the sea, the latter for choice . . . The people in the main are with me . . .' He added that by selling tickets for his lectures he had managed to clear his expenses in New Zealand, which he put at about £3,000. 'I think I should be able to earn another £1,000 which I can hand over to the Cause and strengthen their rather weak hands. They are splendid folk and worth helping – but very poor. It has been a thousand times worthwhile to come here.'[15]

Later, Conan Doyle wrote again to say that he had attended a seance in Dunedin at which contact was made with Jean's mother, Selina Leckie who had died the previous year. 'I had a sitting with one Mrs Roberts who has a name as a medium. She said "I see an elderly lady with you who is now a very high spirit. She gives the name Selina. Does that mean anything to you?" I said "Yes, it does." She said "She will give a message through me." She became slightly convulsed and unconscious. Then a voice spoke through her with considerable emotion. It said "Thank God! Thank God to be in touch once more. I can! I can! Give my love to Jean!" I said "Dear Mother, it is good to hear you. We never forget you. Have you a message for Pater [Jean's father]?" The power was waning and I only got disjointed words like "eternal – love – remembrance". It was very convincing.'[16]

On his return to Melbourne Conan Doyle learned that his own mother had died on 30 December. She was 83 and had been ill and almost totally blind for some years, so it was hardly a surprise. She had been the most powerful influence in his life, his sage and counsel, someone to whom he poured out his heart and whose advice he always respected. And even when he had been suspicious of her relationship with Bryan Waller, his dependance on her never waned. Conan Doyle was deeply saddened by her passing but not grief-stricken. How could he be? He now knew without any doubt that she would be waiting for him on the other side, with Kingsley and Innes. Once again he did not consider cutting short his tour. The Mam was buried at Grayshott, next to Touie and Kingsley, without her favourite child being present. 'For my own psychic work she had, I fear, neither sympathy nor understanding,' Conan Doyle wrote, 'but she had an innate faith and spirituality which were so natural to her that she could not conceive the needs of others in that direction.'

From Melbourne they moved on to Brisbane, where he laid the foundation stone for a spiritualist church and found 'the more bigoted clergy to be very vituperative and unreasonable', although the 'general public were amazingly friendly and packed the theatre' for his lecture. As a goodwill gesture he invested £2,000 in Queensland Government Bonds. A government photographer took his photograph as he handed over the cheque on the steps of Parliament House, but when the film was developed his face was obscured by what he called a 'cloud of ectoplasmic light'. Always ready to find psychic phenomena all around him, he took it as an indication that he was in the presence of 'those great forces for whom I act as a humble interpreter'.[17]

Back in Sydney they had a short holiday in the Blue Mountains, went sightseeing and attended a number of seances – including another with Charles Bailey at which 2 tortoises and 56 Turkish coins were produced – before leaving for home on 1 February 1921, again on board the SS Naldera. Conan Doyle was well satisfied with the tour: he estimated that he had addressed about 50,000 people at 25 well-attended meetings across Australia and New Zealand. Somewhat to his surprise, the tour made a profit of £700 after all the expenses had been paid, which he handed over to the movement, asking for £500 to be set aside to guarantee expenses for the next visiting lecturer. The Australian media remained implacably hostile to the end. 'The one thing clear,' Life newspaper reported, 'is that Sir Conan Doyle's mission to Australia was a mournful and complete failure, and it has left him in a very exasperated state of mind.'

As the SS *Naldera* set a course for Colombo and Bombay, Conan Doyle had little idea that his reputation at home had taken a severe battering in his absence. For in the Christmas 1920 issue of the *Strand*, Sir Arthur Conan Doyle had revealed that he believed in fairies.

CHAPTER 21

THE CURIOUS CASE OF THE COTTINGLEY FAIRIES

OTTINGLEY WAS A VILLAGE OUTSIDE Bradford in Yorkshire which would have remained in deserved obscurity were in not for 16-year-old Elsie Wright and her 10-year-old cousin Frances Griffiths. In the summer of 1917 Frances and her mother, both recently returned from Cape Town, South Africa, were staying with the Wright family at their home at 31 Main Street, Cottingley. The two girls played frequently together along the beck, a narrow brook which ran behind the garden and it was there, in July, that Elsie took a remarkable photograph of Frances playing with 'fairies'.

A few days earlier Frances had slipped on rocks and fallen into the water. She scrambled up the bank with Elsie's help and, fearful of a scolding from her mother, tried unsuccessfully to slip back into the house unnoticed. When her mother demanded to know why her dress was soaked, a tearful Frances offered the excuse that she fallen into the stream while she was 'playing with the fairies'. Her mother, unamused, sent her up to the attic bedroom she shared with Elsie, where that afternoon the two girls hatched a childish prank that would eventually make headlines around the world, severely damage the reputations of eminent public figures and generate a controversy that endured for generations.

Elsie suggested they should take photographs of the 'fairies' in order to prove to Frances's mother that she had been telling the truth. Elsie liked to draw fairies and had been a student at Bradford Art College. When she left college she found work in the photographic laboratory of a greeting card factory where her job was to create composite pictures of fallen soldiers with their loved ones. Thus she knew about photography and was familiar with plate cameras. Indeed, her father, an electrical engineer and a keen amateur photographer, owned one.

By happy circumstance, the family also possessed *Princess Mary's Gift Book*, published in 1914 by Hodder & Stoughton to raise funds for charity. Beautifully illustrated, it was a collection of drawings, poems and stories from a range of distinguished contributors, including Sir Arthur Conan Doyle. The girls flicked through its pages and found suitable fairy pictures in the illustrations for a poem by Alfred Noyes, 'A Spell for a Fairy', which they cut out and pasted onto cardboard. With a few long hatpins on which to mount their 'fairies' and a roll of zinc oxide bandage tape they were ready.

Arthur Wright willingly agreed to lend his daughter his Midg quarter-plate camera when she said she wanted to take a photograph of Frances by the stream; he set it at 1/50th and f11, and loaded it with a single glass plate. The girls set off, blissfully unaware that they were about to create one of the most reproduced photographs in history. They arranged the four fairies – three with wings and one playing a piped instrument – in front of Frances, who put flowers in her hair, cupped her chin in her hand and, curiously, stared intently at the camera rather than the fairies when Elsie took the picture. Arthur Wright developed the exposed plate in the darkroom he had built for himself under the stairs, and the image that emerged was a sweet picture of Frances with what he at first thought were 'bits of paper' in front of her. When he asked Elsie what they were she told him that they were the fairies that she and Frances played with by the beck. Wright dismissed it as girlish nonsense, filed the plate away and forgot about it.

A month later, the girls produced another 'fairy' photograph. This time it was taken by Frances and showed Elsie sitting on the grass with her skirt spread around her, reaching out to a gnome-like figure about a foot high who appeared to be prancing on the hem of her skirt. Wright was irritated that the girls refused to admit it was a joke and as a punishment said they could no longer borrow his camera. Unabashed, Elsie and Frances stuck by their story with admirable, if ill-advised, persistence.

In November 1918 Frances sent a copy of the first photograph to her friend Johanna Parvin in Cape Town. 'Dear Joe,' she wrote. 'I hope you are quite well. I wrote a letter before, only I lost it or it got mislaid. Do you play with Elsie and Nora Biddles? I am learning French, Geometry, Cookery and Algebra at school now. Dad came home from France the other week after being there ten months, and we all think the war will be over in a few days. We are going to get flags to hang upstairs in our bedroom. I am sending two photos, both of me, one of me in a bathing costume in our back yard. Uncle Arthur took that. While the other is me with some fairies up the beck, Elsie took that . . .' On the back of the fairy photo she had written: 'Elsie and I are very friendly with the beck Fairies. It is funny I never used to see them in Africa. It must be too hot for them there.'[1] This letter, and the casual way she mentions the fairies, with no more surprise or emphasis than her father, the war and her dolls, would later be used to bolster the case for the girls' credibility.

Polly Wright, Elsie's mother, and her sister, Annie Griffiths, Frances's mother, faced with the photographs, were less inclined to dismiss the girls' story. Both women were interested in theosophy and in the spring of 1919 Polly Wright attended a Theosophical Society meeting in Bradford at which the topic of discussion was 'fairy life'. At the end of the lecture she approached the speaker and asked him if he thought that 'fairies were really true', and said she had two photographs that might be of interest. At another meeting of the Theosophical Society in Harrogate she was persuaded to produce the photographs, where many of those present believed, with barely suppressed excitement, that the pictures offered the first evidence that countless accounts of fairy 'sightings' were true.

This was the heyday of 'spirit photography', when the spiritualist movement fed the insatiable hunger of the war bereaved and unscrupulous photographers made a handsome living producing portraits with ghostly images of a loved one lost in the war hovering in the background. Knowledge of photography was not widespread and few understood that a 'spirit' could be introduced by a simple double exposure. As a result, many spiritualists were encouraged to believe that the camera could 'see' what the naked eye could not, which helped to legitimise the Cottingley fairy photographs. That Elsie and

Frances were young and pretty also undoubtedly helped; within the spiritualist movement it was widely believed that adolescent girls and young women often possessed psychic powers.

In May 1920 the photographs were sent to Edward L. Gardner, a leading theosophist, in London, for his opinion. 'The post brought me two small prints,' he recalled, 'with a covering letter from a friend asking for my opinion. One print showed a group of fairy-like figures dancing on the bank of a stream in front of a little girl, and on the other was a winged gnome-like creature near a girl's beckoning hand. The letter merely stated that they were taken some time since by two girls in Yorkshire . . .'[2] Gardner was a 49-year-old building contractor who devoted his spare time to lecturing on theosophy and, as a committed theosophist, was inclined to believe in the existence of 'nature spirits'.

He wrote excitedly to Polly Wright to tell her that the first picture was 'the best of its kind I should think, anywhere', adding 'I am keenly interested in this side of our wonderful world and am urging a better understanding of nature spirits and fairies.' As the prints were faded and poorly developed he asked to see the original plates. The Wrights were happy to oblige and Gardner sent them to his friend Harold Snelling, a spiritualist and an expert on photographic retouching. Snelling confirmed their authenticity, at least inasmuch as he considered they were not produced by artifice. Each plate, he reported on 31 July 1920, was a single exposure; the dancing figures were not made of paper or fabric and had not been painted onto a photographed background; most important of all, it was his opinion that the figures were *moving* at the time of the exposure. 'In my opinion,' he concluded, 'they are both straight, untouched pictures.'[3] Gardner asked Snelling to make new negatives, retouching and cleaning up the images. 'The result,' Gardner reported, 'was that [he] turned out two first class negatives which are the same in every respect as the originals except that they are sharp cut and clear and far finer for printing purposes.'[4] In fact Snelling's work only served, probably unconsciously, to add confusion, for in 'improving' the images he removed a number of shadows and lines indicating the fairies were two-dimensional cut-outs.

Increasingly energised, Gardner took the improved negatives to Kodak for scientific analysis but their report was not encouraging.

While it could find no indication that the pictures had been faked, this could not be construed as evidence that they were genuine, since photography, with its multitude of processes, lent itself to the possibility of trickery. It was certainly not prepared to provide a certificate of authenticity, as Gardner had hoped. Kodak's studio chief did offer one theory of how they could have been created, first by photographing the girl by the stream, then enlarging a print and painting in the fairies, then rephotographing that print, first with a half-plate camera, then with a quarter-plate. He did admit, however, that this would have involved considerable technical skill and time.

This was the key for Gardner. How could a 16-year-old girl with very limited photographic experience produce an image so convincing that even experts at Kodak could not, with confidence, declare it bogus? He was also struck by a casual remark made by a Kodak technician as he was leaving the laboratory; as fairies do not exist, the man said, it stood to reason that the photographs were faked, even if they could not discern how. But Gardner was by no means convinced that fairies did not exist. His provisional theory was that 'elemental spirits' used ectoplasm emanating from the girls to form fairy figures visible only to the girls themselves and to a camera; their exact form was probably created, he thought, by the girls' subconscious minds.

———————◆———————

By happy coincidence word of the photographs reached Conan Doyle, through the editor of *Light*, when he was writing an article about fairy sightings for the Christmas issue of the *Strand*. It could fairly be said that Conan Doyle was genetically programmed to believe in fairies: his Celtic heritage was populated by countless stories about the 'little people'. His unhappy father Charles had filled page after page of a sketchbook with fantastical drawings of fairies, elves, goblins and sprites while he was an inmate at the Montrose Royal Lunatic Asylum. One caption read, 'This fairy knows a heep [*sic*] more than you do', and he had scrawled under another drawing, 'I have known such a creature.' Conan Doyle's uncle Richard wrote in his journal that when he was young he was kept awake at night by visions of fairies and gnomes. He made his reputation as an artist with his fairy paintings; even his design for the cover of *Punch,* which he first drew in 1844, showed swarms of 'little people' in various poses and occupations. He illustrated a new translation of one of Grimm's tales, 'The Fairy Ring' in 1846, prompting William Thackeray to declare that Dick Doyle was the new 'master of fairyland', supplanting the artist Cruikshank. His *Wood Elves Watching a Lady* was acquired by the Victoria and Albert Museum in London, and *The Triumphant Entry – a Fairy-tale Pageant,* a monumental work containing several hundred figures, is included in the permanent collection of the National Gallery of Ireland. After Richard's death in 1883, Conan Doyle wrote a charming poem, titled 'In Memoriam', imagining the reaction of the twittering fairies in the paintings lining his uncle's studio as his body was laid out:

> The little elves upon the walls
> Cried 'What's this before us?
> Why should the Master lie so still,
> And why should he ignore us?'
> 'Oh what is this and why is this?'
> They whispered in a chorus
>
> And one behind a heather bell,
> A gentle nymph and slender,
> Said 'What if we have made him cross,
> 'And I be the offender!'
> 'Nay, nay' they cried, 'he will not chide,
> The master's heart is tender.'

On 22 June 1920 Conan Doyle wrote to Gardner: 'I am greatly interested in the "fairy" photographs, which really should be epoch-making if we can entirely clear up the circumstances.' He asked for copies and offered to have them formally copyrighted. 'Very willingly will I assist you in any way that may be possible,' Gardner replied. 'The children who are concerned are very shy and reserved. They are of a working class family in Yorkshire and . . . have played with fairies and elves in the woods near their village since babyhood.' The two men met at the Grosvenor Hotel in London to discuss the matter over lunch. With his neat demeanour, trimmed beard and bow tie, Gardner gave the impression to his dining companion of being 'quiet, well balanced and reserved – not in the least a wild and visionary type'.[5]

Conan Doyle was, nevertheless, wary when first shown the photographs and sought the opinion of others. An artist, May Bowley, examined them with a magnifying glass and declared that the hands did not look like human hands and the 'beard in the little gnome seems to me to be some sort of insect-like appendage'. In a letter to Conan Doyle she ventured the view that 'the whiteness of the fairies may be due to their lack of shadow, which may also explain their somewhat artificial-looking flatness'.

His friend Sir Oliver Lodge, shown the photographs at the Athenaeum Club, immediately declared them fakes and advised him to drop the whole matter, but Conan Doyle found it hard to believe that two young girls would resort to such duplicity. He told Lodge he thought that 'two children of the artisan class' were incapable of such 'photographic tricks'. As a gentleman, it was virtually inconceivable to him that the girls would be lying. He was also undoubtedly sorely tempted by the opportunity of illustrating his article for the *Strand* with photographs of real fairies. What harm could there be in contacting the Wright family?

It was Conan Doyle's characteristically parsimonious habit to collect headed stationery from clubs and hotels and use it for his personal correspondence at home, striking out the printed address and substituting 'Windlesham, Crowborough'. On 30 June Conan Doyle wrote separate registered letters to Elsie and her father on the headed notepaper of the Athenaeum Club. His letter to Arthur Wright was entirely businesslike: 'Dear Mr Wright, I have seen the very interesting photos which your little girl took. They are certainly amazing. I was writing a little article for the Strand upon the evidence for the existence of fairies, so that I was very much interested . . .'[6] He asked permission to use the photographs to accompany his article, offering a fee of £5 or a five-year subscription to the magazine, and guaranteeing the family anonymity so that they would not 'be annoyed in any way'. Conan Doyle's proposal was hardly generous, since he would be receiving £500 for the article.

His letter to Elsie was friendly and flattering and clearly designed to recruit her cooperation at some later time. 'Dear Miss Elsie Wright, I have seen the wonderful pictures of the fairies which you and your cousin Frances have taken and I have not been so interested for a long time. I will send you tomorrow one of my little books for I am sure you are not too old to enjoy adventures. I am going to Australia soon, but I only wish before I go that I could get to Bradford and have half an hour's chat with you, for I should like to hear all about it. With best wishes. Yours sincerely . . .'[7]

Arthur Wright was suitably awed to receive a communication from the great author and perhaps on this account forbore to mention any doubt about the pictures' authenticity. As Conan Doyle had no time to visit Cottingley before his departure for Australia, Gardner went instead and was impressed by the Wright family, particularly by the fact that none of them was seeking either notoriety or money. Elsie explained that she and her cousin had no power over the fairies and that the only way to ''tice them' was to sit quietly. When 'faint stirrings or movements in the distance heralded their presence', the girls beckoned them welcome. 'Extraordinary and amazing as these photographs may appear,' Gardner wrote in his report, 'I am now quite convinced of their genuineness, as indeed would everyone else be who had the same evidence of transparent honesty and simplicity that I had.'[8]

Gardner went on to Scarborough to meet Mrs Griffiths and Frances, then 13, who he immediately decided was 'mediumistic': 'She had loosely knit ectoplasmic material in her body. The subtle ectoplasmic or etheric material of the body, which with most people is very closely interwoven with the denser frame, was in her case unlocked or, rather, loosened, and on seeing her I had the first glimpse of how the nature spirits had densified their own normal bodies sufficiently to come into the field of the camera's range.'[9]

By the beginning of August, a deal had been done; Conan Doyle agreed to pay each of the girls £20 in bonds. 'I saw Mr Gardner today and everything is now in order,' he wrote to Wright on 3 August, 'I hope to get a small wedding dowry for Elsie from the fairies. Also for the little girl. I go to Australia next week but my agent is in touch with Mr G. and you will hear from the latter. Meanwhile I have altered all names and places. [Elsie and Frances became Iris and Alice.] We can always let the cat out of the bag, but when he is out you can't put him back. I don't want you all to be worried by curiosity hunters. I can foresee 100 charabancs a day if the press gets hold of it . . .'[10]

Conan Doyle put his original article aside and delivered a new one to the *Strand,* describing how the photographs were taken. Meanwhile, Gardner was determined to obtain more pictures. The girls, now 13 and 19, were apparently unbothered by the sudden attention they were receiving, and willingly agreed to try to take more pictures by the stream during their summer holiday, using Cameo quarter-plate folding cameras supplied by Gardner. 'I went off to Cottingley again,' he wrote, 'taking the two cameras and plates from London, and met the family and explained to the two girls the simple working of the cameras, giving one each to keep. The cameras were loaded, and my final advice was that they need go up to the glen only on fine days as they had been accustomed to do before and 'tice the fairies, as they called their way of attracting them, and see what they could get.'[11]

Gardner returned to London, praying for good weather that would encourage the fairies to emerge. It rained for two weeks, but towards the end of August he received momentous news from Polly Wright: the girls had managed to take three more pictures of fairies. As agreed, Arthur Wright packed the plates in cotton wool and dispatched them to Gardner in London. One showed a fairy offering a posy of flowers to Elsie, the second, slightly out of focus, captured a fairy in flight and the third portrayed a 'fairy bower' in a tree. Gardner took them straight to Harold Snelling, who pronounced them completely genuine. Gardner was ecstatic and untroubled by what looked like a hatpin holding the fairy in flight and the remarkably fashionable bobbed hairstyle worn by the fairy with the flowers. He was similarly unconcerned that only the girls were present when the pictures were taken, believing that the fairies were probably shy and would not make an appearance in the presence of adults.

On 6 September he wrote to Conan Doyle in Melbourne, enclosing three prints: 'My dear Doyle, Greetings and best wishes! Your last words to me before we parted were that you would open my letter with the greatest interest. You will not be disappointed – for the wonderful thing has happened . . . !' Surely, he said, the 'flying fairy' and the 'fairy bower' were 'the most amazing photographs the modern eye has ever seen'.[12] Conan Doyle agreed enthusiastically. Having examined them he decided they were 'altogether beyond the possibility of fake' – 'beyond any doubt' was a phrase he would use many times over the coming years, usually in connection with dubious psychic phenomena. 'My heart was gladdened,' he replied on 21 October,

> when out here in far Australia I had your note and the three wonderful pictures which are confirmatory of our published results. You and I needed no confirmation but the whole line of thought will be so novel to the ordinary busy man who has not followed psychic inquiry, that he will need that it be repeated again and yet again before he realises that this new order of life is really established and has to be taken into serious account, just as the pigmies of Central Africa . . . They [sceptics] can't destroy fairies by antediluvian tests and when once fairies are admitted other psychic phenomena will find a more ready acceptance. Goodbye, my dear Gardner, I am proud to have been acquainted with you in this epoch-making incident. We have had continued messages at séances for some time that a visible sign was coming through – and perhaps this was what was meant.[13]

Although Conan Doyle knew Lodge, a man he greatly respected, thought the first two pictures fakes, he could not resist sharing this development with him: 'Is it not marvellous?' he gushed in a letter written from Sydney. 'I can't think what the materialists will make of them. We will draw their fire with the first two, and then produce these other three, one of which is a fairy bower, showing them asleep in cocoons! It should mark an era . . .'[14]

In the meantime, Gardner had returned to Cottingley for further information about the pictures from Elsie – Frances had returned to school in Scarborough – to bolster their authenticity. Elsie was exceptionally forthcoming and explained in detail how each picture was taken. The leaping fairy was particularly difficult, she claimed: it had jumped from a bush five or six times and seemed to hover at the top of its spring; at one point Frances thought the fairy was going to jump onto her face and tossed her head back, and it was then that Elsie clicked the shutter. Gardner noted that the movement of Frances's head could be detected in the print; the grace and poise of the fairy itself, he thought, made it seem like a 'super-Pavlova in miniature'. The truth was that it had been hand-drawn by Elsie and fixed to the branch of a tree with a hatpin. She described the colours of the dress of the fairy offering harebells to Elsie – pastel shades of mauve and yellow – and when Gardner quizzed her about the fairy's bobbed hair, she quickly pointed out that it was not bobbed at all but closely curled.

It was the bower picture that most excited Gardner. By Elsie's account they had not seen the bower at all. They had noticed a wreath of faint mist alongside a fairy in long grass and without waiting to get into the picture herself, Elsie had pushed the camera through the grass and pressed the shutter. 'Never before,' Gardner gushed, 'has a fairy's bower been photographed! The central ethereal cocoon shape, something between a cocoon and an open chrysalis in appearance, lightly suspended amid the grasses, is the bower or cradle. Seated on the upper left-hand edge with wing well displayed is an undraped fairy apparently considering whether it is time to get up. An earlier riser of more mature age is seen on the right possessing abundant hair and wonderful wings. Her slightly denser body can be glimpsed within her fairy dress. Just beyond, still on the right, is the clear-cut head of a mischievous but smiling elf wearing a close-fitting cap . . .'[15]

On his return from Cottingley, Gardner wrote again to Conan Doyle to say that he was 'more convinced than ever' of the Wright family's honesty and the genuineness of the photographs. Conan Doyle briefly entertained a doubt – not that the photographs were not authentic but that the 'fairies' might somehow have been conjured up by the girls as occult 'thought forms' – but quickly decided that such a possibility was 'far-fetched and remote':

> The fact that they are so like our conventional idea of fairies is in favour of the idea [that they could be 'thought forms']. But if they move rapidly, have musical instruments, and so forth, then it is impossible to talk of 'thought-forms,' a term which suggests something vague and intangible. In a sense

we are all thought-forms, since we can only be perceived through the senses, but these little figures would seem to have an objective reality, as we have ourselves, even if their vibrations should prove to be such that it takes either psychic power or a sensitive plate to record them. If they are conventional it may be that fairies have really been seen in every generation, and so some correct description of them has been retained.[16]

On 12 December the validity of the pictures was further confirmed by Fred Barlow, a leading authority on psychic photography and honorary secretary of the Society for the Study of Supernatural Pictures, in a letter to Gardner: 'I am returning herewith the three fairy photographs you very kindly loaned to me and have no hesitation in announcing them as the most wonderful and interesting results I have ever seen.'[17]

By then the first two Cottingley pictures had been published in the *Strand*, which blazoned across its cover the headline: 'Fairies Photographed – An Epoch Making Event Described by A. Conan Doyle'. Inside, the picture of 'Iris and the Dancing Gnome' was captioned as 'one of the most astounding photographs ever published'. Although Conan Doyle opened his article in non-committal fashion, calling for the scenes portrayed to be repeated before a 'disinterested witness' in order to 'remove the last faint shadow of doubt', by the end the reader was left in little doubt where he personally stood: 'It seems to me that with fuller knowledge and with fresh means of vision these people are destined to become just as solid and real as the Eskimos.'

He explained that he had examined the photographs 'long and earnestly' with a high-powered lens, rather in the manner of Holmes, and went on to recount, in effusive prose, what he had found in the first picture: 'There is an ornamental rim to the pipe of the elves which shows that the graces of art are not unknown among them. And what joy in their complete abandon of their little graceful figures as they let themselves go into the dance! They may have their shadows and trials as we have, but at least there is a great gladness manifest in the demonstration of their life.'

Obviously intent on using the fairies to advance the spiritualist cause, Conan Doyle concluded that there was a strong prima facie case for the authenticity of the pictures and presciently predicted that more photographs would soon come to light. Seemingly carried away by the implications of the 'discovery', he speculated about how the world would change: 'These little folk who appear to be our neighbours, with only some small difference of vibration to separate us, will become familiar. The thought of them, even when unseen, will add charm to every brook and valley and give romantic interest to every country walk. The recognition of their existence will jolt the material twentieth century mind out of its heavy ruts in the mud, and will make it admit that there is a glamour and mystery to life. Having discovered this, the world will not find it so difficult to accept that spiritual message supported by physical facts which has already been so convincingly put before it.'

The 'Fairies' edition of the *Strand* sold out across the country in three days. Conan Doyle had hoped that his article would cause a sensation, and it certainly provoked a heated debate as to whether the photographs were genuine or crude fakes. There was also some surprise that a respectable magazine should publish such material, but only from those unaware of the considerable debt the *Strand* owed Conan Doyle.

Early into the fray was Major John Hall-Edwards, an expert on radium and a pioneer of X-ray treatment: 'I criticise the attitude of those who declared there is something supernatural in the circumstances attended to the taking of these pictures because, as a medical man, I believe that the inculcation of such absurd ideas into the minds of children will result in later life in manifestations and nervous disorder and mental disturbances . . .'

'It is easier to believe in faked photographs,' *John O'London's* weekly sensibly pointed out, 'than fairies.'

Social reformer Margaret McMillan begged to differ: 'How wonderful that to these dear children such a wonderful gift has been vouchsafed.'

'Look at Alice's, look at Iris's face,' novelist Henry de Vere Stacpoole noted. 'There is an extraordinary thing called TRUTH which has ten million faces and forms – it is God's currency and the cleverest coiner or forger can't imitate it.'

The *Yorkshire Weekly Post* was equally positive: 'When one considers that these are the first photographs these children ever took in their lives it is impossible to conceive that they are capable of technical manipulation which would deceive experts.'

'For the true explanation of these photographs,' *Truth* magazine asserted, 'what is wanted is not a knowledge of occult phenomena but a knowledge of children.'

The *City News* sat on the fence: 'It seems at this point that we must either believe in the almost incredible mystery of the fairy or in the almost incredible wonders of faked photographs.'

Conan Doyle was untroubled by the criticism and urged Greenhough Smith to publish his original article, 'The Evidence for Fairies', along with the new pictures. It appeared in the March 1921 issue with the explanation that it was written 'before actual photographs of fairies were known to exist' and was illustrated by Elsie with the fairy holding harebells and Frances with the leaping fairy. The captions did not equivocate: 'The fairy is leaping up from leaves below and hovering for a moment – it had done so three or four times. Rising a little higher than before, Alice thought it would touch her face and involuntarily tossed her head back. Fairy is in close-fitting costume, with lavender-coloured wings.'

In the article, largely a collection of accounts by individuals who claimed to have glimpsed fairies, Conan Doyle revealed that his own children had seen them: 'My younger family consist of two little boys and one small girl, very truthful children, each of whom tells with detail the exact circumstances and appearance of the creature. To each it happened only once, and in each case it was a single little figure, twice in the garden, once in the nursery.' His thesis was that the world was very much more complex than we imagine and that it was highly possible that 'there may be upon its surface some very strange neighbours who will open up inconceivable lines of science for our posterity, especially if it should be made easier for them, by sympathy or other help, to emerge . . .'[18]

All five Cottingley fairy pictures were featured in an exhibition mounted later that year by Gardner at the Theosophist Hall in Brompton Road, London. It was not an unqualified success. While theosophists and spiritualists hailed the pictures as a historic breakthrough, cynics sneered. Why, they asked, did the fairies conform so precisely to traditional illustrations in fairy tales? Why were they so fashionably attired and coiffed? Why did the 'gnome' appear to have a hatpin stuck in his midriff? Why, in the first picture, was 'Alice' looking directly at the camera and not at the alleged fairies prancing in front of her? The candle makers, Price & Son, joined the debate by issuing a statement remarking that the Cottingley fairies bore a striking similarity to the fairies they used in advertisements for their night lights.

Conan Doyle, however, refused to budge and in another article for the *Strand* attempted to elaborate on the fairy world as revealed by the photographs. It revealed more about his extreme credulity and his willingness to use his imagination to fill in the details: 'Elves are a compound of the human and the butterfly, while the gnome has more of the moth. This may be merely the result of under-exposure of the negative and dullness of the weather. Perhaps the little gnome is really of the same tribe, but represents an elderly male, while the elves are romping young women. Most observers of fairy life have reported, however, that there are separate species, varying very much in size, appearance and locality – the wood fairy, the water fairy, the fairy of the plains, etc. . . .'

As the controversy raged on, Gardner sent a well-known clairvoyant, Geoffrey Hodson, back to Cottingley in the summer of 1921 armed with an array of exotic psychic investigation tools, including a stereoscopic camera and a cine camera in an attempt to uncover further evidence. Aside from his years with the Tanks Corps on the Western Front, Hodson had devoted his life to spiritualism, clairvoyance, yoga and healing. He was just the man to believe in fairies, and the girls soon discovered that their impressionable visitor was prepared to believe he was seeing whatever they said they were seeing and enjoyed a great deal of quiet fun teasing him. They took him for walks in the woods pointing out 'fairies' here and there and were delighted when he claimed to be able to see them as well. No fairies were photographed during Hodson's two weeks there, but he reported that the Cottingley area was swarming with elemental life, undines, wood elves, brownies and fairies wearing long semi-transparent skirts floating slowly about to the accompaniment of tinkling music. 'I am personally convinced of the bona fides of the two girls who took these photographs,' he reported.

In 1922 Conan Doyle, as always utterly unmoved by the potential for embarrassment or the prospect of public ridicule, wrote *The Coming of the Fairies,* undoubtedly the nadir of his non-fiction work, in which the story of the Cottingley fairies was knitted into his fanciful theories about fairy life, supported by numerous sightings from around the world. The Cottingley photographs, he wrote, represented 'either the most elaborate and ingenious hoax ever played upon the public or else they constitute an event in human history which may in the future appear to have been epoch-making in its character'. He made it clear which he believed: 'I have convinced myself that there is overwhelming evidence for the fairies.'

His medical training had not entirely deserted him, and he strove to find a pseudo-scientific rationale for his conjectures, speculating that fairies could exist beyond the spectrum of light visible to human beings and suggesting that 'some sort of psychic spectacles' might be invented which would allow everyone to see them. 'It is hard for the mind to grasp,' he wrote, 'what the ultimate results may be if we have actually proved the existence upon the surface of this planet of a population which may be as numerous as the human race, which pursues its own strange life in its own strange way, and which is only separated from ourselves by some difference of vibrations.'

Completely blind to any evidence that the pictures might not be genuine, where detractors saw a hatpin on the gnome, Conan Doyle saw a 'navel', implying that births in the fairy kingdom were not dissimilar to others on earth. This apparently did not strike him as odd. He also bolstered his case with a new phenomenon: the 'fairy observers' who in Scotland and the New Forest were familiar with the bower in the fifth photograph and described it as a 'magnetic bath, woven very quickly by the fairies and used after dull weather, in the autumn especially. The interior seems to be magnetised in some manner that stimulates and pleases.'

The publication of *The Coming of the Fairies* convinced many that Sir Arthur Conan Doyle was no longer a man who could be taken seriously; some even questioned his mental state. While his ardent espousal of spiritualism could be tolerated or politely ignored by his friends, it was difficult to accept his increasingly bizarre views had any connection with real life and the brilliant creator of Sherlock Holmes began to be seen as a gullible old man who had been duped by two silly schoolgirls. One joke doing the rounds was that when J. M. Barrie's Peter Pan asked everyone in the audience who believed in fairies to clap their hands to revive the dying Tinker Bell, it was Conan Doyle who led the applause.

Many commentators made the point that Holmes would surely have dismissed the Cottingley fairies instantly; *Punch* contributor J. E. Wheelwright lampooned Conan Doyle:

> If you, Sir Conan Doyle, believe in fairies,
> Must I believe in Mister Sherlock Holmes?
> If *you* believe that round us all the air is
> Just thick with elves and little men and gnomes,
> Then must I now believe in Doctor Watson
> And speckled bands and things? Oh, no! My hat!
> Though all the t's are crossed and i's have dots on
> I simply can't Sir Conan. So that's that!

As always, Conan Doyle remained impervious to criticism and in a second edition of *The Coming of the Fairies* published in 1928, he went even further asserting that 'the discovery by Columbus of a new terrestrial continent is a lesser achievement than the demonstration of a completely new order of life inhabiting the same planet as ourselves'. It was his belief that the Cottingley Fairies would be 'recognised some day as opening a new vista of knowledge for the human race'.

Ironically, *The Coming of the Fairies* was published by Hodder & Stoughton, who had also published *Princess Mary's Gift Book* only eight years earlier. If anyone had compared the illustrations for 'A Spell for a Fairy' in *Princess Mary's Gift Book* with the 'fairies' that featured in the first photograph with Frances Griffiths, the hoax would have been instantly exposed.

'Among all the notable persons attracted to Spiritualism,' said psychic investigator Harry Price, 'he [Conan Doyle] was perhaps the most uncritical. His extreme credulity, indeed, was the despair of his colleagues, all of whom, however, held him in the highest respect for his complete honesty. Poor, dear, loveable, credulous Doyle! He was a giant in stature with the heart of a child.'[19]

Controversy over the Cottingley Fairies continued for decades, long after Conan Doyle's death. Arthur Wright died in 1926 puzzled that the world could have been bamboozled by 'our Elsie, and her at the bottom of the class'. Elsie emigrated to the United States, where she met her husband, Frank Hill. After living in India for some years, they returned to Britain, to the Midlands, with their son and daughter, in 1949. Frances married a soldier, Sydney Way, and after several postings overseas they settled in Ramsgate.

In 1966 reporters from the *Daily Express* tracked down and interviewed Elsie, then aged 65, in an attempt to determine the Truth. She proved cooperative but elusive, admitting only that the fairies might have been 'figments' of her imagination and suggesting that this was what they had photographed. In 1971 she was persuaded to appear on the BBC television programme *Nationwide* and repeated the same story: 'I've told you that they're photographs of figments of our imagination and that's what I'm sticking to.'

In 1976 both Elsie and Frances agreed to be interviewed by Austin Mitchell for Yorkshire Television's *Calendar* programme. They were taken back to Cottingley, but revealed nothing. When Elsie was asked if she would swear on the Bible that the photographs were genuine she simply replied: 'I'd rather leave that open if you don't mind.'

Not until March 1983, when she was 76 years old, did Frances finally confess to a reporter from *The Times* that the fairies in four of the five pictures had been cut-outs traced from *Princess Mary's Gift Book* and secured by hatpins. 'I'm fed up with all these stories,' she complained. 'I hated those photographs and cringe every time I see them. I thought it was a joke, but everyone else kept it going. It should have died a natural death 60 years ago.'

Elsie at first refused to comment, but two weeks later confirmed her cousin's story: 'I have never even told my son and my husband how I did it at all. I will swear on the Bible that my father had nothing to do with it, but I will not swear on the Bible that they are real fairies . . . I do not want to die and leave my grandchildren with a loony grandmother to remember. But I am sorry someone has stabbed all our fairies dead with a hat pin.'

Not quite. Frances continued to claim, contrarily, that she *had* seen fairies and that the fifth photograph – the fairy bower – was authentic. She died in 1986; Elsie died two years later. 'The joke was only meant to last two hours,' Elsie said towards the end of her life, 'and it lasted seventy years.'

CHAPTER 22

THE SPIRITUALIST AND THE MAGICIAN

N THE SPRING OF 1922 Conan Doyle and his second family embarked on another major spiritualist crusade, this time to the United States. They arrived in New York on 9 April on board the White Star liner RMS *Baltic* at the start of a daunting tour schedule that covered the cities of New York, Boston, Washington, Philadelphia, Buffalo, Toronto, Detroit, Toledo and Chicago.

Conan Doyle's name on the passenger list had alerted the New York media, and a press conference had been arranged in his suite at the Ambassador Hotel. The reporters perched around the sitting room and Conan Doyle occupied an armchair in the centre of the room while he talked about spiritualism and then took questions. Speaking with his usual confidence, the soft burr of his Scots accent still pronounced, he told the assembled media that he had absolutely no doubt about the existence of the other world.

He explained that the other world was made up of a series of Spiritual planes at differing levels. The plane called 'Paradise' was where normally respectable people arrived after death. The average length of stay in Paradise was about 40 years, after which they floated higher. Bad people were initially sent to a much lower plane than Paradise and continued to sink lower and lower until they repented; after a considerable probationary period they might then be able to begin the ascent to Paradise. He knew all this, he said, from messages received from mediums.

When it came to questions, Conan Doyle recalled that he was

'subjected to a fine raking fire which would have shot me to pieces had I been vulnerable'. Actually, he *was* vulnerable, since he was questioned closely on delicate subjects such as whether sex was available in the next world, and whether spirits ate, or smoked cigars, or enjoyed hard liquor – of great interest in a country gripped by Prohibition. Despite believing he had acquitted himself well enough, he was mocked the following day in headlines such as 'High Jinks in the Beyond' and 'Do Spooks Marry?' and 'Doyle Says They Play Golf in Heaven'. Actually, he had said no such thing. In response to a facetious question, 'Do they have golf in the next world?', he had replied, 'No. I have no reason to say that.' The reporter had persisted: 'Well, you said they had amusements.' 'Yes, they say they have more than we.' 'Well, maybe golf is among them.' 'I never heard them say so.'

The outspoken Mayor of New York, John F. Hylan, joined in the fun, publicly deriding Conan Doyle for spreading 'airy nothings'. He had, said the mayor, found a 'new line of business, and from all reports the shekels are rolling in to him as fast as when he told how easy it was for the famous detective of fiction to get out of tight corners'. His Honour was not just being uncharitable but unjust: Conan Doyle was not making money; any surplus, after his expenses had been met, would be handed over to the spiritualist cause. Lady Conan Doyle, incensed, hit back in a newspaper interview saying that she had only seen one city in the world with dirtier streets than New York – Constantinople – and that the Mayor would be well advised to spend his time cleaning up the city rather than abusing a guest.

A number of public figures also rose to Conan Doyle's defence, among them Public Service Commissioner William Prendergast, who observed that such a distinguished visitor deserved hospitality, 'even if here on a misguided mission'. But there was, in truth, a distinct lack of public enthusiasm for Conan Doyle's crusade: Americans had become cynical about spiritualism – too many mediums had been exposed as charlatans and crooks – and burgeoning movements like theosophy and Christian Science offered alternative sources of solace.

This notwithstanding, advance sales for his lectures, at between 50 cents and $3.50 per ticket, were encouraging. The first of a planned series of six lectures at the Carnegie Hall was held on 12 April with 3,500 people in the audience, braving an unseasonably early heatwave.

Many were women wearing mourning and gold stars to indicate they had lost someone in the war. Conan Doyle always spoke first of his own experiences, of making contact with his mother, his son and other members of his family at seances. 'Can you wonder that after such experiences,' he boomed, 'I do not say that I think, but I say that I KNOW that the dead live and come back to us. I have seen them. I have heard them. I have touched them. If I did not believe the evidence of my own senses I should not be sane.'[1] He went on to explain what was to be expected after death and how people would be reunited with their loved ones. When a curious, high-pitched whistling could be heard in part of the auditorium, many wondered if a spiritual manifestation was taking place, but it turned out to be an aberrant hearing aid.

The *New York Times* reported next day that Sir Arthur offered the prospect of a new and finer religion which would 'clear out the weeds in the old religions' and show the human race 'what God has written down as His eternal law'. But an editorial was much less sympathetic. Under the headline 'Such a Man on Such a Mission!', his crusade was roundly condemned. That a man who had given so much pleasure to the English-reading world should devote himself to the promotion of spiritualism was 'simply pathetic' and his descriptions of audible and visible visits from the dead generated little more than pity.

Between lectures the family had plenty of time for sightseeing: they took a carriage ride through Central Park, visited the major museums and enjoyed an aerial view of the metropolis from the top of the Woolworth Building, then the world's tallest skyscraper. One afternoon New Yorkers on Fifth Avenue were treated to the sight of the 63-year-old author chasing a taxi in which he had left his brief-case. When the cab turned into a side street, Conan Doyle leapt onto the running board with such vigour that the driver thought he was about to be robbed.

Although heartened by the audiences he was attracting, Conan Doyle cannot have been very pleased to read, in the New York *Independent,* a damning review of his book about his Australian tour, *The Wanderings of a Spiritualist.* The reviewer, Joseph Jastrow, professor of psychology at the University of Wisconsin, described it as a 'pathetic human document' and suggested 'The Maunderings of a Spiritualist' as a more suitable title. It was not the author's beliefs that prevented serious consideration of the book, 'but the puerile (or is it senile?) credulity that pervades the pages'. He singled out Conan Doyle's seance with Bailey and the production of various exotic objects for particular derision: 'It seems to Sir Arthur "perfect nonsense to talk about these things being the result of trickery," just as it seems quite as perfect nonsense to the rest of us to talk about them as being anything else.'

One unwelcome and unexpected side effect of the publicity surrounding the tour was that newspapers began reporting suicides by those impatient to see the next world. Much of this was a media invention, but a New Jersey woman, Maude Fancher, murdered her baby son and then killed herself by swallowing a bottle of Lysol cleaner, leaving a note claiming she had been guided by spirits after hearing Conan Doyle talk on the radio. Asked by reporters for his reaction, Conan Doyle claimed that it was the result of a 'misunderstanding' of spiritualism which demonstrated the great danger of spiritual ignorance. He emphasised that suicide was considered a desperate and very grave offence on the other side and that 'the hand of providence cannot be forced'.[2]

Conan Doyle then travelled alone to Boston, where his audience at the Symphony Hall was said to be 'spellbound'. He laid flowers on the grave of his 'Spiritual and literary Godfather', Oliver Wendell Holmes, who was buried in Mount Auburn Cemetery in nearby Cambridge, and spent time in the library at Harvard University 'consulting some old alchemical books which seemed to allude directly to ectoplasm, showing that these medieval philosophers were really a good deal ahead of us in some phases of psychic knowledge'.[3] He also met Mina Crandon, a medium known as 'Margery', who would soon be embroiled in one of the most bitter controversies in the history of American psychic research.

Next stop was the capital, Washington DC, via New York, where Conan Doyle was reunited with his family and local spiritualists had arranged for him and his wife to attend a number of seances. The country's first spiritualist church, established in 1853, featured prominently in their itinerary, as did the recently completed Lincoln Memorial. It had long been rumoured that Abraham Lincoln, the sixteenth and most famous president, had been interested in the spirit world and had held seances in the White House. In Britain a music sheet called 'The Dark Séance Polka' had been illustrated with a picture of Lincoln holding a candle, while violins and tambourines flew about his head over a caption 'Abraham Lincoln and the Spiritualists'. Conan Doyle was happy to believe that Lincoln was a 'convinced Spiritualist' and would later claim in his massive work *The History of Spiritualism* that it was a medium who persuaded the president to issue the historic Emancipation Proclamation in 1863, freeing the slaves in Confederate territory.

The tour continued with two lectures in Philadelphia and another back in New York, then the family travelled west, passing Hydesville, the home of the notorious Fox sisters and the birthplace of the modern spiritualist movement. Conan Doyle, perhaps inspired by the impressive Lincoln Memorial, believed it should be the site of 'one of the greatest monuments in the world' (despite the fact that the Fox sisters had been exposed as frauds). Enthused by the idea, he launched an appeal in the *International Psychic Gazette* for subscriptions for a 'fine inscribed obelisk' at Hydesville, offering to start it off with a contribution of £50. Five years later he was obliged to admit he had only managed to raise 22s. 6d. 'Is this,' he asked despairingly, 'to be the British contribution?'[4]

In Chicago he lectured to a 'completely sold-out crowd' but did not much like the city and was irritated when a local newspaper reported that his children were clearly 'bored stiff' with spiritualism. Actually all three younger children had been indoctrinated into spiritualism and regularly attended seances with their parents. Conan Doyle claimed in an interview with the *American* magazine that it was his children's faith in spiritualism that made them exceptionally happy and well adjusted. 'Everybody who sees them speaks of their high spirits and happy faces. And why not? There is no fear in their lives; they know that if their mother and I should pass over tomorrow, it would be no occasion for sorrow. They know we would be happier than we have ever been, and that we would be waiting for them on the other side.'[5]

He reported 'splendid results' from a seance at the Blackstone Hotel with Mrs Pruden, a medium from Cincinnati, who had travelled

to Chicago to hear him. Mrs Pruden's gift was slate-writing. Partici-
pants were invited to write a question on a piece of paper, fold it and
drop it under a table draped with a cloth. The medium held a slate
and pencil under the cloth, and after 'about an hour and a half' the
slate began to vibrate. 'It was the strangest feeling,' Conan Doyle
reported, 'to hold the slate and to feel the thrill and vibration of the
pencil as it worked away inside.' Everyone received a message. Conan
Doyle's was from Kingsley, who told him 'Trust Dr Gelbert'. His question had been whether it was wise for him to become involved with
a French inventor he had met earlier in the day to discuss a business
proposition, but he had not mentioned the man's name. Lady Conan
Doyle received a message from a dear friend which ended with a
convincing replica of her signature. 'Altogether,' Conan Doyle
concluded, 'it was a most utterly convincing demonstration.'[6]

But then he *wanted* to be convinced, was always ready to ascribe
psychic explanations for everyday events and almost never accepted
that he had been tricked, although back in New York at the end of
his tour, he suffered considerable embarrassment after a seance at the
home of Dr Leonard J. Hartman, a trustee of the First Spiritualist
Church of New York. It was conducted by William Thompson and
his wife, Eva, who was a 'materialising medium' and her speciality
was to bring back spirits of the dead in human form. Sitters were
required to abide by strict rules, though this was not unusual. While
Mrs Thompson was hidden in a cabinet, in a deep trance, they were
to sing hymns 'industriously', were not to stare too closely at any
spirits who materialised and were to give such spirits plenty of 'elbow
room'. While the hymns were being sung in the darkness, a spirit
emerged from the cabinet which Conan Doyle instantly recognised
as his mother. Almost overcome with emotion, he asked if he might
be allowed to touch her hand, which he did briefly before the spirit
withdrew into the cabinet. Afterwards he told Dr Hartman that he
was greatly moved: 'The chance to touch my mother's hand and feel
the substance there . . . was very precious to me.'

Three days later the Thompsons were arrested and charged with
fraud after a police sting. Two undercover officers had attended a
second seance at Dr Hartman's home and unmasked the apparition
as none other than the medium herself, garbed in iridescent robes.

New York newspapers had their moment. Under the headline 'How the Mediums "Brought Back" Sir Conan Doyle's Dead "Mother"', *American Weekly* published photographs of Mrs Thompson in her 'spirit robes', a drawing of Conan Doyle kissing the 'spirit's' hand and an article by Dr Hartman expressing his anger. 'When I think now,' he wrote, 'how the feeling of that son for that little old mother long dead was played upon by those charlatans I feel indignant clear through.'

Conan Doyle would claim later that he had not been deceived by the Thompsons at all and only refrained from expressing his doubts out of a wish not to offend his host: 'Both my wife and I were of the opinion that the proceedings were very suspicious and we came away deeply dissatisfied, for there were no test conditions and no way of checking such manifestations as we saw.'[7]

———————◆———————

While Conan Doyle and his wife were still in the city, a welcome invitation arrived from the famous magician and escape artist, Harry Houdini, to attend the annual banquet of the Society of American Magicians on Friday, 2 June, at the Hotel McAlpin on Broadway and 34th Street. Conan Doyle had met Houdini two years earlier when he was touring Britain and they had become friends. Conan Doyle at first refused the invitation when he learned that the after-dinner entertainment was to feature demonstrations of how magic could replicate psychic phenomena. 'I fear that the bogus Spiritual phenomena must prevent me from attending the banquet which you have so graciously proffered,' he wrote to his friend. 'I look upon this subject as sacred, and I think that God's gift to man has been intercepted and delayed by the constant pretence that all phenomena are really tricks, which I know they are not. I should be in a false position, for I must either be silent and seem to acquiesce, or else protest, which a guest should not do.'[8]

Houdini, who was to be master of ceremonies, rapidly changed the programme to accommodate Conan Doyle's sensibilities. 'I assure you,' he replied, 'it was only with a view of letting you see the mysterious effects and only for your special benefit that this was being put on; therefore I assure you as a gentleman that there will be nothing performed or said which will offend anyone.'⁹

Conan Doyle relented, although the fortuitous arrival of a package from Chicago might have encouraged his decision. It was a long-standing tradition at the Society's annual meeting that members demonstrated their 'magical' abilities, each trying to outdo the other. Conan Doyle and his wife watched, enthralled, as Houdini, undoubtedly one of the greatest magicians and illusionists of all time, performed his famous 'metamorphosis' trick. First, he borrowed and donned Conan Doyle's dinner jacket, then was bound, gagged and tied into a sack, which was placed into a locked trunk and concealed in a tent. In seconds he emerged from the tent, and when the trunk was unlocked and the sack untied, it revealed Houdini's diminutive wife, Bess, wearing Conan Doyle's dinner jacket!

Conan Doyle had let it be known that he would be participating in the evening's entertainment, and after the magicians had all performed he was invited onto the stage. While a movie projector and screen were being set up, he engendered an appropriate air of mystery by stating that he would not be taking any questions about what they were about to see. 'These pictures are not occult,' he explained, 'but they are psychic because everything that emanates from the human spirit, or human brain, is psychic. It is not supernatural – nothing is. It is preternatural in the sense that it is not known to our ordinary senses. It is the effect of the joining on the one hand of imagination, and on the other hand of some power of materialisation. The imagination, I may say, comes from me – the materialising power from elsewhere.'

With this obtuse and tantalising introduction, the lights were dimmed, the projector whirred and there appeared on the screen flickering images of prehistoric monsters brought to life. Great slavering dinosaurs, including an iguanodon, a tyrannosaurus and a brontosaurus lumbered through primeval forest, apparently unaware of the camera, searching for food, or basking in sunlit clearings, or fighting over territory. The audience was rapt and when the lights went up there was bafflement. Had Conan Doyle somehow used his psychic powers to conjure up a lost world? He would not be drawn.

The following day the *New York Times* front-page headline read: 'DINOSAURS CAVORT IN FILM FOR DOYLE'. The subheading explained: 'Spiritist Mystifies World-famed Magicians With Pictures Of Prehistoric Beasts – Keeps Origin A Secret – Monsters Of Other Ages Shown, Some Fighting, Some At Play, In Their Native Jungles'. The reporter candidly admitted that he did not know what to make of the pictures and could not decide if the 'sober-faced Englishman was making merry with them' or was 'lifting the veil' on some new world discovered in the ether. 'Whether these pictures were intended by the famous author as a joke on the magicians or genuine pictures, like his photographs of fairies, was not revealed.' Either way, the reporter noted, the monsters were 'extraordinarily life-like. If fakes, they were masterpieces.' Conan Doyle was delighted by the attention – his sense of mischief had not been entirely eradicted by his obsession with the spirits – and did not confess until later that day that it was test footage for an upcoming feature film being shot in Chicago based on his novel, *The Lost World*. The animation was the work of Willis O'Brien who would later go on to make the acclaimed original version of *King Kong*.

Conan Doyle and Houdini were unlikely friends. The two men could hardly have been more unalike physically, as photographs of them together testify: Houdini barely reached the other's shoulder. The magician was bandy-legged, wiry and bushy-haired; the author now portly, with thinning hair, fleshy features and a large walrus moustache. They also came from very different backgrounds, enjoyed very different careers and held diametrically opposing views about spiritualism. The difference between them was simple, yet profound. Conan Doyle wanted to believe and did, Houdini wanted to believe but could not; about all they shared was an unshakeable belief in their own view.

Born Ehrich Weisz in Budapest in 1874, the son of a rabbi, Houdini's family emigrated to Appleton, Wisconsin, when he was 4 years old. At the age of 8 Ehrich was selling newspapers on the street and working as a shoeshine boy. Four years later he left home and worked in Kansas City, then returned to join his family after they had moved to New York, where he got a job as a messenger at a tie factory in the garment district and developed an interest in athletics, training hard in his spare time and winning medals in both swimming and track events. But his life changed forever when he happened upon the autobiography of a well-known magician with a grandiloquent title: *The Memoirs of Robert Houdin – Ambassador, Author and Conjuror, Written by Himself.* Ehrich was captivated and began performing card tricks for his workmates. Soon he progressed to simple magic, first calling himself 'Eric the Great', then 'The King of Cards' and finally adding an 'i' to his mentor's name. Harry came from 'Ehrie', his family's pet name for him.

After the death of his father in 1890 he decided to try to make a living as a professional entertainer. With his brother Theo as his assistant, and billed as 'The Houdini Brothers', they began appearing at amusement parks, beer halls, dime museums and travelling circuses around the country; in 1893 they gave several performances at the Chicago World's Fair. The following year, in Coney Island, Houdini met Wilhelmina Beatrice Rahner, who was part of a singing and dancing act called 'The Floral Sisters'. Within two weeks they were married; Bess took Theo's part and the couple toured as 'The Houdinis'. Houdini moved to ever more extraordinary escape acts, wriggling out of handcuffs, leg irons, straitjackets and chains, usually in full view of the audience. Soon he was offering a reward to anyone who could restrain him. He successfully escaped from a prison cell, a mail pouch, a packing crate, a milk can, an iron boiler, a coffin and a giant paper bag – without tearing the paper.

In 1899 he came to the attention of Martin Beck, the booking agent for the Orpheum Circuit, the largest chain of vaudeville theatres in the country. Beck booked Houdini as a 'challenge escape artist' and put him on as a supporting act. He was an instant success and was soon headlining shows. The following year he completed his first European tour to great acclaim, and thereafter, as his fame grew, he regularly shuttled backwards and forwards between Europe and the United States, always with Bess as his loyal assistant. In Britain he challenged police forces to restrain him: he would be stripped, searched, handcuffed and locked into the most secure cell, only to escape with ease. After his demonstration at Liverpool's Bridewell jail, the *Police Review* reported, only half tongue in cheek, that he was admired by the burgling profession but that its members sorrowed deeply for his 'wasted abilities'.

Many imitators followed, but he remained ahead of the pack, using his great strength and agility to invent ever more ingenious, difficult and dangerous escapes, including being buried six feet under the ground in a coffin and the legendary 'Chinese Water Torture Cell' in which he was suspended, upside down, in a glass cabinet full of water which was then padlocked while an assistant stood ready with an axe to break the glass if something went wrong. It never did. He also added illusion tricks to his act and in 1918, on the stage at the Hippodrome Theatre in New York City, he made a 10-tonne elephant by the name of Jenny disappear into thin air.

Houdini had flirted with spiritualism for many years, particularly since the death of his much loved mother in 1913, to whom he had an obsessive attachment. He dedicated his book *A Magician among the Spirits* to her memory:

In worshipful homage

I

Dedicate this book

To the memory of my sainted mother

If God

In His infinite wisdom

Ever sent an angel upon earth in human form

It was my

Mother.

Surprisingly for a showman, Houdini was extremely well read and owned an impressive library of books about spiritualism, magic and the supernatural. He eventually concluded that the movement was based on fraud and turned his energies to debunking self-proclaimed psychics and mediums, and campaigning against 'mediumistic parlour tricks'.

Conan Doyle might have been expected to loathe Houdini were it not that, like a number of spiritualists, he believed the magician, either knowingly or unknowingly, was himself a medium and used supernatural powers to accomplish his astounding feats. To Conan Doyle there could be no other explanation: he clearly 'dematerialised' to escape from the traps he set himself. Houdini's ability to unbolt locked doors, Conan Doyle said, was due to his 'mediumistic powers' and not to any normal operation of the lock. Houdini vigorously denied it and continually asserted that his stunts were achieved by pure trickery; Conan Doyle was unpersuaded.

Paradoxically, Conan Doyle also approved of Houdini unmasking charlatans because they gave the spiritualist movement a bad name – he described them as 'human hyenas' – although he remained ambivalent about the magician's ability to replicate psychic manifestations by trickery. Just because Houdini could do it, he argued, did not mean that spiritual manifestations were not real. The gentleman in Conan Doyle was always reluctant to accept that mediums might resort to fraud, and when they did he endeavoured to justify their behaviour, often blaming the pressure of expectation. Conan Doyle's fervent desire to *believe* could not be crushed by a mere magician.

When the two had first met in 1920, their shared interest in spiritualism – although from opposite sides of the fence – brought them together. Houdini sent Conan Doyle a copy of his book in which he exposed the tricks used by the Davenport Brothers in their 'psychic' stage act; Conan Doyle did not believe the Davenports were frauds and said so in his letter of thanks. They began corresponding and when Houdini was performing at the Brighton Hippodrome, not far from Windlesham, he received a note from Conan Doyle: 'Why not run up and see me? I would come down, but this is my one resting week, amid many lectures, and my wife holds me to it . . . We lunch at one, but you can't come too early – any day.' At Windlesham the magician charmed Lady Conan Doyle and the children with tricks and jokes about life in New York. 'Visited Sir A. Conan Doyle at Crowborough,' Houdini wrote in his diary on April 14. 'Met Lady Doyle and the three children. Had lunch with them. They believe implicitly in Spiritualism. Sir Arthur told me he had spoken six times to his son. No possible chance of trickery. Lady Doyle also believed and has tests that are beyond belief. Told them all to me.'[10] The following month Houdini and his wife joined the Conan Doyles for lunch at the Royal Automobile Club in London. Conan Doyle told him that a few days earlier they had been sitting at that same table when it began to move – much to the astonishment of the waiter.

Presenting himself as a 'seeker after truth', Houdini asked Conan Doyle to recommend mediums, promising to go with a clear and open mind and a willingness to believe. He was being duplicitous. After a seance with Mrs Annie Brittain, one of Conan Doyle's favourite mediums, he wrote in his diary: 'All this is ridiculous stuff.' Another medium wrote to Conan Doyle warning him that Houdini was out to make trouble, but Conan Doyle would not believe it. Instead, he wrote to Houdini urging him to acknowledge his 'wonderful occult power': 'Such a gift is not given to one man in a hundred million that he should amuse the multitude or amass a fortune. Excuse my frank talking but you know this is all very vital to me.'[11]

Conan Doyle constantly encouraged his new friend to look at the subject of spiritualism more positively: 'I see that you know a great deal about the negative side of Spiritualism,' he wrote. 'I hope more on the positive side will come your way. But it wants to be approached not in the spirit of a detective approaching a suspect, but in that of a humble and religious soul yearning for help and comfort . . .'[12]

It is probable that Conan Doyle hoped to convert Houdini to spiritualism since the magician frequently stated that he would do so if anyone could prove beyond doubt genuine psychic manifestation. To Conan Doyle the little showman was an enigma. 'In a long life which has touched every side of humanity,' he wrote, 'Houdini is far and away the most curious and intriguing character whom I have ever encountered. I have met better men, and I have certainly met very many worse ones, but I have never met a man who had such strange contrasts in his nature, and whose actions and motives it was more difficult to foresee or to reconcile.'[13] He recalled Houdini railing against being charged two shillings to have a suit pressed and the next moment paying for hundreds of barefoot children to be fitted with boots. He was also impressed by the magician's conspicuous courage. 'Nobody has ever done, and nobody in all human probability will ever do,' he noted, 'such reckless feats of daring.' Houdini in turn valued his friendship with Conan Doyle: 'Whatever one's views on the subject [of spiritualism], it is impossible not to respect the belief of this great author who has wholeheartedly and unflinchingly thrown his life and soul into the conversion of unbelievers.'[14]

Not long after the Conan Doyles arrived in New York, they were entertained to lunch by Houdini and his wife at their elegant brownstone at 278 West 113th Street, where the host proudly showed his visitors his library and his collection of spiritualist material. In June the Conan Doyles reciprocated, inviting the couple for the weekend at the

Ambassador Hotel in Atlantic City, New Jersey, then a fashionable seaside resort. The children were thrilled to meet Houdini again, who entertained them with simple magic tricks and a demonstration of how long he could stay submerged in the hotel swimming pool. The weekend promised to be a great success until the magician was persuaded, on Sunday afternoon, to attend a private seance in the Conan Doyles' suite in an attempt to make contact with his late mother. Conan Doyle would later claim that the seance was held 'entirely at his [Houdini's] urgent request'.[15] Houdini insisted that the suggestion came from Sir Arthur, that his host had come down to the beach and said his wife 'had a feeling a message might come through' and that she would give him a special seance if he was agreeable. Lady Conan Doyle had by then, fortuitously, developed mediumistic powers.

Despite his misgivings, the temptation proved too great and Houdini found himself sitting around a table with Conan Doyle and his wife in a room with the blinds drawn to exclude the afternoon sun. Conan Doyle opened the proceedings with a prayer, head bowed, calling on the Almighty for a sign from our 'friends from beyond.' He placed his hands tenderly on his wife and asked if she was ready. Her hand, trembling violently, struck the table three times – a sign for 'yes' in spiritualist practice – and in a quavering voice she called on the spirits to give her a message.

'I made up my mind,' Houdini wrote later, 'that I would be as religious as it was in my power to be and not at any time did I scoff during the ceremony. I excluded all earthly thoughts and gave my whole soul to the seance. I was *willing* to believe, even *wanted* to believe. It was weird to me and with a beating heart I waited, hoping that I might feel once more the presence of my beloved mother . . .'[16]

Lady Conan Doyle, breathing heavily, her eyelids fluttering, her body trembling, picked up a pencil and her hand began to move, as if of its own volition, at extraordinary speed across a notepad in front of her. Such was her agitation that her husband constantly attempted to soothe her. 'It was a singular scene,' Conan Doyle later recalled, 'my wife with her hand flying wildly, beating the table while she scribbled at a furious rate, I sitting opposite and tearing sheet after sheet from the block as it was filled up, and tossing each to Houdini, while he sat silent, looking grimmer and paler at every moment.'[17]

It was a message from the magician's mother and began: 'Oh my darling, thank God, thank God, at last I am through. I've tried, oh so often – now I am happy. Why, of course, I want to talk to my boy – my own beloved boy – friends, thank you, with all my heart for this . . .' She assured her son that she was happy, that he would soon 'get all the evidence he is so anxious for' and that she was busy 'preparing so sweet a home for him' for the day when they would be reunited. 'I am so happy in this life – it is so full and joyous – my only shadow has been that my beloved one hasn't known how often I have been with him all the while, all the while – here away from my heart's darling – combining my work thus in this life of mine. It is so different over here, so much larger and bigger and more beautiful – so lofty – all sweetness around one – nothing that hurts and we see our beloved ones on earth – that is such a joy and comfort to us – Tell him I love him more than ever – the years only increase it – and his goodness fills my soul with gladness and thankfulness . . .' The message ended: 'I have bridged the gulf, that is what I wanted, oh so much – now I can rest in peace.' Houdini and Conan Doyle would later disagree about its length; Houdini claimed it covered five pages, Conan Doyle fifteen.

Conan Doyle asked Houdini if he wanted to ask his mother a question. Her reply, he said, 'will prove that she is at your side'. By Conan Doyle's account, Houdini sat pale and shivering and appeared too upset to talk, so Conan Doyle asked if he should suggest a question. The magician nodded. Conan Doyle asked Houdini's mother if she could read her son's mind. Once again, Lady Conan Doyle began writing at a furious pace:

> I *always* read my beloved son's mind, his dear mind, there is so much that I want to say to him, but . . . I am almost overwhelmed by this joy of talking to him once more . . . it is almost too much to get through . . . the joy of it . . . thank you, thank you friend, with all my heart for what you have done for me this day. God bless you, too, Sir Arthur, for what you are doing for us, for us over here, who so need to get in touch with our beloved ones on the earth plane . . . If only the world knew this great truth – how different – life would be for men and women – Go on, let nothing stop you – great will be your

reward hereafter – Goodbye – I brought you, Sir Arthur, and my darling son together – I felt you were the one man who might help us pierce the veil – and I was right – Bless him, bless him, bless him, I say from the depths of my soul . . .

When it seemed that Lady Conan Doyle was inspired to write no more, Houdini picked up a pencil and asked how to hold it for 'automatic writing', then jotted 'Powell' on a pad. Conan Doyle was stunned. Dr Ellis Powell, editor of the *London Financial News,* his friend and 'dear fighting partner in Spiritualism', had died three days earlier. Conan Doyle immediately assumed he was trying to make contact via Houdini. 'I am the person he is most likely to signal to,' Conan Doyle explained, 'and here is his name coming through your hands. Truly Saul is among the prophets.' The magician demurred and explained that he had been thinking of Frederick Eugene Powell, a magician friend with whom he had recently been corresponding, but Conan Doyle would hear none of it.

What happened at that seance would become a matter of bitter dispute when their friendship foundered. Aware of Houdini's feelings for his mother, Conan Doyle claimed it was act of 'pure humanitarian pity'[18] on his wife's part to offer the seance to try to comfort their friend. They had no doubt that Houdini was deeply moved by the occasion; in fact he told them three days later that he had been 'walking on air' ever since. For his part, Houdini asserted that he was 'serene' throughout and while he had hoped to feel his mother's presence, there was no semblance of it.

What Houdini had not told the Conan Doyles was that his mother could only speak broken English and certainly could not write it. The day of the seance, 17 June 1922, was her birthday and he was convinced that had she really 'come through' she would have mentioned it. Finally, he could not understand why Lady Doyle had drawn a cross on the top of each sheet of paper since his mother, as a Jew, would never have used such a symbol. The seance was his final proof that spiritualism was a fraud. Houdini did not think, however, that his friends were deliberating deceiving him, rather that they were deceiving themselves. For the time being, he decided to keep silent out of respect for his hosts and a desire not to embarrass Lady Conan Doyle.

Curiously, Houdini's dilemma was reflected in 'The Parasite', a short story Conan Doyle had written nearly thirty years earlier about an evil female mesmerist, in which the protagonist, a Professor Gilroy, is reluctantly persuaded to attend a seance at the home of a friend. Houdini would have sympathised with his views: 'I like none of these mystery-mongers, but the amateur least of all. With the paid performer you pounce upon him and expose him the instant that you have seen through his trick. He is there to deceive you, and you are there to find him out. But what are you to do with the friend of your host's wife? Are you to turn on a light suddenly and expose her slapping a surreptitious banjo? Or are you to hurl cochineal over her evening frock when she steals round with her phosphorous bottle and her supernatural platitude? There would be a scene, and you would be looked upon as a brute.'

Houdini brooded on what had happened in Atlantic City for several months. While he was reluctant to betray his friends, he did not want people to think he believed he had been in contact with his mother; in some way the incident seemed to make a mockery of his deep feelings for her. On 30 October 1922, he wrote an article for the *New York Sun* under the headline 'Spirit Compacts Unfulfilled' that comprehensively debunked the seance and claimed that there was not the slightest evidence that his mother had contacted him through Lady Conan Doyle. He had not sensed her presence, he could not understand how she had suddenly mastered the English language and when the seance ended he felt as alone and lost as on the day she died.

Conan Doyle was affronted by what he considered both a betrayal of his trust and an insult to his wife and sent a bristling reply: 'I have no fancy for sparring with a friend in public . . . but none the less I felt rather sore about it. You have all the right in the world to hold your own opinion, but when you say that you had no evidence of survival, you say what I cannot reconcile with what I saw with my own eyes. I know by many examples the purity of my wife's mediumship, and I saw what you got and what the effect was upon you at the time . . . However, I don't propose to discuss this subject any more with you, for I consider you have had your proofs and that the responsibility for accepting or rejecting it is with you.'[19]

To Conan Doyle the fact that Houdini's mother could not write

English and failed to mention her birthday was entirely irrelevant. Language and earthly dates meant nothing to spirits; the communication came as thoughts in his wife's head rather than as a verbatim message in a foreign language, though this rather contradicted the spiritualist belief that during 'automatic writing' the pen was entirely controlled by the spirit. He explained to Houdini that the spirit becomes more educated the longer it is departed and it was thus quite likely that his mother had learned English in heaven. Privately, he believed that Houdini was too overwhelmed by the encounter to admit it was genuine, that he was both wilfully blind and utterly ungrateful. He described the magician's rejection of the message as 'an abnormal frame of mind which may be called Conjuror's Complex or Houdinitis'.

Houdini continued to protest, ingenuously, that he had no desire to discredit spiritualism: 'I am willing to be convinced; my mind is open, but the proof must be such as to leave no vestige of doubt that what is claimed to be done is accomplished only through or by supernatural power. So far I have never on any occasion, in all the séances I have attended, seen anything which would lead me to credit . . . that it is possible to communicate with those who have passed out of this life. Therefore I do not agree with Sir Arthur.'[20] This schism notwithstanding, the two men contrived to maintain the façade of their friendship.

Conan Doyle's American tour had greatly revived interest in spiritualism in the United States, and in December 1922 the respected *Scientific American* magazine offered a prize of $2,500 to anyone able to demonstrate genuine psychic phenomena, under rigorous test conditions before a committee of experts, and a further $2,500 to the first person to produce a visible psychic manifestation. One of the judges was Houdini, included to serve as a 'guarantee to the public that none of the tricks of his trade have been practiced upon the committee'. Conan Doyle was deeply unhappy about the contest and particularly about Houdini's participation. He wrote to Orson D. Munn, editor of *Scientific American*, warning him that offering money would 'stir up every rascal in the country' and dispatched another letter to Houdini, asking how the judging committee could be considered impartial when he had made clear his scepticism. 'I fear some of your recent comments,' he wrote, '. . . would not only keep away every decent medium – for they are human beings, not machines, and resent insult – but it would make spirit approach impossible, for they also do not go into an atmosphere which is antagonistic.'[21]

Among those competing was Margery, the medium Conan Doyle had met in Boston: Margery was Mina Crandon, the beautiful wife of a prominent Boston surgeon, Le Roi Goddard Crandon, whose followers claimed she was one of the greatest mediums in history. She was certainly notorious for her bizarre and risqué seances, sometimes conducted in the nude, using her brother, Walter – a fireman who had been crushed to death in a railway accident in 1911 – as her spirit guide. Margery was said to be able to produce ectoplasm from her vagina and obtain her spirit guide's thumbprint in dental wax placed on the seance table. Houdini's suspicions had been aroused early: over dinner in New York with Conan Doyle he had patiently explained in precise detail how Margery created a 'teleplasmic hand', but Conan Doyle steadfastly refused to believe trickery was involved.

In the summer of 1924 Margery met members of the *Scientific American* judging committee in Boston and made a good impression, although Houdini remained implacably unconvinced. An exasperated Le Roi Crandon wrote to Conan Doyle that it was a 'war to the finish', that his wife's supporters would 'crucify' Houdini and prove Margery to be 'the most extraordinary medium in history'. Such fighting talk sat uncomfortably with Conan Doyle's view that the Crandons were 'the most patient and forgiving people in the world, treating the most irritating opposition with a good-humoured and amused tolerance'.[22]

In August Houdini arrived in Boston to attend two seances with Margery, and what happened would be the subject of fierce debate throughout the spiritualist world. The Crandons claimed, not without some justification, that Houdini arrived determined and equipped to sabotage the seances, while he insisted that he had exposed Margery as a fraud. All agreed that Walter played a key role.

At earlier seances Walter had moved screens around the room and rung a bell operated by a battery in a box on the floor. During the first seance, Walter's voice came through, but he complained he was unable to ring the bell. When the session ended, the bell box was examined and it was found that a rubber eraser had been inserted between the clapper and the bell. The Crandons believed Houdini was responsible.

The next night, at Houdini's insistence, Margery was padlocked into a large wooden 'control cabinet' with one hole for her head and holes on each side so she could join hands with two sitters. Two minutes after the lights had gone down, Houdini put his hand through one of the armholes, ostensibly to ensure that the medium was all right. Walter broke in immediately: 'What did you do that for, Houdini? You God-damned son of a bitch! You cad you! There's a ruler in this cabinet, you unspeakable cad. You won't live forever Houdini, you've got to die. I put a curse on you now that will follow you every day until you die.' The lights went on immediately, the cabinet was opened and on its floor was found a folding ruler which could have been used to effect fake psychic phenomena by moving objects around the room. Houdini, of course, denied that he had planted it, but spiritualists were convinced he had been exposed by the estimable Walter. Most agreed with Conan Doyle, who concluded that Margery's reputation had been saved and Houdini's ruined by the 'miraculous' interference of Walter, 'a very real and live entity, who was by no means inclined to allow his sister to be made the laughing stock of the continent'.[23]

Initially Conan Doyle had doubted that Houdini would resort to such tactics. 'I hear from New York,' he wrote to Harry Price at the Society for Psychical Research, 'that Houdini is accused of dropping objects into a medium's cabinet in order to discredit her . . . He is a very conceited self-opinionated man but I should not have thought he would have descended to that.'[24] But on 10 September he wrote to tell Lodge of the 'great Spiritual doings in Boston' and had clearly decided that Houdini was guilty and unrepentent: 'Houdini must know in his own heart that the thing is true and his conscience must gnaw at him. He was terrified, I heard.'[25]

Far from being troubled, Houdini stepped up his anti-spiritualist campaign. He toured the United States, dazzling audiences by reproducing all the 'tricks' of the seance room. He posted $5,000 in bonds for any medium who could produce physical phenomena he could not replicate. He testified before a Congressional committee in support of an anti-fortune telling bill: 'This thing they call Spiritualism, wherein a medium intercommunicates with the dead, is a fraud from start to finish. There are only two kinds of mediums, those who are mental degenerates and who ought to be under observation, and those who are deliberate cheats and frauds.' In a speech at Symphony Hall in Boston, where once Conan Doyle had presented a persuasive case for spiritualism, Houdini attacked him and Lodge and men like them as 'menaces to mankind', provoking gasps of shock from the audience. They were great and much to be respected in their own fields, but they were not qualified to pass judgement on 'pickpockets and burglars'. He was not denouncing spiritualism, he said, he was exposing frauds.

When Houdini published a pamphlet, 'Houdini Exposes the Tricks Used by the Boston Medium Margery', Conan Doyle rose to defend her in a long article for the *Boston Herald*. He reprimanded the *Scientific American* committee for failing to fight for truth, expose evil and defend 'the honour of a most estimable lady' and for similarly failing to disown Houdini, whom Conan Doyle criticised as being ignorant and motivated by a desire for publicity. The *Boston Herald* reported that Conan Doyle's accusations had 'aroused the famous magician's mirth', but Houdini's stinging response was far from humorous: 'My opinion of Sir Arthur Conan Doyle is that he is a menace to mankind, because the public thinks that he is just as great a man in the Spiritualistic field as he is at writing stories . . . I have personally warned Sir Arthur of a number of things, but it seems he will not protect himself. He has not enough mentality left to use good judgement . . . I am really sorry for him. It is a pity that a man with such a reputation in the literary field should, in his old age, do such really stupid things.' Houdini later threatened legal action, accusing his former friend of being 'a bit senile' and 'easily bamboozled'.

In a final manoeuvre, Houdini deliberately upstaged the *Scientific American*'s conclusions about spiritualism by issuing a statement immediately before it was published, asserting that everything that took place at the five seances he attended with Margery was 'a deliberate and conscious fraud, and that if the lady possess any psychic power, at no time was the same proven in any of the above dated séances'.

Scientific American issued its verdict on 11 February 1925: 'We have observed phenomena the method of production of which we cannot in every case claim to have discovered. But we have observed no phenomena of which we can assert that they could not have been produced by normal means.' Margery's case was not helped by the revelation that all the 'psychic thumbprints' exactly matched those of her husband's dentist, Dr Kerwin, a ruse discovered when a researcher for the American Society for Psychical Research began collecting the thumbprints of everyone known to have attended Margery's seances.

As Walter had predicted, Houdini did not have long to live. That, at least, was true. On 22 October 1926 he was in Montreal, where he was due to deliver a lecture. Relaxing in his dressing room backstage at the theatre, he was visited by a group of students from McGill University, one of whom asked if it was correct, as had been reported, that he could withstand any blow to his stomach. Before Houdini had an opportunity to tighten his stomach muscles, the student hit him several times. Though Houdini did not know it, his appendix was ruptured. He finished his engagement and then travelled to Detroit, where he gave one performance before collapsing. He died in hospital of peritonitis on 31 October.

After his death, Conan Doyle revealed that on the evening of the infamous Atlantic City seance he and Lady Doyle had attended another seance at which Houdini's mother again came through mourning the premature end she foresaw for her brilliant son. 'As we were all on friendly terms with Houdini at the time, we were shocked at the message. We did not pass it on to him, as we hoped it might prove mistaken, but that hope has now been dissipated.'[26]

In a placatory gesture, Bess Houdini offered her husband's large collection of books on spiritualism and the supernatural to Conan Doyle, but he was reluctant to accept. Bess hastened to assure him that her husband had admired and respected Conan Doyle and secretly never gave up on the possibility of contacting his mother. 'He would have been the happiest man in the world,' she wrote, 'had he been able to agree with your views on spiritism.' Conan Doyle responded affectionately, assuring Bess he would never again say any unkind things about her husband. 'Any man who wins the love and respect of a good woman,' he told her, 'must himself be a fine and honest man. I am sorry that shadows grew up between us.'

Conan Doyle continued to view Houdini's antagonism towards spiritualism with sadness: 'His anti-Spiritualist agitation became more and more unreasoning until it bordered upon a mania which could only be explained in some quarters by supposing that he was in the pay of certain clerical fanatics, an accusation which I do not believe. It is true that in order to preserve some show of reason he proclaimed that he wished only to attack dishonest mediums, but as in the same breath he would assert that there were no honest ones, his moderation was more apparent than real.'[27]

To the end of his life, Conan Doyle doggedly insisted that Houdini possessed supernatural powers. Two years after the magician's death he wrote a two-part article for the *Strand* insisting that dematerialisation was the only explanation for his most baffling feats: 'I contend that Houdini's performance was on an entirely different plane and that it is an outrage against common sense to think otherwise.'

In the end, Houdini hedged his bets about spiritualism. Shortly before his death, he made a pact with Bess to reach her from the 'other side' if it was at all possible and to deliver a prearranged coded message. For ten years, on the anniversary of his death, Bess Houdini held a seance in the hope that he would make contact. No message came through.

CHAPTER 23

PHENEAS SPEAKS

EAN CONAN DOYLE HAD ACQUIRED what her husband called 'the great gift of inspired writing' some time during 1921. 'In her intense honesty and deep modesty,' he noted, 'she somewhat retarded it at first by holding back her impulses in the fear lest they should come from her own subconscious self. Gradually, however, the unexpected nature of the messages, and the allusions to be found in them, showed both her and me that there were forces at work which were outside herself.'[1]

Early messages arriving through Jean's mediumship tended to be from friends and family: innocuous, comforting, encouraging – and almost always entirely what Conan Doyle wanted to hear, particularly in regard to approval of his work on earth. His mother, Kingsley and Innes all communicated their regret at not supporting spiritualism during their lifetimes. Willie Hornung, who had died of pneumonia as Conan Doyle was returning from Australia, expressed similar sentiments: 'I am so glad to be here, Arthur, this is wonderful. If only I had known this on earth, how much I could have helped others . . . It is a wonderful life, so high and fine in all ways. Worth living for. If only people knew!' Malcolm Leckie assured Conan Doyle that he found 'life' very full and interesting on the other side and that he and Jean would be very happy when they arrived: 'We are helping to prepare your home. We know just what you both like. It is already looking sweet.' Lily Loder Symonds came through to chide her friend gently for once having been a sceptic: 'Jean, you are awful at not believing. It is really wrong, old girl. It is NOT your subconscious self. Do, for Heaven's sake, get that out of your head. Trust more.'[2]

Loder Symonds went on to describe her home. 'It is lovely. I never saw any home on earth to compare with ours. So many flowers, a blaze of colour in all directions and they have such wonderful scents, each one different, and all blending so deliciously . . . Every home is an oasis, as it were. Beyond is wonderful scenery and other sweet homes, full of dear, sweet, bright people, full of laughter . . . No earthly mind can conceive the light and wonder of it all. We have rooms as on earth, but so much lovelier. The colours are so much daintier, and the fabrics so much more delicate. The whole scheme of the house is so much more radiant.'

Conan Doyle's mother spoke through her daughter-in-law at a seance at Windlesham when the children were present. 'Oh my dears, I am so glad to be with you all. God bless you, darlings . . . I am so glad, dearie, that you brought the lambs [the children] tonight to meet us. My son, you are tired. It grieves me to see you so. Do rest more. But I know Jean will see to that. God bless her for taking care of my dear, beloved son.'

Strangers occasionally intruded, heartening Conan Doyle in his mission. 'Soon great things will happen,' offered one, 'so that the whole world will see for itself how true all this is. No one will laugh then. Only regret will be felt for the foolish stupidity of the ignorant . . . For God's sake, Sir Arthur, strike hard at these people, these dolts who will not believe.'

One voice conspicuously and curiously absent in these sessions, however, was that of Lady Conan Doyle's predecessor, Touie, the first Lady Conan Doyle. During the nine years that Jean would record messages from the spirit world Touie never once attempted to make contact with her former husband, despite her devotion to him when she was alive. If Conan Doyle thought this odd, he forbore to mention it, though the natural reluctance of a first wife to talk to her husband through the dubious offices of her replacement perhaps explains her silence. His neglected alcoholic father similarly failed to 'cross the divide' and share his thoughts on life in the hereafter.

Five months after the family had returned from the United States, a message came through from the Mam that a 'spirit guide' would soon be introducing himself and would take control of their circle. 'The name is Pheneas,' Lady Conan Doyle wrote on her message pad. 'He is a very, very high soul sent especially to work through you on the earth plane. He died thousands of years ago in the East, near Arabia. He was a leader among men. He wants me to say, dear one, that there is much work before you.' Conan Doyle queried: 'In this world?' 'Well, of course, my darling, it is here on this grey earth that you are needed.'

Pheneas first made contact on 10 December 1922 and thereafter would be Conan Doyle's direct, if capricious, link to the spirit world. 'There have been months on end when we have longed for Pheneas,' he wrote, 'and sat awaiting him with every condition favourable, and yet he has not come. Then at another time, unexpected, unannounced, in the midst of conversation, in the course of a meal, he will suddenly, with altered voice and sweeping Oriental gestures of greeting, make his presence known.'[3] Pheneas had been a scribe in the city of Ur, 140 miles south of Babylon, capital of the Sumerian civilisation, 3,000 years before the birth of Christ. By a strange coincidence, a joint expedition mounted by the British Museum and the University of Pennsylvania under Sir Leonard Woolley had recently begun an excavation of Ur. Its departure and early progress were widely reported in British newspapers.

Cynics studying Pheneas's many messages could be forgiven for concluding some of them aligned very closely with the kind of advice a loving wife and mother on an earthly plane might offer her family. The children were encouraged to work hard and behave properly; their father was told to rest more, not to drink tea, to take a mile-long walk morning and afternoon, whatever the weather, and to take bismuth, an indigestion potion, twice a day. Conan Doyle was reassured that the spirits approved of his views, that he was doing good work, that opponents of spiritualism would eventually be 'swept away' when 'people from all nations' realised how utterly they had been failed by conventional religion. 'England is to be the centre to which all humanity will turn,' said Pheneas. 'She is to be the beacon of light in this dark, dark world.'

Pheneas was also at pains to point out, frequently, how wonderful Lady Conan Doyle was. 'She is a medium of rare and wonderful vibration, through whom I can work in perfect harmony of one accord. It is like virgin soil. You put the plant in, and it grows a beautiful specimen. So with our power, the vibrations between us of harmony are complete. Therefore I can come to you without fear of any outside force polluting or touching my channel.' The children Denis, 13, Adrian, 11, and Jean, 9, now regularly attended seances with their parents and Pheneas was similarly lavish in his praise of them, particularly the boys. He told Denis that 'We are proud of the efforts you are making', and advised Adrian 'You have a great work set apart for you to do ... If you do it, it will bring you enormous advancement of soul.' Not all his messages were on a higher plane: 'You can't get an apple dumpling, until you have the apples.'

Soon after Pheneas first came through, Conan Doyle asked him if he should return to America to continue his crusade.

'Go,' Pheneas allegedly replied, 'and God's blessing go with you every mile of the way.'

'Shall we take the children?'

'You could *not* leave them. They, too, in their own way work well for the cause.'

This was good news, since Lady Conan Doyle always wanted to travel with her husband and had a marked aversion to leaving the children behind.

So it was that on 3 April 1923 the family arrived back in New York, accompanied by a nanny and twenty pieces of baggage. It had been a stormy crossing and halfway across the Atlantic Conan Doyle slipped on the wet deck, twisted his knee and was obliged to rest in his cabin for two days, which reminded him to tell reporters in New York that Kingsley had arrived during a seance and massaged the limb with highly beneficial results.

An even more ambitious itinerary had been planned, taking in both east and west coasts, the Midwest and Canada, but Jack Bowman, the owner of the Biltmore Hotel, had generously put his personal suite at the disposal of the family and agreed that Jean and the children could remain there while Conan Doyle worked from New York to Chicago.

The hostility of the established church towards spiritualism in general and Conan Doyle in particular was now even more pronounced in the United States than in Britain, and the New York-based *Truth* magazine used his visit to publish a stinging attack on the 'knighted prophet of the New Revelation' by the Reverend P. J. Cormican, a Jesuit priest whose claim to fame was having written 'True Son of God, Eternal Light', a hymn in *American Hymns, Old & New*. Cormican accused Conan Doyle of dissembling and of ignoring 'the evil consequences, physical intellectual and moral, to those who dabble in Spiritism'. He claimed there were more than 30,000 lunatics in England alone who had 'lost their mind through this modern necromancy', not to mention 'the countless cases of insanity and suicide, of blasphemy and obscenity, of lying and deception, of broken homes and violated truth, all caused by Spiritism'. To suppose that God was speaking through the new medium of spiritualism was 'blasphemy pure and simple' and to suggest that Christianity was a worn-out creed both gratuitous and absurd. 'Christianity will last till the crack of doom,' the Reverend concluded, adding a final dig at Conan Doyle, 'when titled prophets shall have ceased to cross the Atlantic in quest of American shekels'.

Lady Conan Doyle leapt to the defence of her husband in a radio broadcast from the Ritz Carlton Hotel extolling the many blessings of spiritualism. 'If I were offered all the wealth of New York in exchange for the knowledge which Spiritualism has brought me,' she said, 'I would rather live in a two-room shack than part with the intense comfort, the glorious vision of that wonderful future world I know lies ahead.' Her doting husband drank in every word: 'As I listened to those great truths ringing out in her beautifully modulated voice it was more like an angel message than anything I could imagine. Her deep convictions sent a thrill into her words which could not have been lost upon her unseen audience of 500,000 souls.'[4]

Everywhere he looked, Conan Doyle found more evidence interlinking this world with the next. While he was in New York, news arrived of the death of Lord Carnarvon, the patron of the British expedition which had discovered the tomb of Tutankhamen in the Valley of the Kings in November 1922. Carnarvon's death gave rise to frenzied newspaper stories around the world about a 'Pharaoh's Curse' and, like other spiritualists, Conan Doyle fanned the fire by asserting publicly that it was a 'dangerous game' to desecrate ancient graves. 'We were, of course, laughed at for our pains,' he would write later. 'But look at the sequel. Lord Carnarvon, the director of the expedition, is dead. The Hon. Aubrey Herbert, who was present, is dead. Sir Douglas Reid, who had undertaken to X-ray the mummy, is dead. Professor Laffleur, who investigated the tomb, is dead. The two French Egyptologists, Benedite and Cassanova, who helped in the work, are both dead . . . It is impossible for any reasonable man to doubt that there is a malign psychic influence connected with some of these old objects when used for sepulchral purposes.'[5] Actually, the 'curse' was a media invention: subsequent research indicated that those involved in the expedition lived an average of more than twenty years after the opening of the tomb.

Conan Doyle travelled alone on a tour of the Midwest, and while he was away, he wrote frequently to Jean and made it clear he longed to be reunited with her, though their separation lasted only seven days: 'Oh my love it will be good to see your dear kind eyes once more.' He arrived in Cleveland as a non-stop dancing contest was drawing to a close after more than sixty hours: 'repulsive in a way, as all pain which one cannot relieve is repulsive, but it was fine too as an exhibition of pluck'. He was depressed by the industrial city of Pittsburgh: 'Personally I am of the opinion that God sent a man into this world that he might improve in mind and spirit, and not that he should make screws and rivets.' In Chicago, where he was reunited with Jean and the children, he visited a jail and was appalled by the medieval conditions in which the inmates lived.

In Toledo, Ohio, a sitting was arranged with a well-known medium Ada Besinnet, whose speciality was to bring forth mask-like 'phantom faces' which appeared in an illuminated patch in front of the sitters. It was held in the darkened dining room of a local doctor's house and among those present was J. Malcolm Bird, a young journalist from *Scientific American* who had been assigned to investigate psychic phenomena. Once the medium had established the presence of her spirit control, a Native American named Black Cloud, the seance got under way with a cacophony of different voices, male and female, singing and whistling.

After about half an hour, faces began to appear in a 'psychic light' and Conan Doyle made desperate attempts to identify them, asking for them to be produced again and again, and eventually satisfied himself that the faces were those of his mother and his nephew, Oscar Hornung, killed at Ypres. Bird, who was sitting next to Conan Doyle, wondered how he could be so sure. 'I saw these particular apparitions almost as well as he did; and it was my best judgment that they were not sufficiently clear to be identified at all, save by a liberal contribution of desire and imagination on the part of the sitter.'[6]

Conan Doyle later told the Toledo *News-Bee* that he had seen 'beyond all doubt or question' his mother and could 'count the very wrinkles' on her face. Miss Besinnet, he added, should be 'guarded and looked after very carefully, for she is very valuable'. Two months later Samri Frikell, a journalist working for McFadden Publications, also attended one of her seances. He kept his foot pressed against that of the medium as the lights were extinguished and was certain she had left her chair. When a 'spirit' lightly touched his cheek, he was pretty sure that he could also feel Miss Besinnet's bosom touching the back of his head and, to him, the spirit 'voices' bore a strong resemblance to that of the medium. 'Sir Arthur Conan Doyle has told you what he saw,' he concluded. 'I have told you what I saw. I ask you to judge for yourselves.'

The following year *Scientific American* published a long article explaining how fraudulent mediums made use of paraffin masks dipped in phosphorus to create spirit manifestations. (Conan Doyle would have been familiar with this technique as he had used it to create the spectral appearance of the Baskerville hound.) Fixed to the end of a long pole and waved over the heads of the sitters in the darkness of the seance room, it was not hard for those present to 'recognise' the disembodied faces.

After stops in Kansas City and Denver, the family arrived in Salt Lake City, Utah, spiritual home of the Church of Jesus Christ of Latter Day Saints – the Mormons whom Conan Doyle had portrayed in such an unforgiving and unflattering light in *A Study in Scarlet*. He was nervous about how they would be greeted and impressed by their cordial welcome. Their journey continued west to the culture shock of California. While in Los Angeles, the family toured Hollywood film studios and met Douglas Fairbanks and his wife, Mary Pickford, whom Conan Doyle found to be 'intensely psychic'. Later he sent her some 'psychic notes', for which Fairbanks wrote to thank him and expressed the hope they would have 'many more meetings'.[7]

Conan Doyle was photographed with child star Jackie Coogan, aged 8, and entertained him with a 'gruesome Sherlock Holmes tale'. The family also visited Catalina Island, then owned by William Wrigley, the chewing-gum king. Conan Doyle had little time for Mr Wrigley's product. He thought that even Venus would appear vulgar if she chewed gum: 'There was never so hopelessly undignified a custom. A man may drink and look a king among men, he may smoke and look a fine fellow and a sportsman, but the man, or, worse still, the woman, who chews becomes all animal at once.' The next stop was San Francisco, then Portland, Tacoma and Seattle, where they took a ferry to Vancouver to continue the tour in Canada.

Arriving in Winnipeg on Dominion Day, 1 July, in time to attend a baseball game between the local side and Minneapolis, Conan Doyle found himself harbouring, as a cricketer, an heretical thought. 'I wish more and more,' he would write later, 'that this game could acclimatise in Britain, for it has many points which make it the ideal game both for players and spectators. I have all the prejudices of an old cricketer, and yet I cannot get away from the fact that baseball is the better game.'[8] The Canadian tour finished in Montreal, where he gave two lectures and investigated the case of a poltergeist haunting which he naturally pronounced as genuine. Conan Doyle calculated that he and his family had travelled 15,000 miles in a little more than three months, during which time he had delivered forty lectures. Before returning home on 4 August, the family spent three weeks on vacation at Loon Lake, in upper New York state, where Conan Doyle drafted his account of the tour, *Our Second American Adventure*.

———◆———

Throughout his years on the stump for spiritualism, Conan Doyle never stopped writing. After his return from his second tour of the United States, however, his literary output became more eclectic and erratic. In late 1923 he was moved to write a cloyingly intimate portrait of family life at Windlesham when the children were aged between 5 and 9. If proof were needed that *anything* Conan Doyle wrote would be published, it was *The Three of Them – A Reminiscence*. The author resorted to reproducing his daughter's lisp phonetically ('woses wustle'), and composed a doting description of an idyllic childhood with 'Daddy, an impish person with some gift for playing Indian games when he is in the mood' and his 'Lady Sunshine'.

Denis was 'Laddie', an 'unselfish, gallant and innocent soul set to bring an extra shine to the earth, housed in a tall, slight, graceful body, with a face as clean-cut and well favoured as a Greek cameo and eyes that are grey and wise and captivate the heart of all he meets.' Adrian, known in the family by his second name, Malcolm, was 'Dimples . . . full of fun and naughtiness" and Jean, who liked to be called Billie, was 'dainty and elfin'. 'The boys are but shallow, sparkling pools compared with this little girl with her self-repression and dainty aloofness . . . As a rule she sits quiet, aloof, affable, keenly alive to all that passes and yet taking no part in it save for some subtle smile or glance. And then suddenly the wonderful grey-blue eyes under the long black lashes will gleam like coy diamonds, and such a hearty little chuckle will come from her that everyone else is bound to laugh out of sympathy.'

The children clearly reciprocated Conan Doyle's gushing affection: 16-year-old Denis wrote on his father's birthday in 1925: 'My darling Daddy, Very many happy returns of the day!!! And all the best in the coming year! . . . I am so looking forward to Saturday, when I will see you, Darling . . .'[9]

While *The Three of Them* revealed more than any reader could reasonably want to know about the Conan Doyle children, his next book, his autobiography, did not reveal enough. *Memories and Adventures*, published in 1924, was a curiously anodyne work, revealing little of the inner man or of his talents as a writer. He had an instinctive Victorian distaste for exposing his private life, and thus the book was more a dry chronicle of his experiences than an autobiography. Much was omitted. There was not a word about the shadow cast over the family by his father's alcoholism and incarceration, no mention of Bryan Waller, his mother's long-time benefactor, no hint of falling in love with Jean Leckie while his first wife was still alive. And spiritualism, which by now entirely dominated his life, occupied only thirteen pages at the very end of the book, although he emphasised its importance: 'the work which will occupy, either by voice or pen, the remainder of my life'.

Most remarkable about *Memories and Adventures* was the author's candour about the quality of his own early work. He considered *The Firm of Girdlestone* (1890) to be 'worthless'; *The Doings of Raffles Haw* (1892) was a 'not very notable achievement'; *Beyond the City* (1892) and *The Parasite* (1894) he dismissed as 'very inferior'. He made little of his most famous characters – Sherlock Holmes, Brigadier Gerard and Professor Challenger – but advanced *Sir Nigel* (1906) as representing his personal 'high-water mark in literature'.

In fact Conan Doyle had not entirely abandoned his old friend. The booming silent film industry had revived interest in Sherlock Holmes. Between 1921 and 1923 the actor Eille Norwood played the detective in no fewer than 45 'one-reelers' and 2 'two-reelers', including *The Hound of the Baskervilles*. Acceding to continual pleas from Greenhough Smith for more Holmes stories, Conan Doyle had produced 'The Adventure of the Three Gables' in 1920 and 'The Adventure of the Mazarin Stone' the following year. The latter was the most disappointing of all, written in the third person without Dr Watson as the narrator. Adapted from an earlier play, *The Crown Diamond*, it showed every sign of being dashed off by an uninterested author. Over the next few years Conan Doyle would produce ten more Holmes stories, but even the most ardent fans were forced admit that they lacked the sparkle and verve of the earlier work.

The truth was that Conan Doyle's heart was no longer in writing fiction. The days when he would abort a round of golf if a good idea for a story struck him were long gone. Even when he decided to bring back the irrepressible Professor Challenger in 1926 in a new novel, *The Land of Mist*, his first for ten years, it was only as an opportunity to propagate spiritualism further. 'I keep you in touch with my plans so you know what is coming,' he wrote to Greenhough Smith. 'I have for years had a big psychic novel in me which shall deal realistically with every phase of the questions, pro and con. I waited and knew it would come. Now it has come, with a full head of steam, and I can hardly hold onto my pen it goes so fast – about 12 or 15,000 words in three days . . . I don't think it has ever been done by anyone who had the subject thoroughly at his fingers before. So far I am very satisfied with it . . .'[10]

The Land of Mist was semi-autobiographical, as the author explained in the preface: 'There is no incident in this volume which has not come within the immediate ken of the writer, or else has happened to those in whom he has full confidence . . . Accuracy of statement has been cultivated throughout, and some of the seance-room conversations are absolutely transcriptions of stenographic reports.'

Of the engaging quartet who had made their debut in *The Lost World* only three survived, Professor Summerlee apparently having died in Naples the year before. The journalist Edward Malone is commissioned to write an article on spiritualism in partnership with Challenger's feisty daughter, Enid. Professor Challenger naturally dismisses the subject as nonsense. 'Death ends all, Malone,' he snorts. 'This soul-talk is the animism of savages. It is superstition, a myth.' But when Summerlee sends a message from the other side, Malone is rapidly converted. The dashing Lord John Roxton turns up, initially sceptical, but experiences a change of heart after a night in a haunted house, an episode in which Conan Doyle let rip: 'They only knew that the black shadows at the top of the staircase had thickened, had coalesced, had taken a definite, batlike shape. Great God! They were moving! They were rushing swiftly and noiselessly downwards! Black, black as night, huge, ill-defined, semi-human and altogether evil and damnable . . .' But neither the pace nor the suspense is sustained, thanks to the tedious appearance of numerous spiritualists intent on spreading propaganda in the guise of 'teaching' Malone, Roxton and Challenger. Mr Algernon Mailey, 'with his athletic proportions, which had run a little to seed but were still notable, and with his virile voice and strong if homely face', is recognisable as Conan Doyle when he declares that the spirit message was 'infinitely the most important thing in the world'.

Challenger is finally persuaded to attend a seance at which two former patients, who died many years earlier after he had administered an experimental drug, come through to absolve him of any blame. A 'cloud of guilt' lifts from his shoulders. No living soul had known of their fate and so the chastened professor is forced to accept the 'incontrovertible evidence'. 'It is incredible, inconceivable, grotesquely wonderful,' he says, 'but it would seem to be true.' The novel ends with a 'gentler, humbler, and more spiritual' Challenger affirming his new faith.

Many readers felt they were being manipulated by *The Land of Mist* and reviewers objected to the book's overt propagandising. 'Too much pill,' *The Times* sniffed, 'too little sugar-coating'. 'It may be good Spiritualist propaganda,' said the *New Statesman*, 'but as an essay in imaginative fiction, in which guise it is presented, it is unworthy of so skilled a story-teller as Sir Arthur Conan Doyle.' Reaction in the United States was similar. 'The characters in *The Land of Mist* are scarcely more than props for Sir Arthur's propaganda,' the *New York Times* noted.

Writing *The Land of Mist* had provided Conan Doyle with a break from a major new literary project – a massive two-volume history of spiritualism – yet he still found time to fulfil his many other commitments. He remained heavily involved in the movement's activities in Britain, lecturing around the country and lending his presence at important events. He worked hard to set up a spiritualist church in London, served as president of the London Spiritualist Alliance and the British College of Psychic Science, and was elected chairman of the International Spiritualistic Congress in Paris. There were frequent rumours that he would have been offered a peerage were it not for his advocacy of spiritualism;[11] yet he was neither concerned nor deterred from his mission.

It would soon become clear that spiritualism was a lost cause as interest in it rapidly faded, but Conan Doyle continued to believe he was at the forefront of the greatest religious revival the world had seen for 2,000 years. His claims for the movement became increasingly intemperate, sometimes preposterous. He spoke with dark foreboding about an impending disaster threatening to engulf the world which only spiritualism could avert. He said he felt closer now to Kingsley than if the young man were still alive. 'There is never a month, often never a week, that I do not communicate with him. Is it not evident that such facts as these change the whole aspect of life, and turn the grey mist of dissolution into a rosy dawn?'

He experimented with making contact with spirits by wireless after Oliver Lodge suggested that a tall aerial ascending into 'etheric' forces would bring those on earth closer to the spirit world. 'The spirits speak of "receiving stations" on the other side,' he explained, 'and repeatedly compare their messages to "electrical transmissions".

One senses that by fine-tuning some electrical device it might be possible to pick up transmissions from heaven itself without ever leaving one's fireside.'[12] He was also in serious correspondence with a fellow spiritualist who professed to be in touch with Mars by means of a 30,000-metre wireless band.[13]

Ridiculed, reviled and attacked from all sides, it was little wonder that Conan Doyle kept largely to himself details of the most serious message vouchsafed thus far by his spirit guide.

CHAPTER 24

FAREWELL TO HOLMES

N THE SUMMER OF 1924, at a seance in the old nursery at Windlesham, Pheneas first communicated the alarming news that the end of the world was nigh. Lady Conan Doyle had by this time acquired a talent for 'semi-trance inspirational talking' in addition to her 'inspired writing'; she would sit with her eyes tightly closed and allow the spirit to speak directly through her mouth. By these means Pheneas delivered a doom-laden prediction that the world was on the brink of a catastrophe of biblical dimensions – war, famine, earthquakes, tidal waves, poison clouds and massive death tolls were to be expected. The recent war would be 'as nothing, nothing, nothing compared with what lies ahead'. Humanity was 'sinking into a slough of evil and materialism' and 'God's own light must descend and burn up the vile fumes.'[1]

Considerable detail was provided, all of which Conan Doyle diligently recorded in a small leather-bound notebook with 'Prophesied Course of Events' written on the first page. The apocalypse would begin at harvest time in 1925, with a great storm tracking from west to east, followed by a 'terrific convulsion' and worldwide destruction of civilisation by fire and flood. America would face a civil war during which New York would be utterly destroyed by fire; Africa and Japan would be submerged by tidal waves; Russia, that 'black mark upon the map of humanity' would cease to exist; Brazil would suffer an 'eruption of an extraordinary kind' and the Vatican, 'that sink of iniquity' from which 'countless veins of poison flow to humanity' would be 'wiped off the face of the globe'.

Although millions would die, spiritualists were 'the Elect' and would be spared in order to establish a Spiritualist Utopia. Conan Doyle speculated that some kind of poison gas would be released – as in his story *The Poison Belt* – to which spiritualists would be immune. Pheneas foretold that England would be a 'beacon of light' in this new dark world and said that Conan Doyle's task was to 'prepare men's minds so that when the awakening comes they shall be more ready to receive it'. Conan Doyle noted that the process might be very lengthy but 'I shall survive to the end, then pass over with my whole family.'

Mediums had been predicting a global apocalypse for years – some suggested that the carnage wrought by the war was but the first act in the drama – but Conan Doyle had such faith in Pheneas and in his wife's talents as a medium that he faithfully followed Pheneas's instructions to have his predictions typed out and circulated in a four-page mimeographed memorandum in confidence to a few spiritualist friends, including Sir Oliver Lodge. 'These various forecasts of the immediate future of the world should be used with the utmost discretion,' he pointed out. 'We have, above all, to avoid sensationalism and undignified newspaper stunts.'[2] While admitting that previous apocalyptic warnings had come to nothing, he considered it very significant that Pheneas's predictions had been confirmed, independently, by other mediums. There had also been a notable increase in seismic activity in those areas of the world most at risk. 'These warnings have come unsought and often unwelcome in many quarters, and are all roughly to the same effect . . . It is impossible, in my opinion, not to take them seriously, for they represent in themselves a psychic phenomenon for which I know no parallel . . .'

Pheneas had predicted, he continued, that the crisis would come in an instant and that the general destruction and utter dislocation of civilised life would be beyond belief. The good news for spiritualists was that the havoc would be accompanied by 'a complete rending of the veil', so that the spirit world and the material world would for the first time be face to face. When they separated again a 'great number of those who have worked in the cause will be privileged to pass over with their spirit friends and without death in the ordinary sense of the word'. Others of the 'Elect' would be obliged to stay behind to establish a new world order with spiritualism as the basis of all future religions. The object of the movement was to prepare for this crisis, and it would be the duty of all spiritualists to devote themselves entirely to the comfort and instruction of the terrified and bewildered human race. But, Conan Doyle warned, 'hopeless material', presumably the criminal classes and unbelievers, would be swept away.

'I need not ask you to handle this paper with discretion,' he concluded. 'We want no hysterical developments, nor do we wish to commit the Spiritualistic movement to a prophecy which may not materialise. At the same time, without publicly committing the movement in any way I should wish to let individuals know my own individual point of view so that they may now watch the course of events for themselves and form their own conclusions and the line of action. Let those hear who have an ear to hear but let it not be broadcast. ACD.'[3]

The autumn of 1925 passed without bringing Armageddon. Pheneas explained, through Lady Conan Doyle's willing lips, that preparations were taking longer than expected, since the strength of 'the enemy' had been underestimated. Conan Doyle, unusually pragmatic, thereafter no longer forecast a date for the calamity, but suggested instead that it would come 'soon'. He never stopped believing the truth of these warnings, however, and held meetings with fellow spiritualists at his home to discuss how to handle the crisis, including how to distribute their literature in the event of 'interruption of railway communication'.

While waiting for the apocalypse, Conan Doyle could often be found pottering around his own bookshop in London. In January 1925 he had opened the Psychic Bookshop at 2 Victoria Street, just round the corner from Westminster Abbey, which he hoped would become a 'central depot' for psychic knowledge. He felt it was needed because 'the most important literature in the world, found hardly any place upon the shelves of the ordinary bookseller'.[4] At the same time he also launched his own publishing house, the Psychic Press, which would churn out much of his spiritualist writings as mainstream publishers were showing less and less interest despite his fame as a writer. Among the services on offer at the bookshop – which boasted the telegraphic address 'Ectoplasm, Southwest' – was a 'circulating library' available for a subscription of 2s. 6d. a month or 1 guinea a year, and information about the spiritualist movement, as well as advice on which mediums to consult. In the basement was a small museum where Conan Doyle displayed some of his vast collection of spirit photographs and spiritual artefacts.

His older daughter, Mary, by now a convert, was in charge of running the enterprise but her father liked to be involved and had bought a lease on a flat nearby at 15 Buckingham Palace Mansions so that he could 'keep an eye on the shop' (and also watch the cricket at Lord's). His friend John Lamond recalled his surprise when he dropped into the shop to find the owner in his shirtsleeves stacking books and was humbled by 'great joy he felt in seeing the parcels of books going forth to the ends of the earth'.[5]

The American publisher George H. Doran also never forgot his visit to the Psychic Bookshop. Doran, who had published many Sherlock Holmes stories, arranged to meet Conan Doyle at the bookshop to try and persuade him to write a 'biography' of Doctor Watson. Conan Doyle listened to the proposal courteously, said he thought the idea was good but insisted that he could not be distracted from his psychic work. Doran recalled: 'He took me gently by the arm and said, "Let me show you my museum, but first you must look at this." With that he took me to the forepart of the shop and showed me a water colour painting that looked for all the world like a sublimated and idealized picture of the Riviera between Nice and Monte Carlo – the blue sea in the foreground, the marble and white stone palaces and chalets, the beautiful foliage, the grandeur of the mountains in the background and the opalescent sky. This, Doyle explained to me, was a picture of a section of Heaven given under guidance to an inspired artist. And Doyle was convinced of its validity and reality.'[6]

It was Conan Doyle's hope that he would recoup the £1,500 annual running costs from sales, but the venture never made money. He was unconcerned and would tell friends that while other successful writers enjoyed yachts and racehorses, he chose to have a psychic bookshop. Conan Doyle estimated that, including the profits from his spiritualist books and lecture tours, he probably contributed around £250,000 – a phenomenal sum now equivalent to many millions – to the movement.

He remained, nevertheless, a wealthy man. In addition to the London flat and the bookshop, he also purchased Bignell Wood, a large thatched house near Minstead in the New Forest, as a birthday present for his wife, who had always loved the area. With all modern conveniences including central heating, seven bedrooms, four reception rooms, staff quarters, a trout stream running through the garden and a gate leading directly into the forest, the idea was that it would provide a haven for them from the pressure of their busy lives. The gardener, Ezra, was soon put to work building chicken coops, a ducks' house and a run for goats to provide food when the catastrophe struck.

Not long after they had completed the purchase of Bignell Wood, Pheneas indicated that he would like his own seance room there, painted mauve. It was during a sitting in this newly decorated room, with the American violinist Florizel von Reuter and his wife, that Charles Dickens came through, expressing regret that he had 'gone across' before finishing *The Mystery of Edwin Drood* and suggesting that Conan Doyle might like to take it on. 'I shall be honoured, Mr Dickens,' Conan Doyle replied reverentially. 'Charles, if you please,' the spirit apparently responded, 'we like friends to be friends.' Despite this exchange, Conan Doyle did not finish the book and also claimed he turned down a proposal from Joseph Conrad, who had died in August 1924, that he might consider completing his unfinished novel, *Suspense*.[7]

Many of Conan Doyle's literary colleagues, baffled by what he was doing, by now felt obliged to distance themselves from him. Jerome K. Jerome went public with an attack on the 'puerile' events of the seance room and the 'insipid logic' behind them. After his death in 1927, Conan Doyle maintained Jerome sent him a message: 'Tell him [Conan Doyle] from me that I know now that he was right and I was wrong. We never know our greatest mistakes at the time we make them.' J. M. Barrie, while disdaining to fall out with Conan Doyle in public, was not willing to discuss spiritualism with him in private.

Edgar Wallace, the crime writer, penned a carping article in the *London Opinion* about the 'dreary nonsense' of the séance. 'I do not believe,' he wrote, 'that anyone by falling into an epileptic fit, or a good imitation of one, secures the mysterious power of bringing themselves into touch with those personalities which have no longer habitation in the human frame . . . why should spirits blow horns and tin trumpets, and pick up tambourines and shake them? When we depart this mortal life do the sanest of us become clowns? Why is all this dreary nonsense necessary if it is not that it is tricks which are easily performed by an unscrupulous medium?'

When G.B. Shaw weighed in with a description of using seance tricks to fool his friends, Conan Doyle hit back with a familiar refrain. 'His argument,' he wrote, 'is that he himself has cheated at the seance table and has successfully deceived trusting friends, and that therefore all phenomena are suspect and worthless. To put this argument into concrete form, I have in the presence of witnesses unquestionably seen my mother since her death. But what I say must be false because Bernard Shaw cheated his friends. Was there ever a more absurd non sequitur than that?'

Conan Doyle's mammoth two-volume project, *The History of Spiritualism*, was ready for publication by 1926. Writing to Lodge for permission to dedicate the work to him, 'for I think no one has shown greater courage in the matter than you', Conan Doyle promised it would be 'a dignified and balanced book, never extreme in statement'.[8] Reviewers tended not to agree. While conceding his 'absolute sincerity', *The Times* pointed out: 'His tone in the present book often approximates more to that of the Hebrew prophet denouncing the wrath to come than to that of the apologist anxious to conciliate opponents . . . Sir Arthur hardly seems to suspect that there may be honest people who find things which are incredible and even nauseating in the Spiritualist theology . . .'[9]

Professor Joseph Jastrow, who had reviewed *The Wanderings of a Spiritualist*, returned to the attack in the *New York Times*: 'It is very easy to show that Sir Arthur has been repeatedly and grossly deceived by the most vulgar kind of spirit-séance that is designed to prey upon the emotions of the gullible . . . if there is any one member of the very small modern group of distinguished men who for one reason or another have gone over to the delusion of the supernormal, who is thoroughly discredited by his versatile and eager credulity and his readiness to ignore all the exposure of fraud that has been accumulated, it is Sir Arthur Conan Doyle.'[10]

Despite its manifest bias, the 684-page *History of Spiritualism* was an impressively researched work. The blurb on the dust jacket stressed that the book was aimed at the general reader: 'The story of Modern Spiritualism is here told with such obvious sincerity and is invested with such vibrant interest, that its appeal is by no means confined to professional Spiritualists . . .' Certainly there was profuse detail, about the nature of ectoplasm and how it could be 'moulded by the mind', the reasons some people saw ghosts and others did not, how spirit transmissions were similar to those by wireless, how the war was part of a divine plan and how Armageddon would cleanse and purify the world before the emergence of a utopian state.

As always untroubled by self-doubt, Conan Doyle dismissed critics as 'bumptious and ignorant'. He responded to the 'charge of credulity which is invariably directed by the unreceptive against anyone who forms a positive opinion upon this subject', by asserting that in the course of his long career as an investigator he could not recall a single case where it was clearly shown that he had been mistaken upon any serious point or had 'given a certificate of honesty to a performance which was afterwards proved to be dishonest'. On 19 November 1926 he addressed a spiritualist rally at the Albert Hall in London and once again asked all those present who had definitely been in contact with the dead to stand up. More than half did so. 'It would have rejoiced your heart,' he wrote to Oliver Lodge, adding with his usual tendency to glorify such events: 'Rightly judged I should say it was one of the most remarkable things that ever occurred in London.'[11]

The following month Conan Doyle became peripherally involved in the mysterious disappearance of another famous detective-story writer, Agatha Christie, whose car had been found abandoned with the headlights still burning at Newlands Corner, Surrey, some miles from her home in Sunningdale, Berkshire on the morning of 4 December. The massive police search for her made headlines in all the national newspapers and when no trace had been found after a week, it was widely assumed that she had met her end, either by accident, suicide or even murder. When the chief constable of Surrey approached Conan Doyle for advice, he no doubt assumed the novelist would employ the Sherlockian talents he had demonstrated in the cases of George Edalji and Oscar Slater. Instead, Conan Doyle sought to solve the mystery by psychic means. As early as 1920, in 'A New Light On Old Crimes', in the *Strand*, Conan Doyle had advanced the theory that psychic science should be used by the police: 'It should be possible at every great police-centre to have the call upon the best clairvoyant or other medium that can be got, and to use them freely, for what they are worth. None is infallible. They have their off-days and their failures. No man should ever be convicted upon their evidence. But when it comes to suggesting clues and links, then it might be invaluable.'

Conan Doyle called on the services of Horace Leaf, a medium whose speciality was psychometry, the ability to derive psychic information from physical objects. 'An article worn or handled by an individual,' Leaf explained in *The Psychology and Development of Mediumship*, 'held in the hand of the psychometrist or pressed against the forehead may call up in his mind thoughts, feelings, and even visions related to that individual.' Indeed, when one of Mrs Christie's gloves was placed in Leaf's hand, he immediately produced the name 'Agatha', which Conan Doyle considered to be extremely encouraging, as Leaf had not been told whose glove it was or why he was being asked to examine it. (That the disappearance of Mrs Christie had been on the front pages for a week, perhaps offered a clue.) Leaf went on to claim that there was 'trouble' associated with the glove and that 'the person who owns it is half dazed and half purposeful. She is not dead, as many people think. She is alive. You will hear of her, I think, next Wednesday.'

He proved to be absolutely correct. On the morning of Wednesday, 15 December, every newspaper in Britain carried the sensational story that Agatha Christie had been discovered staying at the Hydropathic Hotel in Harrogate, Yorkshire, where she had checked in under the name of Teresa Neele – her husband had asked for a divorce in order to marry a Nancy Neele, with whom he had fallen in love – and had enjoyed, among other facilities, dancing in the evenings to the music of the 'Happy Hydro Boys'. Agatha Christie never explained why she had chosen to disappear and many theories were propounded, from a sudden loss of memory, to depression on the discovery that her husband had been having an affair, to nothing more than a publicity stunt.

To Conan Doyle, Horace Leaf's predictions were, of course, further endorsements of psychic science. 'The Christie case has afforded an excellent example of the use of psychometry as an aid to the detective,' he wrote in a letter to the *Morning Post*. 'It is, it must be admitted, a power which is elusive and uncertain, but occasionally it is remarkable in its efficiency. It is often used by the French and German police, but if it is ever employed by our own it must be *sub rosa*, for it is difficult for them to call upon the very powers which the law compels them to persecute.'

In June 1927 the last twelve Holmes stories Conan Doyle would ever write were published in a book as *The Casebook of Sherlock Holmes*. In the preface Conan Doyle bade him a dignified farewell: 'I fear that Mr Sherlock Holmes may become like one of those popular tenors who, having outlived their time, are still tempted to make repeated farewell bows to their indulgent audiences. This must cease and he must go the way of all flesh, material or imaginary . . . And so, reader, farewell to Sherlock Holmes! I thank you for your past consistency, and can but hope that some return has been made in the shape of that distraction from the worries of life and stimulating change of thought which can only be found in the fairy kingdom of romance.'

Fairy kingdom! Sherlockians undoubtedly cringed at the term and while they tried to put the best face on the new collection, they could hardly but be disappointed. There were glimpses of his former talent as a storyteller, notably in the intricate plotting in 'The Problem of Thor Bridge', and of the humour that laced his work, such as the famous telegram in 'The Adventure of the Creeping Man' ('Come at once if convenient – if inconvenient come all the same'), but it was abundantly clear that Conan Doyle had lost his touch. Some of the story lines were ludicrous and Holmes's self-confidence and assurance occasionally gave way to asinine philosophising, as in 'The Adventure of the Retired Colourman', where Holmes muses to Watson: 'Is not all life pathetic and futile? Is not his story a microcosm of the whole?

We reach. We grasp. And what is left in our hands at the end? A shadow. Or worse than a shadow – misery.' Conan Doyle confessed to creative fatigue. After finishing the final Sherlock Holmes story, 'The Adventure of Shoscombe Old Place', he wrote to Greenhough Smith: 'It's not the first flight and Sherlock, like his author, grows a little stiff in the joints, but it is the best I can do. Now farewell to him forever.'[12]

'The Adventure of Shoscombe Old Place' appeared in the January 1927 issue of the *Strand* with an appropriate valedictory: 'Sherlock Holmes began his adventures in the very heart of the later Victorian era, carried them all through the all-too-short reign of Edward, and has managed to hold his own little niche even in these feverish days. Thus it would be true to say that those who first read of him as a young man have lived to see their grown up children following the same adventures in the same magazine. It is a sterling example of the patience and loyalty of the British public.'

Punch magazine resorted to verse when reviewing *The Casebook of Sherlock Holmes*, lamenting his departure:

> What though these last adventures show
> No weakening of the magic vigour
> Which centuries (it seems) ago
> Informed that fascinating figure,
> How can we measure them or urge
> Our stricken souls to jubilation
> When every phrase is like a dirge
> Each tale a funeral oration?

Though Conan Doyle always publicly insisted that he thought the final stories withstood comparison with their predecessors, few critics agreed. T. S. Eliot remarked on the great detective's 'mental decay', and P. G. Wodehouse thought that Conan Doyle had simply fallen victim to hubris. The truth was that Sherlock Holmes was facing formidable competition: the twenties marked the beginning of the golden age of modern detective fiction and a new generation of fictional detectives was becoming hugely popular. Dorothy L. Sayers introduced readers to the suave, aristocratic figure of Lord Peter Wimsey; Agatha Christie created the fastidious little Belgian detective Hercule Poirot and the gentle spinster, Miss Marple; and G. K. Chesterton gave them the endearing Father Brown, always preoccupied with the moral and religious aspects of the crimes he was solving. Not to mention Bulldog Drummond, Maigret, Albert Campion, Charlie Chan and many others. As Raymond Chandler would conclude, the tradition of the 'grim logician' and his 'exhausting concatenation of insignificant clues' no longer appealed.[13]

All these dashing newcomers rendered Sherlock Holmes irrelevant, faintly absurd and obsolete, a description that might fairly be applied to his creator. Conan Doyle's increasingly dogmatic views on spiritualism had alienated many of his friends. As he grew older he also grew markedly less tolerant. He was furious when he stayed at the Royal Bath Hotel in Bournemouth and discovered it was half empty while hotels on the French Riviera were reportedly packed with British holidaymakers. He dashed off a letter to the *Daily Express* suggesting that citizens should be forced by law to spend their money at home and that tax 'shirkers' who lived abroad should be deprived of all rights of citizenship.

In the same year *The Casebook of Sherlock Holmes* appeared in the bookshops, Conan Doyle decided, against the advice of friends, to publish transcripts of the messages received from Pheneas. *Pheneas Speaks, Direct Spirit Communications In The Family Circle Reported By Arthur Conan Doyle M.D., LL.D*, published by the Psychic Press, was unquestionably the most ludicrous volume to which he had ever put his name and served only to illustrate the extent to which he was now suffering from self-delusion. In the preface Conan Doyle admitted that 'great excisions' had had to be made in the manuscript, but did not elaborate, presumably for fear of causing widespread public panic, although there was much dark, Old Testament-style foreboding: 'Those who have stood in the way of God's truth are being swept aside. Soon, very soon, the light will be seen in the sky, and great will be the fear. Great also the rejoicing of those who kept their lamps burning [i.e. spiritualists] against the coming of the bridegroom. Tell the people this that they will be forced to realise God and life immortal. The autumn leaves of the world's history have fallen, the winter's frosts are approaching . . .'

Since Conan Doyle sincerely believed that Pheneas's opaque offerings were a matter of world importance, he felt impelled to send copies out to prominent individuals with a covering letter: 'Dear Sir, I venture to send you a copy of "Pheneas Speaks". It is so often stated that other world communications carry no message of importance that I think every leader of public opinion should have the opportunity of judging for himself.' The reaction of most recipients was one of disbelief.

Pheneas Speaks was trounced by the critics. H. G. Wells's savage judgement in the Sunday Express was that Pheneas was a 'platitudinous bore'. He forbore to mince his words: 'This Pheneas, I venture to think, is an imposter, wrought of self-deception, as pathetic as a rag doll which some lonely child has made for its own comfort ... We are told of floods of spiritual light, and, behold! "Pheneas Speaks!" Wonderful prophecies are spoken of. Where are they?' Irritated at being so casually dismissed by a fellow writer, Conan Doyle insisted that many of Pheneas's predictions had, in fact, already been fulfilled, citing the unrest in Russia since the Bolshevik Revolution as one of many examples: 'In spite of all your scientific veneer, you are still in the exact position of the cardinals who jested at Galileo's telescope, even as you jest at our mediums.'

Harry Price, Conan Doyle's nemesis at the Society for Psychical Research, contemptuously dismissed his apocalypse theories: 'The cataclysmic disaster of cosmic magnitude with which Doyle has been trying to make our flesh creep for the past two years still hangs fire and the dawn of 1927 finds us sleeping serenely in our beds, giving little heed to the devastating seismic catastrophe with which – says Sir Arthur – we are threatened by evil spirits on both sides of the veil ... We are now promised a new Armageddon for 1928!'[14]

Even Conan Doyle's dwindling band of supporters were becoming uneasy about his activities. 'I rather regret Doyle's decision, if it is a decision, to set up a Spiritualistic Church in London,' Sir Oliver Lodge wrote, somewhat despairingly, to a friend. 'But I suppose it is a natural outcome of his missionary activity. I suppose he regards himself as a sort of Wesley or Whitefield [two of the founders of Methodism].'[15]

Neither the disparagement of his peers, nor public ridicule, nor abusive letters – one addressed to 'The Devil' found its way to Windlesham – could divert Conan Doyle, yet he was fighting a losing battle. Despite his heroic efforts, spiritualism was in inexorable decline. The Jazz Age, a term coined by the American writer F. Scott Fitzgerald, had arrived and with it the frenzied pursuit of frivolity. American popular culture began to capture the world's imagination and the 'flapper' became a symbol of an age intent on pleasure, anxious to forget the past and happy to ignore the future. Memories of the war were fading; the need to contact departed loved ones was no longer so desperate. Sir Arthur Conan Doyle, the drumbeating prophet of spiritualism, still reasonably fit in his late 60s but increasingly hard of hearing, was beginning to resemble one of the characters from his medieval novels – swashbuckling but bumbling, quaint but irrelevant, and outdated, a dinosaur.

CHAPTER 25

THE FINAL JOURNEY

S CONAN DOYLE APPROACHED HIS seventieth year, he could look back with satisfaction on a life which, as he wrote in *Memories and Adventures*, 'for variety and romance, could . . . hardly be exceeded'. If he was disappointed that the world was not yet ready to embrace spiritualism, he had much else to be thankful for in a material sense: extraordinary success as a writer, wealth, reasonable health, a loving wife and family and a comfortable life at Windlesham.

He still doted on Jean, searching the garden at Windlesham every spring for the first snowdrops which he would bring into the house and present to her to mark the anniversary of their first meeting and sending her adoring little notes whenever they were apart for more than a few hours. From Buckingham Palace Mansions to Windlesham, January 1927: 'Darling, you are always my wonder woman in every way. I really did dream of you last night.' From Buckingham Palace Mansions to Bignell Wood, April 1927: 'Just a word of love, my own sweet girl. I have one hour to get my speech finished and be off so excuse this scrawl. Yours ever, A.' She was as much in love with him. 'After twenty three years of married life,' she wrote in 1930, 'whenever I heard my husband's dear voice in the distance, or he came into the room, something radiant seemed to enter and permeate the atmosphere.'[1]

Although he had been forced to give up cricket, he still enjoyed a daily round at Crowborough Beacon Golf Club, playing nine holes instead of eighteen as a concession to his doctor. He indulged his sons inordinately, buying them a sports car which they raced around the narrow lanes of Crowborough and occasionally crashed, much to the irritation of the neighbours. Conan Doyle paid all the bills and made little attempt to rein them in, although when Adrian was reported for dangerous driving he did threaten to deny him access to the car unless he promised to drive more slowly.

Domestic staff at Windlesham remembered their employer as an amiable individual of mostly gentle disposition. 'He was kind and fair, at times quiet and thoughtful,' Bill Latter, the chauffeur, recalled:

> He could get in a temper if he thought you had disobeyed his orders. He would like to talk to almost anybody, especially if they interested him. Often, if we were driving back from Lewes or Brighton, we would see tramps on the road between Uckfield and Pembury, going from workhouse to workhouse . . . he would get me to stop, then he would get out and ask the tramp if he minded if he walked along with him. They always seemed to agree. He would then tell me to go along and wait for him. In this way he asked the tramps all about their lives, and what had brought them to a life on the road. He seemed to like the idea of their way of freedom. He would give them five bob and then get in the car and we would drive home. Once, when it was very cold and snowy he told me not to wait but to go straight back, and he came home in his socks, having given the tramp his boots.[2]

He also retained his sense of humour. William Foyle, co-founder of the famous bookshop in Charing Cross Road, London, was a frequent visitor to Windlesham, often with his teenage daughter, Christina. When she was fifteen, she asked Conan Doyle if he had ever contacted any famous people during his seances. Conan Doyle agreed that he had and mentioned the name of Oscar Wilde. 'What did he tell you?' she asked. 'That it was very boring being dead!' Conan Doyle replied with a guffaw.

He liked young people and enjoyed their company until the end of his life, but he was quick to anger if any of his own children broke his code of honourable behaviour. 'Father had an iron will,' Adrian recalled, 'that could neither understand nor forgive any deviation from the singular code that was his own.'[3] Yet he was tolerant of youthful high spirits, intrigued by his sons' passion for 'hot jazz', enjoyed being driven by Denis in his sports car at 100 miles an hour and allowed Jean to smoke one cigarette a month from the age of 10. About all he required of his sons was that they should be gentlemen. The only occasions the boys could recall their father losing his temper was when Adrian was rude to a housemaid, and when Denis, at age 16, commented on a train that a woman passenger was ugly. His furious father hit him round the head, and said, 'No woman is ugly. Every woman is beautiful. But some are more beautiful than others.'

He was fascinated by new technology, posing with a radio and headphones for the cover of *Popular Wireless Weekly*. Yet in many ways he remained firmly rooted in the past. He was offended by much of what was happening to society in the 1920s – women smoking in public, for example – and clung determinedly to cherished Victorian values. He was not in the least interested in modern art, thought the post-Impressionists were mad and was among the signatories to a letter demanding the removal of a bas-relief by the sculptor Jacob Epstein from Hyde Park on the basis that it was a piece of 'artistic anarchy'. He was shocked by the General Strike of 1926, regarding socialism as both un-English and undesirable. As a writer, he remained resolutely unimpressed by the Bloomsbury set, and still much preferred Scott and Thackeray to emerging writers like D. H. Lawrence, James Joyce, F. Scott Fitzgerald, Ernest Hemingway or Virginia Woolf, even during the decade which saw the publication of *Lady Chatterley's Lover*, *Ulysses*, *The Great Gatsby*, *A Farewell to Arms* and *To The Lighthouse*. The post-war generation of writers, with their sexual freedom and cynicism about much he held sacred mocked the very foundation of his beliefs.

In 1927 the *Strand* conducted a poll of its leading writers asking which of all the characters of literature they would most liked to have created. H. G. Wells and John Buchan chose Falstaff, Compton Mackenzie Don Quixote and others suggested D'Artagnan, Don Juan and Robinson Crusoe. No one selected Sherlock Holmes, although Greenhough Smith pointed out that Holmes was, without question, the most familiar and widely known character in English fiction and his creation was a 'feat any author might feel proud of'. Conan Doyle's choice was characteristic of him as a writer and a man: he proposed

Thackeray's Colonel Newcome, because he was 'an ideal English gentleman'.

That year Conan Doyle began work on a science-fiction novel, *The Maracot Deep*, in which Professor Maracot sets out to explore the deep ocean floor in a diving bell which breaks its cable and is plunged into a trench several miles deep, where it settles into 'thick elastic ooze'. Maracot and his fellow explorers are eventually rescued by the citizens of the lost world of Atlantis. There they discover that the inhabitants had failed to heed the warnings of reformers, 'grave and earnest men, reasoning and pleading with the people', and had thus been enslaved by an inferior race. Priests led the opposition to the reformers, who were 'scorned and jeered at by those whom they were trying to save', a painfully heavy-handed parallel with those on earth who scorned spiritualism and jeered at its disciples. One critic described it as 'incredibly muddled . . . a hastily written, confusing story that unsuccessfully mixes adventure with Spiritualism'.[4]

While some wondered what a man nearing seventy was doing writing this bizarre nonsense, Conan Doyle had still more flights of science-fiction fancy in his repertoire. He brought back Professor Challenger for two more adventures in 'The Disintegration Machine' and 'When the World Screamed'. In the latter Challenger drills a tunnel into the earth's crust to prove his theory that the planet was a living organism and discovers underneath a 'greyish material, glazed and shiny, which rose and fell in slow palpitation'. When it is harpooned it emits a terrible scream and sets off volcanoes all round the earth. Conan Doyle apparently had few qualms about the quality of his work. When he wrote to Greenhough Smith to tell him he had finished 'When the World Screamed', he added: 'I am not sure it is not the best short story I have ever done.'[5]

Not long afterwards he tried to persuade Greenhough Smith to publish a follow-up to his notorious fairies article, having acquired more photographs from Germany. 'How would it do to have an article "The Fairies Again"?' he asked. 'You had the courage to do the first article that ever treated the matter. This second one would rub in the fact that it was no hoax and that your judgement was right. It would have to be largely quotations from witnesses but I would put it together in an interesting way . . .'[6]

This time the editor demurred, but Conan Doyle pressed ahead with a second edition of *The Coming of the Fairies*, and included the new German photographs in an appendix. More cautious men might have paused for reflection before submitting themselves to further derision, but he was now more than ever convinced of the existence of fairies and claimed to be mystified that there were 'thousands of people who still believe the wild assertion made years ago that the fairy photographs were taken from a well-known advertisement'.

Most of the objections to the Cottingley photographs were 'palpably absurd'. The one which merited closest attention was that they were cleverly cut out figures which had been held up by invisible threads and, while such an explanation was conceivable, he conceded, 'the balance of probability seems to me to be greatly against it'. His book, he claimed, was the 'first serious treatment of what may prove to be a new order of life upon this planet' since *The Secret Commonwealth*, Robert Kirk's seventeenth-century monograph devoted to Celtic fairy lore.

***

In July 1928 Conan Doyle gave evidence for the defence at Westminster Police Court when two spiritualists were prosecuted under the Vagrancy Act of 1824 which stated quaintly that 'every person professing to tell fortunes or using any subtle craft, means or device to deceive and impose on any of His Majesty's subjects shall be deemed a rogue and a vagabond'. Mrs Claire Cantlon, a well-known medium and a member of the London Spiritualist Alliance, had been separately visited by three policewomen in plain clothes posing as clients and subsequently charged with fortune telling. Miss Mercy Phillimore, the secretary of the London Spiritualist Alliance, was charged with aiding and abetting. The three undercover policewomen all gave evidence that Mrs Cantlon's spirit control, a North American Indian by the name of White Chief, was wildly inaccurate in his predictions, and there was some hilarity when one policewoman said that towards the end of the seance White Chief asked the time and said he could only give her ten minutes more. The magistrate, while not doubting the defendants' guilt, dismissed the charges and strongly advised Mrs

Cantlon to get rid of a 'disembodied spirit who wants to know the time when the hour of lunch or tea approaches'.

Despite both women being released, Conan Doyle was incensed that the charges had been brought in the first place. 'That the police should be employed upon such a matter is deplorable,' he wrote in a letter to *The Times* on 26 July 1928, 'especially as their activities take the hateful shape of *agents provocateur* . . .' He took up the matter with the Home Secretary Sir William Joynson-Hicks, but received short shrift and was told there was no hope of changing the law. He refused to accept defeat and mounted a campaign for the repeal of both the Vagrancy Act and the Witchcraft Act, a piece of legislation dating back to James I which he claimed was also being used to persecute mediums.

Conan Doyle wisely steered clear of controversy when, in October 1928, he agreed to be interviewed on camera by Movietone News in the garden at Windlesham, on the condition he would be allowed talk about spiritualism as well as Sherlock Holmes. He was filmed strolling out of the house with his Irish terrier, Paddy, at his heels, then he took off his hat, settled himself in a garden chair and spoke directly to the camera for about twenty minutes in a deep gruff voice, still with a marked Scots accent. It was, in many ways, a faultless performance and his sincerity was evident. He began by saying there were two things people always wanted to know about him, how he came to write Sherlock Holmes and his psychic experiences. Holmes, he said, was a 'monstrous growth from a comparatively small seed . . . The curious thing is how many people there are in the world who are perfectly convinced that he is a living human being. I get letters addressed to him. I get letters asking for his autograph. I get letters addressed to his rather stupid friend, Watson. I've even had ladies writing to say that they'd be very glad to act as his housekeeper . . .'

Turning to the 'psychic matter' he continued in the same genial and confiding tone, explaining that he had had his first experiences at about the time he started writing Holmes stories, in 1886 or 1887, 'so nobody can say that I formed my opinions of psychic matters very hastily'. Since then he had never passed up any opportunity to study the subject. 'People ask me will I write any more Sherlock Holmes stories? I certainly don't think it is at all probable. But as I grow older the psychic subject always grows in intensity, and one becomes more earnest upon it, and I should think that my few remaining years will probably be devoted much more in that direction than in the direction of literature . . .'

On the subject of spiritualism he described himself as a 'gramophone' trying to explain that 'this is not the foolish thing which is so often represented, but that it really is a great philosophy'. It was the war that finally convinced him.

> When all these splendid young fellows were disappearing from our view, the whole world was saying 'Well, what's become of them? Where are they? What are they doing now? Have they dissipated into nothing, or are they still the grand fellows that we used to know?' It was only at that time that I realised the overpowering importance to the human race of knowing more about this matter. Then it was that I flung myself more earnestly into it, and that I felt the highest purpose that I could devote the remainder of my life to was trying to bring across to other people something of that knowledge and assurance which I had acquired myself. Certainly the results have justified me. I'm quite sure I could fill a room of my house with letters that I have received from people telling me of the consolation which my writings on this subject have given to them.

With that he stood up, called the dog, smiled at the camera and said, 'Well, goodbye', then wandered back into the house. As propaganda for spiritualism, it was a tour de force. His critics were deriding him as a sad and deluded old man, but there he was on the screen exuding bonhomie and common sense. Cinemagoers everywhere could hardly fail to be impressed.

In November 1928 Conan Doyle embarked on what he described as a 'journey of psychic research and exposition' to Africa, actually another gruelling lecture tour. A few days out from Southampton, their ship, the RMS *Windsor Castle,* was caught in a fierce storm in the Bay of Biscay and several passengers were badly cut or bruised by the ship's pitching and rolling. While the ladies kept to their cabins, the 69-year-old author could be seen standing at the weather rail, marvelling at the surging sea. In calmer weather further south Conan Doyle lectured separately to all three classes on his psychic experiences, and the children proved adept at deck games. Both boys were in the tug-of-war team, Denis was champion of deck tennis, while Jean was in the final of the deck bowls championship and caused something of a stir by choosing to bowl overarm in the ladies' cricket.

After dropping anchor in Table Bay, off Cape Town, on Monday, 12 November, Conan Doyle was whisked ashore for a radio interview but he would not, in Africa, be received with the same enthusiasm as in the United States, and he reported that the audience of 1,750 at his first formal engagement, a lecture at the City Hall, 'listened with indulgence if not with acquiescence'.[7] The questions were markedly unsympathetic. One man asked why it was, if the other world was so wonderful, that spiritualists didn't precipitate their journey to it by committing suicide and a woman wondered if she would be obliged to endure the same husband in the other world. Conan Doyle assured her that where there was no sympathy between married partners there would be no reunion.

The family remained for two weeks in Cape Town, staying at the venerable Mount Nelson Hotel. Conan Doyle played golf with Denis on the city's main course, but was wisely dissuaded from joining his sons on a climb up Table Mountain. He attended a seance at which the actress Ellen Terry, who had died only three months previously, was manifested, and another in which a female medium said to be controlled by the Italian opera singer Vincenzo Sabatini went into a trance and sang Handel's 'Lascia ch'io pianga' in a fine baritone voice which the music critic Ashton Jonson, who was also present, confirmed was of exceptional quality and undoubtedly male. 'What are we to say of such a performance as that?' Conan Doyle noted. 'I do not readily ascribe things to psychic causes if there can be any normal explanation. Personally, I can see none . . .'[8]

Reaching the capital of the Orange Free State, Bloemfontein, Conan Doyle was able to visit the cricket pavilion in which he had set up a field hospital during the Boer War, almost thirty years earlier. He found it little changed, but the war was still a cause of lingering resentment. At a memorial commemorating the 26,000 women and children who had died in British concentration camps, he was told that the inscription, in Afrikaans, blamed the British for their deaths. He objected loudly. It was a disgraceful assertion, he said; the women and children were being fed even while the British were fighting the men. The incident was widely reported in the local newspapers, one even claiming that Conan Doyle had said the wives and children had no right to a memorial, as a result of which several hundred outraged young Afrikaners gathered outside his hotel threatening violence, though nothing came of it. Conan Doyle subsequently wrote to the *Cape Times* to apologise, explaining that he had misunderstood the inscription.

At another event a heckler accused Conan Doyle of using the death of his own son as propaganda for the spiritualist cause and Conan Doyle had to be restrained from attacking the man with his umbrella. Later, on a big game hunt with his sons, he found another use for it. When the beaters offered to drive a rhinoceros into their line of fire, Conan Doyle suggested distracting the beast by suddenly opening his umbrella to give the boys time to fire. The rhinoceros was not inclined to take advantage of this arrangement and survived.

After stops at Pietermaritzburg, Durban, Pretoria and Johannes-burg, which he described as a 'hellish place',⁹ they went to Rhodesia, now Zimbabwe. Conan Doyle had received a psychic communication in Cape Town that Cecil Rhodes, who died in 1902 and whom he greatly admired as an empire builder, had a message for him, and he was anxious to visit his grave, in the Matopo Hills, not far from Bulawayo. On a fearsomely hot day, they laboured up the winding path to the hilltop grave and found a simple iron slab engraved 'Here lie the remains of Cecil Rhodes', surrounded by a circle of large stones. Conan Doyle first took a series of photographs with a camera with a quartz lens which he had been told had a 'broader psychic radius' than crystal, in the hope that psychic phenomena would appear on the prints. In this, he confessed later, he was 'entirely disappointed'. He then asked his wife to sit with pencil and paper on one of the stones surrounding the grave. At first her gift for automatic writing appeared to have deserted her, but suddenly her hand became 'strongly agitated' and she began scribbling messages from Rhodes. Soon she was able to write replies to her husband's questions, while their bemused Xhosa guide looked on in silence.

Conan Doyle only reported a brief extract of their conversation for fear of appearing immodest, since Rhodes seemed intent, through the good offices of Lady Doyle, on heaping plaudits on her husband:

'Is it really you Mr Rhodes?

'Yes, it is I.'

'It is indeed a privilege to speak with you. Your work on earth was wonderful.'

'No, sir. It can never be as wonderful as religious work – not by many leagues. Religious work is world work. My energies affected only a small area . . . I have been wanting to get in touch with you for I value the effect such teaching will have upon the world's ultimate destiny. Your own burial place will be in the souls and hearts of men. We shall meet anon and what talks we shall have . . .'[10]

He continued in this adulatory vein for some time, somewhat to Conan Doyle's subsequent embarrassment. 'I got a long and very moving message from Rhodes,' he wrote to a friend. 'It was beautiful in parts, but too kindly to my own work to bear much publicity.'[11]

In a letter to Stewart Leckie, his brother-in-law, from the Grand Hotel Bulawayo, Conan Doyle described Rhodesia as a 'great country' and the white population as a 'very cheerful and patriotic crowd'. He prophesied optimistically that in a hundred years Rhodesia would be the 'very finest dominion that flies the British flag'. His attitude to the black majority was paternalistic; he was not in favour of educating them, even though 'they educated very easily', because he felt it would breed discontent.

His poor health had become a constant refrain in letters: 'I have not got my full strength, no golf yet' and 'Nearly well but not yet fit to smoke – the supreme test.' While sightseeing in Victoria Falls, Conan Doyle complained of chest pains and dizzy spells, but there was to be no respite in their schedule, despite the heat and the strain of constant travelling. He lectured to packed audiences in what was then North and South Rhodesia, and Uganda, Tanganyika and Kenya before sailing for home from Mombasa on the east coast of Africa. The party left behind them a trail of more than 2,000 books and pamphlets.

A tour of mixed success concluded with an embarrassing incident during Conan Doyle's last lecture in Nairobi when he showed a photograph taken of a ghost at a country house in Somerset and the 'ghost' turned out to be sitting in the audience. Arthur Spencer Palmer, a British dental surgeon working in Nairobi, was astonished to see a picture of himself covered in a gauze sheet flashed up on the screen as one of the 'spirit photographs'. He immediately stood up and called out, 'I am that ghost!' Lady Conan Doyle, sitting on the stage with her husband, could hardly conceal her fury at this undignified interruption, but Conan Doyle invited Spencer Palmer on the platform. He explained precisely how, where and when it had been taken by his brother years earlier as a student prank, and since, in the picture, the dentist's features were discernible under the sheet, Conan Doyle had little choice but to accept it was a fake and promise to withdraw it. He would later complain bitterly about psychic research being hampered by 'irresponsible buffoonery', perhaps because of the extensive and inconvenient publicity such an incident generated.[12]

Despite not feeling particularly well on the homeward bound voyage, Conan Doyle delivered a lecture on the ship to a large audience of passengers – mainly colonial officials, planters and their families returning home – and another to members of the crew. At Suez they had time to motor a hundred miles across the desert to visit the pyramids before passing through the canal and into the Mediterranean. They disembarked in Marseilles and travelled overland through France to the English Channel and home. 'We come back,' he wrote, 'stronger in health, more earnest in our beliefs, more eager to fight once more in the greatest of all causes, the regeneration of religion and of the restoration of that direct and practical spiritual element which is the one and only antidote to Spiritualism.'[13]

The trip resulted in another book, *Our African Winter*, and another long and extravagant polemic: 'I see more clearly that this revelation is the most important that mankind has ever had and that we who are spreading it are doing the most vital work that is done in the world today . . .' It was not published in the United States, as George Doran explained in a letter to his agent, A. P. Watt: 'Our Winter in

Africa [*sic*] gives us two very difficult problems. In the first place, the political and economic questions of Africa concern America little or not at all. Secondly, we can do almost nothing with Sir Arthur's psychic books . . .'[14] Doran's view was that Conan Doyle's other books would be 'disadvantaged' by the publication of yet another psychic tome.

The family recuperated from the trip in the peace and quiet of Bignell Wood, which had been modernised and extended, and where Conan Doyle celebrated his 70th birthday on 22 May 1929. Some locals were suspicious of the Conan Doyles and gossiped about the house being used for mysterious spiritualist rituals. It was well known that 'life-size' pottery gnomes were dotted around the garden to encourage fairies out of the woods. The gardener's 8-year-old daughter was occasionally persuaded to sit on the stump of an old tree, on the forest side of the garden gate, while Conan Doyle played ethereal music on a portable gramophone and waited with a camera, poised to capture images of the elusive sprites the moment they appeared.

Everyone rallied round, however, when in August 1929, the house caught fire. Conan Doyle returned from his morning stroll to see flames leaping from the roof of the 200-year-old house. The alarm had been raised by the head gardener after sparks from the kitchen range had set light to the thatch. It took half an hour for the fire brigade to arrive from Southampton by which time local villagers were helping the family and staff to retrieve what they could. 'Luckily this is only my country home and not my headquarters,' Conan Doyle told a reporter from *The Times* afterwards, 'so that such valuable things as my library were not endangered. We have saved a great deal, but I regret that my son Denis has lost the collection of photographs and skins brought back by him from many parts of the world which he visited with me when on my lecturing tours. He was so unselfish that he did not think for a moment of saving his own collection, but busied himself assisting to save other property.' Conan Doyle also wrote to the local newspaper to thank the villagers for their help in dragging furniture and valuables onto the lawn. 'One or two, I regret to say,' he added, with a flash of his old wit, 'showed a disposition to remove the goods even further, but the greater number gave me invaluable assistance.' After the fire Lady Conan Doyle received a message asserting that a 'bad psychic cloud' had infected parts of the property and that it needed to be cleansed, leading her husband to conclude that the incident was the work of psychic forces.

A few weeks later, Conan Doyle and his wife were invited to spend the weekend with Barrie, by then Sir James Barrie, one of a dwindling number of literary friends. Every summer Barrie took a large house near Cheltenham, Stanway Court, to entertain friends but was apprehensive Conan Doyle would bore the other guests by preaching spiritualism. While Conan Doyle did raise the subject, it did not dampen spirits, and the main entertainment of the evening was flicking moistened stamps onto the library ceiling with coins. In his diary, Conan Doyle made notes of the conversation at dinner, during which Barrie complained that George Bernard Shaw's plays were all about 'town councillors and sanitation'. 'Barrie said Shaw gets up every morning and cries out, "Hurrah! I am Shaw." He [Barrie] said he was out of touch and sympathy with the present generation of writers. They were too sexual. At the same time we had to stand aside and see what the youngsters could do. It was a pity women took the same line. He thought well of [D. H.] Lawrence, of a new man called [John Cowper] Powys, and of Lacon Watson.'[15]

Even now Conan Doyle still smarted over the way his literary reputation had been dominated by one character. The four Holmes novels had been published in a single volume that year and were enthusiastically reviewed by Hesketh Pearson in *G.K.'s Weekly*. A few days later Pearson received a letter from Conan Doyle thanking him for the review but going on to say how he sometimes hated Holmes and wished he had never created him because his popularity had prevented 'a proper appreciation' of his more serious work, although he did concede that he had 'much to be thankful for'.

Conan Doyle's Psychic Press – now one of the most significant dents to his literary reputation – continued to churn out a stream of sixpenny pamphlets written by the proprietor, ramming home his message. He could still frequently be found in his bookshop, although the years were taking their toll. Reginald Pound, a future editor of the *Strand*, never forgot his disappointment when he finally met the man who had set his imagination alight as a boy:

> Meeting him, then, I had expected an heroic hospitality of heart and mind. He disclosed himself as petulant and patronising. His attitude was that of a man who considers it perverseness which challenges his opinions. I did not challenge them because I was not primarily interested in his Spiritualistic activities, but his way of describing the various objects in his museum was distinctly of the take-it-or-leave-it order. Besides, his handshake lacked warmth and his greeting was perfunctory. Of course, he may very well have been weary by that time of meeting anyone new. I remember the shortness of his arms. I remember the grizzled old-campaigner moustache enclosing his mouth and much of his chin. I remember the lifeless look in his eyes, as if disillusion had clouded his vision of things.[16]

In October 1929 Conan Doyle set forth on yet another lecture tour, this time to Holland, Denmark, Sweden and Norway. His ambition, he told a friend, was to lecture in every non-Catholic capital in Europe, but his health was rapidly deteriorating. 'Twelve years of our lives have now been spent in trying to impart our knowledge to others in the course of which we have travelled 75,000 miles and we have addressed a quarter of a million people,' he wrote to John Lamond. 'The work has now been too much for me. It has weakened my heart and I am temporarily disabled . . .'[17]

In Copenhagen he was crippled by agonising chest pains, yet refused to cut short the tour and battled on in more or less constant pain. Returning to England in early November, he had to be carried ashore from the cross-channel ferry at Dover by two sailors and was wheeled from Victoria Station to his flat in Buckingham Palace Mansions in a bath chair. His doctor diagnosed angina pectoris and advised him to rest, but Conan Doyle explained that he had two engagements the following day, Armistice Sunday, to speak in the morning to a spiritualist assembly at the Royal Albert Hall and in the evening at the Queen's Hall. His doctor warned him he would be putting his life at risk and that he could not be held responsible. As a doctor himself, Conan Doyle knew the implications of the diagnosis, that angina was caused by coronary heart disease, but decided to go on anyway. In the taxi on the way to the Albert Hall he suffered another violent attack and had to be helped into the hall, leaning heavily on Denis and Adrian, and received treatment before going onto the stage. Unsteady on his feet, clinging to the lectern for balance, he nevertheless managed to struggle through both engagements.

Back at Windlesham his doctor now ordered complete bed rest, but he insisted on dealing with his correspondence and dictated letters to the faithful Woodie from his sickbed. His daughter Mary recalled that he stayed alert and active mentally. 'He took up painting and wanted to learn something of music, became interested in the reincarnation theory and wrote an article on it. He often spoke to me of passing over, and told me one of the things he was looking forward to in the future life was time to cultivate friendships. He still talked Spiritualism to everyone he met, and would get slightly irritated with those who professed an "open mind". He would say: "Their minds are so open everything falls out of them."'[18]

Early in the New Year he summoned sufficient energy for one last fight with the Society for Psychical Research. The January 1930 issue of its *Journal* carried a critical review of a book called *Modern Psychic Mysteries*, which included a description of a series of seances held at the medieval Millesimo Castle in Italy, the home of the Marquis Centurione Scotto, who had turned to spiritualism after losing a son in an aeroplane accident. The reviewer, the SPR librarian Theodore Besterman, complained that the marquis had taken no precautions against fraud and suggested that the author, Ernesto Bozzano, had been duped. For Conan Doyle, who had been highly critical of the society in his *History of Spiritualism*, this was too much. He had long believed that it fostered an antagonistic and destructive attitude towards mediums and wrote a letter lodging a formal complaint over the 'insolence', 'gratuitous offensiveness' and 'insulting innuendos' contained in the Besterman review and asserting that the Marquis Scotto, with whom he was acquainted, was conducting psychical research 'at the very highest level'. It was ludicrous to imagine, he said, that 'an Italian nobleman, a member of the legislative body, has invited a circle of friends to his home to practise a succession of complicated frauds on them'.

But the society refused to back down. In a formal statement it pointed out that it had always been committed to a critical and even-handed investigation of psychic phenomena and that had the seances at Millesimo Castle been conducted in a scientific manner they would not have been subjected to censure: 'It is, however, to be noted that sittings held in complete darkness, for the most part without control and without any searching of those present, sittings at which phenomena were produced which cannot be paralleled in the records of any sittings held under good conditions, are described by Sir Arthur as "on the very highest possible level of psychical research". Further comment is superfluous.'

Conan Doyle was left with no option but to resign. In his resignation letter he warned he would be making 'some sort of public protest against the essentially unscientific and biased work of a Society which has for a whole generation produced no constructive work of any kind, but has confined its energies to the misrepresentation and hindrance of those who have really worked at the most important problem ever presented to mankind'.[19] It took the form of an intemperate circular distributed to other members, complaining that the society had become an anti-spiritualist organisation: 'Everything which tends to prove the truth of that cult, no matter how honourable or sane the source may be, is assailed by suppression, misrepresentation and every sort of unreasonable and vicious opposition . . . I have waited long in the hope of some reform but I have now concluded that it is not to be expected and that the influence of the Society is entirely for evil.'[20] Conan Doyle called on other members to join him, but if he was expecting mass resignations in sympathy with his own, he was disappointed. Only six members followed his example.

Despite the stress of this battle Conan Doyle's health improved during the early months of 1930. He updated his autobiography and wrote the introduction to his arcane collection of spiritualist essays, *The Edge of the Unknown*. 'One cannot help feeling admiration,' the *Journal of the Society for Psychical Research* noted in its review, 'for the persistence with which Sir Arthur continued to advocate the most hopeless causes.'

As a committed spiritualist he was, of course, serene before the looming prospect of death. 'There is a chance that I may talk it over with Houdini himself before very long,' he wrote to a friend in the United States. 'I view the prospect with perfect equanimity. That is one thing that psychic knowledge does. It removes all fear of the future.'[21]

One afternoon at Windlesham he completed a small pen-and-ink cartoon very much in the style of his father's work in which he depicted himself as an old workhorse pulling a heavy cart, piled high with neatly labelled bundles of his life's work – books, travels, campaigns, lectures and sporting interests – '500 Lectures' teeters above possibly the heaviest load of all 'Sherlock Holmes'. The horse and cart have travelled a winding road from Edinburgh in 1859 to his sickbed at Windlesham in 1930. Three top-hatted vets, discussing its condition, reach the conclusion that the horse has 'pulled a heavy load a long way, but he is well cared for and with six weeks' stable and six months' grass he will be on the road once more'. It proved to be an optimistic assessment.

On 1 July Conan Doyle gathered sufficient strength for a trip to London, to lead a deputation to the Home Secretary John R. Clynes to lobby for the reform of the Witchcraft Act and the Vagrancy Act. He presented a pitiful sight, hobbling along Whitehall, leaning heavily on his wife. When the deputation was ushered into the Home Secretary's office and Conan Doyle struggled to rise to his feet to present his case, a concerned Clynes said 'Pray sit down, Sir Arthur.' Fighting for breath, with his wife at his side proffering a bottle of smelling salts, Conan Doyle began, 'I beg you to stop the persecution of our religion . . .' He insisted on finishing his prepared speech, urging the repeal of these antiquated statutes and demanding legal protection for mediums.

The strain was too much. He returned to Windlesham with some difficulty and would never leave again. He now needed frequent doses of oxygen and his condition steadily deteriorated. Attempts were made to contact Mary to warn her that her father was dying but it proved impossible. For two days and nights his wife sat by his bedside. At two o'clock on the morning of 7 July Denis and Adrian were sent to a hospital in Tunbridge Wells to fetch more oxygen. At half-past seven Conan Doyle said he wanted to get out of bed to look out over the Sussex countryside. They wrapped him into a dressing gown and sat him in a big basket chair by the window. 'There ought to be a medal struck for you,' he whispered to Jean, who was stroking his brow, 'inscribed "to the best of all nurses".' Two hours later, with Jean and their three children by his side, he died, aged 71. According to Lady Conan Doyle, his last words to her were: 'You are wonderful.'

EPILOGUE

IN THE DAYS FOLLOWING THE death of Sir Arthur Conan Doyle, 620 letters of condolence and 83 telegrams arrived at Windlesham.

'Sir Arthur Conan Doyle sets before us an example which must inspire all the best in us. It is by knowing great men and learning to love and admire them that we can shape our own characters. Conan Doyle stands out as an example to all men of activity, intelligence and noble thought.' General Sir Hubert Gough, GCB, GCMG, KCVO (Commander in Chief, Fifth Army, 1916–18)

'Conan Doyle was one of the best men I have ever known. There can never have been a more honourable.' Sir James Barrie

'His passing from this earth leaves a very great gap. It is of him as a man, even above all his triumphs of the pen, that we feel his going most.' Lord Gorell, Chairman of the Society of Authors

'Though Sir Arthur's fame as a writer is secure, he will be remembered no less as a defender of the defenceless.' R. Hodder Williams, publisher

'Literature has lost a great figure. The Strand is proud that it was the means of bringing Sir Arthur's genius to an appreciative world.' Sir Frank Newnes, proprietor, *Strand* magazine

'One of the most fearless and honest men that I ever knew. His friendship was a precious jewel.' H. E. Gwynne, editor of the *Morning Post*

'The recollection I cherish is of the impression of courteous strength and the tremendous loyalty that made him the pattern of modern knight-errantry. He was indeed a very gentle knight.' Francis Hiley, artist and illustrator

'Only a big man, big of brain, big of heart, big of human understanding could have written such a letter to a lifer in prison.' A convict serving a life sentence in Sing Sing prison

'Big-bodied, big-brained, big-hearted Conan Doyle.' Jerome K. Jerome

'Just as a headland juts out dominatingly into the sea, dwarfing its immediate surroundings, so does Conan Doyle stand out in my memory as a very headland of honesty and helpfulness to others, among some of us, his contemporaries, with our small insincerities, our small mean-nesses and our small self-seekings.' Coulson Kernahan, novelist

'How thankful we were to receive them [the swimming collars] on the destroyer I was serving in. I know only too well many a poor sailor thanks you, although he didn't know it was you he was blessing.' Able Seaman L. Micham, served on a destroyer in 1915

'His methods are not mine, he regarded himself as a missionary, a trustee of a great truth which he felt bound to share with others, whether they would receive it or whether they would reject and ridicule it, but one cannot but admire the completeness and self-sacrificing character of his life and doctrines. Occasionally, I think, he lacked the wisdom of the serpent, but the goodness of his motives must be manifest to all.' Sir Oliver Lodge

———◆———

Three hundred people – family, friends and fellow spiritualists – attended the funeral, held on 11 July, in the rose garden at Windlesham, where the oak coffin rested on trestles on the lawn. The family had let it be known that there should be no mourning, rather a celebration. None of the blinds in the house was drawn and the ceremony was conducted on a gloriously sunny day in a cheerful garden-party atmosphere with most of those present wearing everyday clothes. Mary Conan Doyle accompanied hymns on the piano and the 121st Psalm was read ('I will lift up mine eyes unto the hills from whence cometh my help . . .'), with some of Conan Doyle's favourite biblical quotations. Then Lady Conan Doyle, in a grey chiffon summer dress with a crimson rose pinned to the shoulder, read the tribute she had written herself: 'God bless him for his beautiful and unselfish life, for his courage and fearlessness, for his never failing championship of those suffering injustice, and for the help he gave to those in sorrow. No man more truly walked in his Master's footsteps . . .'

The gathering followed the coffin across the tennis court and down a garden path to the graveside, close to the rough-hewn garden hut where Conan Doyle often worked. Inside, his chair was drawn up to his desk and a notepad still bore the indentations of his last written words. Flowers sent in his memory covered the grass all around. As the coffin, decked in red roses, was lowered slowly into the ground, Lady Conan Doyle stepped forward and dropped a single red rose into the grave. The moment was almost too much and she looked close to fainting; Adrian stepped forward to support her. Later she assured friends that her husband would stay in touch with those he loved: 'We know that it is only the natural body that we are committing to the ground. The etheric body, or as Saint Paul said, the spiritual, is the exact duplicate and lives on and is able, when the psychic conditions are attuned to the spiritual, even to show itself to earthly eyes.'

Two days later, on the evening of Sunday, 13 July, a memorial service was held at the Albert Hall in London, organised by the Marylebone Spiritualist Association. Long before the service was due to begin at seven o'clock the hall was packed and throngs of people, many in evening dress, milled outside. Not all were friends or fellow spiritualists – a rumour had spread that Sir Arthur might make an appearance, in voice or perhaps even in body, and it was an event no one wanted to miss. Newspapers the following day would estimate that 10,000 people were present, almost twice the capacity of the hall.

A row of chairs was lined up on the flower-filled stage and propped on the seat of the centre chair was a large card bearing the name 'Sir Arthur Conan Doyle'. By the time the family appeared, Denis and Adrian in tail suits and carrying top hats, Lady Conan Doyle, Mary and daughter Jean in formal evening dresses, it was standing room only within the great concert hall and there were still many stranded outside. Lady Conan Doyle took the seat to the left of the chair reserved for her late husband, the place she had faithfully occupied at countless spiritualist rallies around the world for more than a decade.

George Craze, chairman of the Marylebone Spiritualist Association, opened proceedings, welcomed those present and read a statement from Lady Conan Doyle: 'At every meeting all over the world I have sat at my beloved husband's side, and at this great meeting to which people have come with respect and loving thoughts to do him honour, his chair is placed here, as I know that in psychic presence, he will be next to me, although our earthly eyes cannot perceive beyond the earth-obvious. Only those with the God-given extra sight, called clair-voyance, will be able to see his beloved form in our midst. I want in my children's name and my own and my husband's to thank you all from my heart for the love for him which brought you here tonight.'

After a hymn, an invocation by the Reverend C. D. Drayton Thomas, a two-minute silence and the recitation of the Lord's Prayer, friends and colleagues stepped up to offer their memories. They spoke of his great qualities as a spiritual leader, his devotion to the cause, the sacrifices he and Lady Conan Doyle had made in travelling to the ends of the earth to deliver their message, the labour expended writing letters of condolence to thousands of bereaved people. He had suffered for his beliefs, receiving venomous letters and attracting derision, but in assuming leadership of the movement he felt he was answering a call from heaven.

One speaker made the audience laugh with a jocular tale about Sir Arthur's love of cricket; another reduced many to tears when he suddenly looked upwards, raised his hands and cried: 'We thank you! God bless you, Doyle!' Fellow spiritualist Ernest Hunt referred to the rumours that Conan Doyle would be materialised during the course of the evening. Pointing at the vacant chair, he said: 'It would be a very trifling thing if any people here with hectic imagination were to persuade themselves imaginatively that they could see Sir Arthur's form there . . . But it would be a great thing for you to see in the vacant chair a symbol of God's call to you to qualify for being Doyle's successors.' Sir Oliver Lodge could not attend but sent a stirring message: 'Our great-hearted champion will still be continuing his campaign on the Other Side with added wisdom and knowledge. *Sursam corda!* [Lift up your hearts!]'

The tributes ended with an organ voluntary and a collection for the spiritualist movement. Then Craze returned to the microphone and generated a ripple of excited murmurs through the audience with an announcement: 'This evening we are going to make a very daring experiment with the courage implanted in us by our late leader. We have with us a spirit sensitive who is going to try and give impressions from this platform. One reason why we hesitate to do it in such a colossal meeting as this is that it is a terrific strain on the sensitive. In an assembly of ten thousand people a tremendous force is centred upon the medium. Tonight, Mrs Roberts will try to describe some particular friends, but it will be the first time this has been attempted in such a tremendous gathering. You can help with your vibrations as you sing the next hymn, "Open My Eyes".'

As the final notes of the mystical hymn died away, Estelle Roberts stepped up to the microphone wearing a long black dress with a white collar and a bouquet of roses pinned to the shoulder. Then 41 years old, she was one of the best-known mediums in London and a favourite of Conan Doyle. The audience waited expectantly as she stood for a moment or two with her arms outstretched, communing with the other world. 'There are vast numbers of spirits here with us,' she said eventually, 'they are pushing me like anything.' Later in the performance, she would stagger about the stage, as if being jostled by invisible forces. 'All right,' she snapped at thin air. '*All right!*' Shielding her eyes from the lights, she began pointing at members of the audience: 'There is a gentleman over there with hardly any hair. Yes, there! That's right. I see standing there in front of you a spirit form of a young soldier. He looks to be about 24, in khaki uniform. Upright. Well built. Broad. Mouth droops a little at the corners. He passed suddenly. He gives me 1916 as the year of his passing. He calls you Uncle, Uncle Fred. Is that correct?' Each time she rapped out 'Is that correct?', she received a nod or a wave of assent.

After half an hour of this, some members of the audience were restless; they had not come for a public demonstration of clairvoyance but to see the still conspicuously empty seat occupied. A few people got up to leave. 'I am afraid I cannot go on with people walking in and out,' Mrs Roberts complained. When her words had no discernable effect on the increasing numbers heading for the exit, she suddenly stopped them in their tracks by shouting, 'He's here!' There could be no doubt who she meant: everyone switched their attention to the empty chair and Lady Conan Doyle jumped to her feet, eyes sparkling. The medium appeared to be following with her eyes an invisible figure moving towards her. 'He's wearing evening clothes,' she said, inclining her head as if to listen to something being said very quietly. Only those sitting nearby overheard the exchange that followed. 'Sir Arthur tells me that one of you went into the hut this morning. Is that correct?' Lady Conan Doyle, beaming, agreed it was so. 'I have a message for you,' the medium said. At this point someone signalled for the organist to strike up. Estelle Roberts could be seen whispering urgently to Lady Conan Doyle, who was smiling and nodding, for several minutes. She was still smiling broadly as the service broke up with a closing hymn and benediction.

After the service, Mrs Roberts, still in a highly nervous state, spoke to reporters and claimed she had first seen Sir Arthur 'in a flash' during the two-minute silence, that he had walked across the stage and taken a seat in the chair reserved for him, from where he later silently encouraged her clairvoyance. 'I received a message from Sir Arthur Conan Doyle and I gave it to the family,' she said. 'It was a message to Lady Conan Doyle and her family, especially to one of them. I shall not divulge more. It was a perfectly happy message.'

'I am perfectly convinced,' Lady Conan Doyle confirmed, 'that the message is from my husband. I am as sure of the fact that he has been here with us as I am sure that I am speaking to you. It is a happy message, one that is cheering and encouraging. It is precious and sacred. You will understand that it was secret to me.'

She never revealed its nature.

———◆———

CHRONOLOGY

———————

1859 Arthur Conan Doyle born, 22 May
1868 Enrols at Hodder preparatory school
1870 Enters Stonyhurst College
1875 Passes matriculation exam with honours, spends a year at
      Feldkirch
1876 Enrols at University of Edinburgh Medical School, meets
      Joseph Bell, inspiration for Sherlock Holmes
1879 Early stories published anonymously
1880 Signs on to Arctic whaler as ship's surgeon
1881 Graduates as doctor; his father Charles Altamont Doyle sent
      to Blairerno
1882 Joins practice of friend George Budd in Plymouth, then
      moves to Portsmouth and establishes own practice in
      Southsea
1885 Marries Louise (Touie) Hawkins
1887 *A Study in Scarlet*, first Sherlock Holmes novel, published
1889 Daughter Mary Louise born, 28 January; *The Sign of Four* and
      Micah Clarke published
1891 First Sherlock Holmes stories appear in *Strand* magazine;
      abandons medicine for full-time career as writer
1892 Son Kingsley born, 15 November; Holmes 'dies' at Reichenbach
      Falls
1893 Father dies, 10 October; Touie diagnosed with tuberculosis
1896 War correspondent in Egypt; publishes *Brigadier Gerard* and
      Rodney Stone
1897 Meets, and falls in love with, Jean Leckie
1900 Serves in field hospital in South Africa during Boer War

1901   *The Hound of the Baskervilles* published; Queen Victoria dies

1902   Knighted

1903   Second Holmes series begins in *Strand*

1906   Fights to clear name of George Edalji; Touie dies, 4 July.

1907   Marries Jean Leckie

1909   Son Denis born, 17 March

1910   Son Adrian born, 19 November; takes up case of Oscar Slater

1912   Daughter Jean born, 21 December; *The Lost World* published

1914   Outbreak of First World War; forms local volunteer force

1915   Begins six-volume history of the war

1916   Visits fronts in France and Italy

1918   Kingsley dies, 28 October

1919   Brother Innes dies, 19 February; begins worldwide crusade to promote spiritualism

1920   Tours Australia; his mother Mary Josephine Doyle dies, 30 December

1922   Lecture tour of United States; publishes *Coming of the Fairies*

1923   Second lecture tour of the United States and Canada

1926   *History of Spiritualism* published

1927   *Pheneas Speaks* published

1928   Tours South Africa promoting spiritualism

1930   Dies, 7 July, at Windlesham

NOTES

NSOURCED QUOTATIONS ARE TAKEN FROM Conan Doyle's less-than-reliable autobiography, *Memories and Adventures*, published in 1924. Just as he was unbothered by inconsistencies in the Sherlock Holmes stories, he did not trouble to check dates and details for his autobiography. Where I am aware of mistakes, I have noted them. Extracts from Conan Doyle's letters, diaries and journals and other family correspondence are used with the kind permission of Charles Foley, the executor of his estate.

Abbreviations used below

ACD = Arthur Conan Doyle
BL = British Library
RCS = Royal College of Surgeons
RLG Archive = Richard Lancelyn Green Archive, City of Portsmouth
SML = *Stark Munro Letters*
SPR = Society for Psychical Research

Sources cited by surname, and initials and titles where needed. For full information see Select Bibliography.

Chapter 1
1. G. M. Trevelyan (ed.), *The Seven Years of William IV: A Reign Cartooned by John Doyle* (London: William Heinemann, 1952)
2. RLG Archive
3. G. Doyle

4. *Dictionary of National Biography*
5. G. Doyle
6. Letter to Dr James Rutherford at Crichton Royal Asylum, 3 December 1892
7. Dr Allan Beveridge, *Journal of Royal College of Physicians*, September 2006
8. Ibid.

Chapter 2

1. Stevenson, 'Edinburgh: Picturesque Notes'
2. *SML*
3. Ibid.
4. RLG Archive
5. Conan Doyle's essay in 'My First Book VI – Juvenilia', *Idler*, January 1893, Vol. 2. This essay so impressed Robert Louis Stevenson that he submitted his own article on *Treasure Island*
6. *Memories*
7. RLG Archive
8. ACD interviewed by the *New York World*, 27 July 1907
9. RLG Archive
10. *Strand*, September 1909
11. RLG Archive
12. Ibid.

Chapter 3

1. Carr
2. Clement Bryse Gunn, *Leaves from the Life of a Country Doctor* (Edinburgh: Moray Press, 1935)
3. H. E. Jones
4. RLG Archive
5. Edward W. Harnargel, 'Joseph Bell MD – the Real Sherlock Holmes', *New England Journal of Medicine*, 5 June 1958
6. RCS, Edinburgh
7. In 1942 *Blackwood's* handed an archive to the National Library of Scotland and the manuscript was discovered among works and correspondence from some of the greatest names in literature, including George Eliot, Anthony Trollope and Henry James. ACD's daughter, Jean, vetoed publication for fear it would damage her father's reputation and only after her death was it finally brought to light in a limited edition published by the Arthur Conan Doyle Society. It begins: 'Looking back now at the events of my life that one dreadful night looms out like

some great landmark. Even now, after the lapse of so many years, I cannot think of it without a shudder. All minor incidents and events I mentally classify as occurring before or after the time when I saw a ghost . . .' The story has intimations of the future, as the narrator, Jack, has manifest touches of Watson and his friend, Tim Hulton, with 'his strange speculative way of thinking', could be the forerunner of Holmes.

8. *New York World*, 28 July 1907
9. D. Marinus, *Experiences and Some Reflections of a Medical Practitioner* (1928)

Chapter 4

1. ACD, 'On the Slave Coast with a Camera', *British Journal of Photography*, 7 April 1882
2. Ibid.
3. Gibson and Green, *Essays on Photography*
4. National Library of Scotland
5. Lellenberg, Stashower and Foley (eds), *Arthur Conan Doyle: A Life in Letters*
6. *SML*
7. *SML*
8. *SML*
9. *SML*

Chapter 5

1. *SML*
2. *SML*
3. Conan Doyle Estate
4. Letters to Mrs Charlotte Thwaites Drummond, Hinch Collection, University of Minnesota
5. *SML*
6. *Idler*, January 1893
7. Speech at the Author's Club, July 1896
8. *Westminster Gazette*, 13 December 1900
9. RLG Archive

Chapter 6

1. Edgar Allan Poe, 'Murders in the Rue Morgue', *Graham's Magazine*, 1841
2. ACD, *A Study in Scarlet*
3. ACD, *Through the Magic Door*
4. *Scotsman*, 19 December 1887
5. National Library of Scotland
6. Ibid.

7. Ibid.

8. *Parish Magazine*, August 1994

Chapter 7

1. *World, A Journal for Men and Women*, 3 August 1892

2. RLG Archive

3. 'Index to the Periodical Literature of the World', *Review of Reviews* (1893)

4. *Strand*, December 1930

Chapter 8

1. Leslie G. Klinger, *The Annotated Sherlock Holmes* (New York: W. W. Norton, 2006)

2. RLG Archive

3. BL

4. G. K. Chesterton papers, British Library

5. RCS, Edinburgh

6. Smith, *Authors*

7. Stoker

8. Jerome

9. Ibid.

10. Barrie

11. Hocking

12. Beveridge

13. *New York World*, 27 July 1907

Chapter 9

1. Speech at the Author's Club, July 1896

2. RLG Archive

3. *Strand*, December 1894

4. *Strand*, September 1909

5. *English Literature in Translation 1880–1920*, Vol. 33, I, 1990

6. Stoker

7. *Cincinnati Commercial Gazette*, 10 June 1894

8. Pond

9. *New York Times*, 3 October 1894

10. *Ladies Home Journal*, 12 March 1895

11. Pond

12. *New York Times*, 3 October 1894

13. *Union & Advertiser*, Rochester, New York, 21 November 1894

14. Pond

15. Toronto Public Library
16. Samuel S. McClure, *My Autobiography* (New York: 1914)

Chapter 10
1. *Strand*, September 1909
2. Toronto Public Library
3. G. Doyle
4. Ibid.
5. Ibid.
6. *Saturday Review*, 26 December 1896
7. *Saturday Review*, 2 January 1897
8. Stoker

Chapter 11
1. G. Doyle
2. RLG Archive
3. Toronto Public Library
4. Thompson
5. Smith, *Authors*
6. RLG Archives
7. Toronto Public Library
8. *Literature*, 1 April 1899
9. *Quarterly Review*, July 1904

Chapter 12
1. *The Times*, 18 December 1899
2. *The Times*, 22 February 1900
3. *Friend* (Bloemfontein: 4 April 1900)
4. Menpes
5. ACD, *Boer War*
6. *British Medical Journal*, 7 July 1900
7. Nevinson

Chapter 13
1. RLG Archive
2. Ibid.
3. *Scotsman*, 16 October 1900
4. National Library of Scotland
5. *Westminster Gazette*, 12 November 1900
6. Letter to *Glasgow Evening News*, 19 December 1900

7. *Grocers' Assistant*, January 1901
8. *New York World*, 2 February 1901
9. *The Times*, 5 September 1901
10. RLG Archive
11. RLG Archive

Chapter 14

1. G. Doyle
2. Toronto Public Library
3. RLG Archive
4. Toronto Public Library
5. Toronto Public Library
6. G. Doyle
7. Letter to *The Times*, 12 April 1906
8. *Victoria Club Magazine*, 2 July 1903
9. *Motor Cycle*, 27 February 1905
10. Letter to Greenhough Smith, 14 May 1903, Toronto Public Library
11. Toronto Public Library
12. RLG Archive
13. *Bookman*, January 1907
14. G. Doyle
15. Ibid.
16. Ibid.

Chapter 15

1. Home Office File 989, Part 2, National Archives
2. Home Office File 990
3. *Daily Telegraph*, 11 January 1907
4. Home Office File 989, Part 2
5. Ibid.
6. Ibid.
7. RLG Archive
8. Home Office File 989

Chapter 16

1. BL
2. G. Doyle
3. Ibid.
4. BL
5. BL

6. ACD, Letter to US newspaper editor
7. *Bookman*, November 1912
8. RLG Archive
9. Morel, Introduction
10. RLG Archive
11. *Referee*, September 1910
12. *Strand*, September 1909
13. BL
14. ACD, *The Case of Oscar Slater*
15. Ibid.
16. Mitchell Library, Glasgow
17. Ibid.
18. Ibid.
19. Ibid.
20. Ibid.

Chapter 17
1. Toronto Public Library
2. RLG Archive
3. Ibid. French boxing prodigy Georges Carpentier knocked out the British challenger, Billy Wells, to win the European heavyweight title in June 1913.
4. Gibson/Green, Letters to the Press
5. Toronto Public Library
6. *New York American*, 21 May 1914
7. Toronto Public Library
8. BL

Chapter 18
1. *The Times*, 4 August 1916
2. BL
3. RCS, Edinburgh
4. RLG Archive
5. Ibid.
6. Ibid.
7. Ibid.
8. ACD, *A Visit to Three Fronts*
9. BL
10. Toronto Public Library
11. Casement Petition Papers, BL

12. Ibid.
13. Ibid.
14. Ibid.
15. Taylor
16. RLG Archive
17. *The Times*, 3 October 1918
18. Ibid.
19. *The Times*, 11 March 1920
20. ACD, *Pheneas Speaks*

Chapter 19

1. ACD, *New Revelation*
2. Oliver Wendell Holmes, *Speeches* (Boston: Little Brown, 1900)
3. ACD, *New Revelation*
4. SPR Report, 1884
5. ACD, *New Revelation*
6. Sir Henry Dickens, *Recollections* (London: William Heinemann, 1934)
7. *Light*, 2 July 1887
8. Ibid.
9. Southsea notebooks
10. BL
11. ACD, *New Revelation*
12. SPR Archive, Cambridge University
13. Jerome
14. ACD, *New Revelation*
15. Undated letter to Innes, BL
16. RLG Archive
17. *Light*, March 1916
18. Oliver Lodge, *Raymond: Or Life & Death, with Examples of the Evidence for Survival of Memory and Affection after Death* (London: Methuen, 1916)
19. ACD, *New Revelation*
20. SPR Archive, Cambridge University
21. BL
22. BL
23. G. Doyle
24. Ibid.

Chapter 20

1. Toronto Reference Library
2. RLG Archive

3. G. Doyle
4. BL
5. *Truth Magazine*, June 1919
6. ACD, *The Vital Message*
7. *Living Age*, 3 January 1920
8. RLG Archive
9. Malcolm Payne and Philip Weller, *Recollections of Sir Arthur Conan Doyle by Residents of Crowborough* (Conan Doyle (Crowborough) Establishment, 1993)
10. RLG Archive
11. Letter to *The Times*, January 1920
12. *Two Worlds Christmas Supplement*, 19 December 1919
13. BL
14. ACD, *The Wanderings of a Spiritualist*
15. BL
16. BL
17. ACD, *Wanderings*

Chapter 21

1. ACD, *The Coming of the Fairies*
2. Gardner
3. Brotherton Collection, Leeds University
4. Ibid.
5. ACD, *Fairies*
6. James Randi Educational Foundation
7. Ibid.
8. Brotherton Collection
9. Ibid.
10. ACD, *Fairies*
11. Brotherton Collection
12. Ibid.
13. ACD, *Fairies*
14. SPR Archive, Cambridge University
15. Brotherton Collection
16. ACD, *Fairies*
17. Brotherton Collection
18. ACD, *Fairies*
19. Harry Price Library, University of London

Chapter 22

1. Handwritten lecture notes, Toronto Public Library
2. RLG Archive
3. ACD, *Our American Adventure*
4. *Light*, 26 November 1927
5. *American* Magazine, September 1922
6. ACD, *Our American Adventure*
7. Ibid.
8. Houdini
9. Ibid.
10. Polidoro
11. Houdini
12. Ibid.
13. ACD, *The Riddle of Houdini*
14. Houdini
15. ACD, *On the Edge of the Unknown*
16. Houdini
17. ACD, *Our American Adventure*
18. Letter to *Westminster Gazette*, 22 November 1926
19. Houdini
20. Ibid.
21. Ernst
22. ACD, *On the Edge*
23. Ibid.
24. Harry Price Library, University of London
25. SPR Archive, Cambridge University
26. Letter to *Westminster Gazette*, 22 November 1926
27. ACD, *Riddle*

Chapter 23

1. ACD, *Pheneas Speaks*
2. Ibid.
3. Ibid.
4. ACD, *Our Second American Adventure*
5. Herries
6. Bird
7. BL
8. ACD, *Second*
9. RLG Archive
10. Toronto Public Library

11. RLG Archive
12. ACD, *Pheneas*
13. SPR Archives, Cambridge University

Chapter 24

1. RLG Archive
2. SPR Archive, Cambridge University
3. Ibid.
4. ACD, *Pheneas Speaks*
5. Lamond
6. Doran
7. RLG Archive
8. SPR Archive
9. *The Times*, 10 June 1926
10. *New York Times*, 2 September 1923
11. SPR Archive
12. Toronto Public Library
13. Raymond Chandler, *The Simple Art of Murder* (London: Hamish Hamilton, 1950)
14. *Journal of the Society for Psychical Research*
15. RLG Archive

Chapter 25

1. BL
2. Malcolm Payne and Philip Weller, *Recollections of Sir Arthur Conan Doyle by Residents of Crowborough* (Conan Doyle (Crowborough) Establishment, 1993)
3. Adrian Doyle, *The True Conan Doyle*
4. Cox
5. Toronto Reference Library
6. Ibid.
7. ACD, *Our African Winter*
8. Ibid.
9. Letter to Stewart Leckie, 22 January 1929, BL
10. ACD, *African Winter*
11. RLG Archive
12. Author's interview H. J. Spencer-Palmer
13. ACD, *African Winter*
14. RLG Archive
15. Ibid.

16. Pound
17. Lamond
18. G. Doyle
19. SPR Archive, Cambridge University
20. Ibid.
21. RLG Archive

SELECT BIBLIOGRAPHY

Arnold, Julian. *Giants in Dressing Gowns* (London: Macdonald, 1944)

Baker, Michael (ed.). *The Last Great Conan Doyle Mystery* (London: Paddington Press, 1978)

Barrie, James M. *The Greenwood Hat, Being a Memoir of James Anon 1885–1887* (London: Peter Davies, 1937)

Bayley, Harold (ed.). *The Undiscovered Country: A Sequence of Spirit Messages Describing the Death and the After-world Selected from Published and Unpublished Automatic Writing, 1874–1918* (London: Cassell & Co., 1918)

Bell, Joseph. *Mr Sherlock Holmes* (1893)

Bird, J. Malcolm. *My Psychic Adventures* (London: Allen & Unwin, 1924)

Booth, Martin. *The Doctor, the Detective and Arthur Conan Doyle: A Biography of Arthur Conan Doyle* (London: Hodder & Stoughton, 1997)

Brandon, Ruth. *The Spiritualists* (New York: Alfred A. Knopf, 1983)

Brooks, Peter. *Reading for the Plot* (London: Random House, 1985)

Brown, Ivor. *Conan Doyle: A Biography of the Creator of Sherlock Holmes* (London: Hamish Hamilton, 1972)

Carr, John Dickson. *The Life of Arthur Conan Doyle* (London: John Murray, 1949)

Citron, Gabriel. *The Houdini–Price Correspondence* (London: Legerdemain Publications, 1998)

Conan Doyle, Arthur. *Arthur Conan Doyle on Sherlock Holmes: speeches at the Stoll Convention Dinner: An Exchange of Rhymed Letters* (London: Favil Press, 1981)

Arthur Conan Doyle's Book of the Beyond (Liss: White Eagle Publishing Trust, 1994)

—. *The British Campaigns in Europe, 1914–1918* (London: Geoffrey Bles, 1928)

—. *The Coming of the Fairies* (London: Pavilion, 1997)

—. *The Crime of the Congo* (London: Hutchinson, n.d.)

—. *The Early Christian Church and Modern Spiritualism* (Cambridge: Rupert Books, 1998)

—. *The German War* (London: Hodder & Stoughton, 1914)

—. *The Great Boer War* (London: Thomas Nelson & Sons, 1900)

—. *The History of Spiritualism* (London: Cassell & Co., 1926)

—. *In Quest of Truth: Being a Correspondence between Sir Arthur Conan Doyle and Captain H. Stansbury* (London: Watts & Co., 1914)

—. *Memories and Adventures* (London: Hodder & Stoughton, 1924)

—. *The New Revelation* (Cambridge: Rupert Books, 1997)

—. *An Open Letter to Those of My Generation* (London: Psychic Press, 1929)

—. *Our African Winter* (London: John Murray, 1929)

—. *Our American Adventure* (London: Hodder & Stoughton, 1923)

—. *Our Reply to the Cleric: Sir Arthur Conan Doyle's Lecture in Leicester, October 19th 1919, Following the Church Congress* (Cambridge: Rupert Books, 1998)

—. *Our Second American Adventure* (London: Hodder & Stoughton: 1924)

—. *Pheneas Speaks. Direct Spirit Communications . . . Reported by A. C. Doyle* (London: Psychic Press, 1927)

—. *Psychic Experiences* (London and New York: G. P. Putnam Sons, 1925)

—. *Sir John French: An Appreciation* (Cambridge: Rupert Books, 1998)

—. *Spirit Return* (Kizhanattam: Indian Academy of Science, 1925)

—. *Spiritualism and Rationalism; with a Drastic Examination of Mr. Joseph Mcabe* (London: Hodder & Stoughton, 1920)

—. *The Spiritualists' Reader: A Collection of Spirit Messages from Many Sources . . . Compiled by Sir A. C. Doyle* (Manchester: Two Worlds Publishing Co., 1924)

—. *The Story of Mr. George Edalji* (London: Grey House, 1985)

—. *To Arms!* (Cambridge: Rupert Books, 1999)

—. *Three of Them: A reminiscence* (London: John Murray, 1923)

—. *Through the Magic Door* (London: John Murray, 1920)

—. *The True Conan Doyle* (London: John Murray, 1945)

—. *Verbatim Report of a Public Debate on The Truth of Spiritualism between Sir A. C. Doyle . . . and Joseph McCabe* (London: Watts & Co., 1920)

—. *A Visit to Three Fronts, June, 1916* (London: Hodder & Stoughton: 1916)

—. *The Vital Message* (London: Hodder & Stoughton, 1919)

—. *The Wanderings of a Spiritualist* (London and Glasgow, Wm. Collins Sons & Co., 1922)

—. *The War in South Africa: Its Cause and Conduct* (London: Smith, Elder & Co., 1902)

—. *Western Wanderings* (Penyffordd: Arthur Conan Doyle Society, 1994)

—. *What Does Spiritualism Actually Teach and Stand for?* (London: Psychic Bookshop, 1928)

—. *A Word of Warning* (London: Psychic Press, 1928)

Cooke, Ivan (ed.). *The Return of Arthur Conan Doyle* (Hampshire: White Eagle, 1961)

Cooper, Joe. *The Case of the Cottingley Fairies* (London: Robert Hale, 1990)

Coren, Michael. *Conan Doyle* (London: Bloomsbury, 1995)

Costello, Peter. *The Real World of Sherlock Holmes* (London: Robinson Publishing, 1991)

Cox, Don Richard. *Arthur Conan Doyle* (New York: F. Ungar, 1985)

Crookes, William. *Research in the Phenomena of Spiritualism* (Manchester and Psychic Bookshop: Two Worlds Publishing Co., 1926)

Debates on the Meaning of Life, Evolution and Spiritualism (Buffalo, New York: Prometheus Books, 1993)

Doran, George H. *The Spiritualists' Chronicles of Barabbas 1884–1934: Further Chronicles and Comment* (New York: Rinehart, 1952)

Doyle, Georgina. *Out of the Shadows: The Untold Story of Arthur Conan Doyle's First Family* (Ashcroft, British Columbia: Calabash Press, 2004)

Edalji, Reverend S. *A Miscarriage of Justice: The Case of George Edalji* (1905)

Edwards, Owen Dudley. *The Quest for Sherlock Homes* (Edinburgh: Mainstream, 1983)

Elliott, Douglas, *The Curious Incident of the Missing Link: Arthur Conan Doyle and Piltdown Man* (Toronto Bootmakers: 1988)

Engel, Howard, *Mr Doyle & Dr Bell, A Victorian Mystery* (London: Viking, 1997)

Ernst, Bernard M. L. *Houdini and Conan Doyle. The story of a Strange Friendship* (London: Hutchinson & Co., 1933)

Frank, Lawrence. *Victorian Detective Fiction and the Nature of Evidence: The Scientific Investigations of Poe, Dickens & Doyle* (New York: Houndmills, 2003)

Gardner, Edward L. *Pictures of Fairies: The Cottingley Photographs* (London: Theosophical Publishing, 1966)

Gibson, John Michael and Richard Lancelyn Green (eds). *The Unknown Conan Doyle*: Essays on Photography (London: Secker & Warburg, 1982)

—. (eds). *The Unknown Conan Doyle*: *Letters to the Press* (London: Secker & Warburg, 1982)

—. (eds). *The Unknown Conan Doyle*: *Uncollected Stories* (London: Secker & Warburg, 1982)

Goldfarb, Clifford S. *The Great Shadow: Arthur Conan Doyle, Brigadier Gerard & Napoleon* (Ashcroft, British Columbia: Calabash Press, 1997)

Green, Richard Lancelyn (ed.) *Arthur Conan Doyle on Sherlock Holmes: Speeches at the Stoll Convention Dinner* (London: Favil Press, 1981)

—. *Conan Doyle of Wimpole Street* (Chester: Arthur Conan Doyle Society, 1994)

— and John Michael Gibson *A Bibliography of A. Conan Doyle* (Oxford: Clarendon, 1983)

Haining, Peter (ed.). *The Supernatural Tales of Sir Arthur Conan Doyle* (London: Foulsham, 1987)

Hall, Trevor H. *Sherlock Holmes & His Creator* (New York: St Martin's Press, 1977)

Hansen, Ferdinand. *The Unrepentant Northcliffe: A reply to the London Times of October 19, 1920* [i.e. to its review of the author's *An Open Letter to an English Officer*] . . . *Together with a correspondence with Sir Arthur Conan Doyle* (Hamburg; Overseas Publishing Co., 1921)

Hardwick, John Michael and Mollie. *The Man Who Was Sherlock Holmes* (London: John Murray, 1964)

Harrison, Michael. 'The World of Sherlock Holmes (New York: E. P. Dutton & Co. Inc., 1975)

Herries, James William. *Other World People with a foreword by Arthur Conan Doyle* (Edinburgh and London: Hodge & Co., 1926)

Higham, Charles. *The Adventures of Conan Doyle: The Life of the Creator of Sherlock Holmes* (London: Hamilton, 1976)

Hines, Stephen (ed.). *The True Crimes Files of Sir Arthur Conan Doyle* (New York: Berkley Prime Crime, 2001)

Hocking, Silas. *My Book of Memory: A String of Reminiscences and Reflections* (London: Cassell, 1923)

Holroyd, James Edward. *Baker Street By-ways* (London: Allen & Unwin, 1959)

Houdini, Harry. *A Magician among the Spirits* (New York: Harper & Bros, 1924)

Jaffe, Jacqueline A. *Arthur Conan Doyle* (Boston: Twayne Publishers, 1987)

Jann, Rosemary. *The Adventures of Sherlock Holmes: Detecting Social Order* (Oxford: Maxwell Macmillan International, 1995)

Jerome, Jerome K. *My Life and Times* (New York: Harper & Row, 1926)

Jolly, Martyn. *Faces of the Living Dead: The Belief in Spirit Photography* (London: British Library, 2006)

Jones, Dr Harold Emery. *The Original of Sherlock Holmes* (Windsor: Gaby Goldscheider, 1980)

Jones, Kelvin I. *Conan Doyle and the Spirits: The Spiritualist Career of Sir Arthur Conan Doyle* (Wellingborough: Aquarian, 1989)

Lamond, John. *Arthur Conan Doyle: A Memoir* (London: John Murray, 1931)

Lasting impressions: the 25th anniversary of the Bootmakers of Toronto, the Sherlock Holmes Society of Canada (Toronto: Metropolitan Reference Library, 1997)

Lellenberg, Jon (ed.). *The Quest for Sir Arthur Conan Doyle: Thirteen Biographers in Search of a Life* (Carbondale: Southern Illinois University Press, 1987)

Lellenberg, Jon, Daniel Stashower and Charles Foley (eds). *Arthur Conan Doyle: A Life in Letters* (London: HarperPress, 2007)

Liebow, Ely. *Dr Joe Bell: Model for Sherlock Holmes* (Bowling Green, Ohio: Bowling Green University Popular Press, 1982)

Lycett, Andrew. *Conan Doyle: The Man Who Created Sherlock Holmes* (London: Weidenfeld & Nicolson, 2007)

Magnusson, Magnus. *Fakers, Forgers and Phoneys* (Edinburgh: Mainstream Publishing, 2006)

McCrum, Robert. *Wodehouse: A Life* (London: Viking, 2004)

McDonald, Peter. *British Literary Culture and Publishing Practice 1840–1914* (Cambridge: Cambridge University Press, 1997)

Menpes, Mortimer. *War Impressions: Being a Record in Colour by Mortimer Menpes* (1901)

Milbourne, Christopher. *Houdini: The Untold Story* (London: Cassell & Co., 1969)

Morel, Edmund. *Great Britain and the Congo; The Pillage of the Congo Basin* (London: Smith, Elder & Co., 1909)

Nevinson, Henry W. *Changes and Chances* (London: Nisbet & Co. Ltd, 1923)

Nichols, Beverley. *Are They the Same at Home? Being a Series of Bouquets Diffidently Distributed by Beverley Nichols* (New York: George H. Doran, 1927)

Nollen, Scott Allen. *Sir Arthur Conan Doyle at the Cinema* (Jefferson, North Carolina: McFarland & Co. Inc., 1996)

Nordon, Pierre. *Conan Doyle* (London: John Murray, 1966)

O'Connell, Maurice (ed.). *Daniel O'Connell, Political Pioneer* (Dublin: Institute of Public Administration, 1991)

Orel, Harold (ed.). *Sir Arthur Conan Doyle, Interviews and Recollections* (London: Macmillan, 1991)

Park, William, *The Truth about Oscar Slater: With the Prisoner's Own Story* (London: Psychic Press, 1927)

Pearsall, Ronald. *Conan Doyle: A Biographical Solution* (London: Weidenfeld and Nicolson, 1977)

—. *The Table Rappers* (New York: St Martin's Press, 1972)

Pearson, Hesketh. *Conan Doyle: His Life and Art* (London: Methuen, 1943)

Polidoro, Massimo. *Final Séance: The Strange Friendship between Houdini and Conan Doyle* (Amherst, New York: Prometheus Books, 2001)

Pond, Major J. B. *Eccentricities of Genius: Memories of Famous Men and Women of the Platform and Stage* (1901)

Pound, Reginald. *A Maypole in the Strand* (London: Ernest Benn, 1948)

Redmond, Christopher. *Welcome to America, Mr Sherlock Holmes: Victorian America Meets Arthur Conan Doyle* (Toronto: Simon & Pierre, 1987)

Redmond, Donald A. *Sherlock Holmes: A Study in Sources* (Kingston, Ontario: McGill-Queen's University Press, 1982)

Richard Doyle and His Family (London: Victoria & Albert Museum, 1983)

Richards, Jeffrey. *Sherlock Holmes, Conan Doyle and the British Empire: An Investigation into Conan Doyle's Links with the British Empire as Expressed through his Sherlockian and Other Literature* (Halifax: Northern Musgraves Sherlock Holmes Society, 1997)

Rodin, Alvin E. and Jack D. Key. *Medical casebook of Doctor Arthur Conan Doyle: From Practitioner to Sherlock Holmes and Beyond* (Malabar, Florida: Robert E. Krieger Publishing Co., 1984)

Roughead, William (ed.). *The Trial of Oscar Slater* (Edinburgh: William Hodge & Co., 1929)

Saxby, Jessie E. *Joseph Bell: An Appreciation by an Old Friend* (1913)

Simpson, James Gordon. *A Commentary and Questionnaire on Micah Clarke* (1928)

Smith, H. Greenhough. *Authors I Have Known* (1925)

—. *'What I Think': A symposium on Books and Other Things by Famous Writers of Today* (1927)

Stashower, Daniel. *Teller of Tales: The Life of Arthur Conan Doyle* (London: Allen Lane, 2000)

Stavert, Geoffrey. *A Study in Southsea: The Unrevealed Life of Doctor Arthur Conan Doyle* (Portsmouth: Milestone, 1987)

Stoker, Bram. *Personal Reminiscences of Henry Irving* (1907)

Stone, Harry. *The Case-book of Sherlock Doyle: True Mysteries Investigated by Conan Doyle* (Ramford: Ian Henry Publications, 1991)

Symons, Julian. *Conan Doyle: Portrait of an Artist* (London: G. Whizzard, 1979)

Taylor, A. J. P. (ed.). *Lloyd George: A Diary by Frances Stevenson* (London: Hutchinson, 1971)

Thompson, Flora. *Heatherley* (Bordon: John Owen Smith, 1995)

Trevelyan, W. R. (ed.). *The Seven Years of William IV: A Reign Cartooned by John Doyle* (London: William Heinemann, 1952)

Von Reuter, Florizel. *Psychical Experiences of a Musician* (1928)

Walsh, John Evangelist. *Unravelling Piltdown: The Science Fraud of the Century and Its Solution* (New York: Random House, 1996)

Weaver, Gordon. *The Edalji Case* (Cambridge: Vanguard Press, 2006)

Weller, Philip (ed.). *Recollections of Sir Arthur Conan Doyle* (Fareham: Sherlock Publications, 1993)

Whitt. J. F. *The Strand Magazine, 1891–1950: A Selective Checklist Listing All Material Relating to Arthur Conan Doyle . . .* (London: J. F. Whitt, 1979)

Whittington-Egan, Richard. *The Oscar Slater Murder Story: A New Light on a Classic Miscarriage of Justice* (Glasgow: Neil Wilson, 2001)

Wilson, James Maurice. *Life after Death . . . Two lectures on Christianity and Spiritualism . . . With replies by Sir A. Conan Doyle and Sir Oliver Lodge* (1920)

Wynne, Catherine Elizabeth. *Bram Stoker, Arthur Conan Doyle and the Colonial Gothic* (Oxford: University of Oxford, 1999)

—. *The Colonial Conan Doyle: British Imperialism, Irish Nationalism, and the Gothic* (London: Greenwood, 2002)

INDEX